Presidential Administration and Justice	Political Party	Home State	Years on Court	Age at Nomination	Number of Years of Previous Judicial Experience
Johnson appointees					
Abe Fortas	Democrat	Tennessee	1965–1969	55	0
Thurgood Marshall	Democrat	New York	1967–1991	59	4
Nixon appointees					
Warren E. Burger	Republican	Minnesota	1969–1986	61	13
Harry A. Blackmun	Republican	Minnesota	1970–present	61	11
Lewis F. Powell Jr.	Democrat	Virginia	1971–1987	64	0
William H. Rehnquist	Republican	Arizona	1971–1986	47	0
Ford appointee					
John Paul Stevens	Republican	Illinois	1976–present	55	5
Reagan appointees					
Sandra Day O'Connor	Republican	Arizona	1981–present	51	6.5
Antonin Scalia	Republican	Illinois	1986–present	50	4
Anthony Kennedy	Republican	California	1988–present	51	12
George H.W. Bush appointees					
David H. Souter	Republican	New Hampshire	1990–present	50	13
Clarence Thomas	Republican	Georgia	1991–present	43	1
Clinton appointees					
Ruth Bader Ginsburg	Democrat	New York	1993–present	60	13
Stephen G. Breyer	Democrat	Massachusetts	1994–present	56	14
George W. Bush appointees					
John Roberts[c]	Republican	New York	2005–present	50	2
Samuel Alito	Republican	New Jersey	2006–present	56	16

[a]Died in office.

[b]Prior to appointment to associate justice.

[c]Appointed Chief Justice in 2006 by George W. Bush.

Source: Harold W. Stanley and Richard G. Niemi. *Vital Statistics on American Politics.* Washington, DC: CQ Press, 1994, pp.294–299. Table adapted by SOURCEBOOK staff. Reprinted by permission.

Updated by the authors.

FOURTH EDITION

CONSTITUTIONAL LAW
AND THE
CRIMINAL JUSTICE SYSTEM

J. SCOTT HARR, JD
Concordia University Saint Paul

KÄREN M. HESS, PhD
Normandale Community College

with contributions from **Christine Hess Orthmann, MS**

WADSWORTH
CENGAGE Learning™

Australia • Brazil • Japan • Korea • Mexico • Singapore • Spain • United Kingdom • United States

Constitutional Law and the Criminal Justice System, Fourth Edition
J. Scott Harr, Kären M. Hess

Acquisitions Editor: Carolyn Henderson Meier

Assistant Editor: Meaghan Banks

Editorial Assistant: Beth McMurray

Technology Project Manager: Amanda Kaufmann

Marketing Manager: Terra Schultz

Marketing Assistant: Emily Elrod

Marketing Communications Manager: Tami Strang

Project Manager, Editorial Production: Matt Ballantyne

Creative Director: Rob Hugel

Art Director: Vernon Boes

Print Buyer: Linda Hsu

Permissions Editor: Roberta Broyer

Production Service: Graphic World Inc.

Photo Researcher: Terri Wright

Copy Editor: Graphic World Inc.

Cover Designer: Yvo Riezebos

Cover Image: istockphoto.com/ ©Stefan Klein

Compositor: ICC Macmillan Inc.

For product information and technology assistance, contact us at
Cengage Learning Customer & Sales Support, 1-800-354-9706

For permission to use material from this text or product, submit all requests online at **www.cengage.com/permissions**
Further permissions questions can be emailed to
permissionrequest@cengage.com

Library of Congress Control Number: 2007922063

Student Edition:
ISBN-13: 978-0-495-09543-9
ISBN-10: 0-495-09543-5

Wadsworth
10 Davis Drive
Belmont, CA 94002-3098
USA

Cengage Learning is a leading provider of customized learning solutions with office locations around the globe, including Singapore, the United Kingdom, Australia, Mexico, Brazil, and Japan. Locate Your local office at: **international.cengage.com/region**

Cengage Learning products are represented in Canada by Nelson Education, Ltd.

For your course and learning solutions, visit **academic.cengage.com**

Purchase any of our products at your local college store or at our preferred online store **www.ichapters.com**

Printed in Canada
3 4 5 6 7 11 10 09

Dedicated to Captain Steven Simmons (1943–1995), Minneapolis Police Department. Steve Simmons lived the law and upheld the U.S. Constitution through his work as a police officer and educator. But more importantly, Steve was a friend. He embodied every attribute of the professional law enforcement officer, and he is sorely missed by the community he served, his students, his friends and his family.

May you always have blue skies, a pleasant breeze and good sailing.

About the Authors

J. Scott Harr's interest in the law spans over 30 years from varied perspectives. He has been employed as a social worker in youth diversion programs, has proudly served as a police officer for three Twin Cities metropolitan communities and as public safety director and chief law enforcement officer of one of these. He has taught classes in all areas of the law for more than 20 years. While attending William Mitchell College of Law in St. Paul, Minnesota, he received the Warren E. Burger Award given in honor of the former chief justice of the U.S. Supreme Court. He also attended Emmanuel College, Cambridge University (England), where he studied law. Harr has worked as a staff investigator for a preeminent Twin Cities law firm and is a member of the U.S. Supreme Court bar, placing him among attorneys permitted to practice before the Supreme Court. He is a licensed attorney, police officer and private investigator. He founded Scott Harr Legal Investigations, which has been in business for over 20 years. In addition to this text, he has coauthored and contributed to numerous other titles. Scott has taught at Normandale Community College in Bloomington, Minnesota, and Metropolitan State University School of Law Enforcement and Criminal Justice in St. Paul, Minnesota. He is presently the chair of the criminal justice department at Concordia University, Saint Paul, Minnesota, and sits on the Minnesota Peace Officer Standards and Training (POST) Board, where he also chairs the board's training committee.

Kären M. Hess holds a PhD in English and in instructional design from the University of Minnesota and a PhD in criminal justice from Pacific Western University. Other Wadsworth texts Dr. Hess has coauthored are *Careers in Criminal Justice and Related Fields* (Fifth Edition), *Criminal Investigation* (Eighth Edition), *Criminal Procedure, Corrections in the 21st Century: A Practical Approach, Introduction to Law Enforcement and Criminal Justice* (Eighth Edition), *Introduction to Private Security* (Fifth Edition), *Juvenile Justice* (Fourth Edition), *Management and Supervision in Law Enforcement* (Fourth Edition), *Community Policing: Partnerships for Problem Solving* (Fourth Edition), and *Police Operations: Theory and Practice* (Fourth Edition).

She is a member of the Academy of Criminal Justice Sciences, the American Association of University Women, the American Correctional Association, the American Society for Industrial Security, the American Society for Law Enforcement Trainers, the American Society of Criminologists, the Association for Supervision and Curriculum, the International Association of Chiefs of Police, the Minnesota Association of Chiefs of Police, the Police Executive Research Forum and the Text and Academic Authors Association, which has named Dr. Hess to their Council of Fellows.

Brief Contents

Contents

Chapter 2   An Overview of the U.S. Legal System   35

Chapter 3   The Supreme Court of the United States: The Final Word   58

Chapter 4   **Researching the Law**   76

Chapter 7   The Second Amendment: The Gun Control Controversy   149

SECTION III

CONSTITUTIONAL AMENDMENTS INFLUENCING THE CRIMINAL JUSTICE SYSTEM   171

Chapter 8   The Fourth Amendment: An Overview of Constitutional Searches and Seizures   173

Chapter 9   Conducting Constitutional Seizures   202

Chapter 10   Conducting Constitutional Searches   228

Chapter 11   The Fifth Amendment: Due Process and Obtaining Information Legally   266

Chapter 12   The Sixth Amendment: Right to Counsel and a Fair Trial   298

Chapter 13   The Eighth Amendment: Bail, Fines and Punishment   323

SECTION IV

COMING FULL CIRCLE   349

Chapter 14   The Remaining Amendments and a Return to the Constitution   351

Foreword

Jim Ramstad, Minnesota, 3rd District
U.S. House of Representatives

More than two centuries ago, our nation's brilliant and visionary founders wrote a truly remarkable document that has withstood the test of time and flourished as an example for new democracies around the world—our Constitution. All Americans should be very proud of our nation's steadfast approach to upholding the guiding principles as written in the Constitution.

Today our 200-plus-year-old Constitution is just as relevant as it was in 1787. The new, fourth edition of *Constitutional Law and the Criminal Justice System* does a masterful job of explaining why. As this tremendous resource clearly shows, we must give great credit to the visionaries who drafted our Constitution. Although you can read the Constitution in a matter of minutes, you will not appreciate its wonders until you examine each word, phrase and clause. That's what *Constitutional Law and the Criminal Justice System* accomplishes so well. One person's interpretation of the Constitution will differ greatly from another's. So, too, does one generation's interpretation differ from another's. That is why the study of constitutional law is a never-ending process. The America of the 21st century differs markedly from that of 1787. The challenges America faces today simply didn't exist in earlier times. And the challenges of change are occurring at a faster rate and are affecting more and more people because of technology.

As a Member of Congress and former constitutional law professor at American University, I am a firm believer in our Constitution and how it has worked to help all people receive fair and just treatment. I am filled with wonder at how our Constitution still applies so effectively to Americans' lives today.

I highly commend J. Scott Harr and Kären M. Hess for writing this fourth edition of *Constitutional Law and the Criminal Justice System*. This outstanding text on constitutional law will greatly expand readers' appreciation for our Constitution's amazing durability. The authors have done all Americans a tremendous public service.

William Finney
St. Paul (Minnesota) Chief of Police (retired)

The authors of this text have accomplished something that was heretofore difficult to achieve: combining the philosophy of a complicated subject with its practical application. The U.S. Constitution, as important as it is to every citizen—
especially those employed in the criminal justice system—is not easy to fully
grasp. The mountains of case law arising from efforts to interpret the Constitution's "true meaning" are evidence to this. It can be even more challenging for
those working in the field to apply it properly, often with only a split second to
evaluate the circumstances and react.

Young police officers may think that comprehension of the U.S. Constitution
is beyond them because they are not lawyers. Others might think the odds are
against their being immersed in an action or incident that could evolve to the
level of review by the U.S. Supreme Court. They would be wrong on both counts.
Criminal justice professionals are expected to know the law and to apply it, as the
very next call could result in a pivotal case before the Court. This is part of the
excitement and responsibility of our profession.

Professor Harr and Dr. Hess have succeeded at presenting this lofty subject in
an understandable, hands-on manner that would, frankly, benefit every American
to review. It is apparent they have lived, worked and taught what they write
about. Criminal justice professionals, whether newly hired or seasoned cops, correctional officers, probation officers or employed in any other area of our criminal justice system, will particularly benefit from the subject matter of this book
and the masterful way it is presented.

Preface

This text is unlike most traditional legal works and was prepared this way intentionally.

Our teaching experience and feedback from students and educators alike gave us the strong sense that there was a need for something other than a traditional casebook approach to learning "con law." While there is certainly a place for traditional texts, people with whom we consulted wanted a text that fell between basic civics books and law school-level casebooks to use in their introductory undergraduate courses on constitutional law or search and seizure. For those who want an easy, painless journey through the fascinating study of American constitutional law, *Constitutional Law and the Criminal Justice System* will, we believe, prove an ideal solution.

Approach

We created this text with the express intent of making the learning of constitutional law as enjoyable and productive as possible. We have developed a natural progression to help students build their knowledge. Even the layout was done in a way that will make the learning less tedious. You will notice lots of white space to make the reading easier, with enough space to make notes or references as you proceed. Plain language is preferred to legalese. Court opinions are important, and you will have opportunities in this text to learn how to read them and, in fact, read and brief some.

Finally, be aware that mastering the basic concepts of constitutional law is only the beginning. American law is unique in that it can, and does, change to meet the changing needs of the society it serves. A part of the knowledge you will acquire is how to keep current with this changing, constantly evolving area of law. American constitutional law is not a stagnant, boring subject; it is a vital, stimulating topic that is arguably the duty of every American to know . . . and to appreciate.

Organization

Section I provides a foundation for understanding constitutional law beginning with an historical overview of how the Constitution came to be (Chapter 1). This is followed by an overview of our legal system (Chapter 2) and an explanation of the Supreme Court of the United States as the final word on any legal issues (Chapter 3). The section concludes with a description of how to research the law (Chapter 4).

Section II focuses on the guarantees of the Constitution to citizens: their civil rights and civil liberties. The discussion first focuses on equal protection under the law and efforts to balance individual, state and federal rights (Chapter 5). The focus then shifts to the basic freedoms guaranteed by the First Amendment (Chapter 6). This section concludes with a discussion of the gun control controversy arising from the Second Amendment (Chapter 7).

Section III describes in depth the constitutional amendments influencing the criminal justice system. It begins with an overview of constitutional searches and seizures as required by the Fourth Amendment (Chapter 8). A detailed look at conducting constitutional seizures is presented next (Chapter 9), followed by an equally detailed look at conducting constitutional searches (Chapter 10). Next is a discussion of due process and obtaining information legally as required by the Fifth Amendment (Chapter 11), followed by citizens' right to counsel and a fair trial as required by the Sixth Amendment (Chapter 12). The section concludes with a discussion of bail, fines and punishment as regulated by the Eighth Amendment (Chapter 13).

The final section of the text provides a discussion of the remaining amendments and how additional amendments might come to be in the future (Chapter 14).

New to This Edition

The fourth edition of *Constitutional Law and the Criminal Justice System* has been completely updated with the most recent Supreme Court decisions and references available. Each chapter has been revised and updated as follows:

- **Chapter 1: An Historical Overview**   This chapter covers important background information on events leading up to and viewpoints shaping the Constitution, including the Mayflower Compact, the concept of the Great Melting Pot, the influence of English and French philosophers (Thomas Hobbes, John Locke, Montesquieu, Voltaire), the issue of slavery, and the establishment of a balance of power through federalism. Expanded material is also provided on the Articles of the Constitution (*Clinton v. Jones*, 1997; *Nixon v. United States*, 1993).
- **Chapter 2: An Overview of the U.S. Legal System**   This updated summary of the U.S. criminal justice system includes expanded coverage of the components of this system, particularly courts and corrections, trends in the juvenile justice system and a new discussion of how U.S. constitutional law is being challenged by the blurring of jurisdictional boundaries worldwide.
- **Chapter 3: The Supreme Court of the United States: The Final Word**   The concept of federalism is explored in greater detail, as well as how the separation of powers impacts the workings and opinions of the court. The chapter also includes a new section on the controversy over and alternatives to judicial review, a comparison of the Rehnquist and the Warren Courts, and a profile of the current Supreme Court and the politics of recent decisions.
- **Chapter 4: Researching the Law**   Expanded coverage of LEXIS/NEXIS is included in this chapter, as well as additional discussions on the methodology of legal writing in general and case briefs in particular, the growing importance of "information literacy" in relation to current computerized research methods, and the limitations of the Internet and distinguishing between good and bad Web sites.

- **Chapter 5: Equal Protection under the Law: Balancing Individual, State and Federal Rights** This chapter has been expanded to reflect the myriad constitutional challenges presented by our increasingly diverse society, including more in-depth discussions on race-based admissions policies, affirmative action and the struggle for equality (*Bradwell v. Illinois*, 1873), and greater coverage of discrimination and civil rights laws pertaining to other social statuses such as age (*Massachusetts Board of Retirement v. Murgia*, 1976), disability, sexual orientation, religion (*Ansonia Board of Education v. Philbrook*, 1986), immigration and residency status (*Shapiro v. Thompson*, 1969; *Plyler v. Doe*, 1982; *Sugarman v. McDougall*, 1973; and *Hampton v. Mow Sun Wong* (1976), and pregnancy policies. Other relevant cases include *Duncan v. Louisiana* (1968), *Gratz et al. v. Bollinger et al.* (2003) and *Grutter v. Bollinger et al.* (2003).

- **Chapter 6: The First Amendment: Basic Freedoms** Updated topics include difficulties in defining "religion," the Establishment Clause and the ongoing struggle between changing norms and constitutional interpretations, including court-ordered treatment in which an element of religion exists (*Abinton School District v. Schempp*, 1963; *Murray v. Curlett*, 1963; *Wallace v. Jeffries*, 1985; *Griffin v. Coughlin*, 1998; *Kerr v. Farrey*, 1996; *Warner v. Orange County Dept. of Probation*, 1999), freedom of speech and the Internet (*United States v. American Library Association*, 2003), free speech restrictions (*Gertz v. Robert Welch, Inc.*, 1974), cross burning (*Virginia v. Black*, 2003) and flag burning (*Street v. New York*, 1969; *Texas v. Johnson*, 1989), freedoms of expression and association (*Richmond Newspapers, Inc. v. Virginia*, 1980; *Chicago v. Morales*, 1999; *Kelley v. Johnson*, 1976; *Wilson v. Swing*, 1978), and the First Amendment rights of prisoners.

- **Chapter 7: The Second Amendment: The Gun Control Controversy** In addition to updated coverage concerning state and federal legislation, new topics include the effect of concealed carry laws on crime, the Law Enforcement Officers Safety Act, and joint government and community efforts to respond to gun-related violence. Newly cited cases involve the issues of gun ownership by persons convicted in foreign courts (*Small v. United States*, 2005) and anonymous tips where gun possession is reported (*Florida v. J.L.*, 2000; *Pennsylvania v. D.M.*, 2000).

- **Chapter 8: The Fourth Amendment: An Overview of Constitutional Searches and Seizures** Updates to this chapter include discussions on individuals' right to privacy (*Eisenstadt v. Baird*, 1972; *Griswold v. Connecticut*, 1965; *Roe v. Wade*, 1973), fleeing from police; internal sanctions: civil and criminal liability of government agents; the evolving challenges to privacy rights in the wake of terrorist attacks and debates over means of obtaining information. New material also involves the cases of *Illinois v. McArthur* (2001); *Maryland v. Garrison* (1987); *Taylor v. Alabama* (1982) and *United States v. Arvizu* (2002).

- **Chapter 9: Conducting Constitutional Seizures** New coverage includes a look at the authority that grants police the power to do what they do; more in-depth coverage of investigatory stops; how concerns over terrorism have impacted border stops and checkpoints; de facto arrests; changes to the knock-and-announce rule; the intertwined issues of racism, police brutality and use of force; the rights of those held in custody; and the cases of *Almeida-Sanchez v. United States* (1973), *Saucier v. Katz* (2001), *United States* *v. Flores-Montano* (2004), *United States v. Montoya de Hernandez* (1985), *Atwater v. City of Lago Vista* (2001), *Kaupp v. Texas* (2003), *Minnesota v. Carter* (1998) and *Hudson v. Michigan* (2006).

- **Chapter 10: Conducting Constitutional Searches**   Updated and expanded material is included on the constitutionality of thermal imaging; profiling terrorists; the Fourth Amendment; institutional and community corrections; *Kyllo v. United States* (2001); *Maryland v. Dyson* (1999); *Morrissey v. Brewer* (1972) and *United States v. Hambric*, (1999*)*. New material includes the burgeoning area of law concerning electronic privacy, privacy rights of parolees (*Samson v. California*, 2006), and Court rulings on third-party consent (*Georgia v. Randolph*, 2006), vehicle searches (*Thornton v. United States*, 2004; *Illinois v. Caballes*, 2005), warrantless entry into a home (*Brigham City, Utah v. Stuart*, 2006). Other cases new to this chapter are *Illinois v. Caballes* (2005), *Konop v. Hawaiian Airlines* (2002), *Thornton v. United States* (2004), *United States v. Councilman* (2005) and *United States v. Haley* (1982).

- **Chapter 11: The Fifth Amendment: Due Process and Obtaining Information Legally**   Heavily updated with more than two dozen new court cases, expanded material in this chapter includes whether citizens are constitutionally required to provide proper identification to police upon request (*Hiibel v. Nevada*, 2004); the use of force to elicit confessions and other due process rights involved in obtaining information of confessions from suspects (*Beecher v. Alabama*, 1967; *Mincey v. Arizona*, 1978; *Greenwold v. Wisconsin*, 1968; *McNabb v. United States*, 1943; *Mallory v. United States*, 1957; *Brewer v. Williams*, 1977; *United States v. Guarno*, 1987; *United States v. Ballard*, 1978; *Evans v. Dowd*, 1991; *United States v. McClinton*, 1992); *Miranda* issues (*United States v. Patane*, 2004; *Muehler v. Mena*, 2005; *Davis v. United States*, 1994), waiving one's rights (*Burket v. Angelone*, 2000; *United States v. Banks*, 2003; *Diaz v. Senkowski*, 1996; *Dormire v. Wilkinson*, 2001; *Clark v. Murphy*, 2003; *Mincey v. Head*, 2000); double jeopardy (*North Carolina v. Pearce*, 1969; *Sattazahn v. Pennsylvania*, 2003; *United States v. Lara*, 2004; *Seling v. Young*, 2001); and renewal of the USA PATRIOT Act,. New material includes beachheading or "question first" tactics (*Oregon v. Elstad*, 1985; *Missouri v. Seibert*, 2004), a more detailed comparison between trial and grand juries, just compensation rulings in *Hawaii Housing Authority v. Midkiff* (1984) and *Kelo v. City of New London* (2005).

- **Chapter 12: The Sixth Amendment: Right to Counsel and a Fair Trial**   New to this chapter are the topics of jury nullification (*United States v. Moylan*, 1969) and whether juveniles have Sixth Amendment rights. Expanded material includes the grounds for change of venue; basic differences between the *Miranda* and *Massiah* provisions; incorporation of the right to a jury trial, the right to counsel of indigent defendants seeking direct appeals (*Halbert v. Michigan*, 2005); the "offense specific" nature of right to counsel (*Texas v. Cobb*, 2001); the issue of perjury (*Harris v. New York*, 1971; *Michigan v. Harvey*, 1990); the presumption of effective counsel as applied to public defenders; and the freedom to waive one's right to counsel (*Patterson v. Illinois*, 1988).

- **Chapter 13: The Eighth Amendment: Bail, Fines and Punishment**   Expanded discussions in this chapter include asset forfeiture; proportionality review and updated statistics on capital punishment; juveniles and the death penalty (*Roper v. Simmons*, 2005); capital punishment for the mentally ill; DNA testing; the role of juries in capital punishment cases (*Ring v. Arizona*, 2002; *Schriro v. Summerlin*, 2004); and punishment in corrections and prisoner treatment (*Overton v. Bazetta*, 2003): smoking bans, chain gangs, lashing to a whipping post. Other relevant court cases include *Arave v. Creech* (1994); *Bell v. Cone* (2002); *Charles L. Singleton v. Norris* (2003); *Ewing v. California* (2003); *Lockyer v. Andrade* (2003); *Maynard v. Cartwright* (1988); *Morgan v. Illinois* (1992); *Pulley v. Harris* (1984); and *Simmons v. South Carolina* (1994).

■ **Chapter 14: The Remaining Amendments and a Return to the Constitution** This final chapter includes additional cases concerning other provisions contained in additional amendments, such as the Seventh Amendment and jury trials (*Thomas v. Union Carbide*, 1985; *Curtis v. Loether*, 1974; *Colgrove v. Battin*, 1973), and the Ninth Amendment and unenumerated rights (*Griswold v. Connecticut*, 1965; *United States v. Darby*, 1941). The chapter concludes with a discussion of ongoing efforts to pass further constitutional amendments, including a victims' rights amendment and a constitutional ban on gay marriage.

How to Use this Text

Constitutional Law and the Criminal Justice System, Fourth Edition provides a carefully structured learning experience. The more actively you participate in it, the greater your learning will be. You will learn and remember more if you first familiarize yourself with the total scope of the subject. Read and think about the Contents, which provides an outline of the many facets of constitutional law. Then follow these steps for *triple-strength learning* as you study each chapter:

1. Read the objectives at the beginning of the chapter. These are stated as "Do You Know?" questions. Assess your current knowledge of the subject of each question. Examine any preconceptions you may hold. Look at the key terms, and watch for them when they are used.

2. Read the chapter, underlining, highlighting or taking notes—whatever is your preferred study method.

   a. Pay special attention to all information highlighted like so:

   ■ In the supremacy clause, the U.S. Supreme Court declared itself the supreme law of the land.

   The key concepts of the text are spotlighted in this way and answer the chapter-opening "Do You Know?" questions.

   b. Pay special attention to all the words in bold print. The key terms of the chapter appear this way the first time they are used.

3. When you have finished reading the chapter, read the summary—your third exposure to the chapter's key information. Then return to the beginning of the chapter and quiz yourself. Can you answer the "Do You Know?" questions? "Can You Define?" the key terms?

4. Finally, read the Discussion Questions and be prepared to contribute to a class discussion of the ideas presented in the chapter.

By following these steps, you will learn more information, understand it more fully and remember it longer.

Ancillaries

To further enhance your study of constitutional law, several supplements are available:

- **Instructor's Manual/Test Bank**   Available to adopting professors in both print and electronic form, the Instructor's Resource Manual and Test Bank has been extensively updated and revised for this edition. The instructor's manual for each chapter includes learning objectives, detailed chapter outlines, key terms and definitions, class discussion exercises, and student activities. Each chapter's test bank contains approximately 60 multiple-choice, true-false, fill-in-the-blank, and essay questions, along with a full answer key.
- **Book Companion Web Site**   www.thomsonedu.com/criminaljustice/harr   Includes further case content tied to the chapter materials and numerous study aids, including chapter outlines, learning objectives, glossary, flashcards, crossword puzzles, and more.
- *Handbook of Selected Supreme Court Cases,* **Third Edition**   This supplementary text provides briefs of key cases that have defined the administration of justice in this country, along with citations and commentary.
- *The Wadsworth Criminal Justice Video Library*   So many exciting, new videos—so many great ways to enrich your lectures and spark discussion of the material in this text. View our full video offerings and download clip lists with running times at www.cj.wadsworth.com/videos. Your Thomson Wadsworth representative will be happy to provide details on our video policy by adoption size. The library includes these selections and many others:

  - *ABC Videos:* Feature short, high-interest clips from current news events as well as historic raw footage going back 40 years. Perfect for discussion starters or to enrich your lectures and spark interest in the material in the text, these brief videos provide students with a new lens through which to view the past and present, one that will greatly enhance their knowledge and understanding of significant events and open up to them new dimensions in learning. Clips are drawn from such programs as *World News Tonight, Good Morning America, This Week, PrimeTime Live, 20/20* and *Nightline,* as well as numerous ABC News specials and material from the Associated Press Television News and British Movietone News collections. Your Thomson Wadsworth representative will be happy to provide a complete listing of videos and policies.
  - *60 Minutes DVD:* Featuring 12-minute clips from CBS's *60 Minutes* news program, this DVD will give you a way to explore a topic in more depth with your students without taking up a full class session. Topics include the Green River Killer, the reliability of DNA testing and California's Three Strikes Law. Produced by Wadsworth, CBS and Films for the Humanities.
  - *The Wadsworth Custom Videos for Criminal Justice:* Produced by Wadsworth and Films for the Humanities, these videos include short 5- to 10-minute segments that encourage classroom discussion. Topics include white-collar crime, domestic violence, forensics, suicide and the police officer, the court process, the history of corrections, prison society and juvenile justice.

- *Oral History Project:* Developed in association with the American Society of Criminology, the Academy of Criminal Justice Society and the National Institute of Justice, these videos will help you introduce your students to the scholars who have developed the criminal justice discipline. Compiled over the last several years, each video features a set of Guest Lecturers— scholars whose thinking has helped to build the foundation of present ideas in the discipline. Vol. 1: Moments in Time; Vol. 2: Great Moments in Criminological Theory; Vol. 3: Research Methods.
- *COURT TV Videos:* One-hour videos presenting seminal and high-profile cases, such as the interrogation of Michael Crowe and serial killer Ted Bundy, as well as crucial and current issues such as cybercrime, double jeopardy and the management of the prison on Riker's Island.
- *A&E American Justice:* 40 videos to choose from, on topics such as deadly force, women on death row, juvenile justice, strange defenses, and Alcatraz.

- *Films for the Humanities:* Nearly 200 videos to choose from on a variety of topics such as elder abuse, supermax prisons, suicide and the police officer, the making of an FBI agent, domestic violence and more . . .

Acknowledgments

The authors would like to thank the reviewers of this edition for their insightful comments and suggestions:

Morris Jenkins, University of Toledo
Russ J. Pomrenke, Gwinnett Technical College
Pamella Seay, Florida Gulf Coast University

We would also like to thank the reviewers of previous editions: Mitch Chamlin, University of Cincinnati; Bill Kitchens, University of Louisiana–Monroe; Wayne Logan, SUNY–Albany; Milo Miller, Southeast Missouri State; John Wyant, Illinois Central College; Caryl Lynn Segal, University of Texas–Arlington; Gene Straughan, Lewis and Clark State College; Bob Diotalevi, Florida Gulf Coast University; Wayne Durkee, Durham Technical Community College; Jill Jasperson, Utah Valley State College; Mark Jones, Atlantic Cape Community College; Jerry Maynard, Cuyahoga Community College; Leanna Rossi, Western New Mexico University; Vincent Russo, City Colleges of Chicago; James Sanderson, Robeson Community College; and Robert Wiggins, Cedarville University.

Scott wishes to acknowledge each of his students from around the United States and world who have taught him even more, with special recognition of Officer Kirk Wetzlich, M.A., who embodies the spirit of education. As is always the case, thank you to Henry Wrobleski, his mentor (*and friend to both authors*), to whom Scott remains committed to return the favor bestowed upon him by doing the same for others (a true mentor like Hank is a rarity everyone should be blessed with). Thank you to Professor C. Paul Jones, Esq., former Minnesota Public Defender, for teaching what the law is truly about. Thank you to professors Joe Arvidson, Nancy Bode, Esq., and Dr. David Woodard for their research assistance with this new edition. Thank you to Professor Laurel Forsgren for her untiring research assistance and to both her and Professor Mike Conner for their encouragement, support and invaluable contributions to the Concordia Criminal Justice

Department, as well as to Dr. Jim Ollhoff, who recognized the future of criminal justice studies as a legitimate discipline. A special thank you to Christine Hess Orthmann for her thorough research, writing and overseeing of the production process.

Finally, Scott has a special thank you for his wife, Dr. Diane Lacy Harr; daughter Kelsey and son Ricky, with whom he has always shared his dreams; father, Reed S. Harr; and parents-in-law, Richard and Marie Lacy. And from Kären, a special thank you to husband and best friend, Sheldon, and to Christine and Tim— a family whose support and encouragement have been invaluable.

Both authors wish to thank our executive editor, Carolyn Henderson Meier, assistant editor Rebecca Johnson, and production editor Matt Ballantyne, at Thomson Wadsworth; production editor Mike Ederer at Graphic World Publishing Services; our photo consultant, Bobbi Peacock; and photo researchers Terri Wright and Austin MacRae at Terri Wright Design.

A Foundation for Understanding Constitutional Law

Constitutional law—no other subject guides our daily lives as does the Constitution of the United States. Each of us can go about our business in a fairly predictable, safe way because of the guarantees and personal freedoms assured by our Constitution. And yet how many Americans know much about it? Most have never read it. Few have studied it. Even fewer have taken the time to contemplate the implications of this incredible document . . . one many have died for.

Walk into any law library and the sheer volume of material is overwhelming. Yet to remain law, every one of these books must balance ever so delicately on one other, much smaller, document—the U.S. Constitution. This is a heavy burden for the Constitution to bear, yet it has done so admirably for over two centuries. And all you have to do to see that it continues to do so is to maintain an awareness of current events. The American living law changes before your eyes.

When the document was drafted in 1787, it was never meant to be an all-inclusive compendium of legal answers. It was intended as a basic framework within which all other law must remain. It is so powerful a document that any laws people try to impose on it that do not meet its tenets are simply void. However, the difficulties faced by Rosa Parks and other American heroes who have stood up for their constitutional rights remind us that the process is not quite that easy.

Those drafting the Constitution had a timeless vision. They knew society would change, as would its needs. They realized they could never foresee all the issues their country would confront (and what issues there are!). But the framers of our Constitution successfully developed the charters that established our uniquely *American* legal system. The basic organizational structure is created so no one person, royalty or dictator, shall ever have total rule, and so that a handful of precious basic rights are assured. *This* is what the U.S. Constitution is about. It is really quite simple. So why does a course in constitutional law strike fear in the hearts of students of all ages? Because anything that has worked so well for so many, for so long, *must* have some built-in complexity. And it does—*interpretation*.

Myriad forces affect interpretation of the Constitution: the time, societal norms and politics. Indeed, constitutional interpretation is political, explaining why any president wants to exercise the powerful right to appoint justices to the U.S. Supreme Court. This text addresses the awesome power the Court has in being the final arbiter of which laws are constitutional and which are not. In this role, the Supreme Court becomes the ultimate maker of law. In the famous case of *Marbury v. Madison* (1803) the Court considered whether it had the authority to review laws passed by the Congress—and the Court declared that it did. Some argue that by so doing, the U.S. Supreme Court has become the de facto ultimate lawmaking body in our country. So it becomes very important to political leaders to have justices on that bench whose ideologies are in accord with theirs. Politics does play a very real part in interpreting laws.

The Constitution works because those who wrote it more than 200 years ago provided only basic tenets, leaving the challenge of interpreting them as they relate to *current* issues. For example, free speech issues are decidedly different today than two centuries ago—but the basic idea remains. The Fourth, Fifth and Sixth Amendments still guide government investigations, but such matters as the use of very sophisticated electronic eavesdropping and computer equipment now become an issue.

Thus it is how people *interpret* the Constitution that can cause confusion. For all who are certain how the Constitution should be read (in their favor, of course), others are just as sure it should be interpreted differently. And today's issues of abortion, gun control and the environment *beg* for interpretation, flip-flopping back and forth, up and down, through our legal system, always searching for a final interpretation. Most often, the U.S. Supreme Court, as the final arbiter of law, tells us what the interpretation is—until the Court makes a change itself. Or until another case with a slightly different twist than previous cases is decided differently.

Before you look ahead, it is important to take time to reflect on the past. History seems to be an accurate predictor of the future, as it has a unique way of repeating itself. Yet history is often overlooked. That is why this text starts with a brief, but important, review of what led up to the U.S. Constitution, re-establishing the foundation on which the subsequent information neatly rests and making the study of the Constitution logical, perhaps even enjoyable. This point is reinforced by two statues positioned at the rear exit of the National Archives in Washington, DC. Most visitors would never see these imposing statues unless they went out the wrong door. Those who do so may stop to look around to get their bearings and see the crucial advice of these statues, one of which is shown on page 3.

A review of the historical evolution of the Constitution is important in developing not only a basic working knowledge of it, but also in learning to critically review how the Constitution plays into modern society and how it will shape our future. This section begins with a discussion of the events leading up to the drafting of the U.S. Constitution and a broad overview of the Constitution and the Bill of Rights (Chapter 1). This is followed by an overview of our legal system (Chapter 2), including the system as it exists at both the state and federal levels. Next an up-close look at the Supreme Court—the highest court in the land—is presented (Chapter 3). The section concludes with an explanation of how to find the law and the resources available (Chapter 4). The remainder of the text focuses on the amendments making up the Bill of Rights and how they have evolved during the past two centuries.

CHAPTER 1

An Historical Overview

GIVE ME LIBERTY, OR GIVE ME DEATH!
—PATRICK HENRY

What is past is prologue.

Courtesy of J. Scott Harr

DO YOU KNOW . . .

- What law is?
- What the Mayflower Compact was?
- What pluralism contributes to our society?
- Which empires were vying for control over territories in North America that led to bloody confrontations?
- Why American colonists rebelled at Great Britain's taxes?
- What the Boston Tea Party symbolized?
- What resulted from the First Continental Congress? The Second Continental Congress?
- What the Declaration of Independence is?
- What the Articles of Confederation were?
- What the Magna Carta is?
- What important role the Magna Carta played in framing the U.S. Constitution?
- What the primary purpose of the Constitution is? How it is achieved?
- What the first three articles of the Constitution accomplished?
- How the balance of power was established?
- What the supremacy clause established?
- When and where the Constitution was signed?
- Who the Federalists were? The Anti-Federalists?
- Why some states were reluctant to accept the Constitution?
- What the Bill of Rights is and how it was included with the Constitution?
- What serious omission occurred in the Bill of Rights?
- Where the Constitution and the Bill of Rights are housed?

CAN YOU DEFINE?

amendments	Federalists	Patriot
Anti-Federalists	Great Compromise	pluralism
charters	law	Quartering Act
compacts	Loyalist	ratify
constitution	Mayflower Compact	Stamp Act
constitutionalism	minutemen	supremacy clause

Introduction

It has been said that the best way to know where you are going is to look where you have been. As discussed in the introduction to this section, constitutional law can become complicated. Any endeavor becomes easier, however, if a firm base is established from which to proceed. This is why the historical evolution of the Constitution is the best place to start. This history helps you develop a working knowledge of the Constitution and an ability to critically review how it plays into modern society and will shape the future.

Although you might think an historical review is unnecessary, or that you took a wrong turn when opening a Con Law text to begin reading about the colonists, you should gain some important insights. By looking back, events become more focused. So start your study of constitutional law at the logical point: *the beginning*. Because what is past is prologue.

This chapter begins with a discussion of the roots of the U.S. Constitution and contributions from the past. This is followed by an examination of how the United States of America developed, including the convening of the First Continental Congress. Next, the Revolution itself is described, including the convening of the Second Continental Congress, which resulted in the Declaration of Independence. Then, the Articles of Confederation, which established the first model for the U.S. government and the move toward the Constitution, are described. This is followed by the development of the Constitution, the debates that occurred, the ratification process and the addition of the Bill of Rights. The chapter concludes with a discussion of the Constitution, including the Bill of Rights, as a living law, and where the Constitution and Bill of Rights are currently archived.

Where It All Began

A **constitution** is a system of basic laws and principles that establish the nature, functions and limits of a government or other institution. The American Constitution (always written with a capital "C") is youthful, which makes it all the more impressive. Consider other nations that rely on many more centuries, even thousands of years, of tradition and law that has been fine-tuned to serve them. And although our Constitution may be young, the history that influenced it can be traced back to when people first began forming groups throughout the world.

constitution • a system of basic laws and principles that establish the nature, functions and limits of a government or other institution

Recognize that every culture that has made its way to America has been influenced by other cultures, and all of these have contributed to the uniqueness of American law. Rules that become laws are a part of any society.

> ■ **Law** is a body of rules promulgated (established) to support the norms of that society, enforced through legal means, that is, punishment.

law • a body of rules promulgated (established) to support the norms of a society, enforced through legal means, that is, punishment

The laws that the framers of our Constitution were familiar with, many of which served them well, helped form what would become the new law of the new country. American law continues to be influenced by all law that preceded it, including that of many other cultures. The land that now comprises North America has always held an attraction. As long ago as 30,000 B.C., people began traversing the continent to seek something that held the promise of more than they had. And whether the motivations for these incredible journeys were as basic as food or as complicated as a search for political and religious freedoms, people came hoping for something better. This basic desire to seek out something more is the essence of the individuals who have contributed to the society that now exists.

Contributions from the Past

Compared with the series of events that have contributed to and led up to the drafting of the Constitution, American law is young. But its history cannot be ignored, as this is the base on which our law has been constructed. The earliest visitors to North America left their mark, which archaeologists study to better understand social and cultural development. Similarly, by investigating the events that have led to our present laws, you are better able to understand both how and why we have the laws we do.

When the pilgrims first came to America, they realized they needed to band together for their own security, so even before landing, as the ship *Mayflower* was anchored off Cape Cod, Massachusetts, 41 male adults aboard the ship signed the Mayflower Compact.

The Mayflower Compact

■ The **Mayflower Compact** was a written agreement for self-government signed in 1620.

Mayflower Compact • signed on November 11, 1620, by 41 passengers aboard *The Mayflower,* this document is considered to be the first formal document by the Pilgrims establishing a self-determining government upon arriving in the area of New England

This document was the colonists' first attempt at self-government. According to Gundersen (2003), the original compact has disappeared. However, a version of the compact is contained in *Of Plymoth Plantation,* written between 1630 and 1651 by William Bradford, second governor of the colony, following the spelling and punctuation of the period:

> In ye name of God Amen. We whose names are underwritten, the loyall subjects of our dread soveraigne Lord King James, . . . having undertaken, for ye glorie of God, and advancements of ye Christian faith and honour of our King & countries, a voyage to plant ye first colnie in ye Northerne parts of Virginia, doe by these presents solemnly & mutually in ye presence of God, and one of another, covenant, & combine ourselves togeather into a Civill body politick; for our better ordering, & preservation & furtherance of ye ends aforesaid.

The Great Melting Pot

Representatives from every culture that has come to America, regardless of when they arrived or where they came from, share in the historical development of our country and legal system. It is the common thread that binds all who have come here—the desire for something better—that makes American law so unique in serving the pluralistic society that created it.

■ **Pluralism** refers to a society in which numerous distinct ethnic, religious or cultural groups coexist within one nation, each contributing to the society as a whole.

pluralism • a society in which numerous distinct ethnic, religious or cultural groups coexist within one nation, each contributing to the society as a whole

Before the colonization of the United States, the Native-American tribes had their distinct territories, languages and cultures. Pluralism existed long before the colonists "discovered" America. When the colonists arrived and began taking over the land occupied by the Native Americans, the Native Americans began to band together in self-defense.

The colonists came from various countries and were of varied religions and cultures. Initially they settled in specific areas and maintained their original culture, for example, the Pennsylvania Dutch. They, too, represented pluralism.

A pluralistic society challenged the colonists to exercise tolerance and respect for the opinions, customs, traditions and lifestyles of others. Their diversity enriched early American life and strengthened the emerging nation. Often, the distinct culture within a given colony influenced other colonies. For example, in 1682 William Penn, a Quaker and founder of Pennsylvania, set forth the "Great Law of Pennsylvania," abolishing corporal punishment, introducing fines and founding the first penitentiary—"dedicated to God." Penn's great law significantly influenced the development of corrections in America. As more and more individuals inhabited North America, they were forced by necessity to interact. Established Native-American cultures interacted with very foreign ways of life, and people became aware that there were different ways of developing a system for their lives. The following list shows the ethnic population of the colonies in 1775 by percentage:

48.7 English	2.7 Dutch
20.0 African (slaves)	1.4 French
7.8 Scots-Irish	0.6 Swedish
6.9 German	5.3 Other
6.6 Scottish	(Armento et al., 1991, p. 49)

Cultural and ethnic diversity has always been an attribute of America, with a rich blend in the 1700s. Interestingly, the Native Americans are absent from this chart because they were not considered part of the colonies. Also of interest is the 20 percent African population, slaves brought to this country primarily to labor on Southern plantations.

In many Southern states, slaves outnumbered the colonists. For example, in 1720 South Carolina's population was 30 percent white and 70 percent black (Simmons, 1976, p. 125). Concerned over the dangers the oppressed slaves could create, some of the first new laws colonists wrote were slave laws. Most Southern colonies not only established a special code of laws to regulate the slaves, they also established special enforcement officers, known as slave patrols, to assure that these laws were obeyed unquestioningly.

While Native Americans and African Americans are not always given the recognition they are due, they, too, have played an important part in the development of America. In 1775, three large groups coexisted in the United States: the Native Americans, the African slaves and the colonists. The history of the United States, however, has generally focused on only the colonists.

Over time, interaction and, eventually, assimilation occurred among the colonists, commonly referred to as a "melting pot" because several different nationalities combined into what was known as "the American colonist." Such assimilation was encouraged by the vast, apparently unlimited resources available, as well as by the struggle for survival. Colonists faced the threat of foreign countries wishing to control them, the dangers posed by the Native Americans they were displacing and the often rebellious slaves in the South. Therefore, it was natural that they should band together. As noted by Miller and Hess (2005, p. 145):

> The "melting pot" was accomplished relatively painlessly because of the many similarities among the colonists. They looked quite similar physically, they valued religion and "morality," most valued hard work, and, perhaps most important, there was plenty of land for everyone. The "homogenization" of the United States was fairly well accomplished . . . with the formerly distinct cultures blended into what became known as an American culture.

The colonists with the most wealth and power, white male property holders, were sometimes referred to as a "seaboard aristocracy." They created the basic structure of our country as it still exists in the twenty-first century.

Colonies developed and organized in unique ways. The emerging nation saw different priorities and different norms. Some colonies banded together for security in ways not unlike modern businesses. Massachusetts Bay and Virginia,

charters • businesslike agreements to establish a cooperative government

compacts • documents with primarily a religious purpose in establishing how a community or colony chooses to govern itself

for example, entered into businesslike agreements, or **charters,** establishing cooperative government. Virginia was founded in 1607 by the Virginia Company of London, under a grant from the English government. The establishment of Massachusetts Bay was influenced by Puritan beliefs reflecting the role of religion in that community's organization. Other colonists entered into **compacts** with primarily a religious purpose in establishing how they chose to govern themselves, as was the case with Plymouth, Rhode Island, Connecticut and New Haven.

Regardless of how unique the states were allowed, in fact encouraged and demanded, to be, it was undeniable that benefits remained in working *together* rather than *separately.* A fragmented beginning was developing into a single nation. The terms *liberty* and *limited government* were ideals that compelled all that was necessary for establishing a new country. (Imagine the complexities of creating a new household, a new business, a new community, but a new *country?* It almost defies the imagination.) But what did these terms mean, and how could a new country be effectively governed for the good of all while ensuring individual liberty and limited government? The task was daunting, but the promise of what could be was highly motivating.

Levy and Mahoney (1987, p. 35) explain how this new country was forging the law to come: "To keep government limited—that is, to remain a constitutional society, Americans took sovereignty away from government and lodged it with the people . . . with separation of powers. Because the people, rather than government at any level, must be sovereign, they can delegate some powers to their state governments and others to a national government."

Development of the United States of America

Despite the colonists' desire for freedom, America was viewed as an attractive area for expansion by the world powers.

◼ In addition to others, Spain, France and England saw great importance in adding the "New World" to their growing empires.

This desire for existing nations to make America a part of their government planted the tiny seed of what was to grow into independence. Just as Native Americans had seen their freedom threatened by the colonists and the African-American slaves had been stripped of their freedom, the colonists realized their freedom was in jeopardy from abroad.

The independence of the colonists in America, particularly at that time, established an identity that has made America a world leader. Americans were not willing to sit idly by while those asserting power attempted to coerce them into submission. When the colonies were confronted with attempts, primarily by Great Britain, Spain and France, to consume and control the New World, resistance grew, exemplifying the spirit associated with the United States.

Colonial Dissension Grows

As the colonies' populations began to grow, so did serious differences between those who saw themselves as free, independent colonies and those who wanted to fly a foreign flag over them. As existing empires positioned themselves politically and militaristically to expand their boundaries into the New World, conflict was inevitable.

In 1750, French troops began arriving from Canada, building forts and laying claim to land that Native Americans were occupying and that England was eyeing. This competition between the British and the French was part of a larger, general European conflict—the Seven Years War. A showdown eventually occurred in 1754, when British leaders ordered the Virginia governor to forcibly repel the French. George Washington and about 150 colonists marched against the French. By 1763, after the French and Indian War (1755–1763), French resistance was defeated, and the Treaty of Paris resulted in France losing most of the land it had claimed in America. But British problems were far from resolved.

Great Britain confronted two significant problems, the first being continued westward settlement by the colonists (Divine et al., 1991, p. 42). This was problematic for Great Britain because the Native-American tribes fought to protect their land from the colonists, and the British army was not able to protect the isolated frontier settlements. Nearly 2,000 colonial men, women and children died during Pontiac's Rebellion. In December 1763, British and colonial troops finally crushed the Native American's defense of their territory. When King George III learned of the fighting, he issued the Proclamation of 1763, closing the western frontier to colonial settlement and placing it under military rule. Settlers already there were ordered to leave.

The second major problem facing Great Britain was the huge debt resulting from English military action to expand the empire. The British Parliament felt the colonists should share this debt. The colonies resisted the restrictions to westward settlement and to paying for Great Britain's war debts. Significant leaders began emerging, including George Washington, Benjamin Franklin, Paul Revere and Thomas Jefferson. These leaders had found strength in cooperating to resist the French. Now the resistance was redirected toward Parliament's efforts to control America.

Because Parliament thought it only fair that the American colonies share in the expenses incurred, they passed acts to collect money from the colonists. In 1765, Parliament passed the **Stamp Act,** requiring stamps to be purchased and placed on legal documents such as marriage licenses and wills, as well as several commodities, including playing cards, dice, newspapers and calendars.

Stamp Act • passed by Parliament in 1765, it required stamps to be purchased and placed on legal documents such as marriage licenses and wills, and several commodities, including playing cards, dice, newspapers and calendars

■   The colonists resisted increased taxes because they felt it was taxation without representation.

Further resentment grew when, in 1765, Parliament passed the **Quartering Act,** which required colonists to feed and shelter British troops in America. The colonists abhorred the demands on them to shelter and feed the 10,000 British troops. Protests against the increasing British attempts to rule the colonies intensified, but demands that Parliament repeal these laws were rejected. Objections to the Quartering Act found their way into the Third Amendment. In addition, when the king's troops marched out of Boston on their way to Lexington and Concord, they were searching for munitions; hence the Second Amendment, as discussed shortly.

Quartering Act • passed by Parliament in 1765, requiring colonists to feed and shelter British troops in America

In 1766, the Stamp Act was finally repealed but was replaced by other taxes on commodities the colonists needed to import from England. New York resisted the Quartering Act, and Parliament again found itself trying to rule from abroad.

It was not working. Dissension increased, as did tensions between the colonists and the British soldiers sent to enforce Parliament's demands.

Finally, in 1770, after 4,000 armed British troops had come to Boston from Nova Scotia and Ireland, colonists began taunting British soldiers and throwing snowballs and ice at them. The soldiers fired on these colonists in what became known as the Boston Massacre. Attempting to quell the volatile situation, Parliament eventually repealed most of the taxes and duties, except those on tea. For both sides, this remaining tax was a symbol of British rule over the colonies. In December 1773, disguised as Native Americans, colonists boarded three British ships in Boston Harbor and dumped the cargos of tea overboard.

■ The Boston Tea Party, in which colonists boarded British ships and threw their cargos of tea in the harbor, represented the colonists' unwillingness to pay taxes without representation.

As a result of the tea dumping, Parliament passed several laws in retaliation for such an open act of defiance, including the following:

- Town meetings were restricted to one a year.
- The king was required to appoint people to the governmental court rather than have them elected.
- The Quartering Act was expanded, requiring soldiers to be housed in private homes and buildings (which seemed like spying to the colonists).
- British officials accused of crimes in the colonies were permitted to be tried in England, away from angry American colonists.

Again the colonists were not complacent. They met to address the situation.

The First Continental Congress

In September 1774, 55 delegates from 12 colonies met in Philadelphia to address their mounting complaints against Great Britain. At this First Continental Congress, such leaders as Samuel Adams and Patrick Henry resolved to resist British rule.

■ The First Continental Congress resulted in the first written agreement among the colonies to stand together in resistance against Britain.

The Congress agreed on three important actions. First, they adopted a set of resolutions defining the rights, liberties and immunities of the colonists and listing actions of the British government that violated these rights. Second, they drew up an address to King George III and another to the citizens of Britain, presenting American grievances and calling for a restoration of American rights. Third, they called for each community to establish a boycott committee to prevent colonists from buying British goods until the Congress' demands were met. In general, someone who bought British goods was branded a **Loyalist** or Tory. One who supported the boycott was called a **Patriot** or rebel.

The Tension Mounts

By the beginning of 1775, the colonies were actively preparing for what many saw would be an inevitable confrontation with the British. **Minutemen,** the name given to the colonial soldiers, were drilled and equipped to respond at a minute's notice to protect American lives, property and rights. In March 1775, Patrick Henry delivered his famous plea for freedom:

Sir, we have done everything that could be done to avert the storm which is now coming on. We have petitioned; we have remonstrated; we have

Loyalist • a colonist who did not support the boycott of British goods in the colonies and who still paid allegiance to the British monarchy

Patriot • a colonist who supported the boycott of British goods in the colonies and who owed allegiance to America rather than to the British monarchy

supplicated; we have prostrated ourselves before the throne and have implored its interposition to arrest the tyrannical hands of the Ministry and Parliament. Our petitions have been slighted; our remonstrances have produced additional violence and insult; our supplications have been disregarded; and we have been spurned, with contempt, from the foot of the throne. In vain, after these things, may we indulge the fond hope of peace and reconciliation.

There is no longer any room for hope. If we wish to be free; if we mean to preserve inviolate those inestimable privileges for which we have been so long contending; if we mean, not basely to abandon the noble struggle in which we have been so long engaged, and which we have pledged ourselves never to abandon, until the glorious object of our contest shall be obtained; we must fight! I repeat it, sir, we must fight!! . . . It is vain, sir, to extenuate the matter. Gentlemen may cry, peace, peace; but there is no peace. The war is actually begun! The next gale that sweeps from the north will bring to our ears the clash of resounding arms! Our brethren are already in the field! Why stand we here idle? What is it that gentlemen wish? What would they have? Is life so dear or peace so sweet as to be purchased at the price of chains and slavery?

Forbid it, Almighty God—I know not what course others may take, but as for me, give me liberty, or give me death! (Brown and Bass, 1990, p. 140).

The Revolution Begins

The American Revolution was led, financed and designed by and for those with social and economic power. Ironically, some African-American slaves joined the fight for freedom. With tensions at their flash point, **minutemen** in Lexington and Concord were alerted by William Dawes that the British soldiers were coming. (Paul Revere is often incorrectly credited with spreading the alert.)

minutemen • colonial soldiers

On April 19, 1775, the waiting minutemen in Lexington saw the British Redcoats approaching. Shots were exchanged, and the British killed eight Americans that morning and then moved on to Concord. Here, they were fired upon by the minutemen in a battle later immortalized by poet Ralph Waldo Emerson's "Concord Hymn":

> By the rude bridge that arched the flood,
> Their flag to April's breeze unfurled,
> Here once the embattled farmers stood
> And fired the shot heard round the world.

In a mere 25 years, the colonists had come a long way in their march toward independence. The battles at Lexington and Concord strengthened the colonists' resolve and also prompted them to meet again to determine how to proceed.

The Second Continental Congress

In 1775 the Second Continental Congress convened in Philadelphia.

■ The Second Continental Congress established the Continental Army and named George Washington its commander.

The Congress also made plans to raise money and buy supplies for the new army and to seek support from other countries by opening diplomatic relations with them. The colonists were now prepared for all-out war with the British.

George III denounced the American leaders as "rebels" and ordered the British military to suppress the disobedience and punish the authors of the "treacherous" resolves. The ensuing battles of Ticonderoga, Bunker Hill, Trenton and Saratoga, among others, showed the American people's commitment to fight for what they held so dear—their independence. As the war continued, prospects for a reconciliation with Great Britain dimmed.

In May, the Congress instructed each colony to form a government of its own, assuming the powers of independent states. The movement for a break with Great Britain spread upward from the colonies to the Continental Congress, with the desire for independence firmly resolved.

The Declaration of Independence

In July 1776, after arduous debate, delegates at the Second Continental Congress voted unanimously in favor of American independence. Thomas Jefferson was selected to coordinate writing the formal announcement—the Declaration of Independence. It listed the complaints the people had against Britain and justification for declaring independence.

■ On July 4, 1776, the President of the Congress signed the American Declaration of Independence, which formally severed ties with Great Britain.

This historic work consists of six important sections.

First, the opening paragraph explains why the Declaration was issued, that is, the compelling necessity for the colonists to break their political ties with Great Britain.

> When in the course of human events it becomes necessary for one people to dissolve the political bands which have connected them with another, and to assume among the powers of the earth the separate and equal station to which the laws of nature and of nature's God entitle them, a decent respect to the opinions of mankind requires that they should declare the causes which impel them to the separation.

The second paragraph, the crucial statement of the purposes of government, declares all men to be equal and to have equal claims to "life, liberty, and the pursuit of happiness."

> We hold these truths to be self-evident, that all men are created equal, that they are endowed by their Creator with certain unalienable rights, that among these are life, liberty, and the pursuit of happiness.
> No government can deny its people these rights.

This paragraph also states that a government's right to rule is based on the "consent of the governed."

> That to secure these rights, governments are instituted among men, deriving their just powers from the consent of the governed. That whenever any form of government becomes destructive to these ends, it is the right of the people

to alter or to abolish it, and to institute new government, laying its foundation on such principles and organizing its powers in such form as to them shall seem most likely to effect their safety and happiness.

Third, charges against the British king were reviewed in a long list that enumerated how the king's government had denied the American colonists their rights. Fourth, the Declaration describes the colonists' attempts to obtain justice and the British lack of response. Fifth, the last paragraph proclaimed independence.

We, therefore, the representatives of the United States of America, do, in the name, and by authority of the good people of these colonies, solemnly publish and declare, that these United colonies are, and of right ought to be free and independent states; that they are absolved from all Allegiance to the British Crown, and that all political connection between them and the State of Great Britain is, and ought to be totally dissolved.

The final paragraph also lists actions the new United States of America could take as a country. The last sentence asserts the signers' resolve to pledge their lives and everything they owned to support the cause of independence: "*And for the support of this Declaration, with a firm Reliance on the Protection of divine Providence, we mutually pledge to each other our Lives, our Fortunes, and our sacred Honor.*" The entire text of the Declaration of Independence is contained in Appendix A.

What It Cost the Signers

The men who signed the Declaration were the elite of their colonies, men of wealth and social standing. They were, indeed, risking all. To sign the Declaration of Independence was an act of treason—punishable by death. Because it was so dangerous to publicly accuse their king, the names of the signers were kept secret for six months. Although most of the 56 signers survived the war and many went on to illustrious careers, including two presidents, as well as vice presidents, senators and governors, not all were so fortunate.

Jacoby (2000, p. A11) notes that nine of the fifty-six signers died during the Revolution, never tasting American independence. Five were captured by the British. Eighteen had their great estates looted or burned by the British. Carter Braxton of Virginia, an aristocrat who invested heavily in shipping, had most of his ships captured by the British navy and his estates ruined. He became a pauper. Richard Stockton, a New Jersey supreme court judge, was betrayed by his Loyalist neighbors, dragged from his bed and imprisoned, brutally beaten and starved. His estate was devastated. Although he was released in 1777, his health was ruined, and he died within five years, leaving his family to live on charity. John Hart, the speaker of the New Jersey Assembly was forced to flee in 1776 at the age of 65 from the bedside of his dying wife. He hid in forests and caves while the British destroyed his home, fields and mill and ran off his 13 children. When he returned, his wife was dead, his children missing and his estate destroyed. He never saw his children again and died, shattered, in 1779.

Indeed, Americans owe much to those 56 signers of the Declaration of Independence. Because of their commitment to liberty, the colonists were able to move forward in establishing the foundation for their new, free country.

The Articles of Confederation

The Second Continental Congress not only acted to declare independence for America but also set about to determine how government should be developed. Richard Henry Lee, the delegate who made the resolution for America to be independent, encouraged a confederation of independent states.

In 1777, the delegates to the Second Continental Congress agreed, and the Articles of Confederation created a governmental model for this new country. The 13 states were cherishing their independence and resisted agreeing to a single government of any kind. The tension over whether to secede from Great Britain in the first place, both for fear of the Crown's power and fear of the unknown, was replaced with a new tension. Once the break was made, might not a new government be even worse? Might they create a monster? Could any single government meet their needs? The colonists' solution was a confederation of independent states.

■   The Articles of Confederation formally pledged the states to "a firm league of friendship," and "a perpetual union" created for "their common defense, the security of their liberties" and their "mutual and general welfare."

These Articles were important because after they were approved in 1781, the duties of government were divided among the states and the government. During the eight years that America operated under them, great strides were made toward unifying a group of states that had, by their own desire, become separate. And although the inadequacies of this document eventually led to the Constitution itself, the Articles of Confederation were an important steppingstone. The Articles established a congress to conduct the necessary tasks of a central government, including waging war and making peace, controlling trade with the Indians, organizing a mail service and borrowing money.

Reflection on the reasons for the events that led up to this point can easily explain why this preliminary attempt to establish a federal government left Congress with much weaker powers than would eventually be established. *The founders feared a concentrated, centralized political power.* Therefore, Congress was *not* empowered to

■   Regulate trade—internally or externally.
■   Levy taxes. They could ask but could not compel.
■   Draft soldiers. Again, they could ask but could not compel.
■   Establish a court system.
■   Regulate money.

Nevertheless, Benjamin Franklin commented: "Americans are on the right road to improvement [with the Articles of Confederation], for we are making experiments." George Washington, however, cautioned that the Articles did not have the necessary strength to run a new country, and as the Confederation stood, it was little more than the "shadow without the substance."

The colonists were faced with the formidable task of governing themselves and holding together their agreed-upon union. As noted by Beard and Beard (1968, p. 123): "No longer could disputes within and between colonies be carried to London for settlement. No longer did loyalty to the British King or the need for common action in the war against him constitute a unifying principle for Americans."

Loyalists, who had opposed the Revolution, called for re-establishing a monarchy for America. Others called for a military dictatorship. The need for some sort of strong leadership became more apparent as complaints against state governments grew in number and strength. In some states, such as Massachusetts, the right to vote was restricted to property owners and taxpayers. Creditors could sue debtors and take property away from farmers who could not pay what they owed. In 1786, a band of debt-burdened farmers in Massachusetts was led by Captain Daniel Shays in an attempt to shut down the courts through armed force, as described by Beard and Beard (p. 125):

> It was only with difficulty and some bloodshed that the state government put down "Shays' Rebellion." Even then popular sympathies with the uprising remained so strong that the state officials did not dare to execute Shays or any of his followers. Whatever the merits of this popular revolt, it increased the fears of property owners and conservatives in general, inciting them to work harder than ever for a powerful national government.

According to Woodard: "Shays' Rebellion is one of the most important catalysts, if not the most important, in bringing about the Constitution." The rebellion reflects the impact of individuals in forging the shape of their government. Another strong influence came from England—the Magna Carta.

The Influence of the Magna Carta

The U.S. Constitution has important ties to what is perhaps the most important instrument of English government—the Magna Carta. This document, which King John was forced to sign on June 12, 1215, ensured feudal rights and guaranteed that the king could not put himself above the law.

■ The Magna Carta established the supremacy of the law over the ruler and guaranteed English feudal barons individual rights and "due process of law," including trial by jury.

The British, to this day, have never operated their government under a centralized "constitution." Rather, they work under tradition, and at the heart of that tradition is the historic Magna Carta, guaranteeing, among other things, basic due process.

The Influence of English and French Philosophers

Thomas Hobbes (1588–1679), an English philosopher and political theorist, was a leading figure of eighteenth century Enlightenment. He and John Locke (1632–1704), another English philosopher, argued over the size and scope of government and who should run it. Locke believed that common people had the capacity to govern themselves. During the Age of Enlightenment, when philosophers started to ask whether certain universal truths existed outside of science, Locke wrote that certain truths such as "life, liberty and property" should be paramount. He would greatly influence Jefferson, an anti-Federalist. Hobbes, on the other hand, believed that for government to work, it needed to be centralized like a monarchy. Hobbes would influence Hamilton, a Federalist.

The British government established a tripartite balance of power between Sovereign, Lords and Commons. This tripartite balance was praised by French historian and philosopher Charles Louis de Secondat, Baron de la Brede et de

Montesquieu (1689–1755). Montesquieu's most influential work, *The Spirit of the Laws* (1748), was a scientific study that compared various forms of government. Montesquieu wrote that the British subjects' sense of liberty, as well as their feelings of safety and security, sprang from separating governmental powers into three parts with the king holding only executive power, Parliament alone being able to make laws and the judiciary functioning independently of them both. This tripartite division of power and Montesquieu's theory of checks and balances found their way into the U.S. Constitution.

Another French philosopher and writer, François-Marie Arouet Voltaire (1694–1778), spent two imprisonments in the French Bastille (1717 and 1726), which fostered a hatred of arbitrary absolutism and an admiration for English liberalism. Voltaire wrote, "I may disagree with what you say, but I defend to the death your right to say it," an obvious influence on the First Amendment freedom of speech.

The 1787 Convention of Delegates—A Move toward the Constitution

Those who came to America in 1620 and their descendants, through the American Revolution, ultimately rejected rule under the British Crown and what it had come to symbolize. Nonetheless, present-day American law has deep roots in what Great Britain had established as a legal system. This explains the importance of continuity of law. Consistency must run through all law to develop predictability. The framers of our Constitution sought to develop such a format that would guarantee the continuation of basic rights as specific law developed.

■ Americans continued to believe in the principles contained in the Magna Carta, which was a precedent for democratic government and individual rights, as well as the foundation for requiring rulers to uphold the law. It greatly influenced the writers of the U.S. Constitution.

At least some stability in life is assured by holding on to our past. And although the colonists rejected British rule, they recognized that a document such as the Magna Carta provided a stable framework from which to start. First, the Magna Carta was a step away from total rule by a single individual. Second, it had a fairly long history of success by the time the New World began to receive visitors from abroad seeking to colonize. And finally, it provided some security in that not everything needed to start from scratch.

For some 20 years, the British Magna Carta significantly influenced the development of other documents drafted in response to colonists' ever-growing desires for fairer treatment by their government. The revision of the Articles of Confederation was one such example.

The Articles of Confederation had established "a firm league of friendship" between the states. However, they were inadequate as the foundation for effective government because they lacked a balance of power between the states and the central government. Therefore, in 1787, the Congress of the Confederation called for a convention of delegates from the original states to meet in Philadelphia to revise the Articles of Confederation.

During the convention, what might be considered a political revolution occurred, changing the form of government created during the violence of the break with England to a true union. It was a long, arduous process with much conflict and debate. One primary debate was between those who favored holding on to tradition and those who advocated a complete break with the past.

George Mason, who wrote the Virginia Declaration of Rights, recognized the importance of basing the new American government on tradition. Mason expressed his position by saying that there would be much difficulty in organizing a government on this great scale and at the same time reserving to the state legislatures a sufficient portion of power to promote and secure the prosperity and happiness of their respective citizens (Atherton and Barlow, no date, p. 2).

Mason sought to lean upon the traditions established by the Magna Carta because of the fundamental rights that should not be threatened regardless of what government or governments would come and go in the United States. He advocated using the Magna Carta as a single stabilizing force in the growth of this country: "No free government, or the blessings of liberty, can be preserved to any people, but . . . by frequent recurrence to fundamental principles" (Atherton and Barlow, p. 2).

George Mason and James Madison, both delegates from Virginia, had significant roles in shaping the direction of the new Constitution. Their views combined an anchor for stability from the past encouraged by Mason with a vision of the future provided by Madison. Clearly evident, even in the yearning this country had to be new and independent, was the fact that connections with the past cannot be discounted (Atherton and Barlow, pp. 2–7). Again, continuity and predictability provided security, and security was what our ancestors were thirsting for.

In May 1787, delegates to the Constitutional Convention met at Independence Hall in Philadelphia. George Washington was elected to preside over the meetings. The public was not permitted in the meetings so the delegates could speak more freely. Arduous debate occurred during this Constitutional Convention. The summer of 1787 was one of record heat, and because of the standard dress of the day, the framers worked for only a few hours in the mornings. Afternoons were filled with much camaraderie and imbibing of favorite beverages.

The delegates decided how many votes each state would have and that a new document was preferable to merely amending the Articles of Confederation. The challenge of drafting the Constitution began.

■ The purpose of the Constitution was to establish a central government authorized to deal directly with individuals rather than states and to incorporate a system of checks and balances that would preserve the fundamental concepts contained in the Magna Carta, that is, to limit the power of the government.

Bearing in mind the combined difficulties of communication and travel, the willingness and persistence of the delegates who gathered to shape what was to become the Constitution speaks directly to their need for such a tool. For without it, even the most revered and capable politicians and leaders of the time would have been doomed to failure. Instead, the most incredible chapter of U.S. history was slowly being opened.

The Constitution Takes Shape

It can be difficult to grasp all that lies behind the Constitution unless one keeps in mind the underlying reason for the Constitution, that is, to provide a system of government that would prevent one individual from having complete power.

Understandably, such a system would, of necessity, have complexities built in to achieve such a lofty goal, but the basic reasoning is simple.

Issues that became prominent were the structure and powers of Congress, of the executive branch and of the judicial system. What was sought was an array of checks and balances that would allow the system to work, while achieving the primary goal of limiting power to any individual or section of the government.

The delegates at the Constitutional Convention, who came from varied backgrounds, rose to the challenge. Individual power was never their objective, but rather societal cohesiveness and democratic power to achieve... "one nation, with liberty and justice for all." The delegates who would help make the Constitution came that year with differing views, but all were advocates of **constitutionalism.** That is, they believed in a government in which power is distributed and limited by a system of laws that must be obeyed by those who rule. According to that principle, constitutions are a system of fundamental laws and principles that prescribe the nature, functions and limits of a government or other body. Constitutions are distinguished from ordinary acts of legislation in that they are drafted by special assemblages and ratified by special conventions chosen by the people. A constitution is supreme law, not to be annulled by legislation. Constitutionalism is one of the most original, distinctive contributions of the American system of government.

Like those who wrote the Articles of Confederation, the framers of the Constitution recognized that the people are the power. The delegates to the First Continental Congress in Philadelphia had been selected by the people of the colonies, not by existing colonial governments. Likewise, the delegates to the Constitutional Convention represented the people.

All states except Rhode Island were represented at the Constitutional Convention, which met at the State House in Philadelphia from May 25 to September 15, 1787. The 55 delegates included many of the most influential men in the country. Eight had signed the Declaration of Independence, seven were governors of their states and 39 were Congressmen. More than half were college graduates, and at least one-third were lawyers. Most held prominent positions in the Revolutionary War, and all were highly respected property owners of substance.

Although unanimously elected president, George Washington took a limited but effective role in the deliberations. Of greatest influence were Governor Morris and James Wilson of Pennsylvania, James Madison of Virginia and Roger Sherman of Connecticut, each speaking more than 100 times.

Despite some talk of the larger states getting more votes than the smaller states, the Convention followed the procedures used to develop the Articles of Confederation, giving each state one vote, with seven states constituting a quorum.

Any vote could be reconsidered, as many were during the convention. The convention was also governed by a rule of secrecy, requiring that nothing said during the deliberations be printed, published or otherwise communicated without permission. Such secrecy was vital to unbiased discussion and to prevent rumors and misconceptions. The official journal was closed until 1819.

The Convention first debated the Virginia resolution, calling for a national government with a bicameral legislature, an executive and a judiciary branch. The smaller states, however, backed the New Jersey Plan, calling for only modest revisions in the Articles of Confederation. In addition, the larger states supported representation proportional to a state's population, while the smaller states wanted one or two votes per state. A threatened deadlock was averted by the

constitutionalism • a belief in a government in which power is distributed and limited by a system of laws that must be obeyed by those who rule

Great Compromise, which gave each state an equal vote in the Senate and a proportionate vote in the House.

Great Compromise • the agreement reached in drafting the Constitution giving each state an equal vote in the Senate and a proportionate vote in the House

After lengthy debate, the delegates also decided to strengthen the central government and to clearly define federal powers. All other powers were entrusted to the individual states and to the people. Specifically, the country was to be governed by a president to be chosen by electors in each state, a national judiciary and a two-chamber legislature. The House of Representatives was to be popularly elected. The Senate, however, which shared certain executive powers with the president, was to be chosen by individual state legislatures. Under the Great Compromise between the large and small states, representation in the House was to be proportional to a state's population; in the Senate each state was to have two votes. The national plan for government agreed to by the Convention delegates clearly separated the powers of the three branches of government and created a system of checks and balances among these three branches, as well as between the federal and state governments and the people both were to serve.

James Madison explained the delicate relationship between the federal and state governments and the division of power within the system (*The Federalist*):

> In the compound republic of America, the power surrendered by the people is first divided between two distinct governments, and then the portion allotted to each subdivided among distinct and separate departments. Hence a double security arises to the rights of people. The different governments will control each other at the same time that each will be controlled by itself.

The Issue of Slavery

The issue of slavery was omitted during the constitutional debates. Although none of the framers knew whether this radical document would be ratified, they knew it would have zero chance of getting southern ratification if it dealt with the slavery issue. At the time, slavery was on its way out in many states. Some plantation owners in the South had their doubts about slavery as well. It was not until Eli Whitney's invention of the cotton gin six years later that the demand for slaves greatly increased. As Thomas Jefferson said, "Slavery is like holding a wolf by its ears. You don't like it, but you're afraid to let it go." The Tenth Amendment, by default, left the slavery issue up to each state. This omission from the Constitution, and indirectly the failure to compromise, would lead to civil war.

Drafting the Constitution

After all issues had been debated and agreement reached, a committee was formed to draft the Constitution based on those agreements. On Tuesday, August 7, 1787, a draft Constitution was ready for a clause-by-clause review (Armento et al., p. 140). After four months, what had developed is nothing short of amazing. The material was old, connected back to the Magna Carta, but it was new—with some rather brilliant concepts. It was the brainchild of a relatively select few, but if it were to work, it had to be accepted by all. The task was monumental, as was noted by Mitchell (1986, pp. 1–2):

> In the Constitution that emerged from these deliberations, the concept of government by consent of the governed formed the basic principle; accountability was the watchword. The rights of the people were to be protected by diffusing power among rival interests.

The final document was put before the Convention on September 17. Following are the provisions of the articles contained in the final draft of the Constitution.

The Constitution of the United States: An Overview

Descriptions of the debates that forged the Constitution during the summer of 1787 in Philadelphia are fascinating, and this is certainly worthwhile reading for those who wish to pursue it further. The following condensation describes the results of those debates—the articles contained in the final draft of the Constitution (Lieberman, 1976, pp. 33–41).

The Constitution is both a structure for government and a set of principles, a method for making law and a law itself. Of all the principles in this 7,000-word document, the single most important principle is that the government has been delegated its powers by the people. The government is not superior to them; its powers come only from them.

■ The first three articles of the Constitution establish the legislative, executive and judicial branches of government and the country's system of checks and balances.

Article 1—The Legislative Branch

Article 1 establishes the legislature: "All legislative Powers herein granted shall be vested in a Congress of the United States." This legislature may pass laws, but it has no power to enforce or interpret them. This article contains the Great Compromise. Congress has two chambers, a Senate and the House of Representatives, each acting as a check against the other. Senators are chosen by each state's legislature, with each state having two senators, and each senator having one vote. (Senators are no longer chosen by state legislatures.)

Membership in the House is based on state populations. The House has the "Power of Impeachment," the Senate the "sole Power to try all Impeachments." The House and Senate determine their own rules of procedure and conduct. They publish a journal, the *Congressional Record*, containing discussion, debate and a record of the members' votes.

Laws of the United States—in the form of bills—may originate in either house. The sole exception is that only the House of Representatives may first consider "bills for raising revenue." The cry "no taxation without representation" was still strong. Only the popular body, the house representing the people, was given the power to initiate taxes.

All bills must clear three hurdles before they can become laws. They first must pass each house in identical form and then meet the approval of the president. The president has the power to veto, but Congress, in turn, can override that veto if each house, by a two-thirds vote, chooses to do so.

Section 8 of Article 1 grants specific powers to Congress, including coining money and establishing post offices, as well as the power to

■ Lay and collect taxes.
■ Borrow money on the credit of the United States.
■ Regulate international and interstate commerce.
■ Naturalize foreign-born citizens.
■ Raise and govern the military forces.
■ Declare war.

In what has come to be known as the "elastic clause," Congress also was given the power "to make all Laws which shall be necessary and proper for carrying into effect the foregoing Powers, and all other Powers vested by this Constitution in the Government of the United States, or in any Department or Officer thereof." In other words, Congress was granted an enormous potential reserve of power to do what was "necessary and proper" to pass laws for the nation. For the first time, the new Congress could do what the old Congress could not: enact laws that directly affected the people.

The Supreme Court addressed the necessary and proper clause in *McCulloch v. Maryland* (1819), establishing the authority of the federal government to address national issues. Historically, the clause caused considerable debate because of concern that it was too open-ended and could lead to excessive federal authority. However, the need to permit Congress to make necessary laws and carry out their enumerated powers was acknowledged in *McCulloch v. Maryland*. This need to allow Congress to pass necessary and proper laws was later reinforced in *Kinsella v. Singleton* (1960). In this case, the clause was not considered a grant of federal power, but a declaration that Congress does possess the means needed to carry out its authority as set forth in the Constitution to run the country by enacting laws that are necessary and proper.

Article 1 is just one building block of our national government. Like the other Articles and the Bill of Rights, none are exclusive and, in fact, work together to prevent any one branch of government from having excessive or exclusive power. For example, Article 1 provides that if a public official is to be removed from office, both the House of Representatives and Senate are involved. In the case of *Nixon v. United States* (1993), a challenge was brought regarding these procedures by the impeached judge. Becoming involved in this case but not usurping congressional authority, Chief Justice Rehnquist wrote: "Judicial involvement in impeachment proceedings...would eviscerate the 'important constitutional check' placed on the Judiciary by the Framers." Although Congress is a powerful element of American law, it remains but one component required to lawfully interact with the others.

Article 2—The Executive Branch

The office of president was created to carry out the law; to provide a commander in chief of the military forces; to carry out the nation's foreign policy, including entering into treaties with other nations; and to appoint the ambassadors, judges and officials needed for the government to function. The president is chosen through a complex system that utilizes "electors," who are selected by procedures that vary from state to state. The number of electors equals each state's number of senators and representatives in Congress. Therefore, it is possible for a president to be elected without receiving a majority of the popular votes. Whether an electoral college is needed is a continuing controversy.

As a check against the president's power, many of the president's most significant actions must be approved by the Senate. Treaties require a two-thirds vote. Judges and appointed executive officials need a majority vote to be confirmed. In addition, the president must report periodically to Congress on the state of the Union and may recommend laws Congress should enact. The president's most important duty is phrased, characteristically, in very general language requiring that the president "shall take care that the laws be faithfully executed."

Like the other articles and elements of our legal system, the presidency is not immune from limitations. Nowhere are absolute rights or privileges guaranteed because of the ever-present tension between the people's rights and the government's needs. Individuals do not have boundless freedoms, and their government does not have boundless power, including the presidency. Although the president has great power, it is not absolute. A president can be impeached or removed from office. Although two presidents have been impeached (Andrew Johnson and Bill Clinton), none have actually been removed from office. No public figure can completely escape public or private accountability, as evidenced by the Supreme Court permitting the sexual harassment suit by Paula Jones to proceed, *Clinton v. Jones* (1997). Students of the Constitution should be ever mindful of the balance of individual and government authority and responsibility.

Article 3—The Judicial Branch

The third article completes the national government structure, vesting judicial power in the U.S. Supreme Court, as discussed in depth in Chapter 3. Congress is also empowered to create lower courts. Federal court judges are appointed by the president and hold office for life.

As a check against judicial power, Congress is authorized to regulate the courts' dockets by deciding what kinds of cases the Supreme Court may hear on appeal. This power of Congress to regulate the courts' jurisdiction further illustrates how each branch of government is given significant power to affect the others. Congress enacts laws, but the president may veto them, and the courts may interpret them.

■ The balance of power was established vertically through the separation of power between the federal government and the states and laterally through the three branches of government with its system of checks and balances.

Federal versus State Power   The fact that powers not specifically delegated to the federal government were reserved for the states and the people has been a big issue. Many court cases and policy debates revolve around that issue. Slavery, segregation, education, transportation and environmental concerns, such as migrating waterfowl versus nonmigratory birds and the like, are all issues that at one time or another would inspire debate on the role of the federal government versus that of state government.

Checks and Balances   The Constitution established an effective system of checks and balances on the power of any one of the three branches of government. The president has veto power, but Congress can override with two-thirds majority vote. The president nominates Supreme Court justices, but the legislative branch confirms or denies the nomination. The president is commander in chief, but the legislative branch declares war and pays for it.

Article 4—Other Provisions

Article 4 contains a variety of provisions, some taken over from the Articles of Confederation, further describing the creation of the federal union. The article also deals with criminal extradition, formation of new states and Congress' power to govern in territorial lands not yet states.

Article 5—The Amendment Process

Article 5 dictates how the Constitution may be amended. An amendment must first be approved by a two-thirds vote in each house of Congress. It is then submitted to the states for ratification, requiring the approval of three-fourths of the states to pass the amendment. The people may also begin the amendment process if the legislatures of two-thirds of the states call for a constitutional convention. This article was extremely important in allowing the Bill of Rights to be added to the Constitution, as discussed shortly.

Article 6—The Constitution as the Supreme Law

The second section of Article 6 contains the famous supremacy clause:

> The Constitution and the Laws of the United States which shall be made in Pursuance thereof; and all Treaties made, or which shall be made, under the Authority of the United States, shall be the supreme Law of the Land; and the Judges in every state shall be bound thereby, anything in the Constitution or Laws of any state to the Contrary notwithstanding.

> Here, in a stroke, was the solution to the problem of dual sovereignty of the federal and state governments. It was denied. In matters over which the Constitution grants the federal government authority, the states must concede.

■ In the **supremacy clause,** the Constitution declared itself the supreme law of the land.

> **supremacy clause •** Constitutional doctrine that federal law will reign when there is conflicting state law (U.S. Const. Art. VI, Paragraph 2)

This clause establishing the supremacy of federal law did something else momentous: it permitted the Supreme Court to become the ultimate decision maker in whether laws and actions of the government circumvent the Constitution and to invalidate them if they do so. This article also requires the allegiance of every federal and state official to the Constitution.

The Signing of the Constitution

Once the overall format was agreed upon, the next step was to seek approval of the document by the delegates. After hearing the debate over the final version of the Constitution, Benjamin Franklin, on Saturday, September 15, 1787, eloquently urged the Convention to respect the spirit of compromise:

> I confess that there are several parts of this Constitution which I do not at present approve. But I am not sure I shall ever approve them. For having lived long, I have experienced many instances of being obliged by better information or fuller consideration, to change opinions even on important subjects, which I once thought right, but found to be otherwise. . . . I consent, Sir, to this Constitution because I expect no better and because I am not sure that it is not the best (Lieberman, 1987, p. 447).

Franklin urged: "Every member of the Convention who may still have objections to it [the Constitution], would, with me, on this occasion doubt a little of his own infallibility, and . . . put his name to this instrument." He moved that the Constitution be approved unanimously and signed by those states present. The delegates voted to accept the Constitution, and the following Monday, September 17, it was ready to be signed.

■ The U.S. Constitution was signed in Philadelphia on September 17, 1787.

Forty-two of the 55 delegates were present on September 17 to sign the Constitution, with only three members refusing to sign, including George Mason, who cited the lack of a bill of rights as a remaining concern. He proposed adding a bill of rights, but other delegates argued that the individual states' declarations of rights would sufficiently protect individual liberties. They voted against adding a bill of rights. James Madison was quoted (The Records of the Federal Convention of 1787):

> Whilst the last members were signing it, Doctor Franklin looking towards the President's chair, at the back of which a rising sun happened to be painted, observed to a few members near him, that painters had found it difficult to distinguish in their art a rising from a setting sun. I have, said he, often in the course of the session . . . looked at that [sun] behind the President without being able to tell whether it was rising or setting. But now at length I have the happiness to know that it is a rising and not a setting sun (Armento et al., p. 133).

The delegates agreed that the Constitution should next be submitted to special conventions of the states for ratification.

Ratification

ratify • approve a constitutional amendment

Although the delegates to the Constitutional Convention had agreed to the makeup of the Constitution, each state had to approve, or **ratify,** it. Delaware was the first state to do so. New Hampshire cast the decisive vote, but ratification was not a sure thing. Many people had grave reservations. Although they were all supportive of the Constitution, the dispute tended to be more about how strong or weak the central government should be.

Federalists • colonists who favored a strong federal government

Anti-Federalists • colonists who opposed a strong federal government

■ The **Federalists** favored a strong central government. They were greatly challenged by the **Anti-Federalists,** who favored a weaker central government.

Political leaders such as Alexander Hamilton, James Madison and John Jay wrote powerful essays in a newspaper called *The Federalist Papers,* which encouraged the ratification of the Constitution and the formation of a strong national government. For example, Madison wrote the following passage in one issue (*The Federalist,* No. 51):

> If men were angels, no government would be necessary. If angels were to govern men, neither external nor internal controls on government would be necessary. In framing a government which is to be administered by men over men, the great difficulty lies in this: you must first enable the government to control the governed; and in the next place oblige it to control itself. A dependence on the people is, no doubt, the primary control on the government; but experience has taught mankind the necessity of auxiliary precautions.

The Anti-Federalists, however, feared such a strong federal government—what would assure the country that this attempt would not fail, too? Further, they were reluctant to ratify the Constitution without a bill of rights to guarantee individual liberties. The Anti-Federalists were not successful in blocking the final ratification of the Constitution, but they did raise awareness regarding the need for a bill of rights. Because the Constitution primarily addressed the formation of a government with limited and distributed powers, a bill of rights to protect individuals was not considered necessary.

■ Some states opposed the Constitution because it did not contain a bill of rights.

After the Philadelphia convention, most of those who drafted the Constitution could not understand why a bill of rights was such an issue for many states. They believed the Constitution could stand on its own. Nonetheless, most Federalists were willing to compromise on this issue to ratify the Constitution and establish a new government. Fearing defeat in the Massachusetts ratifying convention, Federalist leaders sought support by drafting a list of **amendments,** additions to improve the Constitution. They enlisted John Hancock, the most popular man in Massachusetts, to present these amendments to the state convention. The proposed amendments made the Constitution acceptable to many who had opposed ratification.

amendments • changes to a constitution or bylaws

The compromising strategy of the Massachusetts Federalists turned the tide of ratification. As other states debated ratification, they also insisted on amendments that would guarantee individual rights.

The Bill of Rights became part of the Constitution in 1791 by the addition of 10 amendments designed to ensure that the national government would not interfere with individual liberties. By December 15, 1791, the states had ratified 10 of the 12 proposed amendments to the Constitution and the United States had a bill of rights. Figure 1.1 illustrates the timeline of events occurring in the United States between the 1620 landing of the Mayflower and the 1791 ratification of the Bill of Rights.

A Balance Is Struck with the Bill of Rights

The framers of the Constitution sought to balance the powers of the legislative, executive and judicial branches of government. The proposed amendments aimed at balancing the rights of the states and of individual citizens against the powers of the central government. In December 1791, the 13 states had passed the 10 amendments that constitute the Bill of Rights. Proof of how well the Constitution would work was seen by the fact that it could, as a single document, embrace the additions that those it was drafted to serve determined necessary. Thomas Jefferson's comment on this process was of great significance: "The example of changing a Constitution by assembling the wise men of the State instead of assembling armies."

■ In 1791, 10 amendments, known as the Bill of Rights, were added to the Constitution to ensure the individual rights of American citizens.

The Bill of Rights is intriguing because, whereas the Constitution was general, the amendments were specific. However, even these directives have offered enough room for interpretation to keep a steady flow of constitutional cases before courts at all levels.

The Bill of Rights continues as an outgrowth of the Magna Carta. The English, including those who left to establish the United States, found that documenting their laws reduced the likelihood of abuse, misunderstanding or being forgotten.

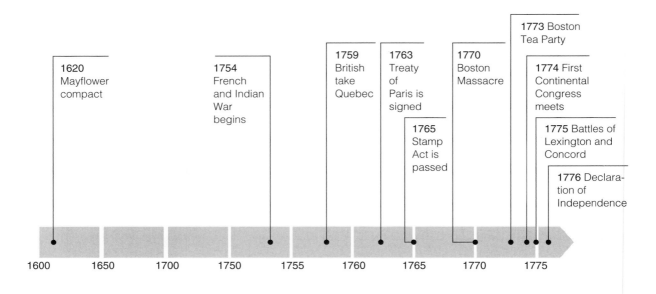

Figure 1.1 Timeline of Events

Adapted from: Robert A. Devine, et al., *America: The People and the Dream*. Copyright © 1991 by Scott, Foresman and Company. Used by permission of Pearson Education, Inc.; and Richard C. Brown and Herbert J. Bass. *One Flag, One Land*. Morristown, NJ: Silver Burdett and Ginn, 1990, p. 175.

Because the charters and compacts of the colonies were all different, the benefits of some uniformity in a national set of laws made sense.

It was illogical for civil liberties to be safe from an overly strong federal government, only to be abused by the states. And it made even less sense for some states to have a version of a bill of rights and others to have none. James Wilson of Pennsylvania suggested: "An imperfect bill of rights was worse than none at all because the omission of some rights might justify their infringement by implying an unintended grant of government power" (Levy, 1999, p. 21).

Americans were becoming more comfortable with a clearly established, written law. Documented agreements worked. Recognizing that certain rights were so important to the country to ensure that no government, state or federal, could infringe upon them, the Bill of Rights was finally agreed upon. To this day, amendments are not taken lightly, and adding or deleting amendments is extremely difficult.

Had the Constitution been ratified without a bill of rights, it would have taken several years for those protections to be passed. By taking the form of amendments, these provisions became an integral part of the Constitution that

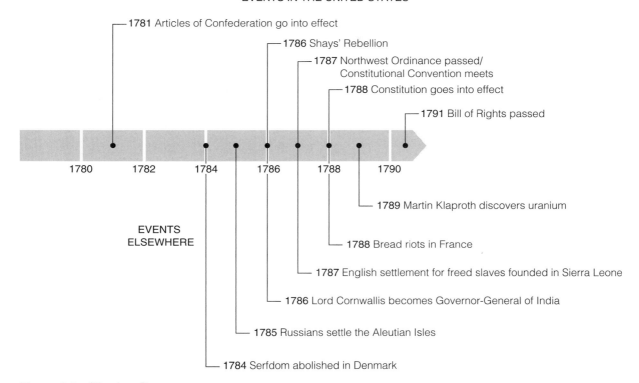

EVENTS IN THE UNITED STATES

1781 Articles of Confederation go into effect

1786 Shays' Rebellion

1787 Northwest Ordinance passed/
Constitutional Convention meets

1788 Constitution goes into effect

1791 Bill of Rights passed

1780   1782   1784   1786   1788   1790

EVENTS
ELSEWHERE

1789 Martin Klaproth discovers uranium

1788 Bread riots in France

1787 English settlement for freed slaves founded in Sierra Leone

1786 Lord Cornwallis becomes Governor-General of India

1785 Russians settle the Aleutian Isles

1784 Serfdom abolished in Denmark

Figure 1.1   (*Continued*)

many had argued be included originally. As noted by the Honorable Warren E. Burger during the Constitution's bicentennial (Armento et al., p. 26):

> The Founders, conscious of the risks of abuse of power, created a system of liberty with order and placed the Bill of Rights as a harness on government to protect people from misuse of the powers. The evils of tyranny even today fall on most of the world's people and remind us of what life would be like without our respect for human dignity and freedom. We must never forget what our strength was meant to serve and what made that strength possible—the Constitution and the Bill of Rights as they stand today.

The Bill of Rights: An Overview

Sections II, III and IV of this text focus on the Bill of Rights, as well as additional amendments made to the Constitution. Most laws and controversies deal with these amendments. The following brief introduction to each of the first 10 amendments provides an overview upon which later discussions can be based.

The *First Amendment* lists important individual liberties, including freedom of religion, speech and the press:

> Congress shall make no law respecting an establishment of religion, or prohibiting the free exercise thereof; or abridging the freedom of speech, or of the press, or the right of the people peaceably to assemble, and to petition the Government for a redress of grievances.

These freedoms are so basic to the American way of life that they are sometimes referred to as "First Amendment rights."

The *Second Amendment* preserves the right of the people "to keep and bear arms":

> A well-regulated militia being necessary to the security of a free state, the right of the people to keep and bear arms shall not be infringed.

The courts have ruled that this is not an absolute right. Laws prohibiting private paramilitary associations and carrying concealed weapons have been upheld.

The *Third Amendment* prohibits the government from housing soldiers in private homes during peacetime without the owner's consent:

> No soldier shall, in time of peace, be quartered in any house without the consent of the owner, nor in time of war but in a manner to be prescribed by the law.

This is the only amendment that the government has never tried to violate (Lieberman, p. 46).

The *Fourth Amendment* is concerned with the right to privacy and security:

> The right of the people to be secure in their persons, houses, papers, and effects, against unreasonable searches and seizures, shall not be violated, and no warrants shall issue but upon probable cause, supported by oath or affirmation, and particularly describing the place to be searched, and the persons or things to be seized.

The Fourth Amendment forbids the government or its agents from searching individuals, their homes or their personal possessions or from seizing them unless the government has "probable cause" to believe a crime has been committed. If such probable cause exists, a search warrant describing in detail what (or who) is to be seized should be obtained. (This capsule description is necessarily loose: the police need not obtain warrants for every arrest or for every search. The past 15 years have seen an enormous volume of litigation over the precise limits of this amendment.)

The *Fifth Amendment* sets forth several restrictions on how the government may treat a person suspected of a crime:

> No person shall be held to answer for a capital or otherwise infamous crime unless on a presentment or indictment of a grand jury, except in cases arising in the land or naval forces, or in the militia, when in actual service, in time of war or public danger; nor shall any person be subject for the same offense to be twice put in jeopardy of life or limb; nor shall be compelled in any criminal case to be a witness against himself; nor be deprived of life, liberty, or

property, without due process of law; nor shall private property be taken for public use without just compensation.

The Fifth Amendment establishes the need for a grand jury indictment for felony cases. It prohibits double jeopardy, meaning a person acquitted by a jury of a crime may not be retried for the same offense. It prohibits the government from forcing a person to testify against himself; hence the expression "pleading the Fifth." It also contains the famous due process clause: "nor shall any person . . . be deprived of life, liberty, or property without due process of law."

The *Sixth Amendment* describes the requirements for a fair trial:

> In all criminal prosecutions, the accused shall enjoy the right to a speedy and public trial, by an impartial jury of the state and district wherein the crime shall have been committed, which districts shall have been previously ascertained by law, and to be informed of the nature and cause of the accusation; to be confronted with the witnesses against him; to have compulsory process for obtaining witnesses in his favor, and to have the assistance of counsel for his defense.

The trial must be convened speedily and must be public. The accused is entitled to an impartial jury in the community where the crime occurred and must be advised of the crimes being charged. Accused individuals must also be allowed to cross-examine witnesses who testify against them. In addition, they can compel witnesses who will testify in their favor to come to court. Finally, they have the right to be represented by a lawyer.

The *Seventh Amendment* preserves the right to trial by jury in common law cases "where the value in controversy shall exceed twenty dollars":

> In Suits at common law, where the value in controversy shall exceed twenty dollars, the right of trial by a jury shall be otherwise re-examined in any Court of the United States, than according to the rules of the common law.

This amendment is one of the few clauses in the Constitution that includes a figure that has lost meaning over the years. By law today, federal courts cannot hear cases where the contested value is less than $10,000, unless a federal law is involved. The amendment also forbids courts to re-examine facts found by juries, except as the common law permits.

The *Eighth Amendment* prohibits excessive bail, excessive fines and cruel and unusual punishment:

> Excessive bail shall not be required, nor excessive fines imposed, nor cruel and unusual punishments inflicted.

It is this amendment that opponents of capital punishment most frequently cite.

The *Ninth Amendment* answered the objections of those who thought that naming some rights but not all might result in the government's claiming more power than was intended:

> The enumeration in the Constitution of certain rights shall not be construed to deny or disparage others retained by the people.

The *Tenth Amendment* further underscores the framers' intent to reserve certain powers to the states and to the people:

> The powers not delegated to the United States by the Constitution, nor prohibited by it to the States, are reserved to the States respectively, or to the people.

This amendment establishes no rights nor takes any away. It is a reminder that the government is for the people, not the reverse.

The U.S. Constitution and its amendments are provided in Appendix B.

A Living Law

The inclusion of the Bill of Rights stands as an example of how the U.S. Constitution lives. It is neither unchangeable nor unresponsive. It is not merely a piece of paper locked away in a vault in Washington, DC. The framers took a lot of good ideas referenced earlier and, with the political skill of compromise, developed a workable form of government that continues to this day. It was designed to grow, develop and be redefined if necessary to best serve the people's needs. Study of the amendments and how they have been interpreted since their inception makes it obvious that the Constitution is a living document that grows with the citizens it was written to protect.

A Nearly Timeless Document

The final draft of the Constitution established a broad framework for the new American government. For more than 200 years, the Constitution has been flexible enough to meet the nation's changing needs without extensive formal revision. Although the framers of the Constitution would find many modern governmental practices quite foreign, the basic system continues to operate as they planned. Recognizing the importance of assuring in practice the division of power, Madison suggested this could best be done "by so contriving the interior structure of the government as that its several constituent parts may, by their mutual relations, be the means of keeping each other in their proper places."

Lieberman (1976, p. 49) notes: "The Constitution has the distinction of being an almost timeless document but for one grievous flaw. It did not abolish slavery."

■ The Constitution and Bill of Rights failed to abolish slavery.

Lieberman continues:

> Those who detested slavery reconciled themselves to this grievous and glaring flaw that contradicted the Declaration of Independence at its most solemn point—that all men are created equal—by assuming that slavery would in time vanish naturally. But it would not go away so easily. The compromise that saved the Union could not be peacefully eliminated, and the amendments that would make the Constitution true to itself could come about only after the bloodiest war in American history.

Although nearly timeless, the Constitution reflects the will and values of the people who originally drafted it and those charged with maintaining it. For example, whereas the Constitution as originally ratified did not prevent slavery and other discriminations, the ability of our law to be amended (in this case by the 14th Amendment) speaks volumes about the American spirit to learn, even from its own mistakes.

Where the Declaration of Independence and Constitution Are Today

The Declaration of Independence, which established the United States as an independent nation, and the Constitution, which established its form of government, have been carefully preserved.

■ The Declaration of Independence and the U.S. Constitution are housed in the Rotunda of the National Archives in Washington, DC.

These valuable documents are contained in helium-filled bronze cases housed in a vault below the Exhibition Hall floor. The vault is 71.2 feet long, 5 feet wide, 6 feet high and weighs 55 tons. The walls are reinforced concrete and steel.

Federalism at Work in the Criminal Justice System

The American system of government is actually two systems operating both together and separately. The very concept of federalism is that a central body of government is needed to guide the United States, but federal power should be limited to only what is necessary to keep the country moving forward. An analogy could be made to federal government being the keel of a ship; it is neither the largest nor most comprehensive component of the vessel but serves a critical part in the overall structure. Everything else is intentionally left to the states. When a differentiation is made between federal and state government, state government includes local government as well: county, municipal and tribal government. Reflecting on why America was built with the Constitution serving as the central document, the framers wanted as little federal government and as much state (and local) control as possible.

As explained elsewhere in this text, *jurisdiction* refers to which branch of government has the authority to enforce laws and call upon those involved to appear in which courts. The emphasis of this text will be on decisions of the U.S. Supreme Court because it is the final arbiter of American law; however, it is important to recognize that very few cases go directly there. These other courts, referred to as "inferior" courts because they do not have the ultimate power of the Supreme Court, have their own definite jurisdictional considerations.

Just as the federal government has limited powers, so do federal courts. Fewer crimes are classified as federal crimes than are defined by the 50 states. This is by intent; excessive *government* was the primary motivator for the creation of The United States, and the framers carefully calculated how much federal power should be allotted, with the formula being simply as little as absolutely necessary.

Cole and Smith (2007, p. 292) explain: "The federal system has no trial courts of limited jurisdiction. In state systems, 13,000 trial courts of limited jurisdiction handle traffic cases, small claims, misdemeanors and other less serious matters. These courts handle 90 percent of all criminal cases. The federal system begins with the U.S. district courts, its trial courts of general jurisdiction." Figure 1.2 illustrates the components of the federal and state systems of government.

A case may find itself in the federal system because the impact of the crime crosses state borders or is broad enough to affect people throughout the country, for example, terrorism, bank robbery or drug trafficking. The next chapter describes this dual system in greater detail.

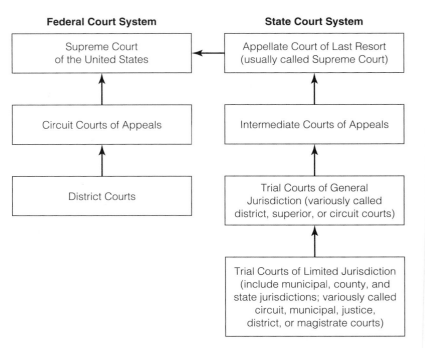

Figure 1.2   The Dual Court System of the United States

Source: George F. Cole and Christopher E. Smith. *The American System of Criminal Justice*, 11th ed., Belmont, CA: Wadsworth Publishing, 2007, p. 292. Reprinted by permission.

SUMMARY

From the very beginning, the colonists sought structure and collaboration. The Mayflower Compact was a written agreement for self-government signed in 1620. The U.S. Constitution was written to serve the needs of a pluralistic society. Pluralism refers to a society in which numerous distinct ethnic, religious or cultural groups coexist within one nation, each contributing to the society as a whole. The most important events leading up to the Constitution were the Declaration of Independence and the colonists' winning of the Revolutionary War.

The history of the Constitution is rooted in the colonists' desire for freedom from foreign rule. In addition to others, Spain, France and Great Britain saw great importance in adding the New World to their growing empires. Most threatening was Great Britain. In 1765, the British Parliament passed the Stamp Act, requiring stamps to be purchased and placed on such items as legal documents and certain commodities. The colonists resisted this act because it was viewed as taxation without representation. That same year, Parliament passed the Quartering Act, requiring that the colonists feed and shelter British troops in America.

Tensions between the colonists and the British army mounted, and in 1770, fighting broke out; this incident became known as the Boston Massacre. In an attempt to lessen the conflict, Parliament repealed most of the taxes, but kept the tax on tea. In 1773, colonists boarded British ships in Boston Harbor and threw the ships' tea cargo into the water. This event, the Boston Tea Party, represented the colonists' unwillingness to pay taxes without representation.

As tension between the British and the colonists increased, the First Continental Congress was called. This Congress resulted in the first written agreement among the colonies to stand together in resistance to Great Britain. The British retaliated by sending more troops to quell the "rebels." In 1775, the Second Continental Congress established the Continental Army and named George Washington as its commander. On July 4, 1776, the President of the Congress signed the American Declaration of Independence, which formally severed ties with Great Britain.

The Congress also drafted the Articles of Confederation. The Articles of Confederation formally pledged the states to "a firm league of friendship," and "a perpetual union" created for "their common defense, the security of their liberties" and their "mutual and general welfare." This loose governmental structure proved unsatisfactory and resulted in the colonists seeking a stronger central government—one established by the Constitution.

The U.S. Constitution was greatly influenced by the Magna Carta, which established the supremacy of the law over the ruler and guaranteed English feudal barons individual rights and "due process of law," including trial by jury. Americans continued to believe in the principles contained in the Magna Carta, which was a precedent for democratic government and individual rights and the foundation for requiring rulers to uphold the law. It greatly influenced the writers of the U.S. Constitution.

The purpose of the Constitution was to provide a system of government that would prevent one individual from having complete power. The first three articles of the Constitution establish the legislative, executive and judicial branches of government and a system of checks and balances. The balance of power was established vertically through the separation of power between the federal government and the states and laterally through the three branches of government with its system of checks and balances. In the supremacy clause, the Constitution declared itself the supreme law of the land.

The U.S. Constitution was signed in Philadelphia on September 17, 1787. The next step was for the individual states to ratify it. The Federalists favored a strong central government. They were greatly challenged by the Anti-Federalists, who favored a weaker central government. Some states opposed the Constitution because it did not contain a bill of rights. In an important compromise, 10 amendments, known as the Bill of Rights, were added to the Constitution in 1791 to ensure the individual rights of American citizens. The Constitution and Bill of Rights had one serious shortcoming: they failed to abolish slavery. The Declaration of Independence and the U.S. Constitution are housed in the Rotunda of the National Archives in Washington, DC.

DISCUSSION QUESTIONS

1. Few people could live together and not have laws. Why?

2. Does pluralism have any negative aspects? Why have some fought so hard against the concept in the United States?

3. Do demonstrations such as the Boston Tea Party have any effect? Are they positive or negative?

4. What factors make it amazing that any organization among the colonies was successful?

5. Were the Articles of Confederation a wasted effort or were they needed?

6. What do you think about the Constitutional Convention being closed to the public? Was this necessary?

7. Why is the Constitution called a living document. Give examples.

8. What do you think the Anti-Federalists were really afraid of?

9. Why shouldn't the Bill of Rights have been left up to each state to develop on its own?

10. If the U.S. Constitution works so well, why don't all countries adopt it?

INFOTRAC COLLEGE EDITION ASSIGNMENTS

- Use InfoTrac College Edition to assist you in answering the Discussion Questions when appropriate.
- Find and outline additional information about the Magna Carta, Shays' Rebellion, *The Federalist Papers* or the Revolutionary War.

INTERNET ASSIGNMENTS

- Use *http://www.findlaw.com* to find *Kinsella v. Singleton.* Outline the key points. OR
- Go to the World Book Online Web site at *http://www.worldbookonline.com* and find what it says about the Mayflower Compact.

COMPANION WEB SITE

- Go to the Constitutional Law and the Criminal Justice System 3e Web site at *http://cj.wadsworth.com/hessharr_constlaw3e* for Case Studies and Study Guide exercises.

REFERENCES

Armento, Beverly J.; Nash, Gary B.; Salter, Christopher L.; and Wixson, Karen K. *A More Perfect Union.* Boston: Houghton Mifflin Company, 1991.

Atherton, Herbert M. and Barlow, J. Jackson, eds. *The Bill of Rights and Beyond.* Washington, DC: Commission on the Bicentennial of the United States (no date).

Beard, Charles A. and Beard, Mary R. *The Beards' New Basic History of the United States.* Garden City, NY: Doubleday & Company, Inc., 1968.

Brown, Richard C. and Bass, Herbert J. *One Flag, One Land.* Morristown, NJ: Silver Burdett and Ginn, 1990.

Cole, George F. and Smith, Christopher E. *The American System of Criminal Justice,* 11th ed. Belmont, CA: Thomson Wadsworth Publishing, 2007.

Divine, Robert A.; Breen, T. H.; Fredrickson, George M.; and Williams, R. Hal. *America: The People and the Dream.* Glenview, IL: Scott, Foresman and Company, 1991.

Gundersen, Joan R. "Mayflower Compact." *World Book Online Reference Centre,* 2003.

Jacoby, Jeff. "56 Who Pledged their Lives, Fortunes, Sacred Honor." *Boston Globe.* Reprinted in (Minneapolis/St. Paul) *Star Tribune,* July 4, 2000, p. A11.

Levy, Leonard W. *Origins of the Bill of Rights.* New Haven, CT: Yale University Press, 1999.

Levy, Leonard W. and Mahoney, Dennis J., eds. *The Framing and Ratification of the Constitution.* New York: Macmillan Publishing Company, 1987.

Lieberman, Jethro K. *Milestones!* St. Paul, MN: West Publishing Company, 1976.

Lieberman, Jethro K. *The Enduring Constitution: A Bicentennial Perspective.* St. Paul, MN: West Publishing Company, 1987.

Miller, Linda S. and Hess, Kären M. *The Police in the Community: Partners for Problem Solving,* 4th ed. Belmont, CA: Wadsworth Publishing Company, 2005.

Mitchell, Ralph. *CQ's Guide to the U.S. Constitution: History, Text, Glossary, Index.* Washington, DC: Congressional Quarterly, Inc., 1986.

Simmons, R. C. *The American Colonies.* New York: McKay, 1976.

Woodard, David. Personal correspondence, 2006.

ADDITIONAL RESOURCES

Dorsen, Norman, ed. *The Evolving Constitution: Essays on the Bill of Rights and the U.S. Supreme Court.* Middletown, CT: Wesleyan University Press, 1985.

Kelly, Alfred; Harbison, Winfred A.; and Belz, Herman. *The American Constitution: Its Origins and Development,* 6th ed. New York: W.W. Norton & Company, Inc., 1983.

Knight, Alfred H. *The Life of the Law: The People and Cases that Have Shaped Our Society, from King Alfred to Rodney King.* New York: Crown Publishers, Inc., 1996.

Swindler, William F. *Magna Carta: Legend and Legacy.* New York: The Bobbs-Merrill Company, Inc., 1965.

Webster, Mary E., ed. *The Federalist Papers: In Modern Language Indexed for Today's Political Issues.* Bellevue, WA: Merrill Press, 1999.

CASES CITED

Clinton v. Jones (1997)

Kinsella v. Singleton, 361 U.S. 234 (1960).

McCulloch v. Maryland, 17 U.S. (4 Wheat.) 316 (1819).

Nixon v. United States (1993)

CHAPTER 2

An Overview of the U.S. Legal System

THE LAW MUST BE STABLE, BUT IT MUST NOT STAND STILL.

—ROSCOE POUND

© Bill Ross/CORBIS

The United States Supreme Court in Washington, DC, welcomes visitors to tour the building and observe the Court in session. As a public place the terrace of the Court is a frequent site of demonstrations.

DO YOU KNOW . . .

- What two prominent theories about the underlying purpose of law are?
- What the basic purpose of the American legal system is?
- What the scales of justice symbolize in law?
- When common law began, what it is based on and what it is synonymous with?
- What *stare decisis* requires?
- How the Constitution ensures individual liberty?
- Why American law is said to be a living law?
- Where statutory law originates?
- The difference between a crime and a tort?
- What two main functions are served by courts?
- On what two levels the judicial system operates?
- Who officers of the court are?
- What doctrines govern whether a case will be heard in court?
- What the three components of the criminal justice system are? The juvenile justice system?
- What the main similarity and difference between the criminal justice system and the juvenile justice system are?

CAN YOU DEFINE?

adversarial judicial system	crimes	promulgate
amicus briefs	exclusive jurisdiction	ripeness doctrine
appellate jurisdiction	general jurisdiction	social contract
case law	jurisdiction	standing
codified law	limited jurisdiction	*stare decisis*
common law	mootness	status offenses
comparative law	ordinances	statutory law
concurrent jurisdiction	original jurisdiction	substantive law
conflict theory	penal codes	tort
consensus theory	petition for certiorari	venue
	procedural law	

Introduction

This chapter describes the American legal system and how it operates. Through understanding *how* it operates comes an appreciation of the crucial role the U.S. Constitution plays in achieving the primary goals of the framers of the Constitution—liberty, freedom and fairness. You will also learn the term that embodies these concepts and assures they will remain: *due process.*

When examining the overall legal system, you may find it, like the Constitution itself, to be overwhelming and complex. It can be, but it doesn't have to be. You learn about something as intimidating as the American legal system one concept at a time. Start with understanding the basic purpose of the legal system. Once you understand the *Why's,* the *What's* will become more logical.

The chapter begins with a discussion of the purpose of the U.S. legal system and a description of law and how it has developed throughout the centuries, including the important development of common law, the concept of *stare decisis* and a discussion of American Law as living law. This discussion is followed by a description of categories of law, often overlapping, found in the U.S. legal system. Next is a discussion of the components of the legal system and the officers of the court. The chapter concludes with an explanation of the adversarial nature of the legal system, a comparison of the criminal and juvenile justice systems, and a look at the emerging influence of U.S. law beyond our borders.

Theories about and the Purpose of the Legal System

Futurist Joel Barker defines a *paradigm* as a boundary or parameter that outlines a rule and is based on experience. Sociologist Max Weber contends that the primary purpose of law is to regulate human interactions—to support social function. Combining these two views leads to the concept that a society's legal paradigm defines the behavioral boundaries of that culture.

As law evolves, different theories emerge to explain its development. People want to know not only *what* the law is but also *why* it exists as such. One theory is natural law, which suggests people should not create law in conflict with the natural order. Legal positivists suggest law is strictly a response to what is occurring at the moment. There are many other theories filling volumes that the reader may wish to explore independently.

To present a solid base from which to develop an understanding of law and its development, this text focuses on the basic premise that throughout history law has regulated human interactions for different reasons: to protect society's interests, to deter antisocial behavior, to enforce moral beliefs, to uphold individual rights, to support those in power and to punish lawbreakers or seek retribution for wrongdoing. Although many theories exist, two very different views address the purpose of laws.

■ Two prominent theories about the underlying purpose of the law are consensus theory and conflict theory.

Consensus theory holds that individuals in a society agree on basic values, on what is inherently right and wrong. Laws express these values. Consensus theory dates back at least to Plato and Aristotle. Society, in general, agrees on what is right and wrong and makes laws to prohibit deviant behavior. Consensus theory was expanded on by French historian-philosopher Montesquieu (1689–1755). His philosophy focused on the **social contract** whereby free, independent individuals agree to form a society and to give up a portion of their individual freedom to benefit the security of the group. Later, Emile Durkheim (1858–1917) described social solidarity as the shared values of a society, its "collective conscience." The Durkheimian perspective saw punishment as revenge and a means to restore and solidify the social order.

A second prominent theory regarding the underlying purpose of the law, conflict theory, is not as humanitarian. **Conflict theory** holds that laws are established to keep the dominant class in power. (Recall that the framers of our Constitution were the socially, politically and economically powerful men in the New World.)

consensus theory • holds that individuals in a society agree on basic values, on what is inherently right and wrong, and that laws express these values

social contract • a philosophy proposed by French historian-philosopher Montesquieu, whereby free, independent individuals agree to form a society and to give up a portion of their individual freedom to benefit the security of the group

conflict theory • holds that laws are established to keep the dominant class in power, in contrast to the consensus theory

The roots of this theory are found in Marx and Engels' *Manifesto of the Communist Party* (1848):

> The history of all hitherto existing society is the history of class struggles. Freeman and slave, patrician and plebeian, lord and serf, guild-master and journeyman, in a word, oppressor and oppressed stood in constant opposition to one another, carried on an interrupted, now hidden, now open fight, a fight that each time ended in either a revolutionary reconstruction of society at large, or in the common ruin of the contending classes.

Rather than regarding punishment as a way to provide social solidarity, Marx regarded punishment as a way to control the lower class and preserve the power of the upper class. This rationale has its roots in the Middle Ages, the Renaissance and the Reformation and into the nineteenth century. During those times, society was divided into a small ruling class, a somewhat larger class of artisans and a much larger class of peasants. Harsh laws kept the "rabble" under control.

Conflict theory is used by some sociologists and criminologists to explain how laws protect the interests and values of the dominant groups in a society. Walker et al. (2004, pp. 19–20) suggest:

> Conflict theory explains racial disparities in the administration of justice as products of broader patterns of social, economic, and political inequality in U.S. society. These inequalities are the result of prejudicial attitudes on the part of the white majority and discrimination against minorities in employment, education, housing, and other aspects of society. . . . Conflict theory explains the overrepresentation of racial and ethnic minorities in arrest, prosecution, imprisonment, and capital punishment as both the product of these inequalities and an expression of prejudice against minorities.

Chapter 1 discussed the challenge facing the framers of the Constitution to balance the rights of individuals against the rights of society. Recollections of the tyranny of British rulers prompted the framers of the Constitution to build in many safeguards against any such tyranny in the United States. Nonetheless, to avoid anarchy, a country of laws had to be established. Consider this challenge: to meet the needs of the individual and the government—a strong, but not excessive, system of law and order.

■ The basic purpose of the U.S. legal system is to ensure fairness in balancing individual and societal rights and needs, while preventing excessive government power.

Achieving a workable system that balances the rights and needs of individuals as well as those of the society being served is no small task. In fact, many have died here, and continue to die in other countries, fighting for a system of government that provides the freedoms U.S. citizens now enjoy.

■ The scales of justice represent keeping individual and societal needs in balance.

Some argue that in striving to balance individual and societal rights and needs, the system itself has become so complicated that justice is compromised. Although the Constitution appears complex, it has been the many laws subsequently enacted to maintain the balance that have created the massively intricate body of law. In fact, to those not educated in the law, it might appear that legal loopholes abound, when in reality it is through the passage of new laws and the continual evolution of existing laws that the crucial balance is struck. Consider this analogy:

> To balance a car tire, technicians put the tire on a machine that spins the tire around at high speed. If the tire wobbles, a lead weight is strategically placed on the tire's edge to counter-balance the wobble. The tire is spun again. The first weight added might cause another more minor wobble elsewhere on the tire, so a second weight is applied to counter-balance that problem. This process of "spin the tire, add a weight" might go on several more times until a balance is achieved. This is how it is with the law. There is a constant effort to achieve a balance that requires counter-balancing with other fine-tuning efforts via additional laws. As societal changes require legal changes, this process proceeds in an endless, cyclic effort to achieve the balance of justice and due process.

Because the Constitution is meant to be basic, it is, by itself, easy to begin to understand. Students of the Constitution need to grasp the "bigger picture" before looking at the developments that have occurred in the past 200 years. Details can get in the way of understanding the system and how it works.

The Law Defined

Laws are rules with the power of the government behind them. In the United States, these rules are created by legislative bodies empowered by the people to pass laws. The term **promulgate** means to make law through such legal process. These laws reflect what the citizenry holds important, and they support the norms of society by enforcing its rules through legal consequences. As our society becomes more complex, so do the rules and the means by which they are enforced. American law must be enforced through legal means, that is, in accordance with the tenets of the Constitution.

promulgate • publish or announce officially a law or rule; to make law through a legal process

Development of the Law

The development of societal rules began the first time people congregated. When people are together, a norm is established so individuals know what is expected of them relative to the group as a whole. Whether via de facto rules, which naturally develop, or de jure results, which are promulgated, some order must arise to prevent chaos. Law generally evolves through four phases:
1. People come together seeking collective security, to collectively gather food and to satisfy other mutual needs.
2. They discover that they need rules to maintain order and their sense of security.
3. Inevitably some individuals break the rules.
4. Consequences are established for breaking the rules.

Of great influence on the American legal system was early Roman law, dealing with basic rules related to economic, religious and family life contained in the Twelve Tables, written about 450 B.C. These rules were based on tradition and a quest for fairness. Another important period in Roman history was the rule of Emperor Justinian I (527–565 A.D.). His Justinian Code distinguished public and private laws and influenced legal thought throughout the Middle Ages.

Another significant influence on the development of the American legal system was the system of common law that evolved in England during the Middle Ages. Rather than smaller groups of people relying completely on local custom to determine their rules or law, the royal judges traveling through the territories began to apply a broader or national norm as cases were decided. In essence, the law became more common throughout the country.

While initially unwritten, the decisions of the cases heard became the basis for how subsequent cases were to be decided. If a current case was similar enough to a preceding case, it was decided on the basis of the ruling in the previous case. Eventually, the cases were written down, and by 1300, recorded decisions were serving as precedent, making it easier to maintain the continuity of the developing legal system.

■ **Common law** began as early English judge-made law, based on custom and tradition that was followed throughout the country. As a term in American law, it is synonymous with **case law.**

This system of common law is the basis for American law, in which the decisions made in past cases are routinely examined when new cases are considered.

As English Parliament took over the role of promulgating law, the role of common-law courts changed. For example, offenses that once were considered personal wrongs, such as murder, rape and burglary, were redefined by English judges as crimes against the state because such transgressions disrupted the security of the entire community, not just the individual victimized. These redefinitions also made offenders subject to state control and punishment.

Similarly, American common law also took on the role of interpreting and defining existing law, resulting in forging of new law. Common law still has the capacity to create law as well as interpret it and is integral to the present legal system. Common law depends heavily on predictability through precedent and the concept of *stare decisis*.

Stare Decisis

American common law has developed by building upon itself. Courts continue to rely on prior cases—directly, by implication or conceptually—to maintain continuity. This continuity not only results in current cases being decided in a way that relates to existing law (from past cases) but also provides the U.S. system of law development a stronger, more predictable basis on which to determine future cases. This concept is termed ***stare decisis,*** meaning that previous rules set forth in other cases shall be used to decide future cases.

■ ***Stare decisis*** is a common law doctrine requiring that precedent set in one case shall be followed in all cases having the same or similar circumstances, thus assuring consistency in the law.

Although this doctrine has its roots in early English law, the court in *Moore v. City of Albany* (1885) set forth: "When a court has once laid down a principle of law as applicable to a certain state of facts, it will adhere to that principle and apply it to all future cases where facts are substantially the same." The idea behind this approach is to permit people to arrange their lives in accordance with the rules of society that can be best understood by knowing existing and past matters with the understanding that future matters will adhere to these concepts.

common law • early English judge-made law based on custom and tradition; a legal system that, as in the United States, decides present cases on past decisions

case law • common law approach, so named because it is based on previous cases; as a term in American law, it is synonymous with *common law*

stare decisis • Latin for "to stand by decided matters"

By deciding each set of facts on a case-by-case analysis, the opportunity remains for law to continue emerging.

Stare decisis is a Latin term that literally means "let the decision stand." When a legal principle has been determined by a higher court, lower courts must apply it to all later cases containing the same or similar facts. Of course, one side will say the facts are the same, and so *stare decisis* dictates that a certain ruling prevail. The other side will assert that the facts are not exactly the same, and so a different result should be reached. The doctrine of *stare decisis* does not, however, prevent the law from growing, changing or even reconsidering itself in matters from which undesirable law resulted. Facts can and will be interpreted by those involved in a manner that will best suit society *and* the parties involved.

The Continuing Need for Law

People need laws to know what behavior is acceptable and to be able to deal with those who do not follow the law. In any society, laws should, in fact must, be obeyed for the good of all. In a sense, obedience to the law is voluntary. At least in countries that enjoy freedom, people are permitted to carry on with life's activities, for the most part, as each sees fit. You perhaps obey traffic laws because you should. You most likely pay taxes because you should. You probably obey the many other laws of our society because you *should,* because as one member of a larger group, you know everyone benefits if laws are obeyed. Because consequences are part of orderly society, if you do exceed the speed limit, you might get a ticket. You have freedom to decide, including the decision to not obey laws.

Rather than being purely punitive, laws set the parameters for social behavior, including the consequences for actions outside these parameters. Consequences for not complying are part of these parameters, but another critical issue arises when those making and enforcing the law act outside the law. Remember, the purpose of the Constitution remains to limit government power. The law itself controls government by restricting how and when government can and cannot interfere with citizens' lives. The Latin phrase *nulla poena sine lege* translates to "no punishment without law." Similarly, *nullum crimen sine lege* means "no crime without law."

▓ The Constitution ensures individual rights by limiting government power.

American Law Lives

Because the needs of any group change as that group itself changes, effective law should be flexible enough to respond to those changing needs, as introduced in Chapter 1. Human nature dictates that different needs are perceived at different times. For example, laws against witchcraft in colonial America are now perceived as unnecessary and inappropriate, as are laws permitting slavery or prohibiting women to vote. Similarly, laws pertaining to the use of drugs have changed as societal norms have changed, as evidenced by laws dealing with certain uses of marijuana (deemed less serious than a decade ago) or the increasing strictness of drunken-driving laws. The constitutional amendments dealing with prohibition provide a concrete example of how law can advance and retreat as needs and expectations change.

American law is referred to as a living law because it is not stagnant. It can be changed, expanded or rescinded to serve the overall system. Constitutional amendments are not easily or frequently added or removed. It takes two-thirds of each house of Congress, or conventions called by two-thirds of the state legislatures, to propose constitutional amendments. For an amendment to be ratified, three-fourths of the state legislatures or special conventions must agree. More than 7,000 amendments have been proposed in Congress, with only 33 of those passed and submitted to the states, where more fell short of the requisite vote.

When amendments are passed, they reflect true societal changes. Since the Bill of Rights was ratified in 1791, 17 amendments have been successfully ratified. Those considered most influential came after the Civil War:

- The Thirteenth Amendment (ratified in 1865) abolished slavery.
- The Fourteenth Amendment (1868) prevented the states from denying former slaves equal protection and due process of law.
- The Fifteenth Amendment (1870) ensured the right to vote regardless of race.
- The Nineteenth Amendment (1920) extended the right to vote to women.
- The Twenty-First Amendment (1933) repealed prohibition, which was ratified as the Eighteenth Amendment in 1919.

■ American law is considered a living law because it can change along with society.

As you develop an understanding of what modern law is and how it developed from the needs of the earliest gatherings of people, it becomes obvious why it has reached its level of complexity. With more than 298 million people in the United States, and with the importance we place on pluralism, our needs are varied. A legal system that responds to such societal diversity and technological change becomes, out of necessity, complex. One of the complexities is that various categories of law exist, often overlapping in an effort to respond to society's changing needs.

Categorizing Law

Different aspects of the law interact in ways that may appear confusing at first. For clarity, go back to the basics: What is the purpose of law? To limit government power and to provide societal guidelines. Why is there so much law? To strive for justice and due process in a growing and increasingly complex society with many different viewpoints. To further clarify, it helps to categorize the law by asking: *Who? What?* and *How?*

Who? (Jurisdiction)

This question is actually twofold: *Who makes the law?* and *Who does the law affect?*

Who makes the law is whichever group has **jurisdiction,** or authority, to promulgate that law. It might be a legislative body, such as the elected or appointed members of the city council, county board and state or federal legislatures. Or it could be a court that makes decisions through case law or common law. Who the law affects are the people over which the law-making group has jurisdiction.

■ **Statutory** (codified) **law** is promulgated by legislatures or governing bodies.

Statutory law can also be referred to as **codified law** because it is set forth in organized, structured codes such as the U.S. Criminal Code or the criminal code

jurisdiction • the authority of a legislative body to establish a law, the authority of a particular court to hear certain types of cases or the authority a law has over a specific group of people

statutory law • law set forth by legislatures or governing bodies having jurisdiction to make such law

codified law • law specifically set forth in organized, structured codes such as the U.S. criminal code, state statutes or local ordinances of a specific state. Local jurisdictions, such as county or municipal levels, also enact their own specific codes, often referred to as **ordinances.** Of crucial importance is the fact that no statutory law, regardless of the level of jurisdiction, can violate the Constitution.

ordinances • laws or codes established at the local level, that is, the municipal or county level

A group need not be elected to have authority to promulgate law. Legislative bodies have the authority to appoint administrative groups to make rules that have the power of law. The reason administrative agencies may do so is twofold. First, legislative groups do not have time to address every issue that arises. Second, they often lack the knowledge to adequately address every issue that arises. So they appoint people who have the time and expertise. Examples of administrative agencies include federal regulatory agencies such as the Food and Drug Administration. Examples of state agencies include the fire marshal's office or the state police licensing board. Other examples include county, city or other local groups, such as a metropolitan council, health department or even a park board.

Remember that courts make law through their holdings that act as rules because of *stare decisis*. Whatever they have decided becomes the law and is relied on in subsequent cases. The fact that courts are making law, but for the most part are not elected to do so as are legislators, stirs debate. This is especially the case at the Supreme Court level and is why the ability of a president to appoint justices is so powerful. The legally enforceable rules that any court, legislative body or administrative agency may make depends on the jurisdiction granted them by law.

How? (Procedural)

Substantive law establishes rules and regulations, as in traffic law. How the law is to be enforced is embodied in **procedural law.** For example, how and when police can stop people is governed by procedural law. The effects of substantive law being enforced in violation of law can result in serious consequences for the government. For example, the exclusionary rule (discussed in Chapter 8) prohibits evidence obtained in violation of a person's constitutional rights (illegal search and seizure) to be used in court, no matter how incriminating. This is why it is crucial for criminal justice professionals to know the law and know when it changes.

substantive law • establishes rules and regulations, as in traffic law

procedural law • how the law is to be enforced, for example, how and when police can stop people

What? (Criminal or Civil)

This question asks whether the wrong considered is a *public* wrong or a *private* wrong. In other words, who is the victim? The answer affects several critical factors.

Criminal law considers society the victim because, whenever a crime is committed, the act disrupts the community. Although one or possibly more than one victim is identifiable, if the community's security is upset, *all* community members are considered victims. Society's welfare has been violated. This is why the caption (name) of a criminal case is the government, representing the people, versus the defendant (e.g., *United States v. Smith, State of Maine v. Jones*). Wrongs that disrupt the status quo of the community are called **crimes**, and criminal laws are found in each state's **penal codes.**

crimes • acts defined by federal or state statute or local ordinance that are punishable; wrongs against the government and the people it serves

penal codes • criminal codes or laws

If a dispute involves only individuals and affects only them, it is considered a civil case, and the wrong is called a **tort.** These cases are captioned with the name of the aggrieved party bringing the legal action, generally referred to as the plaintiff, versus the individual accused of causing the harm, generally referred to as the defendant.

tort • civil wrong by one individual against another, with the remedy most often being either an order by the court for particular action or compensation

Although there may be more than one plaintiff, as in the case of a class-action lawsuit, civil cases involve individuals, and the government usually is not involved.

■ Civil laws deal with wrongs against individuals—called *torts*. Criminal laws deal with wrongs against society—called *crimes*. An act may be both a tort and a crime.

A drunk driver causing a crash, for example, could be guilty of the crime of driving under the influence, as well as be held civilly liable for the injuries caused to others by the tort committed. This example also helps explain other differences between crimes and torts, including the burden of proof required and the desired outcome.

In a criminal action, the government must prove its case *beyond a reasonable doubt*, which one could view as to a 99 percent degree of certainty. It does not mean without *any* doubt, because few decisions in life can be made with no doubts. This is the same standard applied to any of life's major decisions—marriage, having children, divorce, taking a new job or undergoing surgery. Facts are gathered, decisions reached and action taken. The government is required to meet this high standard in proving its case because the consequences for the accused are so significant, including imprisonment or the ultimate sentence imposed, the death penalty. The system wants to be sure, to the highest degree possible, the government is right when the ultimate goal of the criminal justice system is punishment.

In a civil action, the plaintiff has only to prove their case by a *preponderance of the evidence*, which means "more likely than not," or a 51 percent level of certainty. This lower burden of proof exists in the civil arena for several reasons, a primary one being that the defendant does not face the same monumental loss of freedom as they do if they are found "guilty" in criminal court. Because the goal of the civil system is to right the wrong by making the victim or plaintiff "whole" again, civil damages are usually limited to financial awards or injunctions to return the plaintiff to where they were to begin with, for example, paying on a broken contract, removing a fence on someone else's land or paying to compensate for a wrongful injury. The civil system also acknowledges that individuals have limited resources compared with the government and likely could not afford the experts often utilized during a criminal investigation, and their use would not be warranted.

To return to the drunk-driving example, whereas the driver could be charged criminally because of the disruption caused to the community, the person injured in the crash could also sue civilly to recoup medical costs and compensate for injuries sustained. One decision does not depend on the other. In the infamous O.J. Simpson case, the defendant was acquitted on the criminal charges because the government could not prove their case beyond a reasonable doubt, but the plaintiffs in the civil case were successful in proving their case by a preponderance of the evidence.

The Components of the U.S. Legal System

This chapter provides a starting point for studying the Constitution by helping you understand the system that permits the law to serve society. Just like a complicated engine made of many individual parts, the legal system has many components that must work together to produce the desired result.

Recall that Article 3 of the U.S. Constitution established the federal judicial system: "The judicial Power of the United States shall be vested in one Supreme Court, and in such inferior courts as the Congress may from time to time ordain and establish." In addition, the congresses of the individual states have established state supreme courts and inferior courts.

■ The courts' two main functions are to settle controversies between parties and to decide the rules of law that apply in the specific case.

The types of cases a court can hear depend on its jurisdiction. The term *jurisdiction* refers to
■ The authority of a legislative body to establish a law or a court to hear a case.
■ The authority a law has over a specific group of people.

Three levels of jurisdiction exist: federal, state and local. In addition, jurisdiction can be original or appellate. **Original jurisdiction** describes a court authorized to hear cases first, try them and render decisions. Such courts are often called trial courts. **Appellate jurisdiction** describes a court authorized to review cases and to either affirm or reverse the actions of a lower court.

Courts may also have general or limited jurisdiction. As the names imply, courts with **general jurisdiction** may hear a wide range of cases; those of **limited jurisdiction** hear a much narrower range of cases. Further, courts may have exclusive or concurrent jurisdiction. **Exclusive jurisdiction** applies to courts that can hear only specific cases. **Concurrent jurisdiction** refers to two or more courts authorized to hear a specific type of case.

Finally, jurisdiction may refer to a geographical area. A more precise term to describe the geographic area in which a case may be heard is *venue*. **Venue** refers to the place a specific case may come to trial and the area from which the jury is selected.

With this understanding of the terminology describing the authority of specific courts, look next at the court system of the United States, beginning with the lowest level and continuing to the highest—the U.S. Supreme Court.

The Court System

Just as the U.S. Constitution established the federal court system, state constitutions establish their own court systems with many variations from state to state.

■ The U.S. judicial system is two-tiered, consisting of state and federal court systems. Each includes specific levels of courts.

At either tier, three levels of courts function: a lower level or trial court, an appellate court and a court of last resort, or supreme court, as illustrated in Figure 2.1.

The U.S. legal system was designed to provide individuals with a fair and just trial conducted under fair rules of procedure in an atmosphere of objectivity. These levels exist to assure that if either side thinks procedural rules were violated, they can appeal the case to a higher court. This appellate court can uphold the lower court's finding, order a new trial or overturn/reverse/dismiss the charge.

The State Court System

Individual states establish a variety of lower courts with a variety of names. Figure 2.2 illustrates the state court system.

original jurisdiction • courts authorized to hear cases first, try them and render decisions

appellate jurisdiction • describes a court authorized to review cases and to either affirm or reverse the actions of a lower court

general jurisdiction • courts having the ability to hear a wide range of cases

limited jurisdiction • restriction of the types of cases a particular court might hear

exclusive jurisdiction • courts that can hear only specific cases

concurrent jurisdiction • two or more courts authorized to hear a specific type of case

venue • the geographic area in which a specific case may come to trial, and the area from which the jury is selected

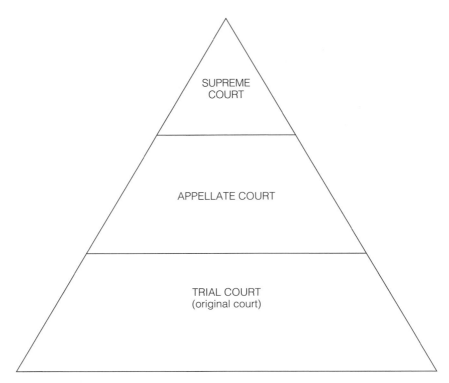

Figure 2.1 Levels in the State and Federal Court System

Lower Courts   Lower courts include municipal courts, inferior courts of limited jurisdiction and county courts. Municipal courts hear ordinance violations, minor criminal cases, traffic cases and sometimes more major cases. Their authority is usually limited to the city or county in which the court is located.

Inferior courts of limited jurisdiction include probate courts, family courts, police courts, justice of the peace courts and traffic courts. A few states still have police courts, courts that try misdemeanor offenses and conduct preliminary examinations to decide whether evidence is sufficient to bring the case to trial in a higher-level court. Some states have established these inferior courts of limited jurisdiction to eliminate the expense and inconvenience of traveling to a county or district court.

County courts often have exclusive jurisdiction over misdemeanor cases and civil cases involving a limited amount of money. In some states, county courts are also probate courts and juvenile courts. Some states have combined various courts under the umbrella of the county courts.

Superior courts are the highest trial courts with general jurisdiction. More than 3,000 such courts exist in the United States. This is where most felony cases enter the system. Some states call them district courts, circuit courts or courts of common plea. These courts may have an appellate department to hear and decide appeals from the municipal courts.

Intermediate Appellate Courts   These courts were created in several states to reduce the caseloads of state supreme courts. Appealed cases generally go to the intermediate appellate court first.

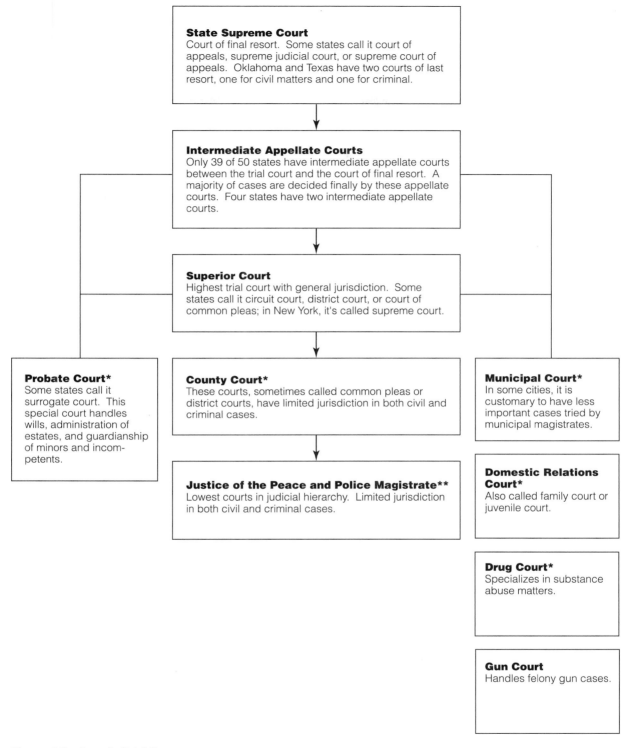

Figure 2.2 State Judicial System

*Courts of special jurisdiction such as probate, family or juvenile courts, and the so-called inferior courts such as common pleas or municipal courts may be separate courts or part of the trial court of general jurisdiction.

**Justices of the peace do not exist in all states. Where they do exist, their jurisdictions vary greatly from state to state. Note: In California all justice courts are municipal courts.

Source: American Bar Association. *Law and the Courts.* Chicago: American Bar Association, 1974, p. 20. Updated information provided by West Publishing Company, St. Paul, MN [Senna and Siegel, 9th ed., 2002, p. 276].

State Supreme Courts   State supreme courts are the highest courts in a state and are generally called supreme courts, although some states call them courts of appeals. These courts are given their power by the individual state constitutions. They generally oversee the intermediate appellate courts and have very few areas of original jurisdiction. If someone petitions the supreme court to review the decision of an appeals court, this is called a **petition for certiorari.** A lower court must abide by the decision of a higher court.

petition for certiorari •
request that the Supreme Court review the decision of a lower court

The Federal Court System

The federal court system consists of a number of specialized courts, a number of district courts with general jurisdiction, 12 circuit courts of appeals and the U.S. Supreme Court (Figure 2.3).

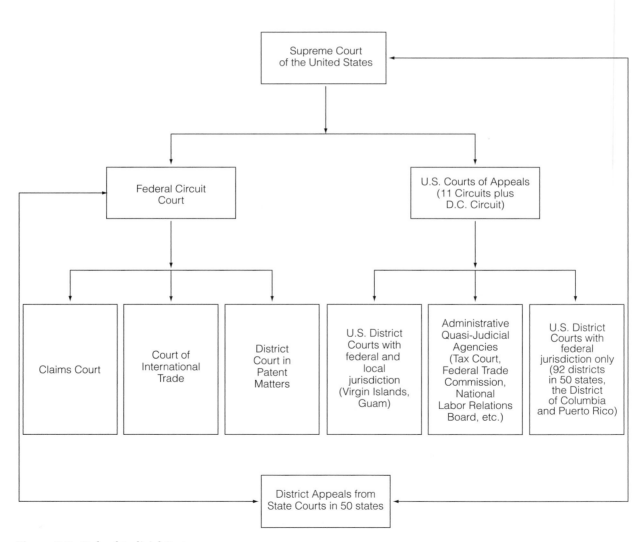

Figure 2.3   Federal Judicial System

Source: American Bar Association. *Law and the Courts.* Chicago: American Bar Association, 1974, p. 21. Updated information provided by the Federal Courts Improvement Act of 1982 and West Publishing Company, St. Paul, MN [Senna and Siegel, 9th ed., 2002, p. 283].

Special U.S. Courts   Congress has created several specialized courts with which you will probably never have any dealings. They include the Court of Military Appeals, the Court of Claims, the Court of Customs and Patent Appeals, the Customs Court and the Tax Court.

U.S. District Courts   The district courts are trial courts with general, original federal jurisdiction. They try both civil and criminal cases. In civil cases, however, the plaintiff and defendant must be from different states, and the amount of the lawsuit must be more than $10,000. The federal district courts try a very limited number of criminal cases. Each state has at least one district court. Some large states have four. The total number of district courts is 94 (92 in the states, one in the District of Columbia and one in Puerto Rico) (Figure 2.4).

U.S. Courts of Appeals   Like the intermediate appellate courts at the state level, the U.S. Courts of Appeals were created to ease the caseload of the Supreme Court. Each state is assigned to one of 11 districts or circuits. The District of Columbia has its own circuit and court. These courts have jurisdiction over final decisions of federal district courts. They are the courts of last resort in most federal cases.

The U.S. Supreme Court   The U.S. Supreme Court is the ultimate court of appeal. Its chief function is as an appellate court. It receives petitions for certiorari from over 6,000 cases a year but usually accepts fewer than 10 percent for review. More than a third of the cases received are from state supreme courts. The Supreme Court is restricted by act of Congress to hear only certain types of appeals

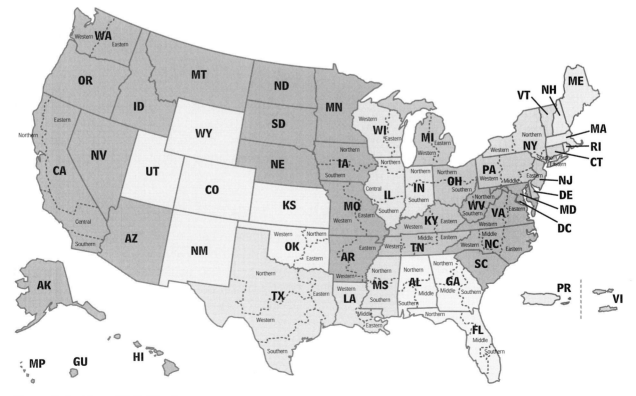

Figure 2.4   Map of U.S. Districts

from federal appeals courts and state supreme courts. Basically, the cases must involve a federal or state statute alleged to be unconstitutional. There is no right to have a case heard by the Supreme Court. It hears only cases of extreme national importance to set important policy.

The Supreme Court has dealt with such controversial issues as abortion, busing and school prayer. Bills have been introduced in Congress to prevent the Supreme Court from ruling on such "moral" issues, leaving it up to the individual states. The Supreme Court is the only court empowered to handle lawsuits between two states. Because of its extreme importance in shaping the country's laws, the next chapter is devoted to the Supreme Court.

Officers of the Court

The legal system does not consist simply of buildings. It is about people. It is there to serve people and does so through those who play important and varied roles in the system. Those whose jobs are to carry out the administration of law are called officers of the court.

▓ The officers of the court are judges, lawyers, clerks of court, sheriffs, marshals and bailiffs.

Judges, sometimes called justices or magistrates, are elected in some states and appointed in others. Judges preside over trials and hearings and render decisions. They also oversee the selection of juries and instruct them during jury cases.

Lawyers represent one side or the other. In a civil case, the plaintiff's lawyer represents the party bringing suit. In a criminal case, the prosecutor represents the state. The lawyer representing the accused or answering party is the defense attorney. The lawyers prepare and present their clients' cases to a judge and sometimes to a jury.

Clerks of court schedule cases, officially record all business conducted by the court, and receive and file all official documents related to a case, for example, summons and complaints. Sheriffs and marshals serve summons and other court documents and enforce court orders. Sheriffs function at the state level and marshals at the federal level. Bailiffs are responsible for keeping the courtroom proceedings orderly and dignified and for protecting everyone in the courtroom.

An Adversarial Judicial System

After a person is charged with an offense, civil or criminal, sides are drawn—*accuser v. accused.* The accusing side has the burden of proof to establish guilt. The defendant is presumed innocent until this has been accomplished. It is expected that each side will assert their positions vehemently, not only so that their situation will be resolved but also so that truth will prevail. This is accomplished by having each side provide the strongest legal response possible, a concept difficult to appreciate by those who lack understanding of the law. For example, a question frequently asked of defense lawyers is: "How can you defend someone accused of such a horrible crime?" The answer is that even the accused has a right to legal representation as aggressive as the law allows. It could be a matter of life and death.

The legal system established in the United States is termed an **adversarial judicial system** because only in an actual conflict will a judicial body hear the case. Theoretically, courts will not entertain "what if" questions. Actual people must have reached an impasse and require a binding decision by a court. In practice, however, the Court has frequently relaxed this barrier, finding exceptions to it and applying it inconsistently. The abortion case *Roe v. Wade* (1973), for example, was decided long after the petitioner's pregnancy had terminated and the controversy ended.

As designed, however, the system places one side against the other, whether the government against a private party or individual against individual. Although the system encourages problems to be settled out of court, the system is prepared to be accessed when necessary.

The overall legal system is organized to provide parties to a case the most accessible tribunal. For example, a matter involving a local building-code dispute is best taken up by a municipal board of adjustments and appeals or the city council. The violation of a state statute, on the other hand, is best dealt with by a state court.

All levels of jurisdiction have avenues of appeals so that matters may be heard by another body of decision makers. This system provides a degree of checks and balances and removes the element of personal involvement sometimes present at the local level.

> **adversarial judicial system** • a legal system such as that used in the United States, which places one party against another to resolve a legal issue, stipulating that only in an actual conflict will a judicial body hear the case

Doctrines Governing What Cases Will Be Heard

■ Three important doctrines govern whether a case will be heard by the court: standing, mootness and ripeness.

Standing   To bring a case or to argue a legal issue in court, one must have **standing,** meaning an actual interest in the matter of dispute. It is not permissible for just anyone to bring a legal action unless they are actually a party to the matter intended to be adjudicated. Someone must have been legally wronged or accused of the wrongdoing to be involved in a legal case. People who are not a party to the action may still have an interest and are permitted to submit **amicus** ("friends of the court") **briefs** arguing their perspective. However, these are only considered at the pleasure of the court and as merely thoughts of a nonparty.

> **standing** • having an actual interest in the matter of dispute
>
> **amicus brief** • a "friend of the court" brief submitted by a person not a party to the action but interested in the outcome

Mootness   exists when the issues that gave rise to a case have either been resolved or have otherwise disappeared so that a court decision would have no practical effect. An example of a case dismissed for **mootness** is one in which a group of students and their parents filed suit challenging the inclusion of two prayers and a hymn during a 1991 public high school graduation ceremony as unconstitutional. Although the federal district court rejected the challenge, the circuit court of appeals declared the practice unconstitutional under the Establishment Clause of the First Amendment. However, the Supreme Court remanded the case, instructing the court of appeals to dismiss it as moot because the students who filed the suit had already graduated. A court can use the mootness doctrine to avoid considering controversial constitutional issues.

> **mootness** • exists when the issues that gave rise to a case have either been resolved or have otherwise disappeared

ripeness doctrine • invoked when a case comes to court too soon, preventing the court from getting prematurely involved in a case that may eventually resolve through other means

Ripeness   The **ripeness doctrine** is invoked when a case comes to court too soon. This doctrine prevents the court from getting prematurely involved in a case that may eventually be resolved through other means.

The Constitution and Criminal Justice in the United States: The Big Picture

This chapter has focused on the legal system and U.S. courts because this is where constitutional issues are decided. However, the courts are only one component of the American system of justice both at the adult and juvenile levels. The Constitution also directly affects what happens before a case comes to court and after the court renders a decision.

■ The criminal justice system consists of law enforcement, courts and corrections.

Law enforcement officers, as the gatekeepers of the criminal justice system, must be thoroughly versed in the Fourth Amendment's guarantee of the right to be free from unreasonable search and seizure. The Constitution applies to the police officer who wants to search the interior of a car stopped for a traffic violation as well as to searches conducted within the walls of a prison by a correctional officer.

Furthermore, these same constitutional constraints apply to nonsworn police, community service officers and animal control personnel, fire and building inspectors, community corrections workers (probation and parole officers), food and drug inspectors and postal inspectors. The number of jobs in the governmental system is huge, and all those working in them are regulated by the Constitution. Finally, those constraints apply to all who work within the juvenile justice system as well.

The Courts, Corrections and Criminal Sanctions

The courts determine what criminal sanctions will be imposed on those who commit crimes. Cole and Smith (2007, p. 384) note: "Criminal sanctions in the United States have four goals: retribution (deserved punishment), deterrence, incapacitation, and rehabilitation. Ultimately, all criminal punishment is aimed at maintaining the social order, but the justifications for sentencing speak to the American values of justice and fairness." Clear et al. (2006, p. 6) explain: "Punishing people who break society's rules is an unfortunate but necessary part of social life. From the earliest accounts of humankind, punishment has been used as one means of social control, or compelling people to behave according to the norms and rules of society."

The manner by which violators have been held accountable has varied over time, and challenges to the Eighth Amendment (forbidding "cruel and unusual punishments") will likely have as many, if not more, challenges in the future as it has in the past, as discussed in detail in Chapter 13.

The Juvenile Justice System

More than 100 years ago, the juvenile justice system was born by the establishment of a separate juvenile court (the Juvenile Court Act of 1899 in Illinois). Reformers believed that the punitive focus of the adult system was not in the "best interest of the child." They sought to establish a court whose purpose was to rehabilitate youthful offenders rather than to punish them. Initially youths coming before the juvenile court had no due process rights whatsoever. But as the court evolved, these rights were instituted, as discussed later in the text. And over time, a juvenile justice system developed to parallel the adult (criminal) justice system.

■ The juvenile justice system has the same three components as the criminal justice system: law enforcement, courts and corrections.

The law enforcement component is directly affected by the establishment of **status offenses,** behavior prohibited by law simply because the person engaging in the behavior is a minor (usually younger than 18). Examples include smoking cigarettes, drinking alcohol, running away from home and truancy. Corrections is affected because most states have enacted legislation prohibiting housing juveniles in adult facilities.

status offenses • offenses deemed to be illegal when committed by juveniles because of their age, which are not unlawful for adults, such as smoking, drinking and curfew

Beginning in 1980, a trend emerged to "get tough" on juvenile offenders, especially those committing more serious crime: "Legislatures passed laws to crack down on juvenile crime, reflecting a widespread reconsideration of juvenile philosophy, jurisdiction, and authority and a more punitive approach to juvenile delinquency" (Burfeind and Bartusch, 2006, p. 45). Such legislative changes include provisions allowing juveniles to be tried in adult courts, increased sentencing options by juvenile courts and a reduction in juvenile court confidentiality: "These initiatives for punishment and accountability have replaced the rehabilitative ideal . . . of the original juvenile court" (ibid). The effectiveness of this approach is yet to be documented.

The Criminal Justice and Juvenile Justice Systems Compared

■ The most important similarity between the criminal justice and the juvenile justice systems is that all constitutional rights apply. The most important difference is that the focus of the criminal justice system is to punish and to deter, whereas the focus of the juvenile justice system is to rehabilitate.

Law Enforcement   Many police departments have a separate juvenile division or at least a few juvenile officers. Many other departments have no such specialists, and all officers are responsible for both juvenile and adult offenders. The terminology usually differs, however. Juveniles are *taken into custody;* adults are *arrested.* Juveniles are accused of *delinquent acts;* adults are accused of *crimes.* Juveniles are directed to appear in court by a *petition;* adults are directed to appear in court by an *information* or *indictment.* Juveniles and adults may be kept in custody before appearing in court to protect the public or to assure their court appearance. In the case of juveniles, this is called *detention;* adults are *jailed.* Adults usually have a right to bail; in most states juveniles do not.

Courts   Juvenile court proceedings are less formal and may be private; adult proceedings are more formal and public. Juvenile identifying information is usually not released to the press; adult information is released. Juveniles have no right to a jury trial, but adults do. Both systems require proof beyond a reasonable doubt and the right to be represented by an attorney, and both allow appeals to a higher court. The initial appearance before a juvenile judge is called a *conference;* before a criminal judge it is called a *preliminary hearing.* In juvenile court, the *adjudication hearing* parallels the adult *trial.* Juvenile court proceedings are quasi-civil and may be confidential; criminal court proceedings are open.

During a juvenile hearing, a youth may be adjudicated *delinquent;* in the adult court, the defendant is declared a *criminal.* In either court, if a guilty decision is rendered, a hearing to determine the outcome is held. In juvenile court, this is the *dispositional hearing;* in adult court, it is the *sentencing hearing.* In either system, the disposition or sentence cannot be cruel or unusual. Although controversy has always surrounded the death penalty, the controversy increases as to whether it should be applied to juveniles.

Corrections   As noted, juvenile and adult correctional facilities are to be separated. Juveniles released from custody receive *aftercare;* adults receive *parole* or *probation.*

The Changing Face of American Criminal Justice and Constitutional Law

This brief overview of the criminal and juvenile justice systems has been provided to stress the importance of the Constitution at every juncture within these systems. Whatever the role of government agents, their power is limited by the constraints of the Constitution. This should never be viewed as a hindrance or something negative. Rather, this provides the government, and those it serves, with clear guidelines that maintain the purpose the framers of the Constitution had in mind more than two centuries ago. This system of reserved power benefits all concerned.

The Constitution is not just about history and theory. It applies to every criminal-justice practitioner. Each is expected to understand constitutional rights and to apply them in any number of situations, including many that have not previously arisen. In fact, U.S. constitutional law is being challenged in myriad unprecedented ways, as technology and travel make crossing international borders an everyday event for millions around the world. Returning to a concept introduced earlier—that American law is living and ever evolving—this chapter concludes with a look at how this blurring of jurisdictional boundaries has an impact on constitutional law.

American Criminal Justice beyond Our Borders

As the entire world continues to become closer for reasons that include electronic communication, the Internet and ease of travel, people find themselves increasingly interested in laws different from their own. The study of **comparative law** is just that, comparing and contrasting laws to expand understanding of law and legal theory. It is fascinating to delve into the historical development of legal systems and compare them with ours, finding some are quite similar and some vastly different.

comparative law • comparing and contrasting laws to expand understanding of law and legal theory

Even more relevant to the study of the American Constitution and criminal justice system is the impact of our Constitution and the laws of other nations when Americans are called on to provide services in foreign lands: "In a shrinking world with a global economy, terrorism, electronic communications, and jet aircraft, much crime is transnational, giving rise to a host of international criminal law enforcement tasks. American law enforcement is being 'exported' in response to increased international terrorism, drug trafficking, smuggling of illegal immigrants, violations of U.S. securities laws, and money laundering, as well as the potential theft of nuclear material" (Cole and Smith, 2007, p. 156).

Because the Constitution serves as the primary roadmap for American law enforcement, primarily involving American citizens, entirely different rules, regulations, policies and procedures are taken into account when foreign governments are involved. It is not as simple as having U.S. law enforcement officials conduct their official duties the same elsewhere as they do at home.

Without more powers, any foreign official may be restricted to lawfully gathering data with no more authority than any other citizen or visitor would have. Cooperative agencies such as the International Criminal Police Organization (INTERPOL) serve as clearing houses but cannot summarily grant expanded police powers.

The U.S. National Bureau of Interpol, the Interpol unit in the United States, operates in Washington, D.C. and directly involves multiple federal agencies and cooperates with foreign police entities, as their mission statement explains: "The U.S. National Central Bureau (USNCB) was authorized by statute (22 U.S.C. 263a) and operates within the guidelines prescribed by the Department of Justice, in conjunction with the Department of Homeland Security. The mission of the U.S. National Central Bureau is to facilitate international law enforcement cooperation as the United States representative with the International Criminal Police Organization (INTERPOL), on behalf of the Attorney General."

The authority by which U.S. law enforcement may act in any official capacity in a foreign country is the result of compacts, treaties or other formal arrangements with those nations. Times of war bring additional rules regulating what is and is not permissible. Recently, the complexities of incorporating such laws as promulgated by the Geneva Convention and Uniform Code of Military Justice have been scrutinized regarding such issues as the treatment of military prisoners at the Abu Ghraib prison in Iraq. The increased practice of combining military and private security during wartime has expanded the complexities of rules that apply during global conflict.

Because the Constitution is considered the basis of U.S. law and that which is considered just, those pursuing further studies of comparative, military and law enforcement on foreign soil are best served by developing an initial understanding of the U.S. Constitution. As with studying other legal theories, you are encouraged to explore comparative and international law as opportunities present themselves. Chapter 4 provides means by which you can pursue your own interest in these areas.

SUMMARY

In the United States, two prominent theories about the underlying purpose of law exist: consensus theory and conflict theory. The basic purpose of the U.S. legal system is to ensure fairness in balancing individual and societal rights and needs, while preventing excessive government power. This balance between individual and societal rights and needs is represented by the scales of justice.

Our legal system has its roots in the common law of England, the early English judge-made law based on custom and tradition and followed throughout the country. In American law, common law is synonymous with case law. Inherent in the common law is the principle of *stare decisis*. *Stare decisis* requires that precedents set in one case be followed in all cases having similar circumstances, thus assuring consistency in the law. The Constitution ensures individual rights by limiting government power. And although the law, in fairness, must be consistent, it is also flexible. American law is considered a living law because it can change along with society.

In addition to common law, the legal system also relies upon case law, statutory law—that is, law passed by legislature or governing bodies—and constitutional law. The U.S. legal system categorizes offenses into two specific areas: civil and criminal. Civil laws deal with personal matters and wrongs against individuals—called torts. Criminal laws deal with wrongs against society—called crimes. An act may be both a tort and a crime. When civil or criminal laws are broken, the courts' two main functions are to settle controversies between parties and to decide the rules of law that apply in specific cases.

The U.S. legal system is made up of a number of necessary components. It is basically a two-tiered system consisting of state and federal courts. Each tier includes specific levels of courts. The officers of the court are judges, lawyers, clerks of court, sheriffs, marshals and bailiffs. Three important doctrines govern whether a case will be heard by the court: standing, mootness and ripeness.

The Constitution affects not only our legal system but also both our criminal and juvenile justice systems. Both systems have three components: law enforcement, courts and corrections. The most important similarity between the criminal and the juvenile justice systems is that all constitutional rights apply. The most important difference is that the focus of the criminal justice system is to punish and to deter, whereas the focus of the juvenile justice system is to rehabilitate.

DISCUSSION QUESTIONS

1. Could a country such as the United States function without a federal constitution? Would it be possible for each state to merely abide by its own constitution?

2. Why shouldn't the Constitution include an overall criminal code specifying crimes and punishments that could apply throughout the United States?

3. Why is society considered the victim of a crime rather than the individual victimized?

4. Why must the legal system provide an appeal procedure?

5. Can you develop an argument against *stare decisis*?

6. Why shouldn't courts be permitted to argue "what if" questions?

7. Which underlying theory about the purpose of law do you feel makes most sense—consensus or conflict theory?

8. If the basic purpose of the U.S. legal system is to ensure fairness in balancing individual and societal rights and needs, is that end best served by an adversarial system in which the person with the best lawyer often comes out on top? Does this system of justice provide equal access to people of different socioeconomic classes?

9. Discuss whether you consider U.S. law a "living law."

10. Should people have a right to a defense attorney?

 INFOTRAC COLLEGE
EDITION ASSIGNMENTS

- Use InfoTrac College Edition to assist you in answering the Discussion Questions when appropriate.

- Search *courts* and list the numerous types of courts in this country. Select one type of court to look at in depth. Outline the main characteristics of that court.

- Use one of the following key words/phrases to locate an article related to this chapter to read and outline: *amicus briefs, common law, mootness, scales of justice, stare decisis, U.S. legal system.*

 INTERNET ASSIGNMENTS

- Use http://www.findlaw.com to find one case discussed in this chapter. Outline the key points.

- Research and outline information on one of the following terms (be sure the material relates to chapter content): *amicus briefs, case law, common law, conflict theory, consensus theory, legal standing, mootness, petition for certiorari, procedural law, ripeness doctrine, social contract, stare decisis, status offenses, statutory law, substantive law, torts.*

- Using the key term *jurisdiction*, find the article "Law about Jurisdiction: An Overview" and outline the main points.

COMPANION WEB SITE

■ Go to the Constitutional Law and the Criminal Justice System 3e Web site at http://cj.wadsworth.com/ hessharr_constlaw3e for Case Studies and Study Guide exercises.

REFERENCES

Burfeind, James W. and Bartusch, Dawn Jeglum. *Juvenile Delinquency An Integrated Approach.* Sudbury, MA: Jones and Bartlett Publishers, 2006.

Clear, Todd R.; Cole, George F.; and Reisigm, Michael D. *American Corrections,* 7th ed, Belmont, CA: Thomson Wadsworth Publishing, 2006.

Cole, George F. and Smith, Christopher E. *The American System of Criminal Justice,* 11th ed. Belmont, CA: Thomson Wadsworth Publishing, 2007.

"Trends in Juvenile Justice and Delinquency." *Criminal Justice Research Reports,* July/August 2003, pp. 89–90.

Walker, Samuel; Spohn, Cassia; and DeLone, Miriam. *The Color of Justice: Race, Ethnicity, and Crime in America,* 3rd ed. Belmont, CA: Wadsworth Publishing Company, 2004.

ADDITIONAL RESOURCES

Whitman, James Q. *Harsh Justice: Criminal Punishment and the Widening Divide between America and Europe.* New York: Oxford University Press, 2003.

Silverman, Ira J. and Vega, Manuel. *Corrections, A Comprehensive View.* New York: West Publishing, 1996.

CASES CITED

Moore v. City of Albany, 98 N.Y. 396, 410 (1885).

Roe v. Wade, 410 U.S. 113 (1973).

CHAPTER 3

The Supreme Court of the United States: The Final Word

THE PRINCIPLE IS THAT OURS IS A GOVERNMENT OF LAWS, NOT OF MEN, AND THAT WE SUBMIT OURSELVES TO RULERS ONLY IF UNDER RULES.

—JUSTICE ROBERT H. JACKSON

YOUNGSTOWN SHEET AND TUBE CO. V. SAWYER (1952)

© AP/Wide World Photos

Current Supreme Court justices pose for their official group portrait. *Front row:* Anthony Kennedy, John Paul Stevens, Chief Justice John Roberts, Antonin Scalia, David Souter. *Back row:* Stephen Breyer, Clarence Thomas, Ruth Bader Ginsburg, Samuel Alito.

DO YOU KNOW . . .

- Under what authority the Supreme Court operates?
- What the jurisdiction of the Supreme Court is?
- How the Supreme Court has effectively created most of its own power and authority?
- Whether the Supreme Court can review acts of Congress? The precedent case?
- Whether the Supreme Court can review cases that are pending in state courts or that have been decided in state courts? The precedent case?
- What certiorari is?
- Why appointments of justices to the Supreme Court are lifetime?
- Whether the current Supreme Court is liberal or conservative?

CAN YOU DEFINE?

certiorari	judicial review	recesses
concurring opinion	liberal	sittings
conservative	opinion	strict construction
dissenting opinion		

Introduction

The U.S. Supreme Court is uniquely American, and like American law itself, its roots extend to the history of why the framers of the Constitution—representing those who came to this country in search of freedom, due process and the possibilities of a better life—created the United States. Visitors to our nation's capitol may be overwhelmed with symbols of the hope, dreams and challenges of creating a new government two centuries ago. Recall the two statues outside the National Archives in Washington: they proclaim *Study the Past* and *What Is Past Is Prologue* and are symbols of the ideals of American government that abound throughout the city.

This chapter has been included not because many of us will ever find ourselves appearing before the Supreme Court, but because what occurs there affects each of us daily. Unfortunately, many Americans take this for granted. Criminal justice professionals cannot. The history of the Supreme Court, including those who make up the Court, combines with its role as defined by the Constitution to create this uniquely effective overseer of the legal system. Therefore, it is imperative that those studying law, and particularly constitutional law, have a working knowledge and understanding of the role the Supreme Court and the justices appointed to it play in the continuing saga of the country's living law.

In the final analysis, the Supreme Court is about people, people who conceptualized such a system, people who risked everything in their effort to make it happen. It is about nominees and those appointed to the Court. It is about individuals named in the cases that gain infamy by having been involved in something that turned out to have broad-reaching effects and those whose seldom-heard stories changed the course of history. And it is about each person affected by the cases the Court hears and those they elect not to hear. Every U.S. citizen is affected by all the Supreme Court does.

> The Supreme Court—by virtue of its exercise of responsibility—has become the most powerful court the world has ever known. It can override the will of the majority expressed in an act of Congress. It can remind a president that in the United States all persons are subject to the rule of law. It can require the redistribution of political power in every state. And it can persuade the nation's citizens that the fabric of their society must be rewoven into new patterns (*The Supreme Court at Work*, 1999, p. 3).

In addition to influencing every U.S. citizen, the Supreme Court has had a profound influence on criminal justice and on law enforcement in particular. Spector (2003, p. 16) notes, "Over the past 50 years, the U.S. Supreme Court has molded law enforcement from a seat-of-the pants job to a highly standardized profession." He (p. 21) notes that in the past 50 years a "flood of Supreme Court cases [has created] the foundation for virtually every action officers take today."

This chapter begins with a discussion of how the U.S. Supreme Court gets its authority and its jurisdiction and the powerful influence it has through judicial review and through certiorari. Next the makeup of the Supreme Court is discussed, including the composition of the present-day court and how the jurists' personal philosophies regarding crime and justice affect the entire system. This discussion is followed by a discussion of the political nature of the Supreme Court. The chapter concludes with a description of some of the Court's traditions, procedures and power.

Authority for the Supreme Court

The law that emanates from the Supreme Court is the law of the land, and no other judicial or political body can overrule decisions it makes. Because American law is a living law, conceivably the Supreme Court could overrule itself, which it has, in fact, done.

The constitutional establishment of authority is found in Article 3, which provides a framework for the federal judiciary. The Federal Judiciary Act of 1789 established the first Supreme Court, and although the number of justices has varied, nine has remained the agreed upon number since 1869.

The Constitution itself is a rather brief document, intended to set forth the framework of the new government rather than to provide the lengthy specifics that others would find themselves having the responsibility of developing. It should not surprise—or trouble—us that this article is brief and to the point as well. Article 3 states the following:

> The judicial power of the United States, shall be vested in one Supreme Court, and in such inferior courts as the Congress may from time to time ordain and establish.

■ The U.S. Constitution ordains in Article 3 that there shall be a Supreme Court.

Section 2 of Article 3 of the Constitution defines the jurisdiction (or boundaries) of the Supreme Court.

Jurisdiction of the Supreme Court

> Section 2. The judicial Power shall extend to all Cases, in Law and Equity, arising under this Constitution, the Laws of the United States, and Treaties made, or which shall be made, under their Authority;—to all Cases affecting Ambassadors,

other public Ministers and Consuls;—to all Cases of admiralty and maritime Jurisdiction;—to Controversies to which the United States shall be a Party;—to Controversies between two or more States; between a State and Citizens of another State;—between Citizens of the same State claiming Lands under Grants of different States, and between a State, or the Citizens thereof, and foreign States, Citizens or Subjects.

In all Cases affecting Ambassadors, other public Ministers and Consuls, and those in which a State shall be Party, the Supreme Court shall have original Jurisdiction. In all the other Cases before mentioned, the Supreme Court shall have appellate Jurisdiction, both as to Law and Fact, with such Exceptions, and under such Regulations as the Congress shall make.

The Court has jurisdiction over two general types of cases: cases that reach it on appeal and cases over which the Court has original jurisdiction, meaning the case can actually start at the Supreme Court. Whether a case begins in the state or federal system, the path to appeal a case to the Supreme Court is the same, as shown in Figure 3.1.

Because the framers of the Constitution did not wish for any individual or body to have excessive authority, the Supreme Court has only specific authority itself. It may hear appeals from lower state and federal courts on issues that involve interpretation of either federal law and/or the applicability of the Constitution to the subject at hand. The Supreme Court can also hear appeals on cases dealing with treaties the United States has entered into, admiralty and maritime cases or those involving certain public officials and political entities.

It should not be assumed, however, that the Supreme Court and inferior (lower) federal courts have carte blanche to do whatever they want. In the post–Civil War case *Ex parte McCardle* (1868), Congress reserved the right to limit the jurisdiction of federal courts, including the Supreme Court. This does not mean that Congress, or any legislature, can override the Constitution by promulgating unconstitutional law. It does mean that Congress retains the authority to determine the types of cases these courts can hear, thus affecting their jurisdictional authority.

United States v. Klein (1871) supported the McCardle decision when the Supreme Court held that Congress, indeed, retains the power under Article 3 to determine which federal courts may hear certain types of cases. These two cases dealt with what types of appeals could be presented to federal courts. This is an excellent example of the natural tension the Constitution creates to prevent any one branch of government from exercising excessive power. These cases show how power with limitations is granted to Congress and the Court to assure the balance sought by a free society through the Constitution.

The Constitution permits the Court original jurisdiction in cases dealing with foreign dignitaries or cases involving legal disputes between states, with the rationale that a state court could not remain unbiased if its state was a party to the suit. All other cases the Court considers only on appeal.

■ The Supreme Court has original jurisdiction in cases dealing with foreign dignitaries and legal disputes between states. All other cases are considered only on appeal.

As noted by Goebel (1971, p. 280): "The brevity of the constitutional description left to Congress and the Court itself the task of filling in much of the substance

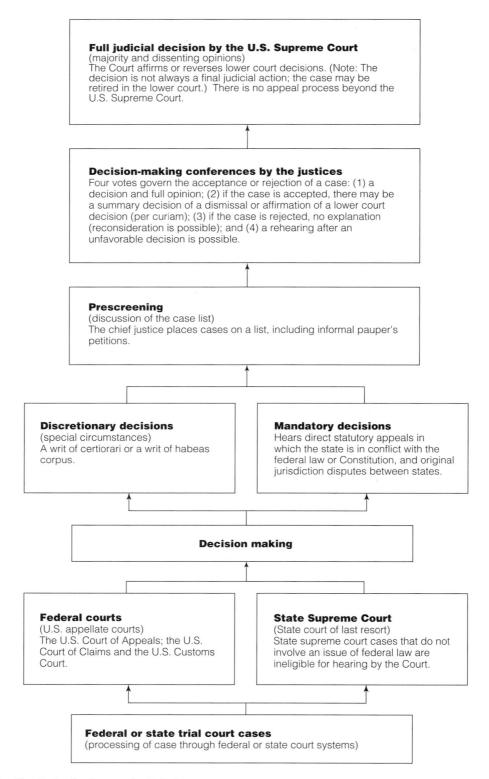

Full judicial decision by the U.S. Supreme Court
(majority and dissenting opinions)
The Court affirms or reverses lower court decisions. (Note: The decision is not always a final judicial action; the case may be retired in the lower court.) There is no appeal process beyond the U.S. Supreme Court.

Decision-making conferences by the justices
Four votes govern the acceptance or rejection of a case: (1) a decision and full opinion; (2) if the case is accepted, there may be a summary decision of a dismissal or affirmation of a lower court decision (per curiam); (3) if the case is rejected, no explanation (reconsideration is possible); and (4) a rehearing after an unfavorable decision is possible.

Prescreening
(discussion of the case list)
The chief justice places cases on a list, including informal pauper's petitions.

Discretionary decisions
(special circumstances)
A writ of certiorari or a writ of habeas corpus.

Mandatory decisions
Hears direct statutory appeals in which the state is in conflict with the federal law or Constitution, and original jurisdiction disputes between states.

Decision making

Federal courts
(U.S. appellate courts)
The U.S. Court of Appeals; the U.S. Court of Claims and the U.S. Customs Court.

State Supreme Court
(State court of last resort)
State supreme court cases that do not involve an issue of federal law are ineligible for hearing by the Court.

Federal or state trial court cases
(processing of case through federal or state court systems)

Figure 3.1 The Path of a Case to the U.S. Supreme Court

Source: Joseph J. Senna and Larry D. Siegel. *Introduction to Criminal Justice*, 9th ed. Belmont, CA: Wadsworth Publishing Company, 2002, p. 286.

and all of the details of the new judicial system. One early observer commented, 'The convention has only crayoned in the outlines. It is left to Congress to fill up and colour the canvas.'" One of the most important ways in which the Court did so was to establish judicial review of laws passed or of cases settled by lower courts.

Judicial Review

The Supreme Court has tremendous power through the process of **judicial review**— the power of the Court to analyze decisions of other government entities and lower courts. Ducat (2004, p. 3) says: "Judicial review is the doctrine according to which courts are entitled to pass upon the constitutionality of an action taken by a coordinate branch of government." That coordinate branch of government is the legislature. And, as Chief Justice Charles Evans Hughes put it: "We are under a Constitution, but the Constitution is what the judges say it is." The Supreme Court can decide which laws and lower court decisions are constitutional.

judicial review • the power of a court to analyze decisions of other government entities and lower courts

■ The Supreme Court has effectively created most of its own power and authority through the process of judicial review.

Initially, the Supreme Court did not review state decisions. It is not surprising that lively debate has occurred over just exactly how far the Supreme Court may go in performing its job or what that job actually is. As with other parts of the Constitution, the brevity leaves room for much interpretation, debate and disagreement.

In 1803, the stage was set when the Court forcefully asserted its right to judicial review in *Marbury v. Madison*, taking advantage of the opportunity to define its own role. William Marbury had been appointed justice of the peace for the District of Columbia in 1801 by President John Adams, just before Adams left office. When Thomas Jefferson became president, his new secretary of state, James Madison, would not acknowledge Marbury's position. Marbury took the case to the Supreme Court, demanding that the new secretary of state recognize his appointment. (See Appendix D for the case.)

Although admittedly a complex case, Chief Justice John Marshall recognized the opportunity to definitively state that, indeed, the Supreme Court had the power to declare an Act of Congress (in this case, the Judiciary Act, passed by Congress in 1789) unconstitutional. Chief Justice Marshall went so far as to say that it was the Supreme Court's responsibility to overturn unconstitutional legislation because of the Court's duty to uphold the Constitution. Chief Justice Marshall forcefully established the Supreme Court's authority as the final interpreter of the Constitution, and his words still ring: "If the courts are to regard the Constitution as superior to any ordinary act of the legislature, the Constitution and not such ordinary act must govern the case to which they apply. . . . It is emphatically the province of the judicial department to say what the law is."

In stating that the Constitution is the supreme law of the land and that the justices are required to follow it rather than inconsistent provisions of legislation, the Court denied Marbury his commission. Some scholars describe *Marbury v. Madison* as the cornerstone of American constitutional law because for the first time the Supreme Court nullified a provision of federal law. Chief Justice John Marshall established that judges are authorized to nullify any law that in their view violates the Constitution.

This case called attention to the conflict between judicial review and political democracy by asking: "Who makes the law—those elected by the people or those sitting on the Supreme Court bench?" The Court's decision was seen as completely opposed to political democracy, with Chief Justice Marshall stating that under the Constitution, "it is emphatically the province and duty of the judicial department to say what the law is."

In short, the legal groundwork (precedent) was established authorizing the Court to maintain a position of the ultimate de facto lawmaker by deciding what legislation is and is not constitutional. Arguably, although Congress could regroup and promulgate additional legislation, the Supreme Court could declare it unconstitutional as well. The Supreme Court does, in fact, have awesome power.

■ *Marbury v. Madison* (1803) established that the Supreme Court has the authority to nullify and void an act of Congress that violates the Constitution.

The Court extended its review authority beyond federal law to state laws through *Fletcher v. Peck* (1810) and again in *Martin v. Hunter's Lessee* (1816), a case that established the power Congress had given the Supreme Court to hear cases involving federal law and constitutional issues. In *Martin*, the Supreme Court determined that it could reverse state court decisions that involved federal legal issues. This case involved a dispute over land ownership. When the Supreme Court heard the case and made a determination, the Virginia state courts refused to follow the Court's decision, arguing that the Supreme Court had no authority to overrule the state court's decision. Again, although the case is complex, the final determination was that the Supreme Court did have the authority to review cases dealing with federal law, even though the case is pending in a state court.

To clarify, Supreme Court Justice Oliver Wendell Holmes asserted that whereas the *Marbury v. Madison* case gave the Supreme Court the power to declare acts of Congress unconstitutional, it was even more important that, in the case of *Martin v. Hunter's Lessee*, the Supreme Court had the authority and power to review and reverse state court decisions to ensure consistent interpretations of federal law.

■ *Martin v. Hunter's Lessee* (1816) held that the Supreme Court can review and reverse state court decisions and can review pending state cases.

Controversy over and Alternatives to Judicial Review

Opponents of judicial review contend judges have too much power: "The main alternative to judicial review is legislative supremacy, and the question is whether the courts have the power to overrule the decisions of elected legislators. Thus, today, opponents of judicial review call for the courts to give up the power to declare state or federal statutes unconstitutional" (Farber, 2003, p. 417).

Proponents of judicial review, on the other hand, argue there must be some watchdog to maintain the constitutionality of law, even if passed by elected bodies of government: "Essentially, judicial review is an attempt to solve a practical problem: how to keep politicians from violating individual rights or undermining the overall system of government for short-term gains" (Farber, p. 443).

Admittedly, judicial oversight is not the only option available. The most basic alternative is for judges to simply refuse to overrule a law, albeit unlikely. Alternative means of resolution could keep cases from finding their way to the courtroom.

One often suggested alternative is mediation. Other alternatives include subgroups within legislatures to provide self-oversight, leaving an obvious potential conflict of interest. Another alternative is to have legislative goodies assess the actions of others. Some have even proposed an individual, such as the president, be the final arbiter. Howeyer: "If Congress is not to be trusted to be the sole judge of its own authority, and if the state governments are eliminated, that leaves only the president as an alternative to judicial review," and even presidential decisions may necessitate judicial oversight (Farber, p. 441).

The debate is not that there needs to be some form of final say as to what law is constitutional. The debate is over *who* should have that final say. And so, the issues set forth in *Marbury v. Madison* more than two hundred years ago persist.

Certiorari: Deciding Which Cases to Hear

The Supreme Court's decision to review a case is almost entirely discretionary. Rarely are cases heard by the Court simply because there is a right to have them heard. The Supreme Court may review a case if a federal appeals court requests the Court to "certify" or clarify a legal point. The Court is also obligated to hear certain cases meeting the requirements for an "appeal of right," although these types of cases occur infrequently. The vast majority of cases heard by the Supreme Court occur through the writ of **certiorari** (certiorari is Latin, meaning "to be informed"), whereby the Court determines which cases are worthy of review on the basis of their national importance.

certiorari • Latin for "to be informed"

Staff attorneys begin the process of deciding which cases will be heard. A "discuss list" is generated and considered during private meetings of the justices. Any case that does not have at least one justice expressing an interest in it is summarily denied. This accounts for the disposition of over 70 percent of cases submitted. At least four of the nine justices must vote in favor of granting certiorari for a case to be accepted for review. Even then, more than 90 percent of all cases submitted for certiorari are denied.

The power that goes with granting certiorari is significant, but so is not "granting cert," as it is also referred to. When certiorari is denied, the Court effectively holds that the previous decision will stand, as will the associated law. Not to decide *is* to decide. Either way, the Court makes a statement.

■ If the Court grants certiorari, it will hear and decide that case. If certiorari is denied, a legal determination has still been made that *previous decisions stand.*

Because some 7,000 cases are submitted to the Court for review annually and that number is rapidly increasing, the Court agrees to hear only about 150 cases a year. This agreement is reached behind closed doors.

In determining which cases to hear, the justices are looking for cases involving matters that directly influence the law and the nation, another example of how powerful this institution is. The justices alone determine on which cases a final decision will be made.

The Supreme Court Justices

The Supreme Court has one chief justice and eight associate justices, nominated by the president of the United States and confirmed by the Senate. Clearly, the framers of the Constitution did not intend for undue influence to be applied to justices serving on the Supreme Court or on any inferior court, as stated in Section 1:

> The Judges, both of the supreme and inferior Courts, shall hold their Offices during good Behavior, and shall, at stated Times, receive for their Services, a Compensation, which shall not be diminished during their Continuance in Office.

No one trying to influence the justices' decisions can ever hold either their jobs or their paychecks over their heads.

■ A Supreme Court appointment is a lifetime appointment so a justice may not be unduly influenced.

Article 2 of the Constitution directs that the president of the United States shall nominate a judge for appointment to the Court, which the Senate must confirm. Article 2 also directs that federal judges, along with all other government officials, could be removed from their offices "on impeachment for and conviction of, treason, bribery, or other high crimes and misdemeanors."

Impeachment is a complex process whereby the House of Representatives brings forth articles of impeachment and the Senate holds the trial. The process, which cannot be based on anything other than actual misconduct, has resulted in only one Supreme Court justice being impeached (Samuel Chase in 1804), but because of the political motivations behind it, he was never actually convicted by the Senate. According to Stephens and Scheb (2003, p. 56): "Barring criminal conduct or serious breaches of judicial ethics, federal judges do not have to worry that their decision might cost them their jobs."

Nominating Supreme Court justices is a particularly powerful responsibility. Although the president will have no authority over a justice once appointed, considerable research is conducted before the president recommends an individual. By scrutinizing a judicial candidate's record, a president is likely to predict how someone might lean when deciding certain politically important issues. A conservative president will seek a conservative judge; a liberal president will seek a liberal judge. The power of a president to potentially mold the makeup of the Court is a most envied political privilege.

Since the origin of the Supreme Court in 1790, more than 100 justices have served, some liberal, some conservative. Smith (2003, p. 164) provides definitions of liberal and conservative modeled on the classifications in the Supreme Court Judicial Database. **Liberal** decisions are pro–person accused or convicted of a crime, pro–civil liberties or civil rights claimants, proindigents, pro–Native Americans and antigovernment. **Conservative** decisions favor the government's interest in prosecuting and punishing offenders over recognition or expansion of rights for individuals.

The 1960s saw a liberal Supreme Court under Chief Justice Earl Warren, with a focus on the rights of the accused. The expansion of criminal procedural rights was slowed in the 1970s and 1980s by President Richard M. Nixon's appointments of conservatives Warren Burger and William H. Rehnquist. However, another Nixon appointee, Harry Blackmun, tended to the liberal side. President Gerald R. Ford's single appointee, John Paul Stevens, tended to be moderate to liberal in his views, rather middle of the road, not greatly influencing the direction of the Court.

liberal • decisions that are pro–person accused or convicted of a crime, pro–civil liberties or civil rights claimants, pro–indigents, pro–Native Americans and antigovernment

conservative • decisions that favor the government's interest in prosecuting and punishing offenders over recognition or expansion of rights for individuals

President Ronald Reagan's three appointments shifted the Court toward a more conservative stance. Sandra Day O'Connor, the first woman to serve on the Court, was seen as moderate to conservative, usually voting to limit prisoners' rights. Antonin Scalia and Anthony Kennedy were both considered very conservative. Also tipping the balance to the conservative side was the appointment of Rehnquist as chief justice at the time.

When conservative David Souter was appointed by President George H.W. Bush to replace liberal William Brennan in 1990, the trend continued, with the Court increasingly favoring the state and law enforcement's position over that of criminal defendants. The conservative nature of the Court was further bolstered when the first President Bush appointed Clarence Thomas (yet another conservative) to replace liberal Thurgood Marshall. President Bill Clinton's 1993 appointment of Ruth Bader Ginsburg is unlikely to change the existing "law and order" Court.

President George W. Bush in his second term not only appointed John Roberts, Jr., to the Court but also appointed him to replace William Rehnquist as Chief Justice after Rehnquist's death. Interestingly, Roberts was nominated by President George H. W. Bush in 1992, but no vote occurred before President Clinton took office. President George W. Bush succeeded with the appointment in 2005. President Bush also appointed Samuel Alito to replace a retiring Sandra Day O'Connor. Table 3.1 compares the records of the justices of the Rehnquist Court and the Warren Court in terms of liberal–conservative voting.

According to Smith (p. 162): "During William Rehnquist's tenure as Chief Justice, the Court has gained a reputation as a consistent supporter of expanded discretionary authority for state legislatures, prosecutors, police officers and corrections officials." This is in sharp contrast to the rights-expanding performance of the Warren Court era. Considering the number of decisions arrived at by a

Table 3.1   Rehnquist Court Justices' Liberal–Conservative Voting Percentages in Decisions from the 1995 Term through the 2000 Term Compared with 1968 Warren Court Justices' Lifetime Voting Percentages

	Rehnquist Court			Warren Court	
Justice	Liberal	Conservative	Justice	Liberal	Conservative
Rehnquist	26.1% (43)	73.9% (122)	White	33%	67%
Thomas	27.9% (46)	72.1% (119)	Harlan	38%	62%
Scalia	30.9% (51)	69.1% (114)	Stewart	45%	55%
O'Connor	31.5% (52)	68.5% (113)	Black	70%	30%
Kennedy	34.5% (57)	65.5% (108)	Warren	74%	26%
Breyer[a]	54.9% (90)	45.1% (74)	Brennan	76%	24%
Souter	57.6% (95)	42.4% (70)	Marshall	80%	20%
Ginsburg	60% (99)	40% (66)	Fortas	83%	17%
Stevens	69.7% (115)	30.3% (50)	Douglas	89%	11%

a. Justice Breyer participated in only 24 of the 25 criminal justice cases during the 2000–2001 term. Thus, his total number of decisions is one fewer than that of his colleagues. He recused himself from participating in *United States v. Oakland Cannabis Buyers' Cooperative* (2001), presumably because his brother is a federal judge who made a decision in the case in the lower courts.

Source: Christopher E. Smith. "The Rehnquist Court and Criminal Justice." *Journal of Contemporary Criminal Justice*, May 2003, p. 171. Reprinted by permission of Sage Publications, Inc.

5-to-4 vote, the change in the makeup of the Court by President Bush's appointees will be followed with keen interest. Although there has been too little time to assess the impact of these two new justices, the fact they were appointed by a Republican president would suggest a more conservative path.

The Influence of the Supreme Court on the Justice System

The influence of the Supreme Court on the justice system is tremendous, as previously noted. Indeed, most criminal procedure has been established not by legislative acts, but by appellate courts, the most important of which is the Supreme Court. However, as Maguire and Pastore (2001) explain, state supreme courts, state intermediate appellate courts and federal courts of appeals throughout the country determine the outcomes in many more cases affecting individual's rights in the criminal justice system than does the Supreme Court.

The Supreme Court hears 25 to 32 criminal justice cases each year. From the 1995 term through the 2000 term, of the 165 total criminal justice cases decided, 78 (47 percent) dealt with constitutional issues; the remaining 87 (53 percent) dealt with statutory and other issues (Smith, p. 166). Among the constitutional issues, those involving the Fourth Amendment were most frequent. Table 3.2 summarizes issues in the U.S. Supreme Court's criminal justice cases from the 1995 term through the 2000 term.

One reason the Court may focus attention on interpretation of federal criminal statutes is that Congress has reacted with increasing frequency to federalize crimes by enacting new statutes defining offenses and punishments (Gest, 2001). Also of interest, as Smith (p. 169) points out: "Despite the Rehnquist Court's reputation for conservatism in criminal justice cases, 37 percent of its decisions supported individuals' claims." Moreover, nearly half of these liberal decisions (28 of 61) were unanimous, as summarized in Table 3.3.

Smith (p. 179) suggests that the production of liberal decisions by a conservative-dominated Court might be partially explained by "consensual norms about statutory interpretation, the need to rein in criminal justice officials by reaffirming limits on authority and the reiteration of symbolic principles (such as *Miranda*). Observers of the Court are eager to see the results of the Roberts' Court.

The Current Supreme Court

It is generally accepted that the current Court's majority consists of conservatives who have "been active in narrowing or overturning many Warren and Burger Court precedents that were favorable to the rights of individuals in the criminal justice system" (Fliter, 2001, p. 181). Smith (p. 169) points out: "The majority of Warren Court members had personal experiences that gave them an empathetic understanding of the risk that suspects and defendants could experience maltreatment at the hands of abusive law enforcement officials. By contrast, most of the Rehnquist Court justices' contacts with criminal justice came through experiences as lawyers on the staffs of county prosecutors, state attorney generals or the U.S. Justice Department (i.e., Sandra Day O'Connor, William Rehnquist, Antonin Scalia, Clarence Thomas, David Souter). Moreover, most of the Rehnquist Court justices were selected by Republican presidents who emphasized 'law and order'

Table 3.2   Issues in the U.S. Supreme Court's Criminal Justice Cases from the 1995 Term through the 2000 Term

Constitutional Issues	78 (47.3%)	Statutory and Other Issues	87 (52.2%)
Fourth Amendment	20	Habeas corpus procedures	25
Due process	11	Federal criminal statutes	21
Sixth Amendment right to counsel	6	Civil rights litigation	13
Capital jury instructions	6	Federal sentencing statute and guidelines	1
Fifth Amendment self-incrimination	5	Federal rules of criminal procedure	5
Fifth Amendment double jeopardy	4	Appellate review standards	3
Ex post facto clause	4	Interstate detainers/extradition	2
Sixth Amendment confrontation clause	3	Forfeiture procedures	2
Equal protection	3	Federal rules of evidence	1
First Amendment	3	Federal prison regulations	1
Sixth Amendment fair trail	2	Lawyer–client privilege	1
Separation of powers	2	Tribal court jurisdiction	1
Sixth Amendment trial by jury	1	Other federal statute	1
Sixth Amendment compulsory process	1		
Eighth Amendment excessive fines	1		
Habeas corpus suspension	1		
Prisoners' access to courts	1		
Appointments clause	1		
Federalism	1		
Fourteenth Amendment right to practice law	1		
Privacy	1		

Source: Christopher E. Smith. "The Rehnquist Court and Criminal Justice." *Journal of Contemporary Criminal Justice,* May 2003, p. 167. Reprinted by permission of Sage Publications, Inc.

Table 3.3   Case Distribution by Vote and Liberal–Conservative Outcomes in U.S. Supreme Court Criminal Justice Decisions from the 1995 Term through the 2000 Term

Vote	Liberal	Conservative	Total
9–0	28	35	63
8–1	4	13	17
7–2	9	15	24
6–3	7	13	20
5–4	13	28	41
Total	61 (37%)	104 (63%)	165

Source: Christopher E. Smith. "The Rehnquist Court and Criminal Justice." *Journal of Contemporary Criminal Justice,* May 2003, p. 170. Reprinted by permission of Sage Publications, Inc.

Table 3.4   The Current U.S. Supreme Court

Justice	President appointing	Political party	Year nominated	Age at nomination	Born	Years of previous judicial experience	Views	Home state
John Paul Stevens	Ford	Republican	1976	55	1920	5	Moderate to liberal	Illinois
Antonin Scalia	Reagan	Republican	1986	50	1936	4	Very conservative	Illinois
Anthony Kennedy	Reagan	Republican	1988	51	1936	12	Very conservative	California
David H. Souter	George H. W. Bush	Republican	1990	50	1939	13	Conservative	New Hampshire
Clarence Thomas	George H. W. Bush	Republican	1991	43	1948	1	Conservative	Georgia
Ruth Bader Ginsburg	Clinton	Democrat	1993	60	1933	13	Moderate	New York
Stephen G. Breyer	Clinton	Democrat	1994	56	1938	14	More liberal	Mass.
John Roberts*	George W. Bush	Republican	2005	50	1955	2	Conservative	New York
Samuel Alito	George W. Bush	Republican	2006	56	1950	16	Conservative	New Jersey

*Chief Justice
Adapted from The Supreme Court Historical Society.

crime control policies." This continued with John Roberts having been a deputy solicitor general arguing cases for the government and Samuel Alito having been a federal attorney. Appendix C details the characteristics of presidential appointees to the U.S. Supreme Court from 1930 to 2006.

■ The current Supreme Court is considered by many to be conservative—a "law and order" court.

Table 3.4 describes the makeup of the current Supreme Court.

Politics and the Supreme Court

It is interesting to listen to laypeople discuss the Supreme Court and try to argue that it is too political or should not be politicized. Comments such as these show a misunderstanding of the Supreme Court. Make no mistake, the Court *is* a political body. The political nature of the Supreme Court is exactly why the Constitution gives the power of appointing justices to the president. The unique twist is that once appointed, justices are beholden to no one and truly are their own people. Although politics may have helped them get the job, that is where party lines end, as illustrated in the preceding discussion.

A president seeks nominees who have political views similar to his and the party. This is common sense. The president is not likely to appoint justices who have vastly different views. Although ability is a factor in selecting justices, the appointment process, as well as the confirmation process, revolves around the appointee's political views.

The confirmation process is difficult for any potential justice because during this process all questions are allowed, and politics become readily apparent. People may argue this is not fair; however, the U.S. legal process is not only fair but logical. The president is elected to perform a job that includes appointing Supreme

Court justices who will support the ideals of the president's party. The argument that holds more weight is this: Once appointed, how are the justices held accountable? This argument becomes more of a "greater good" argument: Is it better for the greater good to have justices who cannot be influenced by anyone rather than putting them in a position to have to consider being re-elected?

This system is not without fault. But given the number of justices on the bench and the process used, the system has proved itself to work extremely well, unless you happen to disagree with the justices' politics. The Supreme Court creates policy through the decisions it makes. Issues are carefully considered by the entire Court, and changes to American law are never taken lightly. It is never one justice's decision alone, and although many decisions come down to a 5-to-4 vote, it can be said that the greatest legal minds in the country have given their best consideration to the decision.

Traditions and Procedures

Although there is certainly definitive authority as to what the Supreme Court can hear, how the Court conducts its business is based to a very large degree on tradition, with respect for the process that has endured, along with the Constitution and the findings of the Supreme Court itself.

By federal statute, a term of the Supreme Court always begins on the first Monday in October, continuing until June or July. Terms are made up of **sittings,** when cases are heard, and **recesses,** during which the Court considers administrative matters at hand and the justices write their opinions. Usually each side has 30 minutes to present its arguments, with 22 to 24 cases presented at one sitting. The 10:00 A.M. entrance of the justices into the courtroom is announced by the marshal and is steeped in history and tradition, as described by the Supreme Court itself:

> Those present, at the sound of the gavel, arise and remain standing until the robed Justices are seated following the traditional chant: "The Honorable, the Chief Justice and the Associate Justices of the Supreme Court of the United States. Oyez! Oyez! Oyez! All persons having business before the Honorable, the Supreme Court of the United States, are admonished to draw near and give their attention, for the Court is now sitting. God save the United States and this Honorable Court!" (*Supreme Court of the United States,* no date, p. 14).

The public is invited to observe the Supreme Court in session, although all Court discussions and decisions occur in private. This tradition has resulted in the Court being one of the most leak-proof organizations in Washington—those who work there abide by this honored tradition. The public can observe the Supreme Court from the visitors' gallery, and when that is filled, additional visitors are ushered into an area at the rear of the courtroom where people are permitted to sit for up to 15 minutes before others are allowed the seats. The remaining seats are reserved for lawyers who are admitted to the Supreme Court bar and members of Congress. Also, a chair is always left open for the president, should he wish to attend.

Strict protocol is followed, and the air of formality encourages the overall respect the Supreme Court demands and deserves. Although the general traditions of courtesy, civility and the utmost professionalism result in a subdued atmosphere most of the time, the scene can change when an emotionally charged

sittings • periods during which the Supreme Court hears cases

recesses • periods when the Supreme Court does not hear cases, but rather considers administrative matters and writes opinions

case is heard or when Americans exert their First Amendment right to speak their mind, often in protest. The abortion issue draws protestors on the anniversary of the *Roe v. Wade* (1973) decision, and when related cases are heard, it can be anticipated that throngs of people on both sides of the issue will be present, as will the media.

The justices sit at a large conference table and discuss each case. The most junior justice is required to present his or her view of that particular case first. This allows the most senior justices to control the decisions as the votes come in. The decisions reached are then cast into opinions.

Opinions

opinion • a written statement by a judge providing a description of the facts; a statement of the legal issues presented for decision, the relevant rules of law, the holding and the policies and reasons that support the holding

concurring opinion • agreeing with the majority

dissenting opinion • a justice's opinion that disagrees with the majority decision of the court

An **opinion** is a written statement explaining the legal issues involved in a case and the precedents on which the opinion is based. The chief justice assigns the writing of the opinion if he voted with the majority. The justice may assign the case to himself. If the chief justice did not vote with the majority, the most senior justice voting with the majority assigns the writing of the opinion. Any justice is free to write an opinion, even if not assigned to do so. This opinion can be a **concurring opinion** (agreeing with the majority) or a **dissenting opinion** (disagreeing with the majority and the reasons underlying the disagreement).

Concurring opinions, a legal tradition dating back to the 1700s, give justices who did not author the opinion a forum to agree in part, or disagree in part, with what was written. Often, a justice will use a concurring opinion to address why they agree with the outcome but not with the reasoning. Any opinion issued by a justice has the power to influence others by simple virtue of the fact that a Supreme Court justice wrote it. These additional opinions might be viewed as "the rest of the story" beyond what the justice writing the majority opinion sets forth and give readers a glimpse into what the other justices were thinking.

Dissenting opinions are included along with the majority opinion to provide the bigger picture and the other perspectives. Although including dissenting opinions is a legal tradition dating back to the King's Bench of Great Britain in 1792, there are more purposeful reasons for continuing the practice. Primarily, justices can use the opportunity to assert their opinions in hopes of influencing future decisions. Dissenting opinions may be referred to in briefs written by other lawyers but carry no legal authority.

Interpretations

The justices not only render decisions, they also interpret the Constitution. The interpretive principles used as the justices deliberate are crucial in accomplishing judicial review.

strict construction • a rigid interpretation of a law not likely to expand the specifically set forth law of the particular statute, particularly in expanding the intent of that law

Strict construction means there is a rigid reading and interpretation of that law. Although there is no formal definition of the term, strict construction would not likely expand the specifically set forth law of the particular statute, particularly in expanding the intent of that law. Others may choose to interpret laws more liberally, often referring to the "spirit of the law" rather than the specific wording of the law.

The justices' personal views regarding the civil rights of victims and criminals influence the day-to-day operations of the entire justice system as they shape the meaning of the Constitution. In addition, interpreting the Constitution is inherently subjective, influenced by the long-term political and social pressures of the times.

Where Supreme Court Decisions May Be Found

Few people read the full text of Supreme Court decisions, relying instead on the news media for such information. These decisions may be found in newspapers and newscasts and in magazines such as *U.S. News & World Report* and *Time*. In addition, the Public Education Division of the American Bar Association, in cooperation with the Association of American Law Schools and the American Newspaper Publishers Association Foundation, publish *The Preview of United States Supreme Court Cases*—an analysis of cases the Court is going to hear. Cases may also be found on the Internet and through Westlaw and Lexis. Chapter 4 explains how to find and research cases.

The Power of the Supreme Court

The Supreme Court is tremendously powerful. It is so powerful that it has been permitted to actually create much of its own immense authority. As Chief Justice Rehnquist reminded us in *The Supreme Court: How It Was, How It Is*, consider that in No. 78 of *The Federalist Papers*, Alexander Hamilton referred to the Supreme Court as the "least dangerous" division of the federal government. Yet, in the cases of *Marbury v. Madison* and *Martin v. Hunter's Lessee*, the Supreme Court was permitted to redefine its powers. Who could stop it? Perhaps diabolical in a sense, perhaps they are merely carrying out the true intentions of the framers of the Constitution. Who else could practically oversee the Bill of Rights?

It can be interpreted from *The Federalist Papers* that the Supreme Court was assigned to this awesome task. As Alexander Hamilton so stated, the interpretation of the Constitution was to become the "proper and peculiar province of the United States Supreme Court." For what other reason would the framers of the Constitution have included a supremacy clause declaring that federal law would outweigh state law?

Any system, including that of the United States, must have a final point. Certainly, many argue that "between here and there" are far too many resting points. For example, there is an effort by many to decrease the number of appeals available to condemned prisoners because of the time and expense involved in the current system. Nonetheless, in the end, the Supreme Court has the definitive say, even if it is by deciding not to hear a particular case.

In many ways, the policies and procedures by which the Supreme Court operates reflect how the American legal system all comes together, quite literally, at the end. It is the appeal of last resort for cases coming before it, reflecting the traditions and complexities of law and the discretion that strongly influences the direction the law takes. Interpretation, application and review of the law gives the Supreme Court tremendous power. However, not even the Court possesses total control over the American legal system. Congress still promulgates law, and the president can still veto. The power of the president to appoint, and Congress to endorse, the makeup of the Court contributes to how the final picture will be painted.

SUMMARY

The Constitution ordained in Article 3 that there shall be a Supreme Court. The Supreme Court has original jurisdiction in cases dealing with foreign dignitaries and legal disputes between states. All other cases are considered only on appeal.

The Supreme Court has created most of its own power and authority through the process of judicial review. Two precedent cases confirmed this power. *Marbury v. Madison* (1803) established that the Supreme Court has the authority to nullify and void an act of Congress that violates the Constitution. *Martin v. Hunter's Lessee* (1816) held that the Supreme Court can review and reverse state court decisions and can review pending state cases. If the Supreme Court grants certiorari, it will hear and decide that case. If certiorari is denied, a legal determination has still been made that former rulings stand.

Because justices decide matters vital to national interest, a Supreme Court appointment is a lifetime appointment so a justice may not be unduly influenced. The current Supreme Court is considered by many to be a conservative "law and order" court.

DISCUSSION QUESTIONS

1. Should any one court be given the final say? Why or why not?

2. Is there a negative side to appointment for life on the Court? Does this and the inability to lessen a justice's salary really prevent influencing a Supreme Court justice?

3. Do you think the Supreme Court is a de facto lawmaker? Why or why not?

4. Is it possible for the justices to provide a fair review of a case when they hear about it so briefly from the lawyers arguing it before them?

5. Should the Supreme Court accept so few cases? Does the fact the justices decide this totally in private concern you?

6. Do you think the current Supreme Court is carrying out the desires of the founders of our Constitution?

7. Explain where you see the real power of the Supreme Court. What makes the justices so powerful as individuals and as a group?

8. Do you believe the Supreme Court acted properly in the 2000 presidential election in *Bush v. Gore* (2000)?

9. If you were sitting on the Supreme Court, what sorts of cases would you look for to review?

10. Do you favor strict construction (rigid reading and interpretation) of the law or a more liberal approach?

INFOTRAC COLLEGE EDITION ASSIGNMENTS

- Use InfoTrac College Edition to assist you in answering the Discussion Questions when appropriate.

- Using InfoTrac College Edition, search for *Supreme Court Justices*. Outline the *Time* article, "The Supremes." OR

- Using InfoTrac College Edition, search for *judicial activism* and *judicial restraint*. Which has more entries? Read and outline one article on each.

INTERNET ASSIGNMENTS

- Use http://www.findlaw.com to find one Supreme Court case discussed in this chapter and outline the key points. OR

- Go to http://oyez.at.nwu.edu/oyez.html to view a multimedia database about the U.S. Supreme Court. Take notes on what you learn.

- On the Internet, research one of the following key terms or phrases (be sure the materials relate to concepts in this chapter): *certiorari, conservative, judicial review, liberal, strict construction, Supreme Court power, Supreme Court procedures, Supreme Court sittings, Supreme Court traditions.*

COMPANION WEB SITE

- Go to the Constitutional Law and the Criminal Justice System 3e Web Site at http://cj.wadsworth.com/ hessharr_constlaw3e for Case Studies and Study Guide exercises.

REFERENCES

Ducat, Craig R. *Constitutional Interpretation*, 8th ed. Belmont, CA: Thomson/ West, 2004.

Farber, Daniel A. "Judicial Review and Its Alternatives: An American Tale." *Lake Forest Law Review*, October 2003, pp. 415–444.

Fliter, K. *Prisoners' Rights: The Supreme Court and Evolving Standards of Decency*. Westport, CT: Greenwood, 2001.

Gest, T. *Crime and Politics: Big Government's Erratic Campaign for Law and Order*. New York: Oxford University Press, 2001.

Goebel, Julius, Jr. "The Oliver Wendell Holmes Devise: History of the Supreme Court of the United States, Volume I." *History of the Supreme Court of the United States: Antecedents and Beginnings to 1801*. (Vol. 1). New York: Macmillan, 1971.

Maguire, K. and Pastore, A. L. *Sourcebook of Criminal Justice Statistics 2000.* 2001.

Smith, Christopher E. "The Rehnquist Court and Criminal Justice: An Empirical Assessment." *Journal of Contemporary Criminal Justice,* May 2003, pp. 161–181.

Spector, Elliot B. "50 Years of Supreme Court Decisions." *Law and Order,* Fiftieth Anniversary Issue 1953–2003, pp. 16–21.

Stephens, Otis H., Jr. and Scheb, John M. II. *American Constitutional Law,* 3rd ed. Thomson/West, 2003.

Supreme Court of the United States. Published with the cooperation of the Supreme Court Historical Society (no date).

The Supreme Court at Work. Washington, DC: Congressional Quarterly Inc., 1999.

CASES CITED

Ex parte McCardle, 74 U.S. 506 (1868).

Fletcher v. Peck, 10 U.S. 87 (1810).

Marbury v. Madison, 5 U.S. (1 Cranch) 137 (1803).

Martin v. Hunter's Lessee, 14 U.S. (1 Wheat.) 304 (1816).

Roe v. Wade, 410 U.S. 113 (1973).

United States v. Klein, 80 U.S. (13 Wall.) 128 (1871).

CHAPTER 4

Researching the Law

KNOWLEDGE IS OF TWO KINDS. WE KNOW A SUBJECT OURSELVES, OR WE KNOW WHERE WE CAN FIND INFORMATION UPON IT.

—SAMUEL JOHNSON

© Jim Arbogast/Getty Images

Attorneys, required to graduate from law school and pass the bar exam for each state in which they practice, spend far more time researching the law and preparing cases than in the courtroom.

DO YOU KNOW . . .

- At what levels information about law may be written?
- What primary and secondary sources are?
- What secondary sources are available?
- What a legal citation is and what it includes?
- What the National Reporter System is?
- What the components of a legal opinion are?
- What skills are needed to read case law?
- What six sections are usually included in a case "brief"?
- How to determine whether a case has been overturned or expanded upon?
- What an invaluable tool in researching the law is?
- How to distinguish between reliable and questionable information found on the Internet?

CAN YOU DEFINE?

affirm	National Reporter System	scholarly literature
brief	popular literature	secondary information sources
caption	primary information sources	shepardizing
concur	professional literature	string cites
dicta	remand	treatise
holding	reverse	
information literacy		
legal citation		

Introduction

Criminal justice professionals are expected to know the law and when it changes. And it *will* change throughout your education and your career. The amount of paper dedicated to recording law is simply enormous. With the increasing use of computer databases, an incredible amount of material is available to research any aspect of the law. In fact, you might think there is *too much* information out there. It can become intimidating, even overwhelming. Because those working in the criminal justice system are professionals, they are expected to know the changes that occur, just as physicians, CPAs, educators and other professionals are. Being unaware of changes in the law could have serious consequences.

Current law may not be the same as the law you are studying. Remember, American law is a living law. Laws do change—sometimes before texts or other sources are updated. For example, the *Miranda* ruling is a staple topic in every criminal procedure and constitutional law text. What if the Supreme Court had reversed itself when granting certiorari during its 1999–2000 term? Every text in use would have been written from the *old* law. As it turned out, the Court did not reverse itself, but criminal justice professionals throughout the country were well aware the ruling was being reconsidered and knew how to find the results the moment the opinion was released. By the end of this chapter, you also will know how to do this.

This chapter explains the resources with which to stay current with changes in the law, as well as where to seek answers to specific law-related questions. Because of the nature of U.S. law, there is seldom a "yes" or "no" answer to legal questions. Rather, the response is usually more of an "it depends," based on the facts in their totality.

Researching constitutional law is not all that difficult. It is a matter of working with it and developing a knowledge base. Be forewarned, however, that legal research can go on ad infinitum. Like a good mystery, legal research can provide a number of avenues to pursue. You will find case references, digest cites and other research possibilities that could immerse you in material with little hope of finding your way out. Most criminal justice professionals need to know only the basics, and that is precisely what this chapter is intended to provide. With practice and experience, your own knowledge and ability will expand.

Also recognize the level of legal research that is reasonable for you to conduct. As a student of the law and as a criminal justice practitioner, you are more likely to be looking for legal basics rather than the detailed information found in legal briefs written by attorneys. Legal research can be exciting because rather than finding specific answers, you are more likely to find yourself asking more questions. Have realistic expectations for yourself.

The chapter begins with a discussion of why it is important to have the skills to research the law and effectively use the variety of sources available, from the most basic to the most sophisticated. This discussion is followed by an explanation of how to read legal citations and how to find and read case law. Next, the process of briefing a case and the skills needed are presented. The chapter concludes with determining the current status of a case through shepardizing and how to conduct computerized research.

The Importance of Knowing How to Research the Law

Researching the law is important because this skill enables you to find answers to legal questions and, perhaps more important, to better understand the judicial system. Knowing how and where to find answers to legal questions is a worthwhile skill, and knowing what goes into researching laws, including reading legal opinions and briefs, helps bring the study of law into focus.

Police officers never know whether the next call they respond to will result in litigation with the potential to dramatically affect the course of future law. The hope is that any decisions will positively affect criminal justice. Not knowing the law could have drastic results, not only with justice not being met but also in tremendous liability exposure.

Basic legal research skills are as important as any of the more traditional job-related skills. Criminal justice professionals are not expected to be legal scholars or expert researchers after this short introduction, but it will be a steppingstone for efforts to find and understand U.S. laws.

Popular, Scholarly and Professional Sources

A wealth of information at a variety of levels is available. You may have already consulted one this morning: your newspaper. This is a very legitimate source of legal information. In fact, newspapers keep most Americans updated on what is happening in the world of law. Whether it is a national newspaper, a local paper or even a community weekly, every edition has something about the law. A basic professional skill is to regularly review newspapers. You may be amazed at the amount of information to be found when you expand your reading beyond the sports and comics sections.

It is important to recognize the intended audience for which information is written, as well as who is doing the writing and editing.

■ Information about law may be written at a popular level for the layperson, at a professional level for the practitioner or at a scholarly level for the researcher.

Popular literature is written for the layperson. It is not necessarily less authoritative; it simply does not go into the depth that professional or scholarly literature does. Examples of popular literature would be articles dealing with constitutional law found in *Time, Newsweek* or even *Reader's Digest*.

popular literature • publications written for the layperson

Although some academicians may not consider magazines and newspapers legitimate sources for finding law, they are, in fact, the most popularly used sources, even if all readers do not realize that is what they are doing. Few people will ever actually conduct formal legal research; however, almost everyone reads about the law in magazines and newspapers.

Keep in mind, however, the potential for inaccuracy in popular sources. Although some larger publications have legal correspondents, some even trained as lawyers, time and space do not permit anything more than a cursory presentation. Even then, editors may cut and paste portions of the story that could skew pertinent facts. Politics can also affect how a story is written, slanting it one way or another. Whatever the case, popular sources are available for most people and can be a starting point.

Anyone using any resource to learn law must understand the limitations of that particular resource. *Reader's Digest* will present material far differently than, for example, *United States Law Week*, one of the best sources for keeping current on law. However, not everyone has the access, or the desire, to keep current on every case being decided. Although there can be no substitute for the carefully detailed research required of lawyers, legislators and academicians, to ignore the popular literature that enables many Americans to learn about the law would be to discount how most Americans do learn about the law.

Many of these sources are sociological and do not report the actual law. Such sources are not to be confused with the official reported volumes of cases and statutes. If you become interested in a case reported in one of these sources, you can pursue your interest further through professional literature.

Professional literature is written for the practitioner in a given field. In criminal justice this would include articles in such publications as *The Police Chief* (published by the International Association of Chiefs of Police), the *FBI Law Enforcement Bulletin, Corrections Today* (published by the American Correctional Association), the *UCLA Law Review*, the *Journal of Municipal Government* and the *NCJA Justice Bulletin*.

professional literature • publications written for the practitioner in the field

Professional periodicals are most likely to keep readers current on the ever-changing constitutional law. These journals frequently contain articles on newly enacted laws and their effect on the criminal justice system. If a criminal justice agency does not subscribe to such magazines, they are affordable enough for individuals to subscribe personally. However, just as newspapers and magazines are not really "the law," professional sources fall a bit short of what you can learn from going to the next level of authority—scholarly sources.

scholarly literature • publications written for those interested in theory, research and statistical analysis

Scholarly literature, as the term implies, is written for people interested in theory, research and statistical analysis. Examples of scholarly literature would be articles in *Justice Quarterly,* an official publication of the Academy of Criminal Justice.

All the preceding sources of information are classified as secondary. The most authoritative information source is primary information—the actual cases and the opinions handed down.

Primary and Secondary Sources

Information may be classified according to whether it is primary or secondary. You will rely on both primary and secondary resources to research a specific aspect of the law.

Primary Information Sources

Sources of primary information for legal research include the U.S. Constitution, the constitutions of the 50 states, the statutes of the U.S. Congress and the statutes of the 50 state legislatures, as well as appellate court decisions of the federal and state courts.

primary information sources • raw data or the original information

■ **Primary information sources** present the raw data or the original information.

Secondary Information Sources

Secondary information involves selecting, evaluating, analyzing and synthesizing data or information. For the nonlawyer, it is usually easier to understand than primary information.

secondary information sources • information based on the raw data or the original information

■ **Secondary information sources** present data or information based on the original information. Among the important secondary information sources for legal research are periodicals, treatises/texts, encyclopedias and dictionaries.

These secondary information sources usually can be found in a general library.

Legal Periodicals   Legal periodicals record and critique the activities of legislators and judges and discuss current case law. Three groups of legal periodicals can provide important information: (1) law school publications such as the *Harvard Law Review,* (2) bar association publications such as the *American Bar Association Journal* and (3) special subject and interest periodicals such as the *Black Law Journal* and the *Women Lawyers Journal.*

treatise • a definitive source of material written about a specific topic or area of study

Treatises/Texts   A **treatise** is a comprehensive document on a legal subject. Treatises or texts go into a specific subject in depth. Such works provide the backbone for a great deal of research by legal professionals. Specialized treatises exist in almost every area imaginable.

Although such works are an invaluable resource, they are frequently multivolume and always expensive. They make ideal additions to agency libraries (law schools, county attorneys' offices, prosecutors' offices) and are readily available at law libraries. It is worth your time to become acquainted with the treatises/texts available. Stop in and browse.

Legal Encyclopedias   Legal encyclopedias are narratives arranged alphabetically by subject with supporting footnote references. The three types of legal encyclopedias are (1) general law, (2) local or state law and (3) special subject. Most are objective and noncritical, simply stating the propositions of law and providing an elementary introductory explanation. Legal encyclopedias are popular, useful research tools.

- *Corpus Juris Secondum* (C.J.S.) is a general legal encyclopedia that restates the entire body of American law (West Publishing Company). It consists of approximately 150 volumes, including supplements and a five-volume index.
- *American Jurisprudence 2d* (AM.Jur.2d) is a general legal encyclopedia that contains 400 topics (Lawyers Cooperative Publishing Company and the Bancroft-Whitney Company). It contains approximately 90 volumes, including an eight-volume index.
- *Encyclopedia of Crime and Justice* (Macmillan) contains authoritative articles on all areas of criminal justice. This four-volume set provides a good overview of the major areas of criminal justice.
- *Guide to American Law* is less voluminous and covers general topics.

Legal Dictionaries   Legal dictionaries define words in their legal sense. Among the most popular American law dictionaries are *Ballentine's Law Dictionary* (Lawyers Cooperative Publishing Company, 1969), *Black's Law Dictionary*, 7th ed. (West Publishing Company, 1999) and *Oran's Law Dictionary for Nonlawyers*, 4th ed. (Thomson Publishing Company, 2000). Whether hardbound or paperback, a legal dictionary makes an excellent addition to a personal library.

Reading Legal Citations

Although they look as if they were designed to bedevil the unwary, legal citations are actually simple to decipher. However, many students and criminal justice practitioners do not use them enough to remember what they are. This introduction can serve as a reference in the future. A valuable resource to enhance understanding of basic legal citations is www.law.cornell.edu/citation/.

- A **legal citation** is a standardized way of referring to a specific element in the law. It has three basic parts: a volume number, an abbreviation for the title and a page or section number.

legal citation • a standardized way of referring to a specific element in the law

Legal citations are usually followed by the date. Following are examples of legal citations:

- U.S. Supreme Court case: *Horton v. California*, 496 U.S. 128 (1990). This means volume 496 of the *United States Reports* (the official reporter for the U.S. Supreme Court opinions), page 128, decided in 1990.
- Federal law: 42 USC 1983. This means title or chapter 42 of the *United States Code*, section 1983.
- Journal: Janice Toran, "Information Disclosure in Civil Actions: The Freedom of Information Act and the Federal Discovery Rules." 49 Geo. Wash. L. Rev. 843, 854–55 (1981). This refers to an article written by Janice Toran that appears in volume 49 of the *George Washington Law Review*, beginning on page 843, and specifically referencing pages 854–855 of the article, which was published in 1981.

string cites • additional legal citations showing where a case may be found in commercial digests

The preceding U.S. Supreme Court citation is to the official United States Reports. Sometimes additional sites will be given. These are called **string cites** or parallel citations. The additional cites show where the case could be found in other commercial reporting services. For example, the official cite for the *Miranda* case is *Miranda v. Arizona*, 384 U.S. 436 (1966). This shows that the case is found in the official United States Report. A string cite for this case would be *Miranda v. Arizona*, 384 U.S. 436, 86 S.Ct. 1602, 16 L.Ed.2d 694 (1966). This shows that in addition to the official United States Report, the case is also in West Publishing Company's *Supreme Court Reporter* (S.Ct.) and the Lawyers Cooperative Publishing Company's *U.S. Supreme Court Reports, Lawyers' Edition* (L.Ed.2d).

Locating provisions of federal and state constitutions does not present a problem. When it comes to case law, however, the situation is very different. Millions of judicial opinions have been written in the United States, with thousands more published each year. Finding case law can be a real challenge.

Case Law

Court decisions are recorded as opinions that describe what the dispute was about and what the court decided and why. The opinion may be written by one member of the court, or there may be many concurring and dissenting opinions. Some landmark cases have eight or nine opinions. The massive number of decisions is an obstacle to finding case law. Decisions of the Supreme Court and of most state appellate courts can be found in their official reports. Cases decided from about 1887 to date can also be found in the unofficial **National Reporter System,** which contains thousands of volumes, each with about 1,500 pages.

National Reporter System • a private publisher's compilation of case law throughout the United States

■   The **National Reporter System** publishes regional sets of cases, as well as individual sets for specific states.

Figure 4.1 illustrates the eight regions of the National Reporter System.

Another system of unofficial reports, the *American Law Reports*, publishes only those cases thought to be significant and of special interest and discusses them in depth, whereas the official reporters do not provide comments in addition to the actual opinion.

Reading Case Law

You may find yourself challenged with attempting to read actual case law at some time. While this text is not written in traditional casebook style (relying heavily on copying case law, followed by analysis), if you take any other classes on law, you will probably find yourself working your way through cases. Most legal writing, in whatever format, uses jargon foreign to most readers, including students. It is helpful to become familiar with some basic concepts and terminology you will encounter.

caption • the title of a case setting forth the parties involved

To begin, the **caption** (title of the case) tells who is involved. It may be the government against a criminal defendant (*State of Washington v. Smith*), or it may be two individuals disputing an issue (*Anderson v. Smith*). The parties to the action may be identified by different titles (defendant, plaintiff, petitioner, respondent), depending on the nature of the case. The particular court and level of legal action (whether it is an appeal, etc.) will determine whose name comes first in the caption. This is usually clarified within the first part of the case.

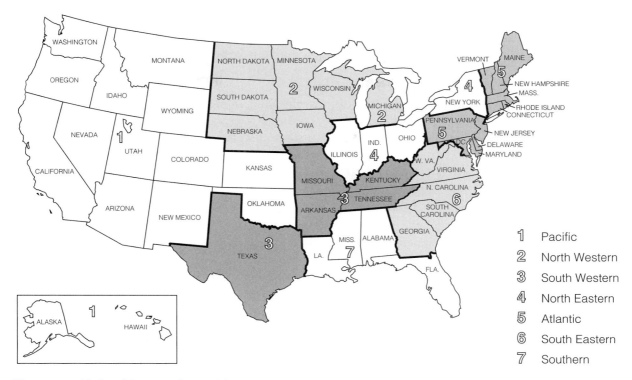

1   Pacific
2   North Western
3   South Western
4   North Eastern
5   Atlantic
6   South Eastern
7   Southern

Figure 4.1   National Reporter System Map

Most cases start in the trial court. The trial court has two basic responsibilities: to find out what happened and to determine which legal rules should be used in deciding the case. The trial court makes its decision on the basis of the facts presented by the lawyers representing both parties (or by the individuals themselves if not represented by legal counsel), using the legal rules the judge determines are appropriate to apply to this case. The party that does not emerge victorious may appeal to a higher court on any number of issues. However, only legal issues will be reviewed on appeal, as new evidence is not permitted. In fact, appeals are considered only by the appellate judges reviewing written arguments from the parties, along with case transcripts and opinions issued by the previous judge involved. (Not all cases produce opinions, particularly at the trial court level.)

Although many issues may be presented in one case, they may not all be addressed by the court deciding the case. Whether to save time or perhaps even to avoid other issues within a case, a court may choose to answer only one issue in its opinion, leaving the others for future cases.

Opinions include more than simply a statement of who won the court case. They tell the story of what occurred, which rules were applied and why the judges decided the case as they did.

■ A legal opinion usually contains (1) a description of the facts, (2) a statement of the legal issues presented, (3) the relevant rules of law, (4) the holding and (5) the policies and reasons that support the holding.

The **holding** of a case is the rule of law applied to the particular facts of the case and the actual decision. A court may **affirm** (support), **reverse** (overturn) or **remand** (return the case to the lower court).

holding • the rule of law applied to the particular facts of the case and the actual decision

affirm • agree with a lower court's decision

reverse • overturn the decision of a lower court

remand • return a case to the lower court for further action

As Bode (2006) explains: "Appellate courts consist of more than one judge or justice. If an appellate judge agrees with the result (to affirm, reverse or remand), but thinks different reasoning should have been used or wants to highlight a certain point, the judge may write a concurring opinion. If one of the judges disagrees with the decision of the majority a dissenting opinion may be written explaining why the judge thinks the majority got it wrong." A concurring or dissenting opinion provides a judge the opportunity to explain why they agree or disagree with the majority but does not constitute a separate action from the majority.

Skills Required to Read a Case

Three skills are required to read case law. First, you must be able to think in reverse. The opinion provides the end result of the deliberations. You must isolate what the dispute involved, what the trial court decided, how it proceeded and what happened on appeal. Second, you must untangle the interplay of the basic components of a judicial opinion. Each affects the others in a process that goes back and forth and around in what may appear to be circles. Third, not all the elements of the judicial opinion may be included. You must infer them from the decisions made.

■ The skills and process needed to read case law are (1) thinking in reverse, (2) untangling the interplay of the basic components and (3) drawing inferences.

Briefing a Case

Once you locate a case, you will want to make some notes to help you decipher it. Because cases are usually rather long, the best way to do this is to outline, or **brief,** the case.

brief • a summary presented to the court that describes the manner in which each side in a legal contest thinks the laws should apply to the facts of the case

■ Most case briefs contain the case name and citation, a summary of key facts, the legal issues involved, the court's decision, the reasons for that decision and any separate opinions or dissents.

Traditionally, law is taught through case law. This is an arduous process by which issues and rules are dissected from court opinions. This discipline is necessary for those intending to become lawyers because case analysis is the cornerstone of understanding how and why cases are decided as they are, and why the law in any particular area developed as it did.

Case law, also known as common law, depends on comparing one case with others. As difficult as the case analysis approach to learning law is, it definitely has its place. However, this complex approach can hinder understanding the basics of constitutional law as they apply to criminal justice—the focus of this text.

You should, however, know what a case opinion looks like, as well as how a brief of that case might be used to analyze the issues and rules drawn from it. Opinions also provide judges with an opportunity to express thoughts on issues not essential to the court's decision, looking at facts or issues other than those needed to determine the case. These are called **dicta** and are not binding on future courts. A dictum is a means for the majority to address other issues beyond the facts before them. Consequently, an opinion holds a great deal of information to be scrutinized.

dicta • statements by a court that do not deal with the main issue in the case or an additional discussion by the court

Two famous, relevant cases have been selected to illustrate opinions and the briefs that might be written from them. *Marbury v. Madison* (1803) was selected because it is the pivotal case of constitutional law granting the Supreme Court authority to review legislation to determine whether it is constitutional—and thus legal. *Miranda v. Arizona* (1966) was selected because it is perhaps one of the most famous constitutional law cases in criminal justice. The opinions for these two cases are contained in Appendix D. You may wish to read them before reading the briefs that follow.

Brief of Marbury v. Madison

Type of Case. This case deals with a petition to the U.S. Supreme Court for a writ of mandamus to compel a government official to deliver a commission, subsequently requiring a determination of whether the Supreme Court may review an act of Congress to determine its constitutionality.

Facts of the Case. Just before President John Adams left office after his defeat by Thomas Jefferson in 1800, Adams made several judicial appointments. While Adams signed these appointments under the authority granted by Congress, some appointments were not officially made before Adams left office, for no reason other than time pressures. President Jefferson ordered his new Secretary of State, James Madison, to withhold delivery of several commissions made by the previous president, including that of justice of the peace to William Marbury. Marbury, along with several others, petitioned the Supreme Court to require Secretary of State Madison to deliver their commissions.

Legal Issue. Does the Supreme Court have the authority to declare congressional acts unconstitutional?

Holding and Decision. Yes. Because the government of the United States is one of laws, not men, the law needs to be able to remedy wrongs that result from acts of Congress. In this case, the Judiciary Act of 1789 as passed by Congress is unconstitutional.

Because the Constitution limits the Supreme Court's original jurisdiction to only certain areas, giving the Court only appellate jurisdiction in all other areas, the Judiciary Act may not grant the Supreme Court original jurisdiction to issue writs of mandamus. It is the Constitution that limits the rights and powers of the legislature, and the legislature cannot change the Constitution, which itself provides that it is the "supreme law of the land."

If an act of the legislature is repugnant to the Constitution, are courts bound by that law? No. If a law is not in accordance with the U.S. Constitution, the Supreme Court may determine which of the conflicting rules will govern the particular case. If the Constitution is to have the power it was meant to have, it must prevail pursuant to Article 3, Section 2.

The framers of the Constitution meant for it to govern courts as well as Congress. Why else are judges required to take an oath to uphold the U.S. Constitution? The Supreme Court has the authority to review acts of Congress, and in this case, Section 13 of the Judiciary Act of 1789 is unconstitutional.

Rule. Under the Supremacy Clause and Article 3, Section 2 of the U.S. Constitution, the Supreme Court has the authority to review acts of Congress to determine whether they are unconstitutional.

Brief of Miranda v. Arizona

Type of Case. This case deals with the issue of whether the police must advise certain criminal suspects who are being questioned of their constitutional right to not speak.

Facts of the Case. After being arrested, the defendant was taken to an interrogation room where he gave a confession to the police. He had not been told of his constitutional right to remain silent or to have a lawyer present because the police assumed he knew about these rights because he had been arrested before.

Legal Issue. Must government agents advise certain suspects of their constitutional Fifth Amendment rights?

Holding and Decision. Yes. Suspects held for interrogation must be clearly informed that they have the right to consult with a lawyer and to have the lawyer with them during interrogation. They must also be advised of their right to remain silent and that anything stated can be used as evidence against them.

If individuals indicate they wish the assistance of counsel before any interrogation occurs, the authorities cannot deny this request. If a person cannot afford legal counsel, it must be provided without cost. Suspects must be advised that they have a right to have legal counsel present during any questioning.

Once the warnings have been given, interrogation must cease at any time before or during questioning if suspects indicate in any way that they wish to remain silent. If the questioning continues, the burden is on the government to demonstrate that the suspect knowingly and intelligently waived the privilege against self-incrimination and the right to retained or appointed counsel.

Rule. When government agents question people in custody, those being questioned must be advised of their specific Fifth Amendment rights dealing with self-incrimination and must knowingly and intelligently waive such privileges.

A great deal more could be addressed regarding the legal process and how to decipher legal cases and their resulting opinions. However, this text was not intended to address these specific issues. The goal in this chapter is to provide the basic information to seek out the law as needed. One last skill is needed by those performing actual legal research: going beyond the case itself to determine if it is still a precedent or if it has been overturned or expanded—a process known as *shepardizing*.

Shepardizing

After a case has been researched, the current status of the case should be determined.

shepardizing • using the resource *Shepard's Citations*

■ **Shepardizing** a case involves using *Shepard's Citations,* a reference that tracks cases so legal researchers can easily determine whether the original holding has been changed through any appeals. *Shepard's* is also available online.

To rely on a case that has been overturned or otherwise rendered invalid could prove disastrous. Shepardizing cases is almost the exclusive domain of attorneys and their clerks. It is improbable that criminal justice practitioners will actually perform this step in the legal research process; however, it is important to know the procedure and the term.

Computerized Legal Research

Computerized legal research is now the norm. Nothing has made the law more accessible to *everyone* than the Internet. While computerized legal research has been in law offices for years, the Internet, along with law-related software, brings more legal sources to homes and offices than ever to allow anyone to locate answers to many legal queries.

Most students and criminal justice professionals use computers for their research. Anyone with basic computer skills has immediate access to a vast array of legal information when studying and working with the law. In a sense, the Internet has truly made the people's law available to them. The following discussion is included as a review for those proficient with technology or to serve as a foundation for those just learning.

CDs and DVD Data

Legal information of all sorts is available for purchase in CD or DVD format. Everything from federal and state statutes to scans of famous legal documents can be purchased on disc. "Do it yourself" programs are available to help nonlawyers meet some of their own legal needs, including software to assist in creating basic business documents such as contracts, drafting simple wills and tax forms and so on. Once thought of as revolutionary, disc memory storage technology is now seen as useful in some cases but having limitations. Although convenient, the usefulness declines as time lapses between when the discs are created and ultimately used by the consumer. Remember, the American living law is constantly changing.

The Internet

Although CDs and DVDs provide easy access to information, they are finite when it comes to the amount of information they have, the breadth of subject matter and how current that material is. The Internet, on the other hand, allows access to data that is almost infinite and far more current than material published in print or disc format.

Around 1990, when the World Wide Web was created, approximately 100,000 computers were accessing the Internet. The number of computers linked via the Internet is now in the hundreds of millions and expanding by the minute.

▓ The Internet is an invaluable tool in researching the law and has made the law accessible to the people it is intended to serve.

The Law on the Web

You might be wondering where and how to start your online legal research. A reasonable starting point, especially for those with only rudimentary legal knowledge, is whatever search engine a person is comfortable with, such as Google, Yahoo or Alta Vista, although there are many others. The limitation with these is not accessing enough sources but often too many. One helpful reference to means of narrowing queries is the *Internet Guide for Criminal Justice*, 2nd ed., by DeJong and Kurland (2003). This brief (68 pages), reader-friendly book discusses keeping current in criminal justice using the Internet as well as doing online criminal justice research.

In addition to developing a personal/professional reference library, students of the law and those working in the field should become familiar with some of the many Internet sources and databases. Experiment with different ones to find several that work for you, and bookmark them. As you become more interested or reliant on information, it may be worthwhile to subscribe to a source that charges a subscription fee such as LexisNexis and Westlaw. Many colleges and even employers subscribe to some of them.

You might also use a legal search engine such as FindLaw or LawCrawler. Following are some Uniform Resource Locators (URLs) or addresses to access criminal justice sources on the Web:

American Bar Association	*http://www.abanet.org/crimjust/*
U.S. Department of Justice, Bureau of Justice Statistics	*http://www.ojp.usdoj.gov/bjs/*
Legal Information Institute at Cornell University	*http://www.law.cornell.edu/*
National Criminal Justice Association	*http://ncja.org/*
U.S. Supreme Court	*http://www.supremecourtus.gov/*
U.S. Federal Judiciary	*http://www.uscourts.gov/*
FindLaw	*http://www.findlaw.com/*
LexisNexis	*http://www.lexisnexis.com/default.asp*

Information Literacy

"Surfing" the Internet can become as frustrating as it can be entertaining. When the Internet was new, it may have been manageable to find things—the cyber equivalent of standing at a bookshelf browsing the material for what might be of use. But that rapidly changed. There is simply too much information available this way now, and a great deal of time is easily wasted. For example, as this text was being prepared, an entry of the word *police* got 22,600,000 hits in 0.13 second. Finding a specific topic related to police would be impossible this way. There will be even more by the time you are reading this. With data on the Internet increasing exponentially, students and all professionals need to develop a strategy for finding information.

information literacy • online research skills that include identifying the issue, narrowing the topic, locating data, discerning fact from fiction and presenting material in an academic and/or professional manner

Information literacy is the ability to effectively identify an issue, narrow that issue, access appropriate online sites, separate fact from fiction and present the findings professionally. Once upon a time people, learned to navigate a library using the card catalog and the Dewey Decimal System (no doubt ancient or unknown terms to many readers). Times change, as do research methods, but the Internet can bring the law to anyone who knows where to look. Throughout your education and careers, you will continue to be exposed to new sources and means of accessing data. By developing your own strategy, you will not only find locating information eminently easier but also be able to remain current on the law, a benefit for the layperson and a necessity for the criminal justice practitioner.

Locating information is only one part of information literacy. Evaluating the validity of the information is also required. How do you tell reliable information from that which is questionable?

■ To evaluate the reliability of information found on the Internet, consider the credibility of the source and the currency of the information.

Most government web sites are credible, as are the sites of nationally recognized organizations and associations. Most sites have a page devoted to "About Us."

Some sites, such as that of the FBI or the Supreme Court, are obviously credible. If in doubt about a site, go to the "About Us" page to see if you find them credible. Most sites also indicate when specific information was last updated. Determine if that date is acceptable to you.

What's Next?

One exciting development is the online discussion group. Electronic bulletin boards and virtual discussion groups exist for every interest, including law, and profession, including all aspects of criminal justice. Questions answered and information shared is available, literally, at a keystroke.

A more recent development is the "blog" (web log) that anyone can start to encourage rolling discussions about a variety of topics. Blogs are proving to be an excellent way to get a variety of perspectives on an even greater variety of topics. Continue developing your information literacy strategy to include these exciting new resources, as well as becoming familiar with the traditional resources. It is a certainty that the law will be constantly developing.

Regardless of what level of legal information you want to locate, it is important to develop an effective strategy to help you optimize your effort. Increasingly laypeople, students and professionals find that the Internet is the most effective and expeditious means of accessing legal information and remaining current with the ever-changing law.

SUMMARY

Information may be written at a popular level for the layperson, at a professional level for the practitioner or at a scholarly level for the researcher. Information may be classified as primary or secondary. Primary information is raw data or the original information. Secondary information is based on the raw data or original information.

Among the important secondary information sources for legal research are periodicals, treatises/texts, encyclopedias and dictionaries. Many legal citations are found within these information sources. A legal citation is a standardized way of referring to a specific legal source. It has three basic parts: a volume number, an abbreviation for the title and a page or section number. The National Reporter System publishes seven regional sets of volumes, as well as individual sets for California, Illinois and New York courts.

As you research the law, you may read legal opinions. An opinion usually contains (1) a description of the facts, (2) a statement of the legal issues presented for decision, (3) the relevant rules of law, (4) the holding and (5) the policies and reasons that support the holding. The skills and process needed to read case law are (1) think in reverse, (2) untangle the interplay of the basic components and (3) draw inferences.

You may also find it helpful to be able to brief, or outline, a case. Most case briefs contain the case name and citation, a summary of key facts, the legal issues involved, the court's decision, the reasons for that decision and any separate opinions or dissents. Sheparding a case involves using *Shepard's Citations,* the set of bound volumes and pocket parts published for each set of official volumes of cases, indicating whether a case's status has changed. An invaluable tool in researching the law is the Internet. To evaluate the reliability of information found on the Internet, consider the credibility of the source and the currency of the information.

DISCUSSION QUESTIONS

1. Why is it necessary to know how to research the law?
2. What is the danger of relying on only texts to learn about the law?
3. What information can be obtained from reading a legal opinion.
4. Why can legal research become frustrating?
5. What are the benefits of actually reading and briefing a case relevant to your specific legal question?
6. Why is a newspaper a legitimate source of legal information?
7. What shortcoming do you think a newspaper might have in providing legal information?
8. What problems could arise for any professional not keeping up with the law?
9. How has the Internet changed legal research?
10. How would you rate your level of information literacy? What could you do to raise it?

 ## INFOTRAC COLLEGE EDITION ASSIGNMENTS

- Use InfoTrac College Edition to assist you in answering the Discussion Questions if appropriate.
- Using InfoTrac College Edition, search *briefs.* Outline two selections of interest to you.

 ## INTERNET ASSIGNMENT

- Use http://www.findlaw.com to find one Supreme Court case discussed in this chapter and outline the key points.

 ## COMPANION WEB SITE

- Go to the Constitutional Law and the Criminal Justice System 3e Web site at http://cj.wadsworth.com/ hessharr_constlaw3e for Case Studies and Study Guide exercises.

REFERENCES

Bode, Nancy. Professor of Criminal Justice. Concordia University, St. Paul. Personal correspondence, March 2006.

DeJong, Christina and Kurland, Daniel J. *Internet Guide for Criminal Justice*, 2nd ed. Belmont, CA: Wadsworth/Thomson, 2003.

RESOURCES

Ballenger, Bruce. *The Curious Researcher,* 5th ed. New York: PearsonLongman, 2007.

The Definitive Guide to Criminal Justice and Criminology on the World Wide Web. (Criminal Justice Distance Learning Consortium) Upper Saddle River, NJ: Prentice Hall, 1999.

Leshin, Cynthia B. *Internet Investigations in Criminal Justice.* Upper Saddle River, NJ: Prentice Hall, 1997.

Maxfield, Michael G. and Babbie, Earl. *Research Methods for Criminal Justice and Criminology,* 4th ed. Belmont, CA: Wadsworth/Thomson Learning, 2005.

Schmalleger, Frank. *The Definitive Guide to Criminal Justice and Criminology on the World Wide Web.* Upper Saddle River, NJ: Prentice Hall, 2001.

Thurman, Quint C.; Parker, Lee E.; and O'Block, Robert L. *Criminal Justice Research Sources,* 4th ed. Cincinnati: Anderson Publishing Company, 2000.

CASES CITED

Marbury v. Madison, 5 U.S. 137 (1803).
Miranda v. Arizona, 384 U.S. 436 (1966).

The Guarantees of the Constitution to Citizens: Civil Rights and Civil Liberties

The essence of the U.S. Constitution is "liberty and justice for all." The significance of these words, generally learned in the Pledge of Allegiance, is what the legal system in the United States strives to achieve and what its system of laws, beginning with the framework provided by the Constitution, is all about: guaranteeing the rights and liberties of the individual.

Section I helped build the framework for understanding how the constitutional machine was conceived and built. Understanding why the Constitution was considered necessary when this country was begun and how the Constitution was worded to address specific idealistic goals enables you to understand what it seeks to achieve: individual rights and liberties.

As you begin an in-depth look at the Constitution and its amendments, remember that the Constitution simply provides a basic framework within which all other laws—whether federal, state or local—must remain. While this basic framework necessarily provides for how the legal system should be constructed (e.g., establishing Congress, the presidency, the Supreme Court, etc.), the guarantees of the Constitution for individual rights and liberties are why those who established the document met in the first place: to protect the individual from the government.

This section begins with a look at two amendments that delineate civil rights and civil liberties, the Thirteenth and Fourteenth Amendments (Chapter 5). This is followed by an up-close look at the First Amendment and the basic freedoms it guarantees (Chapter 6). The section concludes with a discussion of the Second Amendment and the controversial issue of gun control (Chapter 7).

Throughout the section, keep in mind that although the Constitution and its amendments are relatively simple, interpretation of them can become complex. Do not let the complexities obscure the basic purpose of these documents: to prevent government from unnecessarily infringing on citizens' basic rights to liberty and justice.

CHAPTER 5

Equal Protection under the Law: Balancing Individual, State and Federal Rights

ALL PERSONS BORN OR NATURALIZED IN THE UNITED STATES AND SUBJECT TO THE JURISDICTION THEREOF, ARE CITIZENS OF THE UNITED STATES AND OF THE STATE WHEREIN THEY RESIDE. NO STATE SHALL MAKE OR ENFORCE ANY LAW WHICH SHALL ABRIDGE THE PRIVILEGES OR IMMUNITIES OF CITIZENS OF THE UNITED STATES; NOR SHALL ANY STATE DEPRIVE ANY PERSON OF LIFE, LIBERTY, OR PROPERTY, WITHOUT DUE PROCESS OF LAW; NOR DENY TO ANY PERSON WITHIN ITS JURISDICTION THE EQUAL PROTECTION OF THE LAWS.

—FOURTEENTH AMENDMENT TO THE U.S. CONSTITUTION

The role of the jury cannot be overestimated in the American legal system's quest for due process.

DO YOU KNOW . . .

■ What the Thirteenth Amendment provides? The Fourteenth Amendment?

■ How discrimination differs from prejudice?

■ What significance the *Dred Scott* decision had?

■ What the Court held in *Plessy v. Ferguson*?

■ What Jim Crow laws are?

■ What significance *Brown v. Board of Education* has?

■ What legislation in the 1960s and 1970s prohibited discrimination?

■ What the intent of affirmative action programs was?

■ What violations of the Equal Protection Clause have occurred in the criminal justice system?

■ How a right differs from a privilege?

■ What Fourteenth Amendment rights prisoners have?

■ How the incorporation doctrine prevents states from infringing on citizens' rights?

CAN YOU DEFINE?

affirmative action

American Dream

contextual discrimination

discrimination

due process of law

equal protection of the law

incorporation doctrine

Jim Crow laws

prejudice

privilege

racial profiling

reverse discrimination

right

selective incorporation

Introduction

What can now be seen as an obvious shortcoming to the Constitution and Bill of Rights was their failure to abolish slavery; however, the Supreme Court's ultimate decision to reverse itself through ratification of the Thirteenth and Fourteenth Amendments, making slavery illegal, is important for more than the obvious reason. This is an example of our living law at work. Bearing in mind that law serves to support social norms, as hard as it is to imagine, not everyone objected to slavery at the time the *Dred Scott* case was decided in 1856. Social norms changed, and the Constitution and constitutional interpretations have accommodated them. In addition, although the Bill of Rights, as originally drafted and ratified, guaranteed American citizens basic freedoms that the federal government could not infringe upon, it did not apply to the states, each of which had its own constitution and statutes. To assure that the states did not deny the basic rights set forth in the Constitution and the Bill of Rights, Congress passed the Fourteenth Amendment. Keep in mind the Constitution was initially drafted to limit power of the federal government, with later amendments serving to extend this limitation to state and local governments as well.

This chapter begins with a brief look at the abolition of slavery through the Thirteenth Amendment and a discussion of the Fourteenth Amendment, which granted slaves citizenship and required that states abide by the federal Constitution and specific provisions in the Bill of Rights. This is followed by an examination of discrimination and prejudice, the roots of racial discrimination, the issue of "separate but equal" and the struggle for equality. Next, the rise of affirmative action programs is discussed, including the claims of reverse discrimination and the challenges to affirmative action programs mounted in the 1990s. The issue of equal protection and discrimination within the criminal justice system is also explored. The chapter concludes with a discussion of balancing state and federal powers, selective incorporation and a check on federal powers.

The Thirteenth Amendment

The Civil War resulted from a variety of issues, including differing interpretations of the Constitution on the basis of the different norms of a still-developing country. The legal conflict with the emerging Constitution was that although the framers sought to prevent excessive *federal* authority, their desire to give states more authority over their own development resulted in problems the national government simply could not continue to overlook. Among the issues were state banks and money versus national banks and currency, federal aid versus state aid for improving roadways and railways and freedom versus slavery. During debates involving these issues, two theories as to the nature of the Constitution emerged, articulated during the 1830 Great Debate in the Senate between Robert Hayne of South Carolina and Daniel Webster of Massachusetts.

On the one hand, Hayne asserted that the Union created by the Constitution was merely a compact between sovereign states, a league of independent states and, as such, states may lawfully withdraw from the Union if they so wish. Webster, on the other hand, asserted that the Constitution established an indivisible Union with laws binding on the states, and states could not simply leave the Union.

These issues came to a head when Abraham Lincoln was elected president in 1860. That December, South Carolina passed a resolution to withdraw from the Union. Early in 1861, Florida, Georgia, Alabama, Mississippi, Louisiana and Texas did the same.

President Lincoln was faced with the task of trying to keep the Union together. He had been elected on a promise to abolish slavery in the territories, but he conceded that under the Constitution, slavery was legal in the states where it had been established. Lincoln tried to assure the southern states that he had neither the right nor the intent to interrupt their way of life. The Supreme Court had ruled in *Dred Scott v. Sandford* (1856) that even free blacks could not be citizens of the United States and that they "had no rights which a white man was bound to respect." The southern states were not convinced, however, and the Civil War ensued (1861–1865).

The Civil War affected this country in ways no other war could. The casualties were enormous—364,511 dead and 281,881 wounded (Brunner, 1999, p. 398)— and the divisiveness to the nation deep, with impacts remaining to this day. It pitted American against American and sometimes brother against brother. It is a prime example of how important societal norms are and again showed America's resolve to stand firm to the principles on which the country was founded, as so eloquently expressed by Lincoln in his Gettysburg Address, which began with this declaration:

> Fourscore and seven years ago our fathers brought forth on this continent a new nation conceived in liberty and dedicated to the proposition that all men are created equal . . .

and ended with this promise:

> . . . we here highly resolve that these dead shall not have died in vain, that this nation under God shall have a new birth in freedom, and that government of the people, by the people, for the people shall not perish from the earth.

While debating and passing bills regarding such critical issues of a new country as conducting war, taxes, tariffs and banking, Congress also sought to deal with the slavery issue. In April 1862, slavery was abolished in the District of Columbia and two months later in all the territories. In the summer of 1862, Lincoln announced that unless the southern states returned to the Union, he would call for an end to slavery in all rebelling states. In the Emancipation Proclamation, issued January 1, 1863, Lincoln declared free all the slaves in all districts of the United States. In effect, this proclamation did little. Those in the South retained their slaves as did those slave states that remained loyal to the Union. What it did, however, was set a national tone that gained momentum toward abolishing slavery.

In January 1864, a resolution to amend the Constitution to abolish slavery throughout the United States was introduced in Congress. After a year of prolonged discussion, the Thirteenth Amendment was approved by the required two-thirds vote in both houses of Congress and ultimately ratified by the states in December of 1865.

■ The Thirteenth Amendment, ratified in 1865, abolished slavery.

> Neither slavery nor involuntary servitude . . . shall exist within the United States or any place subject to their jurisdiction.

Although the Thirteenth Amendment abolished slavery in 1865, after the Civil War, many southern states continued discrimination by passing "Black Codes," which forbade blacks to vote, serve on juries, hold certain jobs, move freely, own firearms or gather in groups. Racial turbulence ensued, and groups such as the Ku Klux Klan emerged in defiance and bigotry in many communities. To remedy this situation, Congress passed the Fourteenth Amendment, which gave blacks citizenship, a status previously defined only by the states.

The Fourteenth Amendment

■ The Fourteenth Amendment, ratified in 1868, granted citizenship to all persons born or naturalized in the United States.

Citizenship, however, was not the only issue addressed in the Fourteenth Amendment. The looming issue was that states remained able to infringe on due process and equal protection rights that federal government was prohibited from. This necessitated federal intervention to provide freedom from excessive government power at *all* levels of government.

The 1833 land dispute case of *Barron v. Mayor and City Council of Baltimore,* drew further attention to the contradictions caused when different standards applied to federal and state government. In this case, the plaintiff challenged the constitutionality of Baltimore taking his land for public use and not adequately compensating him, as mandated in the Fifth Amendment. The Supreme Court held that such a case involving local government had no place in federal court because the first 10 amendments to the Constitution (the Bill of Rights) were not applicable to state governments.

Chief Justice Marshall offered in his opinion that each state was permitted to draft its own constitution, and that the federal Constitution was intended as a means to maintain a separation of powers. The Bill of Rights was meant to be a check on the new national government by limiting its control of state laws. However, it made no sense to permit states to violate rights the federal government could not.

The Civil War altered the perception that national and state governments needed to be considered so separately that one could do what the other was prohibited from doing. In 1868, the Fourteenth Amendment was promulgated to extend to the states many of the same limits placed on federal power, because abuse at either the state or federal level could assault the very liberties the Constitution sought to protect. The Fourteenth Amendment thus sought to prevent both the federal and state governments from infringing on the majority of constitutionally guaranteed rights.

■ The Fourteenth Amendment also forbids the states to deny their citizens due process of law or equal protection of the law, that is, it made certain provisions of the Bill of Rights applicable to the states.

The Fourteenth Amendment is a significant addition to the Constitution. Section 1 states that all people born or naturalized in the United States are citizens of the United States and of the state in which they reside, effectively overriding the *Dred Scott* decision. It also prevents federal and state governments from abridging the privileges of citizens or to deny any citizen "equal protection of the law . . . or deprive them of life, liberty or property without due process of law." Southern states were required to ratify the Fourteenth Amendment before re-entering the Union.

John Bingham, representative of Ohio and author of the Fourteenth Amendment, argued during congressional debates that the amendment, through its privileges or immunities clause, extended the protection of the Bill of Rights to the states. The Supreme Court, however, initially refused to agree with that interpretation. In 1873, in three cases heard as one known as the *Slaughterhouse* cases (dealing with the rights of slaughterhouse owners), the Court held that the privileges or immunities clause of the Fourteenth Amendment did not apply the Bill of Rights to the states. Doing so would "change the whole theory of the state and federal governments" and "would [make] this court a perpetual censor upon all legislation of the states."

Twenty-four years later, however, the Supreme Court began applying the Bill of Rights to the states by using the due process clause of the Fourteenth Amendment. As Justice William Brennan interpreted it, the Fourteenth Amendment extended to Americans "a brand new Constitution after the Civil War." It extended citizenship to former slaves, promising them equal treatment under the law and requiring states to apply fundamental provisions of the Bill of Rights to their citizens, greatly expanding the scope of citizens' constitutional rights as well as the resultant case load of the Supreme Court.

The Fourteenth Amendment has five sections, some of which dealt with issues that arose from the Civil War, such as paying war debts and barring Confederates from holding public office. But it is Section 1 that has had the most lasting significance, providing that no person shall be denied **due process of law** (fairness

due process of law • the Fifth and Fourteenth Amendments' constitutionally guaranteed right of an accused to hear the charges against him or her and to be heard by the court having jurisdiction over the matter

equal protection of the law • a constitutional requirement that the government give the same legal protection to all people

in government actions) or **equal protection of the law** (a constitutional requirement that like people must be treated in like ways by government). These two rights have been the basis of many modern cases in constitutional law.

Despite the ratification of the Fourteenth Amendment by all states and the Supreme Court's ruling that this amendment made specific provisions of the Bill of Rights applicable to the states, prejudice and discrimination were not automatically eliminated, as evidenced by the following "Great Moments in History" reported by the Associated Press:

Rosa's Refusal. Montgomery, Alabama, December 5, 1955. Rosa Parks refuses to give up her bus seat to a white man and is fined ten dollars. One year later, a federal court banned bus segregation.

Rocking the Boat. Little Rock, Arkansas, September 1957. President Eisenhower orders troops to admit nine black students into a previously all-white, southern school.

King's Crusade. Birmingham, Alabama, April 3, 1963. In a quest for equality and civil rights, Dr. Martin Luther King, Jr. led mass demonstrations down the streets and in the parks of Birmingham. A few years later, King would be shot to death as he stood on the balcony of his hotel suite.

"Liberty and justice for all," although an intellectual ideal, has remained more challenging to achieve. Laws, programs and great leaders continue to strive to achieve equality, but laws cannot summarily change long-held beliefs. They do, however, provide the impetus toward achieving a nation of equal treatment and opportunity.

Discrimination versus Prejudice

Even with the heartfelt ideals and best intentions of lawmakers, individual prejudices cannot be legislated. Ironically, America was founded mainly because people despised being unfairly ruled by others, yet at the time, slavery and racism were accepted as the norm by many. As the Civil War was to prove, some would go to their graves for the belief they were so superior to others that they could dictate over or even own other humans.

The tendency to prejudge can be hazardous. Most people have some preconceived notions, or prejudices, about specific people or groups of people, including members of minority groups and other categories, such as the elderly, teenagers, the disabled, professional athletes, homosexuals and police officers. In a democratic society, individuals are free to think what they want. However, if these thoughts translate into socially unacceptable behaviors, problems arise, sometimes to the point government is justified in intervening.

prejudice • a negative attitude regarding a person or thing

discrimination • an action or behavior based on prejudice

■ **Prejudice** is an attitude; **discrimination** is a behavior.

If prejudices are converted into acts, laws punish the actor and protect the victim.

The Roots of Racial Discrimination

Racial discrimination has existed since before the time of colonial America and the Constitution. To people such as Washington, Hamilton and Jefferson, slavery was an accepted part of life.

■ The *Dred Scott* decision (1856) ruled that a freed slave did not have the right to remain free in a territory where slavery was still legal.

Although the Thirteenth Amendment to the Constitution declared slavery illegal, it could not outlaw unequal treatment or change racial attitudes so prominent in southern states. In 1896, the case of *Plessy v. Ferguson* was brought before the Supreme Court and heightened awareness of racial issues. Plessy had refused to abide by a law that required black people to give up their train seats to white passengers. Plessy brought suit, arguing a violation of his Thirteenth and Fourteenth Amendment rights. One often admires the fortitude of individuals who stand up for their rights, especially when they may not have the financial means or education background others do. However, it is interesting here that *Plessy* was actually orchestrated by railroad companies, who began to realize the economic costs of segregation. The Court ruled against Plessy:

> If the two races are to meet upon terms of social equality, it must be the result of . . . a voluntary consent of individuals. . . . Legislation is powerless to eradicate racial instincts . . . and the attempts to do so can only result in accentuating the difficulties of the present situation.

Only Justice Harlan dissented, saying: "Our constitution is color-blind" . . . and that "in respect of civil rights, all citizens are equal before the law." The Court hardly considered whether the law was a violation of Plessy's civil rights, and if it was, the Court did not get involved, because from their perspective at the time, in its view, discrimination was a problem to be dealt with by society, not the law.

■ *Plessy v. Ferguson* (1896) showed the Court's desire to avoid civil rights issues, declaring discrimination to be outside the realm of the Court.

Racial tension mounted as states passed laws to assure that whites could maintain their privileged status.

■ **Jim Crow laws** strictly segregated blacks from whites in schools, restaurants, street cars, hospitals and cemeteries.

Jim Crow laws • laws that strictly segregated blacks from whites in schools, restaurants, streetcars, hospitals and cemeteries

Jim Crow laws supposedly kept blacks "separate but equal." The compelling question became whether separate could ever really be equal.

The Issue of "Separate but Equal"

The issue of "separate but equal" was eventually addressed head-on in *Brown v. Board of Education of Topeka I* (1954), when a group of black children sought admission to an all-white public school. The plaintiffs claimed they were being denied their constitutional right to equal protection and that the laws of "separate but equal" were in fact not equal. When the quality of black and white facilities were compared, black facilities were found to be of lesser quality.

In a ruling that confronted the direct and indirect tenets of racism, the Court ruled unanimously that "separate educational facilities are inherently unequal," legally ending the years of Jim Crow laws that segregated facilities in the South.

■ *Brown v. Board of Education of Topeka I* (1954) established that "separate but equal" schools were illegal.

The Court's reasoning was that barring children from an educational facility based solely on race was a blow to the "hearts and minds" of those being discriminated against, adding that separation may create "a feeling of inferiority" that could affect children's ability to cope, learn and dream of one day becoming successful. The momentum of the *Brown* decision prompted further legislation regarding equality and led to one of the greatest civil rights advances in our history, the 1964 Civil Rights Act.

Can all people be treated the same? No, because different people have different capabilities. But people can be treated fairly, reasonably accommodated and treated with respect regardless of work or lifestyle limitations or issues. As Dr. Martin Luther King, Jr., one of the nation's most powerful advocates for equality based on both law and social desire, so eloquently expressed when he stood at the foot of the Washington Monument in 1963 and delivered his history-altering "I Have a Dream" speech: "I have a dream that one day this nation will rise up and live out the true meaning of its creed: We hold these truths to be self-evident: that all men are created equal."

The Struggle for Equality

Through the tumultuous challenges of racism and segregation during the 1950s and 60s, America continued its struggle with what *equal* really meant. Some chose to embrace equality, whereas others chose to resist any movement toward equality, sometimes to the point of participating in violence, such as that perpetrated by the Ku Klux Klan. But the Court had spoken, and the tide of public opinion was turning toward a willingness to become a unified country with "equal protection for all."

Racial discrimination has not been the only way segments of American society have been made to feel disenfranchised. Gender discrimination is an issue our law has had to confront as well. As difficult as it is for today's generation to imagine, women were not allowed to vote until 1920, 50 years after discrimination based on race was prohibited by the Fifteenth Amendment, which guaranteed that "The right of citizens in the United States to vote shall be denied nor abridged by the United States or by any State on account of race, color, or previous condition of servitude."

Gender discrimination remained during the 1960s; for example, women often were denied equal pay for equal work. Head-of-household rules granting higher pay applied only to men. Women also often found they would not be promoted, were excluded from certain professions and were permitted to serve only limited roles in the military. Even educational opportunities were denied women in some instances. But, as was the case with people of color who found themselves and their lives limited, eventually laws recognized a changing norm in society.

The 1996, Supreme Court decision in *United States v. Virginia* found the exclusion of females from Virginia Military Institute (VMI) unconstitutional. Ducat (2004, p. 1285) explains:

> The federal government brought suit against both Virginia and VMI, challenging the male-only admissions policy as a violation of equal protection. A federal district court rendered judgment in the defendant's favor, but it was reversed by the appeals court. In response, Virginia proposed a parallel military education program for women, styled the Virginia Women's Institute for Leadership (VWIL). . . . The district court held the state's creation of the VWIL program remedied any denial of equal protection. . . . The Supreme Court then granted certiorari at the request of the federal government.

Justice Ginsburg delivered the opinion of the Court:

> The notion that admission of women would downgrade VMI's stature, destroy the adversative system and, with it, even the school, is a judgment hardly proved, a prediction hardly different from other "self-fulfilled prophec[ies]," . . . once routinely used to deny rights or opportunities. When women first sought admission to the bar and access to legal education, concerns of the same order were expressed. . . .
>
> Medical facilities similarly resisted men and women as partners in the study of medicine. . . . More recently, women seeking careers in policing encountered resistance based on fears that their presence would "undermine male solidarity," . . . deprive male partners of adequate assistance, . . . and lead to sexual misconduct. . . . Field studies did not confirm these fears.

According to Ducat (p. 1274): "To be sure, this was worlds away from the Courts ruling (in 1873) in *Bradwell v. Illinois*, is which it upheld a state's refusal to admit a woman to the practice of law who qualified in every respect except gender." In fact, discrimination against women in the public and private work sectors had already been prohibited for nearly a quarter of a century before the Supreme Court ruled on the VMI case.

■ The Equal Pay Act of 1963, the Civil Rights Act of 1964, the 1972 Equal Opportunity Act and the 1972 Equal Education Act prohibit discrimination based on race, color, religion, sex or national origin in employment and education in public and private sectors at the federal, state and local levels.

Stephens and Scheb (2003, p. 737) explain: "Congress responded to growing demands for legal equality between the sexes by passing the Equal Pay Act of 1963, the 1972 Amendments to Title VII of the Civil Rights Act of 1964 and Title IX of the Federal Education Act of 1972. The first and second of these statutes were aimed at eliminating sex discrimination in the workplace. The third authorized the witholding of federal funds from educational institutions that engaged in sex discrimination."

The Rise of Affirmative Action Programs

Many argued that these antidiscrimination laws were nothing but hollow promises that in reality did little to rid society of discrimination in employment and education opportunities. In response, the Nixon administration formed a coalition to address unequal treatment of minorities and women. The result was **affirmative action** programs.

■ **Affirmative action** was created to spread equal opportunity throughout the diverse American population.

affirmative action • programs created to spread equal opportunity throughout the diverse American population

Affirmative action programs, sometimes referred to as ethnic- and gender-preference programs, were designed to cure discrimination in hiring and eliminate past, present and future discrimination using race, color, sex and age as deciding criteria. The idea was that minorities and women would no longer be discriminated against in employment and educational opportunities and, in fact, would be given extra consideration to meet goals and quotas. Through the decades, this subject has led to intense controversy.

The landmark case in this issue is *Regents of the University of California v. Bakke* (1978) in which the Supreme Court upheld the University of California's use of race as one factor in determining admissions. Alan Bakke, a white male, had twice been denied admission to medical school, even though less-qualified minorities had been admitted. Bakke charged that the University's quota system violated the equal protection clause. In the *Bakke* decision, the Court stated: "Preferring members of any one group for no reason other than race or ethnic origin is discrimination for its own sake. This the Constitution forbids."

The Court reviewed the medical school's racial set-aside program that reserved 16 of 100 seats for members of certain minority groups. Four justices voted to uphold the program, and four voted to strike it down. Justice Powell provided a fifth vote not only to invalidate the program but also to reverse the state court's injunction against any use of race whatsoever: "The diversity that furthers a compelling state interest encompasses a far broader array of qualifications and characteristics of which racial or ethnic origin is but a single though important element." Ducat (pp. 1170–1171) summarizes the Supreme Court's rulings on affirmative action cases since *Bakke:*

- *United Steelworkers of America v. Weber* (1979)—The Court upheld a collective bargaining agreement that voluntarily aimed at overcoming a company's nearly all-white craft workforce by requiring that at least half of the trainees in an in-plant training program be black until the proportion of blacks in the craft workforce matched the proportion of blacks in the local workforce.
- *Fullilove v. Klutznick* (1980)—Congress's enactment of a 10 percent quota of construction contracts to minority businesses was within its authority under either the Commerce Clause or Section 5 of the Fourteenth Amendment.
- *Firefighters Local Union No. 1784 v. Stotts* (1984)—Setting aside least seniority as a basis for laying off workers and substituting race was something not contained in an existing consent decree and was unjustified unless black employees could prove they individually had been victims of discrimination.
- *Wygant v. Jackson Board of Education* (1986)—The preferential protection of minority teachers from layoffs contained in a collective bargaining agreement was unconstitutional.
- *Local 28, Sheet Metal Workers International Association v. EEOC* (1986)—A federal court order imposing a 29 percent nonwhite membership goal (reflective of the proportion of nonwhites in the local workforce) on a union and its apprenticeship committee for discrimination against nonwhite workers in selection, training and admission of members to union was upheld.
- *United States v. Paradise* (1987)—A requirement that 50 percent of promotions throughout Alabama state troopers were to go to blacks, if qualified blacks were available, was upheld.

In 1996, state universities in both Texas and California struck down race-based admissions. However, in 2003, in two significant decisions, the Supreme Court again upheld the use of race as one factor in admissions policies. *Gratz et al. v. Bollinger et al.* involved the University of Michigan's undergraduate school, allowing 20 of 100 points for minority status. Citing the *Bakke* decision, the Supreme Court, in a 6-to-3 vote, upheld the right of universities to consider race in admission procedures to achieve a diverse student body. Argued the same day was *Grutter v. Bollinger et al.* involving the University of Michigan's law school admission policy, again allowing race to be considered. Although the vote was closer, 5 to 4, the policy of allowing race to be a factor in admissions was upheld: "The Law School's narrowly tailored use of race in admissions decisions to further a compelling interest in obtaining the educational benefits that flow from a diverse student body is not prohibited by the Equal Protection Clause, Title VI or §1981."

Those supporting affirmative action believe it helps bring equity to an imbalance in society. Opponents of affirmative action argue that such programs are, themselves, discriminatory.

Reverse Discrimination

Opponents of affirmative action programs have contended that civil rights laws cannot remedy the effects of past discrimination. This position questions whether it is fair or effective to have an affirmative action policy that requires, for example, agencies that receive federal funding to provide training and jobs for minorities who, as a group, have been discriminated against in the past.

Some people charge that this policy leads to reverse discrimination because women or racial minorities are to be hired over white males who may be better qualified. **Reverse discrimination** consists of giving preferential treatment in hiring and promoting women and minorities to the detriment of white males.

reverse discrimination • giving preferential treatment in hiring and promoting to women and minorities to the detriment of white males

Critics of affirmative action programs argue that discrimination cannot be cured by counter discrimination, asserting that affirmative action is contrary to the fundamental American concept of individual rights in favor of group entitlement.

The question then becomes whether admission to a college on the basis of diversity is simply a nice way of saying it is going to take race into account. Something must guide the decisions of those who determine who will be hired, fired or admitted to the college of their choice. Wrobleski and Hess (2006, p. 240) note: "This issue [reverse discrimination] has separated whites from minorities, men from women, and the advocates of affirmative action from those who believe in a strict "merit" principle for employment and advancement. . . . A growing number of majority member workers are complaining bitterly about their own civil rights being abridged, and some are filing reverse discrimination suits in court."

The majority position has been summarized as a concern that for every deserving minority group member provided a job or promotion through preferential quotas, a deserving and often more qualified nonminority person is thereby deprived of a job or promotion. The courts themselves have been deeply divided over the constitutionality of the reverse discrimination that some believe is implicit in minority quotas and double standards.

Those in favor of affirmative action say this is a necessary policy to assure that all citizens have access to the **American Dream,** the belief that through hard work anyone can have success and ample material possessions.

American Dream • the belief that through hard work anyone can have success and ample material possessions

The Civil Rights Act, the Fair Housing Act, the Voting Rights Act, as well as other legislation and numerous court decisions have, on paper, outlawed discrimination in this nation. However, generations of attitudes cannot be so easily changed, but because laws reflect desired social norms, movement toward equality continues.

Other Forms of Discrimination

Religious discrimination has been addressed through various cases, including *Ansonia Board of Education v. Philbrook* (1986).

Discrimination against *people with disabilities* affects criminal justice in a number of ways, including who is hired (or not) and how the system treats those with disabilities. Most efforts to respond to issues of the disabled have come through legislation. Congress has responded with Title V of the Rehabilitation Act of 1973 and the Americans with Disabilities Act of 1990, both of which seek to remove barriers encountered by those living with disabilities.

Criminal justice agencies have responded to legislation by improving accessibility, such as by installing wheelchair ramps, wider doors and height-appropriate counters, as well as accommodations for the vision and hearing impaired. As criminal justice agencies seek to have their personnel be more reflective of the communities they serve, they have opened opportunities for employment to those with disabilities. Obviously not everyone has the physical attributes needed to be, for example, a police officer. But those with disabilities can fill many other positions. All that is needed is a respect for the law requiring reasonable accommodations for those with disabilities.

In many ways the criminal justice system has been more accommodating to those being arrested than to those who want to be a part of the criminal justice team. Hopefully, the years ahead will find the system willing to respond with an understanding and appreciation for what many disabled Americans can contribute.

Discrimination because of *sexual orientation* is a challenge for the criminal justice system regarding equal protection issues for victims, as well as how gay or lesbian criminal justice professionals are treated by their own agencies. The approach used by the American military is a "don't ask/don't tell" policy: service people will not be asked and do not have to tell, but will be discharged if their homosexuality is made public. The criminal justice system has no such policy. Rather, those serving in this field are subject to the same laws pertaining to same-sex relationships but may also find themselves subject to the same discrimination as those who become victims of bias crimes.

Sexual-orientation discrimination and same-sex marriage are issues that continue to garner attention on legislative floors and courtrooms, with changes occurring on both fronts so rapidly that attempts to provide current law finds itself almost immediately outdated. Similarly, laws pertaining to *immigration* and *residency discrimination* are currently in the throes of debate and change.

The Immigration Issue   "Give me your tired, your poor, Your huddled masses yearning to breathe free, The wretched refuse of your teeming shore, Send these, the homeless, tempest-tost to me, I lift my lamp beside the golden door!" are the immortal words of poet Emma Lazaras that appear at the base of the Statue of Liberty in New York. These words once reflected a welcoming philosophy of a country developed in large part by immigrants.

Today, immigration issues challenge our past beliefs and some would say the future of America. An estimated 11 to 12 million illegal immigrants reside in the United States and have become an increasing focus of controversy. The economy, possibly racism and the 9/11 attack on America, carried out by hijackers who entered the country on student or tourist visas, contribute to the changing political climate. Americans recognized the porous borders and lax enforcement of immigration laws as security threats, and in Congress, both parties have pushed for a tougher line (Babington and Murray, 2006, p. A01).

President George W. Bush had made immigration reform a prime issue after winning the presidency, calling for a guest-worker program offering illegal immigrants and foreign workers access to the U.S. labor market. But the House, responding to conservative districts' anger about the flood of illegal immigrants, passed legislation in December 2005 that would build hundreds of miles of fence on the southern border and declare illegal immigrants felons.

In April 2006, masses of illegal immigrants, primarily Hispanics, and their supporters responded. A *Washington Post* headline declared: "Immigration Debate Wakes a 'Sleeping Latino Giant'" (Aizenman, 2006, p. A01). Balz and Fears describe what has been called a "watershed moment": "Hundreds of thousands of pro-immigration demonstrators mobilized on the [Washington, DC] Mall and in scores of cities across the country [April 10, 1006] in a powerful display of grass-roots muscle-flexing that organizers said could mark a coming-of-age for Latino political power in the United States." The demonstrators wore white shirts, symbolic of peace, carried American flags and sang the national anthem. Statements from demonstrators included: "We decided not be invisible anymore," and "We deserve to be here. We work hard. We are immigrants, but we are not terrorists."

Other protests fueled the fire of debate: "There was the scene in Apache Junction, Arizona, in which a few Hispanic students raised a Mexican flag over their high school and another group took it down and burned it. In Houston the principal at Reagan High School was reprimanded for raising a Mexican flag below the U.S. and Texas flags, in solidarity with his largely Hispanic student body. Representative Tancredo (R-Colo.) said his congressional offices were swamped by more than 1,000 phone calls, nearly all from people furious about the protests in which demonstrators 'were blatantly stating their illegal presence in the country and waving Mexican flags'" ("Should They Stay," 2006, p. 32.)

Balz and Fears report on a Washington Post-ABC News poll showing that three-quarters of Americans think the government is not doing enough to prevent illegal immigration, but three in five said they favor providing illegal immigrants who have lived here for years a way to gain legal status and eventual citizenship. However, Tancredo, an advocate of cracking down on illegal immigrants, cautioned: "Today's rallies show how entrenched the illegal alien lobby has become over the last several years. The iron triangle of illegal employers, foreign governments and groups like LaRaza puts tremendous pressure on our elected officials to violate the desires of law-abiding Americas."

Constitutional interpretation also struggles with how to respond: "The Fifth and Fourteenth Amendments do not protect citizens alone from arbitrary or unjust government actions. Rather, the amendments use the broader term 'persons.' The Supreme Court has stressed the text of the Fourteenth Amendment in striking down a number of state laws that differentiate between residents and nonresidents or between citizens and aliens" (Stephens and Scheb, p. 745).

The Supreme Court has held that whether people are considered legal or otherwise, government does not have a legitimate interest in denying certain services. Laws requiring a one-year waiting period before new legal residents could receive welfare benefits were struck down in *Shapiro v. Thompson* (1969). In *Plyler v. Doe* (1982), the Court held that a Texas law denying public education to children of illegal immigrants was unconstitutional. And in *Sugarman v. McDougall* (1973) and *Hampton v. Mow Sun Wong* (1976), the Court held that state and federal laws preventing aliens from being given civil service jobs were illegal.

Attitudes change, and so does the law. Where barriers once did not exist, lines have been drawn. As the Court and all of society struggle with how to combine the richness that immigration has contributed to the United States with challenges brought on by changes over these two centuries, the future cannot help but reflect our past. And this past reflects, in the words of the Pledge of Allegiance, *"one nation . . . with liberty and justice for all."* As this text goes to press, the controversy continues.

Criminal justice students and practitioners will need to use the skills discussed in Chapter 4 to remain current, especially in areas such as these that are subject to frequent change.

Equality in the Twenty-First Century

A look at this nation's history helps explain why affirmative action programs developed. In the 1990s, however, such programs found themselves increasingly challenged as unconstitutional. Although these challenges have yet to successful, the tide seems to be slowly turning as a new Supreme Court bench emerges with older justices retiring and new ones being appointed. Although some more recent decisions by the Court have supported affirmative action programs, others are holding them more accountable than in the past. In *Adarand Constructors, Inc. v. Pena* (1995), a program was not rejected but only by a narrow 5-to-4 vote. Both Justices Scalia and Thomas stated they were against affirmative action. The most recent appointments to the Court will take this issue one direction or the other, although public sentiment seems to be turning against the concept. For example, the California Civil Rights Initiative (CCRI) forbidding the government to use ethnicity or gender as a criterion for either discriminating against or giving preferential treatment to any individual or group passed unanimously. In 1996, California voters banned affirmative action, as did the University of Texas.

As the debates over affirmative action continue, it would seem encouraging that Americans, regardless of their position on the topic, agree people should not be treated differently. It is how to achieve a level playing field for all to work from that remains the challenge. Should affirmative action programs, even though they do treat some differently, continue? Only the results of future challenges will tell, but Justice O'Connor's statement in *Adarand Constructors, Inc. v. Pena* best states the Court's position now: "The unhappy persistence of both the practice and the lingering effects of racial discrimination against minority groups in this country is an unfortunate reality, and government is not disqualified from acting in response to it."

Equal Protection in the Criminal Justice System

Unfortunately, discrimination has been an issue within the criminal justice system itself. Equal protection issues have occurred in such areas as racial profiling, biased jury selection, biased sentencing and prisoner violations.

Some suggest that one result of discrimination is racial disparity, an unfortunate reality of the criminal justice system for both juveniles and adults. A report by the National Council on Crime and Delinquency (NCCD) states: "While 'Equal Justice Under Law' is the foundation of our legal system, and is carved on the front of the U.S. Supreme Court, the juvenile justice system is anything but equal. Throughout the system, minority youths—especially African American youths—receive different and harsher treatment" ("Race Disparity Seen . . . ," 2000, p. 7). The same report (p. 6) notes: "Black youths are overrepresented at every decision point in the juvenile justice system."

Data from the FBI, the Bureau of Justice Statistics (BJS) and the Office of Juvenile Justice and Delinquency Prevention (OJJDP) report that although blacks constitute only 15 percent of all youths under age 18, they make up 26 percent of juvenile arrestees, 31 percent of the cases referred to juvenile court, 46 percent of the cases that juvenile courts waive to adult court and 58 percent of the youths sent to adult prisons (p. 7). While theories persist, so do debates. What was yesterday's pluralism is today's multiculturalism, and although both remain cornerstones of America's unique makeup, challenges within the criminal justice system remain.

Discrimination in Law Enforcement

Considering the wide amount of discretion granted to police officers, it follows that those in law enforcement may be accused of discrimination, whether on the basis of age, gender or race. Hess and Wrobleski (2006, p. 19) note: "Discretion lets officers treat different people differently. This may be seen as discrimination and, in fact, sometimes is. Some officers are harder on minorities or on men or on juveniles. This may be conscious or unconscious discrimination, but it does make for inconsistent enforcement of the laws."

Some officers are perceived as "having it in for" juveniles and may respond more harshly than others to youthful offenders, perhaps attempting to derail a future of criminal behavior. Similarly, some law enforcement officers, particularly males, have been accused of gender discrimination, treating women more leniently than men.

The most frequently alleged form of discrimination by the police is racial discrimination. Some argue that minority overrepresentation in the criminal justice system begins with law enforcement and the discriminatory attitudes and practices some officers apply toward members of racial and ethnic groups. In fact, officers themselves admit that a citizen's race and socioeconomic status can lead to unequal treatment and even unwarranted physical force by the police. Weisburd et al. (2000) asked officers whether the police are more likely to use physical force against blacks and other minorities than against whites in similar situations and found only 5.1 percent of white officers agreed that such unequal treatment occurs. However, 57.1 percent of black officers surveyed thought officers were more likely to use physical force against blacks and other minorities than against whites in similar situations, and 12.4 percent of "other minority" officers agreed with the statement concerning unequal treatment.

The contention that police single out subjects solely on the basis of the color of their skin frequently leads to allegations of **racial profiling,** which Ramirez et al. (2000, p. 3) define as "any police-initiated action that relies on the race, ethnicity or national origin rather than the behavior of an individual or information that leads the police to a particular individual who has been identified as being, or having been, engaged in criminal activity." Such an event may be called "DWB" (Driving while Black), "DWA" (Driving while Asian) or "DWM" (Driving while Mexican). Regardless of the acronym used, the event signals the unethical and illegal practice of racial profiling.

Cohen et al. (2000, p. 15) assert: "Racial profiling is inconsistent with the basic freedoms and rights afforded in our democracy. It erodes the foundation of trust between communities and public authorities. Worst of all, it inflames racial and ethnic strife and undermines America's progress toward color-blind justice."

racial profiling • the process of using certain racial characteristics, such as skin color, as indicators of criminal activity

Fridell (2005, p. 1) reports that about half of the states have adopted legislation related to racial profiling, with most of the laws including data-collection requirements. Similar legislation is pending in other states.

■ The equal protection clause of the Fourteenth Amendment to the Constitution applies to racial profiling. Race-based enforcement of the law is illegal.

The exact prevalence of the problem remains unclear, as research findings thus far lack consensus on the extensiveness of discrimination in police stops, searches and arrests. To help present a more complete picture, many agencies now require the collection of additional racial data about drivers and passengers involved in traffic stops. A study by Meehan and Ponder (2002) concluded that racial profiling by police is a function of both race and place, with an increase occurring as African Americans move farther away from predominantly black neighborhoods into wealthier white communities, termed *the race-and-place* effect.

However, in a study of contacts between police and the public, Durose et al. (2005, p. iv) found: "The likelihood of being stopped by police in 2002 did not differ significantly between white (8.6%), black (9.1%) and Hispanic (8.6%) drivers." They (p.v) also found that during a traffic stop, police were more likely to carry out some type of search on a male (7.1%) than a female (1.8%) and more likely to carry out some type of search on a black (10.2%) or Hispanic (11.4%) than a white (3.5%). Another disturbing finding was that among those with police contact, blacks (3.5%) and Hispanics (2.5%) were more likely than whites (1.1%) to experience police threat or use of force during the contact.

Gallo (2003) stresses the need to "distinguish between profiling as a policing technique and the politically charged term *racial profiling*." Fridell et al. (2001, p. 3) suggest not using the term *racial profiling*, but instead refer to "*racially biased policing*," noting that profiling is a legitimate police practice.

Huntington (2001, p. 19) asks: "In light of the recent World Trade Center and Pentagon attacks, has the public's perception and acceptance of profiling changed? Indeed, should police stand firm and not be afraid to admit that profiling can be a powerful tool in apprehending criminals . . . and terrorists?" He suggests: "For the sake of argument, let's rename profiling 'building a case' and go from there." Nowicki (2002, p. 16) cites a legal trainer who believes it may be "borderline incompetence to not use race if intelligence information points to a particular race. Race may be a factor and it would be ludicrous to ignore the obvious, but race is just one factor and cannot be singled out as the only reason for a stop."

It is possible criminal justice practitioners may encounter allegations of other forms of discrimination as well, sometimes even personally. The Court dealt with *age discrimination* in *Massachusetts Board of Retirement v. Murgia* (1976) by upholding a state law that prohibited uniformed police officers from working beyond the age of 50. The Americans with Disabilities Act of 1990, along with other legislation and case law, seeks to address *disabilities discrimination*.

A developing area of discrimination law affecting police officers deals with pregnancy policies. Acknowledging the contributions of women in law enforcement,. Kruger (2006, pp. 10–11) states: "It is critical, then, for the continued success of the profession that law enforcement agencies successfully recruit and retain women to serve as patrol officers. One important tool in achieving these goals is a favorable policy relating to pregnancy, one that supports parenthood without compromising police operations, without unfairly burdening nonpregnant employees, and without violating antidiscrimination law." The federal Pregnancy Discrimination Act and a series of developing court holdings are cited as sources for this developing area of law.

Discrimination in the Courts

Discrimination also exists in some courts. Even before a defendant appears for trial, discrimination in the jury selection process may negatively affect the outcome of the case.

After the Civil War ended, the equal protection clause of the Fourteenth Amendment was used as a legal tool to abolish statutes excluding African Americans from jury selection. In 1880, the Supreme Court cited the equal protection clause in *Strauder v. West Virginia* (1879) when it struck down a statute explicitly prohibiting African Americans from serving on juries. To get around such rulings and continue excluding racial minorities from jury duty, some states passed new laws requiring all jury members to be landholders or pay real estate taxes. Although such laws appeared race and gender neutral and not overtly discriminating, in actuality only white males met these criteria.

It was not until 1935, in *Norris v. Alabama*, that the Court finally acknowledged that virtual exclusion of African Americans from juries constituted an equal protection violation. Nonetheless, the ruling was seen as ineffectual, little effort was made to correct the discrepancies, and African Americans remained noticeably underrepresented on juries, particularly in the South. Even during the civil rights revolution of the 1950s and 1960s, the Supreme Court did not extend its desegregation rulings to the subject of juries. Consequently, in *Swain v. Alabama* (1965), the Court found no equal protection violations in a county where 26 percent of eligible voters were black, yet only 10 to 15 percent of the jury panels were black. The Court denied that such a statistical pattern precluded a fair jury-selection process, stating: "Neither the jury roll nor the venire need be a perfect mirror of the community or accurately reflect the proportionate strength of every identifiable group."

The Court, however, reversed its position in *Batson v. Kentucky* (1986), when it ruled the use of peremptory challenges to deliberately produce a racially unbalanced jury was unconstitutional. In *Batson*, the defendant was African American, and the prosecutor in the first trial used the state's peremptory challenges to remove all four prospective black jurors, leaving an all-white jury that ultimately convicted Batson. The conviction was upheld by the Kentucky Supreme Court, but the U.S. Supreme Court overturned the lower courts' rulings:

> The State's privilege to strike individual jurors through peremptory challenges is subject to the command of the Equal Protection Clause. Although a prosecutor ordinarily is entitled to exercise peremptory challenges "for any reason at all, as long as that reason is related to his view concerning the outcome" of the case to be tried. . . . The Equal Protection Clause forbids the prosecutor to challenge potential jurors solely on account of their race or on the assumption that black jurors as a group will be unable impartially to consider the State's case against a black defendant.

The Court extended the *Batson* ruling in *J.E.B. v. Alabama* (1994), when it held that gender, as with race, could not be used as a proxy for juror competence. In this case, the state of Alabama, on behalf of a minor child's mother, filed a complaint for paternity and child support. A jury pool of 36 potential jurors was assembled—12 males and 24 females. Two jurors were removed for cause, and peremptory challenges used by both sides removed 18 more. The result was an all-female jury, who found the petitioner to be the child's father. The father appealed. The Supreme Court upheld the petitioner's challenge, stating: "Equal opportunity to participate in the fair administration of justice is fundamental to our democratic system. It not only furthers the goals of the jury system. It reaffirms the promise of equality under the law—that all citizens, regardless of race, ethnicity, or gender, have the chance to take part directly in our democracy. When persons are excluded from participation in our democratic processes solely because of race or gender, this promise of equality dims, and the integrity of our judicial system is jeopardized."

■ The equal protection clause prohibits discrimination in jury selection on the basis of race or gender.

Just as discrimination can affect court proceedings before a trial, it can also affect the stage after trial—sentencing. Prosecutorial discretion may also contribute to sentencing disparity. A common tactic used by prosecutors to secure a guilty plea is to offer the defendant a lesser charge. Consequently, the sentence received is based on the charges brought, not necessarily on the act committed.

It should come as no surprise then that great variation exists among the sentences received by offenders convicted of the same offense. A study by Human Rights Watch ("Report Cites Racial Disparity . . . ," 2000, p. 5) found: "Black men are sent to state prisons on drug charges at 13 times the rate of white men, even though five times as many whites use drugs as blacks."

A study on sentencing disparity by Spohn and Holleran (2000, p. 281) examined four offender characteristics—race/ethnicity, gender, age and employment status—and how they interact to affect sentencing decisions. Their study found the following:

> The four offender characteristics interact to produce harsher sentences for certain types of offenders. Young black and Hispanic males face greater odds of incarceration than middle-aged white males, and unemployed black and Hispanic males are substantially more likely to be sentenced to prison than employed white males. Thus, our results suggest that offenders with constellations of characteristics other than "young black male" [also] pay a punishment penalty.

In an effort to standardize sentencing and eliminate disparity, many state and federal sentencing guidelines have been established. In 1984, Congress passed the Sentencing Reform Act (SRA), the purpose of which was to achieve honesty, uniformity and proportionality in sentencing. However, one of the unpredicted by-products of legislature designed to "equalize" was an inadvertent amplification of sentencing disparity.

Numerous studies have documented sentencing disparities among various races of offenders, with some of the disparity attributed to not the race of the defendant but, rather, to that of the victim. In one well-known study, Baldus and two colleagues found defendants charged with murdering white victims were 4.3 times as likely to receive a death sentence as defendants charged with killing blacks. This result was later used by Warren McClesky, a black man sentenced to death after being convicted of armed robbery and the murder of a white police officer in Georgia. McClesky claimed the state's capital-sentencing process operated to deny him equal protection of the laws in violation of the Fourteenth Amendment. In *McClesky v. Kemp* (1987), however, the U.S. Supreme Court found no evidence of such racial discrimination and affirmed the judgments of the lower courts:

> For this claim to prevail, McClesky would have to prove that the Georgia Legislature enacted or maintained the death penalty statute because of an anticipated racially discriminatory effect. In *Gregg v. Georgia* (1976), this Court found that the Georgia capital sentencing system could operate in a fair and neutral manner. There was no evidence then, and there is none now, that the Georgia Legislature enacted the capital punishment statute to further a racially discriminatory purpose.

Whatever sentencing decisions are made by the courts, the corrections system must then execute. Consequently, any disparity or discrimination generated at the court stage is inherited by corrections.

Discrimination in Corrections

What has been termed the *due process revolution* that emerged during the politically tumultuous 1960s and 1970s affected every area of the law. In addition to the civil rights movement, the plight of groups who had been in many ways ignored by the Bill of Rights—for example, children—gained national attention. The field of corrections changed forever in 1968, when, thanks to television and the media, many Americans had their first look inside prisons. And they were horrified.

The Attica Prison riot, followed by the New Mexico Penitentiary riot and a host of other uprisings in American correctional facilities, shocked the public. Not only the deplorable conditions that spawned much unrest by inmates but also the way law enforcement and correctional personnel were treating inmates reversed roles and made the government look like the criminals. Like every other segment of society in the United States during that period, corrections and the prison system were facing vast changes, including the unprecedented granting of rights to prisoners. And with more than 1 million people now incarcerated in prison and an additional 4 million supervised in other correctional facilities, prisoners' rights continue to greatly affect the judicial system.

Perhaps because few Americans ever saw what prison life was actually like, and maybe did not care, the plight of inmates was ignored. People heard stories about prisons elsewhere, as well as the terrible, often cruel conditions prisoners were subjected to, but remained ignorant about the atrocities happening in U.S. correctional institutions. When Americans learned of them, even a system based on law and order recognized the need for due process here as well.

No one disputes the need for rules and for consequences for those who break them, including imprisonment. However, the question raised is whether segregation from society is the punishment, or if continued harsh treatment within the institutions is what the American corrections system is about. Indeed, determining the purpose of corrections has been a challenge.

It comes as a surprise to many that prisoners have any rights at all. Historically, they had few or none. Once a person was remanded to a correctional facility, what happened to them seemed to be of little concern:

> During his term of service in the penitentiary, he is in a state of penal servitude to the State. He has, as a consequence of his crime, not only forfeited his liberty, but all his personal rights except those which the law in its humanity accords him. He is for the time being the slave of the State. He is civiliter mortuus; and his estate, if he has any, is administered like that of a dead man (*Ruffin v. Commonwealth,* 1871).

The judiciary of that time also believed separation of government prevented them from interfering with executive agencies. In fact, from the 1820s through the early 1940s, prison administrators were essentially sovereign, enjoying enormous power and very little accountability. In the 1940s, however, the attitude in the United States toward corrections began to change as a move toward rehabilitation, rather than strictly punishment, emerged. In *Ex parte Hull* (1941), one of the formative cases affecting the prisoner's rights movement, the Supreme Court acknowledged that even prisoners had rights, and that the previous and routine practice of censoring and discarding prisoners' legal petitions to courts was unconstitutional. The Court also held, not totally dissimilar to the holding in *Marbury v. Madison* (1803), that court officials, not correctional officials, held the decision-making authority regarding what rights prisoners had.

Three years later, *Coffin v. Reichard* (1944) extended prisoner rights to issues of conditions of confinement, making it clear that inmates do not lose all their civil rights, contrary to the ruling in *Ruffin.* The Court further ruled, in *Cooper v. Pate* (1964), that inmates could sue the warden for depriving them of their constitutional rights under Section 1983 of the U.S. Code, thereby opening the door for inmates to seek legal redress in court. And although there was a brief flurry of frivolous lawsuits filed by prisoners (one inmate claimed his religion forbade him from eating "pungent" foods, such as anything cooked with onions or garlic; another sought court permission to engage in sexually deviant behavior by claiming his religion justified such acts), and such frivolities still continue although to a lesser extent, the system sought a balance, reflected in the cases discussed in subsequent chapters.

It is important to differentiate between privileges and rights of inmates, and this is where the public gets confused.

right • a legally protected claim

privilege • a claim that is not legally protected

■ A **right** is a legally protected claim, whereas a **privilege** is not necessarily legally protected.

Although there are different theories on what privileges benefit prisoners and/or prisons (for example, television may be seen by the public as an unnecessary privilege, whereas corrections officials view it as a way to keep inmates occupied and to prevent the moral and behavioral problems that result from total boredom), these should not be confused with rights all Americans, even those incarcerated, have under the Constitution.

■ For prisoners, cases based on Fourteenth Amendment rights involve equal protection on the basis of race, gender and the availability of facilities and services.

Race Discrimination   In *Washington v. Lee* (1966), the court held that the need for security and discipline must be determined on a case-by-case basis and that statutorily imposed racial segregation in correctional facilities, without a compelling state interest, is unconstitutional. Segregating racial groups, assuming they will be in conflict otherwise, violates the equal protection component of the Fourteenth Amendment.

Gender Discrimination   *Mary Beth G. v. Chicago* (1983) found an equal protection violation regarding strip search practices. In this case, only females were required to submit to strip searches and body-cavity examinations; males were not. In *Glover v. Johnson* (1979 and 1987), equal protection violations were found when female prisoners were offered fewer educational and vocational programs than males, and when the limited programs available to women were found to be of less quality than those available to men.

Discrimination against the Disabled   Correctional facilities are required by the Americans with Disabilities Act (ADA) to provide special accommodations, programming and services to disabled inmates. Colbridge (2000, p. 28) explains: "For purposes of the ADA, disability means having a physical or mental impairment that substantially limits one or more major life activities, having a record of such an impairment, or being regarded as having such an impairment." Colbridge (2001, p. 23) contends: "The Americans with Disabilities Act is a difficult statute to understand and implement in the workplace."

The ADA gives inmates with disabilities legal leverage in obtaining special benefits. Not providing adequate services may lead to expensive, time-consuming lawsuits. For example, sign language interpreters are usually required for hearing-impaired inmates. However, as Litchford (2000, p. 15) reports: "The courts have held that the ADA does not prohibit officers [law enforcement or correctional] from taking enforcement action, including the use of force, necessary to protect officer or public safety."

Disciplinary Hearings   The Fourteenth Amendment also covers due process rights during disciplinary hearings. *Wolff v. McDonnell* (1974) involved the claim that Nebraska's disciplinary procedures, particularly those relating to loss of good time, were unconstitutional. As a result, the Supreme Court determined that disciplinary proceedings differed from criminal prosecutions such that prisoners were not owed the full due process rights to which a defendant on trial is entitled. The minimum requirements specified by the Court concerning disciplinary proceedings included the right to receive advanced written notice of the alleged infraction, to have sufficient time to prepare a defense, to present documentary evidence and to call witnesses on his or her behalf, to seek counsel when the circumstances of the case are complex or if the prisoner is illiterate, to have a written statement of the findings of the disciplinary committee and to maintain a written record of the proceedings.

Access to Court   Access to court is another Fourteenth Amendment right issue. Since *Cooper v. Pate* (1964), a lengthy list of "access to court" cases has been generated. The validity of a prisoner's right to court access was solidified in *Crug v. Hauck* (1971), when the court stated "ready access to court is one of, perhaps *the* most fundamental constitutional right." However, few resources were available to inmates faced with preparing a defense. In *Bounds v. Smith* (1977), the Court

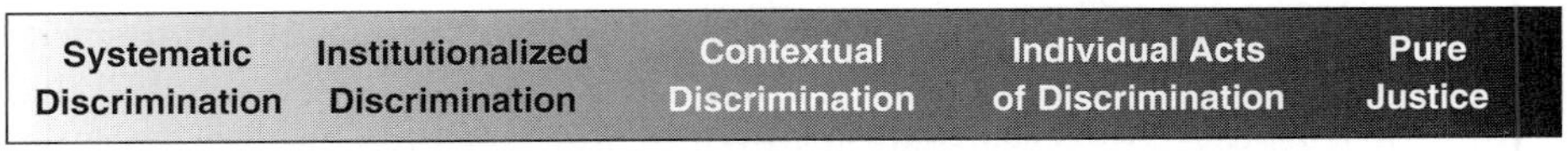

Systematic Discrimination	Institutionalized Discrimination	Contextual Discrimination	Individual Acts of Discrimination	Pure Justice

Figure 5.1 Discrimination Continuum

Source: Samuel Walker, Cassia Spohn and Miriam DeLone. *The Color of Justice: Race, Ethnicity and Crime in America*, 3rd ed. Belmont, CA: Wadsworth Publishing Company, 2004, p. 17. Reprinted by permission.

ruled that North Carolina must furnish each correctional institution with an adequate law library. Some states have even provided law libraries so extensive as to be envied by attorneys.

In *Johnson v. Avery* (1969), the Supreme Court had ruled it acceptable for inmates to help each other with legal work in case preparation, unless the correctional facility provided other reasonable legal assistance. The libraries allowed an inmate with sufficient interest in learning the law to become a "jailhouse lawyer." Some facilities have avoided the extensive use of jailhouse lawyers by establishing legal-assistance programs staffed by practicing lawyers or law students. More constitutional law affecting corrections is included in subsequent chapters.

Is There Systematic Discrimination in the Criminal Justice System?

Walker et al. (2004) address this question. Given the current "get tough" attitude toward criminals by U.S. citizens and the fact that the racial majority in the United States remains white, many have incorrectly assumed that the unspoken sentiment is really "let's get tough on minorities." However, Walker et al. (pp. 17–19) offer a more positive answer. They suggest that there are different types and degrees of racial discrimination, as shown in Figure 5.1.

According to Walker et al.: "At one end of the 'discrimination continuum' is pure justice, which means that there is not discrimination at any time, place or point in the criminal justice system. At the other end is systematic discrimination, which means that discrimination prevails at all stages of the criminal justice system, in all places and at all times." They suggest that the U.S. criminal justice system falls in the middle on the continuum and that the system is characterized by **contextual discrimination.** Contextual discrimination describes a situation in which racial minorities are treated more harshly at some points and in some places in the criminal justice system but no differently than whites at other points and in other places. They (p. 358) conclude, "Although the contemporary criminal justice system is not characterized by pure justice, many of the grossest racial inequities have been reduced, if not eliminated. Reforms mandated by the U.S. Supreme Court or adopted voluntarily by the states have tempered the blatant racism directed against racial minorities by criminal justice officials."

contextual discrimination • describes a situation in which racial minorities are treated more harshly at some points and in some places in the criminal justice system but no differently than whites at other points and in other places

Balancing State and Federal Power and Individual Rights

Although this text specifically addresses the overall importance of the U.S. Constitution and its amendments, state constitutions also play a role in the formation of laws that people are protected by and expected to follow. It is sometimes confusing that two constitutions can be in effect at the same time. In fact, some people are surprised that state constitutions even exist. They do, but they play a different role than the U.S. Constitution.

Like a company's bylaws, a state's constitution sets forth some general guidelines the particular state has chosen to operate under. State constitutions limit and restrict the state government's inherent power; prescribing how the state is to exercise its inherent power; and affirming the existence of certain powers, for example, to use capital punishment. But because the U.S. Constitution is overriding, state constitutions are used more to set forth some specific ideals that the particular state asserts. They also have the more practical use of establishing the organization of a state's governing bodies.

The passage of the Fourteenth Amendment provided through its privileges and immunity and due process clauses that the fundamental provisions of the Bill of Rights would apply to all levels of governmental powers (national, state and local). Some confusion arises here because, for reasons that have confounded many who have argued over the course of history that the entire Bill of Rights should be directly applied to the states, the doctrine of selective incorporation as upheld by the Supreme Court has prevented this from occurring.

Selective Incorporation

Considering the Constitution's primary purpose was limiting the power of *federal* government, it seemed unthinkable that the federal government would be kept in line only to have state authority left unbridled. The **incorporation doctrine,** also known as **selective incorporation,** prevents state or local governments from infringing on people's rights when federal government would not be allowed to.

> ■ The doctrine of selective incorporation holds that only the provisions of the Bill of Rights fundamental to the American scheme of justice are applied to the states through the due process clause of the Fourteenth Amendment.

To identify which rights within the Bill of Rights would apply to state and local government, the U.S. Supreme Court set about the task of determining, through common law case analysis, which rights were protected when the Fourteenth Amendment stated "No State shall make or enforce any law which shall abridge the privileges or immunities of citizens of the United States, nor shall any State deprive any person of life, liberty, or property, without due process of law; nor deny to any person within its jurisdiction the equal protection of the laws." This would prove no small undertaking.

The following question begs to be asked: Why was an amendment not passed that simply applied the Bill of Rights, in its entirety, to the states? The short answer to this immensely complicated, political, philosophical and legal question is that the tremendous changes occurring in the norms of this emerging country had to be given ample time to evolve on their own. Interpreting the Constitution on the basis of societal norms—the essence of a "living law"—is what has allowed the Constitution to remain effective, and this would prove itself as the era of civil rights and liberties continued to emerge. The issue of what rights would be set forth in the Constitution caused much debate, for reasons that included the fear that *only* those rights would be recognized, as well as the idea from the beginning that federal and state law should not be the same.

The opinions of the Supreme Court make it clear they never interpreted the due process clause of the Fourteenth Amendment to mean the entire Bill of Rights

incorporation doctrine • holds that only the provisions of the Bill of Rights that are fundamental to the American legal system are applied to the states through the due process clause of the Fourteenth Amendment; also called **selective incorporation.**

would apply to the states and local government. However, the ultimate result has been that almost all criminal procedure rights in the Bill of Rights have been incorporated into the Fourteenth Amendment. Why? Because of how the Court has analyzed such rights. Justice Harlan I, stated: "There are principles of liberty and justice lying at the foundation of our civil and political institutions which no state can violate consistently with that due process of law required by the Fourteenth Amendment in proceedings involving life, liberty or property" (*Plessy v. Ferguson*, 1896). Justice Cardozo, in *Palko v. Connecticut* (1937), asserted there were rights "so rooted in the traditions and conscience of our people as to be ranked as fundamental," meaning "essential to justice and the American system of political liberty." And in *Duncan v. Louisiana* (1968), the Court used what has become the most frequent standard, "fundamental to the American scheme of justice." For example, if a state law were to abridge freedom of religion, it would be violating the First Amendment as applied to the state through the Fourteenth Amendment.

To answer the question of which rights within the Bill of Rights apply to the states as well, it is easier to answer which do *not*. Of the first eight amendments, only three individual guarantees have not been made applicable to the states by the Supreme Court:

- The Second Amendment guarantee of the right to bear arms.
- The Fifth Amendment clause guaranteeing criminal prosecution only on a grand jury indictment.
- The Seventh Amendment guarantee of a jury trial in a civil case.

The Third Amendment prohibiting the quartering of soldiers in private houses and the Eighth Amendment prohibiting excessive fines have yet to be addressed by the Court.

A Check on Federal Power

Just as states may exceed their power, so too, can the federal government. An example of this is *United States v. Lopez* (1995), in which the U.S. Supreme Court struck down a 1990 federal law aimed at banning firearms in schools, ruling 5 to 4 that Congress had exceeded its power under the commerce clause of the U.S. Constitution when it enacted the law. The U.S. Court of Appeals for the Fifth Circuit ruled that Congress had exceeded its power in enacting the law, and the Supreme Court agreed.

In another case, *Jones v. United States* (1999), the Supreme Court limited the reach of the federal arson law ("Court Limits Federal . . . ," 2000, p. 6). Jones was convicted of throwing a Molotov cocktail into the home of his cousin and was sentenced to 35 years in federal prison. Jones appealed, arguing that the federal arson law did not apply to cases like his. The Supreme Court granted certiorari and ruled the law had, in fact, been misapplied. The federal law, as written, applies only to property used in interstate or foreign commerce, not to the arson of an owner-occupied private residence.

SUMMARY

To assure "liberty and justice for all," two additional amendments were passed. The Thirteenth Amendment, ratified in 1865, abolished slavery. The Fourteenth Amendment granted citizenship to all persons born or naturalized in the United States and forbid states to deny their citizens due process of law or equal protection of the law; that is, it made certain provisions of the Bill of Rights applicable to the states.

These amendments, however, did not eliminate prejudice and discrimination. Prejudice is an attitude; discrimination is a behavior. Racial discrimination in the United States has its roots in our nation's history of slavery. The *Dred Scott* decision (1856) ruled that a freed slave still did not enjoy the right to remain free in those parts of the United States where slavery was legal. *Plessy v. Ferguson* (1896) showed the Court's desire to avoid civil rights issues, declaring discrimination to be outside the realm of the Court. Jim Crow laws strictly segregated blacks from whites in schools, restaurants, street cars, hospitals and even cemeteries by permitting "separate but equal" accommodations.

It was not until the 1950s and 1960s that the Court directly confronted civil rights. *Brown v. Board of Education of Topeka I* (1954) established that "separate but equal" schools were illegal. The Equal Pay Act of 1963, the Civil Rights Act of 1964, the 1972 Equal Opportunity Act and the 1972 Equal Education Act prohibit discrimination on the basis of race, color, religion, sex or national origin in employment and education in public and private sectors at the federal, state and local levels.

Affirmative action was created to spread equal opportunity throughout the diverse American population. Opponents of affirmative action, however, argue forcibly that such measures are, themselves, discriminatory and result in reverse discrimination. And yet, affirmative action may be needed to assure belief in the American Dream.

Unfortunately, even the criminal justice system is unable to achieve total equality, being susceptible to a variety of forms of discrimination. The equal protection clause of the Fourteenth Amendment to the Constitution applies to racial profiling. Race-based enforcement of the law is illegal. The equal protection clause also prohibits discrimination in jury selection on the basis of race or gender.

Some prisoners' rights are recognized as falling within the realm of Fourteenth Amendment protections. A right is a legally protected claim, whereas a privilege is not necessarily legally protected. For prisoners, cases based on Fourteenth Amendment rights involve equal protection on the basis of race, gender and the availability of facilities and services.

The doctrine of selective incorporation holds that only the provisions of the Bill of Rights that are fundamental to the American legal system are applied to the states through the due process clause.

DISCUSSION QUESTIONS

1. Why was the Fourteenth Amendment necessary?
2. Why has the entire Bill of Rights not been embraced by the Fourteenth Amendment?
3. Were the framers of the Constitution racist?
4. Why are people prejudiced? Do you recognize your own prejudices?
5. Do you think employment quota laws improve things or worsen them? For whom?
6. Is "separate but equal" possible?
7. Can it be argued that government has "gone too far" by requiring all people to be treated equally? Can you think of instances in which different people might not be equally able to do a job?
8. What is your definition of the American Dream? Do you think it is within your reach?
9. Can law shape attitude?
10. Should inmates be allowed to file as many petitions as they please, or should a limit be placed so they would be more selective in bringing up their grievances? Is there a potential for corruption in either scenario?

INFOTRAC COLLEGE EDITION ASSIGNMENTS

- Use InfoTrac College Edition to assist you in answering the Discussion Questions when appropriate.
- Find and outline an article on affirmative action, the American Dream, civil rights, Dred Scott, equality before the law, Jim Crow laws or racial discrimination. **OR**
- Read and outline one of the following articles to share with the class:
  - "The Role of Race in Law Enforcement: Racial Profiling or Legitimate Use?" by Richard G. Schott.
  - "Professional Police Traffic Stops: Strategies to Address Racial Profiling" by Grady Carrick.
  - "The Americans with Disabilities Act: The Continuing Search for Meaning" by Thomas D. Colbridge.

INTERNET ASSIGNMENTS

- Use http://www.findlaw.com to find one Supreme Court case discussed in this chapter and brief the case. Be prepared to share your brief with the class.
- Explore three recent Supreme Court cases dealing with "equal rights" at http://www.supremecourtus.gov/

COMPANION WEB SITE

- Go to the Constitutional Law and the Criminal Justice System 3e Web site at http://cj.wadsworth.com/hessharr_constlaw3e for Case Studies and Study Guide exercises.

REFERENCES

Aizenman, N.C. "Immigration Debate Wakes a 'Sleeping Latino Giant.'" *Washington Post*, April 6, 2006, p. A01.

Babington, Charles and Murray, Shailagh. "Immigration Deal Fails in Senate." *Washington Post*, April 8, 2006, p. A01.

Balz, Dan and Fears, Darryl. "'We Decided Not to Be Invisible Anymore.'" *Washington Post*, April 11, 2006, p. A01.

Brunner, Borgna. *The Time Almanac 2000*. Information Please, 1999. (www.infoplease.com)

Cohen, John D.; Lennon, Janet J.; and Wasserman, Robert. "Eliminating Racial Profiling—A 'Third Way.'" *Law Enforcement News*, March 31, 2000, pp. 12, 15.

Colbridge, Thomas D. "Defining Disability under the Americans with Disabilities Act." *FBI Law Enforcement Bulletin*, October 2000, pp. 28–32.

Colbridge, Thomas D. "The Americans with Disabilities Act: A Practical Guide for Police Departments." *FBI Law Enforcement Bulletin*, January 2001, pp. 23–32.

"Court Limits Federal Arson Law." *Criminal Justice Newsletter*, June 8, 2000, pp. 6–7.

Ducat, Craig R. *Constitutional Interpretation*, 8th ed. Belmont, CA: West/Thomson Learning, 2004.

Durose, Matthew R.; Schmitt, Erica L.; and Langan, Patrick A. *Contacts between Police and the Public: Findings from the 2002 National Survey*. Washington, DC: Bureau of Justice Statistics, April 2005. (NCH 207845)

Fridell, Lorie A *Racially Biased Policing: A Guide for Analyzing Race Data from Vehicle Stops*. Washington, DC: Police Executive Research Forum and Community Oriented Policing Services, 2005.

Fridell, Lorie; Lunney, Robert; Diamond, Drew; and Kubu, Bruce. *Racially Biased Policing: A Principled Response*. Washington, DC: Police Executive Research Forum, 2001.

Gallo, Frank J. "Profiling vs. Racial Profiling: Making Sense of It All." *The Law Enforcement Trainer*, July/August 2003, pp. 18–21.

Hess, Kären M. and Wrobleski, Henry M. *Police Operations*, 4th ed. Belmont, CA: Wadsworth Publishing Company, 2006.

Huntington, Roy. "Profiling: Suddenly Politically Correct?" *Police*, December 2001, pp. 18–20.

Kruger, Karen. "Pregnancy Policy: Law and Philosophy." *The Police Chief*, March 2006, pp. 10–11.

Litchford, Jody M. "ADA Decisions Provide Guidance for Enforcement Activities." *The Police Chief*, August 2000, pp. 15–17.

Meehan, Albert J. and Ponder, Michael C. "Race and Place: The Ecology of Racial Profiling African American Motorists." *Justice Quarterly*, September 2002, pp. 399–430.

Nowicki, Ed. "Racial Profiling Problems and Solutions." *Law and Order*, October 2002, pp. 16–17.

"Race Disparity Seen throughout Juvenile Justice System." *Criminal Justice Newsletter*, April 25, 2000, pp. 6–7.

Ramirez, Deborah; McDevitt, Jack; and Farrell, Amy. *A Resource Guide on Racial Profiling Data Collection Systems: Promising Practices and Lessons Learned*. Washington, DC: National Institute of Justice, November 2000. (NCJ 184768)

"Report Cites Racial Disparity in Incarceration of Drug Offenders." *Criminal Justice Newsletter*, June 8, 2000.

"Should They Stay Or Should They Go?," *Time Magazine*, April 10, 2006, p. 32.

Spohn, Cassia and Holleran, David. "The Imprisonment Penalty Paid by Young, Unemployed Black and Hispanic Male Offenders." *Criminology*, February 2000, pp. 281–306.

Stephens, Otis H., Jr. and Scheb, John M. II. *American Constitutional Law*, 3rd ed. Belmont, CA: Thomson/West, 2003.

Tumulty, Karen. "Should They Stay or Should They Go?" *Time*, April 10, 2006, p. 30.

Walker, Samuel; Spohn, Cassia; and DeLone, Miriam. *The Color of Justice: Race, Ethnicity and Crime in America*, 3rd ed. Belmont, CA: Wadsworth/Thomson, 2004.

Weisburd, David; Greenspan, Rosann; Hamilton, Edwin E.; Williams, Hubert; and Bryant, Kellie A. *Police Attitudes toward Abuse of Authority: Findings from a National Study.* Washington, DC: National Institute of Justice Research in Brief, May 2000.

Wrobleski, Henry M. and Hess, Kären M. *Introduction to Law Enforcement and Criminal Justice,* 8th ed. Belmont, CA: Wadsworth Publishing Company, 2006.

CASES CITED

Adarand v. Pena, 515 U.S. 2000 (1995).

Ansonia Board of Education v. Philbrook, 479 U.S. 60 (1986).

Barron v. Mayor and City Council of Baltimore, 32 U.S. 243 (1833).

Batson v. Kentucky, 476 U.S. 79 (1986).

Bounds v. Smith, 430 U.S. 817 (1977).

Bradwell v. Illinois, 83 U.S. (16 Wall.) 130 (1873).

Brown v. Board of Education of Topeka I, 347 U.S. 483 (1954).

Coffin v. Reichard, 143 F.2d 443 (6th Cir. 1944).

Cooper v. Pate, 378 U.S. 546 (1964).

Crug v. Hauck, 404 U.S. 59 (1971).

Dred Scott v. Sandford, 60 U.S. 393 (1856).

Duncan v. Louisiana, 391 U.S. 145 (1968).

Ex parte Hull, 312 U.S. 546 (1941).

Firefighters Local Union No. 1784 v. Stotts, 467 U.S. 561 (1984).

Fullilove v. Klutznick, 448 U.S. 448 (1980).

Glover v. Johnson, 478 F.Supp. 1075 (D.C.Mich. 1979, 1987).

Gratz et al. v. Bollinger et al., 539 U.S.244 (2003).

Gregg v. Georgia, 428 U.S. 153 (1976).

Grutter v. Bollinger et al., 539 U.S.2003 (2003).

Hampton v. Mow Sun Wong, 426 U.S. 88 (1976).

J.E.B. v. Alabama, 511 U.S. 127 (1994).

Johnson v. Avery, 393 U.S. 483 (1969).

Jones v. United States, 527 U.S. 373 (1999).

Local 28, Sheet Metal Workers International Association v. EEOC, 478 U.S. 421 (1986).

Marbury v. Madison, 5 U.S. (1 Cranch) 137 (1803).

Mary Beth G. v. Chicago, 723 F.2d 1263 (1983).

Massachusetts Board of Retirement v. Murgia, 427 U.S. 307 (1976).

McClesky v. Kemp, 481 U.S. 279 (1987).

Norris v. Alabama, 293 U.S. 552 (1935).

Palko v. Connecticut, 163 U.S. 537 (1937).

Plessy v. Ferguson, 163 U.S. 537 (1896).

Plyler v. Doe, 457 U.S. 202 (1982).

Regents of the University of California v. Bakke, 438 U.S. 265 (1978).

Ruffin v. Commonwealth, 62 Va. (21 Gratt.) 790 (1871).

Shapiro v. Thompson, 394 U.S. 618 (1969).

Slaughterhouse Cases, 83 U.S. 36 (1872).

Strauder v. West Virginia, 100 U.S. 303 (1879).

Sugarman v. McDougall, 413 U.S. 634 (1973).

Swain v. Alabama, 382 U.S. 944 (1965).

United States v. Lopez, 514 U.S. 544 (1995).

United States v. Paradise, 480 U.S. 149 (1987).

United States v. Virginia, 518 U.S. 515 (1996).

United Steelworkers of America v. Weber, 443 U.S. 191 (1979).

Washington v. Lee, 263 F.Supp. 27 (D.C.Ala. 1966).

Wolff v. McDonnell, 418 U.S. 539 (1974).

Wygant v. Jackson Board of Education, 476 U.S. 267 (1986).

CHAPTER 6

The First Amendment: Basic Freedoms

CONGRESS SHALL MAKE NO LAW RESPECTING AN ESTABLISHMENT OF RELIGION, OR PROHIBITING THE FREE EXERCISE THEREOF; OR ABRIDGING THE FREEDOM OF SPEECH, OR OF THE PRESS, OR THE RIGHT OF THE PEOPLE PEACEABLY TO ASSEMBLE, AND TO PETITION THE GOVERNMENT FOR A REDRESS OF GRIEVANCES.

—FIRST AMENDMENT TO THE U.S. CONSTITUTION

© AP/Wide World Photos

Freedom of religion remains a cornerstone of not only the Constitution but American ideology, allowing prisoners, even in wartime, the opportunity to worship.

- What basic freedoms are guaranteed in the First Amendment?
- Whether rights guaranteed in the First Amendment are absolute?
- What freedoms are included in religious freedom?
- What the establishment clause guarantees? The free exercise clause?
- What freedom of speech guarantees American citizens?
- What type of speech Congress has passed laws restricting?
- What the "imminent lawless action" test involves and when it is likely to be used?
- Whether symbolic acts are protected under the First Amendment?
- What is included in freedom of the press?
- What basic freedoms prison inmates have?

balancing test

"clear and present danger" test

"clear and probable danger" test

establishment clause

free exercise clause

"imminent lawless action" test

judicial activism

preferred freedoms approach

prior restraint

"rational basis" test

resolution

Introduction

Americans often know more constitutional law than they think. The media, despite criticisms about reporting, present so much about the law that the general public cannot help but develop at least a sense of some basic legal tenets. This notion is certainly the case with the First Amendment, which most people, know has to do with freedom of speech. A generation of Americans witnessed firsthand the influence free speech had during the Vietnam War, the civil rights movement and elections across the country. The downside may be that a generation of Americans take such freedom for granted because of its continual existence.

Being able to speak out, particularly against the government, remains a cornerstone of freedom in the United States. What free speech is there if not in opposition to those in power? No greater right do we have in this country than that of speaking our minds and being able to hear from others. However, even this right is not absolute.

■ The First Amendment prohibits Congress from making any laws that restrict freedom of religion, freedom of speech, freedom of the press or the right to gather or assemble peaceably and to request the government to respond to complaints from its citizens.

Differences and difficulties in interpretation have characterized much of the later history of the First Amendment. For example, despite the apparent absolute prohibition in the phrase "Congress shall make no law . . . ," Congress has, in fact, many times passed laws in the public interest that restrict freedom of religion, speech and press. Keep in mind that the framers of the Constitution intended to construct only the basic framework of American law. Those very general terms such as *religion, speech* and *press* have generated great debate as U.S. law continues to grow and change.

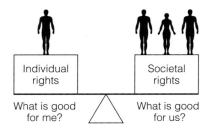

Figure 6.1 Balancing Individual and Societal Rights

In addition, federal agencies and prosecutors have initiated actions that have resulted in certain limitations on freedom of speech and press. In ruling on the constitutionality of various restrictions on these civil rights, the Supreme Court has at times tended to support either individual rights or society's interests. Consider that for a moment: either the interests of the individual or of society. It sounds simple, but it is not. Private versus public interests continue to be at odds while giving courts continual opportunities to provide solutions to best serve all involved, including those who will rely on past law to determine future decisions.

■ No rights are absolute, so government can regulate them when social interests outweigh those of the individual.

Since the early 1950s, the Court has sought a balanced approach whereby both private and public interests are weighed in each case, as illustrated in Figure 6.1.

The framers of the Constitution intended that it be interpreted. If they had intended the document to be an absolute, it would not be as brief as it is. By providing future lawmakers with the cornerstone of what America was to become, law has been able to be the living law desired.

Interpretation plays an important role in constitutional law, and that is why those who drafted the document kept it so fundamental. The basic nature of the Constitution permits courts to continue to interpret law to let it grow along with society.

This chapter provides an in-depth look at how the First Amendment has been interpreted over the years, beginning with freedom of religion, followed by freedom of speech, including such issues as the First Amendment expression rights of police officers. Next, freedom of the press is examined. The chapter concludes with a discussion of the right to peaceful assembly and the basic freedoms prisoners retain.

Freedom of Religion

Freedom of religion is the first right set forth in the Bill of Rights. The colonists who fled religious persecution cherished their right to worship as they saw fit in their new country. Because religions differed from colony to colony, with Episcopalians predominating in one area, Presbyterians in another and Congregationalists and Quakers in still others, the founding fathers wanted to guarantee every individual religious freedom. As Ducat (2004, p. 1045) explains:

The religious wars that battered Europe between the Middle Ages and the Enlightenment and the theological intolerance that blemished the reign of the Tudors and brought down the rules of the Stuarts in the English Civil War provided ample testimony to the importance of not creating political cleavages along such emotional lines. The Establishment Clause was the fruit of a harsh European history lesson that taught that the solder of social cohesion was quite apt to melt under the heat generated by religious conflict.

Freedom of religion is a political principle that strives to forbid government constraint on people's choices of beliefs. It requires also that people be free to act on their beliefs.

■ Religious freedom includes the freedom to worship, to print instructional material, to train teachers and to organize schools in which to teach, including religion.

The concept of separation of church and state is an important legal issue related to freedom of religion. Such a separation is not necessarily present in other parts of the world, and its absence does not necessarily indicate the absence of religious freedom. Many governments attempt to control their society by controlling religion. Some dictatorships have banned certain religions altogether. America, however, has always held such basic freedoms in high regard: "History and current events teach us that human beings are given to zealotry, intolerance, persecution, and even warfare in the name of God. Peaceful coexistence among competing religious groups is one of the major accomplishments of modern democracy" (Stephens and Scheb, 2003, p. 510).

To truly separate church and state is challenging. In fact, it cannot be done totally, even if it was the intent. Churches must conform to building and fire codes. Certain behaviors are not accepted anywhere, including churches. Although some separations are obvious, the line can easily become blurred. Ultimately, the government must decide whether a group claiming to be a religion actually is. The First Amendment demands that in making these decisions, the government neither favors nor is hostile toward one religion over others. Government is to remain neutral.

Freedom of religion is commonly discussed in terms of two clauses: the establishment clause and the free exercise clause.

The Establishment Clause

■ The **establishment clause** of the First Amendment states: "Congress shall make no law respecting an establishment of religion." That is, it cannot create a national church or prescribed religion.

establishment clause • clause in the First Amendment that states: "Congress shall make no law respecting an establishment of religion"

The establishment clause has been interpreted at various times to mean either that government cannot show preference to any particular religion or that church and state must be completely separate. Emotional disputes exist regarding litigation over such issues as government assistance to religiously sponsored schools, devotional practices in public schools and treatment of sectarians, whose religious convictions are not easily accommodated by local law. The cases that follow illustrate how the Court has struggled with religious issues.

An early case regarding religious freedom was *Hamilton v. Regents of the University of California* (1934). This case involved "conscientious objection" to war and pitted student members of a church against the state university they attended. The university required all freshmen and sophomores to complete six units of military training to attain full academic standing as a junior. The students petitioned the university regents to make the military training courses optional or to exempt them as conscientious objectors. Their petition was denied. The students, adhering to their convictions, declined to take the prescribed courses and were suspended. They filed suit, challenging the validity of the state constitution and claiming their suspension violated their constitutional rights. When the students lost and appealed, the court again denied their request, handing down its opinion that under the state's constitution the regents were entitled to include military courses in the required curriculum and that the petitioning students' suspension for refusing to take these compulsory courses involved no violation of their rights under the U.S. Constitution.

The Supreme Court noted the regents' order to take the prescribed courses did not obligate the students to serve in or in any way become a part of the U.S. military establishment. The Court asserted: "Government, federal and state, each in its own sphere owes a duty to the people within its jurisdiction to preserve itself in adequate strength to maintain peace and order and to assure the just enforcement of law. And every citizen owes the reciprocal duty, according to his capacity, to support and defend the government against all enemies."

The establishment clause and separation of church and state was made applicable to the states in *Everson v. Board of Education* (1947), in which the Supreme Court held that a state statute allowing reimbursement to parents for money spent to transport their children to parochial schools on the public bus system did not constitute an establishment of religion. Citing the words of Thomas Jefferson—that the clause against the establishment of religion by law was intended to erect a "wall of separation between Church and State"—and noting the reimbursement policy applied to parents of both public and parochial school students, the Court determined the policy did conform to the separationist intent of the clause and likened the statute to general public-welfare legislation.

In *Engle v. Vitale* (1962), the Court held that prayer, voluntary or otherwise, conducted in public school classrooms was unconstitutional. This decision was also the holding in *Abinton School District v. Schempp* and *Murray v. Curlett* (1963), two cases heard together, regarding schools that began each day by reading Bible verses. In 1985 in *Wallace v. Jeffries,* the Court held that even a "moment of silence for meditation or voluntary prayer" was being used to encourage religious values and was unconstitutional.

Law challenging the establishment clause because of an incidental benefit must meet three standards: it must (1) have a primary secular purpose, (2) have a principle effect that neither advances nor inhibits religion and (3) not generate excessive entanglement between government and religion, as set forth in *Lemon v. Kurtzman* (1971). In this case, Rhode Island was providing a 15 percent salary supplement to teachers of secular subjects in private schools. The Court invalidated the state's attempt to subsidize costs of parochial school education by ruling that the statutes fostered an excessive entanglement between church and state in violation of the establishment clause.

Chief Justice Burger stressed that programs that provided significant ongoing aid to parochial elementary and secondary schools injected an explosive political issue that caused division along religious lines, effectively guaranteeing yearly public debates and political conflicts. In *Lemon,* the Court found that secular and religious education were so tightly intertwined that to support one without supporting the other would be virtually impossible and that separating the two would involve the state so deeply in the religious institution's administration as to impair its independence, generating an "excessive entanglement" in conflict with a central purpose of the establishment clause.

In 1980, the Court struck down a Kentucky law requiring the posting of the Ten Commandments in all classrooms (*Stone v. Graham*, 1980). The "Equal Access" law of 1984, however, gave students the right to hold religious meetings in public high schools outside class hours.

Aguilar v. Felton (1985) began an analytical change by the Court in holding that rather than the specific elements of *Lemon*, the establishment clause barred the City of New York from sending public school teachers into parochial schools to provide remedial education to disadvantaged children pursuant to a congressionally mandated program. The intense state monitoring of public employees who teach in religious institutions to ensure they were not including religion necessitated excessive government entanglement with religion, leading the Court to place a permanent injunction on state aid to parochial schools.

However, the Court's decision in *Agostini v. Felton* (1997) took the opposite direction. At issue was a federally funded remedial education program in New York City, based on Title I of the Elementary and Secondary Education Act of 1965, aimed at economically disadvantaged and educationally deprived children, most of whom attended parochial schools. Public funds were used to purchase materials and supplies and to pay instructors, including those teaching in the private schools. In *Agostini*, the New York City Board of Education sought relief from the injunction resulting from *Aguilar*, contending that the cost of compliance severely restricted the money available to provide remedial instruction to the students who needed it.

In examining its own seemingly opposing interventions involving the time from *Aguilar* to *Agostini*, the Court acknowledged its *Aguilar* ruling had, in fact, been undercut by subsequent decisions, most notably *Zobrest v. Catalina Foothills School District* (1993), which held that public assistance could be used for an interpreter for a parochial school student. The Court admitted the assumptions on which *Aguilar* had relied, such as excessive entanglement, had no support in more recent rulings.

This area of constitutional analysis continues to challenge both students and judges. The Court itself has not been able to define a clear set of rules by which to determine outcomes of these cases. The cases are a struggle between changing norms and constitutional interpretations. The United States was created as a place where all people could worship as they liked. A number of the founders were able to risk what they did because of the courage their faith provided, as proudly proclaimed in much of the Constitution's history. Andrew Jackson pointed out: "The First Amendment to our Constitution was designed to avoid these conflicts by avoiding these beginnings" (*West Virginia State Board of Education v. Barnette*, 1943). The conflicts, however, continue.

In a series of cases that garnered national attention in 2003, Alabama Supreme Court Justice Roy Moore refused to remove a statue of the Ten Commandments from the judicial building and was eventually removed from his position. The statue was put in a storeroom not accessible to the public. While refusing to grant certiorari, supporters of Judge Moore pointed out that even the U.S. Supreme Court begins each session with the words, "God save the United States and this honorable court."

Students and the public may have difficulty understanding why existing displays with religious themes, such as statues, carvings and Christmas displays on public property, are sometimes no longer permitted. There is no easy answer, and courts understand that as norms change along with constitutional interpretations, some people will be upset. Even more challenging for people to understand is how the Court can decide one thing while incorporating religious statements into their rituals, as is the case with other government entities such as Congress, local governments that open meetings with the Pledge of Allegiance and even police agencies that have chaplains on staff. One thing that is predictable is many of these traditions will be challenged.

The Free Exercise Clause

free exercise clause • clause in the First Amendment that declares: "Congress shall make no law . . . prohibiting the free exercise [of religion]"

■ The **free exercise clause** of the First Amendment declares: "Congress shall make no law . . . prohibiting the free exercise [of religion]."

The free exercise of religion involves both the freedom to believe and the freedom to act. In *Davis v. Beason* (1890), the Court described the First Amendment free exercise clause:

> The First Amendment was intended to allow everyone under the jurisdiction of the United States to entertain such notions respecting his relations to his Maker and the duties they impose as may be approved by his judgment and conscience, and to exhibit his sentiments in such form of worship, as he may think proper, not injurious to the rights of others.
>
> In other words, the freedom to believe is an absolute established by the First Amendment.

However, the freedom to act is not so protected, a distinction further clarified when the free exercise clause was made applicable (incorporated) to the states in *Cantwell v. Connecticut* (1940). In this case, three Jehovah's Witnesses were convicted under a statute that forbade the unlicensed soliciting of funds on the representation that they were for religious or charitable purposes. While soliciting in a strongly Catholic neighborhood, the Jehovah's Witnesses had played a phonographic recording that insulted the Christian religion and the Catholic Church in particular, leading to an altercation and a charge of breach of the peace against the Jehovah's Witnesses. Through its ruling, the court helped delineate how beliefs and acts differ with regard to First Amendment protection:

> Freedom of conscience and freedom to adhere to such religious organization or form of worship as the individual may choose, cannot be restricted by law. On the other hand, it safeguards the free exercise of the chosen form of religion. Thus, the Amendment embraces two concepts—freedom to believe and freedom to act. The first is an absolute, but, in the nature of things, the second cannot be. Conduct remains subject to regulation for the protection of society. The freedom to act must have appropriate definition to preserve the enforcement of that protection.

Courts have had to balance the requirements of the free exercise clause against society's legal, social and religious needs. For example, in St. Paul, Minnesota, after a string of bank robberies, thefts and crimes at a mall, the city implemented an ordinance prohibiting people from hiding their identity "by means of a robe, mask or other disguise." Police used the ordinance as a prevention tactic. However, when officers ticketed a Muslim woman for wearing a veil as part of her religious practice, the result was anger among the local Muslim community. The court ruled the ordinance unconstitutional.

In another case, *Employment Division v. Smith* (1990), the Court stated: "We have never held that an individual's religious beliefs excuse him from compliance with an otherwise valid law prohibiting conduct that the State is free to regulate." In this case, two American Indian drug counselors in Oregon lost their jobs because they used peyote, a hallucinogenic drug, as part of a religious ritual in the Native American church. Some states allowed such a practice, but Oregon did not. The court decreed: "Because respondents' ingestion of peyote was prohibited under Oregon law, and because that prohibition is constitutional, Oregon may, consistent with the Free Exercise Clause, deny respondents unemployment compensation when their dismissal results from use of the drug."

Additional examples of how this ruling has affected other religious groups include the performance of autopsies despite families' religious beliefs and the requirement that members of the Amish community put orange reflectors on the backs of their buggies. When Congress passed and President Clinton signed the Religious Freedom Restoration Act (RFRA) in 1993, however, government interference with religious practices was made more difficult.

The free exercise clause has taken some interesting paths as various issues have been presented to the Court. In *West Virginia State Board of Education v. Barnette* (1943), the Supreme Court held that states could not require children to pledge allegiance to the United States each school day. In his opinion, Justice Jackson said that everyone has a First Amendment right to not pledge allegiance because of the "freedom of thought and belief that is central to all First Amendment freedoms."

In *Lynch v. Donnelly* (1984), a government-subsidized Christmas display of a crèche was found not an advancement or endorsement of religion, and, therefore, permitted. In *Wooley v. Maynard* (1977), the Supreme Court held that a state could not punish someone for blacking out the part of his car's license plate that set forth the state's motto, "Live Free or Die," holding that the government is not permitted to compel citizens to advertise government or religious beliefs, or to comply with advertising or asserting them.

However, in balancing this assertion, the Court held in *Wooley* that printing "In God We Trust" on money did not violate the Constitution because money is passed among people, and, therefore, does not indicate that a particular individual agrees with a religious or governmental belief, like a motto on a license plate might. Also, money is transported in such a manner as to not be a public display. These decisions are being made in an effort to strike a very fine balance that sometimes seems out of synch with either social norms or other law.

In effect, the free exercise clause holds that the government may not require people to assert certain religious or political beliefs, and the government may not subsidize activities that would support beliefs favorable to the government but in violation of anyone's First Amendment rights. In *Church of Lukumi Babalu Aye v. Hialeah* (1993), the Supreme Court found itself challenged when a religion that believed in animal sacrifice intended to build a church in a city that had responded, because of pressure from angry citizens, by passing an ordinance prohibiting animal sacrifice. The Court, acknowledging that such activity may offend some and noting that sport hunting was not regulated by the city ordinance, struck down the law. The Court stated that because the law was drafted pursuant to the religious group announcing their plan, its intent was to restrict religious freedom and, as such, was unconstitutional.

In December 1993, the Supreme Court ruled that the Boy Scouts could require applicants to promise to "love God" and to "do my duty to God and my country." The suit was brought by Mark Welsh and his father, Elliott, in 1990, when Mark was denied membership in the Tiger Cub Group because he refused to sign the required pledge. The Court ruled this was not a violation of the First Amendment or of Title III of the Civil Rights Act of 1964, which applied to public accommodations and not the principles of private organizations. Table 6.1 summarizes conduct not protected by the freedom of religion clause.

Table 6.1   **Conduct Not Protected by the Freedom of Religion Clause***

We have never held that an individual's religious beliefs excuse him from compliance with an otherwise valid law prohibiting conduct that the State is free to regulate. United States Supreme Court, *Employment Division v. Smith,* 494 U.S. 110 (1990).

Conduct not protected	Case
Multiple marriages in violation of state polygamy laws, crime of bigamy	*Reynolds v. United States,* 98 U.S. 145 (1879)
Handling poisonous snakes in a public place in violation of state law as part of a religious ceremony	*State v. Massey,* 229 N.C. 734, 51 S.E.2d 179 (1949)
Requirements at airports, state fairs and so on that religious, political and other groups distribute or sell literature only from booths provided for that purpose	*Heffron v. International Society for Krishna Consciousness,* 452 U.S. 640 (1981)
Mailboxes are for mail only. Putting other literature (religious, political and so on) into a mailbox can be a violation of a postal regulation that was upheld by the Supreme Court, which noted that a mailbox is not a "soapbox."	*Council of Greenburgh Civic Assn. v. U.S. Postal Service,* 453 U.S. 917 (1981)
Violation of child labor laws	*Prince v. Massachusetts,* 321 U.S. 158 (1944)
Failure to comply with compulsory military service by defendants who conscientiously objected only to the Vietnam War	*Gillette v. United States,* 401 U.S. 437 (1971)
Air Force officer continued to wear his yarmulke (Jewish skullcap) after repeated orders to remove it. He was dropped from service. Affirmed for Air Force.	*Goldman v. Weinberger,* 475 U.S. 503 (1986)
Illegal importation of aliens in violation of Immigration and Nationality Act 8 U.S.C.A. Sec. 1324	*United States v. Merkt,* review denied, 794 F.2d 950 (5th Cir. 1987)
Members of the Old Order Amish who do not use motor vehicles but travel in horse-drawn buggies would not obey a state law requiring reflecting triangles on the rear of all slow-moving vehicles. Held not exempted from complying with this highway safety law.	*Minnesota v. Hershberger,* 495 U.S. 901 (1990)
There was also no exemption on religious grounds from complying with required vehicle liability insurance. South Dakota law makes it a crime not to carry the insurance.	*South Dakota v. Cosgrove,* 495 U.S. 846 (1989)

The freedom of religion clause could not be used as a defense for: Destroying government property (760 F.2d 447); extortion and blackmail (515 F.2d 112); racketeering (695 F.2d 765, review denied 460 U.S. 1092); refusal to testify before a grand jury (465 F.2d 802, see 409 U.S. 944); photographing of arrested person (848 F.2d 113); putting logging road through area sacred to Indian tribes (108 S.Ct. 1319); nonvaccination of children (25 S.Ct. 358); and not participating in the Social Security system (102 S.Ct. 1051).

*In the 1997 case of *Boerne, Texas v. Flores,* 117 S.Ct. 2157, 61 CrL 2210, the U.S. Supreme Court struck down the Religious Freedom Restoration Act, which was enacted by the U.S. Congress in 1993. The U.S. Supreme Court held that the Act was a legislative encroachment on the judicial right of the courts to interpret the U.S. Constitution.

Source: Thomas J. Gardner and Terry M. Anderson. *Criminal Law: Principles and Cases,* 9th ed. Belmont, CA: Wadsworth Publishing Company, 2007, p. 238.

Another area of controversy is court-ordered treatment that includes religion. In a series of cases, the Court has continued to deny certiorari, thus letting stand the previous rulings, in which judicially mandated involvement in Alcoholics Anonymous (AA) or Narcotics Anonymous (NA) was determined to violate the establishment clause because of the religious components of these 12-step programs that reference God or a higher power. These cases include *Griffin v. Coughlin* (1998), which involved privileges being denied to atheist or agnostic prisoners who refused to participate in AA faith-based treatment; *Kerr v. Farrey* (1996), in which a prisoner had no alternative than to be involved in NA when he objected to the religious component; and, *Warner v. Orange County Dept. of Probation* (1999), in which the defendant objected to the religious content of mandated AA participation.

Interpretations

What, then, exactly did the authors of the First Amendment freedom of religion clause intend? Did they mean, as Justice Black argued, that the statement "Congress shall make no law" meant just that, Congress (and through the Fourteenth Amendment, the states) could not in any way, shape or form do anything that might breech the "wall of separation?" Did they mean that although government could not prefer one sect over another, it might provide aid to all religions equally?

Some scholars believe the historic record is confused and contradictory. At the core of the problem is one's view of the Constitution and its role in American government. Advocates of what they assert is the original intent believe the framers' vision is as good today as it was 200 years ago. They believe any deviation from that view abandons the ideals that have made this country free and great, that judges should go strictly by what the framers intended and that any revisions must be made through the amendment process.

On the other side, defenders of **judicial activism** (allowing judges to interpret the Constitution and its amendments) say that amendments are not necessary. Judges should be allowed to interpret the Constitution and its amendments, and if law is changed, that is what the common law system permits. Such defenders believe that for the document to remain true to the framers' intent, the framers' spirit must reach a balance with modern society realities. They suggest the framers set out a series of ideals expressed through powers and limitations and deliberately left details vague so those who came after could apply the ideals to their world.

judicial activism • allowing judges to interpret the Constitution and its amendments

Freedom of Speech

Freedom of speech is the liberty to speak openly without fear of government restraint. Implicit in this freedom is the right to hear others' ideas. Freedom of speech is closely linked to freedom of the press because this freedom includes both the right to speak and the right to be heard. In the United States, both freedoms, commonly called freedom of expression, are protected by the First Amendment.

■ Freedom of speech/expression includes the right to speak and the right to be heard.

Freedom of speech and the constitutional limits to it have been defined in practice by Supreme Court rulings. The First Amendment right to free speech was the first guarantee to be made applicable to the states through incorporation in *Gitlow v. New York* (1925).

Restrictions on Freedom of Speech

An important understanding of the Constitution is that rights are *not* absolute, and this circumstance is the case with freedom of speech. In balancing personal interests and the public good, reasonable limits, that is, when government has a legitimate interest, are placed on where and when things can be said and, occasionally, on what can be said. Restrictions on speech have occurred most often in time of war and national emergency. The Alien and Sedition Acts of 1798 were the first efforts by Congress to specifically limit actual speech. These acts were passed when war with France threatened and the nation's security was considered to be directly affected. They empowered the president to expel "dangerous" aliens and provided for indicting those who should "unlawfully combine or conspire" against the administration by writing or speaking "with intent to defame" the government, the Congress or the president. Although these laws were never tested in court and expired after several years, what the outcomes *might* have been if tested remain a source of scholarly legal debate.

The first specific test of how far government can limit speech occurred with the Espionage Act (1917) passed by Congress during World War I. This act made illegal interference with recruiting or drafting soldiers or any act that adversely affected military morale. The terms used were obviously broad in interpretation. In *Schenck v. United States* (1919), the Court upheld the conviction of a socialist indicted under the Espionage Act on the grounds that freedom of speech is not absolute. When Schenck was charged with espionage for distributing flyers that encouraged young men to resist the draft, his defense asserted such an act of expression was protected speech. Justice Holmes, however, disagreed, stating: "When a nation is at war, many things that might be said in time of peace are such a hindrance to its effort that their utterance will not be endured." This case is an example of when the good of the greater whole outweighs the rights of the individual. Delivering the Court's unanimous opinion, Justice Holmes went on to say:

> The character of every act depends upon the circumstances in which it is done. The most stringent protection of free speech would not protect a man in falsely shouting fire in a theater and causing a panic. . . . The question in every case is whether the words used are used in such circumstances and are of such a nature as to create a clear and present danger that they will bring about the substantive evils that Congress has a right to prevent.

"clear and present danger" test • the test of whether words are so potentially dangerous as to not be protected by the First Amendment

The Court began to apply this **"clear and present danger" test** to subsequent cases involving freedom of speech. Another test of what speech is protected was *Gitlow v. New York* (1925), in which the Court held that "a state in the exercise of its police power may punish those who abuse this freedom by utterances inimical to the public welfare, tending to corrupt public morals, and incite to crime, or disturbing the public peace." Gitlow had been indicted under a New York State law that prohibited the advocacy of the overthrow of the government by force or violence. In 1940, Congress enacted the Smith Act, which declared advocating the overthrow of the government by force or violence to be unlawful. Being able to speak against the government has always been recognized as an important right of the American people. However, as continuously noted, no right is absolute.

■ Congress has passed laws limiting speech that advocates overthrow of the government by force.

The Court continues to address what is and is not protected speech.

In another speech case, leaders of the Communist Party were convicted under the Smith Act and appealed on the grounds that the act was unconstitutional. The Court upheld the act's constitutionality in deciding *Dennis v. United States* (1951) but not on the grounds of the "clear and present danger" doctrine. Instead, the majority adopted a standard put forward by Judge Learned Hand: "Whether the gravity of the evil discounted by its improbability, justifies such invasion of free speech as is necessary to avoid the danger." This standard has sometimes been called the **"clear and probable danger"** test.

In *Brandenburg v. Ohio* (1969), the Court adopted a new test—the **"imminent lawless action"** test. Although government has a justifiable interest in preventing lawless conduct, the mere discussion of such conduct would not necessarily cause imminent lawless action. The Court in *Brandenburg* created a three-part test that the government must meet if certain communication is not to be protected by the First Amendment: (1) the speaker subjectively intended incitement, (2) in context, the words used were likely to produce imminent, lawless action and (3) the words used by the speaker objectively encouraged and urged incitement.

■ The "clear and present danger" test was replaced by the "imminent lawless action" test to determine when speech should not be protected by the First Amendment.

This approach, modified by other cases, has been termed the **balancing test,** a position taken by the appellate courts to balance society's need for law and order and for effective law enforcement against the privacy rights of individuals. Indeed, a crucial matter with respect to interpreting the Constitution and understanding the conflicting rights and obligations contained within is the concept of substantive due process—the tension between legitimate state interests (e.g., promoting the public health, welfare and/or safety) versus legitimate individual liberty interests (e.g., right to privacy)—and how these interests must be balanced.

Because courts are political institutions and the U.S. legal system is adversarial by design, every case requires a choice between competing social interests. Allowed discretion, judges weigh conflicting social claims, determine each party's rights and obligations and make choices to distribute benefits and burdens based on the judges' values and attitudes. Ducat (p. 86) observes: "This interest-balancing perspective readily translates into judicial self-restraint. When the constitutionality of a law is called into question, judges in a democratic society are duty-bound to respect the balance among interests struck by the statute for the logical reason that, having been passed by a majority of legislators, it presumably satisfies more rather than fewer interests."

When applying the balancing approach to First Amendment free speech cases, the Supreme Court strives to strike a balance between the value of liberty of expression and the demands of ordering a free society. In the case of *Gertz v. Robert Welch, Inc.* (1974), the Court stated: "Under the First Amendment there is no such thing as a false idea . . . however pernicious an opinion may seem, we depend for its correction not on the conscience . . . but on the competition of ideas." According to Stone (2004, p. 76): "The First Amendment, in other words, places out of bounds any attempt to freeze public opinion . . . we don't need to

"clear and probable danger" test • the test of whether the gravity of the evil discounted by its improbability justifies an invasion of free speech necessary to avoid any danger

"imminent lawless action" test • a three-part test that the government must meet if certain communication is not to be protected by the First Amendment

balancing test • a position taken by the appellate courts to balance the needs of society for law and order and for effective law enforcement against the privacy rights of individuals

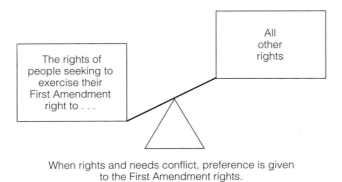

When rights and needs conflict, preference is given to the First Amendment rights.

Figure 6.2　The Preferred Freedoms Approach

preferred freedoms approach • a position that stresses that civil liberties are to take precedence over other constitutional values because they are requisite to a democracy

ban 'bad' ideas, because we are confident the people will not embrace them if they are allowed to consider them in free and open debate . . . The danger of repression is greater than the danger of debate."

The **preferred freedoms approach,** a position originally set forth by Justice Harlan F. Stone, has been important in constitutional law since World War II. This approach stresses that civil liberties have a preferred position among other constitutional values because they are requisite to a democracy. Under this concept, the burden lies largely with the government to prove that clear and present danger exists when a freedom is exercised. This concept tends to change the balance sought in judicial decisions, as shown in Figure 6.2.

Some Supreme Court justices, notably Hugo Black and William Douglas, have argued that free speech is an absolute right, by definition, and not subject to balancing. Justice Black, in *Konigsberg v. State Bar of California* (1961), stated: "I do not subscribe to that doctrine [the balancing approach] for I believe that the First Amendment's unequivocal command that there shall be no abridgement of the rights of free speech and assembly shows that the men who drafted our Bill of Rights did all the 'balancing' that was to be done in the field."

In opposition to this view and in support of the balancing approach, Justice Harlan, in the same case, wrote: "We reject the view that freedom of speech and association . . . as protected by the First and Fourteenth Amendments, are 'absolutes', not only in the undoubted sense that where the constitutional protection exists it must prevail, but also in the sense that the scope of that protection must be gathered solely from a literal reading of the First Amendment."

The difficulty of the absolute approach to free speech was shown in 1978, when a group of American Nazis sought to hold a rally in Skokie, Illinois. The municipality denied them a permit on the grounds that the Nazi rally would incite hostility in the largely Jewish population, which included many survivors of Nazi concentration camps. Lawyers from the American Civil Liberties Union (ACLU) represented the Nazis, arguing that Skokie laws limiting public demonstrations were unconstitutional. A U.S. Court of Appeals agreed with the ACLU, and the Supreme Court upheld that decision by not granting certiorari in *National Socialist Party v. Skokie* (1977). Although many Americans were outraged at the defense of those they considered enemies of free speech, in fact this case illustrated constitutional freedom in action.

The importance of freedom of speech was highlighted during the Free Speech Movement of student protesters in the 1960s and 1970s. Forty years ago, the University of California, Berkeley, banned political activity on campus. Students wanted to raise money and recruit students to do civil rights work, but Berkeley officials said they could not. The students rebelled, claiming their First Amendment rights were being denied. The riot at Berkeley became a catalyst for years of political unrest on the country's college campuses. Ultimately freedom of speech was established in most colleges and universities.

Exclusion of groups with political agendas who want to speak at shopping malls is also a controversial area because such malls, although standing on private property, are essentially public places. Since 1968, when the U.S. Supreme Court first said the public had some speech rights in malls, the issue has gone back and forth between civil libertarians and mall owners, with the current trend being that private property owners can restrict speech but not on the public sidewalks around the property.

A continuing and intensely controversial area surrounds the abortion issue, and antiabortionists' claim that their demonstrations outside abortion clinics are justified, constitutional expressions of free speech. The courts, however, have set limits on such expression. In *Madsen v. Women's Health Center, Inc.* (1994), a state court enjoined Madsen and other antiabortion protesters from blocking or interfering with public access to a Florida abortion clinic and from abusing, intimidating or touching people who enter or leave the clinic. When the clinic returned to court and argued that protesters were still limiting access to the clinic, even greater restrictions were ordered to provide a larger buffer zone around the clinic and even around the residences of clinic employees.

When Madsen and the other demonstrators challenged the injunction on First Amendment grounds, the Florida Supreme Court upheld the injunction in its entirety. The U.S. Supreme Court, however, granted the protesters' petition for certiorari and found parts of the injunction in violation of the Constitution:

> In sum, we uphold the noise restrictions and the 36-foot buffer zone around the clinic entrances and driveway because they burden no more speech than necessary to eliminate the unlawful conduct targeted by the state court's injunction. We strike down as unconstitutional the 36-foot buffer zone as applied to the private property to the north and west of the clinic, . . . the 300-foot no-approach zone around the clinic, and the 300-foot buffer zone around the residences, because these provisions sweep more broadly than necessary to accomplish the permissible goals of the injunction. Accordingly, the judgment of the Florida Supreme Court is affirmed in part, and reversed in part.

Sometimes, multiple freedoms are at issue in a legal dispute, as in the preceding abortion issue, when not only freedom of speech but also freedom to assemble was involved. In another example, *Rosenberger v. Rector and Visitors of the University of Virginia* (1995), both freedom of speech and the establishment clause were involved (Ducat, p. 832). The University of Virginia, a state school, had a policy of using money from the Student Activity Fund (SAF), derived from mandatory student fees, to pay outside vendors to cover printing costs for a variety of publications produced by student organizations. The university, however, denied authorization for payment of printing costs for "Wide Awake," a newspaper put out by a Christian student group, on the grounds that the payments would implicate the school in promoting a religion.

Rosenberger, a founder of the Christian group, sued the university, arguing that the refusal of payment violated freedom of speech. Both the federal district court and the federal appeals court ruled in favor of the school, concluding that the payment withholding was necessary to comply with the dictates of the establishment clause. Rosenberger then petitioned for certiorari, which the Supreme Court granted.

As part of its ruling, the Court declared that no violation of the establishment clause occurs when a public university grants access to its facilities, including computer and printing facilities, on a religion-neutral, first-come-first-served basis to a wide spectrum of student groups. Therefore, there is no difference of constitutional significance between a school using its funds to operate a facility where a religious student organization can itself use a computer, printer or copy machine to generate speech with a religious content or viewpoint and a school paying a third-party contractor to operate the facility on its behalf. In delivering the opinion of the Court, Justice Kennedy stated:

> Government may not regulate speech based on its substantive content or the message it conveys. . . . In the realm of private speech or expression, government regulation may not favor one speaker over another. . . . Discrimination against speech because of its message is presumed to be unconstitutional. . . .
>
> There is no Establishment Clause violation in the University's honoring its duties under the Free Speech Clause. The judgment of the Court of Appeals must be, and is, reversed.

Computers and technology continue to pose new challenges to the law and its interpretation. In *Reno v. American Civil Liberties Union* (1997), the Supreme Court struck down part of the 1996 Federal Communications Decency Act (CDA) as a vague, overbroad restriction on speech. The law made a felony of displaying obscene or "indecent" material on a telecommunications device, in this case the Internet, so that it might be made available to minors.

What is indecent and what should be restricted as unprotected speech continue to spur differences of opinion in and out of the courtroom, not because the courts are too conservative or necessarily prudish, but because society's norms keep changing. What was once considered inappropriate, in poor taste or even obscene a decade ago can now be heard nightly on television during prime time and viewed in movies younger viewers are permitted to see. In free speech areas such as obscenity, fighting words, picketing or demonstrating, symbolic speech and loyalty oaths, the courts have also had to consider the various interests of society in their interpretations and applications of the Constitution. Table 6.2 summarizes some typical fighting words and obscenity violations. Table 6.3 summarizes several types of verbal offenses.

More recently, the Court has been involved in interpreting free speech concerns related to symbolic expression.

■ Symbolic acts are included within the protection of the First Amendment.

Somewhat Protected Speech

Symbolic speech was ruled on in *United States v. O'Brien* (1968), in which the Court considered what actions would be considered protected speech. The case involved draft-card burning and was used by the Court to develop a four-part test

Table 6.2   Fighting Words Violations

Words (or other communication) may be offensive, profane and vulgar but not be fighting words.

Words may be insulting and even outrageous but not be fighting words because they involved no face-to-face confrontation, as in *Falwell v. Hustler Magazine.*

Words may make a person or an audience angry and may be protected by the First Amendment and thus not be forbidden by government.

Words may be rude, impolite and insulting but may fall short of the fighting words violation.

Speech or gestures may be vulgar, profane and obscene but may fall short of being a fighting words violation.

If the person to whom the words are addressed is not angered by the words, no fighting words violation has occurred.

If the person to whom the words are addressed is not likely to make an immediate violent response, no fighting words violation has occurred.

Many states apply a higher fighting words standard to law enforcement officers because they are expected to exercise a higher degree of restraint than the average citizen, but if direct threats to the safety of an officer occur, or if the speech clearly disrupts or hinders officers in the performance of their duty or if the speech tends to incite unlawful conduct by bystanders, such speech is not constitutionally protected.

Fighting Words and Obscenity

Obscenity is a concept different from fighting words. To be obscene, the state must show as a matter of law that (1) the work taken as a whole appeals to the prurient (lustful) interest in sex; (2) the work "portrays sexual conduct in a patently offensive way;" (3) the work "taken as a whole does not have a serious literary, artistic, political or scientific value." *Miller v. California,* 413 U.S. 15, 93 S.Ct. 2607 (1973).

Fighting words and obscenity cause different reactions in people. Fighting words cause people to be come angry, whereas obscenity appeals to the prurient (erotic) interest.

A movie, picture, words, dance or other communication could be sexually explicit without being obscene if the communication has serious "literary, artistic, political or scientific value" (U.S. Supreme Court in *Miller v. California*).

"Dirty words" by themselves are generally not obscene or fighting words.

Although it is absolutely disgusting, it is not necessarily obscene.

Nudity in itself is not obscene or lewd, but a state or community may regulate (1) when nudity is in a place where liquor is sold (see *California v. LaRue,* 409 U.S. 109, 93 S.Ct. 390 [1972]) and (2) when public nudity is forbidden by a specific ordinance or law.

Source: Compiled from Thomas J. Gardner and Terry M. Anderson. *Criminal Law: Principles and Cases,* 9th ed. Belmont, CA: Wadsworth Publishing Company, 2007.

when it supported the constitutionality of a law prohibiting such burning. Chief Justice Burger stated:

> We cannot accept the view that an apparently limitless variety of conduct can be labeled 'speech' whenever the person engaging in the conduct intends thereby to express an idea. . . . A government regulation is sufficiently justified if it is within the constitutional power of the government; if it furthers any important or substantial governmental interest; if the governmental interest is unrelated to the suppression of free expression; and if the incidental restriction on alleged First Amendment freedoms is no greater than is essential to the furtherance of that interest.

In this case, the Court held that the selective service requirement regarding draft cards met these requirements, and the conviction against O'Brien was upheld.

Many symbolic acts fall under First Amendment protection. Such acts range from flag desecration and burning to burning of crosses, to the display of controversial art, from determining what is expressive speech to nude dancing and from proscribing hair and dress styles to sanctioning statements coming from countercultures.

Flag Burning   Two Supreme Court cases involving symbolic expression demonstrate the centrality of such issues and the danger in assuming easy answers to First Amendment dilemmas. In the 1969 case of *Street v. New York,* after an assassination

Table 6.3 Verbal Offenses

Type of verbal offense	To constitute the verbal offense, there must be
fighting words[a]	1. insulting or abusive language
	2. addressed to a person on a face-to-face basis
	3. causing a likelihood that "the person addressed will make an immediate violent response"
obscenity	1. a communication that, taken as a whole, appeals to the prurient (lustful) interest in sex
	2. portrays sexual conduct in a patently offensive way
	3. the communication, taken as a whole, does not have serious literary, artistic, political or scientific value
inciting or urging unlawful conduct	1. language or communication directed toward inciting, producing or urging
	2. *imminent* lawless action or conduct
	3. language or communication likely to incite or produce such unlawful conduct
obstruction of a law enforcement officer or of justice	1. deliberate and intentional language (or other communication) that hinders, obstructs, delays or makes more difficult
	2. a law enforcement officer's effort to perform his official duties (the scienter element of knowledge by the defendant that he or she knew the person obstructed was a law enforcement officer is required)
	3. some states require that "the interference would have to be, in part at least, physical in nature" (see the New York case of *People v. Case*)
defamation (libel and slander)[b]	1. words or communication that are false and untrue
	2. injure to the character and reputation of another person
	3. defamation communicated to a third person
abusive, obscene or harassing telephone calls	1. evidence showing that the telephone call was deliberate
	2. evidence that the calls were made with intent to harass, frighten or abuse another person
	3. and any other requirement of the particular statute or ordinance
loud speech and loud noise	Cities and states may:
	1. forbid speech and noises meant by the volume to disturb others and
	2. forbid noise and loud speech that create a clear and present danger of violence

[a]Many state courts apply a higher fighting words standard to law enforcement officers. Consult a legal advisor for the standard used in your state.

[b]When a public official is the victim, it must also be shown that the words or communications were uttered or published with a reckless disregard for the truth or falsity of the statement. (See also the case of *Falwell v. Hustler Magazine,* as the Rev. Falwell is a public figure.)

Source: Thomas J. Gardner and Terry M. Anderson. *Criminal Law: Principles and Cases,* 8th ed. Belmont, CA: Wadsworth Publishing Company, 2003, p. 222.

attempt on a civil rights leader, Sidney Street burned a flag in protest and was arrested for "malicious mischief," a New York law that made acting out verbally or symbolically a crime. The Warren Court did not act on the flag burning issue in this case, holding only that his words were protected speech, but suggested that the burning of the flag could be prosecutable, even though it, too, was an act of protest. The landmark case in which flag burning as symbolic speech came in *Texas v. Johnson* in 1989. Gregory Johnson, a demonstrator at the 1984 Republic National Convention in Dallas, unfurled an American flag and set it on fire. While the flag burned, the protesters chanted: "America, the red, white and blue, we spit on you."

Johnson was convicted of violating a Texas law prohibiting "the desecration of venerated objects," including the national flag. The Supreme Court ruled: "If there is a bedrock principle underlying the First Amendment, it is that the government may not prohibit the expression of an idea simply because society finds the idea itself offensive or disagreeable." Justice Brennan contended that nothing in the courts' precedents suggests that the state may foster its own view of the flag by prohibiting expressive conduct relative to it. Justice Kennedy concurred, stating: "The ruling [was simply] a pure command of the Constitution. It is poignant and fundamental that the flag perplexes those who hold it in contempt."

Four justices dissented, including Chief Justice William Rehnquist, who wrote a highly emotional opinion stressing that millions of Americans have "a mystical reverence" for the flag and deriding the majority for "bundling off" under the rubric of "designated symbols that inspire deep awe and respect for our flag felt by virtually all of us." Reaction to the ruling was strong and highly negative.

Members of Congress and political candidates continue to demand constitutional action to overrule the Court; some propose an amendment to the First Amendment to deny flag burning as free speech. In 1989, Congress passed a flag protection act that was short lived. On June 11, 1990, the Supreme Court declared it unconstitutional as an unwarranted restriction on symbolic expression. This issue remains volatile, and efforts to enact flag desecration amendments have continued.

Cross Burning and Bias/Hate Crimes   In 1989, St. Paul, Minnesota, like a number of other cities, passed an ordinance against various forms of expression based on bias or hatred to send a message that crimes against people because of their race or religion would not be tolerated. Several months later, in June 1990, a teenager was arrested under the ordinance and charged with burning a cross at the home of the only black family in a St. Paul neighborhood.

A county district judge initially held the ordinance unconstitutional as a violation of the First Amendment. The Minnesota Supreme Court, however, overturned this decision and upheld the ordinance, maintaining that it could be narrowly interpreted to ban acts of bigotry that arouse anger in others and still protect free speech. The state court said: "Burning a cross in the yard of an African-American family's home is deplorable conduct that the City of St. Paul may without question prohibit. The burning of a cross is itself an unmistakable symbol of violence and hatred based on virulent notions of racial supremacy."

The case was subsequently appealed to the U.S. Supreme Court, which held that the ordinance was unconstitutional (*R.A.V. v. City of St. Paul*, 1992). Justice Scalia delivered the Courts' acceptance of the Minnesota court's narrowing of the ordinance to apply only to so-called fighting words, which Scalia termed constitutionally prescribable. Even so, the Court found the ordinance to be unconstitutional on its face because "it prohibits otherwise permitted speech solely on the basis of the subjects the speech addresses." Cross burning and other reprehensible acts, Scalia argued, could be prosecuted under a variety of existing statutes. These means were sufficient for St. Paul to prevent such behavior "without adding the First Amendment to the fire."

Balancing what the Constitution means and what the public wants it to mean at the time is often difficult to effectively accomplish. What the Constitution means to one person is not always what it means to another person. This difference of opinion is why lawsuits occur and why the system is set up to decide which perspective will prevail in a particular case. As the times, politics and values of the United States change, so do legal arguments, holdings and precedents. In *Virginia v. Black* (2003), the Supreme Court held that a law banning cross burning as a hate crime itself is unconstitutional because the law presumes hate is the purpose. Without more evidence to prove a hate crime, cross burning is deemed a protected form of speech.

Nude Dancing   In 1991, the Supreme Court took up the question of nude dancing as a form of symbolic speech. The case involved nude dancers in the Kitty Cat Lounge in South Bend, Indiana, who were arrested for violating the state's public indecency law. A federal appeals court in Chicago had ruled the dancing was inherently expressive, communicating an emotional message of eroticism and sensuality and that the ban, therefore, violated the First Amendment. Five Supreme Court justices voted to reverse but were unable to isolate a single reason for the reversal. The essence of the ruling in *Barnes v. Glen Theatre* (1991) was that requiring dancers to wear at least pasties and a g-string did not violate their freedom of speech. It thus gave local prosecutors a new option to restrict totally nude entertainment in their communities.

Civil liberty lawyers, who had feared that the Court might apply a sweeping analysis that could call into question constitutional protection for many forms of artistic expression, were relieved by the Court's relatively narrow approach. Chief Justice Rehnquist for the majority made clear that nude dancing enjoyed some marginal First Amendment protection. However, because of the state's interest in promoting order and morality, nude dancing *could* be prohibited, just as could other forms of public nudity. He observed that the statute's pasties and g-string requirement was a modest imposition and the bare minimum necessary to achieve the state's purpose.

Yard Signs   Another area of expression some city ordinances seek to limit is use of yard signs. Many cities prohibit such signs altogether. Other cities have restrictions on the size or number of signs that can be placed in a person's yard or window.

Such restrictions were tested in *City of Ladue v. Gilleo* (1994), a case involving Margaret Gilleo, a resident of an exclusive suburb of St. Louis, Missouri. Gilleo put up an antiwar sign in the second-floor window of her home that read "Peace in the Gulf." Ladue's city ordinance prohibits all signs within its boundaries except for real estate signs, road and safety hazards, inspection signs, public transportation markers and business signs in commercially zoned areas. According to officials, the ordinance is intended to protect the community's aesthetics. Lower courts ruled for Gilleo, saying Ladue was wrong in favoring some signs over others, for example, real estate signs over political protest signs.

The Supreme Court agreed. In June 1994, a unanimous Court ruled that cities may not prohibit residents from putting political or personal signs in their yards. Justice John Paul Stevens, writing for the Court, declared: "A special respect for individual liberty in the home has long been part of our culture and our law. That principle has special resonance when the government seeks to constrain a person's ability to speak there."

The fact that some of these cases made their way to any court, especially the Supreme Court, makes one wonder *why*? Often, differing political perspectives are involved, or an ongoing issue between a city, for example, and an individual seen as a "troublemaker." Sometimes, government officials adhere to a strict interpretation policy and do not anticipate the implications of their actions. Sometimes, government believes the issue is worthy of the time and cost to pursue. Sometimes, the results are not anticipated, with law being promulgated that was not the government's intention. These outcomes illustrate why any government employee needs a working knowledge of Constitutional law.

Freedom of Speech and the Internet   A plethora of First Amendment cases have arisen as the Internet continues to make virtually anything available to anyone. The Court began a more definitive review of Internet issues in *Reno v. American Civil Liberties Union* (1997). In this case, the Court struck down a law banning computer-generated or "virtual" child pornography. It acknowledged that in addition to the multifaceted means of disseminating information electronically, much broader community norms had to be considered. Congress responded to the Reno decision by promulgating the Child Online Protection Act, which would, in effect, nullify the Reno decision. That act might also be declared unconstitutional by the Court.

As is the case with the printed and spoken word, not only obscenity will continue garnering both legislative and judicial attention but also business communication, privacy issues and advertising matters will surely be addressed. For example, Congress is currently considering legislation to address the mounting problem of unrequested Internet advertising (spam). As the debate continues over what can be virtually made available to whom, in *United States v. American Library Association* (2003), the Court held that Congress could limit funding to libraries that did not filter Internet access to block obscene material and child pornography without violating the First Amendment.

First Amendment Expression Rights of Police Officers

Because this text is written with an emphasis on the criminal justice system, inclusion of rights as they apply to those working in the field is pertinent. No citizen, regardless of their work, forfeits their constitutional rights; however, how these rights are applied can be different, depending on the circumstances.

Because even how one chooses to dress and groom is expression, the length of an officer's hair has been litigated by the Supreme Court in *Kelley v. Johnson* (1976). Justice Rehnquist held that in an organizational structure that necessitated uniformity, a requirement on hair length did not violate the officer's constitutional rights because it was not arbitrary and had a "rational connection between the regulation . . . and the promotion of safety of persons and property."

In a case involving the First Amendment right of freedom of association, *Wilson v. Swing* (1978), a police sergeant was demoted to patrol officer for reasons that included his having an extramarital affair with another officer while off duty. Among the legal issues argued by the officer was that the rule "members and employees shall conduct their private and professional lives in such a manner as to avoid bringing the Department into disrepute" was unconstitutional because it was vague and overbroad. In this case, the Court did not feel the rule was either and held in favor of the employer.

Police departments commonly seek restrictions on their officers' off-duty activities. However, when such restrictions impinge upon officers' constitutional rights, obvious problems ensue. Such was the case in *Edwards v. City of Goldsboro, N.C.* (1999).

In 1995, North Carolina enacted a conceal/carry handgun bill that enabled citizens to carry concealed handguns after mandatory training and screening. Sergeant Kenneth Edwards, a 20-year veteran of the City of Goldsboro's police department and a firearms instructor, had completed specific training to teach the conceal/carry course. To run his own part-time business, he obtained a business license, scheduled instructional classes to be held during off-duty time at a private location and submitted a request for off-duty employment.

The police chief, a vocal opponent of the conceal/carry law, denied Edwards' request for off-duty employment because of the issues that surround carrying a weapon. Edwards argued that the chief, motivated by personal and political reasons, had issued an illegal/invalid order prohibiting the officer's expression and association. The Fourth Circuit Court of Appeals agreed, observing that the court must "balance the interests of the (public employee), as a citizen, in commenting upon matters of public concern, and the interest of the (government), as an employer, in promoting the efficiency and public services it performs through its employees." The Court concluded the balancing test weighed in favor of Edwards: "We cannot discern any legitimate interest of the defendants in preventing a police officer of the city from conducting a concealed handgun safety course for the public that is a creature of state law."

Freedom of the Press

Freedom of the press *is* integrally related to freedom of speech because speech is not considered only spoken words, but any means of conveying information. As early as 400 B.C., the Greek poet Euripides stated, "The tongue is mightier than the blade," and in 1839, Edward Bulwer-Lytton proclaimed, "The pen is mightier than the sword." Freedom of the press protects the right to obtain and publish information or opinions without governmental control or fear of punishment.

■ Freedom of the press applies to all types of printed and broadcast material, including books, newspapers, magazines, pamphlets, films and radio and television programs.

Historically, freedom of the press has been attached to the general concept of censorship. In countries with extensive censorship, the right to publish news, information and opinions is usually tightly restricted. The British government, for example, was able to restrict almost anything that arguably related to the government through use of the Official Secrets Act. Simply, anything the government wished to remain secret, would—period. Under such a law, for example, news of the Three Mile Island nuclear accident in the United States would not have been released had it happened in the United Kingdom.

Even in the United States, where censorship is light, the right to publish is not absolute. The constraints on freedom of the press in a free society are controversial and are constantly being redefined by the judiciary.

Governments have restricted the right to publish in two ways: by restraining the press from publishing certain materials and by punishing those who publish matter considered seditious, libelous or obscene. The first kind of restriction, often called **prior restraint,** is rare in the United States and most other democratic countries. One of the first attacks on prior restraint can be found in John Milton's essay *Areopagitica* (1644), which was directed against the English licensing and censorship laws enacted in 1534 under Henry VIII. These laws were abolished in England in 1695, but the government was still able to take action on grounds of seditious libel against those who published material, whether true or false, and those who criticized government policies.

In the American colonies, prosecutions of this kind were made more difficult by a jury's decision in *New York v. Zenger* (1735). John Peter Zenger, a New York newspaper publisher, wrote articles critical of the colonial governor. The jury acquitted Zenger on the grounds that his charges were true and, therefore, could not be considered libelous. Not until 1868 did the truth of the published material become an accepted defense in England.

Freedom of the press was protected in the Constitution by including the First Amendment, which states: "Congress shall make no law . . . abridging freedom of speech or the press." This restraint on the federal government was later made binding on state governments via incorporation of the Fourteenth Amendment in *Near v. Minnesota* (1931). In that case, the Court ruled that no newspaper could be banned because of its contents, regardless of how scandalous they might be. Still, freedom of the press has frequently been denied in the areas of obscenity and pornography. The courts have, however, had some difficulty delineating appropriate standards of censorship.

For example, in *Roth v. United States* (1957), the Court ruled that obscenity is not a constitutionally protected freedom of speech. The standard to be used is "whether to the average person, applying contemporary community standards, the dominant theme of the material, taken as a whole, appeals to prurient interest, that is, having a tendency to excite lustful thoughts." In *Miller v. California* (1973), the Court clarified the standards to define obscenity by establishing the following three-part test: (1) Would "the average person applying contemporary community standards" find the work, as a whole, appealing to the prurient interest (meaning it would appeal to one's sexual interests and cause sexual arousal)? (2) Does the work depict or describe, in a patently offensive way, sexual conduct specifically proscribed by the applicable state law? (3) Does the work, in its entirety, lack serious literary, artistic, political or scientific value?

Restrictions on the press have often occurred during national emergencies. Censorship during World War I led to the first clear articulation of the limits to freedom of speech with which free press issues are closely tied. During World War II, freedom of the press was greatly curtailed for security reasons, but the press willingly complied with censorship restrictions. Other than in war time, censorship for national security reasons has been carefully limited.

In 1971, the U.S. government attempted to halt publication of *The Pentagon Papers* on the grounds that it could endanger national security. The Supreme Court ruled (*New York Times v. Sullivan,* 1964) that this case of prior restraint was unconstitutional. Other cases involving national security have concerned attempts to censor or halt publication of books about the Central Intelligence Agency. In 1983, when U.S. troops invaded Grenada, the press was initially barred from the island. The restrictions later imposed were thought to be unprecedented in U.S. practice and generated much controversy.

prior restraint • a restriction on publishing certain materials

Control of the press during the Persian Gulf War (1991) was close to 100 percent. Many criticized the press for accepting conditions that made complete reporting impossible. After the war ended, the accuracy of some press reports was questioned. Constraints upon the press are always controversial.

In Minnesota, reporters promised anonymity to a political campaign worker who gave them information. Later, the editors of the papers revealed his name, and he sued them. The Supreme Court ruled in *Cohen v. Cowles Media Company* (1991) that the First Amendment does not give the press a constitutional right to disregard promises that otherwise would be enforced under state law. The case was returned to the Minnesota Supreme Court for reconsideration. Further complicating the issue, several previous decisions appeared to narrow the newspaper reporters' right to withhold information given to them in confidence. In April 1991, a *Washington Post* reporter was held in contempt of court and jailed for refusing to identify a source.

Zenger had established the precedent that truthful statements were not to be considered libelous. The obvious corollary was that damages could be collected for false statements. In *New York Times v. Sullivan,* however, the Supreme Court held that public officials can win damages only if they can show that a statement defaming them was made with actual malice, that is, knowing it was false or recklessly disregarding whether it was false.

Other court rulings have extended the principle to include public figures not in government office, but involved in public controversy. In 1979, the Supreme Court held that a person who involuntarily receives publicity is not necessarily a public figure and, therefore, need not prove that the statements by the press were made with "actual malice" to obtain liable damages (*Hutchinson v. Proxmire,* 1979).

The Supreme Court has also held in *Zurcher v. Stanford Daily* (1978) that newspapers enjoy no special immunity from searches of their premises by police with warrants. In 1980, however, Congress passed a privacy protection act that required the police in most cases to obtain subpoenas for such searches. In 1979, in a controversial effort to curb prejudicial pretrial publicity, the Court ruled (*Gannett v. DePasquale*) that judges can bar the press and the public from criminal proceedings. In other cases, however, the courts have allowed televised proceedings.

The Supreme Court has further ruled that Americans have a free-speech right to pass out anonymous political pamphlets (*McIntyre v. Ohio Elections Commission,* 1995). In a 7 to 2 decision, the Court said: " 'Anonymous pamphleteering' has a long and honorable history in this country that extends back to the authors of *Federalists Papers* and is deeply ingrained as the secret ballot. 'Anonymity is a shield from the tyranny of the majority.'"

Balancing Freedom of the Press with the Right to a Fair Trial

A delicate balance exists between the people's right to know, the press' right to publish (First Amendment) and the due process rights of those accused of crimes (Sixth Amendment), as well as the needs of the agencies charged with investigating such crimes (Fourth Amendment). A free press, vital to the functioning of a democracy, keeps citizens fully informed and able to discharge their civic responsibilities. However, in this country, defendants in criminal cases are guaranteed due process of law and a fair and impartial trial. These guarantees are jeopardized when the media publish detailed information before a defendant is tried.

The question is whether events reported in the press before the trial may unduly influence jurors. In *Sheppard v. Maxwell* (1966), the defendant, Dr. Samuel Sheppard, was accused of brutally murdering his pregnant wife in their home. The pretrial publicity was intensely prejudicial, and Sheppard was convicted of the crime. On appeal, the conviction was overturned, with the Court quoting the Ohio Supreme Court:

> Murder and mystery, society, sex and suspense were combined in this case to such a manner as to intrigue and captivate the public fancy to a degree perhaps unparalleled in recent annals. Throughout the preindictment investigation, the subsequent legal skirmishes and the nine-week trial, circulation-conscious editors catered to the insatiable interest of the American public in the bizarre. . . . In this atmosphere of a "Roman holiday" for the news media, Sam Sheppard stood trial for his life.

Other high-profile cases include the very political, highly publicized trial of Oliver North, the highly publicized 10-day rape trial of William Kennedy Smith, the trial of Mike Tyson for raping a Miss Black America contestant and the trial of O. J. Simpson.

The court has a duty to protect those who come before it from undue adverse publicity. Failure to do so may result in a higher court declaring that the trial was unfair and overturning the conviction.

The Right to Peaceful Assembly

Within the First Amendment is the "right of the people peaceably to assemble and petition the government for a redress of grievances." This right is often claimed in conjunction with the right to freedom of speech, as seen in abortion protests. Combined with the Fourth Amendment's guarantee to be free from "unreasonable searches and seizures" people do have an expectation they can gather to interact, speak among themselves and make their thoughts and ideas known. Similarly, the right to simply associate with others has been considered to fall under the First Amendment, as well and other amendments. Although no specific references are made to the right of association, it is considered a natural right and, therefore, one to be protected. As stated by Chief Justice Warren Burger in *Richmond Newspapers, Inc. v. Virginia* (1980):

> Notwithstanding the appropriate caution against reading into the Constitution rights not explicitly defined, this Court has acknowledged that certain unarticulated rights are implicit in enumerated guarantees. For example, the rights of association and of privacy, the right to be presumed innocent, and the right to be judged by a standard of proof beyond a reasonable doubt in a criminal trial, as well as the right to travel, appear nowhere in the Constitution or Bill of Rights. Yet these important but unarticulated rights have nonetheless been found to share constitutional protection in common with explicit guarantees . . . . Fundamental rights, even though not expressly guaranteed, have been recognized by the Court as indispensable to the enjoyment of rights explicitly defined.

The right to assemble does not necessarily require an intent to engage in some specific activity, although when it does, the activity cannot be illegal. In the

1999 case of *Chicago v. Morales*, the Court held that an "anti-loitering" ordinance was unconstitutional because its language too vague in defining illegal loitering as "to remain in any one place with no apparent purpose." In response to this ruling and with the intent of combating gang activity, Chicago amended the definition to "remaining in any one place under circumstances that would warrant a reasonable person to believe that the purpose or effect of that behavior is to enable a criminal street gang to establish control over identifiable areas, to intimidate others from entering these areas, or to conceal illegal activities." By being more specific, Chicago hopes to constitutionally address their gang problem without infringing on the rights of others to lawfully assemble.

The right to assemble is an integral part of American culture that allows people to gather and express thoughts and ideas without government interference. Like any other right, however, it is not without limitations. Table 6.4 summarizes several types of property and the types of restrictions that lawfully may be placed on their use for peaceful assembly.

The right to peaceful assembly and, by implication, freedom to petition for redress of grievances, was made applicable to the states via incorporation of *DeJonge v. Oregon* (1937). More than two decades later, the First Amendment protection of freedom of association was extended to the states through *NAACP v. Alabama* (1958). Before concluding this discussion on First Amendment rights, consider how these rights apply to prisoners and the challenges such rights present to corrections.

Table 6.4 Types of Public and Quasi-Public Property

Property	Use by public for communicating and demonstrating	Restrictions that may be placed on use
Publicly owned streets, sidewalks and parks	Such property "has been used for purposes of (public) assembly, communicating thoughts between citizens and discussing public questions."[a]	Reasonable regulations may be imposed to assure public safety and order (for example, traffic regulations).
Government buildings, such as courthouses and city halls	Property used for the business of government during business hours is open to the public at these times so that the public may ordinarily come and go as they wish.	Greater restrictions may be imposed to ensure the functioning of government or the regular use of the facilities by the public. They can accommodate only limited expressions of social protest.
Public hospitals, schools, libraries and so on	Use of these public facilities is ordinarily limited to the specific function for which they are designed.	Because these facilities need more order and tranquility than do other public buildings, they generally have more restrictions concerning use by the public.
Quasi-public facilities, such as shopping centers, stores and other privately owned buildings or property to which the public has access	Many quasi-public facilities are as extensively used by the public as are public streets, sidewalks and parks.	Private owners of quasi-public facilities have greater authority to regulate their property than does the government of public streets and parks.
Public property to which access by the public is limited and restricted	Government may limit and restrict in a reasonable manner the access by the public to jails, executive offices (mayor, police chief and others), and other facilities that must be restricted to permit government to function effectively.	Such restrictions must be made in a reasonable and nondiscriminating manner.

[a]U.S. Supreme Court in *Kunz v. New York*, 340 U.S. 290 (1951).

Source: Thomas J. Gardner and Terry M. Anderson. *Criminal Law: Principles and Cases*, 8th ed. Belmont, CA: Wadsworth Publishing Company, 2003, p. 229.

First Amendment Rights of Prisoners

A result of the "due process revolution" has been the extension of First Amendment rights to prisoners. Using a **"rational basis" test,** the Supreme Court has upheld prison regulations that are, as Justice O'Connor stated in *Turner v. Safley* (1987), "reasonably related to legitimate penological interests." She listed in the opinion four criteria of the "rational basis" test, which continue to be the standard for analyzing not only First Amendment claims by prisoners but also other constitutional claims as well: (1) there must be a rational connection between the regulations and legitimate interest put forward to justify it, (2) alternative means of exercising the right must remain open to prison inmates, (3) the regulations must have only a minimal impact on correctional officers and other inmates and (4) a less restrictive alternative must be available.

"rational basis" test • the standard for analyzing not only First Amendment claims by prisoners but also other constitutional claims as well

■   Prisoners' rights based on the First Amendment involve censorship of mail, expression within the institution, association within the institution, religion, appearance and visitation rights.

Free speech is a right of prisoners, and the burden is on the correctional institution to provide valid reasons for restricting this right. Prisoner correspondence has been the focus of much litigation, often because personal correspondence involves a nonincarcerated person who is protected by the First Amendment. In *Prewitt v. State of Arizona ex rel. Eyman* (1969), the court justified the screening of inmate mail: "Mail censorship is a concomitant of incarceration, and so long as the censorship does not interfere with the inmate's access to the courts, it is a universally accepted practice."

However, the court's ruling in *Procunier v. Martinez* (1974) restricted the censorship of inmates' mail, holding such practices to be permissible only in the event of a compelling government interest in maintaining security. This decision greatly enhanced prisoners' abilities to communicate with the outside world. In *Turner v. Safley,* the Court upheld a restriction on prisoners from different institutions corresponding because of related gang problems and the potential for escape planning. In *Shaw v. Murphy* (2001), the Supreme Court reiterated that "incarceration does not divest prisoners of all constitutional protections . . . [but] the constitutional rights that prisoners possess are more limited in scope than the constitutional rights held by individuals in society at large." In this case, the Court held that a prisoner's rights are not heightened, because the material being read by prison officials happens to be legal advice.

Hearing is as much a part of free speech as speaking or writing, and what individuals are allowed to hear and read has always been part of the First Amendment. This right has concerned corrections because of what might be included with other materials sent to prisoners. In *Thornburg v. Abbott* (1989), the Court held that although prisoners had a right to receive some periodicals, these publications did not have the same First Amendment protections as personal mail, and so periodicals deemed detrimental to the institution's security and order could be banned. Using the "clear and present danger" standard, correctional officials are also required to justify any limitations on mail.

In *Beard v. Banks* (2006) Justice Breyer explained: "While imprisonment does not automatically deprive a prisoner of constitutional protections . . . the Constitution sometimes permits greater restriction of such rights in a prison than it would allow elsewhere." Relying on a previous case (*Turner v. Safley*) Breyer further stated: "Under *Turner*, restrictive prison regulations are permissible if they are 'reasonably related to legitimate penological interests.'" In this case Banks claimed his First Amendment rights were violated by not having free access to non-religious reading material, but the Court disagreed that "a Pennsylvania prison policy that denies newspapers, magazines, and photographs to a group of specially dangerous and recalcitrant inmates violate[s] the First Amendment."

Freedom of religion has also proved challenging for the correctional system. Prisoners have brought an increased number of lawsuits that claim their religious freedoms have been infringed upon when the institution limited such areas as access to faith leaders, special dietary options compatible with their faith's requirements and opportunities to assemble with other prisoners of the same faith to worship. In *Fulwood v. Clemmer* (1962), a federal court ruled that Black Muslims must be recognized as a religion and members be permitted to worship in accordance with their faith. This ruling was also made in the case in *Cruz v. Beto* (1972), which concerned a Buddhist inmate who demanded the right to practice his religion. In such cases, the Court has refused to hold that "different" is synonymous with "clear and present danger."

Disruptive activity in the name of religion, however, has not been permitted. In *O'Lone v. Estate of Shabazz* (1987), the Court refused to force a prison to alter an inmate's work schedule so he could attend certain services, citing the facility's restrictions based on security concerns as "reasonably related to legitimate penological interest." However, reasonable accommodations must be made for prisoners to practice their religious faiths.

An example of the tension within the legal system regarding how far correctional facilities must go to ensure the observance of inmate rights is the Religious Freedom Restoration Act (RFRA), discussed earlier. RFRA aimed to protect religious practices from undue governmental restrictions and had broad applications, such as the regulation of hiring/firing decisions based on an employee's religious practices. The result of RFRA for corrections was an avalanche of lawsuits by inmates claiming their behavior was religious and, therefore, protected. Although some of these lawsuits were justified, many others were frivolous and unnecessarily clogged the court system. Eventually, in *City of Boerne v. Flores* (1997), the Supreme Court declared RFRA unconstitutional, ruling that Congress lacked authority to pass such a law and that, in so doing, had impinged on the power of the judiciary and the states.

Groups arguing for religious freedoms and groups supporting more control by correctional officials disagreed on how this legislation came to be and its demise. The repeal of RFRA does not mean that inmates do not have freedom of religion, but it has limited the types of activities that might be permitted under the name of religious freedom. From a practical standpoint, correctional personnel have a vested interest in promoting the pursuit of religion within their institutions for the positive benefits it yields in the faithful. Both sides have abused the system, and future cases will undoubtedly address this issue further.

SUMMARY

The First Amendment prohibits Congress from making any laws that abridge or restrict freedom of religion, freedom of speech, freedom of the press or the right to assemble peaceably and to petition the government for redress of grievances. However, no rights are absolute, so government can regulate them when social interests outweigh that of the individual.

Religious freedom includes the freedom to worship, to print instructional material, to train teachers and to organize schools in which to teach, and to be free of government control or interference. The establishment clause of the First Amendment states: "Congress shall make no law respecting an establishment of religion." That is, it cannot create a national church or prescribed religion. The free exercise clause of the First Amendment declares that "Congress shall make no law . . . prohibiting the free exercise [of religion]."

Freedom of speech/expression includes the right to speak and the right to be heard. Congress has passed laws to limit speech that advocates overthrowing the government by force. The "clear and present danger" test was replaced by the "imminent lawless action" test in determining when speech should not be protected by the First Amendment. Symbolic acts are included within the protection of the First Amendment.

Freedom of the press applies to all types of printed and broadcast material, including books, newspapers, magazines, pamphlets, films and radio and television programs.

Prisoners' rights based on the First Amendment involve censorship of mail, expression within the institution, association within the institution, religion, appearance and visitation rights.

DISCUSSION QUESTIONS

1. Is the First Amendment the most important amendment?

2. Is free speech a right that should be absolute?

3. Speaking from an historical perspective, why do you think the framers of the Constitution placed so much importance on the First Amendment?

4. Should the government tolerate people speaking against or criticizing it?

5. Should an amendment to ban burning the American flag be passed?

6. Imagine you are an attorney asked to defend nude dancing as an act of expression that should be allowed in a small-town bar. What would you say to represent your client's interests? Include an explanation of how nude dancing could ever be considered "speech."

7. Discuss whether Nazi Germany could have gone as far as it did if a similar First Amendment had been present in Germany.

8. Should all schools, public and parochial, receive equal support from the government?

9. Has government gone too far in prohibiting school prayer, prohibiting nativity scenes at public schools and the like?

10. Discuss whether the U.S. government is hypocritical when, on the one hand, freedom of religion is guaranteed, but, on the other hand, Christianity is so obviously stated in the words of the Pledge of Allegiance, the fact that clergy are assigned to Congress and the like.

 ## InfoTrac College Edition Assignments

- Use InfoTrac College Edition to help answer the Discussion Questions when appropriate.

- Use InfoTrac College Edition to find and outline additional information about one basic freedom guaranteed in the First Amendment—freedom of religion, speech, press or assembly.

 ## Internet Assignment

- Use http://www.findlaw.com to find one Supreme Court case discussed in this chapter and brief the case. Be prepared to share your brief with the class.

 ## Companion Web Site

- Go to the Constitutional Law and the Criminal Justice System 3e Web site at http://cj.wadsworth.com/hessharr_constlaw3e for Case Studies and Study Guide exercises.

REFERENCES

Ducat, Craig R. *Constitutional Interpretation*, 8th ed. St. Paul, MN: West/Thomson Learning, 2004.

Stone, Geoffrey R. *Perilous Times, Free Speech in Wartime*. New York: W.W. Norton & Company, Inc., 2004.

ADDITIONAL RESOURCES

Avery III, Isaac T. and Mary Easely. *Legal Aspects of Police Supervision,* 2d ed. Belmont, CA: Wadsworth Publishing, 2001.

Gardner, Thomas J. and Anderson, Terry M. *Criminal Law,* 9th ed. Belmont, CA: Wadsworth Publishing, 2007.

Ojeda, Auriana. *Civil Liberties—Opposing Viewpoints.* Farmington Hills, MI: Greenhouse Press, 2004.

Pollock, Joycelyn M. *Prisons Today and Tomorrow,* 2d ed. Sudbury, MA: Jones and Bartlett Publishers, 2006.

"Protect the Flag's Meaning." *Chicago Tribune,* September 5, 2005, p. 1.

Rankin, Bill. "New Prison Policy Lets Inmates Wear Religious Headgear." *The Atlantic Journal,* August 4, 2005. p. D3.

"Religion behind Bars." *Chicago Tribune,* June 11, 2005, p. 1.20.

Rossum, Ralph A. and Tarr, G. Alan. *American Constitutional Law, The Bill of Rights and Subsequent Amendments,* 6th ed. Belmont, CA: Wadsworth Publishing, 2003.

Stephens, Otis H. and Scheb, John M. *American Constitutional Law,* 3d ed. Belmont, CA: Wadsworth Publishing, 2003.

Volokh, Eugene. "Free Speech Libertarian?" *Wall Street Journal,* November 12, 2005, p. A7.

CASES CITED

Abinton School District v. Schempp and Murray v. Curlett, 374 U.S. 203 (1963).

Agostini v. Felton, 521 U.S. 203 (1997).

Aguilar v. Felton, 473 U.S. 402 (1985).

Barnes v. Glen Theatre, 501 U.S. 560 (1991).

Beard v. Banks, No. 04-1739 (2006).

Brandenburg v. Ohio, 395 U.S. 444 (1969).

California v. LaRue, 409 U.S. 109 (1972).

Cantwell v. Connecticut, 310 U.S. 296 (1940).

Church of Lukumi Babalu Aye v. Hialeah, 508 U.S. 520 (1993).

City of Boerne v. Flores, 519 U.S. 926 (1997).

City of Ladue v. Gilleo, 512 U.S. 43 (1994).

Chicago v. Morales, 527 U.S. 41 (1999).

Cohen v. Cowles Media Company, 111 S.Ct. 2513 (1991).

Council of Greenburgh Civic Assn. v. United States Postal Service, 453 U.S. 917 (1981).

Cruz v. Beto, 405 U.S. 319 (1972).

Davis v. Beason, 133 U.S. 333 (1890).

DeJonge v. Oregon, 299 U.S. 353 (1937).

Dennis v. United States, 341 U.S. 494 (1951).

Edwards v. City of Goldsboro, N.C., 178 F.3d 231 (4th Cir. 1999).

Employment Division v. Smith, 494 U.S. 872 (1990).

Engle v. Vitale, 370 U.S. 421 (1962).

Everson v. Board of Education, 330 U.S. 15 (1947).

Falwell v. Hustler Magazine, 485 U.S. 46 (1988).

Fulwood v. Clemmer, 206 F.Supp. 370 (D.C. Cir. 1962).

Gannett v. DePasquale, 443 U.S. 368 (1979).

Gertz v. Robert Welch, Inc., 418 U.S. 323 (1974).

Gillette v. United States, 401 U.S. 437 (1971).

Gitlow v. New York, 268 U.S. 652 (1925).

Goldman v. Weinberger, 475 U.S. 503 (1986).

Griffin v. Coughlin, 673 N.E. 2d 98 (1999), *cert. denied,* 528 U.S. 1003 (1999).

Hamilton v. Regents of University of California, 293 U.S. 245 (1934).

Heffron v. International Society for Krishna Consciousness, 452 U.S. 640 (1981).

Hutchinson v. Proxmire, 443 U.S. 111 (1979).

Kerr v. Farrey, 95 F. 3rd 472 (7th Cir. 1996).

Kelley v. Johnson, 425 U.S. 238 (1976).

Konigsberg v. State Bar of California, 368 U.S. 869 (1961).

Kunz v. New York, 340 U.S. 290 (1951).

Lemon v. Kurtzman, 403 U.S. 602 (1971).

Lynch v. Donnelly, 465 U.S. 668 (1984).

Madsen v. Women's Health Center, Inc., 512 U.S. 753 (1994).

McIntyre v. Ohio Elections Commission, 514 U.S. 334 (1995).

Miller v. California, 413 U.S. 15 (1973).

Minnesota v. Hershberger, 495 U.S. 901 (1990).

NAACP v. Alabama, 357 U.S. 449 (1958).

Near v. Minnesota, 283 U.S. 697 (1931).

New York Times v. Sullivan, 376 U.S. 254 (1964).

New York v. Zenger (1735).

O'Lone v. Estate of Shabazz, 482 U.S. 342 (1987).

Prewitt v. State of Arizona ex rel. Eyman, 315 F.Supp. 793 (D.C. Ariz. 1969).

Prince v. Massachusetts, 321 U.S. 158 (1944).

Procunier v. Martinez, 416 U.S. 396 (1974).

R.A.V. v. City of St. Paul, 505 U.S. 377 (1992).

Reno v. American Civil Liberties Union, 521 U.S. 844 (1997).

Reynolds v. United States, 98 U.S. 145 (1879).

Richmond Newspapers, Inc. v. Virginia, 448 U.S. 555 (1980).

Rosenberger v. Rector and Visitors of the University of Virginia, 515 U.S. 819 (1995).

Roth v. United States, 354 U.S. 476 (1957).

Schenck v. United States, 249 U.S. 47 (1919).

Shaw v. Murphy, 121 S. Ct. 1475 (2001).

Sheppard v. Maxwell, 384 U.S. 333 (1966).

South Dakota v. Cosgrove, 493 U.S. 846 (1989).

State v. Massey, 229 N.C. 734 (1949).

Stone v. Graham, 449 U.S. 39 (1980).

Street v. New York, 394 U.S. 576 (1969).

Thornburg v. Abbott, 490 U.S. 401 (1989).

The Trial of John Peter Zenger, 17 Howell's St. Tr. 675 (1735).

Texas v Johnson, 491 US 397 (1989).

Turner v. Safley, 482 U.S. 78 (1987).

United States v. American Library Association, 123 S.Ct. 2297 (2003).

United States v. Merkt, 794 F.2d 950 (5th Cir. 1987).

United States v. O'Brien, 391 U.S. 367 (1965).

Virginia v. Black, 538 U.S. 343 (2003).

Wallace v. Jeffries, 472 U.S. 38 (1985).

West Virginia State Board of Education v. Barnette, 319 U.S. 624 (1943).

Wilson v. Swing (1978).

Wooley v. Maynard, 430 U.S. 705 (1977).

Zobrest v. Catalina Foothills School District, 509 U.S. 1 (1993).

Zurcher v. Stanford Daily, 436 U.S. 547 (1978).

CHAPTER 7

The Second Amendment:
The Gun Control Controversy

A WELL-REGULATED MILITIA, BEING NECESSARY TO THE SECURITY OF A
FREE STATE, THE RIGHT OF THE PEOPLE TO KEEP AND BEAR
ARMS SHALL NOT BE INFRINGED.

—SECOND AMENDMENT TO THE U.S. CONSTITUTION

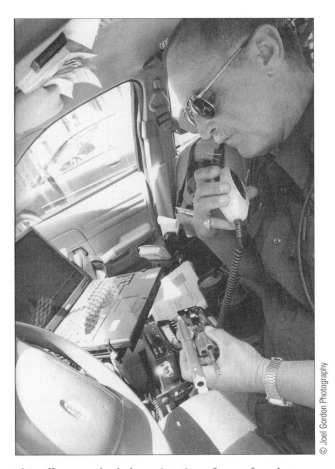

© Joel Gordon Photography

This officer can check the registration of a gun found at a
crime scene using his squad's computer through the FBI's
National Instant Check System (NICS). Registration of gun
purchasers is mandated by the Brady Law, which resulted
in the establishment of the NICS.

DO YOU KNOW . . .

- Historically, who was included in the militia and what was required of them?
- What a central controversy over the Second Amendment involves?
- What opposing interpretations of the Second Amendment have clashed over the years?
- What the primary claim of individuals' rights proponents is? That of states' rights proponents?
- If the Second Amendment has been incorporated into the Fourteenth Amendment and the case that determined this?
- What cases have been important in the gun control controversy?
- Who has nearly absolute authority to regulate firearms?
- How Congress can constitutionally enact federal gun control legislation when this type of legislation is usually left to the states?
- What the Brady Law accomplished?
- Whether the federal courts uphold the view that the Constitution guarantees the right of the individual to keep and bear arms?

CAN YOU DEFINE?

demurrer

dictum

militia

nonincorporated amendment

prohibited persons

sunset clause

Introduction

The Second Amendment protects the "right of the people to keep and bear arms." However, the amendment also begins with a phrase explaining its purpose: that a "well-regulated militia" is "necessary to the security of a free state." At a time when personal freedoms and concerns for self-protection are in political debate with whether more guns means more safety, the Second Amendment is being subjected to careful scrutiny.

What exactly does this brief but controversial amendment mean? Does this phrase mean that the people are allowed to bear arms only if they are part of a militia or defending this country? Does it mean anyone can possess any gun any time? Can guns be used for national defense but not for self-defense? These questions are part of the ongoing debate over gun control and the Second Amendment. One critical question is the definition of a **militia,** a group of citizens who defend their community as emergencies arise.

This chapter begins with a brief historical background on the Second Amendment and a look at how interpretation of this amendment has fueled the debate concerning individual versus state rights in matters of gun control. Next, the current legal status of the nonincorporated Second Amendment is discussed. Then, case law regarding the Second Amendment is presented, followed by a discussion of how the states have addressed Second Amendment issues and the federal regulations aimed at gun control, including the Brady Law and the Violent

militia • an armed group of citizens who defend their community as emergencies arise

Crime Control and Law Enforcement Act of 1994. Then, the controversy surrounding gun control is revisited, with current opinions, facts and actual events presented. The chapter concludes with a consideration of gun control as a political rather than legal issue, as well as examples of how government and communities are working together to address gun-related concerns.

Historical Background

The Second Amendment, like the rest of the Constitution, was drafted in a time when fear of tyranny from a strong central government was uppermost in the new Americans' minds. During the colonial period and the country's earliest years, a permanent army was not possible because of lack of funding and personnel, as well as organizational challenges. In many ways, the colonists were on their own and needed to be prepared, especially with Britain challenging this new country. The result: formation of state militias. Militias consisted mainly of able-bodied adult male civilians and some professional soldiers when available and necessary. They did not encompass the entire national population, but did provide necessary protection and a sense of security.

■ The militia was considered to be the entire adult male populace of a state. They were not simply allowed to keep arms, but were at times *required* to do so by law.

If militia members were called to service, they were to bring their own arms and ammunition. The private populace's arms made up the militia's arms. Most states mandated that all male citizens between certain ages, for instance 18 to 45, be members of the militia. States directed that these males were to be armed and taught basic military skills and protocol. In *Federalist Paper Number 46*, James Madison emphasized to citizens they had "the advantage of being armed, which the Americans possess over the people of almost every other nation."

Some suggest firearms are part of the American fabric. Indeed, the United States' attitude toward weapons arose from the practical need for the pioneers to protect themselves against any number of threats, as well as the philosophical belief that they needed to protect themselves from political tyranny. This reliance on guns reigns to this day, as Wright (2001, p. 63) notes: "Half the households in this country own at least one gun. . . . We are, truly, a gun culture."

One might wonder how an inanimate object evokes such response. To many a gun is much more than just wood and metal. It's a symbol of what was, what has become or what should be. Wright (p. 68) presents an overview of perspectives on guns:

> Guns evoke powerful, emotive imagery that often stands in the way of intelligent debate. To the pro-control point of view, the gun is symbolic of much that is wrong in American culture. It symbolizes violence, aggression, and male dominance, and its use is seen as an acting out of our most regressive and infantile fantasies. To the gun culture's way of thinking, the same gun symbolizes much that is right in the culture. It symbolizes manliness, self-sufficiency, and independence, and its use is an affirmation of man's relationship to nature and to history. The *Great American Gun War*, as Bruce-Briggs has described it, is far more than a contentious debate over crime and the equipment with which it is committed. It is a battle over fundamental and equally legitimate sets of values.

The Debate: Interpreting the Second Amendment

In 1794, the militia was composed of all free male citizens, armed with muskets, bayonets and rifles. Now, the militia is generally considered to consist of National Guard units in every state, armed with government-supplied and owned sophisticated modern weaponry. How might the great differences in today's militia from that in 1794 affect the interpretation of the Second Amendment?

■ A central controversy over the Second Amendment is whether people have a right to bear arms as individuals rather than only as part of a militia.

Confrontations between individuals and government continue to occur in this country involving those some consider the equivalent of modern militia members, only taking a stand for their own freedom. In 1992, at Ruby Ridge in Idaho, the FBI, ATF and U.S. marshals were involved in a standoff with an armed family who refused to obey conventional law and stated, "The tyrant's blood shall flow. . . . Whether we live or die we will not obey you . . . war is upon our land." The ensuing shootout, which ended with the deaths of two family members and one law enforcement official, was a hotly debated action. In 1993, a seven-week standoff occurred between the Branch Davidians religious group and the FBI and ATF. The seige initiated when the government attempted to force access to the Branch Davidian compound while investigating allegations that included polygamy, child abuse and illegal weapons. The ordeal ended with the deaths of 74 compound members, whose chose to burn to death rather than surrender when the compound caught fire.

In 1996, an 81-day standoff occurred between the FBI and the "Freemen," who considered themselves a Christian patriot group in Montana. The Freemen claimed land as their own sovereign nation and refused to abide by laws with which they disagreed. The situation was resolved peacefully. However, the subject will no doubt continue to address the tension between the Constitution and individual rights. Some people feel very much like those more than 200 years ago—that the government has become too powerful and that individuals need to reclaim that power, often with the firearms they believe they are entitled to possess.

Individual Rights versus States' Rights

Two opposing interpretations of the Second Amendment have clashed in past decades.

■ The two opposing interpretations of the Second Amendment involve whether the amendment guarantees individuals' rights to keep and bear arms or whether it guarantees the states freedom from federal government infringement on this right.

Individual Rights   Proponents of "the right to bear arms," including the National Rifle Association (NRA), endorse an individual rights interpretation that would guarantee that right to all citizens. Individual rights proponents see the amendment as primarily guaranteeing the right of the people, not the states. Although they concede that a state right is embodied within the amendment, that right is a product of the more central individual right. By guaranteeing the arms of the individuals who make up the militia, the Constitution guaranteed the militia's arms. The collective right that preserves the states' militia is guaranteed only if the individual right is first maintained.

■ Individual rights proponents claim that the framers intended to preserve individual rights above state rights.

The amendment is placed in close proximity to other individual rights, although the states are not expressly mentioned until the Tenth Amendment. Madison's notes state the amendments were to relate first to private rights. Furthermore, arms were such a pervasive part of colonial life that five state conventions recommended an amendment to guarantee the right to bear arms.

Support for this view may be found in the Los Angeles riots that followed the not-guilty jury verdict in the Rodney King case. Citizens cheered the shopkeepers in Koreatown as they defended their property with weapons. A sobering lesson of the Los Angeles uprising for many people was that the police cannot protect everyone during a citywide emergency. Wright (p. 65) notes: "About a quarter of all gun owners and about 40 percent of handgun owners cite defense against crime as the main reason they own a gun."

Likewise, some activist groups argue that an armed citizenry is the best defense against tyranny and that their thinking is in line with those who wrote the Second Amendment. This view, however, has not been supported by the courts. The courts throughout history have consistently rejected the individual rights view in favor of the states' rights interpretation.

States' Rights   Those favoring a states' rights interpretation see the Second Amendment as protecting and modifying Article 1, Section 8 of the Constitution, which grants Congress the power "to provide for the calling forth of the Militia to execute the laws of the Union." The purpose of the amendment is obviously to "assure the continuation and render possible the effectiveness of such forces" (*United States v. Miller,* 1939). Furthermore, the Second Amendment contains a sort of minipreamble, clearly proclaiming as its purpose the fostering of a "well-regulated Militia," a purpose extraneous to one allowing individual possession of weapons for use against fellow citizens. Consequently, the courts have consistently interpreted the Second Amendment as allowing states to regulate private gun ownership.

■ States' rights proponents claim that the Second Amendment was adopted with the primary purpose of preserving the state militia.

This interpretation is linked to the traditional Whig fear of standing armies. Not only does the amendment preserve the states' power to defend against foreign and domestic enemies, it also reduces the need for a large standing army, which was seen as inherently contrary to preserving a free, democratic people.

Before examining the debate surrounding gun controversy, consider how the courts have interpreted the Second Amendment and the laws resulting from their decisions.

Current Legal Status of the Nonincorporated Second Amendment

An amendment that receives such attention remains a **nonincorporated amendment.** That status means it is one of the few amendments contained within the Bill of Rights that has not been incorporated under the Fourteenth Amendment to apply to both federal and state government, because, presumably, to date the

nonincorporated amendments • when an amendment has not been made applicable (incorporated) to the states under the Fourteenth Amendment

Supreme Court has not considered this right essential to "a scheme of ordered liberty." In *Presser v. Illinois* (1886), the Court refused to incorporate the Second Amendment into the Fourteenth Amendment. Therefore, the Second Amendment does not apply to state government.

This nonincorporation has left the door open for varied interpretations of the Second Amendment and fueled the vigorous controversy surrounding its purpose.

Case Law and the Second Amendment

Federal regulation of firearms possession was virtually nonexistent for more than 140 years after ratification of the Bill of Rights. The first notable case involving the Second Amendment was *United States v. Cruikshank* (1875). The U.S. Supreme Court, in responding to a claim of a right to bear arms for a lawful purpose, ruled: "This is not a right granted by the Constitution. . . . The Second Amendment declares that it shall not be infringed; but this, as has been seen, means no more than it shall not be infringed by Congress."

Despite this decision, more than half a century passed before the federal government made an effort to regulate the possession of firearms, mainly because the Court had little reason to interpret the amendment. The National Firearms Act of 1934 was the first such effort at federal regulation. Section 11 of the act forbade a person "who has not in his possession a stamp-affixed order (from the person requesting the firearm) to ship, carry, or deliver any firearm in interstate commerce."

One of the first important rulings on the Second Amendment involved this act. Jack Miller was convicted of violating the National Firearms Act by feloniously transporting a double-barreled, 12-gauge shotgun (having a barrel less than 18 inches) from Oklahoma to Arkansas (*United States v. Miller*, 1939). The district court granted the defense a **demurrer,** a request that a suit be dismissed because although the facts are true, they do not sustain the claim against the defendant. The United States appealed the demurrer and certiorari was granted. The Supreme Court interpreted the Second Amendment as providing for maintaining a militia: "With the obvious purpose to assure the continuation and render possible the effectiveness of such forces [as outlined in Article 1, Section 8 of the Constitution] the declaration and guarantee of the Second Amendment were made. It must be interpreted and applied with that view in mind."

This case indicates that the amendment protects only arms that bear some relation to preserving the militia. The Court held: "In the absence of any evidence tending to show that possession or use of a shotgun having a barrel of less than 18 inches in length, at this time has some reasonable relationship to the preservation or efficiency of a well-regulated militia, we cannot say that the Second Amendment guarantees the right to keep and bear such an instrument." Therefore, a law prohibiting transportation of unregistered shotguns in interstate commerce is not unconstitutional.

■ In *United States v. Miller* (1939), the Court recognized a state right rather than an individual right to bear arms.

The decision was not intended to be a broadly sweeping decision that designated which arms are protected and which are not. The courts clarified the decision in *Miller* three years later, when a circuit court of appeals held: "The rule

demurrer • a request that a suit be dismissed because the facts do not sustain the claim against the defendant

which it [*Miller*] laid down was adequate to dispose of the case before it and that we think was as far as the Supreme Court intended to go" (*Cases v. United States,* 1942). The Court also clearly stated its position on individual rights and the Second Amendment: "The right to keep and bear arms is not a right conferred upon the people by the federal constitution. Whatever rights in this respect the people may have depend upon local legislation; the only function of the Second Amendment being to prevent the federal government and the federal government only from infringing on that right."

This position was reiterated later in *Stevens v. United States* (1971), when a federal circuit court held that the Second Amendment applies "only to the right of the state to maintain a militia and not to the individual's right to bear arms, there can be no serious claim to any express constitutional right of an individual to possess a firearm."

■ In 1971, the courts ruled that there was no express right of an individual to keep and bear arms (*Stevens v. United States*).

In fact, since *Miller,* lower federal and state courts have interpreted the Second Amendment in more than 30 cases, and in every case except one, the courts have held that the amendment refers to the right to keep and bear arms only in connection with a state militia. The aberrant decision came in *United States v. Emerson* (1999), when U.S. District Judge Sam R. Cummings went against all federal court precedent and restored a domestic abuser's firearms, citing the Second Amendment as guaranteeing the individual's right to keep and bear arms.

The individual involved, Timothy Emerson, was under a domestic restraining order after threatening his estranged wife and child with a firearm and threatening to kill his estranged wife's friends. Because of the threats, federal law prohibited him from possessing a firearm, yet he bragged to friends about owning automatic weapons and needing only to purchase ammunition to prepare for a visit to his wife. The Center to Prevent Handgun Violence asserts:

> This decision flies in the face of years of precedence and jurisprudence and can only be viewed as a renegade decision. In his opinion, Judge Cummings was unable to follow usual judicial practice and cite legal precedents that [validate] his decision because there are none. This ruling is being appealed and since that decision, two federal courts, including a higher Circuit court, have ruled that the Second Amendment does not guarantee an individual right to keep and bear arms (*Gillespie v. City of Indianapolis,* 2000).

States and the Second Amendment

Recall that only those amendments considered *fundamental to the American scheme of justice* apply to state and local government through selective incorporation (*Duncan v. Louisiana,* 1968). The Second Amendment is not among the incorporated amendments and, therefore, does not apply to state or local governments. Provided that a statute does not violate a state's constitution, the federal courts have ruled that a complete ban on certain types of guns is acceptable, even though the federal government could not do so.

■ The states' power to regulate firearms appears to be nearly absolute.

dictum • the statement by a court that does not deal with the main issue in the case or an additional discussion by the court

In *dictum* (the court's side opinion) on a case that involved illegal search and seizure, Douglas summed up the federal position on gun control (*Adams v. Williams*, 1972): "A powerful lobby dins into the ears of our citizenry that these gun purchases are constitutional rights protected by the Second Amendment. . . . There is under our decisions no reason why stiff state laws governing the purchase and possession of pistols may not be enacted."

In 1982, the village of Morton Grove, Illinois, banned from the town all handguns, shotguns with barrels less than 18 inches and guns firing more than eight shots in repetition. Exceptions were made for law enforcement officials and for armed services personnel performing official duties. Several other exceptions were also made (for example, licensed gun collectors and gun clubs), provided the guns were kept securely on the premises.

The village ban on guns was contested by Quilici who brought suit, claiming the ordinance went too far in restricting the right to bear arms according to both the Illinois and U.S. Constitution. He also claimed that the ban violated the Ninth Amendment. The district court upheld the ordinance, which was taken to the U.S. Court of Appeals for the Seventh District.

The Court of Appeals considered the scope of the ban irrelevant and dismissed the issue (*Quilici v. Village of Morton Grove*, 1982): "Since we hold that the Second Amendment does not apply to the states, we need not consider the scope of its guarantee of the right to bear arms." The court went on to conclude that, according to the amendment's plain language: "It seems clear that the right to bear arms is inextricably connected to the preservation of a militia."

Before leaving the issue of the Second Amendment and the states, consider the case of *United States v. Lopez* (1995), which found the federal law banning guns near schools to be unconstitutional. This Supreme Court 5 to 4 decision struck down the Gun-Free School Zones Act. Although Justice Department lawyers argued that the law was a legitimate extension of Congress' power to regulate interstate commerce, Chief Justice Rehnquist found the law "has nothing to do with commerce or any sort of enterprise."

This overturning of the Gun-Free School Zones Act may not have much practical effect, however, because more than 40 states, exercising their right to pass laws controlling guns, have banned possession of handguns near schools.

Concealed/Carry, or Right-to-Carry, Laws

The laws that regulate carrying a concealed weapon (concealed/carry laws), also called right-to-carry (RTC) laws, vary from state to state. Some states have laws that say carrying a concealed weapon is a citizen's basic right. These states allow permits to be easily obtained, provided the gun buyer meets certain background requirements, including not having violated certain laws or been determined to be mentally ill. Some states also require the completion of classroom and range training courses. Other states limit permits to carry a concealed weapon to when employment or personal safety justifies it.

Researchers at Johns Hopkins University Center for Gun Policy and Research, provides examples reflecting the array of past and present legislation, including a Virginia law limiting people to buying only one handgun per month, a Washington, DC, law banning most new handgun sales to the public (since relaxed) and a Maryland law prohibiting sales of low-cost, so-called Saturday-night specials. Although some states require licensing handgun owners or registering guns, or both, other states have sought to require the government to issue a permit unless they have a compelling reason not to. Still others require some employment or personal-safety requirement.

Ferrell (2004, p. 14) points out: "Law enforcement groups have been battling various concealed handgun carry laws for over a decade now and it appears the public and politicians have overwhelmingly decided in a majority of states that concealed handgun laws are a good thing." He notes that more than 35 states now have concealed/carry laws. However, many law enforcement professionals remain steadfastly against concealed/carry laws and will continue to their opposition. More research on this hotly debated issue is needed.

Restrictions on Types of Firearms

Although some weapons, such as fully automatic "machine guns" and those altered to be more conducive to criminal activity, such as sawed-off shotguns, have always been illegal for most people to own (law enforcement personnel and licensed collectors being the exception), what exactly constitutes a *weapon* or *firearm* has not been as easy to define.

Some jurisdictions have included anything that explodes or projects anything, including paintball guns and bow and arrows, whereas others have sought to be more specific. The definition of "assault rifle" has generated its own share of debate with the Federal Assault Weapons Ban (a provision of the Violent Crime Control and Law Enforcement Act of 1994), discussed later in the chapter.

An Evaluation of State Gun Laws

A caution: statistics and laws change—especially in areas as active as gun control. Whatever statistics are presented, and where they are from, they are likely to have changed by the time you are reading this; what is presented here is intended to serve as a snapshot in time.

A 2000 survey by the advocacy group Funders' Collaborative for Gun Violence Prevention asserted that most states were lacking in gun control legislation. According to their report: "Fewer than 10 states have laws requiring the registration of handguns and assault weapons, a minimum age for gun possession, owner licensing, a waiting period, and a 'junk gun' ban" ("Survey Finds State . . . ," 2000, p. 1). Since that time, although some would argue that not enough restrictive legislation has developed, others would point to the laws that have been passed to address these very issues, with commensurate statistical evidence that change is occurring. Another study shows evidence that increasing regulations of guns are resulting in lower crime rates (Webster et al., 2001).

The attention being drawn to the issue of whether people should be permitted to carry handguns in public raises the question as to what this reflects about social norms. Does this reflect a more conservative trend? A greater fear of crime? A greater fear of government? Or is it merely the continuing saga of Americans seeking to retain their rights guaranteed by the Constitution. As one of the most emotionally charged topics in the country, as many opinions exist as people asked.

The Effect of Conceal/Carry Laws on Crime   Lott, in a best seller *More Guns, Less Crime* sets forth the argument that citizens carrying guns makes us safer. This same argument is presented in *The Bias against Guns* (2003, p. 3), in which he asserts that after examining how crime rates change over time in relation to concealed/carry law, he found: "Gun control disarmed law-abiding citizens more than criminals, which meant that criminals had less to fear from potential victims. Guns not only make it easier for people to harm others, guns also make it easier for people to protect themselves."

Donohue (2003, p. 399) presents an opposite finding: "Our best, albeit admittedly imperfect, statistical evidence indicates that increases in permit rate growth may lead to slight increases in crime."

Research by Kovandzic and Marvell (2003, p. 363) found little evidence that increases in the number of citizens with concealed-handgun permits reduce or increase rates of violent crime: "There is little, if any, relationship between the number of RTC permits and violent crime. That is, the level of gun carrying by citizens neither deters nor exacerbates crime." Similar findings were reported by the Centers for Disease Control and Prevention (CDC) (Hann et al., 2003). Their independent task force of public health officials and other scientists found 51 evaluations of gun laws and concluded: "We found insufficient evidence to determine the effectiveness of any of the firearm laws."

Federal Regulation and the Second Amendment

Although the Second Amendment has consistently been interpreted to protect the states' rights from federal intervention, the federal government has passed several gun control laws.

■ Congress, using its broad authority to regulate interstate commerce, has enacted some federal gun control legislation.

In 1938, the Federal Firearms Act was passed, requiring dealers shipping firearms across state lines and importers to be licensed by the federal govern-ment. By the end of the 1980s, more than 230,000 federally licensed firearms dealers existed in the United States. By 2004, that number had dropped to approximately 80,000 stores licensed to sell guns in the United States ("ATF Data Traces," 2004, p. 5).

In 1967, Congress passed the Omnibus Crime Control and Safe Streets Act, a portion of which made possession of firearms by convicted felons unlawful. The constitutionality of this act was called into question in *Stevens v. United States* (1971) and several other cases on the grounds it was unconstitutional because it violated the commerce clause. Stevens, a felon, was convicted under the act and appealed on the grounds that his right to bear arms had been infringed and that Congress did not have the constitutional authority to regulate possession of firearms.

The Court again ruled that the Second Amendment guaranteed no individual right. On the question of constitutional authority, the Sixth Circuit Court of Appeals held that the power to regulate interstate commerce gave Congress the power to regulate firearms: "There can be no serious doubt that the possession of firearms by convicted felons is a threat to interstate commerce." It also ruled that Congress need not wait for "the total dislocation of commerce before it may provide reasonable preventative measures." The Supreme Court denied certiorari on this case.

In 1968, after the assassinations of President John F. Kennedy, the Rev. Martin Luther King, Jr., and Senator Robert Kennedy, the Gun Control Act was passed, which banned federal licensees from selling firearms to **prohibited persons,** anyone they knew or had reasonable cause to believe was or had been:

- Under indictment for or convicted of a felony.
- A fugitive.
- A drug user.
- Adjudicated a mental defective or committed to a mental institution.
- Who fit into other limited categories.

prohibited persons • individuals to whom, under the Gun Control Act, selling a firearm is forbidden

The Supreme Court has ruled that the federal law that bars gun ownership by convicted felons does not apply to those convicted in foreign courts. In *Small v. United States* (2005), the Court overturned the conviction of a man who bought a gun in Pennsylvania after serving more than three years in a Japanese prison for smuggling guns into that country. Justice Stephen Breyer, writing for the majority, said the phrase "convicted in any court" applies only to convictions in U.S. federal or state courts, not to foreign courts.

The Gun Control Act also required the registration of "destructive devices," including cannons, antitank guns and bazookas, and prohibited importation of cheap, "junk" handguns, such as the $6 Saturday-night special that killed Senator Kennedy.

In *United States v. Warin* (1976), the Sixth Circuit Court of Appeals further defined the relation between militia and the right to keep and bear arms. The court heard claims of unconstitutionality of federal taxation on guns and a Ninth Amendment violation. Both claims were rejected.

In this case, Warin was convicted of possessing an unregistered submachine gun. He appealed on several counts. First, he argued that because he was subject to enrollment in (although not actually a member of) the state militia, the amendment granted him the right to bear arms. Second, he argued that the National Firearms Act taxed the right to keep and bear arms. Finally, he argued that as a member of the sedentary militia, he had the fundamental the right to bear and keep arms under the Ninth Amendment.

The court held that being subject to enrollment in the state militia does not grant a special right to keep and bear arms. On the matter of taxation it held: "Even where the Second Amendment is applicable it does not constitute an absolute barrier to congressional regulation of firearms." It also held that the Ninth Amendment confers no additional fundamental right to an "unregistered submachine gun."

In 1986, Congress banned the purchase and sale of all fully automatic weapons. All privately owned automatic weapons bought before 1986 were to be registered but would remain in their owners' hands. This ban was tested by a gun collector, Farmer, who applied for a permit to legally make and register a machine gun for his private collection. The Bureau of Alcohol, Tobacco and Firearms (ATF) denied his application. When the district court ruled in favor of Farmer, the court of appeals stayed the order. The court of appeals ruled that the ATF was not abusing its discretion by denying the permit. In its decision, the court did not consider the constitutional issue of the right to keep and bear arms, but dealt with the case only on its statutory merits (*Farmer v. Higgins,* 1990). Also passed in 1986 was the Firearm Owners' Protection Act, which allowed gun dealers to sell at gun shows and restricted unannounced inspections by the ATF to once annually.

The Brady Act

On November 30, 1993, President Clinton signed the Brady Handgun Violence Prevention Act, and on February 28, 1994, the Brady Act went into effect. The law was named to honor Jim Brady, the press secretary to Ronald Reagan, who was shot during a 1981 assassination attempt on President Reagan. Despite the endorsement of four former presidents (Nixon, Ford, Carter and Reagan) and the active support of President Clinton, seven years were required for the Brady Bill to get through Congress and become law.

The purpose of the law was to prevent prohibited persons from obtaining handguns. The Act imposed a national five-day waiting period and required local law enforcement to conduct criminal background checks on all handgun purchasers. The mandatory waiting period, however, was merely an interim provision and expired on November 30, 1998. It was replaced by the permanent provision of a mandatory, computerized National Instant Criminal Background Check System (NICS), which provides information for criminal background checks on all firearm purchasers.

Until February 2004, the NICS did not include a review of terrorist watch lists, according to the Government Accountability Office (GAO). However, being named on such a list is *not* one of the disqualifying criteria under federal gun control laws. The terrorist watch list was added so that federal officials might determine if terror suspects might be disqualified from buying a gun on other grounds listed in the federal gun control laws ("Brady Act Failing," 2005, p. 4).

■ The Brady Act, passed in 1993, contained the interim provision of a mandatory five-day waiting period on all handgun purchases, phased out and replaced in 1998 with the permanent provision of an instant, computerized criminal background check of all handgun purchasers. Some states still impose a waiting period on firearms purchases.

In 1997, the Supreme Court ruled 5 to 4 in *Printz v. United States* that the federal government was not empowered to require state or local law enforcement agencies to run background checks on prospective gun buyers. According to the Court, the background-check provision violated the principle of separate state sovereignty. Justice Scalia, writing for the narrow majority, stated: "The federal government may neither issue directives requiring the states to address particular problems, nor command the states' officers, or those of their political subdivisions, to administer or enforce a federal regulatory program. Such commands are fundamentally incompatible with our constitutional system of dual sovereignty."

As of November 1, 1998, the Brady Act was modified so applicants can receive immediate clearance to purchase a gun. The issuing law-enforcement agency can contact the FBI by computer and either receive clearance or be denied the permit. Unless federal computer records indicate a felony arrest record, a dishonorable discharge, an illegal alien status or other possible disability, the purchaser may be approved at the time.

From the inception of the Brady Act in 1994 to December 31, 2004, more than 61 million applications for firearm transfers or permits were subject to background checks, with about 1,228,000 being rejected. The most common reason for rejection was a felony conviction or indictment (Bowling et al., 2005, p. 1).

Although acknowledging that any background check is better than no background check, critics of the instant check system say it sacrifices safety for convenience. Because many centralized records are kept only at the state level, and many more records, such as mental health records, may not be computerized. Also, relevant records may not be identified in time, if at all.

The Brady Act does not prohibit states from enacting their own, longer waiting periods. The constitutionality of this act continues to be challenged. Some jurisdictions interpret the law differently. For example, the City of Kenneway, Georgia, passed a law in 1982 mandating the head of each household to own at least one firearm and have ammunition to "protect the safety, security and general welfare of the city and its inhabitants." However, because of what others say is an escalating number of deaths and injuries resulting from guns, including those involving youths, other jurisdictions are becoming increasingly strict.

A study reported in the *Journal of the American Medical Association* ("New Study Questions the Effects of Brady Law," 2000, p. A4) analyzed national homicide and suicide data between 1985 and 1997 and concluded: "Our analyses provide no evidence that implementation of the Brady Act was associated with a reduction in homicide rates." The CDC, in a 2003 report, found insufficient evidence to assess the impact of gun laws on preventing violence (Hann and Bilukha, 2003). Other researchers, however, assert the opposite; their findings show positive impacts from such efforts as licensing and registration, background checks and limitations on what types of weapons can be owned and when and how they can be carried. This debate will undoubtedly continue.

The Violent Crime Control and Law Enforcement Act of 1994

In September 1994, Congress passed and President Clinton signed into law the Violent Crime Control and Law Enforcement Act of 1994. This act banned the manufacture of 19 different semiautomatic guns with multiple assault-weapon features, as well as copies or duplicates of such guns. The act also prohibits transfer to or possession of handguns and ammunition by juveniles, prohibits possession of firearms by people who have committed domestic abuse and provides stiffer penalties for criminals who use firearms to commit federal crimes. Support for such a ban was seen almost 20 years before in *United States v. Warin* (1976): "There can be no question that an organized society which fails to regulate the importation, manufacture and transfer of the highly sophisticated lethal weapons in existence today does so at its peril."

In supporting the ban, Polisar (2004, p. 6) pointed out that weapons banned under the act served no legitimate sporting of hunting purposes and that unless the act was renewed, "The firearms of choice for terrorists, drug dealers and gang members will be back on our streets." Despite strong support, the ban expired with a **sunset clause** (a set ending time for legislation that is not renewed to prevent old law from remaining on the books) in 2004, when Congress did not renew it over significant debate. That same year, federal legislation was passed allowing off-duty and retired police officers to carry concealed weapons, another controversial issue.

sunset clause • a set ending time for legislation that is not renewed to prevent old law from remaining on the books

The Law Enforcement Officers Safety Act

In July 2004, President Bush signed into law the Law Enforcement Officers Safety Act, which allows off-duty and retired officers to carry concealed weapons throughout the country, regardless of state or local firearms restrictions. However, the International Association of Chiefs of Police (IACP) strongly opposed the legislation, concerned about officer and citizen safety, use-of-force and firearm-training standards, officer identification and eligibility issues, supervision of retired police, liability and a "fundamental belief that states and localities should determine who is eligible to carry firearms in their communities" (Boyter, 2004, p. 8). So the gun control debate rages on, with many opposing such measures.

The Current Gun Control Controversy

Both those for and those against gun control effectively argue that any statistical evidence is biased, uses flawed research, is used to prove a specific point or somehow is used to endorse a political point. The plethora of research provides ample data to be interpreted as people wish, and even elected officials have vastly different views of what the law is and should be. Data regarding most controversial issues are to be carefully scrutinized, which is certainly the case with research associated with firearms.

In Opposition to Gun Control

Various philosophies prevail in the gun control opposition camp. Some focus on the issue of constitutionality and rigorously defend individuals' rights to keep and bear arms, whereas others reflect a more passive resignation, believing such legislation is merely a paper tiger that offers no real bearing on any crime control efforts.

A common argument among gun control opponents is the claim that such laws will only put guns where they do not belong—in criminals' hands. The NRA and other advocacy group have captured this philosophy about gun control with phrases suggesting "If guns are outlawed, only outlaws will have guns" and "Guns don't kill people, people do." In May 2001, the *Washington Post* reported: "Attorney General John Ashcroft told the National Rifle Association (NRA) that he 'unequivocally' believes the U.S. Constitution protects the right of individuals to own guns, a position that runs counter to most federal court rulings over the last 50 years that the right is collective instead" ("Constitution Protects," 2001, p. A21). In May 2002, the *Los Angeles Times* reported: "For the first time, the Justice Department has told the Supreme Court, which is considering two cases, that the right to bear arms is not limited to providing for a citizen militia" ("U.S. Brief," 2002, p. A3).

At the 2006 NRA meeting, President Froman stated: "Of all the rights NRA fights for, few are as important as Right-to-Carry. . . . You have the fundamental human right to protect yourself, to not be a victim and to not fear for your safety in your daily life." A similar view is stated by Kopel:

> Many Americans believe that an armed society is a safe society. The reason for this stems form America's unique history. For example, the American Revolution was won due to a sustained popular revolt in which citizen militias took up arms to fight for independence. Later, in the absence of effective law enforcement during the early history of westward expansion, American frontiersmen had to carry guns for personal defense. . . . Americans refused to give up their arms to anyone. Therefore, the American gun culture is deeply rooted in the uniquely American history of survival, independence, and personal freedom (Doyle, 2005, p. 45).

Lee also supports a view held by many: "Owning a firearm is a fundamental, individual right guaranteed by the Constitution. History is full of examples of fascist rulers who sought to disarm the people they intended to enslave. When people are disarmed, government tyranny and oppression thrives. The founding fathers of the United States of America wrote the Second Amendment to protect citizens' right to defend themselves against oppression, whether it be the at the hands of another individual or those of tyrannical government. Therefore, the right to keep and bear arms is arguably the most important constitutionally protected right of all. Laws restricting the keeping and bearing of arms in any way are clearly therefore unconstitutional" (Doyle, p. 58).

Facts to Support This View Data indicate a steady decline in gun violence and associated firearms deaths in the United States since the peak year of 1993. However, a study by Ludwig and Cook (2000) contends that this decline is unrelated to the enactment of the 1994 Brady Law. The researchers found "no evidence that implementation of the Brady Act was associated with a reduction in homicide rates."

Gun control opponents assert the decrease in gun violence may be attributable to many factors other than legislation, including a stronger economy and lower unemployment rates; increased numbers of police in the community; implementation of new, more aggressive and more effective police tactics; and the crackdown on illegal drug trafficking, which invariably involves gun violence ("Brady Act Had No Effect," 2000, p. 3).

Wright (p. 65) cites findings by Kleck that Americans use guns to thwart crime against themselves *millions* of times a year and states: "Whatever the true number of self-defensive uses, about a quarter of all gun owners and about 40 percent of handgun owners cite defense against crime as the main reason they own a gun."

In Support of Gun Control

Among advocates of gun control is Gallegos (2000), national president of the Fraternal Order of Police, who states: "We prefer to refer to the issue as 'crime control'—not 'gun control.' Our members [totaling more than 293,000], the large majority of whom are rank-and-file officers, continue to support the Brady Law and assault weapons ban. The Fraternal Order of Police supports regulations consistent with these laws, but does not support any new firearms legislation. We hope, however, that the next Administration does a better job enforcing the firearms laws we have on the books now."

Blek argues: "The progun lobby repeatedly refers to the Second Amendment to the U.S. Constitution as proof that individuals have the right to own firearms. However, the constitutionality of gun control is supported by numerous court cases ruling that the Second Amendment does not grant individuals the right to own arms. Historical analysis shows that the amendment was written to protect colonists from England's King George III's military forces and contains nothing that could be construed today as prohibiting gun control. . . . For too long, our elected officials have hidden behind the phrase 'our Second Amendment rights' in order to defend the status quo with regard to guns. Guns are not the root cause of violence; but their widespread usage dramatically increases the lethality of the violence" (Doyle, p. 53).

Many advocates of gun control criticize the ability of some to circumvent the law. The Center to Prevent Handgun Violence states, despite legislation now banning the sale of assault weapons, thousands of these firearms are presently "in private hands and available for sale at gun shows because of grandfather clauses in the laws. How about 32-round ammo clips, banned in 1994 as part of the federal assault weapons ban? Just like the assault weapons themselves, clips manufactured before the ban are acceptable to sell—and gun manufacturers like Miami's Navegar (formerly known as Intertec, creator of the infamous 'TEC-9'), stocked up as many as 50,000 of the clips in anticipation of the ban."

Others have expressed, in much harsher language, not so much a strong desire to advocate gun control legislation, but, rather, an intense disdain for those who oppose it through claims that such laws violate their individual constitutional right to bear arms. In 1991, former Supreme Court Chief Justice Warren Burger referred to the Second Amendment as "the subject of one of the greatest pieces of fraud, I repeat the word 'fraud,' on the American public by special interest groups that I have ever seen in my lifetime. . . . [The NRA] has misled the American people and they, I regret to say, have had far too much influence on the Congress of the United States than as a citizen I would like to see—and I am a gun man." Burger continued:

> The very language of the Second Amendment refutes any argument that it was intended to guarantee every citizen an unfettered right to any kind of weapon. . . . There is no support in the Constitution for the argument that federal and state governments are powerless to regulate the purchase of such firearms.

Facts to Support This View According to the FBI's Uniform Crime Reports, of the 16,137 murders in 2004, 70.3 percent involved firearms, with handguns accounting for 77.9 percent of the murder total for which weapon data were submitted (*Crime in the United States*, 2001, p. 26).

Unlike the average citizen, law enforcement officers are well trained in gun safety, yet their training does not exempt them from becoming victims of gun violence. According to the FBI, of the 57 officers feloniously killed during 2004, 54 were shot to death (36 killed with handguns, 13 with rifles and 5 with shotguns). The FBI reports that over the previous decade, 545 law enforcement officers were killed by firearms (*Law Enforcement Officers Killed and Assaulted—2004*).

Finding Common Ground—Is a Compromise Possible?

Despite all the controversy over gun control, where the courts stand is without question. Gun control by the states is not constitutionally prohibited, and under most circumstances, legislation by the federal government is not prohibited.

■ Federal courts to date have held that the Constitution does not guarantee the absolute right of the individual to keep and bear arms.

The Supreme Court has ruled on the amendment relatively few times compared with contests over other amendments. *United States v. Miller* (1939) remains the only Supreme Court case that specifically addresses that amendment's scope. Most of the adjudication has been done at the federal district level and has seldom gone beyond the court of appeals. The Supreme Court has repeatedly denied certiorari in cases in which the individual right to bear arms is at issue.

The history of the courts suggests that they will defer to the discretion of Congress on almost all matters concerning gun control. Thus far, the only actions the courts may find constitutionally offensive are a complete nationwide ban on firearms and acting on reports of gun possession without further evidence.

Cases Governing Response to Gun Possession Reports   Although courts, including the Supreme Court, support efforts of law enforcement to control guns used in crimes, they have been reluctant to relax search-and-seizure requirements of government in cases merely because they may involve weapons. Because in most states, carrying a properly licensed handgun is legal, a report that a person has a handgun, with no additional information regarding criminal activity, may not create reasonable suspicion that a crime is being or will be committed, thus justifying a *Terry* stop (Collins, 2005, p. 10).

A unanimous Supreme Court ruling in *Florida v. J.L.* (2000) established that "in order for an anonymous tip to be reliable enough to justify police action, even when a firearm is reported, it must do more than simply describe a suspect's appearance and location." Writing for the Court, Justice Ginsburg stated: "Firearms are dangerous, and extraordinary dangers sometimes justify unusual precautions, [but] an automatic firearms exception to our established reliability analysis would rove too far. Such an exception would enable any person seeking to harass another to set in motion an intrusive, embarrassing police search of the targeted person simply by placing an anonymous call falsely reporting the target's unlawful carriage of a gun."

Likewise, in *Pennsylvania v. D.M.* (2000), the Supreme Court held that an anonymous tip with a physical description and location that a person had a gun was not enough for reasonable suspicion without anything else to cause suspicion.

Broadening of the Debate

The controversy over the effectiveness of existing gun control legislation and the need to add to that body of legal work has spread into many different occupational venues, pulling in a variety of advocates and opponents from a wide range of professions. The CDC now keep statistics on gun-related injuries and deaths. These statistics include types of weapons, ammunition used, whether the weapon was stolen, information when youths are involved and the relationship between the first person to own the weapon and the victim or assailant. Educators, physicians, the clergy and community groups are concerned as well and, as discussed below, want to participate in finding solutions.

Joint Government and Community Efforts to Respond to Gun-Related Violence

Although some argue any effort to address gun issues is politically based, groups at various levels are attempting to address the problem of gun-related violence. One such effort is Project Safe Neighborhoods, a federally funded program to support local programs. This nationwide effort to reduce gun crime networks existing local programs that target gun crime and provides those programs with additional tools to succeed. The program emphasizes tactical intelligence gathering and more aggressive prosecutions. Although opinions vary as to the success of Project Safe Neighborhoods, Ludwig states (2005): "Project Safe Neighborhoods (PSN), which for the past several years has been the major federal initiative to combat gun violence, includes several elements (such as gun locks and other efforts to reduce gun availability) that research suggests are likely to have at best modest effects on gun crime. . . . Given the substantial social costs of gun violence, an efficiency argument can also be made for increasing funding beyond previous levels."

In conjunction with Project Safe Neighborhood, efforts to hold gun owners liable are underway. California has begun a program to trace legal guns used in criminal activity and to make their legal owners subject to prosecution. According to California, in endorsing Attorney General Lockyer, the goal is to make legal gun owners aware of their responsibilities to maintain control of their weapons ("California Launches Gun Tracing Program," 2005). As reported in *Crime Control Digest* (2005), Attorney General Alberto Gonzales said, in endorsing Project Safe Neighborhood (at the National Sheriff's Association conference): "Federal cooperation with local law enforcement to combat gun and gang crimes is effective in lowering crime rates."

The issue of holding liable those who *make* guns has also been addressed: "We need to know that they aren't putting their personal financial interest above the public safety interest of the neighborhood" ("Taking Aim at Gun Manufacturers," 2006). This article reported on the agreement reached between President Clinton and gun manufacturer Smith & Wesson, which, "facing multiple liability lawsuits, agreed to put safety locks on guns, improve technology to prevent unauthorized usage, and stop selling guns at gun shows where background checks weren't conducted." Attention has also focused on those who *sell* firearms:

> There is a clear relationship between lax gun laws and firearm-related deaths and injuries. The ENFORCE bill . . . is legislation . . . to enhance and improve the enforcement of existing gun violence laws. Because the majority of criminal gun flow moves through . . . gun dealers and gun shows, ENFORCE will require tightening and enforcement of current laws regulating gun dealer transactions and licensing. ENFORCE also asks for effective measures to prevent convicted felons, children, and those with a history of violence from gaining access to firearms. In order to reduce crime and violence, these measures are necessary. The solution is not to arm more Americans and allow greater access to firearms, but to restrict dealer transactions and keep firearms out of the hands of criminals. (Rand, 2000, p. 70)

Teachers groups, including the National Education Association, have developed programs to teach awareness and safety, as has the clergy. In St. Louis, Missouri, the clergy joined with police in a collaborative project called CEASEFIRE to help curb youth violence. This program was modeled after such a program in Boston, Massachusetts, that involved the police, the states attorney's office, community corrections, the mayor's office, educators and clergy.

A Final Consideration: Gun Control as a Political Issue

Thus far, the judiciary has left gun control laws to the states to be determined through the political process. In *Quilici v. Village of Morton Grove* (1982), the U.S. Court of Appeals, 7th District, began its opinion: "While we recognize that this case raises controversial issues which engender strong emotions, our task is to apply the law as it has been interpreted by the Supreme Court, regardless of whether that Court's interpretation comports with various personal views of what the law should be."

Until the U.S. Supreme Court accepts a case to confront these Second Amendment issues, the research, writing, debate and rhetoric will continue. On the one hand, the Constitution provides an opportunity to openly debate the issues. On the other hand, some would suggest the Constitution was also drafted to provide more guidance in resolving issues of national importance.

In a time when crimes committed with firearms continue to draw public attention, what the answers are continues to be debated. Will more guns help deter crime or add to it? Will less restrictive "right to carry" laws make streets safer or more dangerous? Will trigger-lock legislation prevent gun-related injuries or prevent ready access to guns when the need to deter crime suddenly arises? Will "gun-free school zones" affect school-related shooting incidents? Does access to guns increase the likelihood of suicide?

As significant political pressure has been exerted on both sides, the arguments for and against gun control have only become stronger and more emotional. The issue of gun control is sure to remain in the forefront of debate as society examines its needs, rights and desires in the twenty-first century.

SUMMARY

Historically, the militia was considered to be the entire adult male populace. They were not simply allowed to keep arms, but were at times required to do so by law. A central controversy over the Second Amendment is whether people have a right to bear arms as individuals rather than only as part of a militia. A closely related controversy involves opposing interpretations of the Second Amendment as to whether the amendment guarantees the right of individuals to keep and bear arms or whether it guarantees the states freedom from federal government infringement on this right. Individual rights proponents claim that the framers of the Constitution intended to preserve the individual right above the right of the state. States' rights proponents claim that the Second Amendment was adopted with the primary purpose of preserving the state militia.

Court decisions over time reveal how the Court views Second Amendment guarantees. In *Presser v. Illinois* (1886), the Court refused to incorporate the Second Amendment into the Fourteenth Amendment. Therefore, the Second Amendment does *not* apply to state government. In *United States v. Miller* (1939), the court recognized a state right rather than an individual right to bear arms. In 1971, the courts ruled that there was no express right of an individual to keep and bear arms (*Stevens v. United States*). As a result of these decisions, the states' power to regulate firearms appears to be nearly absolute.

However, although federal interpretation of the Second Amendment gives authority over gun control to the states, Congress has been able to enact some federal gun control legislation by using its broad authority to regulate interstate commerce. The federal government has passed legislation regulating the sale of handguns, including the Brady Act. Passed in 1993, the Brady Act contained the interim provision of a mandatory five-day waiting period on all handgun purchases. This provision was phased out and was replaced in 1998 with the permanent provision of an instant, computerized criminal background check of all handgun purchasers. Some states still impose a waiting period on firearms purchases.

Despite all the controversy over gun control, where the courts stand is without question. Federal courts to date have held that the Constitution does not guarantee the right of the individual to keep and bear arms.

DISCUSSION QUESTIONS

1. What makes gun control such a volatile issue?
2. Should the government control the possession of guns?
3. Should the government restrict certain types of firearms?
4. Does the Brady Act serve a legitimate function?
5. Considering the history behind the drafting of the Second Amendment, can any original interpretations reasonably be used today? If so, how?
6. In Great Britain, police officers do not routinely carry firearms because, among other reasons, firearms are not considered the public threat they are elsewhere. Discuss whether you think this could ever occur in the United States.
7. Discuss whether gun control is crime control.
8. Is a "cooling off" period for gun permits reasonable?
9. Does regulating handguns but not rifles and shotguns make sense?
10. Rewrite the Second Amendment as though you were asked to address contemporary concerns.

INFOTRAC COLLEGE EDITION ASSIGNMENTS

- Use InfoTrac College Edition to help answer the Discussion Questions when applicable.
- Find and outline one article for and one against gun control.

INTERNET ASSIGNMENTS

- Find one recent Supreme Court case from the cases in this chapter on the Internet. Brief the case.
- Go to the ATF's Web site, www.atf.gov/firearms/statelaws/, and locate data on the statutory and constitutional provisions relating to the purchase, ownership and use of firearms for the states. Locate your state and answer the following questions:
  - Does your state have any exemptions to the NICS background check requirements?
  - Does your state have waiting period? If so, for handguns, long guns or both?
  - Is a license or permit to purchase required?
  - Is registration required?
  - Is a record of firearms sales sent to police?
  - Are certain firearms prohibited?
  - What are the details of your state's concealed/carry laws?
  - Does your state have a hunter protection law? A range protection law? What do these mean?
  - Does your state have a firearm industry lawsuit preemption?

- Locate several sites that pertain to the Ruby Ridge incident and be prepared to discuss the debate from both the side of the government and the side of those arguing against an overzealous government.

COMPANION WEB SITE

- Go to the Constitutional Law and the Criminal Justice System 3e Web site at http://cj.wadsworth.com/hessharr_constlaw3e for Case Studies and Study Guide exercises.

REFERENCES

"ATF Data Traces Retail Origins of Crime Guns." *Law Enforcement News*, May 2004, p. 5.

Bowling, Michael; Lauver, Gene; Hickman, Matthew J.; and Adams, Devon B. "Background Checks for Firearms Transfers, 2004." *Bureau of Justice Statistics Bulletin*, October 2005.

Boyter, Jennifer. "President Bush Signs Concealed Carry Legislation." *The Police Chief*, September 2004, p. 8.

"Brady Act Failing to Prevent Gun Purchases by Terror Suspects." *Criminal Justice Newsletter*, March 1, 2005, p. 4.

"Brady Act Had No Effect on Homicide or Suicide Rates, Report Says." *NCJA Justice Bulletin*, August 2000, pp. 1–3.

"California Launches Gun Tracing Program." *Juvenile Justice Digest*, September 16, 2006, pp. 3–4.

Center to Prevent Handgun Violence. www.handguncontrol.org.

Collins, John M. "Responding to Gun Possession Reports." *The Police Chief*, December 2005, p. 11.

"Constitution Protects Individuals' Right to Own Guns, Ashcroft Says." *Washington Post* as reported in the (Minneapolis/St. Paul) *Star Tribune*, May 24, 2001, p. A21.

Crime in the United States 2004. Washington, DC: Federal Bureau of Investigation. *Uniform Crime Reports*, 2004.

Donohue, John J., III. "The Final Bullet in the Body of the More Guns, Less Crime Hypothesis." *Criminology and Public Policy*, July 2003, pp. 397–410.

Doyle, Kelly, editor. *Is Gun Ownership a Right?* Farmington Hills, MI: Greenhaven Press, 2005.

Fact Sheet. John Hopkins University Center for Gun Policy and Research, http://www.jhsph.edu/gunpolicy/US_factsheet_2004.pdf Accessed April 25, 2006.

Ferrell, Craig E., Jr. "Law Enforcement Safety Act of 2004." *The Police Chief*, October 2004, pp. 14–20.

Froman, Sandy. *Women, Personal Protection, and Power Politics*. Presented at the 2006 meeting of the National Rifle Association http://www.nra.org/Article.aspx?id=5467 Accessed April 28, 2006.

Gallegos, Gilbert G., National President of the Fraternal Order of Police, quotation as relayed by Timothy M.

Richardson, Legislative Assistant, via e-mail, November 27, 2000. www.grandlodgefop.org/legislat.html.

Hann, R. A.; Bilukham O. O.; Crosby, A.; et al. "First Reports Evaluating the Effectiveness of Strategies for Preventing Violence: Firearms Laws. Findings from the Task Force on Community Preventive Services." *Morbidity and Mortality Weekly Report*, October 3, 2003.

Kovandzic, Tomislav V. and Marvell, Thomas B. "Right-to-Carry Concealed Handguns and violent Crime: Crime Control through Gun Decontrol? *Criminology and Public Policy*, July 2003, pp. 363–396.

Law Enforcement Officers Killed and Assaulted—2004. Washington, DC: Federal Bureau of Investigation, 2004.

Lott, John R., Jr. *The Bias against Guns.* Washington, DC: Regnery Publishing, Inc., 2003.

Ludwig, Jens "Better Gun Enforcement Less Crime." *Criminology & Public Policy*, November 2005, pp. 677–716.

Ludwig, Jens and Cook, Philip J. "Homicide and Suicide Rates Associated with Implementation of the Brady Handgun Violence Prevention Act." *Journal of the American Medical Association*, August 2000, pp. 585–591.

Polisar, Joseph M. "Reauthorization of the Assault Weapon Ban." *The Police Chief*, September 2004, p. 6.

Rand, M. Kristen. Statement before the Crime Subcommittee, House Judiciary Committee, Washington, DC, April 6, 2000, p. 70.

"Survey Finds State Gun Laws Sorely Lacking." *Law Enforcement News*, April 15, 2000, p. 1.

"Targeting Guns, Gangs Works, Says Gonzales." *Crime Control Digest*, July 1, 2005, p. 4.

"U.S. Brief Supports Broad Gun Rights." *Los Angeles Times* as reported in the (Minneapolis/St. Paul) *Star Tribune*, May 5, 2002, p. A3.

Walker, Adrian. "Taking Aim At Gunmakers," *Boston Globe*, March 9, 2006. p. B1.

Webster, D. W.; Vernick, J.S.; and Hepburn, L.M. "Relationship between Licensing, Registration, and Other Gun Sales Laws and the Source of Crime Guns." *Injury Prevention*, September 2001, pp. 184–189.

Wright, J. D. "Ten Essential Observations on Guns in America." *Social Research and Public Policy*, March/April 1995, pp. 63–68.

CASES CITED

Adams v. Williams, 407 U.S. 143 (1972).

Cases v. United States, 131 F.2d 916 (1942).

Farmer v. Higgins, 907 F.2d 1041 (11th Cir. 1990).

Florida v. J.L., 529 U.S. 266 (2000).

Gillespie v. City of Indianapolis, 528 U.S. 1116 (2000).

Pennsylvania v. D.M., 529 US 1126 (2000).

Presser v. Illinois, 116 U.S. 252 (1886).

Printz v. United States, 521 U.S. 898 (1997).

Quilici v. Village of Morton Grove, 695 F.2d 261 (7th Cir. 1982).

Small v. United States, No. 03-750 (2005).

Stevens v. United States, 440 F.2d 144 (1971).

United States v. Cruikshank, 92 U.S. 542 (1875).

United States v. Emerson, 46 F.Supp. 2d 598 (N.D. Texas, 1999).

United States v. Lopez, 514 U.S. 549 (1995).

United States v. Miller, 307 U.S. 174 (1939).

United States v. Warin, 530 F.2d 103 (1976).

Constitutional Amendments Influencing the Criminal Justice System

The preceding section examined amendments to the Constitution that guaranteed citizens' civil rights and civil liberties—basic freedoms promised to everyone. To ensure such freedoms the United States is based on laws that all are expected to obey and has a criminal justice system in place to deal with those who break the law. It also has a Bill of Rights to ensure that the government does not carry its policing powers too far.

This section examines the amendments affecting the criminal justice system, those who are employed in it, those who are protected by it as well as those who become involved with it. At the very core of restrictions on government infringing on citizens' freedom is the Fourth Amendment, which forbids unreasonable search and seizure. Chapter 8 provides an overview of this amendment as well as a discussion of how it and other amendments are enforced—through the exclusionary rule. Chapter 9 provides an in-depth discussion on conducting constitutional seizures, Chapter 10 an in-depth discussion of the restrictions placed on searches. Next, Chapter 11 explains the Fifth Amendment, including its protection for citizens against self-incrimination and their guarantee of due process of law. Chapter 12 discusses the Sixth Amendment and the guarantees of the right to counsel and to a fair trial. The section concludes with Chapter 13 and a discussion of the Eighth Amendment and how it restricts bail, fines and punishment.

CHAPTER 8

The Fourth Amendment: An Overview of Constitutional Searches and Seizures

THE RIGHT OF THE PEOPLE TO BE SECURE IN THEIR PERSONS, HOUSES, PAPERS, AND EFFECTS, AGAINST UNREASONABLE SEARCHES AND SEIZURES, SHALL NOT BE VIOLATED, AND NO WARRANTS SHALL ISSUE BUT UPON PROBABLE CAUSE, SUPPORTED BY OATH OR AFFIRMATION, AND PARTICULARLY DESCRIBING THE PLACE TO BE SEARCHED, AND THE PERSONS OR THINGS TO BE SEIZED.

—FOURTH AMENDMENT TO THE U.S. CONSTITUTION

Courtesy of J. Scott Harr

Facts will determine if a stop or a frisk has occurred, and the Fourth Amendment will then determine what the police are permitted to do.

- What the Fourth Amendment forbids and requires?
- Who is governed by the Fourth Amendment?
- What the reasonableness clause of the Fourth Amendment establishes?
- Whether individuals are constitutionally guaranteed absolute freedom from government intrusion?
- How probable cause relates to searches and arrests?
- What is required for a search or arrest warrant?
- If the Miranda warning must be given in a stop-and-frisk situation?
- What the law of stop and frisk deals with? The precedent case?
- What two consequences police may face if they make an unconstitutional search or seizure?
- What the exclusionary rule is and the precedent case?
- What primary purpose is served by the exclusionary rule?
- What case made the exclusionary rule applicable at the state level?
- What happens to evidence obtained in ways that "shock the conscience?"
- What exceptions to the exclusionary rule exist?
- What other consequences may result from government agency misconduct?

CAN YOU DEFINE?

articulable facts
bright-line approach
case-by-case method
continuum of contacts
conventional Fourth
  Amendment
  approach
exclusionary rule
frisk
fruit of the poisonous
  tree doctrine
furtive conduct

good faith
harmless error
inevitable discovery
  doctrine
litigious
magistrate
nightcap(ped) warrant
no-knock warrant
penumbra
probable cause
reasonable

reasonable expectation
  of privacy
reasonableness Fourth
  Amendment
  approach
reasonable suspicion
search
seizure
stop
Terry stop
totality of
  circumstances

Introduction

If the First Amendment is considered the cornerstone of American freedom, then the Fourth Amendment must be a building block with which freedom continues to develop. The Fourth Amendment is unique because it speaks not only to that desire but also to a need. A prominent theory of human behavior and motivation was set forth by famed psychologist Abraham H. Maslow (1908–1970). In Maslow's hierarchy of needs (Figure 8.1), the need for *security* comes right after the basic physical needs of food, clothing and shelter (Maslow, 1954).

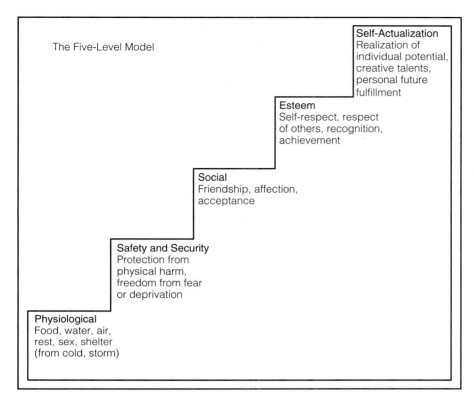

Figure 8.1 Maslow's Hierarchy of Needs

The essence of being an American to many means the right to be left alone by the government—to be "*secure* in their persons, houses, papers, and effects." Although most of us take it for granted, one of the greatest advantages of living in the United States is to be able to live unimpeded by government. A continuing argument in this country, and one the First Amendment permits to be pursued, is whether we, indeed, have "too much" government. Two hundred years after the drafting of the Constitution, governmental controls remain important to Americans.

Governmental controls ensure that citizens can drive to and from their destinations without the fear of being pulled over by an overly zealous police officer who simply does not like the color of their car—or skin. It means that citizens can enjoy the security of their homes without fearing an intrusion by the government seizing assets, property or records just because they are engaged in an unpopular line of work.

Of course, this security does not mean the government is barred from carrying out its responsibility. Limited governmental power is necessary for the laws of the country to be enforced and the government's business to be carried out. However, a balance is required for a democracy such as ours to exist—a balance between the government's powers and the people's freedom; that balance is what the law of search and seizure is all about. Because Americans take this freedom very seriously, U.S. law has developed to firmly regulate how and when government agents can impose on people.

These two key words—*search* and *seizure*—are fundamental to understanding the Fourth Amendment. A **search** is an examination of a person, place or vehicle

search • an examination of a person, place or vehicle for contraband or evidence of a crime

seizure • a taking by law enforcement or other government agent of contraband, evidence of a crime or even a person into custody

for contraband or evidence of a crime. A search, by its very nature, is an intrusion into someone's privacy and, thus, is strictly regulated by the Fourth Amendment. A **seizure** is a taking by law enforcement or other government agent of contraband, evidence of a crime or even a person into custody. It too is regulated by the Fourth Amendment.

■ The Fourth Amendment forbids unreasonable searches and seizures and requires that any search or arrest warrant be based on probable cause.

If a society cannot feel secure from unwarranted invasion by their own government, do any other rights or freedoms really matter? This chapter begins with a discussion of the importance of the Fourth Amendment to law enforcement and who is regulated by the Fourth Amendment. Then, it examines the two main clauses of the amendment, the reasonableness clause and the warrant clause, including the critical concept of probable cause. This discussion is followed by an explanation of warrants and why they are preferred. Next, the continuum of contacts from a simple encounter to an arrest is described. This explanation leads to a discussion of the first Fourth Amendment encounter on the continuum, the law of stop and frisk. The chapter concludes with a discussion of two important results of Fourth Amendment violations by the government: (1) evidence being excluded from court through the exclusionary rule and (2) the officer, the government agent and perhaps department and the agency facing civil liability.

The Importance of the Fourth Amendment to Law Enforcement

The Fourth Amendment is so important that three chapters in this text are devoted to it. It governs much of what police officers are legally allowed to do as they "serve and protect." In addition to its importance to the U.S. scheme of government, the Fourth Amendment provides students of the Constitution with ample opportunity to develop a working understanding of the country's legal system. The Fourth Amendment has continued to evolve constitutionally, substantively and procedurally through common and statutory law. It remains the pivotal area of debate in the field for law enforcement and in the courtroom for the prosecution and the defense, as well as in the classroom for students and legal scholars. Each phrase, each word, within this amendment continues to be reexamined and redefined in the true spirit of the Constitution, as constantly changing human interaction and behavior spawns ever unique circumstances that result in government's intrusion into people's lives.

The idea that citizens can enjoy privacy and freedom from government intrusion with regards to themselves, their possessions, their homes and their businesses is what citizens have come to *expect*, rather than what we consciously *desire*, as was the case more than 200 years ago. The U.S. Constitution has taken the American legal system, its government and those enjoying the freedom a long way in a comparatively short time.

This chapter examines the Fourth Amendment in its entirety and how it affects our lives. Not only the rights assured by the Fourth Amendment but also the consequences of government's violations of this law will be considered.

Before embarking on the substance of the Fourth Amendment, recall the explanation of *procedural law.* This chapter begins to examine those constitutional amendments that make up the body of procedural law, an entire body of law unto itself. It is the law used to enforce other laws and is also known as *criminal procedure.*

In a constitutional democracy, crime control considers both ends and means. The "ends" consists of finding the truth to obtain justice, that is, convicting the guilty *and* exonerating the innocent. The law of criminal procedure seeks this balance. "Criminal law's ultimate ends are dual and conflicting. It must be designed from inception to end, to acquit the innocent as readily at least, as to convict the guilty. This presents the inescapable dilemma of criminal procedure . . . that the easier it is made to prove guilt, the more difficult it becomes to establish innocence" (Hall, 1942, p. 725).

The Fourth Amendment's prohibition against unreasonable searches and seizures by the police is perhaps the most vital component of criminal procedure because of ample opportunities the U.S. Supreme Court has had to set forth when any government agent may and may not act, as well as when they have an expectation, or duty, to do so.

Who Is Regulated by the Fourth Amendment?

As the U.S. Constitution was originally drafted, the Fourth Amendment itself applied to only federal government, but now it is equally applied to state government by the Fourteenth Amendment, as established in *Wolf v. Colorado* (1949). Therefore, any government agent (whether federal, state, county or municipal) is regulated by the Fourth Amendment.

When most people consider search and seizure law, they think of its impact on such agencies as the FBI or local police. Again, any employee of the government at any jurisdictional level is influenced by the constitutional restrictions. This regulation includes all governmental agencies, including but not limited to the Secret Service, the Internal Revenue Service and the Food and Drug Administration. The Fourth Amendment also regulates state agencies, such as state revenue agencies, county sheriffs and local police, public schools and colleges and other regulatory bodies as well as local, county and municipal bodies of government.

■ If a person is an employee of any governmental agency or is an agent of the government in any capacity, that person is bound by the Fourth Amendment.

Private individuals or agencies are not regulated by the Fourth Amendment. When a rebellious teenager angrily informs his parents that they cannot come into his room without a warrant—this statement is inaccurate. Private security guards, such as store detectives, are similarly not controlled by the Fourth Amendment. Why? They are not government agents, and the Constitution was established to limit the power of government and its agents.

Among cases involving the issue of searches conducted by private individuals are the following:

■ *United States v. Parker* (1994) held that United Parcel Service employees could open without warrants packages and inspect their contents whenever a customer insured a package for more than $1,000.

■ *United States v. Claveland* (1994) held permissible a warrantless search by a private electric company employee acting on a tip that a customer was bypassing the electric meter.

- *United States v. Ross* (1982) held that an airline employee who inspected the defendant's luggage according to FAA regulations was acting in a governmental capacity and, thus, was governed by the Fourth Amendment.

Can a private party ever be considered a government agent? Sometimes, yes. An example for discussion would involve individuals who seize evidence of a crime from the home of another—maybe because they were invited into the home, or maybe because they actually broke into the residence. Could that evidence be used in court against the homeowner, although the person who actually seized it did so without a warrant and without permission of the homeowner?

The answer is yes, if the person was not acting as any sort of government agent. This does not, however, make the individual immune from liability for committing an unlawful act while obtaining the information.

- The Fourth Amendment does not apply to private parties.

Similarly, a private store detective could search someone without a warrant or without the other constitutional requirements the police need to comply with because the Constitution does not regulate private police.

In *United States v. Jacobsen* (1984), the Court held that even when a private person had opened a package and then resealed it, the government agent could expose to view that which had previously been observed by the private person without the exposure constituting an illegal search.

What if the private party had agreed to go in and get the item from the house, or the private security guard had agreed to search the person for the police? Then, arguably, this private person, although not employed by the government, has become an agent of the government, and the Fourth Amendment would then apply. Having looked at who is regulated by the Fourth Amendment, consider now the important clauses of this amendment.

The Clauses of the Fourth Amendment

The Fourth Amendment contains two clauses of importance to search and seizure issues:

- The reasonableness clause: "The right of the people to be secure in their persons, houses, papers, and effects, against unreasonable searches and seizures shall not be violated."
- The warrant clause: " . . . and no warrants shall issue but upon probable cause, supported by oath or affirmation, and particularly describing the place to be searched, and the persons or things to be seized."

conventional Fourth Amendment approach • viewing the reasonableness clause and the warrant clause as intertwined

reasonableness Fourth Amendment approach • the reasonableness clause and the warrant clause are interpreted as separate issues

Two Interpretations

These two clauses have been viewed differently by the Supreme Court. Until the 1960s, the Court used the **conventional Fourth Amendment approach,** viewing the two clauses as intertwined and firmly connected. This interpretation holds that all searches not conducted with both a warrant and probable cause are unreasonable and, therefore, unlawful.

Since the 1960s, however, the Court has broadened government's power by adopting what has been called the **reasonableness Fourth Amendment approach.** This interpretation sees the two clauses as separate, distinct and addressing two separate situations. In some instances, searches can be reasonable without either warrants or probable cause.

When a valid warrant has been issued and, thus, judicially determined probable cause, the Supreme Court has continued to find the requirements of the Fourth Amendment satisfied. A great number of cases have developed as the Court has sought to determine under what circumstances searches and seizures are valid without warrants or probable cause.

■ The reasonableness clause of the Fourth Amendment makes warrantless searches and seizures valid and constitutional when they are sensible.

Critical concepts to understanding the Fourth Amendment are reasonableness, reasonable expectation of privacy and probable cause. These terms are considered when deciding what the government, including the police, is permitted to do and when. The terms have also been the basis for many court decisions and remain a viable point of argument in criminal cases.

The Constitution was written in general terms to permit the societies it would continue serving to determine what they consider reasonable, rather than creating a cast-in-stone definition. Such foresight enables this body of law to change along with those it serves. Even the courts have struggled with definitions. They, too, desire to keep the door open for case-by-case interpretation. The guidelines provided through court opinions do not provide any more precise definitions of these terms. Nonetheless, an understanding of key terms such as *probable cause* and *reasonable* are often at the heart of the interpretation.

Reasonableness

How would you define *reasonable*? It is a challenge, but the cases that have sought to do so have come up with the same descriptors most of us would: **Reasonable** means sensible, rational and justifiable. It is one of those terms the framers of the Constitution used to require interpretation and application of a law intended to meet the needs of the people, rather than providing such rigidity that a commonsense application could not be made. Much debate, and much law, has occurred as a result of defining what is reasonable for the government to do. Case definitions for reasonable include:

reasonable • sensible, rational, justifiable

- "What is reasonable depends upon a variety of considerations and circumstances. It is an elastic term which is of uncertain value in a definition" (*Sussex Land & Live Stock Co. v. Midwest Refining Co.*, 1923).
- "Not extreme. Not arbitrary, capricious or confiscatory" (*Public Service Com. v. Havemeyer*, 1936).
- "That which is fair, proper, just, moderate, suitable under the circumstances, fit and appropriate to the end in view, having the faculty of reason, rational, governed by reason not immoderate or excessive, honest, equitable, tolerable" (*Cass v. State*, 1933).

bright-line approach • determining the reasonableness of an action according to a specific rule that applies to all cases

Two approaches have been used to determine reasonableness:

- **Bright-line approach**—Reasonableness is determined by a specific rule applying to all cases.
- **Case-by-case method**—Reasonableness is determined by considering the totality of circumstances in each individual case. This method is most commonly used in U.S. courts.

case-by-case method • determining the reasonableness of an action by considering the totality of circumstances in each case

A key consideration in determining whether a search or seizure is reasonable is the balance between individual rights and the needs of society, as stressed earlier. Another consideration is whether a person's **reasonable expectation of privacy** has been violated by the government.

■ The Constitution does not provide an absolute right to be free from government intrusion, only *unreasonable* interference.

Right to Privacy

The essence of the Constitution is to prevent government from being unnecessarily involved in our lives. Along with a right to be secure from other unreasonable government intrusion is a right to privacy, but this debate has not found answers as readily as those areas police more often find themselves involved with.

Although search and seizure law deals with people and their places and things, cases that address a right to privacy deal with peoples' even more personal relationships, including choices pertaining to sexual relationships, birth control, abortion and sexual preference. Even such personal matters, if determined to be illegal, would involve government.

Constitutional analysis and debate regarding the right to privacy has been emotional because of the intimate matters it addresses and the fact it is not specifically mentioned in the Constitution, but considered, at least by some, to be an implied right. How far government can and should intrude on such personal matters is the focus of this debate.

penumbra • a type of shadow in astronomy with the principle extending to the idea that certain constitutional rights are implied within other constitutional rights

In *Griswold v. Connecticut*, a 1965 case dealing with use of contraceptives, Justice William O. Douglass asserted such a right was within the **penumbra** (shadow) of other specified rights. Justice Brennan explained in *Eisenstadt v. Baird:* "If the right of privacy means anything, it is the right of the individual, married or single, to be free from unwarranted government intrusion into matters so fundamentally affecting a person as the decision whether to bear or beget a child." In the hotly contested *Roe v. Wade* (1973), the Court held, among other things, the right to privacy includes a right to abortion.

As is often the case, new law begs new questions. The inference of these cases is that morality becomes less of a government interest when individuals consent. Can so-called victimless crimes exist when both parties consent to any activity, such as sex between unmarried people, prostitution or homosexuality? What about drug use or sex with a minor? Or does government always have a legitimate interest, and, therefore, authority, to enforce social norms throughout society? These questions reflect the tension of values and beliefs that people look to the Constitution to help address.

In addition to the term reasonable, another key term in the Fourth Amendment is *probable cause*.

Probable Cause

probable cause • stronger than reasonable suspicion

Probable cause (to arrest) exists when the facts and circumstances within the officers' knowledge and of which they had reasonable trustworthy information are sufficient in themselves to warrant a man of reasonable caution in the belief that an offense has been or is being committed. (*Brinegar v. United States,* 1948)

United States v. Riemer, D. C. Ohio (1975) defined *probable cause* as having more evidence for than against or a set of probabilities grounded in the factual and practical considerations that govern the decisions of reasonable and prudent persons and is more than mere suspicion but less than the quantum of evidence required for conviction.

Smith v. United States (1949) defined probable cause as "The sum total of layers of information and the synthesis of what the police have heard, what they know, and what they observe as trained officers. We [the Court] weigh not individual layers but the laminated total." This "laminated total," more often referred to as the **totality of circumstances,** is the principle upon which a number of legal assessments are made, including probable cause. Totality of circumstances is not a mathematical formula for achieving a certain number of factors; rather, it is looking at what does exist to assess whether the sum total would lead a reasonable person to believe what the officers concluded. The more factors present, the more likely a finding of probable cause will be upheld.

totality of circumstances • the principle upon which a number of legal assessments are made, including probable cause

Probable cause is stronger than reasonable suspicion and is a concept crucial to understanding when police may or may not act in the course and scope of their duties. It can legally justify searches and arrests with or, in some cases, without warrants and requires the determining question of: "Would a reasonable person believe that a crime was committed and that the individual committed the offense, or that the contraband or evidence is where it is believed to be?"

The terms *reasonable person* and *believe* are challenging to precisely define, especially when time is of the essence to an officer in the field. Probable cause exists when a reasonable person, in the same or similar situation, would believe that a crime probably has been committed and that the person committing the crime or evidence of it will be found in a particular location.

■ Probable cause determines when officers may execute lawful searches and arrests with or, in some cases, without a warrant. *Probable cause to search* means officers reasonably believe that evidence, contraband or other items sought are where they believe them to be. *Probable cause to arrest* means officers reasonably believe that a crime has been committed by the person whom they seek to arrest.

Probable cause must be established *before* a lawful search or arrest can be made. Note that the terms used here are *arrest* and *search,* not *stop* and *frisk.* Facts and evidence obtained after a search or arrest cannot be used to establish probable cause. They can be used, however, to strengthen the case if probable cause was established before the arrest, making the arrest legal. If probable cause is not present, police cannot act; if they do, consequences will ensue. Without probable cause, seized evidence may be inadmissible in court, arrests determined illegal and officers and others held liable for such illegality, as discussed later in the chapter. Probable cause and its establishment are key elements in motions to suppress in both warrant and warrantless situations.

Sources of Probable Cause

The two basic source categories of probable cause are observational and informational.

Observational probable cause is derived from a government agent's personal experiences—what officers perceive through their own senses of sight, hearing, smell, touch and taste. Officers' experience, training and expertise may lend additional credibility in justifying probable cause, as such things sharpen one's situational awareness and enhance the senses, thereby enabling officers to assess things an ordinary person might be unable to.

furtive conduct •
questionable, suspicious or secretive behavior

The physical actions of an individual may draw the attention of police and lead to probable cause. Observing **furtive conduct,** that is, questionable, suspicious or secretive behavior, will understandably raise an officer's suspicion, and although a person's level of nervousness may not be enough by itself, it can play a part in the totality of the circumstances (*United States v. McCarty,* 1988; *United States v. Ingrao,* 1990).

Fleeing from the police will certainly raise the suspicion of law enforcement and contribute heavily in establishing probable cause. In *Illinois v. Wardlow* (2000) a stop was held lawful when the suspect was in a high-crime area and fled upon seeing the police. The Court cited factors to be considered when establishing probable cause to include whether the area is a high-crime area; nervous, evasive behavior by the suspect; and unprovoked flight upon seeing the police. Such factors viewed as a whole may establish probable cause, whereas any one of them standing alone may not. In *United States v. Arvizu* (2002), the Supreme Court reaffirmed that reasonable suspicion (fleeing from the law) may be part of the totality of the circumstances.

Physical evidence may establish probable cause. In *State v. Heald* (1973), the court held that evidence at a burglary scene, including a distinctive tire tread left in the snow, provided sufficient probable cause to arrest when the police approached the suspect vehicle and the driver drove away.

Admissions made to a police officer, verbally or through actions, may provide sufficient observational probable cause or lead to a finding of probable cause under the totality of the circumstances analysis. In *Rawlings v. Kentucky* (1980), a suspect admitted that the contents of her purse (drugs) belonged to her, and the court found this admission to be sufficient probable cause for the police to arrest her. False or implausible answers may also contribute to probable cause, such as occurred in *United States v. Anderson* (1987), when officers stopped a car on a road known to be used by people transporting drugs and found a large amount of cash wrapped in small bundles, secured with rubber bands. The suspects said they had just won the money in Atlantic City, but the officers did not believe the answers fit their questions.

Presence at a crime scene or in a high crime area may also contribute to probable cause, although alone usually is not sufficient. However, if the suspect is present at a very recent crime, that presence may be sufficient, as was the case in *State v. Mimmovich* (1971), where officers found the suspects of a burglary in suspiciously close proximity to the burglarized dwelling immediately after it occurred. If suspects were crawling out a window during a suspected burglary, that action could be sufficient.

Association with other known criminals is another factor that may contribute to the finding of probable cause. In *United States v. Di Re* (1948), the Court said that "one who accompanies a criminal to a crime rendezvous cannot be assumed to be a bystander," and that one's presence with others engaged in criminal activity can contribute to a finding of probable cause. However, the fact that someone has been involved in *past criminal activity* (*Beck v. Ohio,* 1964) or *fails to protest his or her arrest* is insufficient in itself to infer probable cause to support an arrest.

Often, officers do not personally witness criminal activity and, consequently, must rely on information provided by others. In fact, seldom do the police actually see the crimes being committed. Usually, other sources help establish *informational probable cause* and include official sources such as roll call, dispatch, police bulletins and wanted notices or unofficial sources such as witnesses, victims and informants. A series of Supreme Court decisions set forth the legal requirements for establishing probable cause when working with informants.

In *Draper v. United States* (1959), a narcotics officer received information from a reliable informant that heroin was being transported on a train by a person the informant described in great detail, including what he would be wearing, even the fact he "walked real fast." The officers set up surveillance and arrested a man matching the description. Heroin and a syringe were found in a search incident to the arrest. The Supreme Court at that time held that information from a reliable informant, corroborated by the police, upheld a determination of probable cause.

A more stringent set of requirements for using informants in establishing probable cause was later set forth in *Aguilar v. Texas* (1964), when the court devised a two-pronged test. The first prong tested the informant's *credibility*. Is the person reliable? Is the informant's identity known? Is the informant a law-abiding citizen or a criminal? The second prong tested the informant's *basis of knowledge and reliability of the information* provided. Is the information accurate? Did the informant personally witness the information given? If not, did the information come from another source? Is the information still believable? What is this informant's track record?

In *Spinelli v. United States* (1969), the Court held that the "totality of the circumstances" was to be used and, in this case, held that the FBI's affidavit for a warrant was insufficient to establish probable cause because not enough information was available to adequately assess the informant's reliability, and not enough other supportive information was available to assess the existence of probable cause. Returning to the words of the *Brinegar* opinion, for probable cause to exist, more than bare suspicion is necessary; a belief must also exist.

This two-pronged approach was abandoned in 1983 in *Illinois v. Gates*, which refined the definition of what constitutes probable cause and the "totality of the circumstances" to be considered. In this case, a tip from an anonymous informant led to police obtaining and executing a search warrant for drugs in the defendant's home. Justice Rehnquist held that because "the most basic function of any government is to provide for the security of the individual and of his property," the spirit of the law was better served by determination of the existence of probable cause by consideration of the totality of the circumstances in deciding whether a "reasonable and prudent person" would believe that, in this case, contraband was located in a particular location, thus, indicating criminal activity. Justice Rehnquist noted that "probable cause is a fluid concept—turning on the assessment of probabilities in a particular factual context—not readily, or even usefully reduced to a neat set of legal rules." This "totality of circumstances" test made establishment of probable cause by use of informants easier for police.

In *United States v. Sokolow* (1989), the Court justified a warrantless investigative stop as reasonable under the Fourth Amendment because, given the totality of the circumstances present, sufficient reasonable suspicion existed. Although *Sokolow* dealt with another issue, that of "drug courier profiles," this case demonstrates that the *totality of circumstances* will be relied on in determining the constitutional justification for intrusion by the police.

The preceding cases help explain the common law development of probable cause and show that the more factual information an officer can articulate, the greater the likelihood the existence of probable cause will be upheld in court. In addition, probable cause is the key determination of whether a judge will grant officers a warrant to search or arrest.

Search and Arrest Warrants

magistrate • a judge

Government agents who have probable cause to believe evidence of a crime is located at a specific place or that an individual is involved in a crime must go before a neutral and detached **magistrate** (judge) and swear under oath who or what they are looking for and where they think it can be found.

■ All warrants are to be based on probable cause.

In determining whether probable cause for the warrant exists, the reviewing judge must consider the totality of the circumstances. In other words, all the factors submitted are viewed as a whole in considering whether a reasonable person would believe what the officers claim. The warrant must include the reasons for requesting it, the names of the officers who applied for it, names of others who have information to contribute, what or who specifically is being sought and the signature of the judge issuing it.

As any law enforcement officer will attest, obtaining a warrant is not just a matter of "walking up and getting one." Rather, the officer has the responsibility to provide sufficient data to the judge that the facts provide the necessary probable cause. Because the judge determines whether probable cause exists, the officer must argue the probable cause aspect of the case early on. Not every judge will sign a warrant. The officer may be directed to come back with additional information or be told that a warrant will not be issued on the facts presented.

The fact that an *independent judge* determines the existence of probable cause removes this discretionary decision from the officer involved with the case. Court rulings have delineated this independence as one requirement for judges issuing warrants: "An issuing magistrate must meet two tests. He must be neutral and detached, and he must be capable of determining whether probable cause exists for the requested arrest or search" (*Shadwick v. City of Tampa*, 1972). A valid warrant not only shifts the granting of suppression of evidence to the defendant but also provides a shield against officer liability.

With pagers, fax machines and cellular phones, coordination among police, prosecutors and judges makes obtaining warrants easier than in the past. Many jurisdictions authorize "telephonic warrants," which occur when a judge grants the warrant over the phone.

Special Conditions

Sometimes officers ask for special conditions to be attached to a warrant, such as making an unannounced entrance or carrying out a search at night.

If officers want to make an unannounced entrance because they are afraid evidence might be destroyed or officer safety requires it, they can request a

no-knock warrant. The search warrants for drug busts using bulldozers to crash through the walls of suspected crack houses would have such a provision.

In other cases, the illicit activity occurs primarily at night—illegal gambling, for example. In such cases, the officers can ask the judge to include a provision that allows them to execute the warrant at night—a **nightcap(ped) warrant.**

no-knock warrant • issued when officers want to make an unannounced entrance because they are afraid evidence might be destroyed or officer safety requires it

Executing the Search Warrant

Once signed by a judge, the warrant becomes an order for the police to carry out the search or arrest. Unless special conditions have been included in the warrant, government agents must carry out the warrant during daylight hours and must also identify themselves as officers and state their purpose. The officers may use reasonable force to execute the warrant if they are denied entrance or if no one is home. Police officers also may refuse to allow people to enter their residence while the police obtain a search warrant. In *Illinois v. McArthur* (2001), the Court held that although preventing a suspect from entering their own home constituted a seizure of that person, if the warrant was being obtained as rapidly as possible, such police action was reasonable. The Court explained that exigent circumstances existed and the seizure of the suspect was brief and as unintrusive as possible.

nightcap(ped) warrant • issued when officers wish to execute a warrant at night because that is when the suspected illicit activity is primarily occurring

Having discussed how the Fourth Amendment ensures individual freedom by restricting government's power to intrude, consider next when the government is permitted to search and seize and the broad range of contacts that exist.

The Continuum of Contacts

To understand when government can exercise its immense power, begin by analyzing the variety of contacts people and government may have. These contacts can be viewed as a **continuum of contacts,** as shown in Figure 8.2. The continuum represents the almost limitless variations of contacts between the

continuum of contacts • the almost limitless variations of contacts between the public and the police illustrating how justification for police action increases as their reasons for thinking criminal activity is afoot build

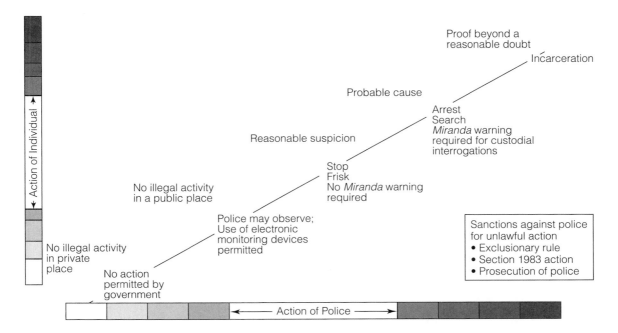

Figure 8.2 The Continuum of Contacts between Individuals and the Police

public and the police and illustrates how justification for police action increases as their reasons build for thinking criminal activity is afoot.

At one end of the continuum, contact consists of nothing more than an individual and an officer crossing paths and exchanging "hello's." Here, the police are unjustified taking any action. At the other extreme, an individual's conduct leads to sufficient probable cause and justifies police in arresting the person, by force if necessary.

Like any continuum, an infinite number of points exist between the two extremes—a middle ground involving the many other daily contacts between the citizenry and the government, where the interactions are not so clearly defined. This realm includes situations when the police or other government agencies are considering, or actually conducting, an investigation, or when an individual or business or other organization is merely suspected of illicit activity. Figure 8.3 illustrates the degree of intrusion on individual liberty and whether the Fourth Amendment is implicated.

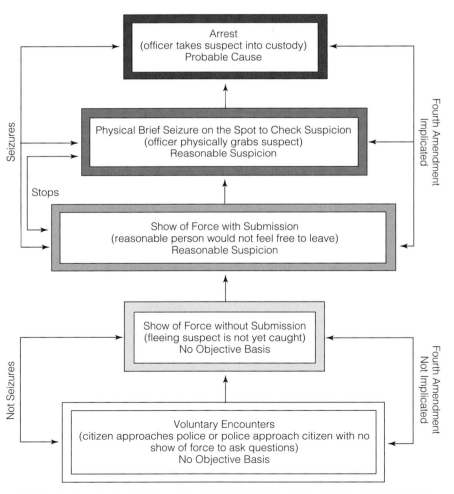

NOTE: Shading shows degree of intrusion and deprivation, from highest degree (darkest) to lowest degree (lightest).
Box size shows number of persons affected, from highest number (largest box) to lowest number(smallest box).

Figure 8.3 Seizures and the Fourth Amendment

Although the intent of the Constitution is to prevent the government from intruding on people's lives when they have done nothing wrong, this freedom, as with all constitutional rights, is not absolute. When police have lawful reason to act, they are expected to do so, and they have the right to do so. The U.S. Supreme Court has clearly stated that police have a responsibility, in fact a duty, to act to prevent crimes and apprehend criminals and has shown continued support for law enforcement. When police are suspicious, they would be foolish to turn their backs until they can acquire more information and then return to try to find the person—the suspect would be long gone.

The police officer's job is to decide, often in a split second, where a particular interaction with a suspect falls along the continuum. The system demands that police make a knowledgeable good-faith decision in accordance with the Constitution. The Supreme Court has continued to recognize the difficult job police have and that, given a proper understanding of law, they often are able to make good decisions under challenging circumstances. The Constitution continues to give law enforcement the tools they need to carry out their duties in an almost limitless number of situations.

As contact between an individual and an officer proceeds upward along the continuum, police acquire increasing justification to seize and search the person, taking away their most valued right—freedom. Chapter 9 addresses this area further, but when probable cause exits, with or without a warrant, the police will be justified in arresting the person. When a person is under lawful arrest, they may be searched and questioned; however, a custodial interrogation requires they be advised of their *Miranda* rights.

As the continuum also shows, searches and seizures cannot be neatly separate. At any point on the continuum of contacts, a situation may escalate to the next level of contact and, thus, change how the police may or may not be permitted to act. For example, the police may have no authority to act when driving by someone who appears to merely be walking along a public sidewalk, but if the officer sees something in the rearview mirror that causes him or her to become suspicious, the situation could justify a stop and possibly a frisk. Depending on what results from these interactions, if probable cause develops, the stop could escalate to the level of an arrest and then a search incident to that arrest, and it could all happen in a matter of moments.

The law of search and seizure defines what authority government has when interacting with the public and how agents can follow up on their suspicions. This authority begins with an examination of the law of stop and frisk. Chapters 9 and 10 will consider these and other forms of seizures and searches.

The Law of Stop and Frisk

The law of stop and frisk is the first point on the continuum of contacts where police have constitutional authority to interfere with a person's freedom. Stop-and-frisk law may be more easily understood by examining its purpose: to balance the rights of an individual and the government's need for tools to carry out its job of protecting society from lawbreakers. Police officers should neither be expected to ignore their reasonable suspicions nor be denied the right to ensure their own safety by checking for weapons. The law of stop and frisk balances the rights of the people and the individual during that "in-between time," when probable cause has not yet developed but officers should be expected to respond, at least in a limited way. The understanding that *any* intrusion on a person's freedom involves Fourth Amendment protections, including stops and frisks, is crucial.

Basic Definitions

The law of stop and frisk gives law enforcement the authority to act in the gray area of the continuum, between the point of no unlawful activity whatsoever and no authority for officers to act and the point of probable cause, when they may arrest. This area of law deals not with reasonable belief, but reasonable *suspicion*. If the officers do not have enough probable cause to arrest, but suspect a person is engaged in illegal activity, what is their recourse?

stop • a brief detention of a person, short of an arrest, based on specific and articulable facts for the purpose of investigating suspicious activity

- A **stop** is a brief detention of a person based on specific and articulable facts for the purpose of investigating suspicious activity. No *Miranda* warning is required.

articulable facts • actions described in clear, distinct statements

Articulable facts are descriptions or actions described in clear, distinct statements. Although the suspect is not free to go just then, without the investigation producing anything more, he or she will be free to go shortly. A stop differs from an arrest, in which the person is not free to go. The Court has held, because this detention is not an arrest (it is a *stop*), no *Miranda* warning need be given. For this reason, a driver stopped by the police for a traffic violation need not be advised of his or her *Miranda* rights—although the driver is not free to go for a short time, he or she will be, so it is not an arrest.

frisk • a reasonable, limited pat down search for weapons for the protection of a government agent and others

- A **frisk** is a limited pat down search for weapons for the protection of the government agent and others. It is not automatically permitted with a stop, but only when the agent suspects the person is armed and dangerous.

Although the words *stop* and *frisk* do not appear in the Fourth Amendment, the Court has found they are tantamount to a search and seizure of the person, with the only differences being the standard required by the police to act, what they may then do and the duration. The constitutional requirement of *reasonableness* is required before one is stopped or frisked, just as it is before one is arrested and searched.

- The law of stop and frisk deals with that time frame during which officers follow up on their suspicions but before the time that the requisite probable cause is established to justify an arrest (*Terry v. Ohio,* 1968).

Law enforcement officers talk about developing a "sixth sense"—an ability to know that something is not right. What they are really talking about are observational skills officers develop. One deputy police chief describes it as "soft vision"—surveying all that is present while on patrol, paying specific attention to those events the officer is trained to note. Tire tracks in fresh snow, furtive conduct by a pedestrian, a discarded parcel, a door ajar, the attendant at an all-night convenience store not visible—to the average citizen such circumstances mean nothing and probably would not even be noticed. To the trained eye of the law enforcement professional, however, they mean an opportunity to delve further into what may be criminal activity. Just what can a government agent do in response to such suspicions? The law of stop and frisk permits officers to act on their suspicions rather than to turn away, awaiting that infrequent, obvious crime to be committed before their eyes.

Terry v. Ohio

The landmark case for stop-and-frisk law is *Terry v. Ohio* (1968), which provides a classic example of how a stop-and-frisk situation may arise and how the law deals with it. In this case, the Court addressed the common law enforcement practice of stopping suspects to ask them questions to assess whether they were involved in criminal activity.

■ The *Terry* decision established that, in what is termed a **Terry stop,** an officer with articulable **reasonable suspicion** may conduct a brief investigatory stop, including a pat down for weapons if the officer has reason to suspect the person is armed and dangerous.

Terry stop • an officer with articulable reasonable suspicion may conduct a brief investigatory stop, including a pat down for weapons if the officer has reason to suspect the person is armed and dangerous

reasonable suspicion • an experienced police officer's hunch or intuition

Detective Martin McFadden had been a police officer with the Cleveland Police Department for 39 years, 35 as a detective. To untrained eyes, the men Detective McFadden saw outside the jewelry store that day were merely standing there talking, but McFadden sensed more. On the basis of his experience, he suspected they were casing the store, planning to rob it and possibly were armed. He watched as the two men walked back and forth, looking into the store window, walking to the corner, and then returning to talk to each other. Another man joined them, then went inside the store, returned and the routine continued.

When the three men were together outside the store, McFadden approached them, identified himself as a police officer, asked their names and grabbed one of the men, placing him between himself and the other two. He quickly patted down the outer clothing of that man, later identified as John Terry, and felt what could be a gun in Terry's pocket, but he could not remove it. He ordered the three into the store at gunpoint, removed Terry's coat and took a .38-caliber revolver from the pocket. When he patted down the other men, he found a revolver in the coat of one. Both men were charged with carrying concealed weapons.

The defense lawyers argued the guns had been seized illegally, so could not be used as evidence. The Ohio trial judge found both suspects guilty, and Terry and the other man appealed their conviction to the U.S. Supreme Court. Before this case reached the Supreme Court, the other man died, so the decision refers to only defendant Terry.

The legal issue before the Court was simply phrased: "whether it is always unreasonable for a policeman to seize a person and subject him to a limited search for weapons unless there is probable cause for an arrest." The U.S. Supreme Court upheld the Ohio court verdict, ruling Detective McFadden had acted reasonably because his experience and training supported his suspicion that the three men were planning a robbery; the robbery would probably involve weapons; and nothing occurred to make him think differently. He had to act quickly when he saw the three men gather at the store. In their opinion, the Court stated:

> Each case of this sort will, of course, have to be decided on its own facts. We merely hold today that where a police officer observed unusual conduct which leads him reasonably to conclude in light of his experience that criminal activity may be afoot and that the persons with whom he is dealing may be armed and presently dangerous, where in the course of investigating this behavior he identifies himself as a policeman and makes reasonable inquiries, and where nothing in the initial stages of the encounter serves to dispel his reasonable fear for his own or others' safety, he is entitled for the protection of himself

and others in the area to conduct a carefully limited search of the outer cloth-ing of such persons in an attempt to discover weapons which might be used to assault him.

Therefore, such a search is reasonable under the Fourth Amendment, and any weapons seized may properly be introduced in evidence against the person from whom they were seized. Guidelines established by *Terry v. Ohio* determining whether a stop or frisk is valid include the following:

- Suspicious circumstances, that is, conduct that leads an experienced officer to believe that a crime is about to be committed and that the person about to commit the crime may be armed and dangerous.
- While investigating the behavior, officers identify themselves as police officers and make reasonable inquiries, for example, "What is your name?"
- If officers are still suspicious and suspect the person may be armed and dangerous, they may conduct a limited search of the person's outer clothing to protect themselves and others in the area.

Consider next what are likely consequences of ignoring the constraints on searches and seizures imposed by the Fourth Amendment.

Consequences of Fourth Amendment Violations

■ An unlawful search or seizure can have two serious consequences: (1) the evidence may be excluded from court and (2) internal sanctions as well as civil and criminal liability may be incurred.

The Exclusionary Rule

exclusionary rule • judge-made case law promulgated by the Supreme Court to prevent police or government misconduct

When police violate a person's constitutional rights by conducting an unlawful stop and frisk, or search and seizure, several consequences may occur. The **exclu-sionary rule** may prevent evidence seized in violation of a person's constitutional rights from being admitted into court; an officer who has violated someone's rights may be sued, together with his or her agency, pursuant to Section 1983 of the United States Code; and an officer could be prosecuted criminally under some cir-cumstances as well. These possible results are discussed later in this text.

■ The exclusionary rule is judge-made case law promulgated by the Supreme Court to prevent law enforcement misconduct. It prohibits evidence obtained in violation of a person's constitutional rights from being admissible in court (*Weeks v. United States*, 1914).

As noted in *United States v. Leon* (1984):

> The Fourth Amendment contains no provision expressly precluding the use of evidence obtained in violation of its commands. . . . This rule thus operates as a judicially created remedy designed to safeguard Fourth Amendment rights generally through its deterrent effect, rather than a personal constitutional right of the person aggrieved.

■ The primary purpose underlying the exclusionary rule is to deter government misconduct.

The exclusionary rule is by far the most frequently used means to address con-stitutional infractions by the government in criminal cases. It is included in this chapter because of its proximity to and absolute effect on searches and seizures found to be unconstitutional because of police conduct.

The exclusionary rule also helps preserve judicial integrity by preventing judicial agreement in denying a person's Fourth Amendment rights, deters police misconduct by making improperly obtained evidence inadmissible in court and protects citizens' constitutional "right to privacy." However, as Wilson (n.d., p. 1) asserts:

> The exclusionary rule is among the most controversial and the most passionately debated rules of law governing our criminal justice system. It is not hard to understand why this is so. The exclusionary rule is the primary means by which the Constitution's prohibition of unreasonable searches and seizures is currently enforced; thus it is seen by some as the primary protection of personal privacy and security against police arbitrariness and brutality. It is also the basis for judges' decisions to exclude reliable incriminating evidence from the trials of persons accused of crime, and is thus considered by others to be little more than a misguided loophole through which criminals are allowed to escape justice.

The exclusionary rule goes back as far as 1886, when the Supreme Court held in *Boyd v. United States* that forced disclosure of papers that evidenced a crime could not be admissible in court:

> The practice had obtained in the colonies of issuing writs of assistance to the revenue officers, empowering them, in their discretion, to search suspected places for smuggled goods, which James Otis pronounced "the worst instrument of arbitrary power, the most destructive of English liberty and the fundamental principles of law, that ever was found in an English law book"; since they placed "the liberty of every man in the hands of every petty officer."

Numerous theories suggest ways the law might respond to unlawful searches and seizures by the police other than preventing evidence, sometimes the only evidence in a case, from getting to a jury. However, the Court has continued to hold that illegally obtained evidence be excluded as the primary means of upholding an individual's constitutional rights.

The exclusionary rule reflects an insistence of American law that the ends do not justify the means. If they did, any means of eliciting evidence would be permissible, including torture. Besides the inherent fact that forced confessions are unreliable, torture is not something the spirit of America condones. However, with America being pushed to its limits with respect to terrorism, new debate over means of obtaining information has arisen, as was the case regarding the prisoner treatment in Abu Ghraib Prison during the Iraq War.

The Supreme Court has stood firm, holding that, especially with regard to domestic law enforcement, unreasonable search and seizure will not be tolerated, even when evidence that would otherwise convict the guilty is not permitted. Some question whether another way can be found to discourage police misconduct without punishing the public.

del Carmen (2004, p. 105) suggests alternatives that have been considered, including an independent review board in the executive branch, a civil tort action against the government, a hearing separate from the main criminal trial but before the same judge or jury, adoption of an expanded good faith exception and adoption of the British system (which admits the evidence but sanctions the officer). Unquestionably a *cost/benefit analysis* is at play, but as Chief Justice Warren Burger stated in *United States v. Calandra,* "The rule is a judicially created remedy designed to safeguard Fourth Amendment Rights generally through its deterrent effect." Although opponents are many, those who support the exclusionary rule believe the risk far outweighs compromising constitutional ideals. *Weeks v. United States* (1914) and *Mapp v. Ohio* (1961) firmly established the exclusionary rule in criminal procedure.

Weeks v. United States   In *Weeks v. United States,* Weeks was charged with using the mail for illegal gambling purposes after officers searched his home on two different occasions without a warrant. The issue was simply whether illegally obtained evidence is admissible in court, to which the Supreme Court held it was not, stating that the right to be free from unreasonable searches and seizures under the Fourth Amendment applies:

> . . . to all invasions on the part of the government and its employees of the sanctity of a man's home and the privacies of life. It is not the breaking of his doors and the rummaging of his drawers that constitutes the essence of the offense; but it is the invasion of his indefeasible right to personal security, personal liberty and private property.

The *Weeks* Court specifically excluded illegally obtained evidence from use in federal prosecutions. *Mapp v. Ohio* (1961) extended the doctrine, through incorporation, to state proceedings.

Mapp v. Ohio   When the Fourteenth Amendment was passed, forbidding states to "deprive any person of life, liberty, or property, without due process of law," the question arose as to whether the exclusionary rule should be applied at the state level. *Wolf v. Colorado* (1949) held that the exclusionary rule was not then applicable at the state level. This precedent was followed for more than a decade. Some evidence was excluded for other reasons, however. For example, *Elkins v. United States* (1960) disallowed the admission of evidence illegally obtained by state officials into federal trials (the silver platter doctrine). In 1961, the *Wolf* precedent was reversed in *Mapp v. Ohio.*

■   *Mapp v. Ohio* made the exclusionary rule applicable at the state level.

In *Mapp v. Ohio,* the defendant refused to allow officers without a warrant into her home. The officers had information that a suspect was hiding in her basement and returned three hours later with reinforcements. When Mapp did not respond, officers broke in and searched the home, finding obscene materials. The Supreme Court, overruling *Wolf,* held that "all evidence obtained by searches and seizures in violation of the Constitution are by the same authority inadmissible in a state court." Reversing the trial court, the Supreme Court stated:

> Since the Fourth Amendment's right of privacy has been declared enforceable against the States through the Due Process Clause of the Fourteenth Amendment, it is enforceable against them by the same sanction of exclusion as is used against the Federal government. Were it otherwise, then just as without the *Weeks* rule the assurance against unreasonable searches and seizures would be "a form of words," valueless and undeserving of mention in a perpetual charter of inestimable human liberties, so too, without that rule the freedom from state invasions of privacy would be ephemeral.

A Further Exclusion   In *Rochin v. California* (1952), the Court held that searches that "shock the conscience" are a violation of due process, and any evidence so obtained will, therefore, be inadmissible. In *Rochin*, the police took the suspect to the hospital and had his stomach pumped after observing him swallow pills. Morphine capsules were recovered in this search, but in invoking the exclusionary rule, the Court stated:

> . . . the proceedings by which this conviction was obtained do more than offend some fastidious squeamishness or private sentimentalism about combating crime too energetically. This is conduct that shocks the conscience. Illegally breaking into the privacy of the petitioner, the struggle to open his mouth and remove what was there, the forcible extraction of his stomach's contents—this course of proceeding by agents of the government to obtain evidence is bound to offend even hardened sensibilities. They are methods too close to the rack and screw to permit constitutional differentiation.

■ Evidence obtained in ways that *shock the conscience* will not be admissible in a court of law.

The exclusionary rule may affect specific illegally obtained evidence, as well as any other evidence obtained as a result of the original illegally obtained evidence. Such evidence is referred to as fruit of the poisonous tree.

Fruit of the Poisonous Tree   *Silverthorne Lumber Co. v. United States* (1920) extended the exclusionary rule. In this case, a U.S. marshal unlawfully entered and searched the Silverthorne Lumber Company's offices and illegally took books and documents. When the company demanded their return, the government did so, but not before making copies of the documents. These copies were later impounded by the district court and became the basis for a grand jury indictment. A subpoena was then served on the company to produce the originals. When the company refused, it was convicted of contempt of court. The Supreme Court, however, reversed the conviction saying: "The essence of a provision forbidding the acquisition of evidence in a certain way is that not merely evidence so acquired shall not be used before the Court, but that it shall not be used at all." In other words, once the primary source (the "tree") is proved to have been obtained unlawfully, any secondary evidence derived from it (the "fruit") is also inadmissible.

The **fruit of the poisonous tree doctrine** states that evidence obtained as a result of an earlier illegality must be excluded from trial. This extension of the exclusionary rule is based on the same rationale as the exclusionary rule itself, that is, to deter illegal police activity and to preserve the integrity of the court. The Supreme Court has, however, permitted such evidence to be used in some proceedings.

fruit of the poisonous tree doctrine • evidence obtained as a result of an earlier illegality (a constitutionally invalid search or activity) must be excluded from trial

In *United States v. Calandra* (1974), the Court ruled that "fruits of illegally seized evidence" could be used as a basis for questions to a witness before a grand jury. In addition, some lower courts have allowed such evidence to be used in sentencing and in probation or parole revocation hearings.

In *Wong Sun v. United States* (1963), the Court held that statements obtained even indirectly as a result of an illegal arrest or search are not admissible in court because they are "tainted fruit of the poisonous tree." In *Wong Sun*, however, the Court also stated that because he voluntarily returned several days after providing what was deemed an inadmissible statement, the subsequent statement had become so *attenuated as to dissipate the taint*. However, a meaningful break in the events must occur, so in *Taylor v. Alabama* (1982), the Court held that even when a suspect was read his *Miranda* rights several times after an unlawful arrest before he confessed, the admission was not admissible.

Is the Court Anti–Law Enforcement?

Any assumption about the exclusionary rule that implies the Supreme Court does not support law enforcement is simply not the case. Most criminal justice practitioners would agree with Michael J. Bulzomi (2005, p. 26), who contends:

> American society has changed dramatically since these early decisions of the Supreme Court. However, despite these dramatic changes, a common thread tying the past with the present has been the importance of personal privacy within the Fourth Amendment. The Supreme Court's opinions indicate a sensitivity on its part to the difficult nature of police work and the great risks routinely confronting law enforcement.

The majority of law enforcement officers do not see rules that support the Constitution they have sworn to uphold as an impediment whatsoever; in fact, they would acknowledge it supports their overall mission by assuring the public that the ends do not justify the means.

Further, as Skogan and Meares (2004, p. 66) point out: "Police compliance with the law is one of the most important aspects of a democratic society. Americans expect the police to enforce laws to promote safety and to reduce crime, victimization, and fear, but no one believes that the police should have unlimited power to do so. We expect police to enforce laws fairly according to law and rules that circumscribe their enforcement powers. The existence of these rules justify the claim that police are a rule-bound institution engaged in the pursuit of justice and the protection of individual liberties, as well as the battle against crime" (p. 66).

Although the Supreme Court has decided cases that eliminated evidence police obtained illegally, it has also established some common-sense exceptions to the exclusionary rule.

Exceptions to the Exclusionary Rule

The exclusionary rule applies only in criminal trials in which a constitutional right has been violated. Several important exceptions to the exclusionary rule exist that have evolved from common law by the U.S. Supreme Court.

■ Among the exceptions to the exclusionary rule are the inevitable discovery doctrine, existence of a valid independent source, harmless error and good faith.

inevitable discovery doctrine • exception to exclusionary rule deeming evidence admissible even if seized in violation of the Fourth Amendment when it can be shown that the evidence would have inevitably been discovered through lawful means

The Inevitable Discovery Doctrine The **inevitable discovery doctrine** resulted from *Nix v. Williams* (1984). To understand how this doctrine came about, one must backtrack to a previous trial, *Brewer v. Williams* (1977). The trials involved the same case and defendant (Williams) but different prosecutors. The case involved in both trials began on Christmas Eve of 1968, when 10-year-old Pamela Powers disappeared while attending an event at a YMCA with her family in Des Moines, Iowa. Shortly after she was reported missing, a 14-year-old boy reported having been asked by a YMCA resident to hold several doors open for him while the man loaded a bundle from the building into a car. The boy reported seeing two skinny white legs within the bundle.

An arrest warrant was subsequently issued for Robert Williams, a YMCA resident and an escapee from a psychiatric hospital. Williams eventually turned himself in to police in Davenport, Iowa. An agreement was reached through Williams' lawyer that the defendant would be returned by police to Des Moines.

All agreed that Williams would not be interrogated in any way during the 160-mile trip. However, during the drive, knowing that Williams was a psychiatric patient and that he possessed a strong religious faith, one officer said the following to Williams (known as the "Christian Burial Speech"):

> I want to give you something to think about while we're traveling down the road. . . . Number one, I want you to observe the weather conditions, it's raining, it's sleeting, it's freezing, driving is very treacherous, visibility is poor, it's going to be dark early this evening. They are predicting several inches of snow for tonight, and I feel that you yourself are the only person that knows where this little girl's body is, that you yourself have only been there once, and if you get a snow on top of it, you yourself may be unable to find it. And since we will be going right past the area on the way to Des Moines, I feel that we could stop and locate the body, that the parents of this little girl should be entitled to a Christian burial for the little girl who was snatched away from them on Christmas Eve and murdered. And I feel we should stop and locate it on the way rather than waiting until morning and trying to come back out after a snowstorm and possibly not being able to find it at all.

The detective told Williams that he did not want an answer, but that he just wanted Williams to think about it as they drove. Williams eventually directed the officers to the little girl's body.

Although the lower courts admitted Williams' damaging statements into evidence, the Supreme Court in *Brewer v. Williams* affirmed the court of appeals' decision that any statements made by Williams could not be admitted against him because the way they were elicited violated his constitutional right to counsel. This case is also discussed in the section dealing with confessions and the right to counsel. The Court said:

> The pressures on state executive and judicial officers charged with the administration of the criminal law are great, especially when the crime is murder and the victim a small child. But it is precisely the predictability of those pressures that makes imperative a resolute loyalty to the guarantees that the Constitution extends to us all.

The Court granted Williams a second trial without his damaging statements being admissible. At this trial (*Nix v. Williams*), the Court allowed the body to be admissible evidence, not because it was found as a result of the improper questioning by the police, but because an independent search party would have eventually discovered it:

> If the government can prove that the evidence would have been obtained inevitably and, therefore, would have been admitted regardless of any overreach by the police, there is no rational basis to keep that evidence from the jury in order to ensure the fairness of the trial proceedings.

Williams was convicted.

Valid Independent Source   If evidence that might otherwise fall victim to the exclusionary rule is obtained from a valid, independent source, that evidence can be admitted. In *Segura v. United States* (1984), although evidence discovered during an illegal entry into an apartment was excluded, evidence later found in the apartment while a search with a warrant was being executed was admissible because the warrant was obtained with information totally unconnected with the illegal entry.

In *Murray v. United States* (1988), the Court again held that evidence initially seen during an illegal search but later recovered under a valid warrant would be admissible. In this case, the police initially broke in without a warrant but returned later with a valid warrant not using what they had seen during the initial break-in to support the probable cause in the warrant.

harmless error • involves the admissibility of involuntary confessions

Harmless Error   The **harmless error** exception refers to instances in which the preponderance of evidence suggests the defendant's guilt and the "tainted" or illegal evidence is not critical to proving the case against the defendant. In *Harrington v. California* (1969), the Court ruled that the evidence should be examined as a whole, and that if overwhelming untainted evidence supported the conviction, or if the error involved a well-established element of the crime, then the error would be considered "harmless."

In *Arizona v. Fulminante* (1991), the Court ruled that the harmless error doctrine applies to cases involving admissibility of involuntary confessions. In this case, Fulminante was accused of murdering his stepdaughter, but the murder could not be proved. While he was in prison on an unrelated charge, he became friends with another inmate, Sarivola, who later became a paid FBI informant. Sarivola told Fulminante that Fulminante was getting hostile treatment from the other inmates because of the rumor that Fulminante was a child killer. He suggested that if Fulminante would tell him the truth, he would protect him. Fulminante confessed to him. At trial, the defense sought to suppress the confession on the grounds it was coerced. The Court agreed. The prosecution then sought to have the confession admitted under the harmless error doctrine, but the Court ruled the error was not harmless, because the confession was likely to contribute to Fulminante's conviction. The confession was not admitted.

good faith • officers are unaware that they are acting in violation of a suspect's constitutional rights

Good Faith   The **good faith** exception involves instances in which police officers are not aware they are violating Fourth Amendment principles. Good faith boils down to whether police followed procedure and who erred (i.e., did a neutral magistrate make a mistake in signing a warrant?). In a dissenting opinion in *Stone v. Powell* (1976), Justice White argued that the exclusionary rule should not disqualify evidence "seized by an officer acting in the good-faith belief that his conduct comported with existing law. . . . Excluding the evidence can in no way affect his future conduct unless it is to make him less willing to do his duty."

United States v. Leon (1984) and *Massachusetts v. Sheppard* (1984), two cases decided on the same day, are, according to del Carmen (p. 97), "arguably the most important cases decided on the exclusionary rule since *Mapp v. Ohio* (1961). They represent a significant, although narrow, exception to that doctrine." He explains:

> In these two cases, the Court said that there were objectively reasonable grounds for the officers' mistaken belief that the warrants authorized the searches. . . . The cases are similar . . . in that judges, not the police, made the mistakes. The

Court said that the evidence in both cases was admissible because the judge, not the police, erred and the exclusionary rule is designed to control the conduct of the police, not the conduct of judges.

In *Leon*, the affidavit failed to establish probable cause. In contrast, in *Sheppard*, the police did establish probable cause, but a typographical error occurred in the warrant (the judge forgot to cross out the words *controlled substance*—an important difference with substantial constitutional implications). Note, however, that *Leon* and *Sheppard* establish a good faith exception only if a warrant has been obtained. The onus is then on the magistrate, not the officer.

The good faith exception often comes into play when the government is executing arrest or search warrants. If such warrants are later found to be invalid, perhaps because of a typographical error citing the wrong address or apartment number, the evidence obtained while the warrants are executed is still admissible because the officers were acting in "good faith."

In 1995, the Court in *Arizona v. Evans* continued the trend to broaden instances when objective good faith on the part of a police officer will save a constitutionally defective search: "The exclusionary rule does not require suppression of evidence seized in violation of the Fourth Amendment where the erroneous information resulted from clerical errors of court employees." In this case, officers observed Evans driving the wrong way on a one-way street. During the traffic stop, officers learned Evans' driver's license had been suspended and an outstanding misdemeanor warrant had been issued for his arrest. While being handcuffed, Evans dropped a hand-rolled cigarette that turned out to be marijuana. More marijuana was found inside Evans' car.

At trial, Evans moved to suppress the evidence as fruit of an unlawful arrest—the arrest warrant for the misdemeanor had been cancelled two weeks before the arrest but had not been entered into the system's database because of a clerical error by a court employee. The Court ruled, however, that because the police did not commit the error, whose conduct the exclusionary rule was meant to control, then the exclusionary rule should not apply. In other words, the police had made an "honest mistake."

In *United States v. Leon* (1984), the Supreme Court specifically addressed the issue of whether the exclusionary rule should be modified so evidence obtained by an officer with a warrant later found to not be based on sufficient probable cause could still be used in court against the defendant at trial. Because no police misconduct occurred, which is what the exclusionary rule seeks to discourage, when an officer lawfully executes a warrant, the possibility that the warrant itself was issued without sufficient probable cause should not withhold valuable evidence from the trial.

The *Leon* case held that the exclusionary rule would be applied to only the following three situations in searches conducted pursuant to a warrant:

- The magistrate abandoned the prescribed detached and neutral role in issuing the warrant.
- The officers were dishonest or reckless in preparing their affidavit or the search warrant.
- The officers could not have harbored an objectively reasonable belief in the existence of probable cause.

Remember that the purpose of having a neutral magistrate is to remove from the police the responsibility of determining probable cause. Obviously, if the police are acting in good faith on the validity of the warrant (which directs an officer to carry out the warrant), the motivation of the exclusionary rule no longer applies because it is not serving to prevent police misconduct.

Whereas the *Leon* case is limited to searches pursuant to a warrant, *Illinois v. Rodriguez* (1990) took this concept a step further by not invoking the exclusionary rule to a search based on an officer's reasonable, albeit mistaken, belief that a third party actually had authority to consent to a search. In *Maryland v. Garrison* (1987), police obtained a warrant to search what they honestly thought was a single apartment unit at a location. However, when the contraband was found in a second apartment there, even though it was not included in the warrant, the evidence was held to be admissible.

Internal Sanction, Civil Liability and Criminal Liability

Government wrongdoing can seldom be excused, and severe consequences may result, in addition to having evidence excluded.

◼ Government misconduct could result in departmental discipline against an officer, civil lawsuits and criminal charges.

del Carmen (p. 385) describes three consequences: administrative liabilities, civil liabilities and criminal liabilities can be incurred at the local, state or federal level, as summarized in Table 8.1.

As noted by del Carmen and Walker (2000, p. 256): "Being sued is an occupational hazard in policing. American society is **litigious** [very prone to suing], and the police are an attractive target because they wield power and are public employees." Because the entire agency or department or the entire jurisdiction

litigious • a tendency toward suing; a belief that most controversies or injurious acts, no matter how minor, should be settled in court

Table 8.1 Administrative, Civil and Criminal Liability

Police legal liabilities came from varied sources, but the whole arena of legal liabilities may be classified as follows:

	Federal law	*State law*
A. Civil liabilities	1. Title 42 of U.S. Code, Section 1983—Civil Action for Deprivation of Civil Rghts 2. Title 42 of U.S. Code, Section 1985—Conspiracy to Interfere with Civil Rights 3. Title 42 of U.S. Code, Section 1931—Equal Rights under the Law	State tort law
B. Criminal liabilities	1. Title 18 of U.S. Code, Section 242—Criminal Liability for Deprivation of Civil Rights 2. Title 18 of U.S. Code, Section 241—Criminal Liability for Conspiracy to Deprive a Person of Rights 3. Title 18 of U.S. Code, Section 246—Violations of Federally Protected Activities	1. State penal code provisions specifically aimed at public officers for crimes like these: a. Official oppression b. Official misconduct c. Violation of the civil rights of prisoners 2. Regular penal code provisions punishing such criminal acts as assault, battery, false arrest, serious bodily injury and homicide
C. Administration liabilities	Federal agency rules or guidelines vary from one agency to another	Agency rules or guidelines at the state or local levels vary from one agency to another

Source: Rolando V. del Carmen. *Criminal Procedure: Law and Practice*, 6th ed. Belmont, CA: Wadsworth, 2004, p. 385.

can be sued, some awards are enormous. del Carmen (p. 384) cites the following examples:

- The City of Los Angeles agrees to pay $15 million to a man who said police officers shot him in the head and chest and then framed him in the attack.
- Jury assesses damages of $256 million for motorist's collision with off-duty police officer that left one child dead, one quadriplegic and one paralyzed on one side with a damaged brain.
- Chicago reaches $18-million settlement with family of unarmed woman shot and killed by officer at the conclusion of an 81-block pursuit of the vehicle in which she was riding.
- Oregon jury awards $8 million, including $4.5 million in punitive damages, against state trooper who allegedly attacked female motorist after stopping her for speeding and then shot her in the shoulder after she attempted to drive away.

del Carmen also lists several instances of lawsuits involving government agencies:

- A municipality may be held liable in a Section 1983 lawsuit and cannot claim the good faith defense (*Owen v. City of Independence*, 1980) (p. 258).
- A police officer is entitled only to qualified immunity, not to absolute immunity if the officer presented a judge with a complaint and a supporting affidavit that failed to establish probable cause (*Malley v. Briggs*, 1986) (p. 260).
- Inadequate police training may serve as the basis for municipal liability under Title 42, Section 1983, but only if it amounts to "deliberate indifference" (*City of Canton v. Harris*, 1989) (p. 261).
- In high-speed vehicle pursuit cases, liability in Section 1983 cases ensues only if the conduct of the officer "shocks the conscience." The lower standard of "deliberate indifference" does not apply (*County of Sacramento v. Lewis*, 1998) (p. 270).

As in a number of other areas of developing law, issues relating to law enforcement liability will continue to receive attention in the media and the courts. Students and practitioners of the law stay current on these issues.

SUMMARY

The Fourth Amendment forbids unreasonable searches and seizures and requires that any search or arrest warrant be based on probable cause. If a person is an employee of any governmental agency or is an agent of the government in any capacity, that person is bound by the Fourth Amendment. The U.S. Constitution ensures freedom by restricting government's power. The Fourth Amendment does not apply to private parties.

The reasonableness clause of the Fourth Amendment makes warrantless searches and seizures valid and constitutional when they are reasonable. The Constitution does not provide an absolute right to be free from government intrusion, only *unreasonable* interference.

Probable cause determines when officers may execute lawful searches and arrests, with or without a warrant. Probable cause to search means that officers reasonably believe that evidence, contraband or other items sought are where they believe them to be. Probable cause to arrest means officers reasonably believe that a crime has been committed by the person whom they seek to arrest. All warrants are to be based on probable cause.

A *stop* is a brief detention of a person based on specific and articulable facts for the purpose of investigating suspicious activity. No *Miranda* warning is required. A *frisk* is a limited pat down search for weapons for the protection of the government agent and others. It is not automatically permitted with a stop, but only when the agent suspects the person is armed and dangerous. The law of stop and frisk deals with that time frame during which officers follow up on their suspicions but before the time that the requisite probable cause is established to justify an arrest (*Terry v. Ohio,* 1968). The *Terry* decision established that, in what is termed a *Terry* stop, an officer with articulable reasonable suspicion may conduct a brief investigatory stop, including a pat down for weapons, if the officer has reason to suspect the person is armed and dangerous.

Unconstitutional searches and seizures by the government may result in sanctions against the officer and the exclusion from court of the evidence obtained. The exclusionary rule is judge-made case law promulgated by the Supreme Court in *Weeks v. United States* to prevent police misconduct. It prohibits evidence obtained in violation of a person's constitutional rights from being admissible in court. The primary purpose underlying the exclusionary rule is deterring government misconduct. *Mapp v. Ohio* made the exclusionary rule applicable at the state level. Evidence obtained in ways that *shock the conscience* will not be admissible in court. The fruit of the poisonous tree doctrine states that evidence obtained as a result of an earlier illegality must be excluded from trial. Among the exceptions to the exclusionary rule are the inevitable discovery doctrine, existence of a valid independent source, harmless error and good faith.

DISCUSSION QUESTIONS

1. Explain why the Fourth Amendment applies to the federal government and also to state, county and municipal governments.

2. Explain the meaning of search and seizure.

3. How does a stop differ from an arrest?

4. How does a frisk differ from a search?

5. At what point does a stop and frisk develop into a search and seizure?

6. What restrictions does the Fourth Amendment put on private security guards, such as store detectives or private investigators?

7. In what ways can government agents be discouraged from violating the Fourth Amendment?

8. Should a case be dismissed because the one piece of evidence that would surely prove the defendant was guilty was not admitted because of a police error in obtaining it?

9. To protect the public, can government ever really go "too far"?

10. Why should a government agent try to get a warrant whenever possible?

INFOTRAC COLLEGE EDITION ASSIGNMENTS

■ Use InfoTrac College Edition to help answer the Discussion Questions when appropriate.

■ Use InfoTrac College Edition to find and outline one of the following articles. Be prepared to share the outline with the class.

   ■ "Origins of the Fourth Amendment," by Leonard Levy.

   ■ "In Defense of the Exclusionary Rule," by Timothy Lynch.

 ## INTERNET ASSIGNMENTS

■ Use http://www.findlaw.com to find one Supreme Court case discussed in this chapter and brief the case. Be prepared to share your brief with the class.

■ Go to http://www.supremecourtus.gov/ to find two recent cases that pertain to *search* and two that pertain to *frisk* and briefly discuss these four cases.

 ## COMPANION WEB SITE

■ Go to the Constitutional Law and the Criminal Justice System 3e Web site at http://cj.wadsworth.com/ hessharr_constlaw3e for Case Studies and Study Guide exercises.

REFERENCES

Bulzomi, Michael J. "Protecting Personal Privacy: Drawing the Line between People and Containers." *FBI Law Enforcement Bulletin,* February 2006, p. 26.

del Carmen, Roland V. *Criminal Procedure: Law and Practice*, 6th ed. Belmont, CA: Wadsworth Publishing Company. 2004.

del Carmen, Rolando V. and Walker, Jeffrey T. *Briefs of Leading Cases in Law Enforcement*, 6th ed. Cincinnati: Anderson Publishing Company, 2006.

Hall, Jerome. "Objectives of Federal Criminal Rules Revision." *Yale Law Journal*, Vol. 51, 1942, p. 725.

Maslow, Abraham H. *Motivation and Personality*. New York: Harper & Row, 1954.

Skogan, Wesley G. and Meares, Tracey L. "Lawful Policing." *The Annals of the American Academy of Political and Social Science*, April 2004, pp. 66–83.

Wilson, Bradford P. *Exclusionary Rule*. Washington, DC: National Institute of Justice, Crime File Study Guide, no date. (NCJ 97222).

ADDITIONAL RESOURCE

Call, Jack E. "The Supreme Court and Police Practices: The Unusually Busy 2003-2004 Term." *American Journal of Criminal Justice*, Spring 2005, Vol.29, Issue 2, p. 247.

CASES CITED

Aguilar v. Texas, 378 U.S. 108 (1964).

Arizona v. Evans, 56 CrL 2173 (1995).

Arizona v. Fulminante, 499 U.S. 279 (1991).

Beck v. Ohio, 379 U.S. 89 (1964).

Boyd v. United States, 116 U.S. 616 (1886).

Brewer v. Williams, 430 U.S. 387 (1977).

Brinegar v. United States, 338 U.S. 160 (1948).

Cass v. State, 124 Tex. Crim. 208, 61 S.W.2d 500 (1933).

City of Canton v. Harris, 489 U.S. 378 (1989).

County of Sacramento v. Lewis, 523 U.S. 833 (1998).

Draper v. United States, 358 U.S. 307 (1959).

Eisenstadt v. Baird, 405 U.S. 438 (1972).

Elkins v. United States, 364 U.S. 206 (1960).

Griswold v Connecticut, 381U.S. 470 (1965).

Harrington v. California, 395 U.S. 250 (1969).

Illinois v. Gates, 462 U.S. 213 (1983).

Illinois v. McArthur, 000 U.S. 99-1132 (2001).

Illinois v. Rodriguez, 497 U.S. 177 (1990).

Illinois v. Wardlow, 120 S.Ct. 6 (2000).

Malley v. Briggs, 475 U.S. 335 (1986).

Mapp v. Ohio, 367 U.S. 643 (1961).

Maryland v. Garrison, 480 U.S. 79 (1987).

Massachusetts v. Sheppard, 468 U.S. 981 (1984).

Murray v. United States, 487 U.S. 533 (1988).

Nix v. Williams, 467 U.S. 431 (1984).

Owen v. City of Independence, 445 U.S. 622 (1980).

Public Service Com. v. Havemeyer, 296 U.S. 506 (1936).

Rawlings v. Kentucky, 448 U.S. 98 (1980).

Rochin v. California, 342 U.S. 165 (1952).

Roe v. Wade, 410 U.S. 113 (1973).

Segura v. United States, 468 U.S. 796 (1984).

Shadwick v. City of Tampa, 407 U.S. 345 (1972).

Silverthorne Lumber Co. v. United States, 251 U.S. 385 (1920).

Smith v. United States, 337 U.S. 137 (1949).

Spinelli v. United States, 393 U.S. 410 (1969).

State v. Heald, 314 A.2d 820 (Me. 1973).

State v. Mimmovich, 284 A.2d 282 (Me. 1971).

Stone v. Powell, 428 U.S. 465 (1976).

Sussex Land & Live Stock Co. v. Midwest Refining Co., 294 F 597 (1923).

Taylor v. Alabama, 457 U.S. 687 (1982).

Terry v. Ohio, 392 U.S. 1 (1968).

United States v. Anderson, 676 F.Supp. 604 (E.D. Pa. 1987).

United States v. Arvizu, 534 U.S. 266 (2002).

United States v. Calandra, 414 U.S. 338 (1974).

United States v. Claveland, 38 F.3d 1092 (9th Cir. 1994).

United States v. Di Re, 332 U.S. 581 (1948).

United States v. Ingrao, 897 F.2d 860 (7th Cir. 1990).

United States v. Jacobsen, 466 U.S. 109 (1984).

United States v. Leon, 468 U.S. 897 (1984).

United States v. McCarty, 862 F.2d 143 (7th Cir. 1988).

United States v. Parker, 32 F.3d 395 (8th Cir. 1994).

United States v. Riemer, D.C. Ohio, 392 F. Supp. 1291 (1975).

United States v. Ross, 456 U.S. 798 (1982).

United States v. Sokolow, 490 U.S. 1 (1989).

Weeks v. United States, 232 U.S. 383 (1914).

Wolf v. Colorado, 338 U.S. 25 (1949).

Wong Sun v. United States, 371 U.S. 471 (1963).

CHAPTER 9

Conducting Constitutional Seizures

THE CONSTITUTION DOES NOT GUARANTEE THAT ONLY THE GUILTY WILL BE
ARRESTED. IF IT DID, § 1983 WOULD PROVIDE A CAUSE OF ACTION FOR EVERY
DEFENDANT ACQUITTED—INDEED, FOR EVERY SUSPECT RELEASED.

—U.S. SUPREME COURT

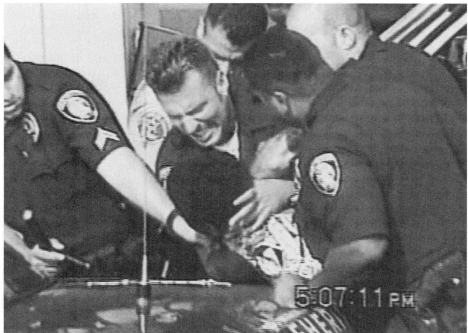

Former Inglewood, California, police officer Jeremy Morse (center) struggles with
16-year-old Donovan Jackson in this image taken from a videotape of the incident
made by a nearby tourist. Jackson and his family brought charges of assault against
Morse, who they claimed used excessive force in detaining the youth. Morse claimed
that Jackson attacked him and the other officers at the scene. The case, which was
reminiscent of the Rodney King incident, clearly showed that the issue of excessive force
is a complicated one; the deadlocked jury was unable to turn in a verdict.

DO YOU KNOW . . .

- Whether a stop constitutes an arrest?
- What factors determine how long a stop may last?
- When vehicles can be stopped?
- Whether *Miranda* must be given during a traffic stop?
- When a person is actually under arrest?
- How *arrest* is usually defined?
- What the elements of an arrest are?
- When an arrest can legally be made?
- Where arrests can be made?
- What the knock and announce rule requires?
- How much force can be used in making an arrest?
- What the only justification for use of deadly force is?
- Who has immunity from arrests?

CAN YOU DEFINE?

arrest	detention tantamount to arrest	hot pursuit
citizen's arrest		police power
de facto arrest	fresh pursuit	pretext stop

Introduction

Chapter 8 discussed how the Fourth Amendment influences searches and seizures. The Fourth Amendment's prohibition of unreasonable searches and seizures applies to people, places and things. The law of seizures refers to governments taking physical control of people or property. Who, what, when, where and why are all factors in the analysis of search and seizure Fourth Amendment criminal procedure law. In this chapter, we address when and how police can seize people and how the Fourth Amendment relates to the seizure of property. The focus is on seizure of people. The next chapter discusses seizure of property.

This chapter looks at the requirements for the ultimate seizure, a lawful arrest. Perhaps one of the most intrusive and powerful of all government actions is the actual taking into physical custody, or the arresting, of an individual. The police have this unique power, which sets them apart from all other professions. The Constitution seeks to control this power through a variety of rules and the courts. Although an area of extreme concern for champions of the Constitution, the necessity for the power to arrest is recognized as a power government requires.

An arrest is a *seizure* of the person, and so the Fourth Amendment applies. Although any citizen may arrest pursuant to their state's laws pertaining to citizen's arrest, these statutes require the suspect to be turned over to a police officer, who then has the authority to determine whether the arrest will be accepted. Because of the power government has through arrest, constitutional limitations are in place to prevent abuse.

This chapter begins with a discussion of how police get their power. It then discusses investigatory stops, including stops of vehicles. This discussion is followed by a look at detention tantamount to arrest. The remainder of the chapter focuses on arrests, beginning with some definitions of arrest and an overview of when arrests may generally be lawfully made. This presentation is followed by a discussion of the elements of an arrest, when an arrest has occurred and where arrests may be made. Next, issues arising from an arrest are examined, including fresh pursuit, use of force and use of deadly force. The chapter concludes with a brief discussion of citizen's arrest, the rights of those in custody and who is immune from arrest in this country.

What Gives Police the Right?

Law always requires some basis in authority. In the case of law enforcement, police power is granted under the Tenth Amendment, which states, "The powers not delegated to the United States by the Constitution, nor prohibited by it to the states, are reserved to the States respectively, or to the people." In turn, state legislatures delegate this authority to the various jurisdictions within their states.

police power • goes beyond criminal law and refers to the government's right to create rules and regulations pertaining to health, safety and welfare

The term **police power** goes beyond criminal law. It refers to the government's right to create rules and regulations pertaining to health, safety and welfare, which includes such areas as zoning, fire, building inspections, education, health, gambling and safety regulations. States have much broader authority to regulate and enforce laws, whereas federal power is only that specifically authorized under the Constitution.

Although case law continues to further clarify the law of criminal procedure over time, this law reflects social norms that are never static. An example, to be discussed in more detail in Chapter 11, is the PATRIOT Act, which was promulgated immediately after and as a direct result of the September 11 terrorist attacks. This law expanded government authority in ways some say is too little, whereas others say is too much. The final answers will result from congressional changes to the law and judicial findings regarding it.

Investigatory Stops

Police have constitutional authority to stop people to investigate even before they can lawfully arrest them. A *stop*, therefore, is considered different than an *arrest*. Both are regulated by the Fourth Amendment and the subject of continuously developing law. In this chapter, we address the stopping and seizure of people by the police and how the Fourth Amendment relates to the seizure of property. This topic will be further discussed in Chapter 10, which specifically addresses searches.

Determining whether the interaction with police constitutes a stop or arrest is crucial because how police proceed with seizing property will determine whether it will be admissible as evidence or excluded. The analysis of whether a search of the person and possible seizure of property is constitutional begins with the determination of whether the intervention by police is considered a lawful *stop* or an *arrest*. To those uninformed about the law, these words may seem synonymous; to the criminal justice system, the differences are critical.

arrest • the detention of an individual

■ The *Terry* case established that the authority to stop is independent of the power to arrest. A stop is not an arrest, but it is a seizure within the meaning of the Fourth Amendment and, therefore, requires reasonableness.

For an investigatory stop to be constitutional, the officer must have articulable reasonable suspicion. In other words, the officer has to be able to explain in detail what specifically was suspicious. Using the totality of the circumstances test, officers must have a particularized and objective basis for suspecting the person stopped (*United States v. Cortez*, 1981). In *Cortez*, the Court described reasonable suspicion this way:

> The totality of the circumstances—the whole picture—must be taken into account. Based upon that whole picture the detaining officers must have a particularized and objective basis for suspecting the particular person stopped of criminal activity. . . . The analysis proceeds with various objective observations, information from police reports, if such are available, and consideration of the modes or patterns of operation of certain kinds of lawbreakers. From these data, a trained officer draws inferences and makes deductions—inferences and deductions that might well elude an untrained person. This process does not deal with hard certainties, but with probabilities. Long before the law of probabilities was articulated as such, practical people formulated certain common-sense conclusions about human behavior; jurors as fact-finders are permitted to do the same—and so are law enforcement officers.

Although the standard is less than the reasonable belief of probable cause, it must be more than a mere hunch or even a general suspicion and cannot be a "fishing expedition" based on a whim or a "gut feeling things were really wrong" (*United States v. Pavelski*, 1986).

Case law has continued to develop this area of criminal procedure. In *Adams v. Williams* (1972), the Court held that information from an informant, and not only personal observation by an officer, may establish the requisite suspicion to make a stop:

> The Fourth Amendment does not require a policeman who lacks the precise level of information necessary for probable cause to arrest to simply shrug his shoulders and allow a crime to occur or a criminal to escape. On the contrary, *Terry* recognized that it may be the essence of good police work to adopt an intermediate response.

However, an anonymous tip, with nothing else, has been held to lack sufficient reliability to establish the reasonable suspicion for a *Terry* stop, given the totality of the circumstances. In *Florida v. J.L.* (2000), the Court held that an anonymous call that told police a young black male wearing certain clothing at a bus stop had a gun was not enough to be considered reasonable suspicion, and the gun the police found on him was held inadmissible because it was the fruit of an illegal search.

This case differs from *Terry* because suspicion did not arise from an officer's personal observations but from an anonymous source. The reasoning here is to not encourage anonymous calls motivated by either grudges or as some sort of joke. Officers must make an effort to assess anything else that would lead to reasonable suspicion. This requirement does not mean the officer cannot stop and talk to the suspect, but without more, the stop would be limited to that.

In the second case, *Illinois v. Wardlow* (2000), the Court addressed the issue of flight as justification for seizure, determining that reasonable suspicion to chase is *not* automatic when people run. In this case, officers observed Wardlow standing on the sidewalk of an area known for heavy narcotics trafficking, holding an opaque bag. When Wardlow saw the police, he immediately fled. Officers gave chase, caught Wardlow and conducted a frisk for weapons based on their experience that weapons were commonly present during drug deals. A loaded gun was found in the bag, and Wardlow was arrested for a weapons violation.

Wardlow moved to suppress the weapon, arguing the stop and frisk were unreasonable under the Fourth Amendment. Several appeals eventually brought the case before the Illinois Supreme Court, which viewed Wardlow's flight as nothing more than a refusal to agree to a voluntary conversation, ruling no inference of reasonable suspicion could be drawn from such action, even in a high narcotics-traffic area. The case was appealed to the U.S. Supreme Court, which ruled that Wardlow's presence in a high-crime area was a relevant fact that officers could consider in deciding whether they had reasonable suspicion that Wardlow was involved in criminal activity. It also held that unexplained flight, upon noticing the police, is a pertinent factor in determining whether reasonable suspicion exists. Justice Rehnquist noted that: "Headlong flight—wherever it occurs—is the consummate act of evasion: it is not necessarily indicative of wrongdoing, but it is certainly suggestive of such."

Although running away itself may not be enough to cause reasonable suspicion, it is a relevant factor overall. As was the case in *Wardlow* and other cases, additional factors contribute to the totality of the circumstances, and merely refusing to talk to the police, as held in *Florida v. Royer* (1983), is not unlawful behavior, either.

Florida v. Royer also addressed how long a person may be detained: "An investigative detention must be temporary and last no longer than is necessary to effectuate the purpose of the stop. Similarly, the investigative methods employed should be the least intrusive means reasonably available to verify or dispel the officer's suspicion in a short period of time."

This issue was also considered in *United States v. Sharpe* (1985): "In assessing whether a detention is too long in duration to be justified as an investigative stop, we consider it appropriate to examine whether the police diligently pursued a means of investigation that was likely to confirm or dispel their suspicions quickly. . . . The question is not simply whether some other alternative was available, but whether the police acted unreasonably in failing to recognize or pursue it."

In this case, the stop took some 20 minutes. The Court held no rigid specific time limit applied, but rather, considerations factored into what a reasonable amount of time would be are (1) the purpose of the stop, (2) the reasonableness of the time used for the investigation that the officers wish to conduct and (3) the reasonableness of the means of investigation used by the officer. Because the detention is allowable, although for only a brief period, reasonable force to stop and detain the suspect is also permissible.

■ How long a stop may last depends on factors that indicate the suspect was not detained an unreasonably long time, including the purpose of the stop and the time and means the investigation required.

In *United States v. Hensley* (1985), the Court held that the existence of a wanted poster or flyer was sufficient reasonable suspicion for the police to stop a person, stating: "In an era when criminal suspects are increasingly mobile and increasingly likely to flee across jurisdiction boundaries, this rule is a matter of common sense: it minimizes the volume of information concerning suspects that must be transmitted to other jurisdictions and enables police in one jurisdiction to act promptly in reliance on information from another jurisdiction."

Traffic Stops

Although the operation of a motor vehicle on public roads is considered a privilege, the driver and occupants remain protected by the Constitution. Being stopped by the police for no or insufficient reason is considered unreasonable and, therefore, a constitutional violation of Fourth Amendment rights. *Delaware v. Prouse* (1979) established that:

> . . . except in those situations in which there is at least clear articulable, reasonable suspicion that a motorist is unlicensed or that an automobile is not registered, or that either the vehicle or an occupant is otherwise subject to seizure for violation of law, stopping an automobile and detaining the driver in order to check his driver's license and the registration of the automobile are unreasonable under the Fourth Amendment.

Motorists, for example, may be stopped if driving a car with expired license plates or burned-out turn signals or headlights/taillights. A vehicle may also be stopped because of erratic driving or if it matches the description of a vehicle seen at or near a crime or coming from the direction of a crime scene.

■ Officers may stop motorists only for violations of the law, which may include equipment violations, erratic driving or invalid vehicle registration.

In *Pennsylvania v. Mimms* (1977), two officers on routine patrol observed Mimms driving a vehicle with an expired license plate. The officers stopped Mimms to issue a traffic ticket. One officer approached and asked Mimms to step out of the car and produce his license and vehicle registration. When the driver stood up, the officers noticed a large bulge under Mimms' jacket. Fearing it was a weapon, one officer frisked Mimms and discovered a loaded .38-caliber revolver. Mimms sought to exclude the evidence during trial, arguing it was obtained illegally. The Court, however, sided with the officers, ruling once a police officer has lawfully stopped a vehicle for a traffic violation, he or she may order the driver out of the car, even without suspicion of other criminal activity or threat to the officer's safety. Once the driver is out of the vehicle, if the officer then reasonably believes the driver may be armed and dangerous, the officer may conduct a frisk. The Court, in *Maryland v. Wilson* (1997), extended *Mimms* by stating:

> An officer making a traffic stop may order passengers to get out of the car pending completion of the stop. . . . As a practical matter, the passengers are already stopped by virtue of the stop of the vehicle. The only change in their circumstances which will result from ordering them out of the car is that they will be outside of, rather than inside of, the stopped car. Outside the car, the passengers will be denied access to any possible weapon that might be concealed in the interior of the passenger compartment.

Ordering the driver out is permitted as a safety precaution for the police once a lawful stop of the vehicle has been made. In the case of passengers, the Court has again conveyed their safety concern for police personnel by permitting the passengers to be ordered out of the vehicle as well.

In *State v. Whitacre* (1992), the court found that the officer had justification to stop and question a vehicle's driver based on the officer's observations that the vehicle stopped behind a stationary car at a stop sign, excessively blew the horn and shouted at the stationary car's driver, leading the officer to suspect the driver was drunk. The smell of an alcoholic beverage on the driver's breath and his responses to the officer's inquiries provided probable cause for continued investigation. These specific, articulable facts justified the stop, which produced the probable cause for the arrest.

An opposite ruling was rendered in *People v. Dionesotes* (1992), where the court held that the officer did *not* have reasonable suspicion to stop a motorist's automobile. The court reaffirmed that mere suspicion or hunch on the officer's part is insufficient to justify a *Terry* stop. In this case, the motorist was driving 10 miles per hour in a 35-mile-per-hour zone. The arresting officer admitted he was not necessarily "suspicious," but found the behavior to be unusual. The officer was unable to identify a particular crime or potential crime that prompted him to stop the defendant. The court concluded that unusual behavior alone does not necessarily support the reasonable suspicion to establish the basis for a *Terry* stop. An articulable, reasonable suspicion of criminal activity must exist.

Ohio v. Wireman (1993) upheld the same reasoning: "Probable cause to arrest and specific articulable facts required for an investigative stop are two separate, distinct legal burdens which are not interchangeable. . . . Specific and articulable facts, not probable cause, are all that is required for an officer to make a reasonable stop of a motorist in order to investigate a traffic violation."

A traffic stop for an offense classified as a petty misdemeanor, for example, a relatively minor driving or equipment violation (not defined by the law as crimes) is just that, a *stop*. Therefore, the *Miranda* warning is not required—the person is not under arrest and is free to go . . . as soon as the officer issues the citation. In *Berkemer v. McCarty* (1984), the Supreme Court held: "Persons *temporarily* detained pursuant to [stops made by police for traffic offenses] are not *in custody* for the purposes of *Miranda*. In addition to the detention being brief, it occurs in public." According to the *Berkemer* Court, these factors "mitigate the danger that a person questioned will be induced to speak where he would not otherwise do so freely." However, the Court cautioned that once the *stop* escalates to an *arrest*, the rules pertaining to arrest will be in effect.

■ Because a traffic stop is brief and occurs in public, it is not considered an arrest, thus, *Miranda* need not be given.

Courts have differed on whether an arrest has actually occurred when the offense for which the party has been stopped constitutes more than a petty violation. Officers have broad discretion in how they will deal with traffic law violations and in many instances may cite the driver, issue a summons for a required court appearance or arrest and jail the defendant. Cases vary across the country regarding at what point the circumstances have crossed from a stop to an arrest with traffic enforcement contacts. The analysis would be the same, whether a stop and frisk has escalated to an arrest by considering the totality of the circumstances and whether the individual reasonably believed he was not free to go. This situation exemplifies the importance of officers' understanding of the law, how they perceive the circumstances and how their actions are recorded in their reports and presented during court testimony.

Whren v. United States (1996) addressed the issue of the **pretext stop,** that is, stopping a vehicle to look for evidence of a crime under the justification of a less-serious traffic stop. In *Whren*, plainclothes officers saw a truck wait at a stop sign unusually long, turn suddenly without signaling and then speed away. The officers stopped the vehicle and, as they approached it, saw the defendant holding bags of crack cocaine. The defendant argued that the police used the traffic stop as a pretext to uncover the drugs. The Court held that as long as probable cause existed to believe a traffic violation occurred, stopping the motorist was reasonable: "Subjective intentions play no role in ordinary, probable-cause Fourth Amendment analysis."

pretext stop • stopping a vehicle to search for evidence of a crime under the guise of a traffic stop

In addition, if police officers make a stop for a traffic violation and are reasonably suspicious that the situation is dangerous, they not only can order the driver out of the car and frisk him or her but also can order any passengers in the car out and frisk them as well (*United States v. Tharpe*, 1976). Furthermore, if a frisk of at least one occupant of a car is permitted, the police may also check the passenger compartment for weapons (*Michigan v. Long*, 1983). However, if only reasonable suspicion exists for nothing more than a traffic *stop*, an arrest is not justified. Although, if the facts escalate so that a crime exists, the rules of arrest come into play. For example, in *Atwater v. City of Lago Vista* (2001), the Supreme Court held that a custodial arrest is lawful when an offense is classified as a misdemeanor, even though no jail time is possible. In this particular case, a woman was arrested and booked into jail for failing to wear her seatbelt, an offense that carried a maximum fine of $50 without the possibility of imprisonment. In this case, a traffic stop escalated into an arrest, exemplifying how a single event can go from a stop to an arrest.

As Walker and McKinnon (2003, p. 39) note: "Before the decision in *Atwater v. Lago Vista*, misdemeanor arrests for minor traffic violations had not been directly addressed by the Supreme Court, although common law (arguably) prevented officers from making warrantless arrests for misdemeanor offenses." According to Urbonya (2001), *Atwater* gave police the authority to arrest a vehicle driver for violations punishable only by a monetary fine. In doing so, the Supreme Court interpreted the Fourth Amendment in a broader sense and widened police authority in traffic-related stops.

In *United States v. Mendenhall* (1980), Justice Stewart wrote: "We conclude that a person has been 'seized' within the meaning of the Fourth Amendment only if, in view of all of the circumstances surrounding the incident, a reasonable person would have believed that he was not free to leave."

Stops at International Borders and Checkpoints

A roadblock stops vehicles *without* suspicion of criminal activity by the person stopped. Although the police have a reason for conducting the roadblock, they are checking everyone, rather than a particular individual. The purposes of the roadblock have been taken into consideration by courts, as have the means.

The increased awareness of and concern over terrorism is affecting police practices and interpretation of the law. As del Carmen (2004, p. 137) states: "Court decisions indicate that the Fourth Amendment is applied differently at immigration borders or their equivalents, such as international airports that are places of entry to the country. Foreigners seeking entry for the first time into the United States hardly have any Fourth Amendment rights at the border itself. They can be stopped and asked questions without reasonable suspicion. Their vehicles and belongings can be searched without probable cause. Once foreigners are legally inside the United States, however, they are entitled to constitutional protection."

How much protection and to where such protection extends are subjects of continuing legal development, especially during these times of increased vigilance, yet precedent cases continue to be the basis on which future decisions are made.

A series of cases, including *United States v. Ortiz* (1975) and *United States v. Martinez-Fuerte* (1976), have concluded that checkpoints at or near international borders need no justification to stop all vehicles to check for illegal entrants into the United States. The Supreme Court has held that the government's compelling interest in protecting the nation's borders alone justifies stopping any vehicle or individual, but stops may not be done on the basis of ethnicity, religion or the like.

Suspects may even be held at international borders longer than would be considered reasonable beyond that point of entry into the United States. In *United States v. Montoya de Hernandez* (1985), the Court held a woman who U.S. Customs agents suspected of being a "balloon swallower (a person who ingests a container of narcotics to be expelled later)" for more than 16 hours while they got a court order to conduct medical tests on her. A rectal examination revealed 88 bags of cocaine. Her detention and search at the border for that period of time, although well beyond what would be considered a normal customs search and inspection, was constitutional because the agents reasonably suspected she was smuggling drugs.

United States v. Flores-Montano (2004), held that 37 kilograms of marijuana was admissible when found by customs agents who took apart a vehicle's gas tank. The defendant argued the government needed reasonable suspicion to remove the gas tank, but Chief Justice Rehnquist disagreed: "The Government's interest in preventing the entry of unwanted persons and effects is at its zenith at the international border. Congress has always granted the Executive plenary authority to conduct routine searches and seizures at the border, without probable cause or a warrant, in order to regulate the collection of duties and to prevent the introduction of contraband into this country."

The same justification that allows searches for no reason at the border is relied on to permit searches with only reasonable suspicion beyond the border but close enough to be considered equivalent. In *Almeida-Sanchez v .United States* (1973), the Court held that a vehicle search 25 air miles from the Mexican border required a warrant because it was not at the border or its functional equivalent.

In *United States v. Brignoni-Ponce* (1975), however, the Court stated that border patrol officers could detain and question, as opposed to actually searching, people in a car if reasonable suspicion existed, adding that within 100 miles of an international border, reasonable suspicion was all that was needed (but that merely "looking Mexican" was insufficient cause). If the stop based on reasonable suspicion produced the probable cause for a warrant, any evidence would be admissible.

Checkpoints farther than 100 miles from an international border are sometimes also made for other reasons, stopping everyone in the name of public safety. This area of law is changing. *United States v. Pritchard* (1981) held that checkpoints to inspect drivers' licenses and vehicle registrations were constitutionally permissible as long as officers did not stop just one vehicle for this purpose, or conduct random checks. In *Brown v. Texas* (1979), the Court created a balancing test:

> The *Brown* balancing test requires that courts evaluating the lawfulness of roadblocks consider three factors: (1) the gravity of the public concerns that are addressed or served by the establishment of the roadblock; (2) the degree to which the roadblock is likely to succeed in serving the public interest; and (3) the severity with which the roadblock interferes with individual liberty.

To combat *drunken driving*, the Michigan State Police established sobriety checkpoints, at which every driver at that location was stopped and checked. In *Michigan Department of State Police v. Sitz* (1990), the police checked drivers at a specific location. They had contact with 126 vehicles, each delayed about 25 seconds, and netted two arrests. When this practice was challenged as violating the Fourth Amendment, the Supreme Court, using the *Brown* balancing test, concurred that sobriety checkpoints are a seizure but one that is reasonable because the "means of intrusion on motorists stopped briefly at sobriety checkpoints is slight." In this case, the severity of the drunken-driving problem combined with the policies in place to limit intrusiveness garnered the Court's approval.

On the other hand, the Supreme Court held in *City of Indianapolis v. Edmond* (2000) that vehicle checkpoints *for drugs* violate the Fourth Amendment. O'Connor, writing for the Court, stated: "We have never approved a checkpoint program whose primary purpose was to detect evidence of ordinary criminal wrongdoing. Rather, our checkpoint cases have recognized only limited exceptions to the general rule that a seizure must be accompanied by some measure of individualized suspicion." Ferdico (2005, p. 321) notes: "The Court said that without drawing the line at roadblocks designed to serve the general interest in crime control, law enforcement authorities could construct roadblocks for almost any conceivable law enforcement purpose and those intrusions could become a routine part of American life."

Checking the safety of vehicles rather than people has been held constitutional. Holtz (2003b, p. 146) stresses that although roadside checkpoints may not be used for general crime control, they can be used to ensure that only those qualified to do so are permitted to operate motor vehicles and that these vehicles are fit for safe operation. Therefore, checkpoints to question oncoming traffic at roadblock-type stops for this purpose are a lawful means of serving and protecting the interest in highway safety (*Delaware v. Prouse*).

While rendering general checkpoints to check people, even if to check for public safety concerns, for the most part unconstitutional, the Court reiterated in *City of Indianapolis v. Edmond* (2000) that their decision did not change the lawfulness of sobriety or border checkpoints or those involving some individualized suspicion. *Illinois v. Lidster* (2004) determined that a roadblock to find a witness to a fatal hit-and-run crash that happened a week before was lawful because it met the balancing test from *Brown* and Sitz. In *Illinois v. Lidster,* the police stopped traffic at the same time the accident occurred, albeit a week later, and going the same direction, hoping to find a witness. A driver approaching the checkpoint was arrested for drunk driving after nearly hitting an officer argued that the checkpoint was unconstitutional pursuant to *City of Indianapolis v. Edmond*, but the Court disagreed:

> The concept of individualized suspicion had little role to play . . . the stop's primary law enforcement purpose was *not* to determine whether a vehicle's occupants were committing a crime, but to ask vehicle occupants, as members of the public, for their help in providing information about a crime in all likelihood committed by others. . . . The relevant public concern was grave. . . . Police were investigating a crime that had resulted in a human death.

In addition, the interference with people's liberty was "minimal . . . Each stop required only a brief wait in line—a very few minutes at most."

Referring again to the changes brought about by increased terrorism around the world, changes in the law, including The PATRIOT Act, will undoubtedly be the issue of future court challenges. According to del Carmen (p. 180): "These cases will doubtless find their way to the United States Supreme Court, which must ultimately strike the balance between national security and constitutional rights, particularly of non-U.S. citizens."

Whatever the purpose of a stop, sometimes circumstances dictate that officers detain a suspect for a more thorough investigation.

An Arrest or Not?

detention tantamount to arrest • middle ground that is technically short of an arrest but more than a simple stop

As noted, a simple stop can escalate into an arrest. A middle ground is technically short of an arrest but more than a simple stop—**detention tantamount to arrest.**

The leading case in this area is *Dunaway v. New York* (1979). In this case, police picked up the defendant based on information that implicated him in a murder. They took him to the police station for questioning. He was never told he was under arrest, but he was not free to leave. Even though he was not booked and, therefore, would have no arrest record, the Supreme Court ruled that the seizure was illegal because the defendant was not free to leave. The seizure was much more than a simple stop and frisk and, as such, should have been based on probable cause. In its ruling, the Court declared: "Hostility to seizures based on mere suspicion was a prime motivation for the adoption of the Fourth Amendment."

Courts will not concern themselves with what the police officer calls the event: a stop, detention or arrest. What does matter is whether, "by means of physical force or show of authority, (the officer) has in some way restrained the liberty of a citizen" (*Terry v. Ohio*, 1968). In *Michigan v. Chesternut* (1988) the Supreme Court stated they would not formulate an exact definition of what constitutes an arrest, rather the analysis would view the totality of the circumstances to determine whether "a reasonable person would have believed that he was not free to leave."

■ An arrest has occurred when a reasonable person believes he or she is not free to leave.

Because of the implications for the arrestee and the arresting officer, the Court has found itself confronted with determining not only when police can seize a person but also what circumstances constitute a seizure. It need not always be what one might imagine—someone handcuffed in the back of a police car. It might be in the course of a defendant being pursued while taking flight or being in the midst of officers causing them to think they are not free to go.

This contention is echoed in *Cupp v. Murphy* (1973): "The detention of the respondent against his will constituted a seizure of his person, and the Fourth Amendment guarantees of freedom from unreasonable searches and seizures is clearly implicated." Detention tantamount to arrest is sometimes called a de facto arrest. A *de facto* **arrest** is a situation in which the police take someone in for questioning in a manner that is, in reality, an arrest. As Rutledge (2003, p. 74) explains: "The tricky part is where you 'bring him in for questioning.' If that takes on the appearance of an arrest without probable cause—even though you don't inform the suspect he's under arrest, and even though you don't personally consider him to be under arrest—the courts will likely find that you've made an illegal *de facto* arrest and suppress all the evidence you get."

Kaupp v. Texas (2003) illustrates this situation. Police officers were investigating the homicide of a 14-year-old girl and had the confessed killer in custody. The killer implicated a friend, Robert Kaupp. The officers did not have enough corroboration to establish probable cause to get an arrest warrant, so they decided to bring him in and confront him with the evidence. At 3 A.M., three officers were admitted to Kaupp's home by his father. The officers woke him with a flashlight, handcuffed him and, without allowing him to get dressed, took him to the station. A statement Kaupp gave them was used to convict him of complicity in the murder. The Supreme Court, however, overturned the conviction, noting that the police lacked probable cause for the de facto arrest, which made it illegal, and, as "tainted fruit," the statement was ruled inadmissible. According to Holtz (2003a, p. 118):

> Because Kaupp was arrested before he was questioned, and because the officers did not have probable cause to detain him at that point, the law requires suppression of the confession unless it was "an act of free will" significant enough to overturn the unlawful arrest. As a matter of law, the administration of *Miranda* warnings alone cannot break the causal connection between the illegal arrest and the confession; and in this case, all other factors point the opposite way. Significantly, there was no indication that any substantial time passed between Kaupp's removal from his home in handcuffs and his confession after only 10 or 15 minutes. Indeed, at no time during this appeal did the prosecution allege "any meaningful intervening event" between the illegal arrest and Kaupp's confession.

> *de facto* **arrest** • when a reasonable person would believe they are not free to leave while in the presence of the police

Arrests

Most state laws define an **arrest** in general terms as the taking of a person into custody, in the manner authorized by law, to present that person before a magistrate to answer for committing a crime.

> **arrest** • taking a person into custody

■ To arrest is to deprive a person of liberty by legal authority; taking a person into custody for the purpose of holding him to answer a criminal charge.

The U.S. Supreme Court has defined the "seizure" of a person as "governmental interference with a person's freedom of movement through means intentionally applied" (*Brower v. County of Inyo*, 1989). The requirement of the Fourth Amendment that searches and seizures be *reasonable* dictates that the physical response by the police must be commensurate with the offense.

The Maine Supreme Court has said: "An arrest in criminal law signifies the apprehension or detention of the person of another in order that he may be forthcoming to answer for an alleged or supposed crime" (*State v. MacKenzie*, 1965). The general guideline is that a person is under arrest if a reasonable person would believe that under the existing circumstances, they were, in fact, being detained by the police and not free to go.

Commonwealth v. Brown (1972) established that "all that is required for an 'arrest' is some act by an officer indicating his intention to detain or take the person into custody and thereby subject that person to the actual control and will of the officer; no formal declaration of arrest is required."

An arrest may involve actual physical detention or a command, verbal or otherwise, by the officer requiring the suspect to stay. If the person reasonably believes he or she is not free to go, he or she is under arrest. Often this situation results from what began as a simple stop based on reasonable suspicion.

An Arrest and a Stop Compared

Law enforcement involves decisions and discretion. Police officers are charged with investigating suspicious circumstances. What begins as a simple stop of a person merely to investigate the possibility of crime may progress to a frisk and then to an arrest and full-body search, as discussed in Chapter 8. The reasonableness of this progression was established in the landmark *Terry* case. The basic differences between a stop and an arrest are summarized in Table 9.1.

The Elements of an Arrest

At what point does an arrest actually occur?

■ The elements of an arrest are (1) intending to take a person into custody, (2) exercising authority to do so, (3) detaining or restraining the person to be arrested and (4) the arrestee understanding what is happening.

When Arrests May Be Lawfully Made

Generally, lawful arrests can be made in one of three ways.

■ Officers can usually make a lawful arrest:

- ■ For any crime committed in their presence.
- ■ For any felony if they have probable cause.
- ■ With an arrest warrant.

In the first two instances, a warrant is not required, although they are preferred by the courts and desirable to protect police from lawsuits. An estimated 95 percent of all arrests are made without warrants.

Table 9.1 Stop versus Arrest

	Stop	*Arrest*
Justification	Reasonable suspicion	Probable cause
Warrant	None	Preferable
Officer's intent	Investigate suspicious activity	Make a formal charge
Search	Pat down for weapons	Full search for weapons and evidence
Scope	Outer clothing	Area within suspect's immediate control
Record	Minimal (field notes)	Fingerprints, photographs and booking

Warrantless Arrests for Crimes Committed in the Presence of an Officer

If police officers observe a crime being committed, they have the authority to arrest the individual(s) involved in committing the crime. "In the presence of" includes any of the officer's senses, for example, hearing a drug buy going down or smelling the odor of marijuana. The information the officer obtains becomes the probable cause for arrest.

As noted in *State v. Pluth* (1923), the officers must know that a crime is being committed before making the arrest. They cannot merely suspect that someone is about to commit a crime. The crime or the attempt must actually take place in the officer's presence.

■ Police may arrest for any crime committed in their presence.

Some laws of arrest depend on whether the violation is a misdemeanor or a felony. The difference, specifically defined within a state's criminal code, is a mathematical one: How much time would a person be sentenced to if convicted of that particular offense? Generally a felony carries a minimum prison sentence of one year.

Officers who come to the crime scene of a misdemeanor after it has been committed usually cannot make an arrest, even though the suspect is still at the scene. State criminal procedure statutes define such limitations. In many states, officers must obtain an arrest warrant to make an arrest for a misdemeanor not committed in their presence.

In some states, however, exceptions exist. For example, officers may arrest for misdemeanors not committed in their presence if the suspect might flee or might conceal or destroy evidence or if the incident involves a traffic accident. In other states, such as Minnesota, officers may arrest for some unwitnessed misdemeanors such as domestic assault, driving under the influence of drugs or alcohol and shoplifting. In fact, in the case of domestic assault, police in Minnesota are mandated to make an arrest if they have probable cause to believe an assault was committed by that person.

Warrantless Arrests Based on Probable Cause

The second type of lawful warrantless arrest is an arrest based on probable cause that the suspect has committed a felony. Referring to the discussion of probable cause discussed previously, if a law enforcement officer has sufficient information to reasonably believe, given the totality of the circumstances, that a crime is occurring or has occurred, and that the suspect is the offender, the officer may arrest without a warrant—but only for a felony-level crime. As with warrantless crimes committed in the presence of an officer, some states have statutory exceptions permitting warrantless arrests based on probable cause for certain lesser crimes, such as driving while intoxicated, domestic assault and shoplifting.

■ Police may arrest for an unwitnessed felony based on probable cause.

United States v. Watson (1976) established that an arrest without a warrant made in a public place is valid if it is based on probable cause, even if the arresting officers had time to obtain an arrest warrant. Recall that probable cause can be based on anything an officer becomes aware of through the senses—observational probable cause—or on information provided by others.

In contrast to warrantless arrests for misdemeanors, which must be made as soon as practical, warrantless arrests for felonies based on probable cause do not need to be made immediately. This differentiation is based on the severity of the felony and society's interest in expediting a felon's arrest, so long as sufficient probable cause exists.

Arrests with a Warrant

A conventional interpretation of the Fourth Amendment requires that to be reasonable, all arrests be made with a warrant based on probable cause. The warrant must name the person making the complaint, the specific offense being charged, the name of the accused and the basis for the probable cause.

The person making the complaint must swear the facts given are true and sign the complaint. Usually the complaint is made by the investigating police officer. In *United States v. Watson* (1976), the Court held: "Law enforcement officers may find it wise to seek arrest warrants where practicable to do so, and their judgments about probable cause may be more readily accepted where backed by a warrant issued by a magistrate." The Court went on to note, however: "We decline to transform this judicial preference into a constitutional rule when the judgment of the nation and Congress has for so long been to authorize warrantless public arrests on probable cause."

Where Arrests May Be Made

Arrests may be made in public places without a warrant if probable cause exists, as established in *United States v. Watson* (1976). Even if a person retreats to a private place, the warrantless arrest based on probable cause is valid, as established in *United States v. Santana* (1975).

Payton v. New York (1980) established that police may not enter a private home to make a routine felony arrest unless exigent circumstances exist, as in hot pursuit, to be discussed shortly. In this case, police gathered evidence sufficient to establish probable cause that Payton had murdered a gas station manager. Without a warrant, they went to his apartment to arrest him. When no one answered the door, they forced it open. Payton was not there, but the police found a .30-caliber shell casing that was used as evidence in Payton's murder conviction. On appeal, the evidence was excluded, with the Court holding: "In terms that apply equally to seizures of property and to seizures of persons, the Fourth Amendment has drawn a firm line at the entrance to the house. Absent exigent circumstances, that threshold may not reasonably be crossed without a warrant." In *Payton,* the Court affirmed the value of having an arrest warrant: "An arrest warrant founded on probable cause implicitly carries with it the limited authority to enter a dwelling in which the suspect lives when there is reason to believe the suspect is within."

The Court held that guests "are entitled to a legitimate expectation of privacy despite the fact that they have no legal interest in the premises and do not have the legal authority to determine who may or may not enter the household." It also held that a person's "status as to an overnight guest is alone enough to show that he had an expectation of privacy in the home that society is prepared to recognize as reasonable."

As recently as 1990, the Supreme Court has changed its earlier position so that now people may have a legitimate expectation of privacy for standing purposes, even without the "right to exclude other persons from access to" the premises in question.

■ Police may make a warrantless arrest based on probable cause in a public place or in a private place that a suspect has retreated to from a public place. They may not make a nonconsentual, warrantless arrest inside a person's home or arrest a guest within that home without exigent circumstances.

Indeed, the founding fathers wanted to assure that a person's home was free from unreasonable searches or seizures, and the courts have upheld this basic freedom.

The Knock and Announce Rule

Officers can break a door or window or break a car window to make an arrest if necessary, but the general rule is that law enforcement officers must first knock and announce their authority and purpose before breaking into a dwelling. This requirement is referred to as the *knock and announce rule*. The intent of this rule is to prevent the occupants from responding with force because they do not know who the intruders are. Depending on the totality of the circumstances and the court having jurisdiction, a violation of the knock and announce rule may make the entry by police unlawful and, thus, invalidate the search and render any evidence found inadmissible—as stipulated by the exclusionary rule.

The knock and announce rule not only protects citizens' rights, it can also enhance officer safety in executing a warrant. For example, a plainclothes police sergeant executing a search warrant was killed by a suspect who claimed to have fired on someone breaking into his house. Although the police asserted they identified themselves as police, the prosecution was unable to prove beyond a reasonable doubt that the resident was not acting in self-defense.

The question of how long officers must wait after knocking and announcing themselves before forcibly entering has been before the courts. *McClure v. United States* (1964) held that "there are no set rules as to the time an officer must wait before using force to enter a house; the answer will depend on the circumstances of each case." However, in *United States v. Banks* (2002), the Ninth Circuit Court ruled that a 15-second to 20-second wait after knocking and announcing before a forcible entry was insufficient to satisfy the Fourth Amendment. Hopper (2003, p. 169) describes the case:

> In the *Banks* case, officers from the North Las Vegas Police Department and FBI agents stood in position outside the front and back doors of Lashawn Banks' small apartment. The officers then followed standard procedure by knocking loudly on the front door and stating, "Police search warrant." After waiting 15–20 seconds without hearing anything from inside, the apartment, police forcibly entered.
>
> Banks, who had just emerged from his shower, was standing naked in the hallway outside of his bathroom when police entered his domicile. He was quickly forced to the floor by officers and handcuffed. Police began questioning him and provided a pair of underwear for Banks to wear during questioning. After a thorough search, police uncovered a significant amount of crack cocaine as well as a firearm.

At the criminal trial, the defense filed a motion to suppress statements made by Banks during questioning on the grounds that the statements were obtained (a) "in violation of *18 U.S.C. § 3109* because the officers failed to wait a reasonable period of time before forcefully entering his residence when executing the search warrant [a Fourth Amendment violation]; (b) in violation of the Fifth Amendment because he did not make a knowing and voluntary waiver of his rights during the interrogation; and (c) in violation of the Fifth Amendment because the interrogation continued after he made an unequivocal request for an attorney."

The District Court denied this motion, but on appeal the Ninth Circuit Court reversed the lower court's decision in favor of Banks.

The Supreme Court granted certiorari and considered the key issue to be not the alleged Fifth Amendment violations but rather the Fourth Amendment violation. *United States v. Banks* was argued on October 15 and decided on December 2, 2003, with the Court unanimously reversing the Ninth Circuit Court's decision. Justice Souter delivered the Court's opinion: "The officers' 15- to 20-second wait before forcible entry satisfied the Fourth Amendment. . . . After 15 to 20 seconds without a response, officers could fairly have suspected that Banks would flush away the cocaine if they remained reticent. . . . This Court's emphasis on totality analysis leads it to reject the government's position that the need to damage property should not be part of the analysis of whether the entry itself was unreasonable. 282F.3d 699 reversed."

In this case, the Court continued to take a case-by-case "totality of the circumstances" approach to deciding the constitutionality of police searches. According to Lane (2003, p. A19): "The unanimous ruling strengthens police powers in cases where loss of evidence or physical danger is a crucial factor."

Hopper (2004, p. 22) notes the comments of a Los Angeles Police Department captain and police tactics consultant regarding the holding: "I would have been shocked if it went the other way. The Court seems to appreciate the difficult challenges that law enforcement faces. This is a very common sense decision that promotes public safety by affirming a reasonable procedure the police use to fight crime." Rutledge (p. 75) suggests that officers might consider making an audio or video recording of knock-notice announcements as evidence of compliance with knock notice as well as the exact amount of time that elapsed before the forced entry.

In *Miller v. United States* (1958), the Court held: "The requirement of prior notice of authority and purpose before forcing entry into a home is deeply rooted in our heritage, and should not be given grudging application. . . . Every householder, the good and the bad, the guilty and the innocent, is entitled to the protection designed to secure the common interest against unlawful invasion of the home." Because the officers did not give notice before breaking into Miller's home, the subsequent arrest was unlawful and the evidence seized should have been suppressed.

A similar finding occurred in *Wilson v. Arkansas* (1995), when the Court stated: "Given the long-standing common-law endorsement of the practice of announcement, we have little doubt that the framers of the Fourth Amendment thought that the method of an officer's entry into a dwelling was among the factors to be considered in assessing the reasonableness of a search or seizure."

Although the Court stated that whether "knock and announce" had occurred would be part of determining the reasonableness of a search, "the Fourth Amendment's flexible requirements of reasonableness should not be read to mandate a rigid rule of announcement that ignores countervailing law enforcement interests." In certain instances, exigent circumstances may justify an entry by police without first announcing their presences, including when victims or hostages may be inside, when a crime is actually in progress, when evidence or contraband may be destroyed or when making the officers' presence known would place them in danger.

■ In arrests, with or without a warrant, the common law rule is that for an entry into a home to be constitutional, police must first knock and identify themselves and their purpose—the knock and announce rule.

However, factors that necessitate entry without complying with the general rule will not automatically cause the arrest to be deemed unreasonable. Exceptions are to be considered on a case-by-case basis, considering the totality of the circumstances. In addition, in some instances officers know in advance that they wish to enter without following the knock and announce rule because they fear the suspect may harm them or others or may destroy evidence.

In such cases they may request a "no-knock arrest warrant" to permit them to enter without first announcing themselves, as discussed in Chapter 8. A warrant with a no-knock provision authorizes the police to enter premises unannounced. They can, for example, break down a door or enter through a window to force entry into fortified crack houses that have barricaded doors and windows, alarms and other protection. A no-knock warrant affords officers the element of surprise and is justified when either officer or citizen safety or the destruction of evidence is a concern. A safety trend is the development of specially trained entry teams to assist in executing such dangerous warrant services.

In a recent change, the Court in *Hudson v. Michigan* (2006) held, in a 5 to 4 decision, that a violation of the knock and announce rule does not automatically invoke the exclusionary rule, if deterrence of police misconduct outweighs the social costs. In an opinion clearly supporting law enforcement, Justice Scalia explained this balance of interests as:

> The social costs to be weighed against deterrence are considerable here. In addition to the grave adverse consequence that excluding relevant incriminating evidence always entails—the risk of releasing dangerous criminals—imposing such a massive remedy would generate a constant flood of alleged failures to observe the rule, and claims that any asserted justification for a no-knock entry had inadequate support. Another consequence would be police officers' refraining from timely entry after knocking and announcing, producing preventable violence against the officers in some cases, and the destruction of evidence in others. Next to these social costs are the deterrence benefits. The value of deterrence depends on the strength of the incentive to commit the forbidden act. That incentive is minimal here, where ignoring knock-and-announce can realistically be expected to achieve nothing but the prevention of evidence destruction and avoidance of life-threatening resistance, dangers which suspend the requirement when there is "reasonable suspicion" that they exist. . . . Massive deterrence is hardly necessary. Contrary to Hudson's

argument that without suppression there will be no deterrence, many forms of police misconduct are deterred by civil-rights suits, and by the consequences of increasing professionalism of police forces, including a new emphasis on internal police discipline (*Hudson v. Michigan*, No. 04-1360, 2006).

Fresh and Hot Pursuit

The pursuit of a suspect does not necessarily end at a border, as often portrayed in the movies. The terms *fresh pursuit* and *hot pursuit* are used to establish this distinction.

The term **fresh pursuit** explains the circumstances in which officers can cross state jurisdictional lines to make an arrest of a felon who committed the felony in the officers' state and then crossed the border into another state. **Hot pursuit** is just that—the police are "hot on the tail" of a suspect.

Many states have adopted the Uniform Act of Fresh Pursuit, which allows police officers of one state to enter another state in fresh pursuit to arrest a suspect who has committed a felony in the state from which the offender is fleeing. Some states require that anyone so arrested be brought immediately before the nearest court. Other states allow the arresting officers to return with their prisoner to their own state. Often, the result of the pursuit will be that the suspect will be charged with crimes in all jurisdictions involved.

Hot pursuit is another issue. In *Warden v. Hayden* (1967), the Court held that police officers in hot pursuit of an armed robbery suspect but lacking a warrant "acted reasonably when they entered the house and began to search for a man of the description they had been given and for weapons which he had used in the robbery or might use against them. The Fourth Amendment does not require police officers to delay in the course of an investigation if to do so would gravely endanger their lives or the lives of others."

United States v. Santana (1975) established that a hot pursuit justifies forcible entry into an offender's home without a warrant. In this case, the police attempted to arrest the defendant in her doorway when she fled into her house and the police followed. The Court found: "We thus conclude that a suspect may not defeat an arrest that has been set in motion in a public place, . . . by the expedient of escaping to a private place."

Minnesota v. Olson (1990) held that "a warrantless intrusion may be justified by hot pursuit of a fleeing felon, or imminent destruction of evidence . . . or the need to prevent a suspect's escape, or the risk of danger to the police or to other persons inside or outside the dwelling."

The intriguing aspect of this case was that the defendant, who was arrested at the home of a friend, where he claimed he had been staying as a guest, challenged the rule up to that point that guests did not have standing to exert a Fourth Amendment defense. In the *Olson* case, the Court held that overnight guests *do* have a reasonable expectation of privacy, and absent fresh pursuit or one of the other exceptions to the warrant requirement, a warrantless search and/or seizure will be the victim of the exclusionary rule. In *Minnesota v. Olson*, sufficient time had elapsed so that the pursuit was no longer hot and, although maybe warm, not of sufficient degree as to justify the warrantless entry.

However, in *Minnesota v. Carter* (1998), the Court further defined when a person is *not* a guest by holding that individuals in a residence solely to conduct

fresh pursuit • a situation in which police are immediately in pursuit of a suspect and may cross state jurisdictional lines to make an arrest of a felon who committed the felony in the officers' state

hot pursuit • the period during which an individual is being immediately chased by law enforcement

a drug deal may not assert a Fourth Amendment defense. Stating that although "an overnight guest in a home may claim the protection of the Fourth Amendment . . . one who is merely present with the consent of the householder may not." The Court considered the following factors: that the defendants were not overnight guests; that they were essentially present for a business transaction; and they were in the apartment for only a few hours.

Use of Force in Making an Arrest

Among events that have startled America was the March 3, 1991, event bystander George Holliday happened to videotape, and that was seen repeatedly by nearly everyone in this country: the aftermath of a 115 mile per hour chase, in which 26-year-old Rodney King was seen being repeatedly subjected to baton blows by police. The question, as stated by *Time Magazine* in their cover story article on May 11, 1992, after the acquittal of the officers involved and ensuing riots across the country, was: "It seemed impossible that any jury could acquit the four officers who were accused of beating Rodney King. How could anyone discount the brutal vision of King being clubbed and kicked on videotape for 81 unforgettable seconds?"

The debate included accusations of racism and police brutality. It also called into question how much force the police are authorized to use. There is legal authority that permits reasonable use of force and consequences when that force becomes excessive. What has sometimes been the source of misunderstanding, debate and even outrage, use of force is a component of the law that courts have sought to articulate and, when necessary, hold accountable those who go too far.

Police brutality tarnishes the image and reputation of the majority of police personnel who do not engage in such unprofessional behavior. Many officers felt the repercussions of the Rodney King incident, as others did after the 1997 assault of Haitian immigrant Abner Louima by at least one New York City police officer. Louima was anally sodomized with a broken broomstick by the officer (three others were acquitted), who threatened to kill him if he told anyone. The prosecutor called the officer's initial claim of innocence a "cowardly, shameful and humiliating fraud he tried to perpetrate on the court, fellow officers of the city police department and the city of New York" (CNN, 1999).

Police know that what may appear to be excessive use of force is not always the case. At citizens' police academies around the nation, ordinary citizens who want a glimpse into what the law enforcement profession is all about experience first hand how hard restraining and handcuffing someone who chooses to resist can be. Suspects on intoxicants or those dealing with mental issues sometimes are unaware of police efforts to subdue them, and what may appear brutal is actually a strategic and controlled escalation of the use of force continuum.

The widespread use of video recorders has resulted in police actions, both on the streets and in police stations, being closely scrutinized. People on both sides argue the images only tell part of the story. Emotions aside, at times reasonable force is necessary and authorized by our law. At other times, government agents must be held accountable for wrongdoing. Law enforcement personnel must understand and abide by the law they have sworn to uphold.

What Is Reasonable Force?

Just how much force is acceptable? The easy answer is that which is reasonable: "By law, the police have the authority to use force if necessary to make an arrest, keep the peace, or maintain public order" (Cole and Smith, 2007, p. 272). A more difficult question surrounds where *necessary* ends and *excessive* starts, and issue can be divisive: "Research has shown that the greatest use of deadly force by the police is found in communities with high levels of economic inequality and large minority populations" (Cole and Smith). People look to the law for unbiased responses.

Tennessee v. Garner (1985) set standards beyond the broad previous standard of any force to make the arrest. In this case, a 15-year-old boy was shot in the back of the head and killed as he began climbing over a fence after being told to stop by police responding to a prowler call. The Court held: "Unless it is necessary to prevent the escape and the officer has probable cause to believe that the suspect poses a significant threat of death or serious physical injury to the officer or others" deadly force was no longer allowed. However, this case begged the question of how an officer would be judged on assessing how dangerous a suspect might have been.

The Court provided further guidance in *Graham v. Connor* (1989). The facts of this case were that Graham, who was diabetic and in need of orange juice to offset a diabetic reaction, had a friend drive him to a store. Because of the long line, he instead rushed back to the car to have his friend take him home. Officers who observed him thought his behavior suspicious and stopped them. In the ensuing interaction with police during which the officers said he would not explain his behavior, Graham alleged he sustained multiple injures at the hands of the police and sued.

In holding for the police and rejecting Graham's complaint, the Court replaced the "substantive due process test" of whether the officer acted "in good faith" or "maliciously and sadistically" with a new test: "objective reasonableness." The Court held: "The calculus of reasonableness must embody allowance for the fact that police officers are often forced to make split-second judgments—in circumstances that are tense, uncertain, and rapidly evolving—about the amount of force that is necessary in a particular situation." The reasonableness of force used must be judged "from the perspective of the officer on the scene rather than with the 20/20 vision of hindsight."

■ When making an arrest, police officers can use only as much force as is needed to overcome resistance. If the suspect does not resist arrest, no force can be used. Excessive force may cause the officer to be sued.

The result of these cases is not that police cannot use force, but that it must be reasonable under the circumstances. When making an arrest, officers may use that force necessary to gain control of the person: "A law enforcement officer making a lawful arrest may use any force reasonably necessary under the circumstances, including deadly force, if the officer reasonably believes that the person to be arrested is about to commit an assault and that the officer is in danger of death or serious bodily injury" (Ferdico, p. 180). The circumstances include when the officer believes deadly force is necessary to prevent the death or serious bodily injury to another.

Officers should be trained in all aspects of use of force, including the law, weapons use and when different degrees of force are appropriate. Force continuums provide graphic representation. Force continuums, such as the one shown in Figure 9.1, provide graphic representation.

According to Grossi (2006): "Use-of-Force Continuum. Control Continuum. Level-of-Force Model. Subject Resistance Matrix. They go by different names, but basically all mean the same thing. They are names for the gradations of force police officers are trained to use when meeting resistance." From the mere presence of an officer to control a situation, to the use of verbal commands, hands, aerosol weapons, batons or electrical weapons, to the use of deadly force, the police have options available, and all are appropriate to implement when reasonable.

Use of Deadly Force

Use of deadly force is restricted to cases of self-defense or to save the life of another. del Carmen (p. 395) defines *deadly force* as "force that, when used, would lead a reasonable officer objectively to conclude that it poses a high risk of death or serious injury to its target." As discussed, the "fleeing felon" rule that allowed police officers to shoot any felon attempting an escape is no longer permissible (*Tennessee v. Garner*, 1985):

> The use of deadly force to prevent the escape of all felony suspects, whatever the circumstances, is constitutionally unreasonable. It is not better that all

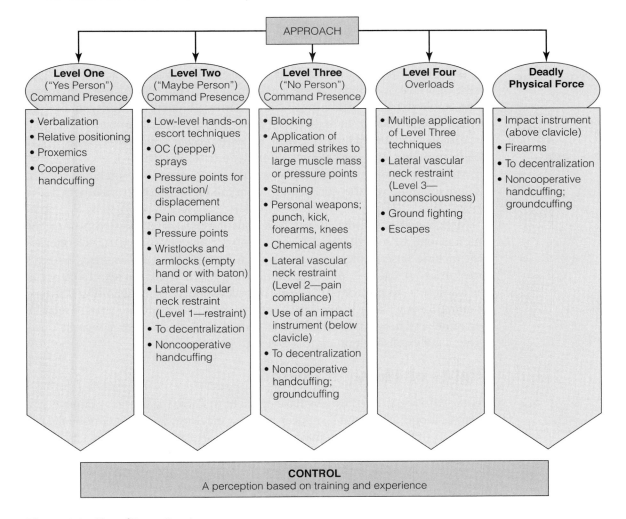

Figure 9.1   Use of Force Continuum

Source: *Police*, November 1995, p. 263. Reprinted by permission of Bobit Publishing, Redondo Beach, CA.

felony suspects die than that they escape. Where the suspect poses no immediate threat to the officer and no threat to others, the harm resulting from failing to apprehend him does not justify the use of deadly force to do so.

As Justice White set forth, even deadly force can be exercised in preventing the escape (i.e., "arresting") of an individual but "only if the officer has probable cause to believe that the suspect poses a significant threat of death or serious physical injury to the officer or others." Thus, no longer can one be shot with justification merely because he or she is a fleeing felon.

■ The only justification for use of deadly force is self-defense or protecting the lives of others.

Citizen's Arrest

citizen's arrest • the detention by a nongovernment agent of one accused of an illegal act

Not all arrests are made by government agents. Common law has held that anyone witnessing certain crimes may make a **citizen's arrest** and then turn that individual over to the authorities. Most states now address this by statute. Although use of force is often not addressed in these statutes, anyone may lawfully use reasonable force to repel an assault, including when making a citizen's arrest. The law of citizen's arrest is what private security officers use. Because of this law, the Fourth Amendment, or any constitutional restraints for that matter, do not bind them.

Any private citizen making a citizen's arrest, however, will be liable if they violate any civil or criminal laws when so doing or do not follow the requirements of the applicable code pertaining to citizen's arrest. Problems that arise in this area include excessive force by individuals making a citizen's arrest, which has been the case in a number of incidents with, for example, bar bouncers who excessively detain someone who has been placed under a citizen's arrest.

Most state statutes do not specify whether a private person making an arrest can use force and whether such a person can call for assistance from others, as the police can.

Most statutes state that the arrestee must be *immediately* turned over to law enforcement. In some cases, a suspect has sued the arresting party for offenses that include false imprisonment and assault. A person who makes a citizen's arrest must use caution, not only for his or her own safety but also to carry out the arrest so as to not commit a crime or become open to civil liability. This type of situation is why an increasing number of states are licensing private security personnel and mandating training, and certainly most professional security operations have extensive training to avoid such problems.

Rights of Those in Custody

People who are arrested usually have the right to know the charges against them, to make a phone call and to appear before a magistrate without "undue delay." Although prisoners give up many of their Fourth Amendment rights by virtue of being under arrest and, thus, have no reasonable expectation of privacy, as previously discussed, prisoners do have the right to be treated reasonably and to make their whereabouts known and to access legal counsel.

Correctional officers are permitted to use reasonable force when called upon as well, including in such situations as self defense, defense of third persons, upholding prison rules, preventing crime and preventing escapes (Cole and Smith, p. 490). The fact prisons are not accessible to the public for security reasons means much of what goes on is behind closed doors. Clear et al. (2006, p. 340) state:

> Although corporal punishment and the excessive use of force are not permitted, correctional officers use force in many situations. They often confront inmates who challenge their authority . . . though unarmed and outnumbered, officers must maintain order and uphold institutional rules . . . correctional departments have detailed sets of polices on the use of force. In confrontational situations, they must defuse hostility yet uphold the rules—a difficult task at best.

Immunity from Arrest

Certain classifications of people have immunity from arrest because of federal or state statutes.

■ Foreign diplomats, including ambassadors, ministers, their assistants and attachés and their families and servants, have complete immunity from arrest. Foreign consuls and their deputies, as well as some legislators and out-of-state witnesses, may also have limited immunity.

Many states have granted their legislators immunity from civil lawsuits. Some states even give legislators immunity from traffic arrests on their way to sessions, as is the case with federal legislators as well. However, a legislator facing criminal charges has no such immunity.

When a witness is subpoenaed to testify in another state, that person will not be subject to arrest for a crime committed in that state before his entrance into that state to testify (but is not immune for arrest for a crime committed while in the state to testify). Such witnesses are also granted a reasonable time to leave the state after testifying without being subject to arrest. Both forms of immunity discussed are matters of public policy, so as not to interfere with the legal process.

In addition to the preceding, officers who use reasonable force in a lawful manner are also immune from arrest because their actions do violate the law. However, officers who use excessive force either against property or people could be subject to criminal or civil sanctions. Whereas in *Saucier v. Katz* (2001), the Court supported police officers by holding they may have qualified immunity in excessive force cases, other cases support the plaintiffs who allege brutality. In addition to civil claims for damages, officers who cross the line could find themselves subject to department discipline or the subject of a criminal complaint.

Although discussed in detail in the next chapter, it is important to remember that any property seized in violation of a person's constitutional rights may be subject to the exclusionary rule and not admissible in court.

SUMMARY

The *Terry* case established that the authority to stop and frisk is independent of the power to arrest. A stop is not an arrest, but it is a seizure within the meaning of the Fourth Amendment and, therefore, requires reasonableness. How long a stop may last depends on factors that indicate the suspect was not detained an unreasonably long time, including the purpose of the stop and the time and means the investigation required.

Officers may stop motorists only for violations of the law, which may include equipment violations, erratic driving or invalid vehicle registration. Because a traffic stop is brief and occurs in public, it is not considered an arrest; thus, *Miranda* need not be given.

An arrest has occurred when a reasonable person believes he or she is not free to leave. To arrest is to deprive a person of liberty by legal authority, taking the person into custody for the purpose of holding him or her to answer a criminal charge. The elements of an arrest are (1) intending to take a person into custody, (2) exercising authority to do so, (3) detaining or restraining the person to be arrested and (4) the arrestee understanding what is happening. Officers can usually make a lawful arrest for any crime committed in their presence, for any felony if they have probable cause and with an arrest warrant.

Police may make a warrantless arrest based on probable cause in a public place or in a private place that a suspect has retreated to from a public place. They may not make a nonconsensual, warrantless arrest inside a person's home or arrest a guest within that home without exigent circumstances. In arrests with or without a warrant, the common law rule is that for an entry into a home to be constitutional, police must first knock and identify themselves and their purpose—the knock and announce rule.

When making an arrest, police officers can use only as much force as is needed to overcome resistance. If the suspect does not resist arrest, no force can be used. The only justification for use of deadly force is self-defense or protecting the lives of others.

Foreign diplomats, including ambassadors, ministers, their assistants and attachés and their families and servants, have complete immunity from arrest. Foreign consuls and their deputies as well as some legislators and out-of-state witnesses may also have limited immunity.

DISCUSSION QUESTIONS

1. Explain at what point a person is considered "under arrest."
2. Explain the difference between a stop and an arrest.
3. Why might states authorize probable cause arrests for certain unwitnessed misdemeanors?
4. How much force can be used by an officer when executing an arrest? How is it determined?
5. When determining whether a stop or an arrest is lawful, how is the term *reasonable* determined?
6. How does the entertainment industry portray arrest situations? Do you think this portrayal is generally realistic?
7. Do you know anyone who has been arrested? If so, what did they have to say about it?
8. Should anyone be immune from arrest, for example, foreign diplomats?
9. Should police officers who are doing their best to enforce the law ever be punished in any way if they are acting in "good faith?"
10. Under what circumstances is someone other than a law enforcement official authorized to make an arrest?

INFoTRAC COLLEGE EDITION ASSIGNMENTS

- Use InfoTrac College Edition to assist you in answering the Discussion Questions when appropriate.

- Use InfoTrac College Edition to find and outline one of the following articles to share with the class:
  - "Flight as Justification for Seizure: Supreme Court Rulings," by Michael E. Brooks
  - "Anonymous Tips and Frisks: Determining Reasonable Suspicion," by Michael J. Bulzomi
  - "Reviewing Use of Force: A Systematic Approach," by Sam W. Lathrop
  - "Investigative Detentions: How Long Is Too Long?" by Jaymes S. Walker

INTERNET ASSIGNMENTS

- Use http://www.findlaw.com to find one Supreme Court case discussed in this chapter and brief the case. Be prepared to share your brief with the class.
- Use your favorite search engine to read accounts of the Rodney King episode and be prepared to discuss the details of what occurred and why you think it escalated to that point.

COMPANION WEB SITE

- Go to the Constitutional Law and the Criminal Justice System 3e Web site at http://cj.wadsworth.com/hessharr_constlaw3e for Case Studies and Study Guide exercises.

REFERENCES

Clear, Todd R.; Cole, George F.; and Reisig, Michael D. *American Corrections.* 7th ed. Belmont, CA: Thomson Wadsworth Publishing, 2006.

CNN http://archives.cnn.com/1999/US/12/13/volpe .sentencing.02/index.html.

Cole, George F. and Smith, Christopher E. *The American System of Criminal Justice.* 11th ed. Belmont, CA: Thomson Wadsworth Publishing, 2007.

del Carmen, Rolando V. *Criminal Procedure Law and Practice,* 6th ed. Belmont, CA: Thomson Wadsworth Publishing, 2004.

Ferdico, John N. *Criminal Procedure for the Criminal Justice Profession.* 9th ed. Belmont, CA: Thomson Wadsworth Publishing, 2005.ww

Grossi, Dave. "Setting the Record Straight on Force Continuums." *PoliceOne.com.* http://www.policeone.com/ writers/columnists/marksman/articles/123080/.

Holtz, Larry. "Transporting Suspects for Questioning." *Law Enforcement Technology,* August 2003a, p. 118.

Holtz, Larry. "Roadside Checkpoints and Crime Control." *Law Enforcement Technology,* September 2003b, p. 146.

Hopper, Joan A. "Waiting—the Knock and Announce Statute." *Law and Order,* October 2003, pp. 169–173.

Hopper, Joan. "Every Second Counts to the U.S. Supreme Court." *Law and Order,* January 2004, pp. 22–24.

Lane, Charles. "Supreme Court Backs Speedy Forced Entry in Drug Investigations." *Washington Post* as reported in the (Minneapolis/St. Paul) *Star Tribune,* December 3, 2003, p. A19.

Rutledge, Devallis. "Avoiding De Facto Arrests." *Police,* August 2003, pp. 74–77.

Urbonya, K. R. "The Fourth Frontier." *ABA Journal,* Vol.87, 2001, pp. 36–38.

Walker, Jeffery T. and McKinnon, Kristi M. "*Atwater v. City of Lago Vista:* Police Authority to Make Warrantless Misdemeanor Arrests." *Journal of Contemporary Criminal Justice,* May 2003, pp. 239–252.

CASES CITED

Adams v. Williams, 407 U.S. 143 (1972).
Almeida-Sanchez v. United States, 413 U.S. 266 (1973).
Atwater v. City of Lago Vista, 532 U.S. 319 (2001).
Berkemer v. McCarty, 468 U.S. 420 (1984).
Brower v. County of Inyo, 489 U.S. 593, 597 (1989).
Brown v. Texas, 443 U.S. 47 (1979).
City of Indianapolis v. Edmond, 531 U.S. 32 (2000).
Commonwealth v. Brown, 187 S.E. 2nd 160 (Va. 1972).
Cupp v. Murphy, 412 U.S. 291 (1973).

Delaware v. Prouse, 440 U.S. 648 (1979).
Dunaway v. New York, 442 U.S. 200 (1979).
Florida v. J.L., 529 U.S. 266 (2000).
Florida v. Royer, 460 U.S. 491 (1983).
Graham v. Connor, 490 U.S. 386 (1989).
Hudson v. Michigan, No. 04-1360 (2006).
Illinois v. Lidster, 540 U.S.419 (2004).
Illinois v. Wardlow, 528 U.S. 119 (2000).
Kaupp v. Texas, 123 S.Ct. 1843 (2003).
Maryland v. Wilson, 519 U.S. 408 (1997).
McClure v. United States, 332 F.2d 19, 21–22 (9th Circ. 1964).
Michigan v. Chesternut, 486 U.S. 567 (1988).
Michigan v. Long, 463 U.S. 1032 (1983).
Michigan Department of State Police v. Sitz, 496 U.S. 444 (1990).
Miller v. United States, 357 U.S. 301 (1958).
Minnesota v. Carter, 000. U.S. 97-1147 (1998).
Minnesota v. Olson, 495 U.S. 91 (1990).
Ohio v. Wireman, 3d Ohio App.3d 451 (1993).
Payton v. New York, 445 U.S. 573 (1980).
Pennsylvania v. Mimms, 434 U.S. 106 (1977).
People v. Dionesotes, 235 Ill.App.3d 967, 177 Ill.Dec. 377, 603 N.E.2d 118 (2 Dist. 1992).
Saucier v. Katz, 533 U.S. 194 (2001).
State v. MacKenzie, 161 Me. 123, 210 A.2d 24 (1965).
State v. Pluth, 157 Minn. 145, 195 N.W. 789 (1923).
State v. Whitacre, 62 Ohio Misc.2d 495, 601 N.E.2d 691 (1992).
Tennessee v. Garner, 471 U.S. 1 (1985).
Terry v. Ohio, 392 U.S. 1 (1968).
United States v. Banks, 02-473, 2003.
United States v. Banks, 282 F.3d 699, 703 (9th Cir. 2002).
United States v. Brignoni-Ponce, 422 U.S. 873 (1975).
United States v. Cortez, 449 U.S. 411 (1981).
United States v. Flores-Montano, 541 U.S. 149 (2004).
United States v. Hensley, 469 U.S. 221 (1985).
United States v. Martinez-Fuerte, 428 U.S. 543 (1976).
United States v. Mendenhall, 446 U.S. 544 (1980).
United States v. Montoya de Hernandez 473 U.S. 531 (1985).
United States v. Ortiz, 422 U.S. 891 (1975).
United States v. Pavelski, 789 F.2d 485 (7th Cir. 1986).
United States v. Pritchard, 645 F.2d 854 (1981).
United States v. Santana, 423 U.S. 890 (1975).
United States v. Sharpe, 470 U.S. 675 (1985).
United States v. Tharpe, 536 F.2d 1098 (1976).
United States v. Watson, 423 U.S. 411 (1976).
Warden v. Hayden, 387 U.S. 294 (1967).
Whren v. United States, 517 U.S. 806 (1996).
Wilson v. Arkansas, 115 S.Ct. 1914 (1995).

Conducting Constitutional Searches

If police have legally stopped a vehicle and have probable cause to believe the vehicle contains contraband, they can conduct a thorough search of the vehicle, including the trunk and any closed packages or containers found in the car or the trunk.

Do You Know . . .

- What limitation is placed on all searches? When general searches are legal?
- What limitations are placed on searches with a warrant? With consent? In a frisk?
- Incident to an arrest?
- What exceptions to the warrant requirement have been established?
- What the plain feel or plain touch ruling allows?
- What the plain view doctrine is?
- When a vehicle can be legally searched and the precedent case?
- What constitutes an exigent circumstance?
- How reasonable expectation of privacy relates to searches, frisks and the Fourth Amendment?
- How searches at international borders and airports are viewed under the Fourth Amendment?
- How electronic surveillance is governed by the Fourth Amendment?
- Whether a physical presence is required to constitute a search?
- What relationship exists between electronic surveillance and one's reasonable expectations of privacy?
- What is required to obtain an electronic surveillance warrant?
- Whether prison inmates, probationers and parolees have full Fourth Amendment protection?

Can You Define?

administrative warrant	functional equivalent	remoteness
contemporaneous	plain feel	standing
contraband	plain touch	voluntariness test
curtilage	plain view	waiver test
exigent	protective sweep	wingspan

Introduction

Nobody has a more sacred obligation to obey the law than those who make the law.
—Sophocles, 495–406 B.C.

Promulgating law and enforcing it are awesome responsibilities that have never been taken lightly. The consequences of good or bad law are enormous, as are the consequences of good or bad law enforcement. Herein lies the criticality of the Fourth Amendment for those who make the law, enforce it and ultimately benefit from its protection.

Fourth Amendment law continues to be a very frequently litigated area. Change continues to occur, and you are expected to know current law. Understanding the history that led up to the change (i.e., previous law) helps you better comprehend these legal transitions that are bound to occur throughout your career.

Search and seizure law is no exception. This area of criminal procedure begins with the presumption that warrantless searches are *unreasonable* and, thus, violate the Constitution. This general assumption begins an analysis of Fourth Amendment search and seizure issues, but the Supreme Court has created a number of exceptions to the warrant requirement. Recall also that the Fourth Amendment is applicable to state and local government via the due process clause of the Fourteenth Amendment.

If evidence seized by the government is to be admissible in court, it must be legally seized; that is, it must have been obtained according to the constitutional requirements developed over the years as the legal system has struggled to determine what is and is not reasonable under the Fourth Amendment.

This chapter begins with the basic tenets of Fourth Amendment search analysis and an explanation of the constitutional scope of searches. The basic tenets are followed by a discussion of searches with warrants and exceptions to this requirement, including consent searches; frisks; plain feel/touch and plain view evidence; incident to lawful arrest; the automobile exception; exigent circumstances; and open fields, abandoned property and public places. Next is a discussion of how the Fourth Amendment and the electronic era, including electronic surveillance, have evolved together. The chapter concludes with a discussion of the Fourth Amendment and corrections, including community corrections.

Tenets of Fourth Amendment Search Analysis

All Fourth Amendment cases begin with two basic conceptual questions: (1) Have the fundamental constitutional rules been met? (2) Does the search fit within one of the permissible realms?

The fundamental constitutional rules are (1) *unreasonable* searches and seizures are not allowed; (2) people's *reasonable expectation of privacy* determines when Fourth Amendment protections apply; and (3) *general searches* are unlawful and restrict government from going beyond what is necessary. An understanding of these three concepts, combined with the ability to analyze search and seizure issues will allow an educated response when someone asks, "Can the government *do* that?" The Constitution ensures the people's rights by *limiting* governmental power. Therefore, people enjoy the right to be free from unreasonable searches and seizures by the government because government is allowed to carry out these intrusive acts only under limited and specific circumstances.

The Scope of Searches

Unrestrained general searches offend our sense of justice today, just as they did when the Constitution was drafted. Limited searches conducted in accordance with established constitutional guidelines serve society's needs, while protecting the individual. No matter under what authority a search is conducted, one general principle is crucial.

■ All searches must be limited in scope. General searches are unconstitutional and never legal.

In *Marron v. United States* (1927), the Court stated: "The requirement that the warrants shall particularly describe the things to be seized makes general searches under them impossible and prevents the seizure of one thing under a warrant describing another. As to what is to be taken, nothing is left to the discretion of the officer executing the warrant."

The legal maxim at the beginning of this chapter refers to narrowing the scope of a search. Looking for "an elephant in a matchbox" suggests that searching for a stolen 24-inch television set in a dresser drawer would be unreasonable. However, police officers may include in the warrant affidavit that they wish to search for receipts as well as documents of title or ownership in addition to the actual items sought. This stipulation allows them to search in much smaller places.

Although the Fourth Amendment generally does not restrict private citizens' actions, it does apply to all government workers. This restriction includes federal, state, county and local governmental bodies. Just as the FBI, state police, county sheriff and local police are bound by the Fourth Amendment, so are the IRS, the Postal Service, fire inspectors, local building officials and code enforcement officials.

Searches with a Warrant

As explained in Chapter 8, government agents who have probable cause to believe evidence of a crime is located at a specific place should go before a neutral judge and swear under oath what they are looking for and where they think it can be found, so the judge can issue a search warrant. The Fourth Amendment requires that all searches conducted with a warrant be "based upon probable cause supported by oath and affirmation, and particularly describing the place to be searched and the persons or things to be seized." See Figure 10.1 for a sample warrant.

The framers of the Constitution no doubt chose those words very carefully to prohibit the general searches they found so abhorrent under British rule. Although they recognized that the government would have a legitimate interest in enforcing law, including executing searches, they limited the scope of any search to only what was necessary and, thus, balanced society's needs with those of the individual.

After officers have obtained their search warrant and gained entrance, they can search only areas where they reasonably believe the specified items might be found.

■ Searches conducted with a search warrant must be limited to the specific area and specific items described in the warrant.

If the warrant states only one specific item is being sought, once it is located the search must end. Sometimes government agents come across items not specifically named in the warrant but similar enough to justify those items being seized as well. For example, if officers were executing a search warrant that specified television sets, VCRs, DVD players, MP3 players and stereos and came across a room filled with television sets, DVD players, stereos *and video cameras,* they could seize the video cameras as evidence, even though not specified in the warrant, because they are similar to the other items.

The government can also seize any contraband or other evidence of a crime found during a search with a warrant, even though it was not specified. **Contraband**

contraband • anything that is illegal for people to own or have in their possession

---

SEARCH WARRANT 2-1

STATE OF ANYWHERE, COUNTY OF _____Hennepin_____ ___Justice___ COURT
TO: _____Edina Police Department any officer_____
_____ (A) PEACE OFFICER(S) OF THE STATE OF ANYWHERE.
WHEREAS, _____Patrick Olson_____ has this day on oath, made application to the said Court applying for issuance of a search warrant to search the following described (premises) (motor vehicle) (person):
_____716 Sunshine Avenue, a private residence,_____
_____

located in the city of _____Edina_____ , county of _____Hennepin_____ STATE OF Minn.
for the following described property and things: (attach and identify additional sheet if necessary)

    One brown, 21" Panasonic Television,
    Serial Number, 63412X

WHEREAS, the application and supporting affidavit of _____Patrick Olson_____
(was) (were) duly presented and read by the Court, and being fully advised in the premises.
NOW, THEREFORE, the Court finds that probable cause exists for the issuance of a search warrant upon the following grounds: (Strike inapplicable paragraphs)
1. The property above-described was stolen or embezzled.
2. The property above-described was used as a means of committing a crime.
3. The possession of the property above-described constitutes a crime.
4. The property above-described is in the possession of a person with intent to use such property as a means of committing a crime.
5. The property above-described constitutes evidence which tends to show a crime has been committed, or tends to show that a particular person has committed a crime.
The Court further finds that probable cause exists to believe that the above-described property and things (are) (will be) (at the above-described premises) (in the above-described motor vehicle) (on the person of _____).
The Court further finds that a nighttime search is necessary to prevent the loss, destruction, or removal of the objects of said search.
The Court further finds that entry without announcement of authority or purpose is necessary (to prevent the loss, destruction, or removal of the objects of said search) (and) (to protect the safety of the peace officer).
NOW, THEREFORE, YOU, _____a peace officer of the Edina Police Department_____
_____
THE PEACE OFFICERS(S) AFORESAID, ARE HEREBY COMMANDED (TO ENTER WITHOUT ANNOUNCEMENT OF AUTHORITY AND PURPOSE) (IN THE DAYTIME ONLY) (IN THE DAYTIME OR NIGHTTIME) TO SEARCH (THE DESCRIBED PREMISES) (THE DESCRIBED MOTOR VEHICLE) (THE PERSON OF _____) FOR THE ABOVE DESCRIBED PROPERTY AND THINGS, AND TO SEIZE SAID PROPERTY AND THINGS AND (TO RETAIN THEM IN CUSTODY SUBJECT TO COURT ORDER AND ACCORDING TO LAW) (DELIVER CUSTODY OF SAID PROPERTY AND THINGS TO _____
_____).

BY THE COURT:

_____Oscar Kuntson_____ ___Justice Court___
JUDGE OF COURT
Dated _____4-14_____ , 20 __00__

COURT-WHITE COPY •PROS. ATTY. -YELLOW COPY •PEACE OFFICER-PINK COPY•PREMISES/PERSON-GOLD COPY

Figure 10.1 Sample Warrant

includes anything that is illegal for people to own or have in their possession, such as illegal drugs or illegal weapons. The contraband does not need to be described in the warrant or be related to the crime described in the warrant. The lawful discovery of additional evidence could lead to additional charges, as discussed under the plain view doctrine.

Cases that deal with search warrant issues have also assessed what actions during the execution of a warrant are acceptable. *Michigan v. Summers* (1981) established that a search with a warrant includes limited authority to detain the occupants of the premises during the search.

In striving to limit government power, the Fourth Amendment begins with the assumption that searches should be conducted with a warrant. In keeping with the assumption that people have the right to be free from unreasonable searches and seizures, the use of a warrant provides a presumption of reasonableness. Subsequent decisions by the Supreme Court have developed legitimate exceptions to the warrant requirement, but law enforcement may prefer to search with a warrant because the burden is on the government agent to articulate probable cause in a warrantless search, whereas a magistrate declares within a warrant that probable cause has already been judicially acknowledged.

The Internet is posing some challenges to officers searching with a warrant, as illustrated in the emerging case of *United States v. Campos* (2000). In this case, a man participating in a gay and lesbian chat room exchanged messages and photos with others, including another participant who sent him e-mail that included child pornography. The man receiving the photos turned this information over to the FBI, including a disk containing the images. Agents identified the sender of the photos as Campos and obtained a warrant to search his home and computer.

The warrant authorized the agents to seize computer equipment "which may be, or is used to visually depict child pornography, child erotica, information pertaining to sexual activity with children or the distribution, possession or receipt of child pornography, child erotica or information pertaining to an interest in child pornography or child erotica," as well as magazines, films, videos and books containing images of minors engaged in sexually explicit conduct. Images of juveniles in sexual scenes were found.

Campos sought to have the evidence suppressed on the grounds that the search warrant was overly broad and the agents should have been permitted to search for only the two images at issue. In refusing to suppress the evidence, the Court held that the police did not expand the scope of their search by looking beyond the two images and that taking the computer was reasonable because the technical complexity of a computer system would make searching the files in the defendant's home unreasonable.

The issue of electronic privacy is a burgeoning area of law, with little precedent to rely on other than cases that can be used by analogy. Whether e-mail and other forms of electronic communiqués can legally be viewed without the permission of those actually sending and receiving them is an issue finding its way to the courts but can first be assessed like any other constitutional question: *is government involved?*

If so and a reasonable expectation of privacy exists, a warrant is needed unless one of the parties involved in the communication consents to having the government see or hear it. *Berger v. New York* (1967) held that electronic equipment used by the government, which in this case was an electronic "bug," to listen to conversations constitutes a search. *Katz v. United States* (1967) held that *any* means of electronic surveillance, in this case wiretapping, constitutes a search if the person had a reasonable expectation of privacy. Although these cases occurred long before today's commonplace e-communications, the analogy is clear. A developing thread of cases includes *United States v. Maxwell* (C.A.A.F. 1996), which suppressed e-mail records obtained beyond the scope of an FBI warrant; *United States v. Lamb* (1996), which held an AOL subscriber had a legitimate expectation of privacy with remotely stored files; and *United States v. Hambrick* (*W.D.Va. 1999*), which stated the need for a subpoena.

If government is not involved, the Fourth Amendment may not apply, but government does have sufficient interest in ensuring people's privacy from others that federal legislation has been passed. Analogous to U.S. Postal Regulations that restrict who can take another's mail to read, Congress enacted the Electronic Communications Privacy Act (Title 18 of the U.S. Code) in 1968. This legislation prohibits anyone from "intentionally intercepting or endeavoring to intercept any wire, oral or electronic communication" by someone not a part of that communication.

In *Konop v. Hawaiian Airlines* (2003), which involved information taken from another's Web site, a federal court held that the statute applied only to data being transmitted, not stored. However, another federal court in *United States v. Councilman* (2005), which involved a company scanning people's e-mails for business research, interpreted the statute to apply to e-mail either being transmitted or temporarily stored en route to the intended recipient. Future cases will likely again address whether stored data falls within the statute.

The issue of whether employers can inspect employee computer use rests on whether the company has a policy in place addressing this issue. Questions regarding whether an employee using company equipment on company time has any expectation of privacy is most easily addressed by well-drafted policies that provide the employees' consent to have their company equipment monitored.

Administrative Warrants

administrative warrant • a search warrant issued to check private premises for compliance with local ordinances

An **administrative warrant** allows civil inspections of private property to determine compliance with government rules, regulations and city ordinances such as fire or building codes. Administrative warrants may also be obtained so government agents can conduct routine inspections when occupants refuse their entry.

At times, the government has a compelling interest that justifies warrantless searches for the public's benefit. Certain strongly regulated businesses may be searched during inspections without a warrant. In *United States v. Biswell* (1972), the Supreme Court reversed a court of appeals ruling that disallowed a warrantless search of a gun shop's locked storeroom, which netted illegal firearms. The Court stated that such inspections pertaining to the sale of illegal firearms are justified and that limited threats such as this inspection to the gun dealer's expectation of privacy are reasonable, adding: "When a dealer chooses to engage in this type of pervasively regulated business and to accept a federal license, he does so with the knowledge that his business records, firearms and ammunition will be subject to effective inspection."

However, in *Marshall v. Barlow's Inc.,* (1978), the Court asserted that government inspectors should not be given unlimited authority and found that OSHA (Occupational Safety and Health Administration) employees would not be permitted to simply wander within a business looking for whatever wrongs they might find, because to do so would be an unreasonable intrusion into the owner's Fourth Amendment rights.

Searches without a Warrant

The Fourth Amendment prefers a warrant because it necessitates judicial review of government action. Thus, the presumption exists that a warrantless search is unreasonable, unlawful and, therefore, invokes the exclusionary rule, with the resulting evidence not permitted in court. However, reasonableness itself dictates that action may become necessary before the government obtains a warrant signed by a judge. Such practical matters as time, emergency circumstances or the probable destruction of evidence or escape of a criminal have resulted in legitimate exceptions being made to the general requirement of a warrant. Through the development of case law, the Supreme Court has defined the following searches without a warrant to be reasonable under Fourth Amendment guidelines.

■ Exceptions to the warrant requirement include:

- Consent search.
- Frisks.
- Plain feel/plain view.
- Incident to arrest.
- Automobile exceptions.
- Exigent (emergency) circumstances.
- Open fields, abandoned property and public places.

Because the preceding have been recognized as lawful exceptions to the warrant requirement, evidence obtained in these circumstances is admissible in court (*Marshall v. Barlow's Inc.,* 1978; *Michigan v. Tucker,* 1974).

Searches with Consent

If an individual gives *voluntary consent* for the police to search his or her person or property, the police may do so without a warrant, and any evidence found will be admissible in court. Although consent makes searching convenient, the downside is the person may revoke consent at any time. Interestingly, the Court has never required police to tell people they have a right to refuse to consent, and the police do not have to tell motorists they are free to go before asking for consent to search (*Ohio v. Robinette,* 1996). See Figure 10.2 for a waiver and consent to search form.

Government agents may conduct a search without a warrant if they are given permission by someone with authority to do so. Usually, the only person who can give consent is the person whose constitutional rights might be threatened by a search. This person is said to have **standing,** that is, the right to object to the unreasonableness of a search because of a reasonable expectation of privacy. Fourth Amendment rights are specific to the person and may not be raised on behalf of someone else or in some abstract, theoretical way. Standing, in constitutional law, must involve a case or controversy.

standing • the right to object to the unreasonableness of a search or seizure because of a reasonable expectation of privacy

Consent to search an individual must be given by that individual. Consent to search any property must be given by the actual owner or, as set forth in *United States v. Matlock* (1974), by a person in charge of that property. If more than one person owns or occupies a building, only one needs to give permission. Thus, if two people share an apartment, all that is required is the consent from one of them (*Wright v. United States,* 1938). However, consent may be given for only

WAIVER AND CONSENT TO SEARCH

The undersigned _____
residing at _____
_____ hereby authorizes
the following named St. Paul Police Officers_____
to search the _____
_____
(insert description of place or auto, lic. number, etc.)

owned by/or in possession of the undersigned.
I do hereby waive any and all objections that may be made by me to said
search and declare that this waiver and consent is freely and voluntarily given
of my own free will and accord.

Signed _____ day of _____ 20 ___ at _____ PM   AM

        Signed _____

    Witnessed _____

Figure 10.2   Waiver and Consent to Search Form

those areas commonly used, not private space of one or the other. Even spouses do not have totality in area of consent if one area is considered to be off-limits to one party.

In some instances, someone else can give a valid consent. For example, in *United States v. Matlock* (1974) the Supreme Court held that if a third party has common authority over the premises of items to be searched, this individual could provide government officials with a valid consent. Examples of relationships where third-party consent may be valid include:

- Parent/Child—A parent's consent to search premises owned by the parent will generally be effective against a child living on those premises. However, if the child uses a given area of the premises exclusively, has sectioned it off, has furnished it with his own furniture, pays rent or has otherwise established an expectation of privacy, the parent may not consent to a search of that area occupied by the child.
- Employer/Employee—In general, an employer may consent to a search of any part of the employer's premises used by an employee (e.g., employees' lockers can be searched with the employer's consent). Recent cases have held that a computer's contents are *not* shielded by employees' right to privacy.
- Host/Guest—The host, owner or primary occupant of the premises may consent to a search of the premises. Any evidence found would be admissible against the guest.
- Spouses—If two people, such as husband and wife, have equal rights to occupy and use premises, either may give consent to a search.

A recent Supreme Court Decision, *Georgia v. Randolph* (2006), affirmed some prior rulings regarding third-party consent but created a new holding that overturns existing rules in many jurisdictions. In this case, Mrs. Randolph called police about marital problems caused by her husband's cocaine use, saying he had drugs in the house. When police arrived, Mr. Randolph refused consent to search, but Mrs. Randolph consented and led the police to the evidence. The state supreme court ruled the wife's consent invalid against her husband's objections, and the state appealed. The Supreme Court affirmed the state ruling that suppressed the evidence. The Court emphasized that in all its previous cases, the co-occupant against whom the evidence was used was not present to object. When both occupants are present and one objects, the other cannot "override" the co-occupants refusal: "A warrantless search of a shared dwelling for evidence over the express refusal of consent by a physically present resident cannot be justified as reasonable."

Rutledge (2006, p. 72) summarizes the general rules on third-party consent after *Randolph*: "(1) property owners cannot validly consent to police entry or search while a tenant or guest has lawful right of possession of the premises; (2) when the suspect is not present or makes no objection, a co-occupant can give valid consent; but (3) if one co-occupant is present and objects, another cannot give valid consent as to evidence incriminating the objector."

The Supreme Court held in *New Jersey v. T.L.O.* (1985) that in a public school, education officials may search a student (including purses, backpacks or other containers) or student lockers without a warrant or probable cause if there is reasonable suspicion to suspect contraband is present at the point to be searched. The justification here is the responsibility of public school officials to maintain a safe environment for students. This responsibility would not apply to adult students, dorm rooms or private schools. The Constitution applies to government officials, which public school personnel are, and not to private school officials.

Examples of instances when individuals *cannot* give valid consent to search include:

- Landlord/Tenant—A landlord, even though the legal owner, has no authority to offer consent to a search of a tenant's premises or a seizure of the tenant's property, including children living at home but paying rent to their parent.
- Hotel Employee/Hotel Guest—The Supreme Court extended the principles governing a landlord's consent to a search of tenant's premises to include consent searches of hotel and motel rooms allowed by hotel/motel employees.

In such instances, only the tenant or hotel guest can give consent. The consent must be free and voluntary. The Supreme Court ruling in *State v. Barlow, Jr.* (1974) stated: "It is a well-established rule in the federal courts that a consent search is unreasonable under the Fourth Amendment if the consent was induced by deceit, trickery, or misrepresentation of the officials making the search."

The request for permission to search must not be stated in a threatening way. It must not imply that anyone who does not give consent will be considered as having something to hide. Failure to give consent cannot be used to establish probable cause. No display of weapons or force should accompany a request to search. In *Weeds v. United States* (1921), police confronted the defendant with drawn guns and a riot gun and said they would get a warrant if they needed. The Court said consent given under these conditions was not free and voluntary. Likewise, in *People v. Loria* (1961), the police threatened to kick down the door of the defendant's apartment if he did not let them in. The court said consent was not free and voluntary.

Usually, the government should not request to search at night. In *Monroe v. Pape* (1961), Justice Frankfurter stated: "Modern totalitarianisms have been a stark reminder, but did not newly teach, that the kicked-in door is the symbol of a rule of fear and violence fatal to institutions founded on respect for the integrity of man. . . . Searches of the dwelling houses were the special object of this universal condemnation of officer intrusion. Nighttime search was the evil in its most obnoxious form." Again, unusual circumstances may require such a search.

Florida v. Jimeno (1991) held that consent can justify a warrantless search of a container in a vehicle if the police reasonably believe the suspect's consent includes allowing them to open closed containers. This analysis uses the "reasonableness" line of argument, and, as discussed, what one person considers reasonable may not be how another would interpret it. *Jimeno* determined that when a person gives consent to search a car, consent is being provided to search everything therein, unless specifically restricted.

■ Consent to search must be voluntary. The search must be limited to the area specified by the person granting the permission. The person may revoke the consent at any time.

Courts typically justify the consent exception by two separate tests: (1) the **voluntariness test**—the consent was obtained without coercion or promises and was, therefore, reasonable, and (2) the **waiver test**—citizens may consent to waive their Fourth Amendment rights. The voluntariness test considers the totality of circumstances to determine whether the consent was given freely and truly voluntarily.

Consent may be revoked at any point. For example, in *State v. Lewis* (1992), a state trooper pulled a defendant over for drunken driving. The trooper offered to drive the defendant home, and the man, after accepting, went to his vehicle to retrieve a bag. The trooper asked permission to check the bag for guns, and the defendant granted it. Inside the bag the trooper found two large brown bags that smelled of marijuana, so he asked permission to check the bags, but the defendant refused. The trooper opened the bags anyway and found marijuana. The court found this search violated the defendant's Fourth Amendment right to privacy.

Although consent may be revoked at any time, if contraband was found before the revocation of consent, probable cause to arrest that person may then exist and a search incident to arrest could ensue, or the police might cease their search, secure the property, detain those present and seek a warrant.

voluntariness test • a determination as to whether one willingly and knowingly relinquished his or her constitutional rights

waiver test • citizens may waive their rights, but only if they do so voluntarily, knowingly and intentionally

Frisks

The elements of stop-and-frisk law were discussed in Chapter 8 but are important to include here as a crucial exception to the warrant requirement for a legal search. Recall that if officers have a reasonable suspicion based on specific and articulable facts that an individual is involved in criminal activity, the officers may make a brief investigatory stop. If the officers reasonably suspect the person is presently armed and dangerous, a frisk may be conducted without a warrant (*Terry v. Ohio*, 1968). A frisk is allowed for the investigating officer's safety:

When an officer is justified in believing that the individual whose suspicious behavior he is investigating at close range is armed and presently dangerous to the officer or to others, it would appear to be clearly unreasonable to deny the officer the power to take necessary measures to determine whether the person is in fact carrying a weapon and to neutralize the threat of physical harm (*Terry v. Ohio*).

Factors contributing to the decision to frisk someone might include a suspect who flees, a bulge in the suspect's clothing, a suspect's hand concealed in a pocket, being in a known high-crime area and when the suspected crime would likely involve a weapon. Whether the frisk is lawful is based on the totality of the circumstances, usually not one factor alone.

> ■ If a frisk is authorized by the circumstances of an investigative stop, only a limited pat down of the detainee's outer clothing for the officer's safety is authorized.

Anything that reasonably feels like a weapon may then be removed and used as evidence against the person if it is contraband or other evidence (*Terry v. Ohio*). If an officer has specific information about where a weapon is on a person, the officer may reach directly for it (*Adams v. Williams*, 1972). Similarly, a vehicle's passenger compartment can be searched if that vehicle is stopped and the person is detained but not arrested. Such a search would have to remain limited to the area where a weapon could be, and it would have to be done with the belief that, as in a frisk situation, the person is presently armed and dangerous. Plain feel is also considered acceptable in a frisk.

Plain Feel/Plain Touch

The Court ruled in 1993 that police do not need a warrant to seize narcotics detected while frisking a suspect for concealed weapons, as long as the narcotics are instantly recognizable by **plain feel** or **plain touch.** The Court's unanimous opinion was the first time the Court has authorized a warrantless pat-down type frisk to go beyond a protective search for weapons.

> **plain feel** • items felt during a lawful stop and frisk may be retrieved if the officer reasonably believes the items are contraband and can *instantly* recognize them as such
>
> **plain touch** • same as *plain feel*

In the precedent plain feel case, *Minnesota v. Dickerson* (1993), two police officers saw Dickerson leaving a known crack house and then, upon seeing the officers, stop abruptly and walk quickly in the opposite direction. The officers decided to stop Dickerson and investigate further. They did so, and as one officer testified later in court: "As I pat-searched the front of his body, I felt a lump—a small lump—in the front pocket. I examined it with my fingers and slid it, and it felt to be a lump of crack cocaine in cellophane. I never thought the lump was a weapon."

When the case was appealed to the Minnesota Supreme Court, however, the conviction was reversed. The court held that the sense of touch is much less reliable than the sense of sight and that it is far more intrusive into the personal privacy that is the core of the Fourth Amendment. The decision was granted review by the U.S. Supreme Court, which upheld the ruling of the Minnesota Supreme Court because the officer did not immediately recognize the object as contraband. However, the Court did support "plain touch" or "plain feel" in frisk situations if contraband is plainly felt by the officer. It held that, when conducting a frisk, if officers feel something they believe to be contraband, rather than being able to seize just weapons as previously set forth in *Terry v. Ohio*, it can be lawfully seized because the situation then escalates to probable cause. As the Court stated in *Minnesota v. Dickerson*: "The (officer's) sense of touch, grounded in experience and training, is as reliable as perceptions from the other senses. Plain feel, therefore, is no different than plain view."

In *Dickerson*, the officer exceeded the scope of a lawful *Terry frisk* by "squeezing, sliding, and manipulating" the object to determine whether it was contraband, rather than just "patting down" as authorized by *Terry*. However, stressing the importance of the ability to *immediately identify* something as contraband, the Court stated in *Dickerson*: "If the officer, while staying within the narrow limits of a frisk for weapons, feels what he has probable cause to believe is a weapon, contraband or evidence, the officer may expand the search or seize the object." *Dickerson* exemplifies how common law works in creating law. Even though the evidence was held inadmissible in this case, the Court created a new "plain touch" doctrine, which holds the force of law, even though Congress never addressed it, because the Supreme Court deemed it law.

If the officer had testified that what he touched did not feel like a weapon, but it was apparent to him, given the totality of the circumstances, including his training and experience, that the object was narcotics, evidence or other contraband, the evidence probably would have been admissible if the initial stop and the frisk were lawful. However, an officer may not simply feel or otherwise manipulate the luggage of a traveler with no other justification (*Bond v. United States*, 2000), for the same reason an officer could not just walk up to someone and frisk them with no justification. The action would be unconstitutional because it violates a reasonable expectation of privacy.

■ If, in the lawful course of a frisk, officers feel something that training and experience causes them to believe is contraband, there is probable cause to expand the search and seize the object—plain feel/touch.

How far the Court will take this line of reasoning by analogy to other senses remains to be seen. The only federal district court case thus far is *United States v. Haley* (1982), which held that odor was sufficient to "bring the contents into plain view." According to Ferdico (2005, p. 431): "The U.S. Supreme Court has not deal with the senses of smell, taste, or hearing in the context of the plain view doctrine, and the question remains open whether these senses would be treated similarly to the sense of touch."

Technology is enabling officers to conduct pat downs without physically touching a subject. A device resembling a blow dryer emits an ultrasound beam that penetrates clothing and soft material and reflects a return beam off hard objects—those made of metal, glass or plastic. The more ultrasound reflected back to the detector, the greater the return signal. The device allows officers the reasonable suspicion to conduct a more intensive search and can alert officers to any concealed weapons. What the future holds will undoubtedly continue to challenge the reasonableness clause of the Fourth Amendment.

Plain View Evidence

The court recognizes that expecting police officers to either ignore or to delay acting on something illegal that they see would be unreasonable. Hunsucker (2003, p. 10) says it well: "Anywhere a law enforcement officer has a right to be, he has a right to see—through the use of any of his unaided senses."

■ The plain view doctrine says that unconcealed evidence that officers see while engaged in a lawful activity is admissible in court.

Objects qualify as **plain view** evidence if officers are engaged in lawful activity when they find the evidence and it is not hidden. Until 1990, discovery of plain view evidence was also a requirement to be "inadvertent." This requirement was overturned in *Horton v. California* (1990), which held that the inadvertence rule gave no added protection to individuals and, therefore, eliminated it as a requirement. In *Coolidge v. New Hampshire* (1971), the Court ruled:

plain view • unconcealed evidence that officers see while engaged in a lawful activity may be seized and is admissible in court

> What the "plain view" cases have in common is that the police officer in each of them had a prior justification for an intrusion in the course of which he came . . . across a piece of evidence incriminating the accused. The doctrine serves to supplement the prior justification—whether it be a warrant for another object, hot pursuit, search incident to lawful arrest, or some other legitimate reason for being present unconnected with a search directed against the accused—and permits the warrantless seizure. Of course, the extension of the original justification is legitimate only where it is immediately apparent to the police that they have evidence before them.

For instance, if a government official is invited into a person's home, and the officer sees illegal drugs on the table, the drugs can be seized. Likewise, an officer carrying out a legal act, such as executing a traffic stop or search warrant, may seize any contraband discovered. Similarly, contraband such as marijuana fields can be legally observed from an airplane over private property without a search warrant. (How privacy expectations relate to searches of open fields, abandoned property and some public places is discussed shortly.)

Even what is considered to be in plain view is in flux. Technology is having an impact on this area of Fourth Amendment law as well, with thermal-imaging devices being used to scan buildings for excessive heat generated, for example, by high-intensity lights used for growing marijuana indoors. Most federal courts that considered this issue ruled that use of thermal-imaging devices was *not* a search within the meaning of the Fourth Amendment and, therefore, did not require a warrant (*United States v. Pinson*, 1994). However, in *Kyllo v. United States* (2001), the Supreme Court again addressed the issue of whether a search warrant was required for police to scan a home from the street and compare that infrared image to other neighboring buildings, ultimately using the results as probable cause to apply for a search warrant. In this case, Kyllo's home was scanned by police from the street and the results used to apply for a warrant. The Supreme Court reversed its position in a 4 to 5 decision, holding that such an act by the police *is* considered a search under the Fourth Amendment and requires a warrant. The effects of this decision may affect law enforcement even further. Because the Court questioned the use of technology when gathering information about the building's interior from the outside, future cases are likely to challenge law enforcement's use of any technology-aided efforts when intruding upon a reasonable expectation of privacy. Heretofore, observations from a public place have been held reasonable, but *Kyllo* has challenged this idea when such tools as infrared-imaging equipment are used to look "inside" a home.

Imagine the framers reading *Kyllo v. United States*. Although the very concept of such technology could never have been conceived at the time the Constitution was drafted, it still serves as the basis for determining when government has gone too far and to secure the people's rights. *Kyllo* also exemplifies how the law of criminal procedure can change. Future cases may well continue to mold the area of warrantless search law. Worrall (2003, pp. 213–215) discusses some problems with *Kyllo:*

> In *Kyllo* the Supreme Court handed down an apparently bright-line rule that the use of thermal imagers constitutes a search that needs to be supported by a warrant or, at least, probable cause. . . .
>
> Perhaps the most important element of the Supreme Court's opinion in *Kyllo* is the notion that for a technological scan to be in violation of the Fourth Amendment, the device must not be in general public use. This is part of the Court's supposed bright-line rule, but the dissent noted that "how much use is general public use is not even hinted at by the Court's opinion, which makes the somewhat doubtful assumption that the thermal imager used in this case does not satisfy that criterion. . . . *Kyllo's* general public use standard is hopelessly vague. . . .

That thermal imaging is not in the public use would appear to be questionable according to Freeborg (2003, p. 28), who notes: "The ability of infrared devices to make images out of heat, which can then be used to prevent potentially catastrophic events, seems like a fascinating prospect. In truth, the possible applications with this technology are vast." Freeborg (p. 30) describes an infrared camera developed for general use in preventive maintenance. Another portable infrared camera has been developed to detect moisture accumulation, targeted for use by roofing, insulation and electrical contractors. Freeborg (p. 51) reports: "*Maxtex,* an infrared news journal, estimates the commercial potential with all infrared products to be more than $1 billion this year with an expected annual growth of 20 percent going forward."

Worrall also contends: "The Court's lack of judicial restraint in *Kyllo* is perhaps its biggest mistake. Judicial restraint is the philosophy of limiting decisions to the facts of each case, deciding only the issues that need to be resolved in a particular situation. Judicial restraint also entails avoiding unnecessary decisions on constitutional questions."

Another potential problem with *Kyllo* is discussed by Woessner and Sims (2003, p. 236):

> Rather than react to the latest shifts in technology, the *Kyllo* decision was aimed at addressing the problem of government intrusion no matter what the method of surveillance. In the creation of a new standard, the Court settles some constitutional questions and raises others. As always, the challenge for law enforcement is to stay within the bounds of established precedent without unnecessarily forgoing powers that the Supreme Court would hold as legitimate. By neglecting to spell out some of the more technical considerations, the difficulty before the government is considerable. Given the serious nature of the current fight against international terrorism, the consequences for legal miscalculations are all the more serious.

Searches Incident to Lawful Arrest

After a person has lawfully been taken into custody by a police officer, U.S. law recognizes the necessity of permitting a complete search. First, officer safety requires that any weapon on or near the defendant be located. Second, any evidence or other contraband should be recovered.

Assume during this discussion that all arrests are legal; if not, the exclusionary rule would prevent any evidence obtained during the search from being used in court. If an arrest is legal, what kind of search can be conducted? The precedent case is *Chimel v. California* (1969), in which police had an arrest warrant for Ted Chimel before they thoroughly searched his home. However, the evidence found during the search was declared inadmissible. The Court said:

> When an arrest is made, it is reasonable for the arresting officer to search the person arrested to remove any weapons that the latter might seek to use to resist arrest or effect an escape.
>
> It is entirely reasonable for the arresting officer to search for and seize any evidence on the arrestee's person in order to prevent its concealment or destruction and the area from within which the arrestee might gain possession of a weapon or destructible evidence.

The key phrases in this statement are *the arrestee's person* and *the area from within which the arrestee might gain possession*. The Court described this area as within the person's immediate control—meaning within the person's reach (also defined as the person's **wingspan**). The fact that the suspect is handcuffed does not restrict the scope of the search. The area remains as if the suspect was not handcuffed, because the belief that the suspect could access a weapon or hidden contraband that had been within reach is reasonable.

wingspan • the area within a person's reach or immediate control

■ Searches after an arrest must be immediate and must be limited to the area within the person's reach (*Chimel*).

After the *Chimel* decision, courts generally insisted that officers making a search incidental to an arrest have a definite idea of what they were searching for, as is required by a search warrant. This knowledge should dictate the scope of the search.

In 1973, however, the Supreme Court expanded the scope of searches allowed after arrests in *United States v. Robinson*. The case involved a full-scale search of an individual arrested for a moving traffic violation. The officer inspected the contents of a cigarette package found on Robinson and discovered illegal drugs. The drugs were admitted as evidence, with the Court stating:

> It is the fact of the lawful arrest which establishes the authority to search, and we hold that in the case of a lawful custodial arrest a search of the person is not only an exception to the warrant requirement of the Fourth Amendment, but is also a "reasonable" search under that Amendment.

Not all states follow this ruling, however. The Hawaiian Supreme Court, for example, limits the warrantless search after a custodial arrest to disarming the person if the officers believe the arrestee to be dangerous and searching for evidence related to the crime for which the person was arrested (*State v. Kaluna*, 1974).

Although a full search is permissible incident to lawful arrest, how far can such a search go? The more intrusive or extreme a search may be, the greater the necessity must be before a judge will authorize it. In *Schmerber v. California* (1966), the Court held that intrusive searches will be upheld only if (1) the process was a reasonable one performed in a reasonable manner (for example, a blood sample taken by a qualified medical professional); (2) there was a clear indication in advance the evidence sought would be found; and (3) there were exigent circumstances (in *Schmerber,* a blood test needed to be taken before the amount of alcohol in the blood lessened). Absent the exigent circumstance, a search as intrusive as drawing blood would not be permissible without a warrant.

Seizures of items from the body, such as hair samples or fingernail clippings, are usually allowed without a warrant incident to arrest if reasonable and painless procedures are used (*Commonwealth v. Tarver,* 1975). During a full search of an arrestee, anything on the person's body may be searched and seized if evidentiary or unlawful. This evidence includes a person's wallet or purse, which according to *United States v. Molinaro* (1989), may be seized and gone through at the time of arrest. Even the numbers on a pager seized on an arrestee may be retrieved from its memory without a warrant (*United States v. Chan,* 1993). Anything arrestees have under their immediate control may be searched and seized, even if unrelated to whatever criminal act they are suspected of committing.

■ A search incident to lawful arrest allows seizure of property or containers not immediately connected with the arrestee's body but under his or her immediate control, including backpacks, brief cases, luggage or other packages.

Even when a full body search may be lawful, police might still be found to have gone too far. This area of law is still being shaped. Since the *Chimel* and *Robinson* cases, state courts have not always been willing to condone full body searches for all offenses and have found some unreasonable. When the offense is petty, such as a traffic offense or other offenses routinely handled by citation rather than formal booking, some courts have held that police cannot conduct full body searches.

remoteness • regarding the unreasonableness and unlawfulness of searches of seized luggage or other personal belongings not immediately associated with the arrestee's body or under his or her immediate control

The issue of **remoteness** may also determine whether a search is unreasonable. In *United States v. Chadwick* (1977), the Court held that the search of seized luggage or other personal belongings not immediately associated with the arrestee's body or under his or her immediate control will not be allowed if that search is remote in time and place from the arrest and no emergency exists. In *Chadwick,* federal narcotics agents had probable cause to arrest the defendants and seize a footlocker they had placed in the trunk of a car. An hour and a half after the arrest, the agents opened the footlocker and found marijuana. The Supreme Court stated:

> The potential dangers lurking in all custodial arrests make warrantless searches of items within the "immediate control" area reasonable without requiring the arresting officer to calculate the probability that weapons or destructible evidence may be involved. . . . However, warrantless searches of luggage or other property seized at the time of an arrest cannot be justified as incident to that arrest either if the search is remote in time and place from the arrest . . . or no exigency exists. Once law enforcement officers have reduced luggage or other personal property not immediately associated with the person of the arrestee to their exclusive control, and there is no longer any danger that the arrestee might gain access to the property to seize a weapon or destroy evidence, a search of that property is no longer an incident of the arrest.

The *Chadwick* Court did, however, include in their opinion that a warrantless search might be reasonable if some emergency situation existed, stating: "Of course, there may be other justifications for a warrantless search of luggage taken from a suspect at the time of his arrest; for example, if officers have reason to believe their luggage contains some immediately dangerous instrumentality, such as explosives, it would be foolhardy to transport it to the station house without opening the luggage and disarming the weapon."

Illinois v. Lafayette (1983) established that police can search the personal effects of a person under lawful arrest if it is standard procedure during booking and jailing. *Maryland v. Buie* (1990) allowed a limited **protective sweep** by officers during an arrest in a home for the officers' safety (to determine whether anyone else was present). The Court held:

> The Fourth Amendment permits a properly limited protective sweep in conjunction with an in-home arrest when the searching officer possesses a reasonable belief based on specific and articulable facts that the area to be swept harbors an individual posing a danger to those on the arrest scene. . . .
>
> We should emphasize that such a protective sweep, aimed at protecting the arresting officers, if justified by the circumstances, is nevertheless not a full search of the premises, but may extend only to cursory inspection of those spaces where a person may be found.

protective sweep • a limited search made in conjunction with an in-home arrest when the searching officer possesses a reasonable belief based on specific and articulable facts that the area to be swept harbors an individual posing a danger to those on the arrest scene

Use of Force in Searching an Arrested Person When government agents search a person incident to arrest, they may use as much force as reasonably necessary to protect themselves, as well as to prevent escape or the destruction or concealment of evidence.

This permission does not apply to the more invasive body searches for evidence, but the reasonable force necessary to control the situation, including stopping the person from destroying or hiding evidence that has been, for example, put into his or her mouth to be swallowed is allowed. In *Salas v. State* (1971), when a police officer applied a choke hold on the suspect, forcing him to spit drugs out of his mouth, the court allowed the drugs to be admitted as evidence. The *reasonableness* of the police action determines the lawfulness of it.

Searching People Other Than the Arrested Person When a person is arrested while with someone else, the associate might be logically assumed to have weapons or contraband. Searches of people who accompany an arrestee are limited to a frisk when the officers reasonably believe the companion may be dangerous or might destroy evidence, and then only if that person was in the immediate area of the arrest (*United States v. Simmons,* 1977). Logically, the area under the companion's immediate control may also be searched (*United States v. Lucas,* 1990).

Searching the Vehicle of an Arrested Person The landmark case for the warrantless search of a vehicle incident to an arrest is *New York v. Belton* (1981). In this case, the Supreme Court said:

> When a policeman has made a lawful custodial arrest of the occupant of an automobile, he may, as a contemporaneous incident of that arrest, search the passenger compartment of that automobile.
>
> It follows from this conclusion that the police may also examine the contents of any containers found within the passenger compartment, for if the passenger compartment is within reach of the arrestee, so also will containers in it be within his reach.

The Court further defined a "container" as any object that can hold another object, including: "Closed or open glove compartments, consoles or other receptacles located anywhere within the passenger compartments, as well as luggage, boxes, bags, clothing, and the like." They added that only the vehicle's interior can be searched incident to arrest, *not* the trunk.

Similar to the ruling that an arrestee may be searched, as well as the area under his or her immediate control, even when the arrestee is in custody and handcuffed, in *United States v. White* (1989), the court authorized the search of a suspect's vehicle while the suspect was handcuffed in the back of a squad car. However, a vehicle may be searched only if the subject of the arrest was in the vehicle when the police contact began (*United States v. Strahan*, 1993).

In *United States v. Ross* (1982), the Court held that when a police officer has probable cause to believe evidence of a crime is concealed in an automobile, the officer may conduct a "search as broad as one that could be authorized by a magistrate issuing a warrant." *Wyoming v. Houghton* (1999) extended the scope of such searches to include the personal effects of passengers also present in the vehicle. The Court noted that the government interest in effective law enforcement would be substantially impaired without the ability to search passengers' belongings because (1) a vehicle's mobility creates the risk that evidence or contraband will be permanently lost while a warrant is sought, (2) a passenger may have an interest in concealing evidence of criminal activity in collusion with the driver and (3) a criminal may hide contraband in a passenger's belongings as readily as in other containers in the car.

Justification to conduct a warrantless search of a vehicle is not present when the vehicle has been stopped for a traffic violation and the driver merely issued a citation, as was the case in *Knowles v. Iowa* (1999), where Knowles was stopped for speeding (43 mph in a 25 mph zone). Although Iowa law allowed the officer the option of arrest, he chose instead to issue a citation and, subsequently, conducted a full search of the vehicle without Knowles' consent. The search produced a bag of marijuana and a pipe, and Knowles was arrested and charged with violating Iowa's controlled substances law.

Although Iowa law stated that issuance of a citation in lieu of an arrest "does not affect the officer's authority to conduct an otherwise lawful search," the U.S. Supreme Court effectively struck down the law as unconstitutional, finding that it violated the Fourth Amendment. *Knowles v. Iowa* made clear that only a lawful custodial arrest justifies a warrantless search incident to arrest. Merely having probable cause to arrest, or issuing a citation when an actual arrest does not occur, does not justify a search. As Ferrell (1999, p. 10) summarizes: "The Supreme Court did note that officers under most circumstances may:

- Order both the driver and any passengers out of a vehicle (*Pennsylvania v. Muniz*).
- Perform a "pat down" of a driver and any passengers, upon a reasonable suspicion that they may be armed and dangerous (*Terry v. Ohio*).
- Conduct a "*Terry* pat down" of the passenger compartment of the vehicle, upon a reasonable suspicion that an occupant is dangerous and may gain immediate control of a weapon (*Michigan v. Long*).
- Conduct a full search of the passenger compartment, including any containers therein, pursuant to a custodial arrest (*New York v. Belton*)."

When an officer may proceed with a vehicle search was addressed in *Thornton v. United States* (2004). In this case, Thornton pulled his vehicle over, got out and was then arrested. The officer proceeded to search his car and found a gun.

Thornton claimed the search was unconstitutional because he was arrested outside the car. The Court held the fact that he had exited the car made no difference, because it was still considered to have been under his control. In *Illinois v. Caballes* (2005), the Court held that having a police narcotics-detection dog simply walk around a vehicle that had been stopped for speeding is not unconstitutional. In this case, the fact that the suspect was stopped only for a traffic violation did not prevent another officer from having the dog walk around the car, and the dog's alert of narcotics provided sufficient probable cause to then search it.

Contemporaneousness   In *James v. Louisiana* (1965), the defendant was arrested for a drug offense, taken to his home, well away from the arrest site, and searched. The Supreme Court held the resulting evidence was not admissible because a search "can be incident to an arrest only if it is substantially **contemporaneous** with the arrest and is confined to the immediate vicinity of the arrest" [emphasis added]. Case law makes clear that the farther away from the area under the defendant's immediate control, the less likely a search incident to the arrest will be considered lawful.

contemporaneous • a concept that holds a search can be incident to an arrest only if it occurs at the same time as the arrest and is confined to the immediate vicinity of the arrest

Inventory Searches   Suspects to be jailed are subject to a warrantless search. This search serves two purposes. First, it protects the prisoner's personal property in that the property is all listed and then held in a safe place until the prisoner is released. Second, it protects officers and other prisoners and helps ensure that no weapons or illegal drugs will be taken into the jail.

In *United States v. Edwards* (1974), the Court stated: "Once the accused is lawfully arrested and is in custody, the effects in his possession at the place of detention that were subject to search at the time and place of his arrest may lawfully be searched and seized without a warrant even though a substantial period of time has elapsed between the arrest and subsequent administrative processing, on the one hand, and the taking of the property for use as evidence, on the other."

Chief Justice Burger wrote in *Illinois v. Lafayette* (1983): "It is entirely proper for police to remove and list or inventory property found on the person or in the possession of an arrested person who is to be jailed. A range of governmental interests supports an inventory process." An impounded vehicle can be inventoried for the same reasons, as discussed shortly.

The Automobile Exception

Because of their *mobility*, automobiles and other vehicles may need to be searched without a warrant. This so-called "automobile exception" has arisen because for law enforcement officers to expect suspects to voluntarily remain in place while the officers returned to the station to prepare the warrant application and then find a judge to sign it would obviously be unreasonable. Detaining suspects that long would also be unreasonable. This exception, like the others, is not difficult to understand if the underlying reason for it is kept in mind. The automobile exception simply states that if a government agent has probable cause to believe the vehicle contains contraband or evidence of a crime, no warrant is needed. Why? Because in the time needed to get a warrant, the car, driver and contraband or evidence could be long gone.

The precedent for a warrantless search of automobiles came from *Carroll v. United States* (1925). During Prohibition in the 1920s, among the 1,500 agents pursuing bootleggers were two federal agents posing as buyers in a Michigan honky-tonk. Two bootleggers, George Carroll and John Kiro, were somewhat suspicious. They said they had to go get the liquor and would return in about an hour. They called later to say they could not return until the next day, but they never appeared.

The agents resumed surveillance of a section of road between Grand Rapids and Detroit known to be used by bootleggers. Within a week after their unsuccessful buy, the agents recognized Carroll and Kiro driving by. They gave chase, but lost them. Two months later they again recognized Carroll's car, pursued it and overtook it. The agents were familiar with Carroll's car, recognized Carroll and Kiro in the automobile and believed the automobile contained bootleg liquor. A search revealed 68 bottles of whiskey and gin, most behind the seats' upholstery, where the padding had been removed. The contraband was seized and the two men arrested.

Carroll and Kiro were charged with and convicted of transporting intoxicating liquor. Carroll's appeal, taken to the U.S. Supreme Court, resulted in a landmark decision defining the rights and limitations for warrantless searches of vehicles:

> If the search and seizure without a warrant are made upon probable cause, that is, upon a belief, reasonably arising out of circumstances known to the seizing officer, that an automobile or other vehicle contains that which by law is subject to seizure and destruction, the search and seizure are valid.

■ *Carroll v. United States* (1925) established that vehicles can be searched without a warrant provided (1) there is probable cause to believe the vehicle's contents violate the law and (2) the vehicle would be gone before a search warrant could be obtained.

Chambers v. Maroney (1970) also held that a vehicle may be searched without a warrant if probable cause is present. Justifications for acting without a warrant were further specified in *Robbins v. California* (1981):

- The mobility of motor vehicles often produces exigent circumstances.
- A diminished expectation of privacy surrounds the automobile.
- A vehicle is used for transportation and not as a residence or repository of personal belongings.
- The vehicle's occupants and contents are in plain view.
- Vehicles are necessarily highly regulated by the government.

For a warrantless search of a vehicle to be valid, law enforcement officers must have probable cause to believe the vehicle contains contraband or evidence. As the Court stated in *United States v. Cortez* (1981): "Based upon [the] whole picture, the detaining officers must have particularized an objective basis for suspecting the particular person stopped of criminal activity." A *seizure* occurs whenever a vehicle is stopped, and so Fourth Amendment prohibitions against unreasonable search and seizure apply.

If police have legally stopped a vehicle and have probable cause to believe the vehicle contains contraband, they can conduct a thorough search of the vehicle, including the trunk and any closed packages or containers found in the vehicle or the trunk. The Court said in *United States v. Ross* (1982): "If probable cause justifies the search of a lawfully stopped vehicle, it justifies the search of every part of the vehicle and its contents that may conceal the object of the search."

Limitations on warrantless searches of automobiles were set in *United States v. Henry* (1980), with the Court stating: "Once these items [for which a search warrant would be sought] are located, the search must terminate. If, however, while legitimately looking for such articles, the officer unexpectedly discovers evidence of another crime, he can seize that evidence as well" (the plain view doctrine).

In *Maryland v. Dyson* (1999), the Court again supported its previous decisions regarding motor vehicle searches by allowing police to search without a warrant when probable cause exists. In this case, Kevin Dyson was stopped by a deputy sheriff who had received a reliable tip, including the make, model, color and license plate of a vehicle suspected of transporting a sizeable amount of cocaine. Dyson argued the evidence should have been suppressed because there was no exigency to the search and no warrant was obtained to search the vehicle. The Court relied upon *Carroll v. United States* (1925) in reaffirming the existence of the motor vehicle exception to the warrant requirement when probable cause exists, adding that exigency need not exist.

Inventory Searches of Impounded Vehicles   Police officers can legally tow and impound vehicles for many reasons, including vehicles involved in accidents, parked in a tow-away zone or abandoned on a highway. When the police impound a vehicle for a legitimate reason, they may lawfully conduct an inventory search. Because the vehicle is now in police custody, officers have a duty to assure personal property is accounted for. If contraband or evidence is found, it will be admissible in court. While inventory searches are more administrative, rather than a traditional Fourth Amendment search for something illegal, these searches still meet the reasonableness requirement.

The precedent case on inventory search is *South Dakota v. Opperman* (1976). Opperman's illegally parked car was towed to the city impound lot and inventoried. During the routine inventory, a bag of marijuana was found in the unlocked glove compartment. The Court concluded that the inventory was not unreasonable under the Fourth Amendment, noting:

> These procedures [inventory of impounded vehicles] developed in response to three distinct needs: the protection of the owner's property while it remains in police custody; the protection of the police against claims or disputes over lost or stolen property; and the protection of the police from potential danger. The practice has been viewed as essential to respond to incidents of theft or vandalism. In addition, police frequently attempt to determine whether a vehicle has been stolen and thereafter abandoned.

Inventory searches are generally accepted as standard procedure for many departments. However, if evidence from a routine inventory search is to be admissible in court, the inventory must be just that: routine. Police cannot decide that some vehicles will be searched when impounded, whereas others are not. Routine inventory searches have been held reasonable; checking only certain vehicles has not. Officers from departments that usually do not conduct inventory searches cannot decide to inventory one particular vehicle.

Two Supreme Court cases illustrate the importance of having standard procedures for conducting inventory searches. In *Colorado v. Bertine* (1987), the Court upheld as lawful the Boulder Police Department's standard inventory policy, stating: "Nothing prohibits the exercise of police discretion to impound a vehicle . . . so long as that discretion is exercised according to standard criteria and on the basis of something other than suspicion of evidence of criminal activity."

The Court's ruling also extended the permissible scope of inventory searches of vehicles to include opening and examining closed containers within the vehicle *if* the police agency has a standard procedure or established routine for such activity. In the absence of such a policy, such a search would violate the Fourth Amendment.

In *Florida v. Wells* (1990), Wells had given the Florida Highway Patrol permission to open his impounded car's trunk. Police found a locked suitcase, which, upon opening, revealed a considerable amount of marijuana. Wells moved to suppress the marijuana on the grounds it was seized in violation of the Fourth Amendment. The Court held that *Colorado v. Bertine* required police agencies to have a policy mandating either that all containers be opened during such searches or that no containers be opened, leaving no room for officer discretion. Noting the absence of any such Florida Highway Patrol policy, the Court ruled: "The instant search was insufficiently regulated to satisfy the Fourth Amendment. Requiring standardized criteria or established routine as to such openings prevents individual police officers from having so much latitude that inventory searches are turned into a ruse for a general rummaging in order to discover incriminating evidence."

California v. Acevedo (1991) held that if police officers have probable cause to believe a container in an automobile holds contraband or evidence of a crime, a warrantless search of the container is justified, even if probable cause to search the vehicle has not been established. The Court also concluded that *Acevedo* was controlled by *United States v. Chadwick* (1977), which held that police could seize moveable luggage or other closed containers but could not search them without a warrant, given the person's heightened expectation of privacy regarding such containers. That is, unless exigent circumstances exist.

Exigent Circumstances

exigent • emergency

Yet another circumstance in which lawful warrantless searches can be made is if an **exigent** (emergency) situation exists. The courts have recognized that sometimes situations will arise that reasonably require immediate action before evidence may be destroyed. Police officers who have established probable cause that evidence is likely to be at a certain place and who do not have time to get a search warrant, may conduct a warrantless search. However, there must be extenuating (exigent) circumstances. Crawford (1999, p. 28) notes:

> Virtually every crime will constitute an emergency that justifies law enforcement's warrantless *entry* to the scene. Traditionally, courts have recognized three different types of emergencies: threats to life or safety, destruction or removal of evidence, and escape. It is difficult to imagine a crime scene that would not automatically present officers with the requisite belief that at least one of these exigent circumstances exists to justify, at the very least, a warrantless entry to assess the situation. Problems arise, however, when officers exceed the scope of the particular emergency that justified the initial entry.

In *United States v. Johnson* (1972), the court upheld a warrantless search of a suitcase because there was probable cause to believe it contained a sawed-off shotgun. Although a warrant is preferred because of the judicial decree that probable cause exists, if a genuinely exigent circumstance exists, such a search is reasonable.

■ Exigent circumstances include danger of physical harm to an officer or others, danger of destruction of evidence, driving while intoxicated, hot-pursuit situations and individuals requiring "rescuing," for example, unconscious individuals.

In the recent case of *Brigham City, Utah v. Stuart* (2006), the Supreme Court unanimously held that police may make a warrantless entry into a home if there is "an objective basis for belief that an exigency or emergency exists." In this case, police responding to a loud party complaint at 3:00 A.M. encountered under-aged drinking outside and saw, through a window, a fight occurring inside the home, during which a juvenile assaulted an adult, who was spitting blood.

With intent to stop the assault, police entered the back door and yelled: "Police!" but were not heard over the noise. Three Utah courts agreed the Fourth Amendment required the police knock first to request entry because they did not have a warrant and the circumstances were not sufficient to be considered exigent.

The Supreme Court, however, reversed, holding that "police may enter a home without a warrant when they have an objectively reasonable basis for believing that an occupant is seriously injured or immediately threatened with injury." Thus, the actual nature of the injuries is irrelevant. Chief Justice Roberts, writing for the Court, stated: "Under these circumstances, there was no violation of the Fourth Amendment's knock-and-announce rule. Furthermore, once the announcement was made, the officers were free to enter; it would serve no purpose to require them to stand dumbly at the door awaiting a response while those within brawled on, oblivious to their presence."

Included in the "danger to life" category are individuals suspected of being armed and dangerous and those who are unconscious. If police officers come across an unconscious person, they are obligated to search the person's pockets or purse for identification and for any possible medical information. If they discover evidence of criminal activity or contraband during this search, they may seize it. For example, in *Vause v. United States* (1931), two officers came upon an unconscious man on a public street. Unable to rouse him, they called for an ambulance and then searched his pockets for identification. During this search, they found 15 cellophane packets that contained narcotics. The Court affirmed the reasonableness of the search: ". . . the search of one found in an unconscious condition is both legally permissible and highly necessary."

Just as a warrant may be challenged, warrantless searches may also be challenged. The most frequent challenges are that the officer did not establish probable cause or that there was sufficient time to obtain a warrant.

Open Fields, Abandoned Property and Public Places

What about instances when someone, known or unknown, abandons property? For example, if a person throws something out of a car window while traveling on a freeway, has he or she forfeited any expectation of privacy? What about a tenant who abandons an apartment or discontinues payment on a storage space and never returns to claim the property inside? What about garbage placed curbside to be transported to a dump and is combined with the trash of others throughout the process? Finally, what about something left in an open field so as to be seen by anyone passing by?

This area of search and seizure does not neatly fit in any of the other exceptions to needing a search warrant. It might be considered a natural extension of the plain view doctrine. In effect, however, the courts have dealt with this area by extending the doctrine that anything held out to the public is not protected by the Fourth Amendment because no reasonable expectation of privacy exists.

■ If there is no reasonable expectation of privacy, Fourth Amendment protections do not apply.

The precedent case for search and seizure of abandoned property and open fields is *Hester v. United States* (1924). In this case, the police were investigating bootlegging operations and went to the home of Hester's father. As they came to the house, they saw a man identified as Henderson drive up to the house. The officers hid and saw Hester come out and give Henderson a bottle. The police sounded an alarm, and Hester ran to a car parked nearby and removed a gallon jug, and he and Henderson ran across an open field.

One officer chased them. Hester dropped his jug, which broke, but retained about half its contents. Henderson threw his bottle away. Officers found another broken jar that contained some liquid outside the house. The officers determined the jars contained illegal whiskey. They seized the evidence, even though they had no search or arrest warrants. Hester was convicted of concealing "distilled spirits," but on appeal, he said the officers conducted an illegal search and seizure. The Court disagreed, stating:

> It is obvious that even if there had been a trespass, the above testimony was not obtained by an illegal search or seizure. The defendant's own acts, and those of his associates, disclosed the jug, the jar and the bottle—and there was no seizure in the sense of the law when the officers examined the contents of each after it had been abandoned.

The Court went on to state: "The special protection accorded by the Fourth Amendment to the people in their 'persons, houses, papers, and effects,' is not extended to the open fields." This exception includes property disposed of in such a manner as to relinquish ordinary property rights.

The "open fields" doctrine holds that land beyond that normally associated with use of that land, that is, undeveloped land, can be searched without a warrant. In *Oliver v. United States* (1984), the Court extended *Hester* by holding that "No Trespassing" signs do not bar the public from viewing open fields; therefore, the owner should have no expectation of privacy and the Fourth Amendment does not apply. In this case, officers, responding to a tip that marijuana was being grown in an open field adjacent to a residence, conducted a warrantless search of the field, which was surrounded by a fence with a "No Trespassing" sign affixed, and found the contraband.

The Court held, because open fields are accessible to the public and the police in ways that a home, office or commercial structure would not be, and because fences and "No Trespassing" signs do not effectively bar the public from viewing open fields, the asserted expectation of privacy in open fields is not one that society recognizes as reasonable. Furthermore, measures taken to protect privacy, such as planting marijuana on secluded land and placing fences, locked gates and "No Trespassing" signs around the property, do not establish a reasonable expectation of privacy required by the Fourth Amendment. The overriding consideration is not whether the individual chose to conceal "private" activity, but whether the government's intrusion infringed on the personal and societal values protected by the Fourth Amendment. Although the government's intrusion on an open field is a trespass at common law, it is not a search in the constitutional sense. The open fields concept is a federal one, and some states hold that "No Trespassing" signs do, in fact, establish a right of privacy requiring a warrant.

Curtilage is the term used to describe that portion of property generally associated with the common use of land, such as buildings, sheds and fenced-in areas. It also includes the property around a home or dwelling directly associated with the use of that property. Because there is a reasonable expectation of privacy within the curtilage, it is protected by the Fourth Amendment.

curtilage • the portion of property generally associated with the common use of land

The concept of curtilage evolved in the Court's attempt to ascertain just how far beyond one's house the reasonable expectation of privacy extended. Inside such areas, the open fields doctrine does not apply. A warrant would be needed to search within the curtilage. In *California v. Ciraolo* (1986), the Court held that police looking from the air into a suspect's backyard does not violate the Fourth Amendment because, although part of the curtilage, it is open to public view from the air. The following year, in *United States v. Dunn* (1987), the Court upheld the warrantless search of a barn that was not part of the curtilage on the same grounds.

Similarly, after a person has discarded or abandoned property, he or she maintains no reasonable expectation of privacy. Thus, something thrown from a car, discarded during a chase or even garbage disposed of (once off the curtilage) becomes abandoned property that police may inspect without a warrant. In *California v. Greenwood* (1988), the Court held that a warrantless search and seizure of trash left curbside for collection in an area accessible by the public does not violate a person's Fourth Amendment rights, as there should be no expectation of privacy. Some states, however, have declared searching through trash a violation of the Fourth Amendment. In most states, garbage searches remain a standard technique for investigators, particularly narcotics investigators.

In *United States v. Diaz* (1994), a district court held that the defendant had no expectation of privacy in a motel parking lot. In *United States v. Garcia* (1994), a district court held that using a drug-detecting dog at an Amtrak station did not violate the defendant's Fourth Amendment rights because the defendant should have no expectation of privacy in the air surrounding his bags.

In contrast to the preceding situations, *United States v. Chun* (1993) held that officers who climbed onto a garage roof so they could look into the second floor window in the defendant's building committed an invalid warrantless search because the occupants had a reasonable expectation of privacy in this circumstance.

Border Searches and Seizures

Border searches are vital to U.S. national security. As discussed in Chapter 9, routine searches of persons, belongings and vehicles at international borders are reasonable under the Fourth Amendment, as the Constitution does not require even a hint of suspicion of criminal activity (*United States v. Ramsey*, 1977; *Carroll v. United States*, 1925; *Boyd v. United States*, 1886).

The Supreme Court held in *United States v. Montoya de Hernandez* (1985) that routine searches at a U.S. international border require no objective justification, probable cause or warrant. In *Quinones-Ruiz v. United States* (1994), the Court stated: "The border search exception applies equally to persons entering or exit-ing the country."

Regarding a person's *reasonable expectation of privacy,* the Court has ruled: "A 'search' occurs when an expectation of privacy that society is prepared to consider reasonable is infringed" (*United States v. Jacobsen,* 1984). A more recent case, *Bond v. United States* (2000), involved a border patrol agent's physical manipulation of a bus passenger's carry-on luggage. Kil (2000, p. 28) explains:

> Bond was a passenger with carry-on luggage on a bus. When the bus stopped at a Border Patrol checkpoint, a Border Patrol agent boarded the bus to check the passengers' immigrant status. In an effort to locate illegal drugs, the agent began to squeeze the soft luggage, which some passengers had placed in the overhead storage space above their seats. The agent squeezed the canvas bag above Bond's seat and noticed that it contained a "brick-like" object. Bond admitted that the bag was his and consented to its search. When the agent looked inside the bag, he discovered a "brick" of methamphetamine.

Bond was indicted for federal drug charges but moved to suppress the drugs, arguing that the agent had conducted an illegal search when he squeezed the bag. The Supreme Court reversed the District Court and Court of Appeals when it held: "A reasonable expectation of privacy exists when the person's subjective expectation is objectively reasonable." According to the Court, a traveler's per-sonal luggage is an "effect" protected by the Fourth Amendment. Because Bond used an opaque bag and placed it directly above his seat, he expressed a subjec-tive expectation of privacy in his bag. Furthermore, his expectation of privacy was objectively reasonable because "although a bus passenger expects other passen-gers or bus employees to handle or move his bag when he places it in an over-head storage area, he does not expect that they will feel the bag in an exploratory manner" (Kil, p. 29). Thus, the agent's manipulation of the bag was an infringe-ment of Bond's reasonable expectation of privacy and constituted a search.

The Court continued by ruling that any search conducted without a warrant is per se unreasonable, unless it falls under a specified exception. Although Bond had consented to the search, the consent was not at issue. The agent's manipula-tion of the bag was at issue, and the government did not assert Bond's consent as a basis for admitting the evidence (Kil, p. 29). This decision directly affects federal and state law enforcement officers' ability to enforce drug laws against those carrying large amounts of narcotics on public transportation.

The complexity of U.S. society has generated an incredible amount of case law pertaining to the Fourth Amendment. What some regard as loopholes that allow the guilty to go free, others see as stringent government control to ensure that either overzealousness or simple error will not result in the innocent being convicted.

functional equivalent • equal or essentially the same

The Supreme Court has also recognized that routine border searches may be carried out not only at borders but also at their **functional equivalent,** meaning being essentially the same, serving the same purpose, for example, airports that receive nonstop flights from foreign countries.

■   The Court has ruled that routine searches at borders and at international airports are reasonable under the Fourth Amendment.

People at airports are increasingly being stopped because they fit a drug courier profile. This profile, developed by the Drug Enforcement Administration (DEA), includes the following characteristics: (1) arriving from a source city,

(2) little or no luggage or large quantity of empty suitcases, (3) rapid turnaround on airplane trip, (4) use of assumed name, (5) possession of large amount of cash, (6) cash purchase of ticket and (7) nervous appearance.

This method is well illustrated in *United States v. Sokolow* (1989), which held that use of a drug courier profile to make an investigative stop was legal. In this case, officers used a profile to detain Sokolow. A drug-detecting dog indicated the presence of narcotics in one of Sokolow's bags. The officers arrested Sokolow and obtained a search warrant for the bag. They found no narcotics but did find documents that indicated involvement in drug trafficking. A second search with the drug-detecting dog turned up narcotics in a second bag that belonged to Sokolow.

At trial, the defense objected to the legality of the investigative stop, but the Court held that the totality of circumstances in the case, the "fit" with the numerous criteria for the drug courier profile, established a reasonable suspicion that the suspect was transporting illegal drugs, which made the investigative stop without a warrant valid.

A profile of a terrorist has also been developed on the basis of the characteristics of the September 11, 2001, hijackers. All were males from the Middle East who spoke Arabic and were in their twenties. Is special attention to individuals who fit this profile constitutional?

The farther a person gets from the border, however, the more traditional search-and-seizure requirements come back into play. Roaming border patrol agents may stop individuals or cars away from the actual border only if they have the traditional reasonable suspicion. Similar to the authorized use of roadblocks elsewhere, border agents can establish roadblocks that stop cars in a certain pattern (every car, every other car, every fifth car, etc.). However, searches may only be conducted according to the traditional rules that apply to vehicles, such as probable cause to believe contraband is present and the like. Figure 10.3 summarizes when searches are "reasonable" and, therefore, constitutional.

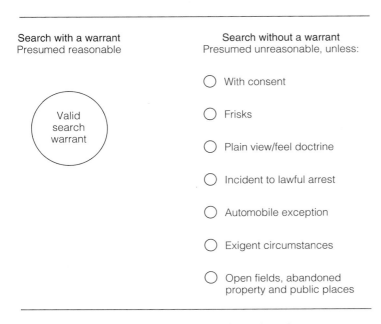

Search with a warrant
Presumed reasonable

Valid search warrant

Search without a warrant
Presumed unreasonable, unless:

◯ With consent

◯ Frisks

◯ Plain view/feel doctrine

◯ Incident to lawful arrest

◯ Automobile exception

◯ Exigent circumstances

◯ Open fields, abandoned property and public places

Figure 10.3 Constitutional Analysis of Search and Seizure

Electronic Surveillance and the Fourth Amendment

The landmark case in the area of electronic surveillance and the issue of the expectation of privacy is *Katz v. United States* (1967).

■ Electronic surveillance is a form of search and seizure and as such is governed by the Fourth Amendment.

In the earlier case of *Olmstead v. United States* (1928), the Court held that in this case, wiretapping was not a "search" within the meaning of the Fourth Amendment because neither was there physical invasion onto someone's property nor was there a taking of tangible items. The *Katz* Court overruled *Olmstead* almost 40 years later, holding that such intrusion into people's lives *does* violate an expectation of privacy, and that a search had, indeed, occurred.

In *Katz*, the defendant had been convicted of gambling violations, and the evidence against him was a conversation heard by FBI agents using an electronic device attached to the public phone booth Katz was calling from. Katz argued that even a public phone booth is a constitutionally protected area because the user expects privacy, and that evidence collected electronically was a violation of the right to privacy of the person using the phone booth. The Supreme Court agreed, holding that any form of electronic surveillance (including recording phone calls) that violates a *reasonable expectation of privacy* constitutes a search. No actual physical trespass is required by the government: "The Fourth Amendment protects people not places. . . . Wherever a man may be, he is entitled to know that he will remain free from unreasonable searches and seizures." The Court's opinion continued:

> The government stresses the fact that the telephone booth from which the petitioner made his call was constructed partly of glass, so that he was as visible after he entered it as he would have been if he had remained outside. But what he sought to exclude when he entered the booth was not the intruding eye, it was the uninvited ear. He did not shed his right to do so simply because he made his calls from a place where he might be seen. No less than an individual in a business office, in a friend's apartment, or in a taxicab, a person in a telephone booth may rely upon the protection of the Fourth Amendment. One who occupies it, shuts the door behind him, and pays the toll that permits him to place a call is surely entitled to assume that the words he utters into the mouthpiece will not be broadcast to the world. To read the Constitution more narrowly is to ignore the vital role that the public telephone has come to play in private communication.

■ For a search to have occurred, government agents need not physically go onto someone's property. Information obtained whenever there is a reasonable expectation of privacy constitutes a search.

Similarly, in *United States v. Karo* (1984), the Court held a warrantless search unconstitutional when the police monitored a homing device (beeper) in a can of material used to make illegal drugs when it was taken into the defendant's home. However, this case needs to be contrasted with situations in which the police put such a device on or in a car to monitor its location on a public road, under which circumstances the Court has determined the police were merely supplementing their sensory faculties, and there is no reasonable expectation of privacy when driving a car on a public road (*United States v. Knotts,* 1983).

The Court-created reasonable expectation of privacy doctrine continues to be how the Court determines whether a search has occurred and has been extended from electronic eavesdropping to searches of people, their luggage (including briefcases, purses and backpacks), where they live and even their bodies. Searches of homes (*Payton v. New York,* 1980), hotel rooms (*Stoner v. California,* 1964) and businesses (*Maryland v. Macon,* 1985), as well as obtaining evidence from a person's body, such as urine testing (*Skinner v. Railway Labor Executives' Association,* 1989), or the surgical removal of a bullet lodged within a person (*Winston v. Lee,* 1985) are all cases that have been held to constitute searches under the Fourth Amendment because in each, the person has a reasonable expectation of privacy. As such, a warrant is generally required.

Can you imagine the framers of the Constitution if they were able to know what marvels of electronic surveillance equipment their Fourth Amendment was limiting? The ability of equipment to listen, record and intrude through electronic surveillance continues to become more incredible. By intruding into people's conversations, or quite literally every aspect of their homes, the potential for abuse is a Fourth Amendment concern.

The *Katz* Court concluded that a Fourth Amendment analysis was to address *privacy* rather than *property.* In *Berger v. New York* (1967), the Court held that a Fourth Amendment search does occur when electronic devices are used to capture conversations.

■ The Fourth Amendment does not limit the use of electronic equipment that merely enhances the officers' senses but does not interfere with a person's reasonable expectation of privacy. Lights, photography from aircraft or telescopes fall within this area.

Wiretapping created sufficient concern about the government eavesdropping on phone conversations that Congress passed Title III of the Omnibus Crime Control and Safe Streets Act of 1965, which prohibits the interception of phone conversations unless one party to the conversation consents. "Interception" is defined within this federal statute as "aural or other acquisition of the contents of any wire, electronic or oral communication through the use of any electronic, mechanical, or other device." Subsequent legislation has brought cellular phones within this definition.

The Omnibus Crime Control Act requires warrants for electronic surveillance and requires states to adopt similar legislation. The application for such a warrant, or wiretap order, must be very detailed and include why less-intrusive means are not practical and show that other investigative means have been attempted (but does not require that *all* other methods be exhausted). The judge who authorizes the wiretap must find probable cause that the suspect has committed or is committing one of a number of specified crimes within the statute and that other means of investigation will not be effective. The order will then be effective for only a specific period, usually no more than 30 days, and the recordings made must be provided to the judge who issued the order, who has control over them.

A series of cases and legislation evolved that sought to come to grips with this complex, powerful new area of obtaining evidence. Most place emphasis on "privacy" rather than on "property." During the 1960s, case law sought to define what uses of technology would be considered "reasonable."

In *Osborn v. United States* (1966), undercover federal agents with a warrant taped a conversation using a hidden recorder in an attempt to prove that labor leader Jimmy Hoffa's lawyer was bribing a juror. The evidence was admitted on the basis that the electronic device was used in "precise and discriminate circumstances" set forth in the warrant.

Berger v. New York (1967) held that using such devices must be limited and that a "two month surveillance period was the equivalent of a series of intrusions, searches and seizures pursuant to a single showing of probable cause." Warrants may be issued for such a redundant period, but beyond that, they must be reviewed or extended.

Other factors contributing to passage of this act included the social unrest caused by the assassinations of Martin Luther King, Jr., and Robert F. Kennedy, as well as the "law and order" presidential campaign of Richard Nixon. Title III called for judicial supervision of all aspects of electronic surveillance.

■ To obtain an electronic-surveillance warrant, probable cause that a person is engaging in particular communications must be established by the court, and normal investigative procedures must have already been tried.

Title III established specific procedures to apply for, issue and execute court orders to intercept wire or oral communications.

The Supreme Court has ruled that the expectation of privacy does not exist when someone voluntarily converses with someone else—the "unreliable ear" exception. The lower courts have held that this expectation does not exist when someone converses in public because others may hear—the "uninvited ear" exception. For instance, a warrant is not required for an undercover officer to converse with suspects and use what they say in court.

Title III also regulates use of electronic devices to tap or intercept wire communications. Such devices are legal under only two conditions: (1) a court order authorizes the wiretap or (2) one person consents to the wiretap. *United States v. White* (1970) held that "the Constitution does not prohibit a government agent from using an electronic device to record a telephone conversation between two parties with the consent of one party to the conversation." In some states, as long as there is one-party consent, a wiretap is not a Fourth Amendment issue.

Title III also does not require a warrant for use of a device to trace telephone calls or devices that record what phone numbers were called from a specific phone because actual conversations are not being monitored. A warrant could be required, however, to install such devices. The federal Electronic Communication Privacy Act (ECPA) of 1986 defines an oral communication as one made by a person exhibiting a reasonable expectation of privacy and stipulates that a warrant is required only when the parties have a reasonable expectation of privacy.

The area of electronic surveillance and expectations of privacy offers additional support for the enduring quality of the Constitution. The explosive development of technology continues to present challenges to which the Fourth Amendment can respond. The incredible increase in the use of computers in our society will surely challenge existing law in this area. Although the computer age presents search-and-seizure issues that Benjamin Franklin and Thomas Jefferson could never have dreamed of, the document they helped draft remains responsive. Telephones, pagers, cellular technology and the Internet all present areas that continue to be further defined by case law.

In addition, pen registers, cordless and cellular phones, digital display pagers and thermal imagers can provide police with needed information but can also raise constitutional issues. Pen registers record every number dialed from a specific telephone. The Supreme Court has ruled that using a pen register to obtain numbers dialed from a phone does not constitute a search and, therefore, does not require a warrant (*Smith v. Maryland,* 1979). Some state courts, however, might view such action as "unreasonable interception of private communication." Likewise, because cordless and cellular phones use radio waves that anyone can receive, the courts have ruled that police may use randomly intercepted cordless and cellular phone conversations as a basis for obtaining a search warrant (*United States v. Smith,* 1992).

A similar situation exists with digital display pagers. Although police often intercept the signals of suspected drug dealers' pagers, one state supreme court has ruled that police must follow the procedures and standards applicable to wiretapping before they may intercept pager signals (*State v. Jackson,* 1995).

The Fourth Amendment and Corrections

In an effort to respond to the issue of dealing with individuals found guilty and sentenced for their crimes, the corrections component of the criminal justice system is made up of two basic sections. The *institutional corrections* component consists of the jails and prisons in which inmates are housed for varying times. The *community corrections* component deals with those still under the court's jurisdiction, who have been sentenced but remain in the community under the supervision and direction of the corrections system.

Institutional Corrections

A surprise to some people is that prisoners have constitutional rights. However, the rights prisoners have are limited. In *Hudson v. Palmer* (1984), the Court stated: "While prisoners enjoy many protections of the Constitution that are not fundamentally inconsistent with imprisonment itself or incompatible with the objectives of incarceration, imprisonment carries with it the circumscription or loss of many rights as being necessary to accommodate the institutional needs and objectives of prison facilities, particularly internal security and safety. It would be impossible to accomplish the prison objectives of preventing the introduction of weapons, drugs and other contraband into the premises if inmates retained a right of privacy in their cells." Searches are a reasonable part of prison life among inmates who have very little expectation of privacy, but how searches are carried out can conceivably challenge the reasonableness clause of the Fourth Amendment.

In *Moore v. People* (1970), the court ruled that searches conducted by correctional personnel "are not unreasonable as long as they are not for the purpose of harassing or humiliating the inmate in a cruel or unusual manner." Likewise, in *Bell v. Wolfish* (1979), the Supreme Court ruled that unannounced cell searches or shakedowns did not require warrants, were not a violation of inmates' Fourth Amendment rights and were justified by a correctional facility's need to maintain order.

Although courts have generally allowed intrusion, within broad limits, into inmates' privacy, some court rulings have extended the degree of privacy to which inmates are permitted. Two cases, *Turner v. Safley* (1987) and *Jordan v. Gardner* (1993), illustrate the conflict among court decisions regarding inmates' constitutional right to privacy. In *Turner*, the Supreme Court ruled in favor of the administrator-defendant and upheld the correctional policy allowing cross-gender searches: "When a prison regulation impinges on inmates' constitutional rights, the regulation is valid if it is reasonably related to legitimate penological interests." In *Jordan*, however, the court sided with the inmate-plaintiff, holding that female inmates subjected to unclothed body searches by male officers had, in fact, been subjected to an unconstitutional search.

■ Prison inmates, probationers and parolees have limited Fourth Amendment rights because while under supervision, they should not expect the degree of privacy enjoyed by law-abiding citizens.

Searches are conducted on visitors, correctional officers and other corrections personnel, as these individuals may smuggle contraband to inmates. The obvious need for prison security is paramount, but courts expect it to be accomplished by lawful, reasonable means.

Community Corrections

Not all people convicted of crimes are sent to prison. The majority of those incarcerated are returned to society, most often under some degree of supervision for a determined length of time, while on either probation or parole. According to Colbridge (2003, p. 22): "Probation is a sentence imposed upon a person after conviction, releasing the person into society in lieu of a prison term. Parole, on the other hand, is the release from prison after actually serving part of a sentence. Both sentences are provisional, depending upon the person's compliance with terms and conditions imposed by the court."

People on probation or parole are protected by the Constitution; however, what is reasonable for them is considered to be different than that for the general population. Convicted criminals do *not* lose their rights entirely. They are limited, to be sure, but not entirely forfeited. The Court in *Morrissey v. Brewer* (1972) asserted: "It is always true of probationers (as we have said it to be true of parolees) that they do not enjoy the absolute liberty to which every citizen is entitled, but only . . . conditional liberty properly dependent on observation of special (probation) restrictions." Whether one considers any sentencing to accomplish rehabilitation or retribution, government obviously has a vested interest in being involved.

Several cases have followed *Morrissey* (which confirmed due process during parole revocation hearings) and further defined to what extent the Constitution protects these individuals from unreasonable government intrusions. In *Griffin v. Wisconsin* (1987), the Supreme Court held that a probationer's residence could be searched by a probation officer if there were reasonable grounds to believe contraband was present. Joseph Griffin was on probation under the jurisdiction of the Wisconsin Department of Health and Social Services, which had a policy permitting, upon approval by a supervisor, a probation officer to search a client's home without a warrant if there were reasonable grounds to believe contraband was present. Such a search was conducted after probation officers learned from police that there "were or might be" guns in Griffin's apartment. During the search, a handgun was found, and he was charged accordingly.

Acknowledging that people on probation have constitutional rights, including protection by the Fourth Amendment, the Supreme Court affirmed that government actions must be reasonable. Recognizing the "special needs beyond normal law enforcement," the Court said that the usual requirements of a warrant based upon probable cause was not necessary, because to so require would "interfere with the operation of the probation system." The Court did not say a warrantless search could be conducted without cause, but that when there was a state policy allowing a search based on reasonable grounds, the search was reasonable under the Fourth Amendment.

More recently, in *United States v. Knights* (2001), the Supreme Court addressed the constitutionality of whether a police officer could search a probationer's home without probable cause or reasonable suspicion; however, the police said they had reasonable suspicion at the time but did not obtain a warrant because they knew that Knights had signed a probation agreement in which he consented to searches at any time. Thus, the Court did not have to deal with suspicionless searches because that was not the case here.

The Court determined that searching Knights' home without a warrant, but with reasonable suspicion, was reasonable under the Fourth Amendment because of the government's interest in regulating and monitoring probationers' behavior. This case, along with *Griffin*, makes clear that individuals on parole or probation have a lesser reasonable expectation of privacy.

In *Knights*, the Court stated: "The reasonableness of a search is determined by assessing on the one hand, the degree to which it intrudes upon an individual's privacy and, on the other hand, the degree to which it is needed for the promotion of legitimate government interest." Here, the Court clearly balanced the government's interests and those of the individual. Colbridge points out that *Griffin* and *Knights* differ because there was a procedural rule in *Griffin*, and the search was conducted by a probation officer. In *Knights*, such a search was conducted by the police and was based on a condition of his probation. Both cases involved searches based on reasonable grounds.

Courts have found that required drug testing of people on parole or probation for drug offenses is reasonable as in *United States v. Leonard* (1991). In *United States v. Thomas* (1984), a parole officer was permitted to require the client to remove his jacket to show fresh needle marks, with a subsequent search of his clothing netting drugs that were admissible as evidence. However, both searches were also based on a recognition that such searches were conditions of parole.

In 2006, in *Samson v. California*, the Court sought to further define what rights those on parole, as differentiated from probation, have by holding: "The Fourth Amendment does not prohibit a police officer from conducting a suspicionless search of a parolee." In this case, an officer searched a parolee only because of his status of being on parole, in contradiction to state law requiring the individual "agree in writing to be subject to search or seizure by a parole officer or other peace officer . . ., with or without a search warrant and with or without cause." Methamphetamine was found, Samson was charged and convicted, and his claim of a Fourth Amendment violation was rejected by the trial court. Samson appealed to the Supreme Court.

Writing for the Court, Justice Clarence Thomas explained how the law sought to balance the interests of the individual and government: "Examining the totality of the circumstances, petitioner did not have an expectation of privacy that society would recognize as legitimate. The State's interests, by contrast, are substantial." Further articulating the state's overwhelming interest in supervising parolees, Justice Thomas continued: "Parolees, who are on the continuum of state-imposed punishments, have fewer expectations of privacy than probationers, because parole is more akin to imprisonment than probation is. . . . The essence of parole is release from prison, before the completion of sentence, on the condition that the prisoner abides by certain rules during the balance of the sentence. . . . The extent and reach of those conditions demonstrate that parolees have severely diminished privacy expectations by virtue of their status alone" [*Samson v. California*, No. 04-9728 (2006)].

The issue of totally suspicionless searches has not, as of yet, been addressed by the Supreme Court. Colbridge (p. 29) states: "The weight of the current case law is against suspicionless searches, requiring some factual justification to search probationers and parolees." Understanding that the Constitution requires searches and seizures to be reasonable and prohibits general searches altogether, this position makes sense. However, until the Supreme Court specifically addresses such a case, the final answer is not known.

SUMMARY

All searches must be limited. General searches are unconstitutional and never legal. The Fourth Amendment forbids unreasonable searches and seizures and requires that any search or arrest warrant be based on probable cause. Searches with a warrant are presumed to be reasonable.

Searches conducted with a warrant must be limited to the specific area and specific items described in the warrant. Although warrantless searches are presumed unreasonable, exceptions to the warrant requirement include the following: (1) with consent, (2) frisking, (3) plain feel/view evidence, (4) incident to arrest, (5) automobile exceptions, (6) exigent (emergency) circumstances and (7) open fields, abandoned property and public places.

In the first exception, consent searches, the consent to search must be voluntary. The search must be limited to the area specified by the person granting permission. The person may revoke the consent at any time. In the second exception, stop-and-frisk situations, if a frisk is authorized by the circumstances of an investigative stop, only a limited pat down of the detainee's outer clothing for the officer's safety is authorized. In the third exception, plain feel/view, if, in the lawful course of a frisk, officers feel something that training and experience causes them to believe is contraband, there is probable cause to expand the search and seize the object—plain feel/touch. In addition, unconcealed evidence that officers see while engaged in a lawful activity is admissible in court—plain view.

In the fourth exception, searches after an arrest, the search must be immediate and must be limited to the area within the person's reach (*Chimel*). A search incident to lawful arrest allows seizure of property or containers not immediately connected with the arrestee's body, but under his or her immediate control, including backpacks, brief cases, luggage or other packages. In the fifth exception, the automobile exception, *Carroll v. United States* established that automobiles can be searched without a warrant, provided there is probable cause to believe the vehicle's contents violate the law and the vehicle would be gone before a search warrant could be obtained. The sixth exception, exigent circumstances, includes danger of physical harm to officers or another person, danger of destruction of evidence, driving while intoxicated, hot-pursuit situations and individuals requiring "rescuing."

The seventh exception, open fields, abandoned property and public places, involves the lack of expectation of privacy; therefore, the Fourth Amendment protection does not apply. The Court has ruled that routine border searches and searches at international airports are reasonable under the Fourth Amendment.

Electronic surveillance is a form of search and seizure and as such is governed by the Fourth Amendment. For a search to have occurred, government agents need not physically go onto someone's property. Information obtained whenever there is a reasonable expectation of privacy constitutes a search. The Fourth Amendment does not limit the use of electronic equipment that merely enhances officers' senses but does not interfere with a person's reasonable expectation of privacy. Lights, photography from aircraft or telescopes fall within this area. To obtain an electronic-surveillance warrant, probable cause that a person is engaging in particular communications must be established by the court, and normal investigative procedures must have already been tried. Electronic surveillance is unconstitutional only when it intrudes on one's reasonable expectations of privacy.

Prison inmates, probationers and parolees have limited Fourth Amendment rights because while under supervision, they should not expect the degree of privacy enjoyed by law-abiding citizens.

DISCUSSION QUESTIONS

1. Explain how a frisk can be a search and a seizure can be an arrest.
2. Discuss why general searches are not permissible.
3. Provide your own definition of reasonable.
4. Discuss the advantages to obtaining a warrant.
5. Should searches of motor vehicles differ from homes?
6. Provide your own definition of *reasonable expectation of privacy.*
7. Do you think the U.S. Supreme Court has been supportive of law enforcement through its rulings in cases involving the Fourth Amendment?
8. Draft a scenario in which an innocent, routine interaction between a citizen in a public place and the police could result in a continuing escalation through reasonable suspicion to probable cause, and what the results to each party would be.
9. Is the exclusionary rule effective in limiting potential abuse of the Fourth Amendment by police when searching. Could another means be more effective?
10. How do you think the Fourth Amendment will be held to apply to e-mail and other data transmitted over the Internet?

 INFOTRAC COLLEGE EDITION ASSIGNMENTS

- Use InfoTrac College Edition to assist you in answering the Discussion Questions when appropriate.
- Use InfoTrac College Edition to locate one of the following articles to outline.
    - "Hi-Tech Surveillance Tools and the Fourth Amendment," by Richard S. Julie (under the heading "searches and seizures")
    - "Anonymous Tips and Frisks," by Michael Bulzomi
    - "Limits of the Frisk," by Craig Bradley
    - "The Fourth Amendment's Iron Triangle," by Craig Bradley
    - "Probationers, Parolees, and the Fourth Amendment," by Thomas D. Colbridge
- You might also find of interest the articles under "border searches."

 INTERNET ASSIGNMENTS

- Use http://www.findlaw.com to find one Supreme Court case discussed in this chapter and brief the case.
- Use your favorite search engine to find a definition of *stop and frisk.*

COMPANION WEB SITE

■ Go to the Constitutional Law and the Criminal Justice System 3e Web site at http://cj.wadsworth.com/hessharr_constlaw3e for Case Studies and Study Guide exercises.

REFERENCES

Colbridge, Thomas D. "Probationers, Parolees, and the Fourth Amendment." *FBI Law Enforcement Bulletin*, July 2003, pp. 22–31.

Crawford, Kimberly A. "Crime Scene Searches: The Need for Fourth Amendment Compliance." *FBI Law Enforcement Bulletin*, January 1999, pp. 26–31.

Ferdico, John N. *Criminal Procedure for the Criminal Justice Professional*, 9th ed. Belmont, CA: Thomson Wadsworth Publishing, 2005.

Ferrell, Craig. "U.S. Supreme Court: Don't Base Car Search Only on Traffic Violation." *The Police Chief*, May 1999, p. 10.

Freeborg, Stacy. "Heat Seekers." *Minnesota Business*, October 2003, pp. 28–30, 51.

Hunsucker, Keith. "Right to Be, Right to See: Practical Fourth Amendment Application for Law Enforcement Officers." *The Police Chief*, September 2003, pp. 10–11.

Kil, Sophia Y. "Supreme Court Cases: 1999–2000 Term." *FBI Law Enforcement Bulletin*, November 2000, pp. 28–32.

Rutledge, Devallis. "Third Party Consent Searches." *Police*, May 2006, pp. 70–72.

Woessner, Matthew C. and Sims, Barbara. "Technological Innovation and the Application of the Fourth Amendment: Considering the Implications of *Kyllo v. United States* for Law Enforcement and Counterterrorism." *Journal of Contemporary Criminal Justice*, May 2003, pp. 224–238.

Worrall, John L. "*Kyllo v. United States:* Why the Supreme Court Has Not Laid the Thermal-Imaging Debate to Rest." *Journal of Contemporary Criminal Justice*, May 2003, pp. 205–223.

ADDITIONAL RESOURCE

Fyfe, James J. "Stops, Frisks, Searches, and the Constitution." *Criminology & Public Policy*, July 2004, pp. 379–396.

CASES CITED

Adams v. Williams, 407 U.S. 143 (1972).

Bell v. Wolfish, 441 U.S. 520 (1979).

Berger v. New York, 388 U.S. 41 (1967).

Bond v. United States, 529 U.S. 334 (2000).

Boyd v. United States, 116 U.S. 616 (1886).

Brigham City, Utah v. Stuart, 547 U.S. ____ (2006).

California v. Acevedo, 500 U.S. 565 (1991).

California v. Ciraolo, 476 U.S. 207 (1986).

California v. Greenwood, 486 U.S. 35 (1988).

Carroll v. United States, 267 U.S. 132 (1925).

Chambers v. Maroney, 399 U.S. 42 (1970).

Chimel v. California, 395 U.S. 752 (1969).

Colorado v. Bertine, 479 U.S. 367 (1987).

Commonwealth v. Tarver, 345 N.E.2d 671 (Mass. 1975).

Coolidge v. New Hampshire, 403 U.S. 443 (1971).

Florida v. Jimeno, 499 U.S. 934 (1991).

Florida v. Wells, 495 U.S. 1 (1990).

Georgia v. Randolph, 547 U.S. ____ (2006).

Griffin v. Wisconsin, 483 U.S. 868 (1987).

Hester v. United States, 265 U.S. 57 (1924).

Horton v. California, 496 U.S. 128 (1990).

Hudson v. Palmer, 468 U.S. 517 (1984).

Illinois v. Caballes, 543 U.S. 405 (2005).

Illinois v. Lafayette, 462 U.S. 640 (1983).

James v. Louisiana, 382 U.S. 36 (1965).

Jordan v. Gardner, 986 F.2d 1521 (9th Cir. 1993).

Katz v. United States, 389 U.S. 347 (1967).

Knowles v. Iowa, 525 U.S. 113 (1999).

Konop v. Hawaiian Airlines, 302 F.3d 868, 878 (9th Cir. 2002).

Kyllo v. United States, 121 S.Ct. 2038 (2001).

Marron v. United States, 275 U.S. 192 (1927).

Marshall v. Barlow's Inc., 436 U.S. 307 (1978).

Maryland v. Buie, 494 U.S. 325 (1990).

Maryland v. Dyson, 527 U.S. 465 (1999).

Maryland v. Macon, 472 U.S. 463 (1985).

Michigan v. Long, 463 U.S. 1032 (1983).

Michigan v. Summers, 452 U.S. 692 (1981).

Michigan v. Tucker, 417 U.S. 433 (1974).

Minnesota v. Dickerson, 508 U.S. 336 (1993).

Monroe v. Pape, 365 U.S. 167 (1961).

Moore v. People, 171 Colo. 338, 467 P.2d 50 (1970).

Morrissey v. Brewer, 408 U.S. 471 (1972).

New Jersey v. T.L.O., 469 U.S. 325 (1985).

New York v. Belton, 453 U.S. 454 (1981).

Ohio v. Robinette, 519 U.S. 33 (1996).

Oliver v. United States, 466 U.S. 170 (1984).

Olmstead v. United States, 277 U.S. 438 (1928).

Osborn v. United States, 385 U.S. 323 (1966).

Payton v. New York, 445 U.S. 573 (1980).

Pennsylvania v. Muniz, 496 U.S. 582 (1990).

People v. Loria, 10 N.Y.2d 368, 179 N.E.2d 478 (1961).

Quinones-Ruiz v. United States, 864 F.Supp. 983 (S.D.Cal. 1994).

Robbins v. California, 453 U.S. 420 (1981).

Salas v. State, 246 So.2d 621 (Fla. Dist. Ct. App. 1971).

Schmerber v. California, 384 U.S. 757 (1966).

Skinner v. Railway Labor Executives' Association, 409 U.S. 602 (1989).

Smith v. Maryland, 44 U.S. 735 (1979).

South Dakota v. Opperman, 428 U.S. 364 (1976).

State v. Barlow, Jr., 320 A.2d 895 (Me. 1974).

State v. Jackson, 650 So.2d 24 (Fla. 1995).

State v. Kaluna, 55 Hawaii 361, 520 P.2d 51 (1974).

State v. Lewis, 611 A.2d 69 (Me. 1992).

Stoner v. California, 376 U.S. 483 (1964).

Terry v. Ohio, 392 U.S. 1 (1968).

Thornton v. United States, 541 U.S. 615 (2004).

Turner v. Safley, 482 U.S. 78 (1987).

United States v. Biswell, 406 U.S. 311 (1972).

United States v. Campos, 221 F.3d 1143 (10th Cir. 2000).

United States v. Chadwick, 433 U.S. 1 (1977).

United States v. Chan, 830 F.Supp. 531 (N.D.Cal. 1993).

United States v. Chun, 857 F.Supp. 353 (D.N.J. 1993).

United States v. Cortez, 449 U.S. 411 (1981).

United States v. Councilman, 418 F.3d 67 (1st Cir. 2005).

United States v. Diaz, 25 F.3d 392 (6th Cir. 1994).

United States v. Dunn, 818 F.2d 742 (10th Cir. 1987).

United States v. Edwards, 415 U.S. 800 (1974).

United States v. Garcia, 42 F.3d 604 (10th Cir. 1994).

United States v. Haley, 669 F.2d 201 (4th Cir. 1982).

United States v. Hambrick, 55 F.Supp.2d 507 (W.D.Va. 1999).

United States v. Henry, 447 U.S. 264 (1980).

United States v. Jacobsen, 466 U.S. 109 (1984).

United States v. Johnson, 467 F.2d 630 (2nd Cir. 1972).

United States v. Karo, 468 U.S. 705 (1984).

United States v. Knights, 534 U.S. 112 (2001).

United States v. Knotts, 460 U.S. 276 (1983).

United States v. Lamb, 945 F.Supp. 441 (N.D.N.Y. 1996).

United States v. Leonard, 931 F.2d 463 (CA8 1991).

United States v. Lucas, 898 F.2d 6060 (1990).

United States v. Matlock, 415 U.S. 164 (1974).

United States v. Maxwell, 45 J.J. 406 (C.A.A.F. 1996).

United States v. Molinaro, 877 F.2d 1341 (7th Cir. 1989).

United States v. Montoya de Hernandez, 473 U.S. 531 (1985).

United States v. Pinson, 24 F.3d 1056 (8th Cir. 1994).

United States v. Ramsey, 431 U.S. 606 (1977).

United States v. Robinson, 414 U.S. 218 (1973).

United States v. Ross, 456 U.S. 798 (1982).

United States v. Simmons, 567 F.2d 314 (7th Cir. 1977).

United States v. Smith, 978 F.2d 171 (5th Cir. 1992).

United States v. Sokolow, 490 U.S. 1 (1989).

United States v. Strahan, 984 F.2d 159 (6th Cir. 1993).

United States v. Thomas, 729 F.2d 120 (CA2 1984).

United States v. White, 401 U.S. 745 (1970).

United States v. White, 871 F.2d 41 (6th Cir. 1989).

Vause v. United States, 284 U.S. 661 (1931).

Weeds v. United States, 255 U.S. 109 (1921).

Winston v. Lee, 470 U.S. 753 (1985).

Wright v. United States, 302 U.S. 583 (1938).

Wyoming v. Houghton, 526 U.S. 295 (1999).

CHAPTER 11

The Fifth Amendment: Due Process and Obtaining Information Legally

NO PERSON . . . SHALL BE COMPELLED IN ANY CRIMINAL CASE TO BE A WITNESS AGAINST HIMSELF; NOR BE DEPRIVED OF LIFE, LIBERTY, OR PROPERTY, WITHOUT DUE PROCESS OF LAW. . . .

—FIFTH AMENDMENT TO THE U.S. CONSTITUTION

The law of criminal procedure, dictated by due process, requires each step made by police to be in accordance with the Constitution.

DO YOU KNOW . . .

- What the Fifth Amendment prohibits the government to do and what it guarantees?
- How the Supreme Court has extended the elements of due process?
- What factors determine the voluntariness of a confession?
- The primary modern case for analyzing confessions?
- What four warnings are included in *Miranda*?
- When the *Miranda* warning must be given?
- What constitutes a valid waiver of *Miranda* rights?
- Whether private security officers need to recite the *Miranda* warning before interrogating suspects?
- What the public safety exception allows police officers to do?
- How expectations of privacy are related to statements, including confessions?
- What the modern-day precedent for establishing probable cause based on an informant's information is?
- What rights in addition to due process are guaranteed by the Fifth Amendment?
- Which rights are not incorporated?
- How the USA PATRIOT Act enhances government's ability to gather information related to suspected terrorist activities?

CAN YOU DEFINE?

beachheading

custodial interrogation

double jeopardy

due process

entrapment

grand jury

harmless error
  doctrine

indictment

just compensation

procedural due process

public safety exception

substantive due
  process

USA PATRIOT Act

waiver

Introduction

Although each amendment to the Constitution is unique, the Fifth Amendment is particularly intriguing. On the one hand, it is perhaps the best known amendment, thanks to movies and television. Everyone knows about "The right to remain silent." On the other hand, it is filled with other rights of which many people are not aware.

The majority of this chapter is devoted to the Fifth Amendment rights of individuals when government is asking them questions. This area of procedural law is vitally important to both sides because so much of law enforcement involves asking people questions. Does the person have to respond? What if they do not? Can the police force someone to talk? What if the police do force a person to talk?

Exactly what does a defendant declaring his or her Fifth Amendment rights mean in the courtroom?

The world revolves around communication. However, as electronic and technological advancements continue to defy the imagination, most of the work the government does is communicating with people the old fashioned way—by talking with them. Interviewing remains an important skill for investigators, as does understanding the rights of the individuals with whom they are talking.

What the government can do with the information it acquires usually is determined by who acquired the data and, if it was the government, how its agents obtained the information. The Constitution recognized that government is capable of letting the ends justify the means. Although the majority of criminal justice practitioners at all levels are professional, some have committed abhorrent acts that necessitate the rules that are in place.

The framers of the Constitution had seen confessions forced through atrocious means. That sort of excessive, intensive government conduct is what compelled the people to forge both a new government and its framework, which continues to define the basics of today's governmental authority. Their goal was to limit government power to ensure freedom for the people. Those who put so much careful thought into developing a document capable of lasting as the world around it changed could have had absolutely no idea how complex crime would become.

Imagine a discussion around 1787 between the likes of James Madison, Thomas Jefferson, George Washington and Benjamin Franklin anticipating the types of crimes that would occur in the future and the means government might use to investigate them. Technology, the education of government officials and criminals, combined with the amount of legal development during the past 200 years have created a legal milieu that was unimaginable to the framers of the Constitution, and yet, their document continues to work, as well as, if not better than, when they provided their final draft.

Technological developments have only increased the challenges of determining how and when government agents can obtain information. Although technology has been addressed elsewhere in this text, the acquisition of information is an important means by which the Constitution may control potential government misconduct.

This chapter introduces the different means by which the government acquires information and the laws that apply. Because a confession by the accused provides the prosecution with powerful evidence, having such an admission rejected by the court for failing to meet the necessary legal requirements can be devastating. What other proof can be as damning as an accused person proclaiming, "I did it!"? Although this area of law is admittedly complex, the basic guidelines are consistent with the spirit of the Constitution, based on fairness and due process.

This chapter begins with a discussion of the government's need to know certain information and how the Fifth Amendment governs this need to know. This discussion is followed by an explanation of two key clauses—the prohibition against self-incrimination and the guarantee of due process. Next, the law surrounding confessions and the well-known *Miranda* decision are explored, including the public safety exception to *Miranda*. This is followed by discussions of the interplay of the Fourth and Fifth Amendments and of using informants to obtain information. Next is a discussion of entrapment. The chapter then examines the other provisions of the Fifth Amendment, as well as how this amendment affects the field of corrections. The chapter concludes with a discussion of the USA PATRIOT Act.

Government's Need to Know

A debate as old as any government has been: "What does the government need to know, and what are the limits by which it is acquired?" In 1790, George Washington's friend and contributor to *The Federalist Papers*, John Jay, wrote: "Let it be remembered that civil liberty consists not in a right to every man to do just what he pleases, but it consists in an equal right to all citizens to have, enjoy, and do, in peace, security and without molestation, whatever the equal and constitutional laws of the country admit to be consistent with the public good."

Enforcing the law depends to a great degree on government agents' ability to obtain confessions from those suspected of committing crimes or knowing who did. The balance lies in doing this within the boundaries of the Constitution.

The Right against Self-Incrimination

■ The Fifth Amendment states: "No person shall . . . be compelled in any criminal case to be a witness against himself."

The right to not be compelled to testify against oneself is what most people think of when they hear about someone's Fifth Amendment rights. Do these rights include the right to refuse to provide identification to the police during a routine law enforcement *Terry* stop? In *Hiibel v. Nevada* (2004), the Supreme Court said no. This case involved the refusal of a stopped motorist to provide proper identification upon request. The refusal and conviction was held to be constitutional and not a denial of Fifth Amendment rights against self-incrimination (Scuro, 2006, p. 36).

Due Process of Law

■ The Fifth Amendment also states: "No person shall . . . be deprived of life, liberty, or property, without due process of law."

The due process clause was made applicable to state governments in *Malloy v. Hogan* (1964). **Due process** is such an important concept of American law that no precise definition accurately suits it, although the concept is simple: basic fairness must remain part of the process. It is the *right to hear and the right to be heard.*

Due process provides rules and procedures to ensure fairness to an individual and to prevent arbitrary government actions. It is a process of rules and procedures by which discretion left to an individual is removed in favor of an openness by which individual rights are protected. Procedural due process and substantive due process work to ensure to everyone the fairness of law under the Constitution.

Procedural due process refers to how laws are applied. Those amendments contained within the Bill of Rights that apply to criminal law set forth procedures

due process • the Fifth and Fourteenth Amendments' constitutionally guaranteed right of an accused to hear the charges against him or her and to be heard by the court having jurisdiction over the matter

procedural due process • constitutionally guaranteed rights of fairness in how the law is carried out or applied

government must follow. Procedural due process applies in both the criminal and the civil arenas and comes into play whenever government seeks to interfere with a person's liberty or a property interest.

■ The Supreme Court has extended the elements of due process through case law beyond the words of the Constitution but in keeping with its spirit.

The 1950s and 1960s have been called the era of the "due process revolution" in the United States. During that time, public sentiment demanded that government be held accountable and that the rights under the Constitution be applied equally to all. Government conduct in general was critically evaluated, and police conduct especially was brought into the public's eye more than ever before. *How* the police were allowed to carry out their work as well as *who* the defendant was were considered to a much greater degree. For example, police actions that would "shock the conscience" were found to violate due process (*Rochin v. California*, 1952).

In *Rochin*, Justice Frankfurter stated: "Due process of law, as a historic and generative principle, precludes defining, and thereby confining these standards of conduct more precisely than to say that convictions cannot be brought about by methods that offend 'a sense of justice.'" In this case, three deputy sheriffs acted on a tip and entered Rochin's home through an unlocked door, forced open the second-floor bedroom door and saw Rochin put two capsules into his mouth. The deputies tried to extract them but could not, so they took him to the hospital and had his stomach pumped. Two morphine capsules were recovered and used as evidence against Rochin. In overturning the conviction, Justice Frankfurter said: "This course of proceeding by agents of government to obtain evidence is bound to offend even hardened sensibilities. They are methods too close to the rack and the screw to permit constitutional differentiation."

Also found to violate the Fifth Amendment were laws, or lack of, that did not provide juveniles with due process in the legal system (*In re Gault*, 1967). In this case, a 15-year-old boy on probation was taken into custody at night for allegedly making obscene phone calls to a neighbor. His parents were not notified. When Mrs. Gault came home and found him missing, she went to the detention home and was told there would be a hearing next day. At that hearing, a general allegation of "delinquency" was made, with no specific facts stated. The complaining neighbor was not present, no one was sworn in, no attorney was present and no record was made of the proceeding. At a second hearing with the same circumstances, the judge sentenced the boy to a state industrial school until age 21—a six-year sentence for which an adult would receive a fine. The Supreme Court overruled this conviction on the grounds that Gault was deprived of his due process rights, as stated by Justice Fortas: "Where a person, infant or adult, can be seized by the State, charged and convicted for violating a state criminal law, and then ordered by the State to be confined for six years, I think the Constitution requires that he be tried in accordance with the guarantees of all provisions of the Bill of Rights made applicable to the States by the Fourteenth Amendment."

substantive due process •
constitutional requirement
that laws themselves be fair

Substantive due process requires the laws themselves be fair—not just how laws are enforced. Laws that unjustly limit a person's freedom or property rights will be found to violate the right to due process. Examples include laws that have permitted segregation and the unjust taking of property by the government.

The Fifth Amendment and Confessions

Whether examined by using a due process analysis or as a strict Fifth Amendment interpretation, this area of law has been the subject of continued judicial examination and has produced a great deal of litigation in an effort to apply constitutional limits. The primary question is: "When will confessions be admissible as evidence in court?" Justice Frankfurter, in *Culombe v. Connecticut* (1961), stated: "Despite modern advances in the technology of crime detection, offenses frequently occur about which things cannot be made to speak. And where there cannot be found innocent human witnesses to such offenses, nothing remains— if police investigation is not to be balked before it has fairly begun—but to seek out possibly guilty witnesses and ask them questions, witnesses, that is, who are suspected of knowing something about the offense precisely because they are suspected of implication in it."

Early common law permitted confessions to be obtained by any manner, including force or the threat of force. This practice continues in some countries and, unfortunately, has been documented in America's more recent past. Wrongdoings by America's military to elicit information from prisoners during wartime, especially regarding terrorism, has spawned new debate over whether the ends can justify the means. For obvious reasons, regardless of the motivation, the reliability of such admissions is to be questioned. By the middle of the eighteenth century, English courts began to limit the admissibility of confessions. The courts increasingly questioned whether the confession was voluntary or provided under improper pressure by the authorities. Thus, although the need for interrogations by law enforcement is acknowledged, not all confessions will be admissible in court.

Voluntariness of Confessions

The exclusionary rule prohibits use of confessions obtained in violation of a person's constitutional rights and those otherwise coerced and, thus, inherently unreliable. Recalling that the judge-made common law exclusionary rule seeks to hold government accountable for misconduct by prohibiting illegally obtained evidence from being admitted into evidence, an understanding of what is legally or illegally obtained information is crucial. To demonstrate that a confession was made voluntarily, many police departments tape record interrogations. Illinois has become the third state to require tape recording interrogations, following the lead of Alaska and Minnesota (Brown, 2005, p. 1).

The first confession case decided by the Supreme Court was *Brown v. Mississippi* (1936), when the Court held that confessions obtained through brutality and torture by law enforcement officials are violations of due process rights. In this case, Brown was accused of murder, and when he denied the accusation, a deputy sheriff and another hung him from a tree, but he insisted on his innocence. He was then tied to the tree and whipped, but still he maintained his innocence. Several days later, Brown was again beaten by the deputy and was told he would continue to receive beatings until he confessed. Finally, Brown confessed.

Two other suspects were also taken to that jail and accused of the murder. They were made to strip, were laid over chairs and were beaten with a leather strap with a buckle. They also finally confessed. The next day, the three were taken to the sheriff where they confessed to the murder. At the trial, which began the next day, the defendants said their confessions were false, obtained through torture. Although rope marks were clearly visible and none of the participants denied that beatings had taken place, the defendants were convicted and sentenced to death.

The Court held the confessions inadmissible, finding them void for violating the defendant's Fourteenth Amendment due process rights and noting that coerced confessions are simply not reliable: "The trial . . . is a mere pretense where the state authorities have contrived a conviction resting solely upon confessions obtained by violence. . . . It would be difficult to conceive of methods more revolting to the sense of justice than those taken to procure the confessions of these petitioners, and the use of the confessions thus obtained as the basis for conviction and sentence was a clear denial of due process."

In the case of *Fikes v. Alabama* (1957), the Supreme Court summarized the standard of that time as "whether the totality of the circumstances that preceded the confessions deprived the defendant of his power of resistance." This standard has been termed the *due process voluntariness test*, and just as consent for an officer to search must be given freely, suspects must make any admission voluntarily. A coerced confession has little credibility. Such a standard requires case-by-case analysis. In a highly publicized murder case in Minnesota, the accused confessed but later recanted his confession. In a letter to a news reporter, he wrote the following explanation of why an innocent person confined in a cell totally alone might confess:

> I got to the point where I didn't care. I just wanted to get the pain over with. I don't believe people understand what it's like to watch your life fall apart and not even have someone to talk to. . . .
>
> Try imagining sitting in a room the size of your bathroom with no window, not knowing when that door will open or what your family is doing outside it. Then picture that for a year. . . .
>
> I thought I was saving my family from more harm. . . . In my twisted thinking at the time I felt I was doing an honorable thing for the people I love more than myself. . . .
>
> They told me many times in many different ways how much better things would be if I cooperated with them. I don't know if I did it [confessed] hoping things would get better or if I just didn't care. . . . I would of sold my soul to the devil not to hear that door bang again, locking me in for another 23 hours by myself.

The courts have identified two factors in assessing the voluntariness of a confession.

■ Voluntariness of a confession is determined by (1) the police conduct involved and (2) the characteristics of the accused.

Police Conduct In *Rogers v. Richmond* (1961), Justice Frankfurter stated that involuntary confessions are "excluded not because such confessions are unlikely to be true, but because the methods used to extract them offend an underlying principle in the enforcement of our criminal law; that ours is an accusatorial and not an inquisitorial system—a system in which the state must establish guilt by evidence independently and freely secured and may not by coercion prove its charge against an accused out of his own mouth." Ferdico (2005, p. 515) lists the following conduct to be among those that violate due process:

- Threats of violence (*Beecher v. Alabama,* 1967).
- Continued interrogation of an injured and depressed suspect in a hospital intensive-care unit (*Mincey v. Arizona,* 1978).
- Physical force or the threat of force (*State v. Jennings,* 1979).
- Promises of any kind (*Bram v. United States,* 1897).
- Unfair and manipulative questioning by a state-employed psychiatrist (*Leyra v. Denno,* 1954).
- Confinement in a small place (*United States v. Koch,* 1977).
- Isolation from family, friends or lawyer (*Davis v. North Carolina,* 1966).
- Deprivation of basic needs such as food, drink and sleep (*Greenwold v. Wisconsin,* 1968)
- Unreasonably long interrogations (*Ashcraft v. Tennessee,* 1944; *Davis v. North Carolina,* 1966).
- Trickery or deception (*Spano v. New York,* 1959).
- Statement obtained during a period of unnecessary delay between arrest and first appearance to a judge (*McNabb v. United States,* 1943; *Mallory v. United States,* 1957)
- Psychological coercion (*Brewer v. Williams,* 1977)

Not all actions by police, even those that may not seem "fair," have been found to violate constitutional rights. Ferdico (p. 516) offers the following examples of police actions that have been found to *not* violate due process:

- Promises of leniency (*United States v. Guarno,* 1987)
- Encouraging a suspect to cooperate (*United States v. Ballard,* 1978)
- Misrepresentations (*Evans v. Dowd,* 1991)
- Promises of psychological treatment (*United States v. McClinton,* 1992)

Arizona v. Fulminante (1991) established that cases involving the admissibility of involuntary confessions could apply the **harmless error doctrine.** If no harm resulted, the confession should be admissible. A key question in this case was whether Fulminante's confession was coerced. In this case, Fulminante was in prison for one crime but was also suspected of having committed murder. A fellow inmate offered to protect Fulminante if he would tell him the truth about the murder, which he did. This inmate later became a state's witness and disclosed Fulminante's confession. The Court ruled that the confession was indeed coerced and, therefore, involuntary. Because it was a key factor in his conviction, the error was not harmless, and the conviction was reversed.

harmless error doctrine • involves the admissibility of involuntary confessions

Characteristics of the Accused   In addition to police conduct, courts will also consider characteristics of the accused when assessing whether a confession was voluntary. Factors such as the defendant's age, education and intelligence levels, emotional problems or mental illness and physical condition (including intoxication) will be considered in determining whether a confession was voluntary, but if it has not been coerced, a confession is presumed to have been voluntarily provided.

A Standard for Voluntariness   In *Haynes v. Washington* (1963), the Supreme Court held that the Fourteenth Amendment due process voluntariness test required examining the totality of the circumstances surrounding each confession.

Was the admission truly voluntary? Were the individual's constitutional guarantees protected? Was the good of the people balanced with the government's and the accused's freedoms? As with all constitutional cases, the balance was delicate, for the final result would vitally affect all concerned, not only in the case at hand but also in all future matters that would depend on the outcome. This case-by-case analysis was becoming cumbersome, with the stakes too high to not have some better standard by which to judge whether the confession was voluntary.

The next year saw a move away from case-by-case voluntariness analyses and the forging of a standard. Two cases decided that year, *Massiah v. United States* (1964) and *Escobedo v. Illinois* (1964) (discussed in Chapter 12), considered a single occurrence: "When the process shifts from investigatory to accusatory—when its focus is on the accused and its purpose is to elicit a confession . . . the accused must be permitted to consult with his lawyer" (*Escobedo*). The court saw interrogation to elicit a confession as a critical stage in the judicial process. The specifics of how the Fifth and Sixth Amendments work together are addressed in the next chapter; the important occurrence was the move toward something different than case-by-case analysis.

Two years after *Massiah* and *Escobedo*, the Supreme Court decided the landmark case of *Miranda v. Arizona* (1966).

Miranda

Miranda is perhaps the best known law enforcement case ever decided. This case, because of its notoriety, has arguably done more to teach constitutional law to the masses than any other source. Most television and movie watchers can recite the requirements set forth by Chief Justice Warren in this pivotal case and understand that the purpose of the warning is to let the accused know they do have rights and to protect themselves.

Miranda is not without critics. The National Center for Policy Analysis says that because of *Miranda* "substantial numbers of criminal convictions are lost each year" and suggests that "*Miranda* may be the single most damaging blow to the nation's crime fighting ability in the past half century" (Garrett, 2003, p. 6). This very important case is discussed in detail because of its historical review of this area of law, the strong position the Chief Justice took in his opinion and the equally strong dissents.

■ *Miranda* remains the precedent case referred to by courts analyzing confession issues.

The Case

Ernesto Miranda was a poor 23-year-old with only a ninth-grade education. He was arrested at his home for rape and was taken to the police station, where the complaining witness identified him. Within two hours, he signed a written confession. Miranda was never informed of his right to consult with an attorney, to have an attorney present during questioning or of his right not to be compelled to incriminate himself.

The legal issue in *Miranda* was whether the police must inform a suspect who is the subject of custodial interrogation of his constitutional rights concerning self-incrimination and counsel before questioning. Chief Justice Warren wrote:

> We hold that when an individual is taken into custody or otherwise deprived of his freedom by the authorities and is subject to questioning, the privilege against self-incrimination is jeopardized. Procedural safeguards must be employed. . . . He must be warned prior to any questioning that he has a right to remain silent, that anything he says can be used against him in a court of law, that he has the right to the presence of an attorney, and that if he cannot afford an attorney one will be appointed for him prior to any questioning if he so desires.

Miranda extended the *Escobedo* decision and shifted the area of inquiry to the Fifth Amendment. *Escobedo* brought the right to counsel to the police station before trial; *Miranda* brought the right to counsel into the street if an interrogation is to take place. *Miranda* also changed the analysis of the Fifth Amendment protection against self-incrimination from a totality of the circumstances test for voluntariness to whether those subjected to a custodial interrogation by police were advised of their rights.

The Miranda *Warning*

Miranda took the unique step of actually directing police officers to tell individuals they had in custody, before questioning them, four specific warnings. The *Miranda* warning itself may be read from a printed card or recited from memory and must include the following:

■ The Constitution requires that I inform you that:

  ■ You have the right to remain silent.
  ■ Anything you say can and will be used against you in court.
  ■ You have the right to talk to a lawyer now and have him present now or at any time during questioning.
  ■ If you cannot afford a lawyer, one will be appointed for you without cost.

Duckworth v. Eagan (1989) held that the *Miranda* warning does not need to be given verbatim—word for word—as stated in *Miranda v. Arizona*. What is required is that suspects' rights as set forth in *Miranda* are clearly conveyed. As stated in *Anderson v. State* (1969), the question is "whether the words used by the officer, in view of the age, intelligence, and demeanor of the individual being interrogated, convey a clear understanding of all *Miranda* rights."

Some officers refer to a "soft *Miranda* warning," which is recited in a less harsh and direct manner than that imprinted on most *Miranda* cards. This version is permissible as long as all elements of the warning are present. *United States v. Patane* (2004) held that a violation does not necessarily occur when police provide the warning in an alternate format or do not finish it (in this case, the suspect interrupted the officer and said he understood his rights).

How an officer provides the warnings becomes a tactical decision. At times, an officer may think the warnings stated directly could be too harsh, such as with younger suspects. Some officers may prefer to not read from a card. The issue is whether all four warnings were adequately conveyed to the suspect. Any officer could become flustered on the witness stand when told by defense counsel to recite verbatim what was said. Could officers say with certainty they were able to remember the exact words months, maybe years, later in court? Many officers find the routine of reading from the card will permit them to state this procedure in court and read from the card on the stand if so requested.

When the Miranda *Warning Must Be Given*

Circumstances that surround an interrogation and whether the situation requires a *Miranda* warning were expanded in *Oregon v. Mathiason* (1977), when the Court said:

> Any interview of one suspected of a crime by a police officer will have coercive aspects to it, simply by virtue of the fact that the police officer is part of a law enforcement system which may ultimately cause the suspect to be charged with a crime. But police officers are not required to administer *Miranda* warnings to everyone whom they question. Nor is the requirement of warnings to be imposed simply because the questioning takes place in the station house, or because the questioned person is one whom the police suspect. *Miranda* warnings are required only where there has been such a restriction on a person's freedom as to render him "in custody." It was that sort of coercive environment, which *Miranda* by its terms was made applicable, and to which it is limited.

custodial interrogation • questioning by law enforcement officers after a person has been taken into custody or otherwise deprived of freedom of action in any significant way

Through the Court's opinion, clarifications have been made to avoid ambiguities. The Court defined **custodial interrogation** as "questioning initiated by law enforcement officers after a person has been taken into custody or otherwise deprived of his freedom of action in any significant way," adding: "This is what we meant in *Escobedo* when we spoke of an investigation which had focused on an accused."

■ The *Miranda* warning must be given to a suspect interrogated in police custody, that is, when the suspect is not free to leave.

Different nuances in different cases may make determining whether the person was actually *in custody* an issue. Even being handcuffed in a squad car may be a *stop* and not an *arrest,* but the difference can be a very thin line. Obviously, when in doubt, an officer should advise the person of their rights; however, this procedure becomes a matter of circumstances and officer discretion. The real problem comes when an officer is not aware of the law and neglects to act accordingly.

Confusion over whether a person is *in custody* may be clarified by making two basic inquiries:

1. Has the person been told by police that he or she is under arrest?
2. Has the person been deprived of freedom in a significant way so that he or she does not feel reasonably free to leave the situation, based on a totality of the circumstances?

In regard to the second question, if the police will not allow the person to leave and if the person tries he or she will be detained by the police, other than in a stop situation during a brief investigatory stop, that person is under arrest, even if the police have not said, "You're under arrest." This circumstance echoes the statement of the court in *California v. Bakeler* (1983) that, for the purpose of *Miranda,* the ultimate determinant of whether a person is "in custody" is "whether the suspect has been subjected to a formal arrest or to equivalent restraints on his freedom of movement." Recall the discussion of detention tantamount to arrest and de facto arrest. No *Miranda* warning is required if there is no seizure of the person, as long as the police do not convey the message that compliance is required. An arrest situation is a much clearer encounter.

Suspect under Arrest   Clearly, an arrested person is in custody and must be given the *Miranda* warning if he or she is to be questioned by police. All detentions may not require the *Miranda* warning.

Even if a person is the suspect of a crime and being questioned, unless the interrogation is done while the suspect is in custody or deprived of freedom in any significant way, the *Miranda* warning need not be given (*Beckwith v. United States,* 1976). This decision was echoed in *Berkemer v. McCarty* (1984), when the Court held: "The . . . noncoercive aspect of ordinary traffic stops prompts us to hold that persons temporarily detained pursuant to such stops are not 'in custody' for the purposes of *Miranda.*"

In addition, *Pennsylvania v. Muniz* (1990) established that police may ask routine questions of individuals suspected of driving under the influence of alcohol or drugs and ask them to perform certain tests without giving them the *Miranda* warning. They may also videotape the responses given.

Suspect at the Police Station   If police direct a suspect to come to the police station for questioning or take the suspect there, this atmosphere is coercive and the *Miranda* warning *is* required. If, however, the suspect voluntarily comes to the station, no warning is required. As noted in *Miranda:* "There is no requirement that police stop a person who enters a police station and states that he wishes to confess to a crime, or a person who calls the police to offer a confession or any other statement he desires to make. Volunteered statements of any kind are not barred by the Fifth Amendment and their admissibility is not affected by our holding today."

The same is usually true of questioning a suspect in a police car. If the suspect is told to get into the car, it is usually a custodial situation, especially if the person cannot get out of the car or will not be let out if they ask.

If, on the other hand, someone flags down a police car and makes a voluntary confession of a crime he or she just committed, no *Miranda* warning is required. If the officer did not ask any questions of the suspect, no *Miranda* is necessary, and the warning is not required if the person just walks up to an officer and is not in custody and confesses (*United States v. Jones,* 1986; *United States v. Wright,* 1993).

Suspect Is in Custody for Another Offense   Because the suspect is obviously in custody, the *Miranda* warning must be given before any questioning begins. All that is required is that a custodial situation exists. What the person is in custody for does not matter.

Other Factors Indicating a Custodial Situation   Most kinds of physical restraint place the situation within the *Miranda* requirement. As found in *People v. Shivers* (1967), if a police officer holds a gun on a person, that person is in custody and not free to leave. If, however, the suspect also has a gun, he or she would unlikely be considered in custody (*Yates v. United States,* 1967).

The Court continues to refine these matters as they hear new cases. In *Muehler v. Mena* (2005), the Court held that a person handcuffed, even for an extended period, while a search warrant is executed at that location is not considered under arrest and, therefore, need not be read *Miranda.*

Waiving the Rights

A **waiver** is a purposeful, voluntary giving up of a known right. Suspects must know and understand their constitutional rights to legally waive them. The Court in *Miranda* set forth that a statement will be admissible only if the government meets its "heavy burden" of demonstrating "that the defendant knowingly and intelligently waived his privilege against self-incrimination and his right to retained or appointed counsel." Further, at any time during questioning, the defendant may choose to exercise the right to remain silent.

■ If after hearing a police officer read the *Miranda* warning, suspects remain silent, this silence is not a waiver. To waive their rights, suspects must state, orally or in writing, that (1) they understand their rights and (2) they will voluntarily answer questions without a lawyer present.

Suspects' competency to understand and waive their rights should always be considered. People who are under the influence of alcohol or other drugs, are physically injured, are in shock or are very young or very old may have difficulty understanding the situation. As noted, suspects may rescind the waiver at any point in the interrogation. People must possess sufficient competence to understand they are waiving a crucial constitutional right. Although television may have exposed many to such rights, the Court in *Tague v. Louisiana* (1980) reemphasized that the government has the "heavy burden" of showing the person was competent to relinquish these rights.

Oregon v. Elstad (1985) established that if police obtain a voluntary admission from a suspect without first being advised of the right to remain silent, a confession made after the *Miranda* warning is given will be admissible: "Absent deliberately coercive or improper tactics in obtaining the initial statement, the mere fact that a suspect has made an unwarned admission does not warrant a presumption of compulsion. A subsequent administration of *Miranda* warnings to a suspect who has given a voluntary but unwarned statement ordinarily should suffice to remove the conditions that precluded admission of the earlier statement."

Colorado v. Spring (1987) established that a waiver of *Miranda* rights is valid, even though the suspect thought the questioning was going to be about a minor crime, but the police changed their line of questioning to inquire about a more serious crime. At this point the suspect could recant the waiver.

Connecticut v. Barrett (1987) established that if a suspect refuses to make a written statement without a lawyer present but does make an oral confession, that confession is admissible.

Finally, *Patterson v. Illinois* (1988) established that a waiver includes waiving the right to counsel in addition to the right against self-incrimination. There is often confusion as to what constitutes a valid waiver and what constitutes an invocation of those rights, especially when the suspect is ambiguous. In *Davis v. United States* (1994), after a fatal attack by one sailor on another with a pool cue over a pool game, the police arrested Davis and questioned him after advising him of his *Miranda* rights. After one and a half hours of talking to the police Davis said, "Maybe I should talk to a lawyer," but then said, "No, I don't want a lawyer," so the questioning continued. "Finding that the statement . . . was not an unequivocal, unambiguous invocation of the right to counsel, the Court upheld admission of Davis's statements and unanimously affirmed his conviction and sentence" (Rutledge, 2006, p. 70). The Court's opinion included: "We decline to adopt a rule requiring officers to ask clarifying questions. If the suspect's statement is not an unambiguous or unequivocal request for counsel, the officers have no obligation to stop questioning him." Rutledge (p. 72) provides specific language that does not require questioning to stop:

"I just don't think that I should say anything." (*Burket v. Angelone,* 2000)
"I don't got nothing to say." (*United States v Banks,* 2003)
"Do you think I need a lawyer?" (*Diaz v. Senkowski,* 1996)
"Could I call my lawyer?" (*Dormire v. Wilkinson,* 2001)
"I think I would like to talk to my lawyer." (*Clark v. Murphy,* 2003)
"Go ahead an run the lawyers." (*Mincey v. Head,* 2000)

Beachheading or "Question First"

Holtz (2005, p. 20) cautions that deliberate "end runs" around *Miranda,* purposely withholding *Miranda* warnings until after a confession is obtained and then giving *Miranda* to re-ask the question, have been found by the Supreme Court to be improper.

The Court rejected the prosecution's argument that a confession repeated using a question-first strategy was admissible in *Oregon v. Elstad,* stating that the failure to preliminarily provide the *Miranda* warning was a "good faith" mistake, not a conscious decision. *Missouri v. Seibert,* in a 5-to-4 vote, rejected the two-step questioning tactic as a deliberate way to sidestep *Miranda.* Therefore, according to Holtz, a "subsequent administration of *Miranda* warnings to a suspect who has given a voluntary but unwarned statement ordinarily should suffice to remove the conditions that precluded admission of the earlier statement." The result is that the previous unwarned admission is excluded, but all admissions made after the proper *Miranda* warnings are given are valid and admissible.

beachheading • the unconstitutional approach of purposely withholding the *Miranda* warnings until after a confession is obtained and then giving *Miranda* to re-ask the question

Miranda *Survives a Challenge*—Dickerson v. United States

If a feature movie were made about the Fifth Amendment right against self-incrimination, it would undoubtedly be based on *Dickerson v. United States* (2000). The case has everything: history, famous people, Congress versus the Supreme Court, police versus criminals, good versus evil, the quest for truth and justice and heated exchanges between Supreme Court justices, *and* it provides a comprehensive review of how this area of criminal procedure developed and why. The entire legal community anxiously awaited the opinion of the Court as to whether *Miranda* would remain the law.

The drama unfolded the morning of June 27, 2000, when Chief Justice William Rehnquist himself delivered the opinion of the Court, which he had written, as had Chief Justice Earl Warren with *Miranda.* Tension was thick, but *Miranda* was upheld by a vote of 7 to 2.

In this case, Dickerson was indicted for bank robbery using a firearm. He moved to suppress his statement made to the FBI based on their not advising him of his rights per *Miranda* before being interrogated. The government relied on a federal law, Section 3501 of the Omnibus Crime Control and Safe Streets Act of 1968, which stated that the admissibility of statements should turn only on whether they were voluntarily made, and not only on whether the *Miranda* warning had been given. The case had two major issues: (1) whether *Miranda* would remain in effect when a federal statute did not require it and (2) whether

Congress could enact a law contrary to that which the Supreme Court had declared to be the constitutional requirement.

Proving again that the various laws are not isolated unto themselves but rely on one another, the Supreme Court returned to a case discussed earlier to address whether Congress could supercede the Supreme Court, *Marbury v. Madison* (1803). In using a precedent set nearly 200 years ago, Chief Justice Rehnquist repeated what was determined by *Marbury*: "*Miranda*, being a constitutional decision of this Court, may not be in effect overruled by an Act of Congress. . . . The law is clear as to whether Congress has constitutional authority to do so. This Court has supervisory authority over the federal courts to prescribe binding rules of evidence and procedure."

The second issue, whether *Miranda* would remain good law, is discussed in great detail that reviews the history of Fifth Amendment self-incrimination law. The federal statute in issue returned to a totality of the circumstances to determine whether the statement was voluntary and not strictly requiring the *Miranda* warnings be given. This action, in effect, was a return to what cases before *Miranda* held. The Court found that: "Stare decisis weighs heavily against overruling it now. Even in constitutional cases, stare decisis carries such persuasive force that the Court has always required a departure from precedent to be supported by some special justification. . . . There is no such justification here. *Miranda* has become embedded in routine police practice to the point where the warnings have become part of our national culture."

The opinion went on to state: "Experience suggests that [this federal statute's] totality-of-the-circumstances test is more difficult than *Miranda* for officers to conform to, and for courts to apply consistently. The requirement that *Miranda* warnings be given does not dispense with the voluntariness inquiry, but cases in which a defendant can make a colorable argument that a self-incriminating statement was compelled despite officers' adherence to *Miranda* are rare."

In sharp dissent, Justices Clarence Thomas and Antonin Scalia accused their colleagues of dismissing previous rulings in which *Miranda's* constitutional underpinnings were questioned ("The Supremes Sing Out . . .," 2000, p. 10): "Since there is in fact no other principle that can reconcile today's judgment with the post-*Miranda* cases that the court refuses to abandon," wrote Scalia, "what today's decision will stand for, whether the justices can bring themselves to say it or not, is the power of the Supreme Court to write a prophylactic, extra-constitutional Constitution, binding on Congress and the states."

Another law that could be deemed to have become "part of our national culture" in the sense *Miranda* has is difficult to imagine. Finding a better example of how American law does what it was intended to so very well is also difficult, yet not without controversy.

Miranda *Issues Continue*

Miranda issues are certainly not over. In *Chavez v. Martinez* (2003), the Court ruled that violating the *Miranda* decision does not subject law enforcement to civil liability if any statements so obtained are not used against the plaintiff in court. According to Judge and Higginbotham (2003, p. 13): "The Court reasoned that although the *Miranda* rule protects important constitutional guarantees, the core Fifth Amendment privilege against self-incrimination does not come into play until trial."

Holtz (2003, p. 162), noting a second issue—could law enforcement officers be held civilly liable under the due process clause of the Fourteenth Amendment—states: "The 5–3 decision [in *Chavez*] produced six opinions, but no majority judgment, leaving the door wide open for the issue to be raised again" ("Supreme Court Hedges Its Bets in Latest Miranda Ruling," 2003, p. 9).

When *Miranda* *Warnings* *Generally* *Are* Not *Required*

Although the *Miranda* decision appears to provide a bright-line rule, case law has continued to guide when the warnings must be given and when they need not. del Carmen (2001, p. 351) lists several instances in which *Miranda* warnings are not normally required:

- When the officer asks no questions
- During general on-the-scene questioning
- When the statement is volunteered
- When questioning a suspect about identification
- When questioning witnesses
- In stop-and-frisk cases
- When asking routine questions of drunken-driving suspects and videotaping the proceedings
- During lineups, showups or photographic identifications
- When the statement is made to a private person
- When the suspect appears before a grand jury
- When there is a threat to public safety

Brief questioning in stores, restaurants, parks, hospitals and other public places is generally considered noncustodial unless the subject is not free to leave. If the suspect is not being detained by the police, the situation is not a custodial situation. The question is: "If the person tried to leave, would the police stop them?"

Likewise, very brief questioning, such as in stop-and-frisk cases and general questioning at a crime scene, is not a custodial situation. Law enforcement officers are allowed to briefly detain witnesses at a crime scene for questioning without *Miranda* warnings. Citizen witnesses directed by an officer not to leave a crime scene are unlikely to consider themselves in custody, and a court unlikely would so consider them (*Arnold v. United States*, 1967).

Another question that arises is whether the *Miranda* warning needs to be given to individuals temporarily detained by the police. This situation arose in *Utsler v. South Dakota* (1969). In this case, police had been alerted to look for a white Mustang with California license plates, believed to be driven by a suspected robber. When officers saw a car fitting that description, they stopped it and asked the driver for identification and whether he had been in the vicinity of the robbery. The driver was convicted of robbery and appealed, stating the officers had not given him a *Miranda* warning before asking questions. The court found nothing in the way the officers handled the case that called for a *Miranda* warning when they initially stopped the car: "In our opinion *Miranda* was not intended to prohibit police officers from asking suspicious persons such things as their names and recent whereabouts without fully informing them of their constitutional rights." The *Miranda* warning need not be given during a stop, as compared with an arrest.

The supreme court of Washington agreed in *State v. Lane* (1997), when it stated: "We hold that it is not a violation of either the letter or the spirit of *Miranda* for police to ask questions which are strictly limited to protecting the immediate physical safety of the police themselves and which could not reasonably be delayed until after warnings are given."

Another exception to interrogation in the absence of a *Miranda* warning is questioning done by a private security officer. Remember, the Constitution exists to regulate the *government's* authority. The regulations set forth by the Constitution apply to government agents, not to private individuals. This stipulation means private security personnel are not bound by constitutional restraints; however, it does not mean they will not be held accountable for wrongful acts, including crimes or civil wrongs. For example, in *State of Minnesota v. Spencer* (1987), the Minnesota Supreme Court relied on the *Miranda* Court that the Fifth Amendment applies only to government agents, and not private security personnel, no matter how much they may look like public police.

■ Private security officers are not required to advise suspects of their *Miranda* rights.

Case law continues to recognize the clear differentiation between public police and private security.

The Public Safety Exception

An important exception to the *Miranda* requirement involves public safety. The precedent case occurred in 1984 in *New York v. Quarles*, when the Supreme Court ruled on the public safety exception to the *Miranda* warning requirement.

In this case, a young woman stopped two police officers and told them she had been raped. She described the rapist and said he had just entered a nearby supermarket, armed with a gun. The officers located the suspect, Benjamin Quarles, and ordered him to stop. Quarles ran, and the officers momentarily lost sight of him. When Quarles was apprehended and frisked, he was wearing an empty shoulder holster. One officer asked Quarles where the gun was, and Quarles nodded toward some cartons, saying, "The gun is over there." The officer retrieved the gun, arrested Quarles and read him his rights. Quarles waived his rights to an attorney and answered questions.

At the trial, the court ruled, pursuant to *Miranda*, that the statement "the gun is over there" and the discovery of the gun as a result were inadmissible. The U.S. Supreme Court, in reviewing the case, ruled that if *Miranda* warnings had deterred the response to the officer's question, the result would have been more than the loss of evidence. As long as the gun was concealed in the store, it was a danger to the public safety: "The need for answers to questions in a situation posing a threat to the public safety outweighs the need for the prophylactic rule protecting the Fifth Amendment's privilege against self-incrimination."

public safety exception • allows officers to question suspects without first giving the *Miranda* warning if the information sought sufficiently affects the officers' and the public's safety

■ The **public safety exception** allows police to question suspects without first giving the *Miranda* warning if the information sought sufficiently affects the officers' and the public's safety.

The Court ruled that in this case, the need to have the suspect talk took precedence over the requirement to read the defendant his rights. As the Court noted,

Table 11.1   A Brief History of Cases Pertaining to the Law of Confessions

■ *Brown v. Mississippi* (1936): Confessions obtained by the government through physical coercion violate the due process clause of the Fourteenth Amendment and are inadmissible.

■ *Rogers v. Richmond* (1961): Coercion, either physical or psychological, violates the due process clause, rendering any resulting confessions inadmissible. ". . . ours is an accusatorial and not an inquisitorial system."

■ *Escobedo v. Illinois* (1964): "When the process shifts from investigatory to accusatory—when its focus is on the accused and its purpose is to elicit a confession . . . the accused must be permitted to consult with his lawyer." In determining whether a confession would be admissible, the *Escobedo* Court moved from a due process analysis to a Sixth Amendment right to have a lawyer present and that the suspect must be advised of this.

■ *Miranda v. Arizona* (1966): Unless government has provided the warnings advising the suspect of his/her Fifth Amendment rights, and that individual has provided a valid waiver, statements will not be admissible.

■ *Edwards v. Arizona* (1981): After a person has been given his *Miranda* warnings and then invokes his right to remain silent and to have legal counsel, he cannot be questioned further until a lawyer is made available.

■ *Berkemer v. McCarty* (1984): Roadside questioning of a motorist during a routine traffic stop is not a custodial interrogation, so no *Miranda* warning is required; however, any custodial interrogation, including those resulting from misdemeanor traffic offenses, do require *Miranda.*

■ *New York v. Quarles* (1984): Created the "public safety exception" to the *Miranda* rule. When public safety necessitates immediate action by police, failure to provide the warnings will not render a statement inadmissible.

■ *Michigan v. Jackson* (1986): If the defendant invokes the right to counsel, police may not initiate interrogation until counsel has been made available.

■ *Arizona v. Roberson* (1988): After a defendant invokes the right to counsel, police may not interrogate him, even about a different crime.

■ *Minnick v. Mississippi* (1990): After a defendant requests a lawyer, the lawyer must be present at all subsequent interrogations, even if the individual had consulted with counsel.

■ *Dickerson v. United States* (2000): *Miranda* stands rather than a return to the totality of the circumstances test.

the material factor in applying this public safety exception is whether a public threat could be removed by the suspect's statement. In this case, the officer asked the question only to ensure his and the public safety. He then gave the *Miranda* warning before continuing questioning. Table 11.1 contains a brief history of key cases related to the law of confessions.

The Interplay between the Fourth and Fifth Amendments

Another important consideration in whether information obtained will be admitted in court is whether it violates a person's Fourth Amendment right to a reasonable expectation of privacy. This information is included to illustrate how different amendments interact and affect one another, as will be even more evident in the next chapter.

The precedent landmark case, *Katz v. United States* (1967), recall, involved such an issue. Recordings of phone calls placed from a public telephone booth were used in obtaining the defendant's conviction. The Supreme Court reversed the California decision, saying: ". . . the Fourth Amendment protects people not places. . . . Wherever a man may be, he is entitled to know that he will remain free from unreasonable searches and seizures." The investigators had probable cause but erred in not obtaining prior approval for their actions in the form of a warrant.

■ Statements, including confessions, will not be admissible in court if obtained while violating a person's Fourth Amendment right to a reasonable expectation of privacy.

Sometimes this reasonable expectation of privacy involves someone conversing with an informant.

Using Informants

Many crimes are solved not because officers stumble on crimes in progress but because they get information from a number of sources that help them learn who may have been involved. An informant is any person who gives government agencies information about criminal activity. Informants remain an important source of information.

The use of informants is interesting for several reasons. An issue is whether incriminating statements made to a third party, who happens to be or becomes a police informant, can be used against that person. Another issue, for a number of obvious reasons, is just how reliable an informant is. Someone may elect to inform for many reasons, not all of which are strictly legitimate.

Officers who use informants to establish probable cause must follow specific legal procedures established by case law. Recall that two Supreme Court decisions, *Aguilar v. Texas* (1964) and *Spinelli v. United States* (1969), formally established specific requirements for officers who use informants' information to prepare complaints or affidavits. These two cases were considered separate and independent of each other.

The *Aguilar* case applied a two-pronged test to determine probable cause. The first prong tested the informant's basis of knowledge. Was the information accurate? Did the informant personally witness the event reported? If not, did the information come from another source? Is there still reason to believe it?

The second prong tested the informant's credibility. Was the person reliable? Was the informant's identity known? Was the informant an ordinary citizen or a criminal?

The two-pronged test to establish probable cause was abandoned in 1983 in the landmark case *Illinois v. Gates.* Here, the Supreme Court said that in the future, they would rely on the totality of the circumstances in judging the trustworthiness of informant information.

■ The current precedent case in most states for determining probable cause based on an informant's information is the totality of the circumstances, as established in *Illinois v. Gates* (1983). In other words, is the information reliable?

In *Florida v. J.L.* (2000), the Supreme Court ruled that an anonymous tip that a person is carrying a gun is not, without more, sufficient to justify a stop and frisk of that person. However, as Reak (2001, p. 10) points out: "The U.S. Supreme Court has held that an anonymous tip can provide that foundation for reasonable suspicion when the tip predicts future activities that the officer is able to corroborate, which makes it reasonable to think that the informant has inside knowledge about the suspect."

Ordinary citizens are presumed credible when they claim to be victims of or witnesses to a crime, or when they express concern for their own safety and expect nothing in return for the information. Citizen informants are also presumed to fear the consequences of committing perjury and would, therefore, be truthful. Hendrie (2003, p. 12) asserts: "To be considered a concerned citizen informant by the courts, an informant must not be involved in the criminal milieu."

Informants who are criminal pose a problem in determining credibility. One way to establish the credibility of criminal informants is to show they have given accurate information in the past. Another way is to show they made admissions or produced evidence against their own interest. A third way is to show they have been informants for a long time. A fourth way is to conduct the investigation with the informant supervised by a law enforcement officer. Use of cellmate informants is discussed later in this chapter.

Entrapment

Due process remains the underpinning of every component of a legal case. Unconscionable or otherwise illegal behavior by the police brings about constitutional issues. Entrapment falls into this category and may be used as a defense to a criminal charge.

Entrapment is discussed here because, although it can be included in any chapter concerning people's rights, the concept of government going too far is what the study of entrapment is about. Like the issues raised in *Miranda*, government going "too far" is not good for either the government or those it serves.

Entrapment, like the *Miranda* rule, is a subject the public believes it is well versed on because of a heavy diet of television police shows. These dramas often depict officers setting up radar in obviously inconspicuous locations and then being assertively informed by the citizens tagged that the police method is a clear case of entrapment. If only it were so easy.

Just what is entrapment? Hess and Wrobleski (2006, p. 275) define **entrapment** as "an action by the police (or a government agent) persuading a person to commit a crime that the person would not otherwise have committed." Another definition is provided in *Sorrells v. United States* (1932): "Entrapment is the conception and planning of an offense by an officer and his procurement of its commission by one who would not have perpetrated it except for the trickery, persuasion, or fraud of the officer." At the same time, however, the Court noted: "Society is at war with the criminal classes, and the courts have uniformly held that in waging this warfare the forces of prevention and detection may use traps, decoys, and deception to obtain evidence of the commission of crime. Nonetheless, when police officers encourage others to engage in criminal activity, this should not be viewed lightly. Such encouragement might, in fact, cause normally law-abiding citizens to commit crime."

entrapment • the act of government officials or agents (usually police) inducing a person to commit a crime that the person would not have otherwise committed

Even when the defendant admits to committing the crime, he may argue that the law enforcement agents themselves brought the crime about. As noted by Justice Frankfurter in *Sherman v. United States* (1958): "The power of government is abused and directed to an end for which it was not constituted when employed to promote rather than detect crime and bring about the downfall of those who, left to themselves, might well have obeyed the law. Human nature is weak enough and sufficiently beset by temptations without government adding to them and generating crime."

If a private person not connected with law enforcement induces someone to commit a crime, no defense of entrapment can be used. The more involved a third party is with the police, as an informant or otherwise, the greater the argument that the individual is an *agent* of the police, which brings in constitutional consideration.

Whether entrapment exists may be determined by *subject* analysis—asking, "Was the suspect predisposed to commit the crime, or was he an unwary innocent party?" (*Hampton v. United States*, 1976). It may also be determined by *objective* analysis—asking, "Was an innocent person induced by the police to commit a crime they never would have otherwise?" (*Sherman v. United States*, 1958).

The leading case is *Jacobson v. United States* (1992), in which the defendant ordered child pornography, which was not illegal at that time. However, a law was subsequently passed making it illegal, and when a postal inspector found Jacobson's name on a mailing list, he was sent a letter from a fictitious group concocted by law enforcement. In his application for membership, Jacobson stated he was opposed to pedophilia but enjoyed sexual material showing preteen sexual photos. For more than two years, a group of government agencies contacted him through different fictitious organizations, and one postal inspector pretended to be a "pen pal" and began communicating with Jacobson. Eventually, Jacobson placed an order through one of these groups, which was not filled. Still later he ordered a magazine from yet another fake catalogue they sent him, and when it was delivered he was arrested.

The Supreme Court held that Jacobson was entrapped because, they argued, the government did so much as to "implant" in his mind the desire to commit the crime. As stated by the Court in *Sorrells v. United States:* "Government agents may not originate a criminal design, implant in an innocent person's mind the disposition to commit a criminal act, then induce commission of the crime so that the Government may prosecute."

No entrapment was found when government agents supplied one of the necessary ingredients for manufacturing a prohibited drug (*United States v. Russell*, 1973) or when they supplied heroin to a suspect predisposed to selling heroin (*Hampton v. United States*, 1976).

Other Rights Guaranteed by the Fifth Amendment

The Fifth Amendment is unique in that it covers such an array of legal areas that apply to both criminal and civil law. This broad range reflects the framers of the Constitution's awareness of the power government has over all aspects of people's lives and how that power needs to be regulated. The Fifth Amendment contains a number of seemingly unrelated elements. Some pertain more to criminal law and others to civil law. Some apply to only the federal government, whereas others apply to the states as well. Although this text addresses law as it pertains to criminal justice, to fully appreciate this amendment, it needs to be considered in total. The right of a person to not be a witness against himself is the component this amendment is best known for, but other important rights are also delineated.

■ In addition to the right to not incriminate oneself, the Fifth Amendment also guarantees:

- ■ The right to a grand jury indictment.
- ■ The prohibition against double jeopardy.
- ■ The right to receive just compensation when government takes private property.

The Right to a Grand Jury

The Fifth Amendment states: "No person shall be held to answer for a capital or otherwise infamous crime, unless on a presentment or indictment of a Grand Jury, except in cases arising in the land or naval forces, or in the Militia, when in actual service in time of War or public danger."

A **grand jury** is a group of citizens that determines whether sufficient evidence exists to send an accused to trial. Like many other aspects of American law, the concept of a grand jury has a rich history, deriving its name from the French meaning "large." Over centuries of evolution, dating back to medieval England, grand juries served two purposes: (1) to investigate a variety of crimes, including official misconduct, as an arm of the king's rule and (2) to ensure that innocent citizens were not wrongfully prosecuted. Both purposes were understandably important to those drafting the Constitution because of their attitude toward the country they had left.

A trial jury (sometimes referred to as a petit jury) differs from a grand jury in a number of ways. A trial jury most often comprises 12 jurors, whereas grand juries have 16 to 23 jurors. A trial jury needs a unanimous vote to convict, whereas a grand jury needs only 12 votes to indict. A jury composed of the defendant's "peers" is not required for a grand jury, and a grand jury may investigate misconduct, whereas a trial jury can address only what is brought before it. The jurors in a trial court hear only one case, whereas those on a grand jury hear numerous cases during their assignment. The outcome of a grand jury is to indict or not, whereas a trail jury convicts or acquits.

Another major difference is a grand jury is not open to the public, and the prosecutor appears to maintain control during the proceedings. In fact, the accused has no right to counsel or to present evidence. Rather than determining guilt or innocence, a grand jury determines only whether the government has enough evidence, whether it will be admissible or not at trial, to justify the matter proceeding to trial. One reason for the secrecy is that if the grand jury returns a "no bill of indictment," the case will not proceed and no one will know the person was involved, at least in theory. In grand jury proceedings, although the rights of a suspect are minimal, the government, in effect, is actually on trial, or at least must convince the jury it has a case. Table 11.2 summarizes the differences between a grand jury and a trial jury.

grand jury • a group of citizens who determine whether sufficient evidence exists to send an accused to trial

Table 11.2   Grand Juries and Trial (Petit) Juries Compared

Grand Jury	*Trial Jury (also known as Petit Jury)*
1 Usually composed of 16 to 23 members, with 12 votes required for an indictment	1. Usually consists of 12 members, with a unanimous vote required for conviction
2. Choice usually determined by state law, with "jury of peers" not a consideration	2. Usually chosen from voter registration list and driver's license rolls, with "jury of peers" a consideration
3. Does not determine guilt or innocence; function is to return indictment or conduct investigations of reported criminality	3. Decides guilt or innocence and, in some states, determines punishment
4. Retains the same membership for 1 month, 6 months, or 1 year; may return several indictments during that period	4. A different jury for every case
5. Hands down indictments based on probable cause	5. Convicts on the basis of evidence of guilt beyond a reasonable doubt
6. May initiate investigations of misconduct	6. Cannot initiate investigations of misconduct

Source: del Carmen, Rolando V. *Criminal Procedure: Law and Practice,* 6th ed. Belmont, CA: Wadsworth, 2004, p. 41.

indictment • a formal accusation of a defendant, usually by a grand jury, that sends the defendant on to trial for prosecution

Today, the primary job of a grand jury is to determine whether sufficient evidence exists to hand down an **indictment** (send an individual accused of a crime on to trial to be prosecuted).

■ The right to a grand jury is the only unincorporated clause of the Fifth Amendment (*Hurtado v. California,* 1884).

Although the Supreme Court has not held the grand jury clause of the Fifth Amendment to be sufficiently essential to the U.S. system of justice to incorporate it under the Fourteenth Amendment due process clause, most states have chosen to use the grand jury process themselves. Depending on the state, prosecutors may be required, or may elect, to have a grand jury evaluate their case. In the states that do not require a grand jury, the prosecutor must convince a judge that sufficient evidence exists to justify a trial. In the other states, a grand jury must indict the defendant for a trial to proceed.

Grand juries have immense power. Nevertheless, debate on the grand jury system's viability continues for several reasons. Only the prosecutor is present during the proceedings; no defendants are permitted to have their lawyers present; everything occurring during the process is kept secret; and evidence that may be inadmissible at trial is permitted. Despite these factors, grand juries are beneficial to the judicial process. The historical roots of the grand jury are noble and are still serving to deflect arbitrary government prosecution. A grand jury provides a step by which, at least in spirit, the innocent are protected. This process also attempts to avoid political or popular pressure on the prosecution in particularly notorious or otherwise sensitive cases.

However, critics assert that the system is too one-sided in favor of the prosecution, and the entire process is contrary to the openness the rest of the criminal justice system demands. Either way, grand juries provide the citizenry with an opportunity for involvement, even in cases that proceed no further, thus removing complete authority over criminal cases from the government, including the prosecution. Notably, England abandoned the grand jury process in 1933.

Double Jeopardy

The double jeopardy clause has been incorporated into the Fourteenth Amendment's due process clause and, thus, applies to the states. Its purpose was explained by Supreme Court Justice Hugo Black in *Green v. United States* (1957): "The underlying idea, one that is deeply ingrained in at least the Anglo-American system of jurisprudence, is that the State with all its resources and power should not be allowed to make repeated attempts to convict an individual for an alleged offense, thereby subjecting him to embarrassment, expense, and ordeal and compelling him to live in a continuing state of anxiety and insecurity, as well as enhancing the possibility that even though innocent he may be found guilty."

double jeopardy • a prohibition against the government from trying someone twice for the same offense

The prohibition against **double jeopardy** prevents the government from trying someone twice for the same offense. del Carmen (p. 440) describes double jeopardy as "the successive prosecution of a defendant for the same offense by the same jurisdiction." As stated in *North Carolina v. Pearce* (1969): "It protects against a second prosecution for the same offense after acquittal. It protects against a second prosecution for the same offense after conviction. And it protects against multiple punishments for the same offense." Double jeopardy requires all three elements: successive prosecution, same offense and same jurisdiction (del Carmen, p. 440).

In a continuing examination of the prohibition against double jeopardy, the Supreme Court in *Sattazahn v. Pennsylvania* (2003) held that there is no double jeopardy when one is sentenced to death at a retrial after receiving a life sentence at the original trial when the jury deadlocked during the sentencing phase. *United States v. Lara* (2004) held that Lara, an Indian who pleaded guilty of assaulting a police officer in the Spirit Tribe Tribal Court, could be tried again in federal court because the courts represented two different jurisdictions. *Seling v. Young* (2001) held that an act considered civil that results in confinement, in this case the civil confinement of a sex offender, does not create double jeopardy to prevent a subsequent criminal trial.

A system of fairness cannot permit inexhaustible resources to be used to continue retrying a defendant. However, this amendment has important nuances. What *is not* double jeopardy? A defendant may be tried again when a jury is unable to reach a verdict resulting in a mistrial or when a mistrial is declared for other reasons. A case may be appealed to a higher court by either side, including the prosecution. If an appeals court grants a defendant a new trial, it is not considered double jeopardy. If an offense is both a state *and* a federal offense, the offenses are considered separate and may be tried independently of each other.

Double jeopardy is said to *attach*, and, thus, prohibit the following: a second prosecution for the same offense after conviction, a second prosecution for the same offense after acquittal and more than one punishment for the same offense. In addition, an illegal act may itself consist of several different criminal acts, each of which could be prosecuted; however, double jeopardy would occur if greater or lesser included offenses were later tried after the initial trial.

Just Compensation

The Fifth Amendment also requires **just compensation**, or fair market value, when government takes property. Sometimes the government needs to take property for the public good. This circumstance would include acts of condemnation by which government acquires property to build roadways, bridges or other public improvements. A "taking" may also occur when government restricts how property may be used, thus limiting its uses. Whether property is actually taken by the government to be used for something altogether different or regulated to the point that owners are no longer able to use it as they wish, fair compensation is required from the government.

just compensation • the requirement that property owners be paid fair market value by the government when government takes their property

On an historical note, the just compensation clause was the first component of the Bill of Rights to be incorporated to apply to the states under the Fourteenth Amendment due process clause (*Chicago, Burlington & Quincy Railroad Co. v. Chicago*, 1897). Subsequent cases have continued to focus on what is considered a taking, what is considered public use and what is just compensation: "The basic problem is to determine the point at which a (government action) goes beyond the legitimate scope of the police power and becomes an (excessive) exercise of eminent domain (the taking of private property for public good)" (Stephens and Scheb, 2003, p. 392).

In *Hawaii Housing Authority v. Midkiff* (1984), the Court held that even when compensated for the taking of land, the taking must always be "rationally related to a conceivable public purpose." *Kelo v. City of New London* (2005) upheld the taking of private property to support a development plan approved by the city that would put the property to a better use and increase taxes, stating, "Promoting economic development is a traditional and long accepted function of government." This case generated great debate, with the feelings of many stated by Justice O'Connor in her sharply worded dissent: "Any property may now be taken for the benefit of another private party, but the fallout from this decision will not be random. The beneficiaries are likely to be those citizens with disproportionate influence and power in the political process, including large corporations and development firms. As for the victims, the government now has license to transfer property from those with fewer resources to those with more. The Founders cannot have intended this perverse result." "That alone is a just government," wrote James Madison, "which *impartially* secures to every man whatever is his *own*. . . . would hold (these) takings . . . unconstitutional."

Fifth Amendment and Corrections

The Fifth Amendment does not arise often in prisoners' rights cases, but it may apply to inmates being questioned about offenses separate from those they are serving time for or those inmates involved in internal disciplinary proceedings. In 1990, the Supreme Court in *Illinois v. Perkins* held that undercover police agents do not have to administer *Miranda* warnings to incarcerated suspects before soliciting incriminating information from them. The Court decided that *Miranda* did not apply because there was no custodial interrogation (not a police-dominated atmosphere) that would necessitate reading the warnings. In *Illinois v. Perkins*, the Court recognized a limitation to *Miranda*, noting that compulsion is "determined from the perspective of the suspect."

Another issue challenged under the Fifth Amendment is compensation for prison labor. Inmates have claimed they are being deprived of property (just wages) without due process. However, the courts have consistently rejected just compensation arguments on Fifth, Thirteenth and Fourteenth Amendment grounds. A third area involving the Fifth Amendment focuses on disciplinary actions. In *Baxter v. Palmigiano* (1976), the Supreme Court ruled: "Prison disciplinary hearings are not criminal proceedings; but if inmates are compelled in those proceedings to furnish testimonial evidence that might incriminate them in later criminal proceedings, they must be offered "whatever immunity is required to supplement the privilege" and may not be required "to waive such immunity."

A fourth Fifth Amendment issue involves the double jeopardy clause. Inmates who commit disciplinary infractions may appear before a disciplinary board and be punished and then find themselves facing criminal prosecution for the same offense. The courts have consistently ruled that this circumstance does *not* constitute double jeopardy.

Before leaving the discussion of the Fifth Amendment, consider another controversial area broadening the government's powers to obtain information: the USA PATRIOT Act.

USA PATRIOT Act

An immediate result of the 9/11 terrorist attacks on the United States was the unity that occurred among Americans, including politicians, which resulted in swift approval of the Uniting and Strengthening America by Providing Appropriate

Tools Required to Intercept and Obstruct Terrorism Act, also known at the **USA PATRIOT Act.** On October 26, 2001, President George W. Bush signed the act into law. Because it was hastily routed through the process, arguably out of necessity, Congress determined that much of it would expire at the end of 2005, so it could be reevaluated.

USA PATRIOT Act •
legislation that significantly improves the nation's counterterrorism efforts

According to Boyter (2003, p. 17): "The Patriot Act dramatically strengthened the ability of the Justice Department and the FBI to monitor suspected terrorists or their associates." This comprehensive, some would say sweeping, law spans much of the specific topics this text addresses. Although coming at a time the country was stunned by the terrorist attacks and joined together in responding, this law has generated controversy because of what some say have eliminated the checks and balances that allowed courts to ensure these powers were not abused.

The Act gives federal officials greater authority to track and intercept communications for law enforcement and foreign intelligence gathering. It gives the Secretary of the Treasury regulatory powers to combat corruption of U.S. financial institutions for foreign money laundering. It further closes our borders to foreign terrorists and allows us to detain and remove terrorists already in our country. It creates new crimes, new penalties and new procedural efficiencies for use against domestic and international terrorists.

■ The USA PATRIOT Act significantly improves the nation's counterterrorism efforts by:

- Allowing investigators to use the tools already available to investigate organized crime and drug trafficking.
- Facilitating information sharing and cooperation among government agencies, so they can better "connect the dots."
- Updating the law to reflect new technologies and new threats.
- Increasing the penalties for those who commit or support terrorist crimes.

The U.S. Department of Justice (www.lifeandliberty.gov) summarizes the elements of this law as follows.

Allowing Use of Already Available Tools

Many tools the Act provides to law enforcement to fight terrorism have been used for decades to fight organized crime and drug dealers and have been reviewed and approved by the courts. As Sen. Joe Biden (D-DE) explained during the floor debate on the Act: "The FBI could get a wiretap to investigate the mafia, but they could not get one to investigate terrorists. To put it bluntly, that was crazy! What's good for the mob should be good for terrorists" (Congressional Record, 10/25/01). Specifically, the act:

- Allows law enforcement to use surveillance against the full range of terrorism-related crimes, including chemical-weapons offenses, the use of weapons of mass destruction, killing Americans abroad and terrorism financing.
- Allows federal agents to follow sophisticated terrorists trained to evade detection by using "roving wiretaps" that apply to a particular suspect rather than to a particular phone or communications device.
- Allows law enforcement to conduct investigations without tipping off terrorists by use of delayed notification search warrants. Notice is always provided, but a reasonable delay gives law enforcement time to identify the criminal's associates, eliminate immediate threats to communities and coordinate the arrests of multiple individuals without tipping them off beforehand.

- Allows federal agents to ask a court for an order to obtain business records in national security terrorism cases. The government can now ask the Foreign Intelligence Surveillance Court to order production of the same type of records available through grand jury subpoenas if the government demonstrates the records concerned are sought for an authorized investigation to obtain foreign intelligence information not concerning a U.S. citizen or to protect against international terrorism or clandestine intelligence activities.

Facilitating Information Sharing and Cooperation among Government Agencies

The act removes the major legal barriers that prevented the law enforcement, intelligence and national defense communities from talking and coordinating their work to protect the American people and the nation's security. Police officers, FBI agents, federal prosecutors and intelligence officials now can protect U.S. communities by "connecting the dots" to uncover terrorist plots before they are completed. As Sen. John Edwards (D-NC) said of the PATRIOT Act: "We simply cannot prevail in the battle against terrorism if the right hand of our government has no idea what the left hand is doing" (Press release, 10/26/01).

Prosecutors can now share evidence obtained through grand juries with intelligence officials—and intelligence information can now be shared more easily with federal prosecutors. Such sharing of information leads to concrete results. For example, a federal grand jury recently indicted an individual in Florida, Sami al-Arian, for allegedly being the U.S. leader of the Palestinian Islamic Jihad, one of the world's most violent terrorist outfits. Palestinian Islamic Jihad is responsible for murdering more than 100 innocent people.

Updating the Law to Reflect New Technologies and New Threats

The United States no longer has to fight a digital-age battle with antique weapons—legal authorities left over from the era of rotary telephones. For example, when investigating the murder of *Wall Street Journal* reporter Daniel Pearl, law enforcement used one of the act's new authorities to use high-tech means to identify and locate some of the killers.

The act allows law enforcement officials to obtain a search warrant *anywhere* a terrorist-related activity occurred. Terrorism investigations often span a number of districts and previously required multiple warrants in multiple jurisdictions, which created unnecessary delays. The act provides that warrants can be obtained in any district in which terrorism-related activities occurred, regardless of where they will be executed.

Increasing Penalties for Those Who Commit or Support Terrorist Crimes

The act creates a new offense that prohibits knowingly harboring people who have committed or are about to commit a variety of terrorist offenses, such as destruction of aircraft; use of nuclear, chemical or biological weapons; use of weapons of mass destruction; bombing of government property; sabotage of nuclear facilities; and aircraft piracy.

The act enhances the inadequate maximum penalties for various crimes likely to be committed by terrorists including arson, destruction of energy facilities, material support to terrorists and terrorist organizations, and destruction of national-defense materials. It also enhances a number of conspiracy penalties, including for arson, killings in federal facilities, attacking communications systems, material support to terrorists, sabotage of nuclear facilities and interference with flight crew members. In addition, the act punishes terrorist attacks on mass transit systems and punishes bioterrorists. Finally, it eliminates the statute of limitations for certain terrorism crimes and lengthens them for other such crimes.

The Renewal of the USA PATRIOT Act

The renewal of this legislation did not occur easily, with a year of contested debate that for some focused on national security and for others on increased government powers no longer needed after the immediate threat seemed to have passed. Questions were raised as to whether the PATRIOT Act needed to be renewed in its entirety. Pike (2006, p. 40) notes some of the controversial provisions of the act:

> Among the most criticized (components) were provisions allowing for "sneak and peek" warrants—issued secretly and without notice until after the search is completed—and expansions in the use of National Security Letters (NSLs), which are warrantless demands for certain records. Of most concern to librarians and others in the informational industry was Section 215, which expanded the definition of business records that could be obtained under a secret warrant to include "any tangible things," a broad definition that would include records form libraries and bookstores. These criticisms were countered by the Bush administration and supporters of the act who believed that it was necessary, that it was working, and that the concerns about civil liberties were misplaced.

Report from the Field: The USA PATRIOT Act at Work (2004, p. 29) states: "The USA PATRIOT Act has played a vital role in the Department of Justice's efforts to preserve America's system of ordered liberty for future generations. After an extension from its expiration at the end of 2005, the Senate cleared the renewal on March 2, 2006, by a vote of 29-10. The House followed suit on March 7, voting 280-13, days before the law was set to expire on March 10" (Greene, 2006, p. 6). On March 9, President Bush signed into law the USA PATRIOT Improvement and Reauthorization Act. Proponents assert the law will keep America safe from threats, whereas opponents fear the real threat is from a nearly unbridled government armed with this law.

When President Bush signed the extension, almost unchanged, he stated: "The law allows our intelligence and law enforcement officials to continue to share information. It allows them to continue to use tools against terrorists that they used against—that they use against drug dealers and other criminals. It will improve our nation's security while we safeguard the civil liberties of our people. The legislation strengthens the Justice Department so it can better detect and disrupt terrorist threats. And the bill gives law enforcement new tools to combat threats to our citizens from international terrorists to local drug dealers." (The reauthorized PATRIOT Act also includes new tools to combat the manufacture and distribution of methamphetamine.)

Other than two provisions, the revised version of the PATRIOT Act will be permanent; it will not expire and will change only if done so through legislation. The sections dealing with business and library records and roving wiretaps will expire at the end of 2009.

The USA PATRIOT Act and a Changing Society

As noted throughout this text, American constitutional law represents the very essence of a living law. Although the reasons underlying passage of the USA PATRIOT Act are most unfortunate, the act provides an ideal example of:

- How U.S. law never remains static.
- The legal system's ability to alter its course in response to change.
- An ability to enact change when many criticize how impossible change is to legislate.
- The ability of legislators to come together in a primarily nonpartisan manner when the country requires.
- How, rather than having legislation continue beyond the time it is needed, it must be renewed, necessitating debate and review.

Renewed debate occurred when the public recently became aware of the National Security Agency monitoring "tens of millions of domestic phone call records of ordinary Americans" (Gordon and Hotakainen, 2006, p. A1). The article also states: "Polls show that most Americans are willing to sacrifice some privacy if it makes them more secure from terrorism." Others contend the risk of an overly intrusive government is no longer as justified as it may have been immediately after 9/11. The debate continues.

SUMMARY

The Fifth Amendment protects against self-incrimination and guarantees citizens due process of law by limiting the federal government's actions. The Fourteenth Amendment made the Fifth Amendment applicable to the states. This protection applies to confessions, which must be voluntary. Voluntariness of a confession is determined by (1) the police conduct involved and (2) the characteristics of the accused.

Miranda remains the precedent case referred to by courts analyzing confession issues. The *Miranda* warning must be given to a suspect interrogated in police custody, that is, when the suspect is not free to leave. If after hearing an officer read the *Miranda* warning, a suspect remains silent, the silence is not a waiver. To waive their rights, suspects must state, orally or in writing, that (1) they understand their rights and (2) they will voluntarily answer questions without a lawyer present.

Private security officers are not required to advise suspects of their *Miranda* rights. The public safety exception allows police officers to question suspects without first giving the *Miranda* warning if the information sought sufficiently affects the officers' and the public's safety. Further statements, including confessions, will not be admissible in court if they were obtained while a person's Fourth Amendment right to a reasonable expectation of privacy were being violated.

Information provided by informants also sometimes involves questions associated with due process. The modern-day precedent for establishing probable cause on the basis of information obtained from an informant relies on the totality of the circumstances (*Illinois v. Gates*).

The Fifth Amendment also guarantees the right to a grand jury indictment, the prohibition against double jeopardy and the right to receive just compensation when government takes private property. The right to a grand jury is the only unincorporated clause of the Fifth Amendment. The prohibition against double jeopardy prevents the government from trying someone twice for the same offense.

The USA PATRIOT Act significantly improves the nation's counterterrorism efforts by (1) allowing investigators to use the tools already available to investigate organized crime and drug trafficking, (2) facilitating information sharing and cooperation among government agencies so they can better "connect the dots," (3) updating the law to reflect new technologies and new threats and (4) increasing the penalties for those who commit or support terrorist crimes.

DISCUSSION QUESTIONS

1. Why should government be limited on how and when it asks questions?
2. How do you feel about police "encouraging" suspects to talk by threatening, using physical force or otherwise intimidating them?
3. Does the *Miranda* decision impede police work?
4. Would a different result occur, given exactly the same circumstances of an interrogation, for what a private security officer could do as opposed to what a city police officer must do?
5. Why shouldn't a stop require *Miranda*?
6. Referencing Justice Holmes' proposition that it is better that some criminals escape rather than have the government involved in playing an ignoble part, what logic can you see in releasing a suspect who has confessed to a crime under circumstances that prohibit use of that admission, when the police know that person committed the crime? Where is the fairness here?
7. What do you think motivates informants, and should their information be considered reliable?
8. Why would it be wise for an officer to read the *Miranda* rights from a card?
9. Why might trickery, innuendo or even falsehoods asserted by police during questioning not be Fifth Amendment violations?
10. Considering the PATRIOT Act, do you think Americans could ever sacrifice too many rights in exchange for national security?

INFOTRAC COLLEGE EDITION ASSIGNMENTS

- Use InfoTrac College Edition to help answer the Discussion Questions when appropriate.
- Use InfoTrac College Edition to find and outline one of the following articles.
  - "Behind the Dickerson Decision," by Craig Bradley (under "*Miranda*")

- "The Supreme Court Revists *Miranda*," by Lisa Regini (under "*Miranda*")
- "Clarifying Entrapment," by Allen et al. (under "entrapment")
- "A Constitutional Guide to the Use of Cellmate Informants," by Kimberly A. Crawford
- "Civil Liability for Violations of Miranda: The Impact of *Chavez v. Martinez*," by Kimberly A. Crawford
- "When an Informant's Tip Gives Officers Probable Cause to Arrest Drug Traffickers," by Edward M. Hendrie

 ## INTERNET ASSIGNMENTS

- Use http://www.findlaw.com to find one Supreme Court case discussed in this chapter and brief the case.
- Use http://www.findlaw.com to find and brief *Dickerson v. United States*. Be prepared to discuss whether you agree with the majority or with the dissenting justices.

 ## COMPANION WEB SITE

- Go to the Constitutional Law and the Criminal Justice System 3e Web site at http://cj.wadsworth.com/hessharr_constlaw3e for Case Studies and Study Guide exercises.

REFERENCES

Boyter, Jennifer. "Attorney General Ashcroft Defends Patriot Act." *The Police Chief*, September 2003, p. 17.

Brown, Cynthia. "Tape the Interview Practice Now Required by Law in Three States." *American Police Beat*, September 2005, p. 1.

del Carmen, Rolando V. *Criminal Procedure: Law and Practice*, 6th ed. Belmont, CA: Wadsworth/Thomson Learning, 2004.

Ferdico, John N. *Criminal Procedure for the Criminal Justice Professional*, 9th ed. Belmont, CA: Thomson Wadsworth Publishing, 2005.

Garrett, Ronnie. "Supreme Court to Revisit *Miranda*." *Law Enforcement Technology*, May 2003, p. 6.

Gordon, Greg and Hotakainen, Rob. "The Issue: Privacy versus Security." (Minneapolis/St. Paul) *StarTribune*, May 14, 2006, p. A1.

Greene, Kevin E. "Congress Reauthorizes Anti-Terrorism Law." *Subject to Debate*, April 2006, p. 6.

Hendrie, Edward M. "When an Informant's Tip Gives Officers Probable Cause to Arrest Drug Traffickers." *FBI Law Enforcement Bulletin*, December 2003, pp. 8–20.

Hess, Kären M. and Wrobleski, Henry M. *Police Operations: Theory and Practice*, 4th ed. Belmont, CA: Wadsworth Publishing Company, 2006.

Holtz, Larry. "Police Interrogation and Civil Liability." *Law Enforcement Technology*, July 2003, p. 162.

Holtz, Larry E. "Deliberate 'End Runs' around *Miranda*." *Police and Security News*, September/October 2005, pp. 20–23.

Judge, Lisa A. and Higginbotham, Jeffrey D. "*Miranda* Revisited." *The Police Chief*, August 2003, p. 13.

Pike, George W. "USA PATRIOT Act: What's Next?" *Information Today*, April 2006, pp. 33, 40.

Reak, Kevin P. "Recent Court Cases Shed Light on How to Deal with Anonymous Tips." *The Police Chief*, April 2001, p. 10.

Report from the Field: The USA PATRIOT Act at Work. Washington, DC: U.S. Department of Justice, July 2004.

Rutledge, Devallis. "*Davis* Rules, What Should You Do When a Suspect Who Waived His Miranda Rights Says He Might Want a Lawyer?" *Police Magazine*, January 2006, p 70.

Scuro, Joseph. "Recent Landmark Decisions." *Law and Order*, April 2006, p. 36.

Stephens, Otis H. and Scheb, John M. *American Constitutional Law*, 3rd ed. Belmont, CA: Wadsworth Publishing, 2003.

"Supreme Court Hedges Its Bets in Latest Miranda Ruling." *Law Enforcement News*, July 31, 2003, p. 9.

"The Supremes Sing Out: You Still Have the Right to Remain Silent." *Law Enforcement News*, June 30, 2000, pp. 1, 10.

CASES CITED

Aguilar v. Texas, 378 U.S. 108 (1964).

Anderson v. State, 253 A.2d 387 (Md. App. 1969).

Arizona v. Fulminante, 499 U.S. 279 (1991).

Arizona v. Roberson, 486 U.S. 675 (1988).

Arnold v. United States, 382 F.2d 4 (9th Cir. 1967).

Ashcraft v. Tennessee, 322 U.S. 143 (1944).

Baxter v. Palmigiano, 425 U.S. 308 (1976).

Beckwith v. United States, 425 U.S. 341 (1976).

Beecher v. Alabama, 389 U.S. 35 (1967).

Berkemer v. McCarty, 468 U.S. 420 (1984).

Bram v. United States, 168 U.S. 532 (1897).

Brewer v. Williams, 430 U.S. 387 (1977).

Brown v. Mississippi, 297 U.S. 278 (1936).

Burket v. Angelo, 208 F.3d 172, 198 (4th Cir. 2000).

California v. Bakeler, 33 CrL 4108 (1983).

Chavez v. Martinez, 538 U.S. 760 (2003) No. 01-1444, Argued December 4, 2002 Decided May 27, 2003.

Chicago, Burlington & Quincy Railroad Co. v. Chicago, 166 U.S. 226 (1897).

Clark v. Murphy, 331 F.3d 1062, 1069 (9th Cir. 2003).

Colorado v. Spring, 479 U.S. 564 (1987).

Connecticut v. Barrett, 479 U.S. 523 (1987).

Culombe v. Connecticut, 367 U.S. 568 (1961).

Davis v. North Carolina, 384 U.S. 737 (1966).

Davis v United States, 512 US 452 (1994).

Diaz v. Senkowski, 76 F.3d 61, 63, n.1 (2nd Cir. 1996).

Dickerson v. United States, 120 S.Ct. 2326 (2000).

Dormire v. Wilkinson, 249 F.3d. 801, 805 (8th. Cir. 2001).

Duckworth v. Eagan, 492 U.S. 195 (1989).

Edwards v. Arizona, 451 U.S. 477 (1981).

Escobedo v. Illinois, 378 U.S. 478 (1964).

Evans v. Dowd, 932 F.2d 739 (8th Cir. 1991).

Fikes v. Alabama, 352 U.S. 191 (1957).

Florida v. J.L., 529 U.S. 266 (2000).

Green v. United States, 355 U.S. 184 (1957).

Greenwold v. Wisconsin, 390 U.S. 519 (1968).

Hampton v. United States, 425 U.S. 484 (1976).

Hawaii Housing Authority v. Midkiff, 467 U.S. 229 (1984).

Haynes v. Washington, 373 U.S. 503 (1963).

Hiibel v. Sixth Judicial District Court of Nevada, 542 U.S. 177 (2004).

Hurtado v. California, 110 U.S. 516 (1884).

Illinois v. Gates, 462 U.S. 213 (1983).

Illinois v. Perkins, 496 U.S. 292 (1990).

In re Gault, 387 U.S. 1 (1967).

Jacobson v. United States, 503 U.S. 540 (1992).

Katz v. United States, 389 U.S. 347 (1967).

Kelo v. City of New London, 545 U.S. ____ (2005).

Leyra v. Denno, 347 U.S. 556 (1954).

Mallory v. United States, 354 U.S. 449 (1957).

Malloy v. Hogan, 378 U.S. 1 (1964).

Marbury v. Madison, 5 U.S. (1 Cranch.) 137 (1803).

Massiah v. United States, 377 U.S. 201 (1964).

McNabb v. United States, 318 U.S. 332 (1943).

Michigan v. Jackson, 475 U.S. 625 (1986).

Mincey v. Arizona, 437 U.S. 385 (1978).

Mincey v. Head, 206 F.3d 1106, 1131 (11th Cir. 2000).

Minnick v. Mississippi, 498 U.S. 146 (1990).

Miranda v. Arizona, 384 U.S. 436 (1966).

Missouri v. Seibert, 124 S. Ct. 2601 (2004).

Muehler v. Mena, 544 U.S. ____ (2005).

New York v. Quarles, 467 U.S. 649 (1984).

North Carolina v. Pearce, 395 U.S. 711 (1969).

Oregon v. Elstad, 470 U.S. 298 (1985).

Oregon v. Mathiason, 429 U.S. 492 (1977).

Patterson v. Illinois, 487 U.S. 285 (1988).

Pennsylvania v. Muniz, 496 U.S. 582 (1990).

People v. Shivers, 21 N.Y.2d 188 (N.Y. Court of Appeals 1967).

Rochin v. California, 342 U.S. 165 (1952).
Rogers v. Richmond, 365 U.S. 534 (1961).
Sattazahn v. Pennsylvania, 537 U.S. 101 (2003).
Seling v. Young, 531 U.S. 250 (2001).
Sherman v. United States, 356 U.S. 369 (1958).
Sorrells v. United States, 287 U.S. 435 (1932).
Spano v. New York, 360 U.S. 315 (1959).
Spinelli v. United States, 393 U.S. 410 (1969).
State v. Jennings, 367 So.2d 357 (La. 1979).
State v. Lane, 937 S.W.2d 721 (Mo. 1997).
State of Minnesota v. Spencer, 414 N.W.2d 528 (1987).
Tague v. Louisiana, 444 U.S. 469 (1980).
United States v. Ballard, 586 F.2d 1060 (5th Cir. 1978).

United States v. Banks, 540 US 31 (2003).
United States v. Guarno, 819 F.2d 28 (2d Cir. 1987).
United States v. Jones, 786 F.2d 1019 (11th Cir. 1986).
United States v. Koch, 552 F.2d 1216 (7th Cir. 1977).
United States v. Lara, 541 U.S. 193 (2004).
United States v. McClinton, 982 F.2d 278, 283 (8th Cr. 1992).
United States v. Patane, 542 U.S. 630 (2004).
United States v. Russell, 411 U.S. 423 (1973).
United States v. Wright, 991 F.2d 1182 (4th Cir. 1993).
Utsler v. South Dakota, 171 N.W.2d 739 (1969).
Yates v. United States, 384 F.2d 586 (5th Cir. 1967).

CHAPTER 12

The Sixth Amendment: Right to Counsel and a Fair Trial

IN ALL CRIMINAL PROSECUTIONS, THE ACCUSED SHALL ENJOY THE RIGHT TO A SPEEDY AND PUBLIC TRIAL, BY AN IMPARTIAL JURY OF THE STATE AND DISTRICT WHEREIN THE CRIME SHALL HAVE BEEN COMMITTED . . . AND TO BE INFORMED OF THE NATURE AND CAUSE OF THE ACCUSATION; TO BE CONFRONTED WITH THE WITNESSES AGAINST HIM; TO HAVE COMPULSORY PROCESS FOR OBTAINING WITNESSES IN HIS FAVOR, AND TO HAVE THE ASSISTANCE OF COUNSEL FOR HIS DEFENSE.

—SIXTH AMENDMENT TO THE U.S. CONSTITUTION

© Joel Gordon Photography

A public defender explains to an incarcerated woman what is likely to happen next. Because this woman has been taken into custody, a critical stage in the criminal justice process, she has the right to have an attorney present.

Do You Know . . .

- What two requirements are set forth for a trial in the Sixth Amendment?
- What four factors are considered in determining whether a trial is sufficiently "speedy?"
- Where the trial is to be held?
- What two requirements for juries are established by the Sixth Amendment?
- Which guarantee of the Sixth Amendment extends beyond the trial?
- What precedent case supports the right to have an attorney present during trial?
- What happens if a defendant facing "deprivation of liberty" cannot afford to hire an attorney? The precedent case?
- When or whether a defendant accused of a misdemeanor offense has the right to an attorney?
- When the Sixth Amendment right to counsel exists?
- How *Miranda* interacts with the Sixth Amendment right to counsel?
- What is required at a lineup?
- Whether there is a Sixth Amendment right to a lawyer during preindictment identification procedures?
- How the court will view pretrial identification procedures to determine whether they are unconstitutional?
- Through how many appeals the right to counsel may be invoked?
- What the Sixth Amendment right to counsel presumes about the attorneys?
- If the right to counsel is waived, what is required?
- If people can defend themselves in a criminal trial?
- Whether juveniles have Sixth Amendment rights?
- How the Sixth Amendment affects corrections?

Can You Define?

adversarial system	functional equivalent	preliminary hearing
arraignment	hearsay	*pro se*
Brady Rule	indigent	showup
compulsory process	jury nullification	subpoena
court trial	lineup	venue
detainer	peremptory challenges	*voir dire*

Introduction

Although the Sixth Amendment is not the most familiar to the public, it deals with the important matter of fairness at trial and the right to a lawyer during the time leading up to and during prosecution.

The Sixth Amendment works well with the Fifth Amendment in that it ensures the defendant has access to legal counsel at certain stages before being tried, as well as a fair trial. In its own right, this amendment stands for protecting the individual against the government's unlimited resources. Article III of the Constitution requires that "a trial of all crimes . . . shall be by jury." The Sixth Amendment exists to ensure a fair trial. However, the results of a prolonged trial prepared for and carried out by government lawyers, preceded by the police investigating the crime, are obvious. Without limitations, government could easily defeat the defendant merely by having the personnel, time and finances. The fact is that very few criminal defendants have anything close to what the government can muster, and the Sixth Amendment strives to balance the contest.

Only a brief review of history is needed to understand why ensuring the right to a *fair* trial was believed necessary. Take, for instance, the *Star Chamber* (2000), created in 1487 by King Henry VII and abolished in 1641, named for the room with stars painted on the ceiling in the royal palace of Westminster, where this court was originally held. The Crown completely controlled this court, which had wide civil and criminal jurisdiction over everyone, including those too powerful to be tried by lesser courts. Under a veil of secrecy, the almost unlimited authority this court enjoyed permitted them to subject individuals to trials without juries and to impose unreasonable fines and prison sentences, as well as terribly cruel torture to compel self-incrimination or as punishment. Unfortunately, some modern cases of police misconduct are reminiscent of days gone by.

Under the system the founders of the U.S. Constitution fled, there were few, if any, rights pertaining to trials for the accused, if trials were even available. This situation remains a reason many people from other countries continue to seek freedom under the law in the United States. The Sixth Amendment embodies the concept of *due process*. Basic fairness is what it is about, including the rights to know what one is accused of and to hear from those accusing.

This chapter begins with a discussion of the Sixth Amendment right to a speedy, public trial where the crime was committed before an impartial, representative jury. This discussion is followed by the rights of being informed of the accusation and confronting witnesses, sometimes through compulsory process. The discussion next turns to the all-important right to counsel, including the right to counsel at critical stages of criminal proceedings and the need for effective assistance of council. Next, waiving the right to legal counsel and the right to represent oneself at trial are described. The chapter concludes with a brief discussion of Sixth Amendment rights and corrections, as well as an explanation of how the Fifth and Sixth Amendments differ.

Speedy and Public Trial

■ The Sixth Amendment requires a *speedy* and *public trial.*

Although few recent cases address speedy or public trials, a speedy, public trial is necessary in a system that places fairness above all else, and an expeditious trial does, indeed, promote fairness. A delayed or prolonged trial is inherently unfair. Beginning with the assumption that a person is innocent until proven guilty, each individual charged with a crime has the right to have this determination made as quickly as possible. Also, the more quickly a trial occurs, the more likely that witnesses can be located and that their memories will be accurate.

Not knowing for certain a trial's outcome causes undue stress on those involved, and some defendants must remain in jail because they are financially unable to secure bail. The system, too, suffers because of the additional backup expenses incurred by the government, and cases do not necessarily improve with time.

Delay that harms the accused's defense may cause the charges to be dismissed. In *Barker v. Wingo* (1972), the Supreme Court held that this right is not established by delay alone and that the conduct of both the defendant and the prosecution must be weighed. It set forth four factors to be used in deciding whether defendants have not been afforded their right to a speedy trial.

■ Whether a trial is sufficiently "speedy" is determined by (1) the length of the delay, (2) the reason for the delay, (3) the defendant's assertion of this right and (4) the harm caused (*Barker v. Wingo*).

In *Barker*, the defendant was charged with murder and tried five years later after numerous continuances by the prosecution. The Court admitted that ascertaining whether a trial failed to be "speedy enough" to meet the requirement of the Sixth Amendment is a "balancing act." Perhaps the most important issue is whether the defendant was unduly harmed because of the delay.

The Sixth Amendment also requires a public trial. America prides itself on having a justice system open to public scrutiny. In *Press-Enterprise Co. v. Superior Court* (1984), the Court held: "Open trials enhance both the basic fairness of the criminal trial and the appearance of fairness so essential to public confidence in the system."

The right to a public trial is a "double-edged sword," however, in that it not only involves the defendant's right to a public trial to avoid the obvious wrong doings possible if conducted in private but also pertains to the media's right to make trials public. This area of law requires a balance between the accused's Sixth Amendment rights and the public's First Amendment rights.

Efforts have been made to achieve this balance by the Court through cases that include *Gannett Co. v. De Pasquale* (1979), in which the Court held that the Sixth Amendment does not permit the public (including the press) to attend every trial, but held in *Richmond Newspapers, Inc. v. Virginia* (1980) that the public does have the right to attend trials unless there is a compelling government interest in doing otherwise, for example, in cases of national security. At play is balancing the interests of the government, the public and the accused.

Although media coverage ensures that trials are public, at times certain trials become so newsworthy as to cause concern that the accused is harmed because of disruption in court or the case being "tried by the media." Closing a trial to the public is often challenged as violating the public's First Amendment rights. However, as ruled in *Estes v. Texas* (1965), if a trial turns into a three-ring circus, losing the dignified atmosphere expected in court proceedings, the defendant can claim a deprivation of due process rights. This area of law continues to be forged, with the rights of the individual and the media, and the limitations placed on access to trials for the benefits of each, being considered in each case.

Where the Trial Is Held

■ The Sixth Amendment requires that the trial occur in the district in which the crime was committed.

The trial is required to at least originate where the crime was committed, and the jury is required to be from "the state and district wherein the crime shall have been committed; which district shall have been previously ascertained by law." This district is referred to as the **venue** of the trial—its geographic location. Historically,

venue • the geographical area in which a specific case may come to trial, and the area from which the jury is selected

this requirement was included to prevent colonists from being returned to England for trial. However, it has remained to permit the defendant from being removed far from home, or at least from where the offense was committed, which could put that much more burden on the accused.

A defendant may seek a change of venue for several reasons, most often because of publicity or emotion in the community that may affect the trial. According to Ferdico (2005, p 69): "Typical grounds for granting a motion for change of venue are:

- Such prejudice prevails in the county where the case is to be tried that the defendant cannot obtain a fair and impartial trial there.
- Another location is much more convenient for the parties and witness than the intended place of trial, and the interests of justice require a transfer of location."

An Impartial Jury

The importance of a jury trial is evidenced by the fact that this is the only right that appears in both the Constitution and the Bill of Rights.

■ The Sixth Amendment requires an impartial and representative jury.

The right to a jury trial was incorporated (applied to the states through the Fourteenth Amendment) in *Duncan v. Louisiana* (1968). Gary Duncan was a 19-year-old black man who slapped a white youth on the elbow and was charged with simple battery, a Louisiana misdemeanor that held a maximum punishment of two years in jail and a $300 fine. He was given a 60-day jail term and fined $150 and, although requested, he was not permitted a jury trial.

Upon review, Justice White, writing for the Court, stated: "Because we believe that trial by jury in criminal cases is fundamental to the American scheme of justice, we hold that the Fourteenth Amendment guarantees a right of jury trial in all criminal cases which—were they to be tried in a federal court—would come within the Sixth Amendment's guarantee." Reflecting on history, Justice White continued: "The Declaration of Independence stated solemn objections to the King's making 'Judges dependent on his Will alone, for the tenure of their offices, and the amount and payment of their salaries,' to his 'depriving us in many cases, of the benefits of Trial by Jury. . . .'"

All crimes involving the potential of jail time do not require a jury trial, however. In *Duncan*, the Court stated that "petty crimes" do not require a jury trial, but the Court did not define what a petty crime was, other than to hold that 60 days in jail was not petty. The Court said, "The penalty authorized for a particular crime is of major relevance in determining whether it is a serious one subject to the mandates of the Sixth Amendment."

Here is an interesting exception to the general rule that once a right has been held to apply to the states and federal government that it be done so equally. While a 12-person jury is required in federal court, state trials are not required to have 12 jurors. Also, while federal juries must reach a unanimous vote for a conviction, states require a unanimous vote only in death penalty cases. The U.S. Supreme Court has, however, declared that state courts must have a minimum of six jurors (*Ballew v. Georgia*, 1978). With six jurors, a unanimous verdict must be reached to find the defendant guilty. The Court has also held that only more serious offenses warrant a jury trial (generally, those whose punishments could exceed jail time of six months).

Codispoti v. Pennsylvania (1974) supports the Sixth Amendment guarantee that a criminal defendant has a right to a jury trial whenever a penalty of incarceration of more than six months is a possibility. The Supreme Court has held that a jury trial is not guaranteed when jail time of less than six months is the maximum possibility (*Baldwin v. New York*, 1970). States may ensure a jury trial for offenses that may result in jail time less than six months, but they would not be constitutionally mandated to do so.

An impartial jury is one not predisposed to prejudice for or against the defendant. The jury must also be representative, that is, a "fair cross section of the community." In *Glasser v. United States* (1942), the Court stated: "The proper functioning of the jury system and, indeed, our democracy itself, requires that the jury be a 'body truly representative of the community,' and not the organ of any special group or class."

Lawyers seek out the most neutral jury during the process of *voir dire*, which is when potential jurors are questioned to determine their impartiality. In addition to a potential juror being removed for reasons of bias, each side has a certain number of **peremptory challenges** they may assert to remove a potential juror for any reason whatsoever. *Batson v. Kentucky* (1986) held that prosecutors' peremptory challenges to exclude from a jury members of the defendant's race based only on racial grounds violates the equal protection rights of both the defendant and the excluded juror. Jury selection goes beyond merely seeking impartial jurors. During the *voir dire* process, both sides also attempt to exclude jurors who may be detrimental to their case and to retain those who may be beneficial. Jury selection experts have created a science of what to ask and look for during this process, leading justifiable inquiries as to whether it truly is about only impartiality.

To try defendants before juries unfairly composed of a group likely to find against them has been held a denial of equal protection. For example, in *Strauder v. West Virginia* (1880), the Court held that a black defendant could not be tried before a jury from which all members of his race were purposely excluded. This finding was also established in *Swain v. Alabama* (1865). Excluding people as jurors based on their profession is also unconstitutional (*Rawlins v. Georgia*, 1906). This determination is the case throughout the legal process—treating people differently or unfairly can be considered a due process violation.

Federal and state courts have a system in place to enable them to randomly compile lists of potential jurors. *Taylor v. Louisiana* (1975) established that the jury panel (those considered eligible to serve on a jury) may not be determined so as to systematically exclude any class of persons, because selection of a jury from a cross section of the community is an important component of the Sixth Amendment.

Although the Sixth Amendment guarantees the right to a jury trial in serious crime, there is no requirement that a person *must* have a trial by jury. A competent individual may voluntarily elect to waive any of their rights. For example, waiving the right to a speedy trial or foregoing a jury trial altogether is not uncommon for defendants.

For tactical reasons, a person might waive the right to a jury trial and select a **court trial,** having the case heard before only the bench (or judge), without a jury.

voir dire • the process of questioning potential jurors to determine their impartiality

peremptory challenges • a specific number of allowances given to each side in a case so that they may assert to remove a potential juror for any reason whatsoever

court trial • when a case is heard before only the bench (or judge) without a jury

For example, a defendant asserting only technical legal claims may have more faith in a judge's comprehension of the law. A defendant previously convicted on other charges may not want to risk that information coming before a jury, which he thinks might give it more weight than a judge would. Some crimes are sufficiently heinous that public opinion in general could make a jury trial less desirable.

Jury Nullification

jury nullification • ability of a jury to acquit a defendant even though they believe that person is guilty

In addition to the better-known options of a jury to convict, acquit or be unable to reach agreement, there is the de facto option called jury nullification. **Jury nullification** is the hotly debated ability of a jury that believes a defendant to be guilty but acquits that person because they do not feel the circumstances would make a conviction fair or they disagree with the law. Such an action taken by a jury *nullifies*, or invalidates, the law.

Although no relevant case has reached the Supreme Court, lower courts have approved jury nullification as within the scope of options available to a jury. In *United States v. Moylan* (1969), the Fourth Circuit stated: "If the jury feels that the law under which the defendant is accused, is unjust, or that exigent circumstances justified the actions of the accused, or for any reason which appeals to their logic of passion, the jury has the power to acquit, and the courts must abide by that decision." Sporadic cases have had to endorse jury nullification, by whatever term used, as an option for juries because otherwise the court would be directing them as to how to decide. However, they have also endorsed not telling juries they have that option because it is not an official nor sanctioned course of action.

Why would a jury nullify a law? Mostly because they do not agree with it or think it unjust. Historically, nullification has probably occurred in such cases as when juries did not want to convict people accused of harboring runaway slaves; juries not agreeing with prohibition or drug laws; and, unfortunately, even juries prompted by racism refusing to convict white defendants accused of murdering blacks. A jury may also feel the penalty is too harsh for the circumstances.

Opponents of nullification assert that if a jury believes a person guilty, the law should be enforced, whereas proponents say that if a jury does not feel a law is just, they need to seek justice.

Being Informed of the Accusation

Fairness dictates that those accused know the charges being made against them and in sufficient detail to respond adequately. The Supreme Court has never formally incorporated this segment of the Sixth Amendment to apply to the states; however, knowing what one is charged with is so fundamentally fair that it has always been considered to fall within the due process clause of the Fourteenth Amendment.

The Right to Confront Witnesses

Experience shows that casting blame is always easier when not facing the accused. The confrontation clause of the Sixth Amendment requires that witnesses be present in court so the defendant can confront them.

Coy v. Iowa (1988) held that a state law allowing closed-circuit television testimony or testimony from behind a screen violated the Sixth Amendment. Although the Supreme Court has voiced strong preference for face-to-face confrontation, issues in this area arise primarily regarding children's testimony and when hearsay evidence may be introduced.

The Supreme Court has supported state laws that seek to protect juvenile victims by permitting child abuse victims, who may be seriously intimidated by an alleged abuser, to testify via one-way closed circuit television (*Maryland v. Craig*, 1990). Here, the system seeks to balance the accused's rights with the children's best interests.

The Sixth Amendment also excludes hearsay evidence. **Hearsay** is a statement given by someone other than the person who actually said it. An example of hearsay is when someone testifies in court they heard someone else confess to a crime. The problem is that the person who supposedly made the statement is not present to be cross-examined. Far too easily, someone can say, "I heard. . . ." This situation is why the general rule is that hearsay evidence is not admissible; however, an entire body of law addresses the exceptions, including when the person who made the original statement is now dead. Similarly, even if the person who allegedly made the statement is present for cross-examination, the defendant may not be able to get that witness to answer if, for example, the witness claims memory loss or invokes a privilege that will not permit them to answer (such as with a doctor/patient, attorney/client or spousal privilege to not testify against the other). Evidentiary law pertaining to hearsay and exceptions is complex and voluminous.

> **hearsay** • testimony made in court about something heard outside of court offered as proof of the matter asserted

Compulsory Process

Compulsory process permits a defendant to require witnesses to appear in court, usually by a court-ordered subpoena. A **subpoena** requires an individual to appear in court to testify or to bring documents or other physical evidence to the court. Subpoenas can be served by an officer of the court, including a sheriff or police officer, or by any other adult who is not a party to the action. Individuals have given many reasons for not wanting to appear in court, but their acceptance by the court is virtually nonexistent.

> **compulsory process** • permits a defendant to require witnesses to appear in court, usually under the issuance by the court of a subpoena

> **subpoena** • requires an individual to appear in court to testify or to bring documents or other physical evidence to the court

Right to Counsel

■ The right to counsel is the only Sixth Amendment guarantee that extends beyond the trial.

The right to legal counsel has been held applicable at federal and state levels and is an important right because individuals' rights are monitored through attorneys. Legal systems in other countries, including England in the past, did not have such a right, because, at best, a neutral judge would watch out for the defendant's rights. Can one remain neutral when a lawyer's job is to aggressively represent his client's? Probably not, and the Sixth Amendment provides an accused with an attorney not only during trial but also at every *critical stage* of the criminal process.

The Role of Counsel

Attorneys seem to be among the most loathed professionals in society . . . until a person needs one. The general public *often* misunderstands what attorneys do, should do and should not do, as well as what they can and cannot do. Among anticipated questions for a defense attorney speaking to any group is, "How can you defend someone you know is guilty?" The answer is quite simple: everyone has the right to legal representation, and every lawyer has an obligation to do everything legally permissible to see that the client's rights are upheld. Their job is not to befriend, support or get the client off. It is to ensure that those accused are afforded their legal rights and that they understand the process in which they are involved.

This obligation does not mean lawyers can instruct their clients to lie on the witness stand or that attorneys can provide misleading or untruthful information to the opposing counsel. To understand the role of a criminal defense lawyer, keep in mind that the defendant is presumed innocent until proved guilty, and the burden of proving guilt beyond a reasonable doubt lies solely on the prosecutor. To prove a case to this level is difficult.

adversarial system • a legal system such as that used in the United States, which places one party against another to resolve a legal issue, stipulating that only in an actual conflict will a judicial body hear the case

A basic premise of the **adversarial system** in American law is that justice is best served when both sides to the conflict give their all. If each side is expected to aggressively assert its position, each side must be able to assert themselves from similar legal footing. Many societal ills are blamed on the lawyers representing their clients' interests. Because the client remains in charge of making the majority of decisions throughout any legal process, the attorney may not even be in total agreement with the direction the client wishes the case to go.

Although representing some accused is distasteful to some attorneys, particularly those clients who are "obviously" guilty or are charged with particularly offensive crimes, the defense counsel's role is crucial. Many people do not know what their rights are and, under the pressure of being accused and tried for a crime, cannot be expected to make the best legal decisions for themselves. The lawyer's role is to know their client's rights and to ensure that any infractions are dealt with according to the law.

Development of the Right to Counsel

England's early legal system did not include the assistance of legal counsel to felons because the government was thought likely to prevail. Undoubtedly this circumstance contributed to the colonists' support of the right to counsel, even before the Sixth Amendment guaranteed it. However, even then, the right to an attorney was for only those who could afford it; those who could not went without. This situation changed as the result of the holding in the infamous "Scottsboro Boys" case (*Powell v. Alabama*, 1932), which established the constitutional necessity of having a lawyer. *Powell v. Alabama* involved a group of African-American youths who fought with a group of whites and threw them off the train they were on. They also were alleged to have raped two white girls. A sheriff's posse arrested the defendants in Scottsboro, Alabama, and the community hostility resulted in their having to be housed in a different city, guarded by a militia that escorted them to the courthouse and back each day for their own protection. Rather than any of these young, illiterate defendants having their own lawyers, the judge appointed "all members of the bar" to render assistance. All the defendants were indicted within a week. Each trial lasted one day and resulted in each defendant being given the death penalty.

The U.S. Supreme Court overturned the ruling, holding that the right to assistance by a lawyer is a basic, fundamental right under the Constitution: "In a capital case, where the defendant is unable to employ counsel, and is incapable of making his own defense because of ignorance, feeblemindedness, illiteracy, or the like, it is the duty of the court, whether requested or not, to assign counsel for him as a necessary requisite of due process of law; and that duty is not discharged by an assignment at such a time or under such circumstances as to preclude the giving of effective aid in the preparation and trial of the case."

The Court went on to explain that even intelligent, educated laypeople have little knowledge of "the science of law" and: "Without counsel, though he may not be guilty . . . [the defendant] faces the danger of conviction because he does not know how to establish his innocence." At the time this case was decided, the Sixth Amendment had not been incorporated; therefore, it was decided under the due process clause of the Fourteenth Amendment. Today it would likely be a Sixth Amendment case.

■ Denying legal counsel for a defendant at trial is a denial of due process (*Powell v. Alabama*).

A series of cases have continued to shape the right to counsel. In *Harris v. South Carolina* (1949), the Supreme Court began to recognize that if a defendant were denied access to an attorney, his or her confession may not have been voluntary. Remember that in determining whether a confession was, indeed, given voluntarily, the court considers the totality of the circumstances to make sure there was due process. *Spano v. New York* (1959) held that there was an absolute right for a defendant to be represented and that a confession was not voluntary if the police ignored a defendant's "reasonable request to contact the attorney he had already retained."

As cases continued to reinforce the right to counsel, *Gideon v. Wainwright* (1963) firmly held that not only was the right to counsel absolute but also, in all serious cases, **indigent** (poor, unable to afford a lawyer) defendants accused of a felony were to be provided with legal counsel. *Gideon* is considered a monumental case because it truly placed a poor, uneducated defendant against the entire governmental system and its almost unlimited resources. Gideon actually submitted his request to the Supreme Court in his own handwritten appeal. To the surprise of many people, the Court granted certiorari and, an even greater surprise, found in his favor.

indigent • poor, unable to afford a lawyer

■ *Gideon v. Wainwright* established that indigent defendants are to be provided lawyers when faced with a "deprivation of liberty."

Justice Black, in writing the *Gideon* opinion, reflected on the *Powell* opinion, which stated: "The right of one charged with crime to counsel may not be deemed fundamental and essential to fair trials in some countries, but it is in ours. . . . The right to be heard would be, in many cases, of little avail if it did not comprehend the right to be heard by counsel."

The *Gideon* Court clarified the existing confusion over which offenses necessitated counsel be provided. In some states, only death penalty cases invoked the right to an attorney; in other states, only felonies and not misdemeanors invoked that right. In a previous case (*Betts v. Brady*, 1942), the Supreme Court had held the requirement of providing poor defendants with legal counsel in felony trials did not extend to the states. This decision was overruled in *Gideon*, which held that any indigent defendant accused of a felony, in federal and state court, be provided a lawyer. See Figure 12.1 for a sample statement of indigency.

FINANCIAL STATEMENT Case No. . . . .
ELIGIBILITY DETERMINATION FOR INDIGENT DEFENSE SERVICES
Presumptive Eligibility:
☐ I currently receive the following type(s) of public assistance in _____
                                                                        City/County

   ☐ AFDC $ _____   ☐ Food Stamps $ _____   ☐ Medicaid _____

   ☐ Supplemental Security Income $ _____   ☐ Other (specify type and amount) _____

   ☐ I currently do not receive public assistance.
Names and addresses of employer(s) for defendant and spouse:
Self _____

Spouse _____

NET INCOME: **Self**   **Spouse**
Pay period (weekly, every second week, twice monthly, monthly) . . . . _____ _____
Net take home pay (salary/wages, minus deductions required by law). . . . . $_____ _____
Other income sources (please specify)—see reverse

_____ . . . . $_____ _____
                                   TOTAL INCOME $_____ + _____ = [COURT USE ONLY] A

ASSETS:
Cash on hand . . . . $_____ _____

Bank accounts at: . . . . $_____ _____
Any other assests: (please specify)

                      with a
_____ value of . . . . $_____ _____
Real estate - $ _____ $_____ _____
        Net Value
                   with net
               value of . . . . . . $_____ _____
Motor { _____
         Year and Make
Vehicles {   with net
       _____ value of . . . . . . $_____ _____
        Year and Make
Other Personal Property: (describe)

_____ . . . . $_____ _____
                                   TOTAL ASSETS $_____ + _____ = [COURT USE ONLY] A

Number in household _____
Number of dependents (spouse/children)
whom you support: _____

EXCEPTIONAL EXPENSES (Total Exceptional Expenses of Family)
Medical Expenses (list only unusual and continuing expenses) . . . . $_____
Court-ordered support payments/alimony. . . . . $_____
Child-care payments (e.g. day care) . . . . $_____
Other (describe): _____
_____ } $_____ [COURT USE ONLY]
                                   TOTAL EXPENSES $_____ = [ ] C
    COLUMN "A" plus COLUMN "B" minus COLUMN "C" equals available funds = [ ]

THIS STATEMENT IS MADE UNDER OATH: ANY FALSE STATEMENT OF A MATERIAL FACT TO ANY QUESTION CONTAINED HEREIN SHALL CONSTITUTE PERJURY UNDER THE PROVISIONS OF §19.2-161 OF THE CODE OF VIRGINIA. THE MAXIMUM PENALTY FOR PERJURY IS CONFINEMENT IN THE PENITENTIARY FOR A PERIOD OF TEN YEARS.

I hereby state that the above information is correct to the best of my knowledge.

Name of defendant (type or print) _____

_____ _____
    Date   Signature
Sworn/affirmed and signed before me this day.

_____ _____ _____
    Date   Signature   Title

FORM DC-333 4/93 (1143-021 5/94)

Figure 12.1 Statement of Indigency

Source: Ronald J. Bacigal. *Criminal Law and Procedure: An Introduction.* St. Paul, MN: West Publishing Company, 1996, p. 155. Reprinted by permission. All rights reserved.

■ In 1972, in *Argersinger v. Hamlin*, the Court extended the right to an attorney to defendants accused of misdemeanor offenses. Any time the penalty could include prison, the defendant must have access to a lawyer.

Many thought *Argersinger*, if implemented, would bankrupt the state. The Supreme Court countered this fear in *Scott v. Illinois* (1979), which made actual, not potential, punishment the trigger for the right to counsel. In *Halbert v. Michigan* (2005), the Court held than indigent defendants, even after pleading guilty, are entitled to have a lawyer appointed when seeking a direct appeal.

As law pertaining to the constitutional right to counsel was changing, questions were necessarily being raised. One key question was whether there were times *before* trial that could require counsel. The case of young Danny Escobedo answered that question, while setting the stage for others, all of which continued to forge Sixth Amendment law.

In *Escobedo v. Illinois* (1964), the police repeatedly refused to permit Escobedo access to the lawyer he had hired. The lawyer was told he could not see his client, and the police told Escobedo his lawyer did not want to see him. Escobedo was 22 years old, had no prior contact with police and was kept handcuffed and standing throughout the interrogation, with testimony affirming that Escobedo was exhausted from lack of sleep. Eventually he admitted to the murder of his brother-in-law. Justice Goldberg stated: "We hold [that when] the investigation is no longer a general inquiry into an unsolved crime but has begun to focus on a particular suspect, the suspect has been taken into police custody, the police [interrogate], the suspect has requested and been denied an opportunity to consult with his lawyer, and the police have not effectively warned him of this absolute constitutional right to remain silent, the accused has been denied the assistance of counsel in violation of the Sixth Amendment to the Constitution as made obligatory upon the states by the Fourteenth Amendment."

■ When police inquiry has begun to focus on a particular suspect, custodial interrogation at the police station entitles a suspect to legal representation (*Escobedo v. Illinois*).

These cases present an excellent example of how common law develops. *Powell* established criminal defendants' right to a lawyer at trial, *Gideon* established that indigent defendants must be provided an attorney at trial and *Escobedo* established that the right to counsel attaches during a criminal investigation when that investigation begins to focus on an individual.

Right to Counsel at Critical Stages of Criminal Proceedings

Through a series of cases, including those discussed, the Supreme Court has held that no one may be imprisoned for any level of crime without legal representation, unless the accused have knowingly and intelligently waived this right (*Faretta v. California*, 1975). Through the additional development of Sixth Amendment law, the Court deemed the right to an attorney applies not only to trial proceedings but also to every critical stage of a criminal proceeding, considered to occur "where substantial rights of a criminal . . . may be affected" (*Mempa v. Rhay*, 1967).

■ The Sixth Amendment right to legal counsel occurs at every critical stage of a criminal proceeding, including during the investigation, at hearings and during the trial.

Critical Stages during the Criminal Investigation

The Supreme Court has determined that several events during a criminal investigation are critical stages that require a lawyer, pursuant to Sixth Amendment protection. *Massiah v. United States* (1964), heard the same year as *Escobedo*, held that statements a defendant makes *after* being charged with a crime, being a critical stage and having retained an attorney, would not be admissible if the attorney is not present. In *Massiah*, after Massiah was indicted, federal agents paid his codefendant to converse with him in the presence of a hidden radio transmitter. Justice Stewart, writing for the Court, stated: "We hold that the petitioner was denied the basic protections of that guarantee when there was used against him at his trial evidence of his own incriminating words, which federal agents had deliberately elicited from him after he had been indicted and in the absence of his counsel."

■ After a defendant has been charged with a crime and retained an attorney, that attorney must be present during any subsequent questioning.

United States v. Henry (1980) established that a defendant's Sixth Amendment right to counsel is violated if police intentionally create a situation likely to result in incriminating statements.

The well-known *Miranda* case (1966), discussed in the preceding chapter, further clarifies when a person has the right to counsel. In this case, the Supreme Court stipulated four warnings to be given to suspects in custody. Two of these warnings deal with the right to counsel. The *Miranda* warning is meant to both safeguard the Fifth Amendment right against self-incrimination and to declare that a person who is questioned while in police custody has a Sixth Amendment right to an attorney.

■ *Miranda* invokes both the Fifth Amendment right against self-incrimination and the Sixth Amendment right to counsel. The exclusionary rule will prohibit confessions obtained in violation of these rights from being used in court.

According to Rutledge (2006, p. 72): "There are some basic differences between *Miranda* and *Massiah*, and the two should not be confused. It is entirely possible that a particular statement might be admissible under *Miranda* but inadmissible under *Massiah*, and vice versa:

- *Miranda* applies only if the suspect is in custody; *Massiah* applies either in or out of custody.
- *Miranda* custody arises at arrest or equivalent physical restraint; *Massiah* attaches by indictment or first court appearance.
- *Miranda* does not prohibit undercover questioning; *Massiah* allows passive listening, but not active undercover questioning."

Questioning after the arraignment may not occur either, unless an attorney representing the defendant is present. In *Brewer v. Williams* (1977), the Supreme Court affirmed what they held in *Massiah*, requiring legal counsel after indictment by requiring it after the arraignment. *Brewer* deserves more careful analysis because it illustrates how law enforcement officials can stray from the confines of the Constitution in a way that may not be physically abusive but psychologically manipulative in an effort to solve a particularly heinous crime. In this case, although the defendant was not interrogated through the usual question-and-answer method, there was a **functional equivalent,** meaning the method used is capable of producing similar or identical effects. What occurred was almost the same as interrogation because the desired result was the same as discussed in Chapter 8 and the Christian Burial Speech.

functional equivalent • equal or essentially the same

This case also shows how multiple legal issues may evolve from one case, including Fifth and Sixth Amendment issues, the use of the exclusionary rule and the creation of the inevitable discovery doctrine, all of which paint a fascinating legal picture of how the Supreme Court finds itself addressing complex issues in particularly troubling factual circumstances.

In holding that the Christian Burial Speech was a de facto interrogation carried out in a way that might have been even more successful than a traditional questioning might have been, the Court found it to be the functional equivalent of custodial interrogation, rendering any evidentiary statements to be inadmissible. Thus, the defendant's statements that lead to the discovery of the victim's body could not be used in the subsequent trial. Although *Brewer* is often considered to be primarily a Fifth Amendment case pertaining to *Miranda* issues, it also stands for the rule of law that questioning of a person after adversarial proceedings have commenced against that person (in this case Williams had been formally charged), he or she has the right to legal representation because it, too, is a critical stage.

Chief Justice Warren Burger authored a blistering dissent, arguing against the use of the exclusionary rule here, stating: "The result in this case ought to be intolerable in any society which purports to call itself an organized society. It continues the Court—by the narrowest margin—on the much-criticized course of punishing the public for the mistakes and misdeeds of law enforcement officers, instead of punishing the officer directly, if in fact he is guilty of wrongdoing. It mechanically and blindly keeps reliable evidence from juries whether the claimed constitutional violation involves gross police misconduct or honest human error."

However, justice was to prevail as described in Chapter 8. When Williams was retried upon appeal, with this case captioned as *Nix v. Williams* (1984), the inevitable discovery doctrine was adopted by the Court to allow the evidence of the victim's body to be admitted. Why? Because at the same time the detective was using an illegally obtained statement to locate the body, volunteer searchers were actually approaching the body and, regardless of the admission by Williams, would have inevitably discovered her.

Herein lies the importance of thoughtful and well-executed work by criminal justice professionals. Can one blame the detective for his motive, when in fact, he testified at the trial, "I was hoping to find out where that little girl was." A child was abducted on Christmas Eve by an escaped mental patient. Probably the last thing on his mind was what the case was evolving toward, eventually being dissected by the U.S. Supreme Court. This case illustrates the importance of thorough investigations, a working understanding of the Constitution and effective report writing skills.

Rights during Identification

In addition to questioning people, police work involves identifying perpetrators in the course and scope of case preparation, with the ultimate hope of a successful prosecution. *If* a suspect is identified during this phase and *how* it occurs are significant pretrial events, which the Supreme Court has considered in assessing when Sixth Amendment right-to-counsel protection occurs.

showup • when only one individual is shown to the victim or witness

lineup • occurs when the victim or witness is shown several people, including the suspect

Terms applicable to this area of criminal procedure define ways police identify suspects to victims or other witnesses. A **showup** is when only one individual is shown to the victim or witness. A **lineup** occurs when the victim or witness is shown several people, including the suspect. In addition to viewing actual people, either can occur with photos, video or even audio recordings when the suspect's voice was a factor.

The Supreme Court has primarily held that right to counsel and due process apply to this area. Because Sixth Amendment protection occurs during critical stages of the criminal proceedings, it makes sense that when someone has been charged with a crime, an identification procedure such as a lineup would necessitate involving the accused's attorney. However, before a suspect has been charged, there is no Sixth Amendment protection of right to counsel. Nonetheless, due process will dictate that any identification process must not be unnecessarily suggestive.

The Supreme Court has decided several important cases that pertain to pretrial identification rights.

■ In the *Wade-Gilbert Rule,* the Court held that pretrial lineups invoke Sixth Amendment protection and require that the suspect have a lawyer.

Because this stage is critical in the legal proceedings, a lawyer will be appointed if the defendant cannot afford one, with failure of the government to so act causing any resulting evidence to be inadmissible (*United States v. Wade,* 1967).

The Supreme Court addressed the inherent unreliability of eyewitness identifications and the potential for prompting in one form or another during the process, surmising that once an identification is made the witness "is not likely to go back on his word later on, so that in practice the issue of identity may . . . for all practical purposes be determined there and then, before the trial" (*Gilbert v. California,* 1967). An attorney's presence will oversee the fairness of the procedure, including making sure the process is not "so unnecessarily suggestive and conducive to irreparable mistaken identification that he was denied due process of law" (*Stovall v. Denno,* 1967). Thus, constitutional challenges could include a Sixth Amendment right-to-counsel defense or a due process claim.

■ Lineups may not be arranged in such a manner as to make the defendant stand out from the others in any unnecessarily suggestive ways.

In *Foster v. California* (1969), a robbery suspect was put in a lineup with two other men, but only Foster was wearing a jacket like the one worn during the robbery, and he was noticeably taller than the others participating in the lineup. Even after speaking in a separate office with only Foster (not the other men in the lineup), the witness still could not identify Foster, but did a week and a half later when viewing a different lineup with four different men. In noting how suggestive these elements were, the Court held that such conditions violate a person's due process rights.

However, there is no right to counsel *before* someone is charged with a crime. In *Kirby v. Illinois* (1972), the Supreme Court held that the right to legal counsel attaches "at or after the initiation of adversary judicial criminal proceedings—whether by way of formal charge, preliminary hearing, indictment, information or arraignment." Because the initiation of criminal proceedings is the beginning of the adversarial system, anything thereafter is a critical stage. However, events that occur beforehand are *not* considered to be critical stages, so there is not a Sixth Amendment right attached.

■ Preindictment, or before being formally charged, identification procedures are not critical stages of criminal proceedings, so there is no Sixth Amendment right to a lawyer.

This circumstance means that when police conduct a showup by having a victim or witness look at an individual, or conduct a photo lineup during their preliminary investigation before the suspect being charged, that suspect has no right to legal representation. Again, however, police may not make such events unnecessarily suggestive, so documentation needs to occur to address such a concern. For example, if a photographic lineup is used, the police should photocopy the entire set of pictures from which the witness could select. Courts have found that one-person showups are not necessarily unconstitutional, because police are expected to occasionally make immediate identifications. The Court has viewed showups as beneficial, allowing for a spontaneous response by a victim while memory is fresh, as long as the police are not unnecessarily suggestive or "aggravate the suggestiveness of the confrontation" (*Johnson v. Dugger*, 1987).

Under Supreme Court guidance, lesser courts continue to view identification issues in light of the totality of the circumstances to determine reliability and whether due process rights were infringed upon. For example, even when there has been a delay in conducting a showup, seven months after the crime in the case in *Neil v. Biggers* (1972), it was not prohibited. The Court considered such issues as the witness's opportunity to see the suspect at the time of the crime; the degree of the witness' attention; the accuracy of the prior description by the witness; the witness' level of certainty; and the length of time that passed since the crime was committed. Even when the suspect has been arrested, the Court has been willing to permit a deviation from the *Wade-Gilbert Rule* if there is a danger of a witness dying or becoming otherwise unable to view the suspect, or if the suspect might die.

Such was the case in *Stovall v. Denno* (1967), when after the suspect was alleged to have stabbed a doctor to death and seriously injured the doctor's wife, the suspect was taken to the victim's hospital room, where she identified him before he was permitted to speak with a lawyer. Here, the court held that whether a due process violation occurred depended on the *totality of the circumstances*, with timing being crucial in such a case.

■ The court will view pretrial identification procedures in the totality of circumstances when determining whether they were unconstitutional.

Critical Stages at Hearings, Trials and Appeals

Legal counsel is required in court at any jurisdictional level for criminal offenses that would result in imprisonment. What about events that occur in court other than an actual trial?

Moore v. Michigan (1957) established that a defendant has the right to counsel while submitting a guilty plea to the court. Later, in *Hamilton v. Alabama* (1961), the Supreme Court held that an **arraignment**, the hearing at which the defendant

arraignment • usually the first court appearance by a defendant during which the accused is advised of his or her rights, advised of the charges and given the opportunity to enter a plea

preliminary hearing • a critical stage of criminal proceedings when it is determined if probable cause exists to believe a crime has been committed and that the defendant committed it

is required to enter a plea, is a critical stage under the Sixth Amendment. In 1970 in *Coleman v. Alabama*, the Court held that a **preliminary hearing** is a critical stage of the criminal prosecution and, thus, invokes the right to counsel because it is a formal adversarial proceeding. The preliminary hearing determines whether probable cause exists to believe a crime has been committed and that the defendant committed it. *Douglas v. California* (1963) held that the first appeal, a right itself, necessitated counsel. This right extends to only the first appeal and no further.

■ Any hearing or trial through the first appeal of right invokes the Sixth Amendment right to counsel, but the right does not extend to any additional appeals.

During the trial itself, both sides must abide by the rules of fairness. The first due process case regarding a trial was *Mooney v. Holohan* (1935), which held that deliberate use of perjured testimony by the prosecutor and deliberate nondisclosure of evidence that would have impeached the perjury violated due process. This holding was reiterated almost 30 years later in *Brady v. Maryland* (1963), which established the rules for "discovery," making unconstitutional "trial by ambush," where the defense learns the identity of prosecution witnesses when they walk down the courtroom aisle.

Brady involved a defendant who admitted participating in a murder but claimed his companion did the killing. Before trial, Brady's lawyer asked the prosecutor to allow him to examine the companion's statements. The prosecutor complied but withheld the statement in which the companion admitted doing the killing. The defense did not learn of this withheld evidence until after Brady was convicted and sentenced. On appeal the Court reversed Brady's conviction saying: "The suppression by the prosecution of evidence favorable to an accused upon request violates due process where the evidence is material either to guilt or to punishment, irrespective of the good faith or bad faith of the prosecution."

Brady Rule • the suppression by the prosecution of evidence favorable to an accused upon request violates due process

This holding is called the **Brady Rule.**

In *Texas v. Cobb* (2001), the Court asserted that the right of counsel applies only to *charged* offenses. In this case, Cobb was charged with burglary, at which time his Sixth Amendment rights attached. Later, however, while Cobb was awaiting trial, the police questioned Cobb about the murder of a mother and her child that occurred during the burglary. Cobb waived his *Miranda* rights and confessed to the murders. Cobb's defense was that his Sixth Amendment rights were violated because he was awaiting trial and should not even have been talked to without his lawyer present, whether he waived his rights or not.

The Supreme Court disagreed, relying on *McNeil v. Wisconsin* (1991), holding that the Sixth Amendment is "offense specific," applying only to the offense charged. Even if another crime arises out of that course of conduct, if the additional crime has even one separate element, it is considered an entirely new set of circumstances for Sixth Amendment purposes. The Court also referred to *Blockburger v. United States* (1932), which held that when the "same act or transaction constitutes a violation of two distinct statutory provisions, the test to be applied to determine whether there are two offenses or only one . . . is whether each provision requires proof of a fact which the other does not."

An example would be a suspect indicted for unlawful possession of a firearm used for a robbery but not yet charged with the offense (Rutledge, p. 70). The "closely related" doctrine would have prevented officers from getting a statement or conducting a lineup without the suspect's lawyer present. In *Texas v. Cobb*,

Table 12.1　**Key Cases Regarding Right to Counsel**

Stage in criminal justice process	Case	When suspect/defendant has a constitutional right to counsel
Investigation	Escobedo v. Illinois (1964)	During any police interrogation
	Miranda v. Arizona (1966)	During any custodial interrogation to secure privilege against self-incrimination
Pretrial	Massiah v. United States (1964)	Once adversary proceedings have begun against defendant
	Brewer v. Williams (1977)	Reaffirmed, once adversary proceedings have begun against defendant
	Hamilton v. Alabama (1961)	During the arraignment
	Coleman v. Alabama (1970)	During the preliminary hearing
	Moore v. Illinois (1977)	During in-court identification at preliminary hearing following criminal complaint
	United States v. Wade (1967)	During pretrial post-indictment lineup for identification
	Moore v. Michigan (1957)	When submitting a guilty plea to the court
Trial	Powell v. Alabama (1932)	During a trial in a state capital case
	Gideon v. Wainwright (1963)	During a trial of an indigent defendant charged with a noncapital felony
	Argersinger v. Hamlin (1972)	During a trial when the defendant might be imprisoned, whether for a felony or a misdemeanor
	In re Gault (1967)	During juvenile delinquency adjudication that may lead to commitment to a state institution
Posttrial	Douglas v. California (1963)	During first appeal after conviction

however, the Supreme Court rejected the closely related doctrine and ruled that the constitutional right to counsel is "offense specific," meaning that it applies only to "the specific charges for which the defendant has been indicted or arraigned . . . and will not prohibit lineup ID or questioning as to other crimes, even though they are related to the charged case" (Rutledge, pp. 71–72).

Table 12.1 summarizes the major Supreme Court cases granting the right to counsel throughout the critical stages of the criminal justice process.

Even when statements are not admissible regarding the charged offense because the person's Sixth Amendment rights were violated, they are still admissible to impeach the witness, meaning to prove that person committed perjury. In *Harris v. New York* (1971), Chief Justice Burger said: "Every criminal defendant is privileged to testify in his own defense, or to refuse to do so. But that privilege cannot be construed to include the right to commit perjury. . . . The shield provided by *Miranda* cannot be perverted into a license to use perjury by way of a defense, free from the risk of confrontation with prior inconsistent utterances. We hold, therefore, that petitioner's credibility was appropriately impeached by use of his earlier conflicting statements." In *Michigan v. Harvey* (1990), Chief Justice Rehnquist stated: "If a defendant exercises his right to testify on his own behalf, he assumes a reciprocal 'obligation to speak truthfully and accurately' and we have consistently rejected arguments that would allow a defendant to turn the illegal method by which evidence in the Government's possession was obtained to his own advantage, and provide himself with a shield against contradiction of his untruths."

The Presumption of Effective Counsel

The right to legal counsel means little if the counsel provided is ineffective. *Powell v. Alabama* (1932), discussed previously, was the first ineffective counsel case.

■ The Sixth Amendment right to counsel presumes counsel is effective.

Understandably, what constitutes effective counsel can be debated, but the Supreme Court has offered this guidance: "The proper measure of attorney performance remains simply reasonableness under prevailing professional norms. . . . The benchmark for judging any claim of ineffectiveness must be whether counsel's conduct so undermined the proper functioning of the adversarial process that the trial cannot be relied on as having produced a just result" (*Strickland v. Washington*, 1984).

Strickland established a two-prong test to establish a claim of ineffective counsel. Defendants must show (1) the counsel's representation fell below an objective standard of reasonableness and (2) there is a reasonable probability that, but for counsel's unprofessional errors, the result of the proceeding would have been different. *Herring v. New York* (1975) asserted: "The very premise of our adversary system of criminal justice is that partisan advocacy on both sides of a case will promote the ultimate objective that the guilty be convicted and the innocent go free."

United States v. Cronic (1984) held that claims of ineffective counsel must point out specific errors of trial counsel and cannot be based on inferences drawn from the defense counsel's inexperience or lack of time to prepare, the gravity of the charges, accessibility of witnesses to counsel or the case's complexity. Although inexperience may not suffice as ineffective representation, failure to take normal and routine steps before and during trial could.

Sixth Amendment law regarding effective counsel continued to evolve in *Lockhart v. Fretwell* (1993), when the Court refined the *Strickland* test to require that not only would a different trial result be probable because of ineffective attorney performance but also the actual result was fundamentally unfair or unreliable. *Strickland* was relied on in *Wiggins v. Smith* (2003), when the Court also held that the trial attorney must thoroughly investigate the life history of a defendant if there is reason to believe it may affect the determination of the death penalty.

If a lawyer has a conflict of interest by representing another client who would prejudice the other, ineffective assistance of counsel would exist, but merely being dissatisfied with the outcome of a trial is not itself sufficient grounds to make such a claim (remember, 50 percent of the parties to a trial are unhappy with the results!). Because the *Strickland* decision places the burden to prove ineffective representation on the claimant, few appeals on such grounds are successful.

Some falsely believe that public defenders assigned to defendants who cannot afford their own lawyers are somehow less effective than private attorneys defendants with money are capable of paying for, or that the more a lawyer costs, the better the representation. Trial lawyers more often respect not only the skills of those who choose to work as public defenders but also their commitment to watch out for their clients' rights, regardless of their financial status. As with any other professionals, attorneys are motivated to specialize for a variety of reasons, and remuneration is second to their commitment to defending those in need.

Public defenders are employed by the government to ensure everyone's Fifth Amendment right to counsel is made available, particularly those who cannot afford their own lawyer. Although many jurisdictions employ their own public defenders, others appoint private practice lawyers who agree to take cases, thus providing these clients with a private practice attorney. This situation occurred in *Gideon v. Wainwright*, in which Abe Fortas, who would later became a justice on the Court, was appointed to represent indigent Clarence Gideon in what would become a landmark Sixth Amendment case.

Waiver of Sixth Amendment Right to Legal Counsel

A suspect cannot be forced to deal with an attorney and so may waive this right. In *Johnson v. Zerbst* (1938), the Court stated: "A waiver is ordinarily an intentional relinquishment or abandonment of a known right or privilege. The determination of whether there has been an intelligent waiver of right to counsel must depend, in each case, upon the particular facts and circumstance surrounding that case, including the background, experience, and conduct of the accused" (*Johnson v. Zerbst*). See Figure 12.2 for a sample waiver.

Patterson v. Illinois (1988) held that a valid waiver of *Miranda* rights not only waives the Fifth Amendment right against self-incrimination but also waves the Sixth Amendment right to counsel. The requirements that a waiver be knowing and voluntary remain the same. A court will consider the totality of circumstances regarding how the waiver was obtained and the competency and age of the person, as well as issues of intelligence, health and ability to understand the language.

For a waiver to be effective, it need not be in writing, but whatever statement is made by the suspect must show there was, in fact, an intentional relinquishment of the known right.

■ A waiver of one's Sixth Amendment right to counsel must be knowing and voluntary.

To have the individual sign a waiver of the right to counsel is tactically preferable. Additionally, a court will assess whether the suspect was competent enough to waive any rights, for which the totality of the circumstances surrounding the waiver will be examined, including education, intelligence, physical and mental condition, language issues and age.

The Right to Act as One's Own Counsel

People may elect to appear in court *pro se*, which is Latin meaning "for himself."

■ Individuals may appear in court without attorneys, representing themselves, that is, *pro se*.

pro se • appearing in court without an attorney, representing oneself

With the complexity of the entire legal process, why anyone would think they were competent to provide their own defense is difficult to understand. However, some defendants distrust attorneys in general or otherwise believe they can handle their defense adequately, or perhaps the expense of hiring a lawyer compels some to defend themselves if they do not qualify for legal aid.

Faretta v. California (1975) set forth three conditions to be met before a person could represent himself or herself: (1) awareness of the right to counsel, (2) a

TRIAL WITHOUT A LAWYER
Va. Code § 19.2-160

CASE NO. . . . .

- -
☐ General District Court
☐ Juvenile and Domestic Relations District Court
☐ Circuit Court

- v. -

WAIVER OF RIGHT TO BE REPRESENTED BY A LAWYER (CRIMINAL CASE)

I have been advised by a judge of this court of the nature of the charges in the cases pending against me and the potential punishment for the offenses, which includes imprisonment in the penitentiary or confinement in jail. I understand the nature of these charges and the potential punishment for them if I am found to be guilty.

I have been further advised by a judge of this court that I have the following rights to be represented by a lawyer in these cases:

    a. I have a right to be represented by a lawyer.

    b. If I choose to hire my own lawyer, I will be given a reasonable opportunity to hire, at my expense, a lawyer selected by me. The judge will decide what is a reasonable opportunity to hire a lawyer. If I have not hired a lawyer after such reasonable opportunity, the judge may try the case even though I do not have a lawyer to represent me.

    c. If I ask the judge for a lawyer to represent me and the judge decides, after reviewing my sworn financial statement that I am indigent, the judge will select and appoint a lawyer to represent me. However, if I am found to be guilty of an offense, the lawyer's fee as set by the judge within statutory limits will be assessed against me as court costs and I will be required to pay it.

I understand these rights to be represented by a lawyer. I understand the manner in which a lawyer can be of assistance and I understand that, in proceeding without a lawyer, I may be confronted with complicated legal issues. I also understand that I may waive (give up) my rights to be represented by a lawyer.

Understanding my rights to be represented by a lawyer as described above and further understanding the nature of the case and the potential punishment if I am found to be guilty, I waive all of my rights to be represented by a lawyer in these cases, with the further understanding that the cases will be tried without a lawyer either being hired by me or being appointed by the judge for me. I waive these rights of my own choice, voluntarily, of my own free will, without any threats, promises, force or coercion.

_____
ADULT

Upon oral examination, the undersigned judge of this Court finds that the Adult, having been advised of the rights and matters stated above and having understood these rights and matters, thereafter has knowingly, voluntarily and intelligently waived his rights to be represented by a lawyer.

-      _____
DATE   JUDGE

CASE NO. . . . .

Figure 12.2 Waiver of Right to Counsel

Source: Ronald J. Bacigal. *Criminal Law and Procedure: An Introduction.* St. Paul, MN: West Publishing Company, 1996, p. 157. Reprinted by permission. All rights reserved.

valid waiver of Sixth Amendment rights and (3) competency. In *Faretta*, the Court held: "To force a lawyer on a defendant can only lead him to believe that the law contrives against him. Moreover, it is not inconceivable that in some rare instances, the defendant might in fact present his case more effectively by conducting his own defense." An accused who represents himself or herself cannot later claim ineffective counsel.

Juveniles and the Sixth Amendment

In re Gault (1967) established that the Constitution applied to juveniles as well as adults. del Carmen and Trulson (2006, p. 253) state: "*In re Gault* is the most important case ever decided by the U.S. Supreme Court in juvenile justice because it signaled a shift from the pure *parens patriae* model in juvenile justice (where juveniles did not have any constitutional right during adjudication) to a due process model (where juveniles are given certain constitutional rights) . . . including the rights against self-incrimination, reasonable notice of the charges, to confront and cross-examine witnesses and the right to counsel."

■ *In re Gault* applied Sixth Amendment rights to juveniles, including the right against self-incrimination, to receive notice of the charges, to confront and cross-examine witnesses and the right to counsel.

del Carmen and Trulson cite research that shows juveniles are not appointed legal counsel in all cases, although the court in *Gault* stated: "We conclude that the Due Process Clause of the Fourteenth Amendment requires that in respect of proceedings to determine delinquency which may result in commitment to an institution in which the juvenile's freedom is curtailed, the child and his parents must be notified of the child's right to be represented by counsel retained by them, or if they are unable to afford counsel, that counsel will be appointed to represent the child." Admittedly, juvenile courts have broad discretion, and such terms as *institutionalization* are not as easily interpreted as terms in the adult system. *In re Gault* applied Sixth Amendment rights to juveniles, with some areas of application remaining to be addressed by the Court. One may anticipate further direction occurring as the Supreme Court addresses them.

The Sixth Amendment and Corrections

Like the Fifth Amendment, the Sixth Amendment is not frequently cited in prisoners' rights lawsuits. *Townsend v. Burke* (1948) held that a convicted offender has a right to counsel at the time of sentencing.

■ For prisoners, cases based on the Sixth Amendment involve the right to a speedy trial and the **detainer** problem.

detainer • document filed against inmates who have other criminal charges pending against them

Often detainers are filed against inmates who have other criminal charges pending against them, ensuring their appearance before the prosecuting jurisdiction for the next trial once their current sentence is complete. For example, in *Smith v. Hooey* (1969), an inmate in a federal institution had state criminal charges pending against him in Texas. He spent six years trying to get his trial, but the detainer process caused the delay.

Other cases regarding right to counsel involve those on probation. *Mempa v. Rhay* (1967) held that a convicted offender has the right to assistance of counsel at probation revocation hearings in which the sentence has been deferred. *Gagnon v. Scarpelli* (1973) held that probationers and parolees have a constitutionally limited right to counsel on a case-by-case basis at revocation proceedings.

Summary

The Sixth Amendment requires a speedy and public trial. Whether a trial is sufficiently "speedy" is determined by (1) the length of the delay, (2) the reason for the delay, (3) the defendant's assertion of this right and (4) the harm caused (*Barker v. Wingo*). The Sixth Amendment also requires that the trial occur in the district in which the crime was committed and that defendants have the right to an impartial and representative jury. The confrontation clause requires that witnesses be present in court so the defendant can confront them.

The right to counsel is the only Sixth Amendment guarantee that extends beyond the trial. Denying legal counsel for a defendant at trial is clearly a denial of due process (*Powell v. Alabama*). *Gideon v. Wainwright* established that indigent defendants are to be provided lawyers when faced with a "deprivation of liberty." Beyond that, when police inquiry has begun to focus on a particular suspect, custodial interrogation at the police station entitles a suspect to legal representation (*Escobedo v. Illinois*).

The Sixth Amendment right to legal counsel occurs at every critical stage of a criminal proceeding, including during the investigation, at hearings and during the trial. After a defendant has been charged with a crime and retained an attorney, that attorney must be present during any subsequent questioning. *Miranda* invokes both the Fifth Amendment right against self-incrimination and the Sixth Amendment right to counsel. The exclusionary rule will prohibit confessions obtained in violation of these rights from being used in court.

In the *Wade-Gilbert Rule,* the Court held that pretrial lineups invoke Sixth Amendment protection and require that the suspect have a lawyer. Lineups may not be arranged in such a manner as to make the defendant stand out from the others in any unnecessarily suggestive ways. Preindictment (before being formally charged) identification procedures are *not* critical stages of criminal proceedings, so there is no Sixth Amendment right to a lawyer. The court will view pretrial identification procedures in the totality of circumstances when determining whether they were constitutional. Any hearing or trial through the first appeal invokes the Sixth Amendment right to counsel.

The Sixth Amendment right to counsel presumes counsel is effective. A waiver of one's Sixth Amendment right to counsel must be knowing and voluntary. Individuals can appear in court without attorneys, representing themselves, that is, *pro se.In re Gault* applied Sixth Amendment rights to juveniles, including the right against self-incrimination, to receive notice of the charges, to confront and cross-examine witnesses and the right to counsel. Finally, for prisoners, cases based on the Sixth Amendment involve the right to a speedy trial and the detainer problem.

DISCUSSION QUESTIONS

1. Does having a lawyer present during a trial ensure fairness?

2. Why would people want to represent themselves in court *pro se*? Would you think more or less of those representing themselves? Why?

3. With the complexity of law, should there be a right to self-representation?

4. When has the line been crossed between a public trial at which the media are present and a "trial by the media"? Could this problem ever justify barring the media from attending trials? Does the media ever have that much influence on the public or jurors?

5. Why would someone choose to be a defense attorney? A prosecutor?

6. Do public defenders provide less of a defense than would a private attorney? What might a private attorney with a wealthy client be capable of that a public defender with an indigent client would not?

7. Why is the adversary system of law a necessity to produce just results?

8. Why could one attorney not represent *both* sides in a trial by providing objective facts?

9. Does the adversary system today encourage, or even demand, that attorneys represent their clients "too vigorously?"

10. If you were a lawyer, would you prefer to represent the prosecution or the defense? Why?

INFOTRAC COLLEGE EDITION ASSIGNMENTS

- Use InfoTrac College Edition to assist you in answering the Discussion Questions when appropriate.
- Use InfoTrac College Edition to find and outline one of the following articles:
  - "The Role of Juries in the Justice System," by Zakaria Erzinclinoglu
  - "Cameras in the Courtroom," by F. Dennis Hale
  - "Constitutional Rights to Counsel during Interrogation: Comparing Rights under the Fifth and Sixth Amendments," by Kimberly A. Crawford OR
- Use InfoTrac College Edition to research either the Sixth Amendment or right to a jury trial. Pick one selection and outline it.

 INTERNET ASSIGNMENTS

- Use http://www.findlaw.com to find one Supreme Court case discussed in this chapter and brief the case.
- Using your preferred search engine, find the facts of the *In re Gault* case and discuss whether you find them compelling enough to justify applying the Constitution to juveniles.

COMPANION WEB SITE

- Go to the Constitutional Law and the Criminal Justice System 3e Web site at http://cj.wadsworth.com/hessharr_constlaw3e for Case Studies and Study Guide exercises.

REFERENCES

del Carmen, Rolando V. and Trulson, Chad R. *Juvenile Justice, The System, Process, and Law.* Belmont, CA: Thomson Wadsworth Publishing, 2006.

Ferdico, John N. *Criminal Procedure for the Criminal Justice Professional*, 9th ed., Belmont, CA: Thomson Wadsworth Publishing, 2005.

Rutledge, Devallis. "Right to Counsel," *Police*, February 2006, pp. 70–72.

"Star Chamber, Court of." *Microsoft Encarta Online Encyclopedia*, 2000.

NOTE: *The Runaway Jury* by John Grisham presents a fictionalized look at jury selection and manipulation that may be of interest to you.

CASES CITED

Argersinger v. Hamlin, 407 U.S. 25 (1972).
Baldwin v. New York, 399 U.S. 66 (1970).
Ballew v. Georgia, 391 U.S. 145 (1978).
Barker v. Wingo, 407 U.S. 514 (1972).
Batson v. Kentucky, 476 U.S. 79 (1986).
Betts v. Brady, 316 U.S. 455 (1942).
Blockburger v. United States, 284 U.S. 299 (1932).
Brady v. Maryland, 373 U.S. 83 (1963).
Brewer v. Williams, 430 U.S. 387 (1977).
Codispoti v. Pennsylvania, 418 U.S. 506 (1974).
Coleman v. Alabama, 399 U.S. 1 (1970).
Coy v. Iowa, 487 U.S. 1012 (1988).
Douglas v. California, 372 U.S. 353 (1963).
Duncan v. Louisiana, 391 U.S. 145 (1968).
Escobedo v. Illinois, 378 U.S. 478 (1964).
Estes v. Texas, 381 U.S. 532 (1965).
Faretta v. California, 422 U.S. 806 (1975).
Foster v. California, 394 U.S. 4400 (1969).
Gagnon v. Scarpelli, 411 U.S. 778 (1973).
Gannett Co. v. De Pasquale, 442 U.S. 368 (1979).
Gideon v. Wainwright, 372 U.S. 335 (1963).
Gilbert v. California, 388 U.S. 263 (1967).
Glasser v. United States, 315 U.S. 60 (1942).
Halbert v. Michigan. 545 US ___ (2005).
Hamilton v. Alabama, 368 U.S. 52 (1961).
Harris v. South Carolina, 338 U.S. 68 (1949).
Harris v. New York 401 U.S. 222 (1971).
Herring v. New York, 422 U.S. 853 (1975).
In re Gault, 387 U.S. 1 (1967).
Johnson v. Dugger, 817 F.2d 726 (11th Cir. 1987).
Johnson v. Zerbst, 304 U.S. 458 (1938).
Kirby v. Illinois, 406 U.S. 682 (1972).

Lockhart v. Fretwell, 506 U.S. 364 (1993).
Maryland v. Craig, 497 U.S. 836 (1990).
Massiah v. United States, 377 U.S. 201 (1964).
McNeil v. Wisconsin, 501 U.S. 171 (1991).
Mempa v. Rhay, 389 U.S. 128 (1967).
Michigan v. Harvey, 494 US 344 (1990).
Miranda v. Arizona, 384 U.S. 436 (1966).
Mooney v. Holohan, 294 U.S. 103 (1935).
Moore v. Illinois, 434 U.S. 220 (1977).
Moore v. Michigan, 355 U.S. 155 (1957).
Neil v. Biggers, 409 U.S. 188 (1972).
Nix v. Williams, 467 U.S. 431 (1984).
Patterson v. Illinois, 487 U.S. 285 (1988).
Powell v. Alabama, 287 U.S. 45 158 (1932).
Press-Enterprise Co. v. Superior Court, 464 U.S. 501 (1984).
Rawlins v. Georgia, 201 U.S. 638 (1906).

Richmond Newspapers, Inc. v. Virginia, 448 U.S. 555 (1980).
Scott v. Illinois, 440 U.S. 367 (1979).
Smith v. Hooey, 393 U.S. 374 (1969).
Spano v. New York, 360 U.S. 315 (1959).
Stovall v. Denno, 388 U.S. 263 (1967).
Strauder v. West Virginia, 100 U.S. (10 Otto.) 303 (1880).
Strickland v. Washington, 466 U.S. 668 (1984).
Swain v. Alabama, 380 U.S. 202 (1865).
Taylor v. Louisiana, 419 U.S. 522 (1975).
Texas v. Cobb, 121 S.Ct. 1335 (2001).
Townsend v. Burke, 334 U.S. 736 (1948).
United States v. Cronic, 466 U.S. 648 (1984).
United States v. Henry, 447 U.S. 264 (1980).
United States v. Moylan 417 F.2d 1002 at 1006 (1969).
United States v. Wade, 388 U.S. 218 (1967).
Wiggins v. Smith, 123 S.Ct. 2527 (2003).

CHAPTER 13

The Eighth Amendment: Bail, Fines and Punishment

EXCESSIVE BAIL SHALL NOT BE REQUIRED, NOR EXCESSIVE FINES IMPOSED, NOR CRUEL AND UNUSUAL PUNISHMENT INFLICTED.

—EIGHTH AMENDMENT TO THE U.S. CONSTITUTION

Families to Amend California's Three-Strikes Law demonstrate at the California Institute for Women. The Supreme Court has ruled that this law does not violate the Eighth Amendment.

- What three rights are protected by the Eighth Amendment?
- What purposes bail serves?
- If the Eighth Amendment guarantees the right to bail? If it applies to the states?
- What the Bail Reform Act of 1984 established?
- What case attempted to define excessive bail and what it established as excessive?
- If the prohibition against excessive bail applies to the states? Excessive fines?
- What may be seized under asset forfeiture laws?
- What restriction is placed on the amount that can be seized through forfeiture?
- Where the meaning of "cruel and unusual punishment" must come from?
- What the general rule under the Eighth Amendment regarding punishments is?
- Whether capital punishment has been found to be constitutional? The precedent cases?
- What is required of proceedings that may involve the death penalty?
- Under what age most states do not consider capital punishment for a juvenile?
- Whether the mentally ill can be executed?
- What Eighth Amendment rights prisoners often claim?

asset forfeiture	compensatory damages	punitive damages
bail	corporal punishment	ROR
bifurcated trial	preventive detention	
commercial bail	proportionality analysis	

Introduction

The Eighth Amendment protects three rights, one which applies before trial, the other two after a person has been convicted of a crime.

- The three rights protected by the Eighth Amendment are:

    - That *excessive bail* shall not be required.
    - That *excessive fines* shall not be imposed.
    - That *cruel and unusual punishment* shall not be inflicted.

Not unlike other brief amendments, this particular one has found itself embroiled in controversy because of interpretations not only about other punishments the government can carry such as fines but also, and most particularly, about whether the death penalty is cruel and unusual. This chapter challenges you to contemplate your perspective about the death penalty. Who does society deem appropriate to put to death—the mentally ill, mentally retarded and juveniles? How is this ultimate punishment to be carried out—by electrocution, hanging or firing squad? In an amendment such as this one, every American is challenged to consider whether the end does justify the means because why the law exists is as important as how it is enforced.

This area of the law is not the only area the high court has been called on to address regarding the Eighth Amendment. For example, what do the terms *cruel* and *unusual* mean as they relate to bail and fines? How is *excessive* defined? With the U.S. Constitution more than two centuries old, can modern standards even begin to match the framers' original constitutional intent?

This chapter begins with a brief history of punishment, followed by a discussion of bail and the Bail Reform Act of 1984. Next, fines are discussed, including asset forfeiture and the prohibition against excessive fines. The chapter concludes with a discussion of cruel and unusual punishment, including capital punishment and how the Eighth Amendment affects corrections.

A Brief History of Punishment

If you found the processes of institutions such as the Star Chamber and the Inquisition revolting, the means by which punishment has been inflicted over the history of the world is, at the very least, as horrific. This description applies not only to medieval tortures we like to think the modern world is incapable of committing but also to public humiliation, branding, amputation and a host of other almost unthinkable means of enforcing the law.

Recognizing a need to somehow ensure human rights, the Massachusetts Body of Liberties, enacted in 1641, provided a right to bail and prohibited cruel and inhumane punishment. The idea of being held in prison for an indefinite time without any opportunity for even temporary release was an abhorrent thought to those who knew how restrictive government could be.

The Massachusetts Bay Colony, founded by the Puritans, sought to eliminate such English punishments as cutting off hands and burning at the stake. The Body of Liberties allowed the death penalty for religious offenses such as blasphemy but not for burglary and robbery, which were capital crimes in England. Society itself determined and continues to decide what is reasonable and unreasonable punishment.

As the colonies considered versions of what was to become the Eighth Amendment, the prohibition on the way things had been done stirred debate, with one representative declaring: "It is sometimes necessary to hang a man, villains often deserve whipping, and perhaps having their ears cut off, but are we in the future to be prevented from inflicting these punishments because they are cruel?" (Monk, n.d., p. 173).

One must wonder what future students will read about in a chapter such as this, when a recommendation was recently made to the Minnesota legislature that public flogging be instituted for drunken drivers. In a society whose thinking about drugs has changed dramatically even in the past decade, what will future scholars think about the current "get tough on drugs" philosophy that, by anyone's account, has significantly contributed to prisons being filled to capacity?

In a sense, the correctional system itself speaks to Eighth Amendment and other constitutional issues overall. Clear et al. (2006, p. 242) state: "Reformers are frustrated by the sheer durability of prisons. For example, the oldest prison in America—New Jersey's Trenton State Prison, opened in 1798 . . . and still houses offenders. Structures of stone and concrete are not easily redesigned when correctional goals change. So, elements of major reform movement can be found within the walls of many older prisons. In line with the Quakers' belief that offenders could be redeemed only if they were removed from the distractions of the city, many correction facilities are found . . . far from most of the inmates' families, friends and communities."

Our legal system reflects norms but cannot by design change overnight. We would not want it changed on a whim or as a result of politics. Instead, our criminal justice system is responsive, not reactive, to social changes. In *Trop v. Dulles* (1958), Chief Justice Warren observed: "The basic concept underlying the Eighth Amendment is nothing less than the dignity of man. . . . The amendment must draw its meaning from the evolving standards of decency that mark the progress of a maturing society."

As has been the case with correctional changes brought on by research, the civil rights movement and different beliefs in how people should be treated and held accountable, Eighth Amendment law has continued to develop to reflect American beliefs, including the tenets of punishment itself, which include "inflicting deserved suffering on evildoers and preventing crime" (Clear et al., p. 64).

Bail

The first part of the Eighth Amendment deals with granting bail to individuals accused of crimes. Bail is actually a verb and a noun, dealing with *pretrial release.* **Bail** is the act of pretrial release of a defendant whose promise to return to trial is secured by some form of collateral, most often money, which is also referred to as bail.

> **bail** • money or property pledged by a defendant for pretrial release from custody that would be forfeited should the defendant fail to appear at subsequent court proceedings

■ Bail serves two purposes. First, it helps to assure the appearance of the accused at court proceedings. Second, it maintains the presumption of innocence by allowing individuals not yet convicted of a crime to avoid continued incarceration.

Bail also allows individuals time to prepare a defense and to continue earning income if employed. Only *excessive* bail is prohibited by the Constitution. Bail itself is not guaranteed, and the Eighth Amendment has never been incorporated under the Fourteenth Amendment to apply to the states. The right to bail has historically been assumed through case law and statutory law rather than a constitutional guarantee.

■ The Constitution does not guarantee a right to bail; it only prohibits excessive bail, which it does not define. The Eighth Amendment does not apply to the states.

Bail may be denied in capital cases (those involving the death penalty) and when the accused has threatened possible trial witnesses. Also, the amount of bail does not have to be something the accused can pay. Some poor people cannot afford any bail and must stay in jail, thus generating debate over whether the system caters to those with money while discriminating against those without resources. State law varies on whether juveniles may be eligible for release on bail.

The Evolution of Legislation and Case Law on Bail

Although bail as an option has been determined legislatively and through common law, a progression of federal law has forged codified bail law. (Note the change in emphasis of this law and who the law is primarily seeking to protect.) The Judiciary Act of 1789 provided for bail in noncapital crimes.

The Bail Reform Act of 1966   The Bail Reform Act of 1966 helped indigent defendants who were unable to post bail in the usual monetary manner. This law was enacted to ensure that poor defendants would not remain in jail only because they could not afford bail, as well as to require judges to consider other ways for defendants to guarantee their return for trial. The Bail Reform Act of 1966 allowed judges to consider the defendant's background, family ties and prior record in setting bail. Under this comprehensive statute, the primary bail condition was for defendants to be released on their own recognizance, or **ROR,** which means the court trusts them to appear in court when required. Some jurisdictions refer to this bail condition as RPR, release on personal recognizance. No bail money is required. Criteria for ROR vary from state to state but usually include the person's residential stability, a good employment record and no previous convictions.

ROR • released on their own recognizance

The Bail Reform Act of 1984   The Bail Reform Act of 1984 (18 U.S.C. § 3141) granted judicial authority to include specific conditions of release for the community's safety. It also eliminated a presumption in favor of pretrial release through the bail process, allowing a court to deny bail for defendants when the prosecution is able to demonstrate, during a hearing, clear and convincing evidence that no conditions will reasonably assure the community's safety.

According to Arvidson (2006): "This legislation is specific to those under federal jurisdiction. The spirit of the Bail Reform Act is to compel federal government to begin with the assumption the accused would be released and to seek the least restrictive means of detention plausible rather than assuming the offender will be incarcerated. These less restrictive means could include outright release or any number of other options including bail, electronic monitoring, halfway house placement, collateral property, third party custody, surrendering one's passport and imposing travel restrictions."

This act also allowed federal courts for the first time to deny bail on the basis of danger to the community or of risk to not appear at trial. Known as **preventive detention,** this practice authorized judges to predict the probability of future criminal conduct by those accused of serious offenses and deny bail on those grounds.

preventive detention • the right of judges to consider the potential criminal conduct of those accused of serious offenses and deny bail on those grounds

■   The Bail Reform Act of 1984 establishes the practice of preventive detention for individuals deemed a threat to society or likely to flee, as well as other options to incarceration.

In *Jackson v. Indiana* (1972), the Court ruled that the government may detain dangerous defendants who may be incompetent to stand trial, and in *Addington v. Texas* (1979), the Court ruled that the government may detain mentally unstable individuals who present a public danger. However, the Jackson Court made clear that these individuals are no less deserving of due process hearings.

Opponents of preventive detention argue that the accused is being punished without trial and that protecting the community is the job of the police, not the purpose of bail. A few months after passage of the Bail Reform Act, in *United States v. Hazzard* (1984), the Supreme Court held that Congress was justified in denying bail to offenders who represent a danger to the community. The Supreme Court also upheld preventive detention in *United States v. Salerno* (1987), stating that pretrial detention under this act did not violate due process or the Eighth Amendment. In this case, the government charged Salerno with 29 counts of racketeering and conspiracy to commit murder. The Court ruled that because the Bail Reform

Act contained many procedural safeguards, the government's interest in protecting the community outweighed the individual's liberty. Strongly dissenting to the *Salerno* majority opinion was Justice Marshall, who said:

> It is a fair summary of history to say that the safeguards of liberty have frequently been forged in controversies involving not very nice people. Honoring the presumption of innocence is often difficult; sometimes we must pay substantial social costs as a result of our commitment to the values we espouse. But at the end of the day the presumption of innocence protects the innocent; the shortcuts we take with those whom we believe to be guilty injure only those wrongfully accused and, ultimately, ourselves.
>
> Throughout the world today there are men, women, and children interned indefinitely, awaiting trials which may never come or which may be a mockery of the word, because their governments believe them to be "dangerous." Our Constitution, whose construction began two centuries ago, can shelter us forever from the evils of such unchecked power. Over two hundred years it has slowly, through our efforts, grown more durable, more expansive, and more just. But it cannot protect us if we lack the courage, and the self-restraint to protect ourselves.

Nonetheless, several states have incorporated elements of preventive detention into their bail systems, for example, excluding certain crimes from eligibility, including crime control factors in release decisions and limiting the right to bail for defendants previously convicted or for those alleged to have committed crimes while on release.

The leading case for bail law is *Stack v. Boyle* (1951), which is interesting for reasons that include the time the case was heard. In *Stack*, the defendants were charged with advocating the violent overthrow of the government during the Cold War, when there was great concern over the threat of communism. In this case, the Supreme Court held that any amount exceeding that necessary to ensure a return to trial violated the Eighth Amendment. Judicial calculation of the appropriate amount would consider such matters as the seriousness of the offense, the government's evidence, the defendant's connection with the community and family, finances, mental condition, criminal record and any history of failing to appear when released on bail. Justice Fred Vinson stated in the Court's opinion:

> From the passage of the Judiciary Act of 1789, to the present . . . federal law has unequivocally provided that a person arrested for a non-capital offense *shall* be admitted to bail. This traditional right to freedom before conviction permits the unhampered preparation of a defense, and serves to prevent the infliction of punishment prior to conviction. . . . Unless this right to bail before trial is preserved, the presumption of innocence, secured only after centuries of struggle, would lose its meaning.
>
> The right to release before trial is conditioned upon the accused's giving adequate assurance that he will stand trial and submit to sentence if found guilty. . . . Like the ancient practice of securing the oaths of responsible persons to stand as sureties for the accused, the modern practice of requiring a bail bond or the deposit of a sum of money subject to forfeiture serves as additional assurance of the presence of an accused.

■ Bail set at a figure higher than an amount reasonably calculated to fulfill its purpose is excessive under the Eighth Amendment (*Stack v. Boyle,* 1951).

In the private bail bonding business, a bail bond provider posts a bond for upwards of 10 percent of the bail amount with the court to be paid if the defendant fails to appear, called **commercial bail.** The bail bond provider will post a person's bond for a fee, in effect making a loan but in a situation that traditional financial institutions may well avoid. If the accused fails to appear in court as ordered, the bail bond provider will often help the police catch the person because the bond company would lose its money. In some states, in fact, bail bond providers and others in the private sector have significant authority to locate "bail jumpers" and bring them before the court.

> **commercial bail** • using the services of a bail bond person to post a defendant's bail for a fee

One issue is who can afford to have bail posted for them or, more importantly, who cannot. This issue is why alternatives have been advocated and accepted, including in appropriate circumstances, release of defendants on their own recognizance if there is sufficient cause to believe their return to court need not be in issue.

■ The excessive bail prohibition has never been formally incorporated to apply to the states under the Fourteenth Amendment, allowing states to deal with it through their constitutions, legislation and case law.

The Court specifically held in *United States v. Salerno* (1987) that pretrial detention without bail does not violate either due process or the Eighth Amendment rights of a defendant. Therefore, even after *Salerno,* state courts are free to forbid preventive detention of state and local prisoners based on excessive bail provisions in the state constitution or through legislation or case law in that jurisdiction.

Fines

After the accused is convicted of a crime, the Eighth Amendment also prohibits punishment by excessive fines. The question then becomes: What is excessive? For example, should the wealthy be fined at a rate concurrent with their financial status? Should the government not be permitted to punish through very high fines, perhaps as an alternative to imprisonment? Until recently, there have been comparatively few cases in this area of constitutional law. Some of these cases have addressed whether there can be excessive fines in civil cases.

■ The prohibition against excessive fines has not been incorporated, so it does not apply to the states.

The Court has continued to uphold the rule that the Constitution regulates government, and because civil cases are, for the most part, between private parties, the excessive fine prohibition does not apply in the civil area. *Browning-Ferris Industries v. Kelco Disposal, Inc.* (1989) questioned whether the Eighth Amendment applied to civil punishments as well as criminal punishments. In criminal law, the government is always involved as a party to the case.

> **compensatory damages** • reimbursement of the plaintiff for actual harm done, such as medical expenses or lost business

In civil lawsuits, the plaintiff usually seeks monetary damages from the defendant to right an alleged wrong. **Compensatory damages** reimburse the plaintiff for actual harm done, such as medical expenses or lost business. Cases that have questioned the amounts awarded have primarily dealt with **punitive damages,** an amount the defendant in a civil case must pay the plaintiff beyond compensatory

> **punitive damages** • fines above and beyond the actual economic loss to punish the defendant in a civil trial

damages. Punitive damages are meant to be just that, additional punishment to the wrongdoer and a warning to others not to engage in similar conduct.

In *Browning-Ferris Industries*, the Supreme Court ruled that the Eighth Amendment applied not only to criminal cases but also to "direct actions initiated by the government to inflict punishment." Punitive damages in civil cases did not involve government actions, the Court said, so the Eighth Amendment did not apply. The Court noted that although it agreed that punitive damages advance the interest of punishment and deterrence, which are also among the interests advanced by criminal law, it failed to see how this overlap required that the excessive fines clause be applied in cases between private parties.

Asset Forfeiture and the Prohibition against Excessive Fines

asset forfeiture • the seizure by the government, without compensation, of money and property connected with illegal activity

An area receiving increasingly significant attention is **asset forfeiture,** the uncompensated government seizure of money and property connected with illegal activity. Researchers Clingermayer et al. (2005) found that asset forfeiture is a common practice in the jurisdictions participating in their research. Over 90 percent of the agencies indicated they used asset forfeiture.

The use of asset forfeiture by law enforcement has become a means by which a great deal of funding is acquired for prevention programs and equipment. According to Worrall (2004, p. 220): "Perhaps the most hardline tool in the war on drugs, and arguably the most controversial, is that state and federal laws have granted police departments and federal law enforcement the authority to not only seize and forfeit assets, but also to receive the proceeds from such activities. This practice, known as 'equitable sharing,' has generated a storm of criticism over the past two decades. . . . Some critics have argued that civil asset forfeiture laws encourage the seizure of assets instead of the suppression of crime. Other critics have clamed that 'policing for profit' has begun to take precedence over policing to reduce crime." Yet another argument is that it is de facto double jeopardy, subjecting the defendant to dual punishments.

■ Property connected with illegal activity may be forfeited when used as a "conveyance" to transport illicit drugs (including aircraft, ships and motor vehicles). Real estate used in association with a crime and money or other negotiable instruments obtained through criminal activity also can be seized and is considered a civil sanction by the government.

While forfeiture is considered a civil action initiated by the government and not a criminal action per se, the high court has recognized it as an area subject to the Eighth Amendment because forfeiture "constitutes payment to a sovereign as punishment for some offense . . . and, as such, is subject to the limitations of the Eighth Amendment's Excessive Fines Clause" (*Austin v. United States*, 1993). Other constitutional questions forfeiture law raise are whether it constitutes cruel and unusual punishment, double jeopardy and a denial of due process.

In *Austin v. United States*, the defendant pled guilty to selling two grams of cocaine, valued at $200, and the government seized property belonging to him (including his business) that netted a profit to the government of $32,000. The Supreme Court unanimously ruled that the Eighth Amendment prohibition against excessive fines applies to civil forfeiture proceedings against property connected to drug trafficking. They held that the amount seized by the forfeiture must bear some relation to the value of the illegal enterprise under the Eighth Amendment prohibition on excessive fines. This decision is the first constitutional limitation on the government's power to seize property connected with illegal activity and could result in challenges to seizures related to criminal activity.

In *United States v. Bajakajian* (1998), the Court ruled that a $357,144 forfeiture for failing to report to U.S. Customs that more than $10,000 was being taken out of the country was "grossly disproportionate" to the offense.

◼ The amount seized through asset forfeiture must bear some relation to the value of the illegal enterprise.

The Supreme Court held in *United States v. Ursery* (1996) that forfeiture is not double jeopardy because it is considered a civil sanction rather than an additional criminal action. Due process requires that property not be forfeited without a hearing (*United States v. Good*, 1993), but the Supreme Court has also held that forfeiture is constitutional even when the owner is not aware of its criminal use. In *Bennis v. Michigan* (1996), Mrs. Bennis argued it was unconstitutional for the government to seize a car of which she was part owner. Her husband was using it when he was arrested for engaging in prostitution, even though she had no knowledge of the crime. In disallowing her claim, the Court referred to "a long and unbroken line of cases in which this Court has held that an owner's interest in property may be forfeited by reason of the use to which the property is put even though the owner did not know that it was to be put to such use."

In 2000, Congress approved the Civil Asset Forfeiture Reform Act, curbing federal law enforcement agencies' asset forfeiture authority and adding due process protections to ensure that property is not unjustly taken from innocent owners. Shortly before the approval, Rep. Henry J. Hyde (R-IL) commented: "Civil asset forfeiture as allowed in our country today is a throwback to the old Soviet Union, where justice is the justice of the government and the citizen did not have a chance." Voegtlin (2000, p. 8) outlines the key changes:

- Burden of proof—In forfeiture cases, the government must establish that the property was subject to forfeiture by a "preponderance of the evidence" rather than the original higher standard of "clear and convincing."
- Statute of limitations—Is reduced from eleven years to five years.
- Destruction of property to prevent seizure—It is a crime to move or destroy property to prevent seizure for forfeiture.

Cruel and Unusual Punishment

The final clause of the Eighth Amendment forbids punishments that are "cruel and unusual," but it does not say what those punishments are. What is "cruel and unusual?"

The easy answer, but the correct one, is that cruel and unusual punishment depends on what a society believes it to be. Just as our previous definition of law includes the idea that law supports the society's current norms, how a society punishes offenders is also directly related to current acceptable norms.

◼ In *Trop v. Dulles* (1958), Chief Justice Warren stated that the cruel and unusual punishments clause "must draw its meaning from the evolving standards of decency that mark the progress of a maturing society."

In *Trop*, the Supreme Court restored a soldier's citizenship he had lost as a result of being found guilty of desertion from the army, finding the punishment too extreme. As Justice Thurgood Marshall noted in a later case: "A penalty that was permissible at one time in our nation's history is not necessarily permissible today." Thus, common punishments during the 1790s, such as whippings and pillories, are no longer constitutional in the twenty-first century.

Although this text emphasizes U.S. law and the events leading to the formation of current law, it is interesting to observe how other countries and cultures, both past and present, determine punishment. Because law in any society seeks to respond to its present needs, always in flux, the punishments considered appropriate also change. Perhaps the "extremity" of the available punishment forms tends to change, as do the society's overall social feelings.

For example, although Americans are steadfast in their belief that crime must be curtailed "at any price," the caning (whipping) of young American Michael Fay in Singapore in 1994, who was found guilty of damage to property, outraged many. Yet, the crime rate in Singapore is considerably lower than that in the United States. So what is appropriate punishment? It is what a society defines it as.

In *Coker v. Georgia* (1977), the Court held that a "punishment is 'excessive' and unconstitutional if it (1) makes no measurable contribution to acceptable goals of punishment and hence is nothing more than the purposeless and needless imposition of pain and suffering or (2) is grossly out of proportion to the severity of the crime." In seeking a more specific answer to what constitutes cruel and unusual punishment, courts have used three inquiries in assessing constitutionality (Clear and Cole, 2006, p. 109):

- Whether the punishment shocks the general conscience of a civilized society
- Whether the punishment is unnecessarily cruel
- Whether the punishment goes beyond legitimate penal aims

proportionality analysis • in essence, making the punishment fit the crime

The Supreme Court established three criteria for **proportionality analysis** of sentences in *Solem v. Helm* (1983):

> A court's proportionality analysis under the Eighth Amendment should be guided by objective criteria, including (1) the gravity of the offense and the harshness of the penalty; (2) the sentences imposed on other criminals in the same jurisdiction and (3) the sentences imposed for the commission of the same crime in other jurisdictions.

- The general rule under the Eighth Amendment is that punishments must be proportional or directly related to the crime committed.

For example, in *Robinson v. California* (1962), the Supreme Court found "excessive" a 90-day jail term for the crime of being "addicted to the use of narcotics." Robinson was not under the influence of drugs when arrested, and the only evidence against him was the scars and needle marks on his arms. The Court believed the defendant was being punished for the mere status of being an addict, not for actual criminal behavior. On the other hand, in *Harmelin v. Michigan* (1991), the Supreme Court upheld a mandatory life sentence without parole for a first-time cocaine conviction.

In *Pulley v. Harris* (1984), the Court held that although many states require proportionality review, nothing in the Court's decisions interpreting the Eighth Amendment requires a state appellate court, before affirming a death penalty, to compare the sentence in that case to penalties imposed in similar cases if the defendant requests such a comparison.

In *Ewing v. California* (2003), the high court considered whether a sentence of 25 years to life imprisonment for felony theft under a "three strikes" sentencing schedule was cruel and unusual. They held 5 to 4 that California's "three strikes" law did not violate the Eighth Amendment. The Court reached the same result in *Lockyer v. Andrade* (2003).

The Supreme Court tackled the issue of **corporal punishment** (causing bodily harm) in *Ingraham v. Wright* (1978). James Ingraham, a junior high school student, had been hit more than 20 times with a paddle for disobeying a teacher's order. He required medical attention and missed 11 days of school. The Court held: "The state itself may impose such corporal punishment as is necessary for the proper education of the child for the maintenance of group discipline." Furthermore, the Court stated: "The school child has little need for protection of the Eighth Amendment because the openness of the public school and its supervision by the community affords significant safeguards against the kinds of abuses from which the Eighth Amendment protects the prisoner." This case is included as an example of the controversy that continues, both in the courtroom and elsewhere, as to what consequences are appropriate in the home, school and court. This does not, however, preclude various civil causes of action a child or parent could bring in court.

corporal punishment • causing bodily harm through physical force, for example, whipping, flogging, beating

Punishment Options

Few dispute the necessity of punishment as a means of social control in an ordered society. As Cicero noted in *Pro Milone* (50 B.C.): "The greatest incitement to crime is the hope of escaping punishment." The challenge is in determining what the most appropriate and effective punishment might be.

The American criminal justice system continues to work with different ways to meet the goals of punishment, incorporating rehabilitation when possible. Many options are available on the continuum of possibilities, as illustrated in Figure 13.1, including probation, parole, length and types of incarceration, restitution and new ideas that continue to evolve from the corrections component of the criminal justice system.

Table 13.1 expands on these sentencing options, showing how they relate to the law on the books and the law in action. Of course, particularly heinous crime does not lend itself to the lesser sanctions, but new possibilities continue to present themselves.

Not all of these options meet the expectations of the public or the politicians. Because new paradigms are not necessarily readily embraced, new correctional concepts are understandably challenged. The real challenge, however, is to honestly inquire whether existing means work and, when they do not, what might? When the prison sanction is selected, the result is often much litigation in this area of Eighth Amendment law that pertains to prisoner treatment.

Physical Forms of Punishment

Modern technology presents several possible treatments for criminals, including Antabuse, a drug used in treating alcoholics by causing nausea and vomiting when alcohol is ingested. Sex offenders have been treated with Depo-Provera, a drug that reduces the sex drive. Use of such drugs and surgical procedures, such as castration and lobotomy, may run counter to the Eighth Amendment's ban on cruel and unusual punishment.

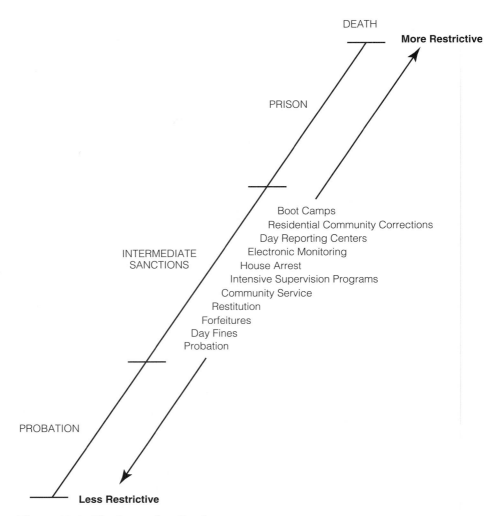

DEATH

More Restrictive

PRISON

Boot Camps
Residential Community Corrections
Day Reporting Centers
Electronic Monitoring
House Arrest
Intensive Supervision Programs
Community Service
Restitution
Forfeitures
Day Fines
Probation

INTERMEDIATE
SANCTIONS

PROBATION

Less Restrictive

Figure 13.1 The Sentencing Continuum

Source: Norman Carlson et al. *Corrections in the 21st Century: A Practical Approach.* Belmont, CA: Wadsworth
Publishing Company, 1999, p. 101.

Although other forms of bodily punishment for criminals have disappeared,
the death penalty remains in use and is controversial. The Supreme Court has
decided many cases on the constitutionality of capital punishment. It has also
defined the nature of cruel and unusual punishment in noncapital cases. However, the death penalty remains the most debated issue under the Eighth Amendment because it concerns the ultimate issue: life or death.

Capital Punishment

Twelve states executed 59 prisoners during 2004, 6 fewer than in 2003 (Bonczar
and Snell, 2005, p. 1). At year end 2004, 36 states and the federal prison system
held 3,314 prisoners under sentence of death, 63 fewer than at year end 2003. Of
those under sentence of death, 56 percent were white, 42 percent were black, and
2 percent were of other races.

The death penalty dates back centuries. History records many brutal methods
of execution, including being buried alive, thrown to wild animals, drawn and

Table 13.1   Sentencing Options

	Law on the Books	*Law in Action*
Prison	A correctional facility for housing adults convicted of felony offenses, usually under the control of state government.	• Almost 1.4 million adults are in prison. • The prison population has doubled in the past decade. • Six percent of inmates are female. • Forty-five percent of prison inmates are black.
Parole	Adults conditionally released to community supervision after serving part of a prison term. The parolee is subject to being returned to prison for rule violations or other offenses.	• Over 700,000 are on parole from state or federal prison. • Twelve percent of parolees are women. • Fifty-three percent of parolees are white.
Probation	Punishment for a crime that allows the offender to remain in the community without incarceration but subject to certain conditions.	• Over 3,775,000 adults are on probation under federal, state, or local jurisdiction. • Half of all offenders on probation committed a felony.
Intermediate Sanctions	A variety of punishments that are more restrictive than traditional probation but less stringent than incarceration.	• Much less costly than imprisonment. • Community service requires offender to perform public service such as street cleaning or hospital volunteer work. • Electronic monitoring ensures that a probationer does not leave home except to go to work.
Fines	A sum of money to be paid to the government by a convicted person as punishment for an offense.	• Often used for misdemeanor offenses. • Recent research shows that it can be effectively used to punish selected felonies.
Restitution	Requirement that the offender pay to the victim a sum of money to make good the loss.	• Most defendants are so poor that they cannot reasonably be expected to make restitution.
Capital Punishment	The use of the death penalty (execution) as the punishment for the commission of a particular crime.	• Over 3,450 prisoners are on death row. • Fifty-five percent of death row inmates are white.

Source: David W. Neubauer. *America's Courts and the Criminal Justice System,* 7th ed. Belmont, CA: West/Wadsworth, 2002, p. 395.

quartered, boiled in oil, burned, stoned, drowned, impaled, crucified, pressed to death, smothered, stretched on a rack, disemboweled, beheaded, hanged or shot.

In biblical times, criminals were stoned to death or crucified. The ancient Greeks, in a much more humane fashion, administered poison from the hemlock tree to execute criminals. The Romans, in contrast, used beheading, clubbing, strangling, drawing and quartering or feeding to the lions. During the Dark Ages, ordeals were devised to serve as both judgment and punishment. These ordeals included being submerged in water or in boiling oil, crushed under huge boulders or forced to do battle with skilled swordsmen. It was presumed the innocent would survive the ordeal; the guilty would be killed by it. Later, in France, the guillotine became the preferred means of execution. Societies have always struggled with balancing societal needs with socially accepted means of punishment.

Although today's methods are said to be more civilized, accounts of witnesses to executions raise doubts as to whether progress has been made. The death penalty has been an established feature of the American criminal justice system since Colonial times, with hanging often the preferred execution, especially on the frontier. Means of execution evolved as states sought more humane ways of killing their condemned—from hangings to the first electrocution in 1890, the invention of the gas chamber in 1923, the use of the firing squad and, finally, the addition of lethal injection, now the predominant method of execution in the United States.

Until the middle of the nineteenth century, the death penalty was the automatic sentence for a convicted murderer. State laws began to draw distinctions between degrees of murder, but the death penalty was still automatic for first-degree murderers. By the early twentieth century, however, state legislatures had given jurors more discretion in sentencing. The jurors were given no guidance by state law in choosing between life and death sentences. Jurors had total discretion in this decision, which could not be reviewed on appeal.

Most criminals were sentenced under state, not federal, law. Thus, the Eighth Amendment's prohibition against cruel and unusual punishment was not relevant to the overwhelming majority of death penalty cases until the Supreme Court incorporated it to apply to the states in *Robinson v. California* (1962).

Is Capital Punishment Cruel and Unusual?

■ Although capital punishment may appear cruel and unusual to some, the Supreme Court has not held this to be the case.

The issue of cruel and unusual punishment has a long history and has given the courts great difficulty in defining it. In *Furman v. Georgia* (1972), the Court's opinion was more than 230 pages. All nine justices wrote separate opinions trying to define the meaning of four words: *cruel and unusual punishment*.

In this case, Furman had broken into a private home in the middle of the night, intending only to burglarize it, although he was carrying a gun. Furman attempted to escape when the home owner awoke. Furman tripped and his gun discharged, hitting and killing the owner through a closed door. Furman was black; the home owner was white. Furman was sentenced to death.

In consolidating three other cases with Furman's (all involving white victims and black defendants but having little else in common), the Supreme Court considered the varied public opinions regarding the death penalty. The court ruled that the death penalty *as then administered* in Georgia was cruel and unusual punishment because it was "wantonly and freakishly" imposed. Judges and juries had far too much unguided discretion under current state laws, and the Court held this led to arbitrary and capricious or random and unreasonable death sentences and violated due process.

■ *Furman v. Georgia* (1972) was the landmark case in which the Supreme Court called for a ban on the death penalty in Georgia, ruling its law as it stood was capricious and, hence, cruel and unusual punishment.

In *Furman*, the Supreme Court did not rule the death penalty was unconstitutional in all circumstances. Rather, the Court held that the states had to give judges and juries more guidance in capital sentencing to prevent discretionary use of the death penalty. It held that Georgia's death penalty law was invalid.

In effect, the *Furman* case put on hold capital punishment statutes in 37 states. Executions across the country were suspended as a result. In response, about three-fourths of the states and the federal government passed new death penalty laws, in many instances instituting a two-step trial procedure: the first step to determine innocence or guilt and the second step to determine whether to seek the death penalty. Such a two-stage trial is often referred to as a **bifurcated trial.** While reviewing these laws, the Supreme Court finally decided whether the death penalty was inherently cruel and unusual punishment.

bifurcated trial • a two-step trial for capital cases

Just four years later, in *Gregg v. Georgia* (1976), the Court sustained a revised Georgia death penalty law by a 7 to 2 margin, stating:

> A punishment is unconstitutionally cruel and unusual only if it violates the evolving levels of decency that define a civilized society. The death penalty today in the United States does not do that—as is proved by public opinion substantially favoring executions, by legislatures enacting death penalty statutes or refusing to repeal them, and by courts willing to sentence hundreds of murderers to death every year.

■ In *Gregg v. Georgia* (1976), the Supreme Court reinstated the Georgia death penalty by sustaining its revised death penalty law.

The Court also affirmed the importance of a bifurcated trial.

■ The death penalty itself is not cruel and unusual punishment, but a capital case requires two proceedings: one to determine guilt or innocence and the other to determine the sentence (*Gregg v. Georgia*, 1976).

In rendering its opinion, the Court recognized the significance of public opinion, citing strong public support for the death penalty. The Court noted that three-fourths of state legislatures reenacted the death penalty after *Furman*; therefore, the death penalty was not "unusual" punishment. In a strong dissent, Justice William Brennan repeated the arguments he had made against the death penalty in *Furman*. Brennan questioned "whether a society for which the dignity of the individual is the supreme value can, without a fundamental inconsistency, follow the practice of deliberately putting some of its members to death. . . . Even the most vile criminal remains a human being possessed of common human dignity." Brennan concluded:

> This Court inescapably has the duty, as the ultimate arbiter of the meaning of our Constitution, to say whether, when individuals condemned to death stand before our Bar, "moral concepts" require us to hold that the law has progressed to the point where we should declare that the punishment of death, like punishments on the rack, the screw, and the wheel, is no longer morally tolerable in our society.

Lengthy Delays in Execution as Cruel and Unusual   The average delay for prisoners under sentence of death before execution is approximately 11 years (Bonczar and Snell, p. l). Justices Stephen G. Breyer and Clarence Thomas have engaged in an unusual public debate over whether long delays in carrying out executions constitute cruel and unusual punishment. Justice Breyer believes the Court should consider this question and dissented when the Court declined to hear arguments in two cases that raised it: *Moore v. Nebraska* (1997) and *Knight v. Florida* (1999). Justice Thomas, on the other hand, is indignant that death row inmates could seek to take advantage of what he called "this court's Byzantine death penalty jurisprudence" and then complain when their appeals cause lengthy delays in their executions.

Justice Thomas said that, in his view, the question of whether long delays in carrying out death sentences are unconstitutional has been decided, and the answer is no: "I write only to point out that I am unaware of any support in the American Constitutional tradition or in this court's precedent for the proposition that a defendant can avail himself of the panoply of the appellate and collateral procedures and then complain when his execution is delayed."

Means of Execution

The five means of execution in the United States are death by hanging, firing squad, electric chair, gas chamber and lethal injection. Figure 13.2 shows the various methods of execution used by states that have the death penalty. (Kansas has since enacted a death penalty statute.)

Of the five means by which the death penalty is carried out in the United States, the Supreme Court has found none of them inherently cruel and unusual, but not without judicial controversy and public dissension. Only hanging has been challenged in federal court and held not to be cruel and unusual (*Campbell v. Wood*, 1994), except in the case of a 400-plus pound man because the result was likely to result in decapitation (*Rupe v. Wood*, 1994).

While executions by means of poisonous gas and electrocution have resulted in quite horrific stories of lingering, painful deaths, including the much publicized execution in 1997 of Pedro Medina, convicted of killing a police officer.

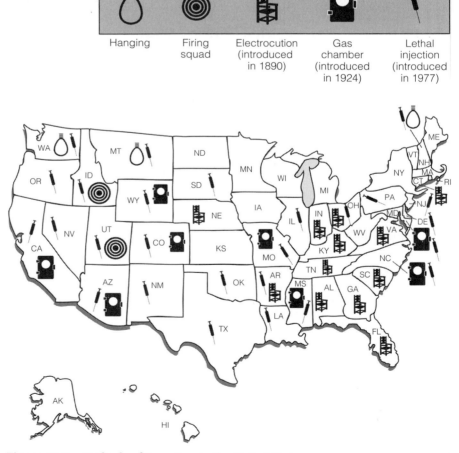

| Hanging | Firing squad | Electrocution (introduced in 1890) | Gas chamber (introduced in 1924) | Lethal injection (introduced in 1977) |

Figure 13.2 Methods of Execution in the United States

Source: *Death Row.* Carlsbad, CA: Glenn Hare Publications, 1995, p. 88. Reprinted by permission.

The 74-year-old electric chair in Florida, referred to as "Old Sparky," shot flames some 12 inches high from Medina's head during the process, but death by such means has not been held to be unconstitutional. Of the 59 men executed in 2004, 58 were executed by lethal injection and 1 by electrocution (Bonczar and Snell, p. 1). Lethal injection is considered by some to be the only politically correct method of capital punishment. Other issues related to capital punishment involve who can legally be executed.

Who Can Be Executed?

As a general rule, the Supreme Court has upheld the death penalty for murder but not for other crimes. Under the Eighth Amendment, the punishment must be related to the crime, so execution is appropriate only in cases of murder—a life for a life. In many states, new death penalty sentencing systems require judges and juries to consider aggravating factors and mitigating factors in each capital case and to apply the death penalty in only the most heinous cases.

Some such sentencing systems were challenged. For example, in *Maynard v. Cartwright* (1988), the Court held that an Oklahoma statute allowing a jury to impose the death penalty if the murder was "especially heinous, atrocious or cruel" was unconstitutional because it did not sufficiently guide the jury's decision. However, in *Arave v. Creech* (1993), the Court upheld an Idaho law identifying as an aggravating circumstance a murderer who showed "utter disregard for human life."

In 2002, in *Bell v. Cone*, the Supreme Court ruled against Tennessee death row inmate Gary Cone, who claimed his lawyer was incompetent. The Court signaled it will take a narrow view of death row inmates' claims that their lawyers were incompetent. However, because the death penalty is involved, claims will be scrutinized.

A series of cases have addressed the eligibility of individuals found guilty of murder or other "heinous crimes" who might be sentenced to death. This arena is where much of the action on the Eighth Amendment has taken place in the past few years. Issues involve age, race, mental retardation and mental illness.

Age   In *Eddings v. Oklahoma* (1982), the Supreme Court vacated the death sentence of a 16-year-old boy by a vote of 5 to 4. In *Thompson v. Oklahoma* (1988), the Court held:

> Less blameworthiness should attach to a crime committed by a juvenile than one committed by an adult because inexperience, less education, and less intelligence make the juvenile less able to appreciate the consequences of his or her conduct while, at the same time, such conduct is more apt to be influenced by peer pressure. Given this lesser culpability, the retributive purpose of the death penalty is not applicable to a 15-year-old offender. Moreover, since 18 states now prohibit imposing the death sentence on an offender less than 16 years old and another 14 states have abolished the death penalty entirely, it is likely there is a national consensus that imposing the death penalty on a 15-year-old today would offend the conscience of the community.

Unlike *Eddings v. Oklahoma, Stanford v. Kentucky* (1989) held: "In the absence of any historical or modern society consensus against imposing capital punishment on 16- and 17-year-old murderers, such death sentences do not violate the Eighth Amendment."

■ Most states will not consider the death sentence for anyone younger than 15 years.

These cases lead to *Roper v. Simmons* (2005), which held that the Eighth and Fourteenth Amendments will not permit executing anyone under 18 years of age for committing a crime. In this case, Christopher Simmons was 17 years old when he received the death sentence for murdering Shirley Crook while burglarizing her home, and then, with the help of an even younger accomplice, throwing her bound body off a cliff in a park. He appealed on the grounds the death penalty was cruel and unusual punishment because of his age when he committed the crime. Simmons gave a full confession, even providing a videotaped reenactment of his crime. In a 5-to-4 vote, Justice Kennedy wrote: "When a juvenile offender commits a heinous crime, the State can exact forfeiture of some of the most basic liberties, but the State cannot extinguish his life and his potential to attain a mature understanding of his own humanity," referring to Justice Stevens quote regarding evolving standards of decency marking a maturing society.

Race   In *McCleskey v. Kemp* (1987), McCleskey presented a thorough statistical study contending that capital punishment in Georgia was filled with racial discrimination. The Court ruled that even if the study was valid, McClesky had not proved the sentence was the result of racial discrimination.

Just as controversy surrounds whether the criminal justice system in general is biased, cases involving the death penalty raise the issue of bias as well: "The percentage of blacks who have been executed far exceeds their proportion of the general population. Particularly interesting is that more than 80 percent of the victims of those executed have been white. What makes this finding interesting is that murders, including capital murders, tend to be intraracial. However the death penalty is imposed primarily on the killers of white people, regardless of the race or ethnicity of the offender" (Bohm and Haley, 2007, pp. 329–330). Although these figures are considered simply factual or disconcerting, the Supreme Court has yet to conclude any constitutional issues are involved.

Mental Retardation   In *Penry v. Lynaugh* (1989), a case involving a mentally retarded defendant possessing an IQ between 50 and 63 and a mental age of a six-and-a-half-year-old, the Court held: "Since mentally retarded individuals vary greatly in their mental attributes and thus their limitations, it is not cruel and unusual punishment to impose the death penalty on a retarded defendant who was found competent to stand trial and whose insanity defense was rejected at trial." The defendant's mental state could be considered, but there was no prohibition against executing the mentally ill convicted of a capital offense. (In an interesting side note, just hours before he was to be executed in 1999, Penry was granted a stay of execution by the U.S. Supreme Court. When told of the stay, his first concern was whether he could still have his last meal of a cheeseburger and French fries. This raises the question: "What is accomplished by executing the mentally retarded?")

In 2002, the Supreme Court amended its position on capital punishment of the mentally retarded in *Atkins v. Virginia*, holding that executing the mentally retarded is cruel and unusual punishment in violation of the Eighth Amendment.

■ The Supreme Court has prohibited executing the mentally retarded.

The Mentally Ill   Closely related to the question of executing those who are mentally retarded is the question of forcing a convicted murderer to take drugs to make him sane enough to be executed. The Supreme Court banned execution of the insane in 1986. In *Singleton v. Norris* (2003), the Supreme Court let stand a ruling by a federal appeals court that allowed Arkansas officials to force a convicted murdered to take drugs to make him sane enough to be executed. According to Lewis (2003): "Scholars in medical ethics have said the issue of medicating patients to improve their mental health to execute them might present formidable obstacles for doctors. In practice, that could mean allowing nonmedical personnel to administer such treatments." The Supreme Court held in *Ford v. Wainwright* (1986) that an inmate who became mentally ill while in prison could not be executed.

Appeals

All but one state that has the death penalty require automatic appellate review of death sentences. South Carolina will allow a competent defendant waive this review. However, there is no such automatic right to have the Supreme Court review every death sentence case, although they are willing to address many issues having merit.

Because capital punishment is the ultimate sanction a government can inflict, appeals are certain and lengthy. Appeals will be heard by the state courts, and a writ of certiorari may be filed with the Supreme Court. Most capital cases originate in the states, and appeals can be filed directly through the state court system. In addition, the defendants may make indirect or collateral appeals of their sentences through the federal court system by arguing that their constitutional rights have been violated.

Juries and Capital Punishment Cases

The Supreme Court continues to hear matters pertaining to the death penalty. Whether potential jurors can be excluded because of their objections to the death penalty has been reviewed in several cases, with the *Lockhart v. McCree* (1986) Court determining that jurors whose opposition to the death penalty is so strong that it would prevent or substantially impair the performance of their duties could be removed.

In *Morgan v. Illinois* (1992), the Supreme Court held that a prospective juror in a capital case who indicates that if the defendant is found guilty the death penalty should be imposed can be challenged for cause and removed.

In *Simmons v. South Carolina* (1994), the Court held that if the prosecution contends a defendant should be put to death because he is too dangerous to ever return to society, without informing the jury of the option of a sentence of life without parole, this action could be considered a denial of due process.

In June 1999, in *Jones v. United States,* the Supreme Court ruled that juries need not be told the consequences of a deadlock. This case involved the first set of issues to reach the Supreme Court regarding the Federal Death Penalty Act of 1994, which re-established capital punishment at the federal level for a number of crimes. In this case, Louis Jones, Jr. was convicted of kidnapping a woman from an Air Force base, sexually assaulting her and beating her to death with a tire iron. Jones appealed on the grounds that the jury was not instructed as to what would happen if they deadlocked. If they had deadlocked, the judge would have sentenced him to life without parole. Justice Thomas, writing for the majority, believed that telling the jury the consequences of deadlock constitutes "an open invitation for the jury to avoid its responsibility and to disagree." Judge Thomas continued: "In a capital sentencing proceeding, the government has a strong interest in having the jury express the conscience of the community on the ultimate question of life and death. . . . We are of the view that a charge to the jury of the sort proposed by [Jones] might well have the effect of undermining this strong governmental interest."

Finally, in *Ring v. Arizona* (2002), the Court ruled that capital punishment can be imposed only by a jury or by a judge following a jury's recommendation. However, in 2004, in *Schriro v. Summerlin*, the Court held that the decision requiring juries, not judges, to impose sentences in capital case need not be applied retroactively to death row inmates whose sentences already had been affirmed on direct appeal. The effect of that decision is that more than 100 death sentences in four states, and potentially more in other states, will *not* be overturned ("Court Declines," 2004, p. 3).

Continuing Controversy

The debate over the cruel and unusual punishment clause is far from over. It has enjoyed a brief period of prominence, although this prominence may have been achieved at some cost in terms of public perception of the legitimacy of the court's decision-making process. In any event, the court's recent concern with the clause is now seriously threatened by attempts to adopt a more traditional authoritarian approach toward interpreting the clause's language. The death penalty has been and remains extremely controversial.

How you personally respond to such circumstances indicates the emotion that goes into determining what sentences are within our legal confines, with the logical question being whether any particular method serves its purpose. To be sure, debate will continue. The death penalty will be an issue for years to come, with strong advocates and opponents, because at the core of the issue is the question of values.

A modern development affecting the law of criminal procedure is DNA testing. Not only prosecutors but also defense attorneys have put this compelling evidence to good use. The impact on past cases has proved particularly troubling because of the number of convicted individual, some awaiting execution, who have since been exonerated through the use of DNA evidence. Ducat (p. 583) states: "Perhaps the worst example . . . occurred in Illinois, where, of 25 prisoners awaiting their fate on death row since 1977, DNA analysis showed a majority could not have committed the murders for which they had been convicted. After the thirteenth prisoner was exonerated, Governor George Ryan in January 2000 announced a moratorium on the death penalty in the state." Ducat also states that more than 100 prisoners have been freed since 1989 because of DNA evidence.

Researchers Unnever and Cullen (2005) found that whether innocent people have been executed is at the center of the debate concerning capital punishment, with public support for the death penalty severely eroding if the public believes innocent people have been executed.

The Eighth Amendment and Corrections

Because corrections is an integral component of the criminal justice system, it must be considered along with law enforcement and courts when one learns about the Constitution, as all components are affected by constitutional law. In addition to the rights of those in prison, the study of criminal justice includes consideration of why people are in prison, who makes up prison populations and whether minorities are disproportionately confined.

The system struggles to understand those who find themselves in prison to better address such issues as prevention, treatment, rehabilitation and the ever-present question as to whether the system is biased. The research is detailed, with 2004 data reflecting the majority of state prison inmates as being male (93.6%); never married (57.1%); 25 to 34 years old (38.1%); having completed only some high school (28.9%); having earned $1,000 to $1,999 in personal income the month before arrest (22.9%); having been employed the month before arrest (68.2%); not being homeless or not having lived on the street during the past year (89.4%); and being black (40.5%) (Bohm and Haley, p. 365).

That the numbers reflect a disproportionate number of inmates who are black begs the question of whether the criminal justice system is racist: "The overrepresentation of blacks in prison is a very heated issue in criminal justice today, and research has not established a consensus on the reasons for that overrepresentation. Currently, however, the weight of the evidence suggests that offense seriousness and prior criminal record generally exert a stronger impact on decisions to imprison than do extralegal factors such as race" (Bohm and Haley, p. 365). The numbers are of concern, as are the questions of why and how society and the system can best respond.

Due process and equal protection issues are significant concerns in corrections because violations of these rights are unconstitutional. Numbers alone do not provide the answer: "People of color, especially young African American and Hispanic men, are vastly overrepresented in the criminal justice system. The reasons for this are disputed" (Clear et al., 2006, p. 491). Clear et al. (p. 490) conclude: "There is no obvious answer. That is one of the reasons recent studies of race and criminal justice find that 'the criminal justice system is neither completely free of racial bias nor systematically racially biased.'" Research, the law and society as a whole continue to seek enlightenment and provide guidance on such issues of importance to criminal justice.

As with the previous amendments, prisoners have limited constitutional rights, but these rights are not entirely suspended and have been the basis for numerous lawsuits. Eighth Amendment violations are typically divided into two categories: (1) actions against individual prisoners, such as solitary confinement, and (2) institutional conditions all inmates are subject to.

■ For prisoners, cases based on Eighth Amendment rights involve cruel and unusual punishment, such as overcrowding, solitary confinement, corporal punishment, physical abuse and the use of force; treatment and rehabilitation; the right not to be treated; and the death penalty.

Prisoner Treatment and the Eighth Amendment

The Supreme Court has been called on to determine whether conditions and actions within correctional institutions constitute cruel and unusual punishment. Clear and Cole (p. 95) describe five cases with selected interpretations of the Eighth Amendment as applied to prisoners. *Ruiz v. Estelle* (1975) ruled that conditions of confinement in the Texas prison system were unconstitutional. In *Estelle v. Gamble* (1976), the Court ruled that deliberate indifference to prisoners' serious medical needs constitutes unnecessary, wanton infliction of pain.

Rhodes v. Chapman (1981) ruled that double-celling and crowding do not necessarily constitute cruel and unusual punishment. The conditions must be shown to involve "wanton and unnecessary infliction of pain" and to be "grossly disproportionate" to the severity of the crime warranting imprisonment. *Whitley v. Albers* (1986) held that a prisoner shot in the leg during a riot did not suffer cruel and unusual punishment if the action was taken in good faith to maintain discipline rather than for the mere purpose of causing harm. *Wilson v. Seiter* (1991) ruled that prisoners must not only prove prison conditions are objectively cruel and unusual but also show they exist because of officials' deliberate indifference.

A more recent case concerned second-hand cigarette smoke. In *Helling v. McKinney* (1993), the Court held that the Nevada Department of Prisons "with deliberate indifference, exposed him [McKinney] to levels of ETS [second-hand smoke] that pose an unreasonable risk of serious damage to his future health." As a result of this case, many correctional facilities have established smoke-free environments or permit smoking only in designated areas or outside. However, many correctional administrators contend that smoking privileges are important in controlling inmate behavior. Not being allowed to smoke may make inmates irritable and aggressive. Ironically, both smokers and nonsmokers claim violation of their Eighth Amendment rights.

Another prisoner management tool, visiting privileges, has also been an Eighth Amendment issue. *Overton v. Bazetta* (2003) held it is not cruel and unusual punishment for a prison to suspend visiting privileges for inmates who have failed more than one drug test. Weight lifting in correctional facilities has also been a management tool to help relieve stress for inmates. However, Arizona, Georgia and North Carolina have banned weight lifting in state prisons and jails, primarily prohibiting use of free weights because they can be used as weapons.

A controversial correctional management tool is the use of chain gangs. Advocates contend that work on a chain gang is appropriate punishment and that it puts criminals to work, giving them the opportunity to make restitution. In addition, the hard work ensures that prison is not pleasant, something society demands. Opponents, however, claim such gangs are a form of cruel and unusual punishment, but courts have not upheld this practice as a violation of the Eighth Amendment.

Some forms of physical punishment have also been challenged. For example, handcuffing a prison inmate to a post as punishment for bad behavior was found to be cruel and unusual punishment. In *Hope v. Pelzer* (2002), the Court held that Alabama prisoner Hope did have his Eighth Amendment rights violated when he was handcuffed on two occasions to a hitching post because his behavior was considered disruptive. His arms were held above shoulder level causing pain and injuries to his arms. Further conduct resulted in Hope spending seven more hours affixed to the post, this time being forced to remain shirtless in the sun. He was provided nothing to drink while at least one guard taunted him about being thirsty. Having previously described cruel and unusual punishment as "unnecessary and wanton pain that is totally without penological justification," the Court held that Hope's Eighth Amendment rights were violated and allowed his civil suit against the guards to move forward.

Summary

The Eighth Amendment protects three rights: a prohibition against excessive bail, excessive fines, and cruel and unusual punishment. Bail serves two purposes. First, it helps to ensure the appearance of the accused at court proceedings. Second, it maintains the presumption of innocence by allowing individuals not yet convicted of a crime to avoid continued incarceration. The Constitution does not guarantee a right to bail; it only prohibits excessive bail, which it does not define.

The Bail Reform Act of 1984 established the practice of preventive detention for individuals deemed a threat to society or likely to flee, as well as other options to incarceration. Bail set at a figure higher than an amount reasonably calculated to fulfill its purpose is excessive under the Eighth Amendment (*Stack v. Boyle,* 1951). The excessive bail prohibition has never been formally incorporated to apply to the states under the Fourteenth Amendment, allowing states to deal with it through their constitutions, legislation and case law. Likewise, the prohibition against excessive fines has not been incorporated, so it does not apply to the states.

One type of fine is asset forfeiture. Property connected with illegal activity may be forfeited when used as a "conveyance" to transport illicit drugs (including aircraft, ships and motor vehicles). Real estate used in association with a crime and money or other negotiable instruments obtained through the criminal activity also can be seized, and such seizure is considered a civil sanction by the government. The amount seized through asset forfeiture must bear some relation to the value of the illegal enterprise.

In *Trop v. Dulles* (1958), Chief Justice Warren stated that the cruel and unusual punishments clause "must draw its meaning from the evolving standards of decency that mark the progress of a maturing society." The general rule for punishment under the Eighth Amendment is that punishment must be proportional or directly related to the crime committed.

Although capital punishment may appear to be cruel and unusual, the Supreme Court has not held this notion to be true. However, in certain instances, the Court has found states to be in violation of its citizens' due process protection. *Furman v. Georgia* (1972) was the landmark case in which the Supreme Court called for a ban on the death penalty in Georgia, ruling its law was capricious and, hence, cruel and unusual punishment. In *Gregg v. Georgia* (1976), the Supreme Court reinstated the Georgia death penalty by sustaining its revised death penalty law. It held that the death penalty itself is not cruel and unusual punishment, but a capital case requires two proceedings: one to determine guilt or innocence and the other to determine the sentence. Most states will not consider the death sentence for anyone younger than 15 years of age. In addition, the Supreme Court has prohibited executing mentally retarded individuals.

For prisoners, cases based on Eighth Amendment rights involve cruel and unusual punishment, such as overcrowding, solitary confinement, corporal punishment, physical abuse and use of force; treatment and rehabilitation; the right not to be treated; and the death penalty.

Discussion Questions

1. What historical background do you suspect led to the Eighth Amendment being included in the Bill of Rights?

2. Why has the Eighth Amendment not been fully incorporated?

3. If the Bill of Rights does not guarantee the right to bail, how can bail be assured for those accused of crimes?

4. Explain the basic need for bail.

5. Does the bail system discriminate against the poor?

6. How would you define cruel and unusual punishment? Can you think of any currently lawful punishments you believe are cruel and unusual?

7. Do you support the death penalty? Why or why not? Could you be an executioner or witness to an execution?

8. Should juveniles or mentally retarded individuals who have committed capital crimes be executed?

9. Does the death penalty deter murder or rape? Why or why not?

10. Should fines be the same for the poor and the wealthy?

InfoTrac College Edition Assignments

■ Use InfoTrac College Edition to help answer the Discussion Questions when appropriate.

■ Use InfoTrac College Edition to complete one of the following assignments:

■ Search *capital punishment* or the *Eighth Amendment*. Because capital punishment has hundreds of entries, narrow your search to a specific topic, for example, capital punishment for juveniles or for the mentally challenged (e.g., John Penry).

■ Find one article in favor of capital punishment and another against it. Outline the articles and indicate which article you think has made the stronger argument.

■ Search *bail* or *bounty hunters*. Pick one selection and outline it.

■ Find "When Feds Say Seize and Desist," by O'Meara to read and outline.

Internet Assignments

■ Use http://www.findlaw.com to find one Supreme Court case discussed in this chapter and brief the case.

■ Examine the site of the Death Penalty Information Center at www.deathpenaltyinfo.org and decide what you interpret to be their mission and whether you perceive a bias that adds to or detracts from their credibility.

Companion Web Site

■ Go to the Constitutional Law and the Criminal Justice System 3e Web site at http://cj.wadsworth.com/hessharr_constlaw3e for Case Studies and Study Guide exercises.

References

Arvidson, Joe. Ramsey County (Minnesota) probation officer. Personal correspondence, 2006.

Bohm, Robert M. and Haley, Keith N. *Introduction to Criminal Justice,* 4th ed. New York: McGraw-Hill, 2007.

Bonczar, Thomas P. and Snell, Tracy L. "Capital Punishment, 2004." *Bureau of Justice Statistics Bulletin,* November 2005. (NCJ 211349)

Clear, Todd R. and Cole, George F. *American Corrections,* 5th ed. Belmont, CA: Wadsworth Publishing Company, 2000.

Clear, Todd R.; Cole, George F.; and Reisig, Michael D. *American Corrections,* 7th ed. Belmont, CA: Thomson Wadsworth Publishing, 2006.

Clingermayer, James C.; Hecker, Jason; and Madsen, Sue. "Asset Forfeiture and Police Priorities: The Impact of Program Design on Law Enforcement Activities." *Criminal Justice Policy Review,* Vol. 16, No. 3, 2005, p. 319.

"Court Declines to Overturn More Than 100 Death Sentences." *Criminal Justice Newsletter,* July 15, 2004, pp. 3–4.

Ducat, Craig R. *Constitutional Interpretation,* 8th ed. St. Paul, MN: Thomson/West, 2004.

Lewis, Neil A. "Ruling Allows Forcible Drugging of an Inmate before Execution." *New York Times,* October 7, 2003.

Monk, Linda R. *The Bill of Rights: A User's Guide.* Alexandria, VA: Close Up Publishing, no date.

Unnever, James D. and Cullen, Francis T. "Executing the Innocent and Support for Capital Punishment: Implications for Policy." *Criminology and Public Policy,* Vol. 4, No. 1, 2005, p. 3.

Voegtlin, Gene R. "Congress Approves Asset Forfeiture Legislation." *The Police Chief,* May 2000, p. 8.

Wilson, John J. *Juveniles and the Death Penalty.* Washington, DC: Coordinating Council on Juvenile Justice and Delinquency Prevention, November 2000. (NCJ 184748)

Worrall, John L. "The Civil Asset Forfeiture Reform Act of 2000: A Sheep in Wolf's Clothing?" *Policing Bradford,* Vol. 27, Issue 2, 2004, pp. 220–240.

Cases Cited

Addington v. Texas, 441 U.S. 418 (1979).

Arave v. Creech, 507 U.S. 463 (1993).

Atkins v. Virginia, 536 U.S. 304 (2002).

Austin v. United States, 509 U.S. 602 (1993).

Bell v. Cone, 535 U.S. 685 (2002).

Bennis v. Michigan, 517 U.S. 1163 (1996).

Browning-Ferris Industries v. Kelco Disposal, Inc., 472 U.S. 257 (1989).

Campbell v. Wood, 978 F.2d 1502 (9th Cir. 1994).

Coker v. Georgia, 433 U.S. 584 (1977).

Eddings v. Oklahoma, 455 U.S. 104 (1982).

Estelle v. Gamble, 429 U.S. 97 (1976).

Ewing v. California, 538 U.S. 11 (2003).

Ford v. Wainwright, 477 U.S. 399 (1986).

Furman v. Georgia, 408 U.S. 238 (1972).

Gregg v. Georgia, 428 U.S. 153 (1976).

Harmelin v. Michigan, 501 U.S. 957 (1991).

Helling v. McKinney, 509 U.S. 25 (1993).

Hope v. Pelzer, 536 U.S. 730 (2002).

Ingraham v. Wright, 430 U.S. 651 (1978).

Jackson v. Indiana, 406 U.S. 715 (1972).

Jones v. United States, 527 U.S. 373 (1999).

Knight v. Florida, 528 U.S. 990 (1999).

Lockhart v. McCree, 476 U.S. 162 (1986).

Lockyer v. Andrade, 538 U.S. 63 (2003).

Maynard v. Cartwright, 486 U.S. 356 (1988).
McCleskey v. Kemp, 481 U.S. 279 (1987).
Moore v. Nebraska, 520 U.S. 1176 (1997).
Morgan v. Illinois, 504 U.S. 719 (1992).
Overton v. Bazetta, 539 U.S. 126 (2003).
Penry v. Lynaugh, 492 U.S. 302 (1989).
Pulley v. Harris, 465 U.S. 37 (1984).
Rhodes v. Chapman, 452 U.S. 337 (1981).
Ring v. Arizona, 536 U.S. 584 (2002).
Robinson v. California, 370 U.S. 660 (1962).
Roper v. Simmons, 543 U.S. 551 (2005).
Ruiz v. Estelle, 503 F. Supp. 1265 (S.D. Texas, 1975).
Rupe v. Wood, 863 F. Supp. 1315 (D.C.W. Wash., 1994).
Schriro v. Summerlin, 542 U.S. 348 (2004).

Simmons v. South Carolina, 512 U.S. 154 (1994).
Singleton v. Norris, 124 S.Ct. 74 (2003).
Solem v. Helm, 463 U.S. 277, 103 (1983).
Stack v. Boyle, 342 U.S. 1 (1951).
Stanford v. Kentucky, 492 U.S. 361 (1989).
Thompson v. Oklahoma, 487 U.S. 815 (1988).
Trop v. Dulles, 356 U.S. 86 (1958).
United States v. Bajakajian, 524 U.S. 321 (1998).
United States v. Good, 510 U.S. 43 (1993).
United States v. Hazzard, 598 F. Supp. 1442 (1984).
United States v. Salerno, 481 U.S. 739 (1987).
United States v. Ursery, 518 U.S. 267 (1996).
Whitley v. Albers, 469 U.S. 928 (1986).
Wilson v. Seiter, 501 U.S. 294 (1991).

Coming Full Circle

Throughout the United States' struggle for freedom and the battles and division of the Civil War, the Constitution has guided Americans forward even when bitter conflicts arise. Since that bloody war, despite numerous conflicts and occasional civil unrest, ours has been a land governed by laws.

Imagine what might have resulted in other countries if they were to experience any number of the crises or controversies considered rather "routine" in the United States. There is seldom panic or a sense of impending doom. Issues are handled by a system of laws with the Constitution remaining the cornerstone of fairness for our country.

Americans can easily take an orderly society and freedom for granted, but some do not. For example, a recently retired physician who had moved to Minnesota and had just gone through one of its worst winters was asked by a long-time Minnesotan, "Why do we live here?" His reply: "I narrowly missed a date with the gas chamber in Germany when I was 12 years old. Frankly, I'm just happy to be alive. There isn't a day I take my freedom here in the United States for granted."

Another example is W. Dunsmore, one of America's quiet heroes. He enlisted in the Marine Corps right after high school and found himself serving as a machine gunner in Vietnam. He doesn't talk about those years much, but when he does it is more than apparent that he learned at a very young age what freedom is—as well as its price. Many of his comrades perished in the defense of democracy. As he surveys what is around him, often from atop his motorcycle touring the country he helped keep free, there is no question he learned why the Constitution is as important as it is.

Still recent history, September 11 continues to affect all of us. If anything positive can be said to come of this horrific chapter in the continuing saga of America, it serves as a grim reminder that freedom and all that accompanies it must *not* be taken for granted—at any time—by any one. It can be lost just that quickly.

Having addressed the components of the Constitution that pertain particularly to law enforcement and criminal justice, this final section addresses the remaining amendments to the U.S. Constitution (Chapter 14) and takes a brief look at what might be anticipated for the future of constitutional law in America (Epilogue).

By design, the text comes full circle, asking you to "study the past" because "what is past is prologue." Maybe it was better said by a student in response to the question of whether the United States could rely solely on tradition as some governments do rather than on a written constitution. He stated that the Constitution *is* our tradition. And what law is being promulgated now will become woven into the rich history of the U.S. Constitution and our way of life.

CHAPTER 14

The Remaining Amendments and a Return to the Constitution

WE JUSTICES READ THE CONSTITUTION THE ONLY WAY WE CAN: AS TWENTIETH CENTURY AMERICANS. THE GENIUS OF THE CONSTITUTION RESTS NOT IN ANY STATIC MEANING IT MIGHT HAVE HAD IN A WORLD THAT IS DEAD AND GONE, BUT IN THE ADAPTABILITY OF ITS GREAT PRINCIPLES TO COPE WITH CURRENT PROBLEMS.

—WILLIAM BRENNAN, FORMER SUPREME COURT JUSTICE

© Jim Bourg/Reuters/Corbis

Protesters for and against gay marriage rights face off in front of the Massachusetts Statehouse in Boston in March 2004. Although a proposal to amend the Constitution to ban gay marriages has been proposed, Congress remains reluctant to make significant changes to the Constitution by adding amendments of any sort.

DO YOU KNOW . . .

- What the Third Amendment established?
- What the Seventh Amendment established?
- What determines whether a person is entitled to a federal jury trial in a civil case?
- What the Ninth Amendment established?
- Whether the Ninth Amendment guarantees the right of privacy?
- What the Tenth Amendment established?
- What amendment allows the Supreme Court to make other amendments applicable to the states?

CAN YOU DEFINE?

delegated powers	reserve powers	unenumerated rights
federalism	selective incorporation	zones of privacy
penumbra	suits at common law	

Introduction

The amount of material generated by constitutional cases, analysis and research is astounding. Of course, because the Constitution affects every American's daily life, the fact that so many are intrigued by it should come as no surprise. The PATRIOT Act, proposed legislation to make flag desecration illegal and what seems like continuing sagas of high-powered business people and celebrities running afoul of the law maintain people's interest in the Constitution and the U.S. legal processes. Although the amendments we have addressed thus far have generated the most attention, in an examination of the Constitution, we must look at the other amendments as well to understand the document as a whole.

The amendments discussed so far are probably the best-known amendments in the Bill of Rights, and those best suited for students beginning their study of this area of law. To complete your understanding of the Constitution and its amendments, turn your attention to the four remaining amendments of the Bill of Rights. That discussion will be followed by a brief look at the other amendments that have been made to the Constitution.

As you read, keep in mind the analogy of the U.S. Constitution as a framework that provides the basis on which all American law is built. Many subareas of the Constitution can be examined. Those selected for inclusion in this text should help tie together your studies at the basic level, as they themselves serve to help tie together this workable, complex document. Remember, however, that there is much more to this fascinating document than time and space allow in this introductory text.

The Remaining Amendments of the Bill of Rights

Four amendments in the Bill of Rights remain to be discussed: the Third, Seventh, Ninth and Tenth.

The Third Amendment

No soldier shall, in time of peace, be quartered in any house, without the consent of the owner, nor in time of war, but in a manner to be prescribed by law.

■ The Third Amendment prohibits housing soldiers in private homes during peacetime without the owner's consent and during wartime without legal process.

While the Third Amendment has never been subjected to Supreme Court review, it holds historical relevance and stands for the general principle that government is to leave people alone without compelling cause. This amendment dates back to colonial times, when England expected the citizenry to feed and shelter British soldiers. Although history, it is history that remains important to the U.S. Constitution as an example of the framer's insistence on curtailing excessive government authority.

The Seventh Amendment

In suits at common law, where the value in controversy shall exceed twenty dollars, the right of trial by jury shall be preserved, and no fact tried by a jury, shall be otherwise re-examined in any Court of the United States, than according to the rules of the common law.

■ The Seventh Amendment establishes the right to a federal jury trial for all "suits at common law" if the value is more than $20.

Recall that the Sixth Amendment guaranteed a jury trial for all criminal proceedings. The Seventh Amendment extends this right to civil proceedings involving more than $20, a large sum in 1791, when the Bill of Rights was passed.

Suits at common law means a legal controversy arising out of civil law as opposed to criminal law. The difference is easiest to observe in the caption (or title) of the case, which, at the trial court level, would always be the government (e.g., the *city, county* or *state v.* or the *United States v.* the specific defendant in a criminal case). In a civil case, the caption would have the name of one party v. the name of the other party. The caption of a case indicates the parties involved. The citation of the case indicates where the judicial opinion could be located, as discussed in Chapter 4. The criminal system ensures the protection of rights everyone enjoys, whereas the civil system ensures rights that one person has against another.

suits at common law • legal controversies arising out of civil law as opposed to criminal law

The issues involved in civil cases become as complex as those for criminal matters, and because of the complexity of our emerging society, civil cases may be more complex. While the importance of the outcome in criminal cases is obvious, civil disputes often involve large sums of money, contracts and other business matters, the ownership of land or other property, the rights to patents, the custody of children, divorces, wills and an almost endless list of other issues that greatly affect those involved.

The Seventh Amendment addresses when an individual (not the government or a criminal defendant) is entitled to a *federal* jury trial (not a local or state court). The reasons people would prefer having their cases heard before one court or another or before a jury or only a judge are tactical. Different procedures can apply at the different levels of courts. Some think a federal court is more impartial and, thus, more fair than courts at a local or state level. Some think that a jury would help their cause; others think it would hinder their cause. Where and how a case is handled is just one example of the many decisions attorneys face in best representing their clients.

This amendment was included in the Bill of Rights out of fairness. At issue was the distinction between types of cases in England, which found their way into American law. It was important to differentiate among the types of cases that might be pursued in actions at law or in equity, affecting which court would have jurisdiction over what type of case. These terms may sound awkward, as they have seldom been used since 1791. However, the Constitution is based on the legal history of those who brought their ideas to America, and subsequent courts tend not to change the basic legal concepts too drastically. The challenge has been for the courts to interpret this amendment in a way that serves a practical purpose, while maintaining its historical significance.

The Supreme Court and others have acknowledged that Seventh Amendment analysis is mostly historical, although cases occasionally arise, mostly dealing with whether certain facts warrant a jury trial at all. Today the practical approach to determining whether there is a Seventh Amendment right to a federal jury trial is based on whether a suit involves legal issues similar to issues raised in cases for which federal jury trials were granted by common law. Whether there is a Seventh Amendment right to a federal jury trial is based mainly on historical analysis of common law.

As recently as 1985, in *Thomas v. Union Carbide*, the Court held there was no right to a jury trial when Congress had created other administrative remedies. On the other hand, in *Curtis v. Loether* (1974), the Court overturned a lower court's ruling that an African-American woman was not permitted a jury trial when a white landlord refused to rent to her contrary to the Fair Housing Act. In *Colgrove v. Battin* (1973), the Court said that six-person juries were permissible in federal civil trials.

These cases illustrate how common law marches on to carve out further nuances of the system, even in areas presumed to be historically dormant.

The Seventh Amendment is an excellent example of how the framers of the Constitution included both what they considered important to them at the time and what they thought would be important in the future, and how even an amendment may be resurrected when the facts of a modern case demand.

■ Cases that involve issues that justify a Seventh Amendment right to a federal jury trial are determined by examining the types of cases heard previously or by a common law analysis.

The common law provides answers by examining previous cases to analyze current-day facts.

The Ninth Amendment

The enumeration in the Constitution of certain rights shall not be construed to deny or disparage others retained by the people.

■ The Ninth Amendment established that the rights of U.S. citizens extend beyond those listed in the Constitution.

The Ninth Amendment highlights the founders' beliefs that government's powers are limited by the rights of the people, not the other way around. The Ninth Amendment's significance is also largely historical. Through the Ninth Amendment, the framers addressed concerns that Americans would retain only those rights enumerated in the Constitution. Among those who did not want a Bill of Rights was James Madison. Madison was against an enumerated Bill of

Rights, but he argued for the Ninth Amendment to ensure that the Bill of Rights would not, in fact, exclude those rights not listed.

The framers made an important statement with the Ninth Amendment, as explained by Supreme Court Justice Potter Stewart in his dissenting opinion in *Griswold v. Connecticut* (1965): "The Ninth Amendment, like its companion, the Tenth, which this Court held (in *United States v. Darby*) 'states but a truism that all is retained which has not been surrendered,' was framed by James Madison and adopted by the States simply to make clear that the adoption of the Bill of Rights did not alter the plan that . . . the *Federal* Government was to be a government of express and limited powers, and that all rights and powers not delegated to it were retained by the people and the individual States."

Rights not specifically listed in the Bill of Rights are known as **unenumerated rights.** They are no less important than specified rights but have been left to develop with our society. Among the unenumerated rights the Supreme Court has recognized are the right to privacy, the right to interstate and international travel, the right to vote and freedom of association.

unenumerated rights • rights not specifically listed in the Bill of Rights

The Ninth Amendment has been referred to on occasion as the forgotten amendment in the Bill of Rights because it is seldom used as a basis for Supreme Court decisions. Some believe that judges have been reluctant to rely on the Ninth Amendment because its language is vague, never defining what specific rights are protected. The Court has referred to the Ninth Amendment in a handful of cases, but the Ninth Amendment has never been the basis of a decision by a majority of the justices. Although the Supreme Court has protected rights not listed in the Bill of Rights, it has not used the Ninth Amendment to do so. This amendment, again, serves as an example of the discussion and interpretations the Constitution continues to generate, particularly by those who assert that the interpretation be made in their own favor.

The Ninth Amendment has also generated significant controversy and much scholarly debate as to what the framers meant and intended with this amendment, serving as an example of how the Constitution does not always provide specific or easy answers.

Whereas most unenumerated rights have, in fact, been protected through the use of the due process clause in the Fourteenth Amendment (no one shall be deprived of life, liberty or property without due process of law), the Ninth Amendment has been used to infer the right of privacy. Many parts of a right to privacy have been recognized by the Supreme Court, including the right to marry, to have children, to have an abortion and of parents to send their children to private schools.

■ The right of privacy has been referred to by the Supreme Court and has been used to infer such a right, but the Ninth Amendment does not guarantee this right.

Griswold v. Connecticut (1965) is considered the first case in which the Supreme Court addressed the Ninth Amendment. In this case, the Court addressed whether contraception was permitted by law, with the issue being whether an 1897 state law prohibiting contraception was lawful. In the Court's opinion, Justice Goldberg stated: "The Ninth Amendment shows a belief of the Constitution's authors that fundamental rights exist that are not expressly enumerated in the first eight amendments and an intent that the list of rights . . . not be exhaustive." Three justices finally agreed on a right protected by the Ninth Amendment: the right to marital privacy or privacy within the marriage relationship. Justice Goldberg devoted several pages to the Ninth Amendment in rendering the decision:

> The language and history of the Ninth Amendment reveal that the framers of the Constitution believed that there are additional fundamental rights, protected from governmental infringement, which exist alongside those fundamental rights specifically mentioned in the first eight constitutional amendments. . . . To hold that a right so basic and fundamental and so deep-rooted in our society as the right of privacy in marriage may be infringed because that right is not guaranteed in so many words by the first eight amendments to the Constitution is to ignore the Ninth Amendment and to give it no effect whatsoever.

penumbra • a type of shadow in astronomy with the principle extending to the idea that certain constitutional rights are implied within other constitutional rights

zones of privacy • areas into which the government may not intrude

Most of the concurring justices, however, did not rely on the Ninth Amendment. Justice Douglas held that "specific guarantees in the Bill of Rights have penumbras, formed by emanations from those guarantees that help give them life and substance." In astronomy, a **penumbra** is a type of shadow. Douglas used astronomy as an example to show how certain rights in the Bill of Rights have other rights implied in or along with them. Justice Douglas went on to write that various guarantees in the Bill of Rights, among them the Third, Fourth and Fifth Amendments, created **zones of privacy,** safe from governmental intrusion. The intimacy of the marriage relationship, said Douglas, involved a "right of privacy older than the Bill of Rights." The Connecticut law was struck down as unconstitutional.

Griswold led to other cases in which the Supreme Court upheld privacy rights and issues pertaining to sexual relations for unmarried as well as married individuals, with an increasing number of cases concerning homosexual relations being considered by the Court. Also, the Supreme Court referenced the right to privacy in support of a woman's right to an abortion in *Roe v. Wade* (1973).

In *Roe v. Wade,* the Court stated: "This right to privacy, whether it be founded in the Fourteenth Amendment's concept of personal liberty and restrictions upon state action, as we feel it is, or, as it was determined by the (lower court), in the Ninth Amendment's reservation of rights to the people, is broad enough to encompass a woman's decision whether or not to terminate her pregnancy." The decision continues to draw protesters and demonstrators to the steps of the Supreme Court every year.

The Supreme Court's decisions, whether under the Ninth or the Fourteenth Amendment, continually upheld the right to sexual privacy until the case of *Bowers v. Hardwick* (1986). An Atlanta police officer arrested Hardwick in his bedroom on the basis of an expired warrant for a minor offense—engaging in sodomy with a consenting male adult. Hardwick challenged the Georgia sodomy law on the grounds that, among other things, it violated his rights under the Ninth Amendment.

The Supreme Court, however, upheld the Georgia law, saying that Hardwick was asking the Court to recognize "a fundamental right to engage in homosexual sodomy." Justice Blackmun dissented, pointing out the Georgia law applied to heterosexuals as well as homosexuals. Under the Court's current rulings on sexual privacy, the law would not be constitutional as applied to heterosexuals, Blackmun argued, so it should not be constitutional when applied to homosexuals. The Court upheld the Georgia law against homosexual sodomy on a 5 to 4 vote, declaring there was not a fundamental right to so engage. Justice Powell later said he believed his swing vote in this case was an error on his part, and in 1998, the Georgia court itself held that state law violative of the state constitution's right to privacy. Change remains a strong possibility, even at the level of the U.S. Supreme Court.

Although seldom relied on, the Ninth Amendment will remain grounds for the belief that rights not specifically referred to within the Constitution are no less protected. Take a moment to consider all the choices people make during their lifetimes: marriage; raising children; how families are created; what the definition of a family is; where to live, travel and recreate; the business entered or begun; and, quite literally, every step throughout life. There is no way anyone could list them or the framers of the Constitution could have predicted what the future would hold. However, through the Ninth Amendment's existence, Americans are assured they will continue to be free to pursue those interests that government does not demonstrate a compelling reason to restrict.

> The makers of our Constitution undertook to secure conditions favorable to the pursuit of happiness. They recognized the significance of man's spiritual nature, of his feelings and his intellect. They knew that only a part of his pain, pleasure, and satisfactions of life are to be found in material things. They sought to protect Americans in their beliefs, their thoughts, their emotions and their sensations. They conferred, as against the Government, the right to be let alone—the most comprehensive of rights and the right most valued by civilized men (*Olmstead v. United States*, 1928).

The Tenth Amendment

The powers not delegated to the United States by the Constitution, nor prohibited by it to the states, are reserved to the states respectively, or to the people.

■ The Tenth Amendment embodies the principle of **federalism,** reserving for the states those powers not granted to the federal government or withheld from the states.

federalism • a principle whereby power is shared by the national government and the states

Stephens and Scheb (2003, p. 142) explain: "The Bill of Rights is generally considered to be the first ten amendments to the Constitution. But the Tenth Amendment is of a fundamentally different character from the nine amendments that precede it. . . . Unlike other provisions of the Bill of Rights, and despite its reference to 'the people,' the Tenth Amendment recognized the powers of the states vis-à-vis the federal government and does not directly address individual rights. However, the Framers of the Constitution and Bill of Rights believed that the federal structure guaranteed by the Tenth Amendment was conducive to the maintenance of freedom generally."

Under federalism, power is shared by the national government and the states. The U.S. Constitution established a federal system to preserve the existing state governments, while creating a new national government strong enough to deal with the country's problems. A controversial question at the Constitutional Convention was just how much power the national government should have. A primary limit was that the government was one of the enumerated powers, powers specifically listed in the Constitution. However, the Constitution also included an elastic clause stating that Congress had the power to make all laws "necessary and proper" to carry out its enumerated powers. The necessary and proper clause became the basis for the implied powers, those powers not specifically listed in the Constitution that are implied by the enumerated powers.

delegated powers • powers of the national government, both enumerated and implied by legal authority, delegated or entrusted to the national government by the states and the people

The powers of the national government, both enumerated and implied, are known as the **delegated powers** because they were delegated or entrusted to the national government by the states and the people. The powers kept by the states are known as the **reserve powers.** The Tenth Amendment refers to both types of

reserve powers • powers retained by the states

powers. A primary reserve power is police power, which enables the state to pass laws and regulations that involve the public health, safety, morals and welfare.

Although the Constitution recognizes both the powers of the states and the federal government, it contains the supremacy clause in Article 6, which states that the Constitution of the United States is "the supreme law of the land." The Tenth Amendment attempted to strike a balance between the federal government's power and that of the states, while maintaining individual freedom. That balance has not always been easy to maintain throughout American history. During one such very difficult period, only a bloody Civil War finally resolved the question of federal versus state power. Since the Civil War, the Supreme Court has worked hard to find the proper balance of the Tenth Amendment.

Madison's version of the Tenth Amendment made clear that any powers not delegated to the federal government belonged to the states or to the people. However, some members of Congress wanted the Tenth Amendment to limit the federal government to those powers specifically listed in the Constitution, just as the Articles of Confederation had done. They wanted the Tenth Amendment to say that powers not expressly delegated to the U.S. government were reserved to the states. Madison believed it was impossible to confine a government to the exercise of expressed powers and that there must necessarily be powers by implication.

Unlike the other amendments, the Tenth Amendment does not ensure specific individual rights. Rather, it seeks to ensure to all people that the federal government will not get too powerful. Historically, the Constitution came to be as a result of fear that federal government might become too powerful. Recognizing the need for a balanced government, a government that could run the nation but leave individualism to the states and their people, the Tenth Amendment sought to strike this balance. However, achieving such a lofty ideal would prove more difficult than imagined.

The concept behind the Tenth Amendment was important enough that it was the only amendment agreed upon by all the states recommending a Bill of Rights. Like the Ninth Amendment, the Tenth Amendment shows the colonists' concern that specific limitations on the federal government could mean such a government *had* control over all other areas.

The Tenth Amendment's road has been rocky compared with that of other amendments. The question of *what* power federal government has and what goes to the states has challenged the government. Before the Constitution was ratified, the states were sovereign governmental bodies that acted much like separate countries. They issued their own money, set their own tax plans and interacted with the other states as they saw fit. Although unity had benefits, the concern of "too much" national power had to be addressed before the country could agree on a central constitution. The framers addressed this issue through the Tenth Amendment, together with equal representation in the Senate, which was of particular importance to the smaller states.

Over the years, the federal government became stronger, and although concerns of there being excessive power continue today, a series of Supreme Court cases carved out the role of national government. In 1819, in *McCulloch v. Maryland*, the Court made its strongest assertion of the government's broad national power when it held that Congress had the authority to establish a national bank pursuant to the necessary and proper clause of Article I, Section 8 of the Constitution. Before this decision, the supremacy clause of Article VI authorized only specific authority.

The national government's authority and power continued to grow, much to the concern of some. *United States v. Darby* (1941) upheld the Fair Labor Standards Act of 1938, and the limits the Tenth Amendment was intended to set on expansion of federal authority seemed to have been forgotten.

Like a pendulum, more recent cases have indicated the high court's willingness to reconsider, or at least limit, a never-ending expansion of federal power. A significant case in 1992 involving federal regulations of radioactive waste, *New York v. United States,* resulted in the Court stating: "No matter how powerful the federal interest involved, the Constitution simply does not give Congress the authority to require the states to regulate."

The crucial issue of federalism was addressed in *United States v. Lopez* (1995), in which the Court invalidated an act of Congress for the first time in 50 years, raising important issues of federal versus states' rights. When Congress enacted the Gun-Free School Zones Act of 1990, it made a federal offense of anyone knowingly possessing a firearm in an area the person knows to be a school zone. A 12th-grade student was convicted under this law for carrying a concealed .38 caliber handgun and bullets at school. The Fifth Circuit Court of Appeals reversed the conviction, holding the act was invalid because Congress had exceeded its authority. Chief Justice Rehnquist delivered the Court's opinion, which said, in part:

> To uphold the Government's contentions here, we would have to pile inference upon inference in a matter that would bid fair to convert congressional authority under the Commerce Clause to a general police power of the sort retained by the States. . . . The broad language in these opinions has suggested the possibility of additional expansion, but we decline here to proceed any further. To do so would require us to conclude that the Constitution's enumeration of powers does not presuppose something not enumerated . . . and that there never will be a distinction between what is truly national and what is truly local.

In *Printz v. United States* (1997), the Supreme Court struck down that portion of the Brady Bill compelling local law enforcement to perform background checks on applicants for handgun ownership. The Court held the requirement violated "the very principle of separate state sovereignty."

Those studying the Constitution will find it of interest in which direction future cases will call the Tenth Amendment into consideration and how these cases will be decided. Before moving on to amendments that follow the first ten, consider the statement in *West Virginia State Board of Education v. Barnette* (1943), in answer to what makes up the Bill of Rights: "We set up government by consent of the governed, and the Bill of Rights denies those in power any legal opportunity to coerce that consent. Authority here is to be controlled by public opinion, not public opinion by authority."

Although the Ninth and Tenth Amendments are not considered guarantees of specific individual freedoms, some refer to the first eight amendments as the Bill of Rights. However, the Bill of Rights presents a "package" of rights that remain viable because of the balance of the system at the federal and local levels. As eloquently described by Cardozo (Hall, 1928): "Bills of Rights give assurance to the individual of the preservation of his liberty. They do not define the liberty they promise."

Amendments beyond the Bill of Rights

The Bill of Rights lays a foundation for individual freedoms, but these freedoms do not stop with the Tenth Amendment. From 1791, when the first ten amendments were ratified, until the present, our Constitution continues to evolve. As proof of the Constitution's ability to respond to America's needs, additional amendments have come, and some have gone. Following is a brief overview of the remaining amendments, including those that have been repealed.

The Eleventh Amendment (1798)

The Eleventh Amendment deals with the extent of the judicial power of the United States:

> *The Judicial power of the United States shall not be construed to extend to any suit in law or equity, commenced or prosecuted against one of the United States by Citizens of another State, or by Citizens or Subjects of any Foreign State.*

This amendment is the only one that deals with the judicial power of the federal government and is actually more an administrative directive. The history of the Eleventh Amendment is noteworthy in that it was introduced the day after the high Court ruled that a citizen of one state had the right to sue another state.

The Thirteenth Amendment (1865)

A key amendment to the Constitution is the Thirteenth Amendment, which abolished slavery, as previously discussed:

> *Neither slavery nor involuntary servitude, except as a punishment for crime whereof the party shall have been duly convicted, shall exist within the United States, or any place subject to their jurisdiction.*
>
> *Congress shall have power to enforce this article by appropriate legislation.*

The Thirteenth Amendment overturned the Supreme Court's *Dred Scott* decision (1857). Using an amendment to overturn a specific Supreme Court decision is rare, dramatic and a good illustration of the checks and balances in the U.S. government. Closely related to this amendment is the Fourteenth Amendment.

The Fourteenth Amendment (1868)

To review from Chapter 5, the Fourteenth Amendment asserts:

> *All persons born or naturalized in the United States, and subject to the jurisdiction thereof, are citizens of the United States and of the State wherein they reside. No state shall make or enforce any law which shall abridge the privileges or immunities of citizens of the United States; nor shall any State deprive any person of life, liberty, or property, without due process of law; nor deny to any person within its jurisdiction the equal protection of the laws.*

selective incorporation • holds that only the provisions of the Bill of Rights that are fundamental to the American legal system are applied to the states through the due process clause of the Fourteenth Amendment

The Supreme Court has chosen, through case law and common law, to selectively apply certain amendments to both federal and state governments through **selective incorporation,** as stipulated in the Fourteenth Amendment.

As has been addressed throughout this text, a significant portion of the Bill of Rights amendments has been made to apply to the states as well. Table 14.1

Table 14.1 Cases Incorporating Provisions of the Bill of Rights into the Due Process Clause of the Fourteenth Amendment

First Amendment

Establishment of religion	*Everson v. Board of Education*	1947
Free exercise of religion	*Cantwell v. Connecticut*	1940
Freedom of speech	*Gitlow v. New York*	1925
Freedom of the press	*Near v. Minnesota*	1931
Freedom to peaceably assemble	*DeJong v. Oregon*	1937
Freedom to petition government	*Hague v. CIO*	1939

Second Amendment

Right of the militia to bear arms	*Presser v. Illinois,* 1886	NI

Fourth Amendment

Unreasonable search and seizure	*Wolf v. Colorado*	1949
Exclusionary rule	*Mapp v. Ohio*	1961

Fifth Amendment

Grand jury	*Hurtado v. California,* 1884	NI
No double jeopardy	*Benton v. Maryland*	1969
No self-incrimination	*Malloy v. Hogan*	1964
Compensation for taking private property	*Chicago, Burlington and Quincy Railroad v. Chicago*	1897

Sixth Amendment

Speedy trial	*Klopfer v. North Carolina*	1967
Public trial	*In re Oliver*	1948
Impartial jury	*Parker v. Gladden*	1966
Jury trial	*Duncan v. Louisiana*	1968
Venue	Implied in due process	NI
Notice	*Cole v. Arkansas*	1948
Confrontation of witnesses	*Pointer v. Texas*	1965
Compulsory process	*Washington v. Texas*	1967
Assistance of counsel	*Gideon v. Wainwright* (felony)	1963
	Argersinger v. Hamlin (some misdemeanors)	1972

Seventh Amendment

Jury trial in civil cases	*Walker v. Sauvinet,* 1875	NI

Eighth Amendment

No excessive bail	*U.S. v. Salerno,* 1987	NI
No excessive fines		NI
No cruel and unusual punishment	*Robinson v. California*	1962

Ninth Amendment

"Privacy"*	*Griswold v. Connecticut*	1965

*The word privacy does not appear in the Ninth Amendment (nor anywhere in the Constitution), but in *Griswold* several justices viewed the Ninth Amendment as guaranteeing that right.

NI—Not incorporated.

Source: David W. Neubaurer. *America's Courts and the Criminal Justice System,* 7th ed. Belmont, CA: West/Wadsworth Publishing Company, 2002, p. 36.

summarizes the cases incorporating provisions of the Bill of Rights into the due process clause of the Fourteenth Amendment, as well as those that remain unincorporated.

The Fourteenth Amendment's due process clause and the concept of selective incorporation are especially important in considering individual civil liability issues. As Worrall (2001, p. 49) points out: "There is no better time than the present to acknowledge that mental state matters."

Amendments Related to Elections and Structure of Congress

Not all amendments and other portions of the Constitution deal directly with specific rights and liberties. Any successful entity needs basic administrative guidelines to function properly, and these are found in the Constitution as well.

Seven amendments deal in detail with numerous matters related to how the federal government is to be structured and its officials elected. Following is a brief summary of these amendments. The full text of each is presented in Appendix B.

The Twelfth Amendment (1804) established the electoral system by which the president and vice-president are chosen. Given the extreme controversy generated by the 2000 presidential election—with Al Gore winning the popular vote and George W. Bush the electoral college vote and, therefore, the presidency—this system is likely to come under close scrutiny in the next few years. *Bush v. Gore* (2000) is an apt illustration of the struggle to maintain the balance of power and to determine which branch of government at what level has the power to do what during elections.

The Fourteenth Amendment (1868) established how representatives are apportioned and what their qualifications are.

The Seventeenth Amendment (1913) describes how the U.S. Senate is to be composed, the qualifications required and how vacancies are to be filled.

The Twentieth Amendment (1933) established that the terms of the president and vice-president end at noon on the 20th day of January and that the terms of senators and representatives end at noon on the 3rd day of January. It also established how often Congress meets and the chain of succession if the president is no longer able to carry out the responsibilities of the office.

The Twenty-Second Amendment (1951) restricted the term of presidency to two terms.

The Twenty-Third Amendment (1961) gave representation to the district that constitutes the seat of government of the United States, that is to the District of Columbia.

The Twenty-Fifth Amendment (1967) established procedures for filling vacancies and for actions to take should the president be unable to "discharge the powers and duties" of the office. Considering American presidents are larger-than-life figures, the unthinkable first occurred when William Harrison died after just one month as president in 1841 and Vice-President John Tyler simply took it upon himself to assume the presidency. According to Stephens and Scheb (p. 166): "The eight other individuals who have succeeded to the office because of the death or resignation of an incumbent president have followed this practice." Stephens and Scheb (p. 166) also address the issue of the president being disabled, as was the case when Woodrow Wilson was stricken by a stroke and his wife took over because there was no official plan in place for such a circumstance.

The Twenty-Fifth Amendment was first proposed after President Kennedy's assassination and provides an official process by which the vice president may assume power if the president is unable.

The Twenty-Seventh Amendment (1992) states: No Law, varying the compensation for the services of the Senators and Representatives, shall take effect, until an election of Representatives shall have intervened." This amendment's purpose is to prevent Congress from setting its own salary because of the apparent conflict of interest. Nonetheless, Congress has continued to give itself cost-of-living raises, which has not been considered the same as an actual raise.

The preceding amendments, along with portions of the Constitution, are important in that they provide the basic administrative and operational bases through which an orderly government will operate. Above all, it remains important to understand that, like a set of directions for any piece of complex machinery, these guidelines provide people with the ability to make something work that would not be possible without such a reference.

Voting Rights

The ability of the Constitution to reflect society's changing needs is well illustrated in the amendments broadening the right to vote, which, initially, was reserved for white males older than 21 years.

The Fifteenth Amendment (1870) required that the right to vote shall not be denied or abridged because of race, color or previous condition of servitude. In other words, black males were given the vote.

The Nineteenth Amendment (1920) required that the right to vote should not be denied on account of sex. Women finally got the vote, 50 years after black males.

The Twenty-Fourth Amendment (1964) requires that the right to vote should not be denied or abridged by reason of failure to pay any poll tax or other tax.

The Twenty-Sixth Amendment (1971) lowered the voting age, giving the vote to U.S. citizens 18 years of age and older.

Taxes

The Sixteenth Amendment (1913) established the federal income tax: "The Congress shall have power to lay and collect taxes on incomes, from whatever source derived, without apportionment among the several States, and without regard to any census or enumeration."

Prohibition

An excellent example of how the Constitution, through the amendment process, can adjust and change to reflect society's wishes is the Eighteenth Amendment (1919), which prohibited the sale and purchase of "intoxicating liquors." This prohibition was ignored by many, with speakeasies opening and gangsters profiting from the illegal sale of liquor. Hundreds of thousands of law enforcement hours and dollars were spent trying to enforce this amendment, but in the end, enforcement was seen as hopeless because it was not what the people wanted. Therefore, the Twenty-First Amendment (1933) was ratified, repealing the "eighteenth article of amendment to the Constitution."

Attempts at Other Amendments

Over the years, various amendments have been proposed espousing different views considered important. For example, Congress has considered amendments prohibiting the burning of the American flag and amendments establishing victims' rights. Although both proposals have been repeatedly defeated, they are likely to be brought up again and serve as yet another example of how change in constitutional law comes about.

California was the first state to pass a victims' rights constitutional amendment in 1982, followed by Florida in 1988. Since then, 27 other states have passed victims' rights constitutional amendments, as shown in Table 14.2.

In 2000, a constitutional amendment failed to win Senate approval, but it was reintroduced in 2003. On June 12, 2003, a Senate subcommittee approved a proposal to amend the Constitution to guarantee rights to crime victims. According to Boyter (2003, p. 8): "Supporters argue that only a constitutional amendment will elevate the rights of crime victims and ensure that judges and prosecutors heed them. Some critics, including the ranking Democrat on the subcommittee, Russell Feingold of Wisconsin, would rather see Congress first try to enact victims' right protections statutorily instead of through a constitutional amendment, which would be more difficult to change later on." Boyter notes: "Proposed constitutional amendments require a two-thirds vote of approval by each chamber. If cleared by Congress and ratified by at least 38 states, the proposal would be the 28th amendment to the Constitution and the first since 1992."

Table 14.2   History of State Victims' Rights Constitutional Amendments

State	Year Passed	Electoral Support	State	Year Passed	Electoral Support
Alabama	1994	80%	Nevada	1996	74%
Alaska	1994	87%	New Jersey	1991	85%
Arizona	1990	58%	New Mexico	1992	68%
California	1982	56%	North Carolina	1996	78%
Colorado	1992	86%	Ohio	1994	77%
Connecticut	1996	78%	Oklahoma	1996	91%
Florida	1988	90%	Oregon	1996	59%
Idaho	1994	79%	Rhode Island	1986	*
Illinois	1992	77%	South Carolina	1996	89%
Indiana	1996	89%	Texas	1989	73%
Kansas	1992	84%	Utah	1994	68%
Maryland	1994	92%	Virginia	1996	84%
Michigan	1992	84%	Washington	1989	78%
Missouri	1992	84%	Wisconsin	1993	84%
Nebraska	1996	78%			

*Passed by Constitutional Conversion.

Source: 1998 NCVRW Resource Guide.

In 2003, a proposal to amend the Constitution to prohibit gay marriages was being talked about. Up until now, individual states, not the federal government, have been responsible for deciding their own family law and policy. However, some argue that this tradition has resulted in a confusing patchwork of laws. An additional argument against such an amendment is that for the first time in our history, an amendment would deny rights to a group of people rather than expand them.

However, because of the extraordinary importance a basic document such as our Constitution holds, Congress has been, and continues to be, reluctant to make significant changes by adding amendments.

> The life of the law has not been logic; it has been experience. The felt necessities of the time, the prevalent moral and political theories . . . even the prejudices which judges share with their fellow men . . . have a good deal in determining the rules by which men should be governed.
> —Chief Justice Oliver Wendell Holmes, Jr., U.S. Supreme Court

SUMMARY

Four additional important amendments of the Bill of Rights are the Third, Seventh, Ninth and Tenth Amendments. The Third Amendment prohibits housing soldiers in private homes during peacetime without the owner's consent and during wartime without legal process. The Seventh Amendment establishes the right to a federal jury trial for all suits at common law if the value is more than $20. Cases that involve issues that justify a Seventh Amendment right to a federal jury trial are determined by examining the types of cases heard previously or by a common law analysis. The Ninth Amendment establishes that the rights of Americans extend beyond those listed in the Constitution. The Tenth Amendment embodies the principle of federalism, reserving for the states those powers not granted to the federal government or withheld from the states.

The Supreme Court has chosen, through case law and common law, to selectively apply certain amendments to both federal and state governments through selective incorporation, as stipulated in the Fourteenth Amendment.

DISCUSSION QUESTIONS

1. Discuss why the framers of the Constitution probably thought it necessary to include the Ninth and Tenth Amendments.

2. With reference to Question 1, would only one or the other have been sufficient? If you were to eliminate the Ninth or Tenth Amendment, which would it be and why?

3. Could the United States not have a federal government? What about a much less powerful federal government, and if so, what would this government do?

4. Having come this far in your study of constitutional law, do you think the United States could ever get along without a written constitution?

5. Does the Constitution works as well as it was meant to? Why or why not?

6. Is there any way an internal military dictatorship could take over the present government in America and be successful?

7. Is there a present-day concern that the national government is too powerful?

8. If you were to eliminate any portions of the Constitution, which would they be? Why?

9. If you were to propose any new amendments, what would they be?

10. Imagine that a time machine would permit those who conceived the Constitution to be present today. What would they think about how their prescription for freedom has endured the challenges of time? What might they not be pleased with, constitutionally?

InfoTrac College Edition Assignments

- Use InfoTrac College Edition to help answer the Discussion Questions when appropriate.
- Use InfoTrac College Edition to search the Tenth, Eleventh or Thirteenth Amendment. Pick one selection to outline.

Internet Assignments

- Use http://www.findlaw.com to find one Supreme Court case discussed in this chapter and brief the case.
- Use http://www.findlaw.com to find and brief *Bush v. Gore*.

Companion Web Site

- Go to the Constitutional Law and the Criminal Justice System 3e Web site at http://cj.wadsworth.com/hessharr_constlaw3e for Case Studies and Study Guide exercises.

References

Boyter, Jennifer. "Subcommittee Approves Victims' Rights Amendment." *The Police Chief*, July 2003, p. 8.

Hall, Margaret E., ed. "Paradoxes of Legal Science." In *Selected Writings of Benjamin Nathan Cardozo*, 1928.

Stephens, Otis H., Jr. and Scheb II, John M. *American Constitutional Law*, 3rd ed. Belmont, CA: Thomson West Publishing, 2003.

Worrall, John L. "Culpability Standards in Section 1983 Litigation against Criminal Justice Officials: When and Why Mental State Matters." *Crime & Delinquency*, January 2001, pp. 28–59.

Cases Cited

Argersinger v. Hamlin, 407 U.S. 25 (1972).
Benton v. Maryland, 395 U.S. 784 (1969).
Bowers v. Hardwick, 478 U.S. 186 (1986).
Bush v. Gore, 531 U.S. 98 (2000).
Cantwell v. Connecticut, 310 U.S. 296 (1940).
Chicago Burlington and Quincy Railroad v. Chicago, 166 U.S. 226 (1897).
Cole v. Arkansas, 333 U.S. 196 (1948).
Colgrove v. Battin, 413 U.S. 149 (1973).
Curtis v. Loether, 415 U.S. 189 (1974).
DeJong v. Oregon, 299 U.S. 353 (1937).
Dred Scott v. Sandford, 60 US 393 (1857).
Duncan v. Louisiana, 391 U.S. 145 (1968).
Everson v. Board of Education, 330 U.S. 1 (1947).
Gideon v. Wainwright, 372 U.S. 335 (1963).
Gitlow v. New York, 268 U.S. 652 (1925).
Griswold v. Connecticut, 381 U.S. 479 (1965).
In re Oliver, 333 U.S. 257 (1948).
Hague v. CIO, 307 U.S. 446 (1939).
Hurtado v. California, 110 U.S. 516 (1884).
Klopfer v. North Carolina, 386 U.S. 213 (1967).
Malloy v. Hogan, 378 U.S. 1 (1964).
Mapp v. Ohio, 367 U.S. 643 (1961).
McCulloch v. Maryland, 17 U.S. 316 (1819).
Near v. Minnesota, 283 U.S. 697 (1931).
New York v. United States, 505 U.S. 144 (1992).
Olmstead v. United States, 277 U.S. 438 (1928).
Parker v. Gladden, 385 U.S. 363 (1966).
Pointer v. Texas, 380 U.S. 400 (1965).
Presser v. Illinois, 116 U.S. 252 (1886).
Printz v. United States, 521 U.S. 898 (1997).
Robinson v. California, 370 U.S. 660 (1962).
Roe v. Wade, 410 U.S. 113 (1973).
Thomas v. Union Carbide, 473 U.S. 568 (1985).
United States v. Darby, 312 U.S. 100 (1941).
United States v. Lopez, 514 U.S. 549 (1995).
United States v. Salerno, 481 U.S. 739 (1987).
Walker v. Sauvinet, 92 U.S. 90 (1875).
Washington v. Texas, 388 U.S. 14 (1967).
West Virginia State Board of Education v. Barnette, 319 U.S. 624 (1943).
Wolf v. Colorado, 338 U.S. 25 (1949).

Epilogue

An inescapable conclusion to be drawn from studying the history of the U.S. Constitution is that it will not remain static. The American people would not allow that. Americans are demanding of their law, and the fact that the Constitution has the built-in ability to change as demanded by its citizens reflects this very important component of the nation's law.

The basic freedoms set forth in the Constitution shall remain, for they are the cornerstones on which the United States was built. Freedom of speech and religion, the right to assemble and speak up, and freedom from unreasonable government intrusions will stand the tests of time. But change itself will continue. It has to. As the country and the needs of its people have changed with time, so will the laws that support this society.

However, the basic mechanisms by which law can change will be maintained. That's what the Constitution is about—providing the predictability that ensures a continuation of America's ideals but including the ability to permit law to flow with natural changes brought on by society. But as those who have tried have learned, changing the Constitution is not easy. Nor should it be. Anything as powerful as this document should be altered only when intense scrutiny, evaluation and input from every stakeholder have been used to weigh the need for change. Although politicians speak of constitutional change as part of their platforms, true scholars understand the importance of maintaining it apolitically. Should the Constitution cater to one side, its effectiveness is lost. Its goal is to serve everyone.

Consider societal desires as a pendulum. On one end of the arc is a conservative perspective; on the other end, a liberal one. These perspectives influence how society perceives its country. It answers such questions as "Why do people act the way they do?" and "How should society respond?" The perspective a society responds from says a lot about how that society views life at any point in time.

This is illustrated by the two primary schools of thought on the causes of delinquency. The classical theory, developed by Cesare Beccaria, sets forth the concept that people are responsible for their own behavior because they act on their own free will. The positivist theory, developed by Cesare Lombroso, operates on the premise that people's personal and background characteristics are to answer for their behavior, which suggests that these individuals are, in effect, "victims of their society." How you perceive the issues will influence how you will respond. Classicalists would argue for accountability and punishment for delinquent behavior, whereas positivists would argue for treatment. Delinquency trends reflect whether society is leaning more toward a conservative or liberal view at that time.

Similarly, the various laws of governments in the United States (be they municipal, county, state or federal) will reflect whether society sees itself as being on the more liberal or more conservative side of the pendulum's arc. Prohibition. Marijuana. Flag desecration. Women voting. Slavery. Abortion. Guns. Religion. The laws addressing important social issues reflect how Americans see themselves and what they think is important at the time. Although change is inevitable, the changes reflect the pendulum's position between conservative and liberal ideals for society at any given moment in history. The pendulum tends to go back and forth, back and forth . . . which is all the more reason that changes to the Constitution come about only after sincere debate.

What conclusions can be drawn from the pendulum analogy? Simply that change will continue. The ability to adapt to change is what has kept American law so viable, and this viability is what the study of the U.S. Constitution is all about. Begin by considering the complex simpleness on which the Constitution was conceived; it continues to provide stability for one of the most complicated societies to ever develop.

Could we, as a society, operate without a written constitution, as some other societies have? Doubtful. Why can the United Kingdom, for example, operate so efficiently simply on tradition, whereas Americans demand a written document? It is the nature of Americans. It was the questioning and demanding nature of those who left England that led to the U.S. Constitution. Citizens want to know why things are the way they are and to know exactly what is expected of them and what can be expected of others. "Because your government knows best" would never be an acceptable answer here. The only answer that appeases the American people's critical nature is that an approach, an issue or a law is constitutionally permissible. The Constitution is our tradition.

Not everyone agrees with the Constitution in full or in part, and people will continue to challenge it and consider changing it. The document can be changed, but because of the importance of maintaining the premises on which subsequent law will be built, changes to the Constitution itself will continue to come with great debate and consideration. This is the way it should be. As history has proved, even this great document can change when the people it serves so demand. Fairness. Justice. Due process. Freedom. These ideals are what our Constitution is about.

The liberties of our country, the freedoms of our civil Constitution are worth defending at all hazards; it is our duty to defend them against all attacks. We have received them as a fair inheritance from our worthy ancestors. They purchased them for us with toil and danger and expense of treasure and blood. It will bring a mark of everlasting infamy on the present generation—enlightened as it is—if we should suffer them to be wrested from us by violence without a struggle, or to be cheated out of them by the artifices of designing men.

Samuel Adams

It is the genius of our Constitution that under its shelter of enduring institutions and rooted principles, there is ample room for the rich fertility of American political invention.

Lyndon Johnson

To live under the American Constitution is the greatest political privilege that was ever accorded to the human race.

Calvin Coolidge

The Declaration of Independence

JULY 4, 1776

(F. N. Thorpe, ed. *Federal and State Constitutions*, Vol. I, p.3 ff. The text is taken from the version in the Revised Statutes of the United States, 1878 ed., and has been collated with the facsimile of the original as printed in the original Journal of the old Congress.)

On June 7, 1776, Richard Henry Lee of Virginia introduced three resolutions one of which stated that the "colonies are, and of right ought to be, free and independent States." On the 10th a committee was appointed to prepare a declaration of independence; the committee consisted of Jefferson, John Adams, Franklin, Sherman and R. R. Livingston. This committee brought in its draft on the 28th of June, and on the 2nd of July a resolution declaring independence was adopted. July 4 the Declaration of Independence was agreed to, engrossed, signed by Hancock, and sent to the legislatures of the States. The engrossed copy of the Declaration was signed by all but one signer on August 2. On the Declaration, see C. L. Becker, *The Declaration of Independence*, esp. ch. v. with its analysis of Jefferson's draft; H. Friedenwald, *The Declaration of Independence*; J. H. Hazelton, *Declaration of Independence*; J. Sanderson, *Lives of the Signers to the Declaration*; R. Frothingham, *Rise of the Republic*, ch. xi.; C. H. Van Tyne, *The War of Independence, American Phase*.

IN CONGRESS, JULY 4, 1776

The Unanimous Declaration of the Thirteen United States of America

When in the Course of human events, it becomes necessary for one people to dissolve the political bands which have connected them with another, and to assume among the Powers of the earth, the separate and equal station to which the Laws of Nature and of Nature's God entitle them, a decent respect to the opinions of mankind requires that they should declare the causes which impel them to the separation.

We hold these truths to be self-evident, that all men are created equal, that they are endowed by their Creator with certain unalienable Rights, that among these are Life, Liberty and the pursuit of Happiness. That to secure these rights, Governments are instituted among Men, deriving their just powers from the consent of the governed. That whenever any Form of Government becomes destructive of these ends, it is the Right of the People to alter or to abolish it, and to institute new Government, laying its foundation on such principles and organizing its powers in such form, as to them shall seem most likely to effect their Safety and Happiness. Prudence, indeed, will dictate that Governments long established should not be changed for light and transient causes; and accordingly all experience hath shown, that mankind are more disposed to suffer, while evils are sufferable, than to right themselves by abolishing the forms to which they are accustomed. But when a long train of abuses and usurpations, pursuing invariably the same Object evinces a design to reduce them under absolute Despotism, it is their right, it is their duty, to throw off such Government, and to provide new Guards for their future security.—Such has been the patient sufferance of these Colonies; and such is now the necessity which constrains them to alter their former Systems of Government. The history of the present King of Great Britain is a history of repeated injuries and usurpations, all having in direct object the establishment of an absolute Tyranny over these States. To prove this, let Facts be submitted to a candid world.

He has refused his Assent to Laws, the most wholesome and necessary for the public good.

He has forbidden his Governors to pass Laws of immediate and pressing importance, unless suspended in their operation till his Assent should be obtained; and when so suspended, he has utterly neglected to attend to them.

He has refused to pass other Laws for the accommodation of large districts of people, unless those people would relinquish the right of Representation in the Legislature, a right inestimable to them and formidable to tyrants only.

He has called together legislative bodies at places unusual, uncomfortable, and distant from the depository of their Public Records, for the sole purpose of fatiguing them into compliance with his measures.

He has dissolved Representative Houses repeatedly, for opposing with manly firmness his invasions on the rights of the people.

He has refused for a long time, after such dissolutions, to cause others to be elected; whereby the Legislative Powers, incapable of Annihilation, have returned to the People at large for their exercise; the State remaining in the mean time exposed to all the dangers of invasion from without, and convulsion within.

He has endeavoured to prevent the population of these States; for that purpose obstructing the Laws of Naturalization of Foreigners; refusing to pass others to encourage their migration hither, and raising the conditions of new Appropriations of Lands.

He has obstructed the Administration of Justice, by refusing his Assent to Laws for establishing Judiciary Powers.

He has made Judges dependent on his Will alone, for the tenure of their offices, and the amount and payment of their salaries.

He has erected a multitude of New Offices, and sent hither swarms of Officers to harass our People, and eat out their substance.

He has kept among us, in times of peace, Standing Armies without the Consent of our legislature.

He has affected to render the Military independent of and superior to the Civil Power.

He has combined with others to subject us to a jurisdiction foreign to our constitution, and unacknowledged by our laws; giving his Assent to their acts of pretended legislation:

For quartering large bodies of armed troops among us:

For protecting them, by a mock Trial, from Punishment for any Murders which they should commit on the Inhabitants of these States:

For cutting off our Trade with all parts of the world:

For imposing taxes on us without our Consent:

For depriving us in many cases, of the benefits of Trial by Jury:

For transporting us beyond Seas to be tried for pretended offences:

For abolishing the free System of English Laws in a neighbouring Province, establishing therein an Arbitrary government, and enlarging its Boundaries so as to render it at once an example and fit instrument for introducing the same absolute rule into these Colonies:

For taking away our Charters, abolishing our most valuable Laws, and altering fundamentally the Forms of our Governments:

For suspending our own Legislature, and declaring themselves invested with Power to legislate for us in all cases whatsoever.

He has abdicted Government here, by declaring us out of his Protection and waging War against us.

He has plundered our seas, ravaged our Coasts, burnt our towns, and destroyed the lives of our people.

He is at this time transporting large armies of foreign mercenaries to complete the works of death, desolation and tyranny, already begun with circumstances of Cruelty & perfidy scarcely paralleled in the most barbarous ages, and totally unworthy the Head of a civilized nation.

He has constrained our fellow Citizens taken Captive on the high Seas to bear Arms against their Country, to become the executioners of their friends and Brethren, or to fall themselves by their Hands.

He has excited domestic insurrections amongst us, and has endeavoured to bring on the inhabitants of our frontiers, the merciless Indian Savages, whose known rule of warfare, is an undistinguished destruction of all ages, sexes and conditions.

In every stage of these Oppressions We have Petitioned for Redress in the most humble terms: Our repeated Petitions have been answered only by repeated injury. A Prince, whose character is thus marked by every act which may define a Tyrant, is unfit to be the ruler of a free People.

Nor have We been wanting in attention to our British brethren. We have warned them from time to time of attempts by their legislature to extend an unwarrantable jurisdiction over us. We have reminded them of the circumstances of our emigration and settlement here. We have appealed to their native justice and magnanimity, and we have conjured them by the ties of our common kindred to disavow these usurpations, which, would inevitably interrupt our connections and correspondence. They too have been deaf to the voice of justice and of consanguinity. We must, therefore, acquiesce in the necessity, which denounces our Separation, and hold them, as we hold the rest of mankind, Enemies in War, in Peace Friends.

We, therefore, the Representatives of the United States of America, in General Congress, Assembled, appealing to the Supreme Judge of the world for the rectitude of our intentions, do, in the Name, and by Authority of the good People of these Colonies, solemnly publish and declare, That these United Colonies are, and of Right ought to be Free and Independent States; that they are Absolved from all Allegiance to the British Crown, and that all political connection between them and the State of Great Britain, is and ought to be totally dissolved; and that as Free and Independent States, they have full Power to levy War, conclude Peace, contract Alliances, establish Commerce, and to do all other Acts and Things which Independent States may of right do. And for the support of this Declaration, with a firm reliance on the Protection of Divine Providence, we mutually pledge to each other our Lives, our Fortunes and our sacred Honor.

New Hampshire

Josiah Bartlett
Wm. Whipple
Mathew Thornton

Massachusetts-Bay

John Hancock
Saml. Adams
John Adams
Robt. Treat Paine
Elbridge Gerry

Rhode Island

Step. Hopkins
William Ellery

Connecticut

Roger Sherman
Sam'el Huntington
Wm. Williams
Oliver Wolcott

New York

Wm. Floyd
Phil. Livingston
Frans. Lewis
Lewis Morris

Pennsylvania

Robt. Morris
Benjamin Rush
Benja. Franklin
John Morton
Geo. Clymer
Jas. Smith
Geo. Taylor
James Wilson
Geo. Ross

Delaware

Caesar Rodney
Geo. Read
Tho. M'Kean

Georgia

Button Gwinnett
Lyman Hall
Geo. Walton

Maryland

Samuel Chase
Wm. Paca
Thos. Stone
Charles Carroll of Carrollton

Virginia

George Wythe
Richard Henry Lee
Th. Jefferson
Benja. Harrison
Ths. Nelson Jr.
Francis Lightfoot Lee
Carter Braxton

North Carolina

Wm. Hooper
Josph Hewes
John Penn

South Carolina

Edward Rutledge
Thos. Heyward, Junr.
Thomas Lynch, Junr.
Arthur Middleton

New Jersey

Richd. Stockton
Jno. Witherspoon
Fras. Hopkinson
John Hart
Abra. Clark

The United States Constitution and Amendments

CONSTITUTION OF THE UNITED STATES

We the People of the United States, in Order to form a more perfect Union, establish Justice, insure domestic Tranquility, provide for the common defence, promote the general Welfare, and secure the Blessings of Liberty to ourselves and our Posterity, do ordain and establish this Constitution for the United States of America.

Article I

Section 1. All legislative Powers herein granted shall be vested in a Congress of the United States, which shall consist of a Senate and House of Representatives.

Section 2. The House of Representatives shall be composed of Members chosen every second Year by the People of the several States, and the Electors in each State shall have the Qualifications requisite for Electors of the most numerous Branch of the State Legislature.

No Person shall be a Representative who shall not have attained to the Age of twenty five Years, and been seven Years a Citizen of the United States, and who shall not, when elected, be an Inhabitant of that State in which he shall be chosen.

[Representatives and direct Taxes shall be apportioned among the several States which may be included within this Union, according to their respective Numbers, which shall be determined by adding to the whole Number of free Persons, including those bound to Service for a Term of Years, and excluding Indians not taxed, three fifths of all other Persons.]* The actual Enumeration shall be made within three Years after the first Meeting of the Congress of the United States, and within every subsequent Term of ten Years, in such Manner as they shall by Law direct. The number of Representatives shall not exceed one for every thirty Thousand, but each State shall have at Least one Representative; and until such enumeration shall be made, the State of New Hampshire shall be entitled to chuse three, Massachusetts eight, Rhode-Island and Providence Plantations one, Connecticut five, New-York six, New Jersey four, Pennsylvania eight, Delaware one, Maryland six, Virginia ten, North Carolina five, South Carolina five, and Georgia three.

When vacancies happen in the Representation from any State, the Executive Authority thereof shall issue Writs of Election to fill such Vacancies.

The House of Representatives shall chuse their Speaker and other Officers; and shall have the sole Power of Impeachment.

Section 3. The Senate of the United States shall be composed of two Senators from each State, [chosen by the Legislature thereof,]* for six Years; and each Senator shall have one Vote.

Immediately after they shall be assembled in Consequence of the first Election, they shall be divided as equally as may be into three Classes. The Seats of the Senators of the first Class shall be vacated at the Expiration of the second Year, of the second Class at the Expiration of the fourth Year, and of the third Class at the Expiration of the sixth Year, so that one third may be chosen every second Year; [and if Vacancies happen by Resignation, or otherwise, during the Recess of the Legislature of any State, the Executive thereof may make temporary Appointments until the next Meeting of the Legislature, which shall then fill such Vacancies.]†

---

*Changed by Section 2 of the Fourteenth Amendment.

*Changed by the Seventeenth Amendment.
†Changed by the Seventeenth Amendment.

No Person shall be a Senator who shall not have attained to the Age of thirty Years, and been nine Years a Citizen of the United States, and who shall not, when elected, be an Inhabitant of that State for which he shall be chosen.

The Vice President of the United States shall be President of the Senate, but shall have no Vote, unless they be equally divided.

The Senate shall chuse their other Officers, and also a President pro tempore, in the Absence of the Vice President, or when he shall exercise the Office of President of the United States.

The Senate shall have the sole Power to try all Impeachments. When sitting for that Purpose, they shall be on Oath or Affirmation. When the President of the United States is tried, the Chief Justice shall preside: And no Person shall be convicted without the Concurrence of two thirds of the Members present.

Judgment in Cases of Impeachment shall not extend further than to removal from Office, and disqualification to hold and enjoy any Office of honor, Trust or Profit under the United States: but the Party convicted shall nevertheless be liable and subject to Indictment, Trial, Judgment and Punishment, according to Law.

Section 4. The Times, Places and Manner of holding Elections for Senators and Representatives, shall be prescribed in each State by the Legislature thereof; but the Congress may at any time by Law make or alter such Regulations, except as to the Places of chusing Senators.

The Congress shall assemble at least once in every Year, and such Meeting shall be [on the first Monday in December,]* unless they shall by Law appoint a different Day.

Section 5. Each House shall be the Judge of the Elections, Returns and Qualifications of its own Members, and a Majority of each shall constitute a Quorum to do Business; but a smaller Number may adjourn from day to day, and may be authorized to compel the Attendance of absent Members, in such Manner, and under such Penalties as each House may provide.

Each House may determine the Rules of its Proceedings, punish its Members for disorderly Behavior, and, with the Concurrence of two thirds, expel a Member.

*Changed by Section 2 of the Twentieth Amendment.

Each House shall keep a Journal of its Proceedings, and from time to time publish the same, excepting such Parts as may in their Judgment require Secrecy; and the Yeas and Nays of the Members of either House on any question shall, at the Desire of one fifth of those Present, be entered on the Journal.

Neither House, during the Session of Congress, shall, without the Consent of the other, adjourn for more than three days, nor to any other Place than that in which the two Houses shall be sitting.

Section 6. The Senators and Representatives shall receive a Compensation for their Services, to be ascertained by Law, and paid out of the Treasury of the United States. They shall in all Cases, except Treason, Felony and Breach of the Peace, be privileged from Arrest during their Attendance at the Session of their respective Houses, and in going to and returning from the same; and for any Speech or Debate in either House, they shall not be questioned in any other Place.

No Senator or Representative shall, during the Time for which he was elected, be appointed to any civil Office under the Authority of the United States, which shall have been created, or the Emoluments whereof shall have been encreased during such time; and no Person Holding any Office under the United States, shall be a Member of either House during his Continuance in Office.

Section 7. All Bills for raising Revenue shall originate in the House of Representatives; but the Senate may propose or concur with Amendments as on other Bills.

Every Bill which shall have passed the House of Representatives and the Senate, shall, before it becomes a Law, be presented to the President of the United States; If he approves he shall sign it, but if not he shall return it, with his Objections to that House in which it shall have originated, who shall enter the Objections at large on their Journal, and proceed to reconsider it. If after such Reconsideration two thirds of that House shall agree to pass the Bill, it shall be sent, together with the Objections, to the other House, by which it shall likewise be reconsidered, and if approved by two thirds of that House, it shall become a Law. But in all Cases the Votes of both Houses shall be determined by yeas and Nays, and the Names of the Persons voting for against the Bill shall be entered on the Journal of each House respectively. If any Bill shall not be returned by the President within ten Days (Sundays excepted) after it shall have been presented to him, the Same shall be a Law, in like Manner as if he had signed it, unless the Congress by their Adjournment prevent its Return, in which Case it shall not be a Law.

Every Order, Resolution, or Vote to which the Concurrence of the Senate and House of Representatives may be necessary (except on a question of Adjournment) shall be presented to the President of the United States; and before the Same shall take Effect, shall be approved by him, or being disapproved by him, shall be repassed by two thirds of the Senate and House of Representatives, according to the Rules and Limitations prescribed in the Case of a Bill.

Section 8. The Congress shall have Power To lay and collect Taxes, Duties, Imposts and Excises, to pay the Debts and provide for the common Defence and general Welfare of the United States; but all Duties, Imposts and Excises shall be uniform throughout the United States;

To borrow Money on the credit of the United States;

To regulate Commerce with foreign Nations, and among the several States, and with Indian Tribes;

To establish an uniform Rule of Naturalization, and uniform Laws on the subject of Bankruptcies throughout the United States;

To coin Money, regulate the Value thereof, and of foreign Coin, and fix the Standard of Weights and Measures;

To provide for the Punishment of counterfeiting the Securities and current Coin of the United States;

To establish Post Offices and post Roads;

To promote the Progress of Science and useful Arts, by securing for limited Times to Authors and Inventors the exclusive Right to their respective Writings and Discoveries;

To constitute Tribunals inferior to the supreme Court;

To define and punish Piracies and Felonies committed on the high Seas, and Offenses against the Law of Nations;

To declare War, grant Letters of Marque and Reprisal, and make Rules concerning Captures on Land and Water;

To raise and support Armies, but no Appropriation of Money to that Use shall be for a longer Term than two Years;

To provide and maintain a Navy;

To make Rules for the Government and Regulation of the land and naval Forces;

To provide for calling forth the Militia to execute the Laws of the Union, suppress Insurrections and repel Invasions;

To provide for organizing, arming, and disciplining, the Militia, and for governing such Part of them as may be employed in the Service of the United States, reserving to the States respectively, the Appointment of the Officers, and the Authority of training the Militia according to the discipline prescribed by Congress;

To exercise exclusive Legislation in all Cases whatsoever, over such District (not exceeding ten Miles square) as may, by Cession of particular States, and the Acceptance of Congress, become the Seat of the Government of the United States, and to exercise like Authority over all Places purchased by the Consent of the Legislature of the State in which the Same shall be, for the Erection of Forts, Magazines, Arsenals, dock-Yards and other needful Buildings;—And

To make all Laws which shall be necessary and proper for carrying into Execution the foregoing Powers, and all other Powers vested by this Constitution in the Government of the United States, or in any Department or Officer thereof.

Section 9. The Migration or Importation of such Persons as any of the States now existing shall think proper to admit, shall not be prohibited by the Congress prior to the Year one thousand eight hundred and eight, but a Tax or duty may be imposed on such Importation, not exceeding ten dollars for each Person.

The Privilege of the Writ of Habeas Corpus shall not be suspended, unless when in Cases of Rebellion or Invasion the public Safety may require it.

No Bill of Attainder or ex post facto Law shall be passed.

[No Capitation, or other direct, Tax shall be laid, unless in Proportion to the Census or Enumeration herein before directed to be taken.]*

No Tax or Duty shall be laid on Articles exported from any State.

No Preference shall be given by any Regulation of Commerce or Revenue to the Ports of one State over those of another: nor shall Vessels bound to, or from, one State, be obliged to enter, clear, or pay Duties in another.

No Money shall be drawn from the Treasury, but in Consequence of Appropriations made by Law; and

*Changed by the Sixteenth Amendment.

a regular Statement and Account of the Receipts and Expenditures of all public Money shall be published from time to time.

No Title of Nobility shall be granted by the United States: And no Person holding any Office of Profit or Trust under them, shall, without the Consent of the Congress, accept of any present, Emolument, Office, or Title, of any kind whatever, from any King, Prince, or foreign State.

Section 10. No State shall enter into any Treaty, Alliance, or Confederation; grant Letters of Marque and Reprisal; coin Money; emit Bills of Credit; make any Thing but gold and silver Coin a Tender in Payment of Debts; pass any Bill of Attainder, ex post facto Law, or Law impairing the Obligation of Contracts, or grant any Title of Nobility.

No State shall, without the Consent of the Congress, lay any Imposts or Duties on Imports or Exports, except what may be absolutely necessary for executing its inspection Laws: and the net Produce of the Duties and Imposts, laid by any State on Imports or Exports, shall be for the Use of the Treasury of the United States; and all such Laws shall be subject to the Revision and Control of the Congress.

No State shall, without the Consent of Congress, lay any Duty of Tonnage, keep Troops, or Ships of War in time of Peace, enter into any Agreement or Compact with another State, or with a foreign Power, or engage in War, unless actually invaded, or in such imminent Danger as will not admit of delay.

Article II

Section 1. The executive Power shall be vested in a President of the United States of America. He shall hold his Office during their Term of four Years, and, together with the Vice President, chosen for the same Term, be elected, as follows

Each State shall appoint, in such Manner as the Legislature thereof may direct, a Number of Electors, equal to the whole Number of Senators and Representatives to which the State may be entitled in the Congress: but no Senator or Representative, or Person holding an Office of Trust or Profit under the United States shall be appointed an Elector.

[The Electors shall meet in their respective States, and vote by Ballot for two Persons, of whom one at least shall not be an Inhabitant of the same State with themselves. And they shall make a List of all the Persons voted for, and of the Number of Votes for each; which List they shall sign and certify, and transmit sealed to the Seat of the Government of the United States, directed to the President of the Senate. The President of the Senate shall, in the Presence of the Senate and House of Representatives, open all the Certificates, and the Votes shall then be counted. The Person having the greatest Number of Votes shall be the President, if such Number be a Majority of the whole Number of Electors appointed; and if there be more than one who have such Majority, and have an equal Number of Votes, then the House of Representatives shall immediately chuse by Ballot one of them for President, and if no Person have a Majority, then from the five highest on the List the said House shall in like Manner chuse the President. But in chusing the President, the Votes shall be taken by States, the Representation from each State having one Vote; A quorum for this Purpose shall consist of a Member or Members from two thirds of the States, and a Majority of all the States shall be necessary to a Choice. In every Case, after the Choice of the President, the Person having the greatest Number of Votes of the Electors shall be the Vice President. But if there should remain two or more who have equal Votes, the Senate shall chuse from them by Ballot the Vice President.]*

The Congress may determine the Time of chusing the Electors, and the Day on which they shall give their Votes; which Day shall be the same throughout the United States.

No Person except a natural born Citizen, or a Citizen of the United States, at the time of the Adoption of this Constitution, shall be eligible to the Office of the President; neither shall any person be eligible to that Office who shall not have attained to the Age of thirty five Years, and been fourteen Years a Resident within the United States.

[In Case of the Removal of the President from Office, or of his Death, Resignation, or Inability to discharge the Powers and Duties of the said Office, the Same shall devolve on the Vice President, and the Congress may by Law provide for the Case of Removal, Death, Resignation or Inability, both of the President and Vice President, declaring what Officer shall then act as President, and such Officer shall act accordingly, until the Disability be removed, or a President shall be elected.]†

*Changed by the Twelfth Amendment
†Changed by the Twenty-First Amendment.

The President shall, at stated Times, receive for his Services, a Compensation which shall neither be increased nor diminished during the Period for which he shall have been elected, and he shall not receive within that Period any other Emolument from the United States, or any of them.

Before he enter on the Execution of his Office, he shall take the following Oath or Affirmation:—"I do solemnly swear (or affirm) that I will faithfully execute the Office of President of the United States, and will to the best of my Ability, preserve, protect and defend the Constitution of the United States."

Section 2. The President shall be Commander in Chief of the Army and Navy of the United States, and of the Militia of the several States, when called into the actual Service of the United States; he may require the Opinion, in writing, of the principal Officer in each of the executive Departments, upon any Subject relating to the Duties of their respective Offices, and he shall have Power to grant Reprieves and Pardons for Offenses against the United States, except in Cases of Impeachment.

He shall have Power, by and with the Advice and Consent of the Senate, to make Treaties, provided two thirds of the Senators present concur; and he shall nominate, and by and with the Advice and Consent of the Senate, shall appoint Ambassadors, other public Ministers and Consuls, Judges of the Supreme Court, and all other Officers of the United States, whose Appointments are not herein otherwise provided for, and which shall be established by Law: but the Congress may by Law vest the Appointment of such inferior Officers, as they think proper, in the President alone, in the Courts of Law, or in the Heads of Departments.

The President shall have Power to fill up all Vacancies that may happen during the Recess of the Senate, by granting Commissions which shall expire at the End of their next Session.

Section 3. He shall from time to time give to the Congress Information of the State of the Union, and recommend to their Consideration such Measures as he shall judge necessary and expedient; he may, on extraordinary Occasions, convene both Houses, or either of them, and in Case of Disagreement between them, with Respect to the Time of Adjournment, he may adjourn them to such Time as he shall think proper; he shall receive Ambassadors and other public Ministers; he

shall take Care that the Laws be faithfully executed, and shall Commission all the Officers of the United States.

Section 4. The President, Vice President and all civil Officers of the United States, shall be removed from Office on Impeachment for, and Conviction of, Treason, Bribery, or other high Crimes and Misdemeanors.

Article III

Section 1. The judicial Power of the United States, shall be vested in one supreme Court, and in such inferior Courts as the Congress may from time to time ordain and establish. The Judges, both of the supreme and inferior Courts, shall hold their Offices during good Behaviour, and shall, at stated Times, receive for their Services, a Compensation, which shall not be diminished during their Continuance in Office.

Section 2. The judicial Power shall extend to all Cases, in Law and Equity, arising under this Constitution, the Laws of the United States, and Treaties made, or which shall be made, under their Authority;—to all Cases affecting Ambassadors, other public Ministers and Consuls:—to all Cases of admiralty and maritime Jurisdiction;—to Controversies to which the United States shall be a Party;—to Controversies between two or more States; [between a State and Citizens of another State;—]* between Citizens of different States—between Citizens of the same State claiming Lands under Grants of different States, [and between a State, or the Citizens thereof, and foreign States, Citizens or Subjects.]*

In all Cases affecting Ambassadors, other public Ministers and Consuls, and those in which a State shall be Party, the supreme Court shall have original Jurisdiction. In all the other Cases before mentioned, the supreme Court shall have appellate Jurisdiction, both as to Law and Fact, with such Exceptions, and under such Regulations as the Congress shall make.

The Trial of the Crimes, except in Cases of Impeachment; shall be by Jury; and such Trial shall be held in the State where the said Crimes shall have been committed; but when not committed within any State, the Trial shall be at such Place or Places as the Congress may by Law have directed.

Section 3. Treason against the United States, shall consist only in levying War against them, or in adhering

*Changed by the Eleventh Amendment.

to their Enemies, giving them Aid and Comfort. No Person shall be convicted of Treason unless on the Testimony of two Witnesses to the same overt Act, or on Confession in open Court.

The Congress shall have Power to declare the Punishment of Treason, but no Attainder of Treason shall work Corruption of Blood, or Forfeiture except during the Life of the Person attained.

Article IV

Section 1. Full Faith and Credit shall be given in each State to the public Acts, Records, and judicial Proceedings of every other State, And the Congress may by general Laws prescribe the Manner in which such Acts, Records and Proceedings shall be proved, and the Effect thereof.

Section 2. The Citizens of each State shall be entitled to all Privileges and Immunities of Citizens in the several States.

A Person charged in any State with Treason, Felony, or other Crime, who shall flee from Justice, and be found in another State, shall on Demand of the executive Authority of the State from which he fled, be delivered up, to be removed to the State having Jurisdiction of the Crime.

[No Person held to Service or Labour in one State, under the Laws thereof, escaping into another, shall, in Consequence of any Law or Regulation therein, be discharged from such Service or Labour, but shall be delivered up on Claim of the Party to whom such Service or Labour may be due.]*

Section 3. New States may be admitted by the Congress into this Union; but no new State shall be formed or erected within the Jurisdiction of any other State; nor any State be formed by the Junction of two or more States, or Parts of States, without the Consent of the Legislatures of the States concerned as well as of the Congress.

The Congress shall have Power to dispose of and make all needful Rules and Republican respecting the Territory or other Property belonging to the United States; and nothing in this Constitution shall be so construed as to Prejudice any Claims of the United States, or of any particular State.

Section 4. The United States shall guarantee to every State in this Union a Republican Form of Government, and shall protect each of them against Invasion; and

*Changed by the Thirteenth Amendment.

on Application of the Legislature, or of the Executive (when the Legislature cannot be convened) against domestic Violence.

Article V

The Congress, whenever two thirds of both Houses shall deem it necessary, shall propose Amendments to this Constitution, or, on the Application of the Legislatures of two thirds of the several States, shall call a Convention for proposing Amendments, which, in either Case, shall be valid to all Intents and Purposes, as Part of this Constitution, when ratified by the Legislatures of three fourths of the several States, or by Conventions in three fourths thereof, as the one or the other Mode of Ratification may be proposed by the Congress; Provided that no Amendment which may be made prior to the Year one thousand eight hundred and eight shall in any Manner affect the first and fourth Clauses in the Ninth Section of the first Article; and the no State, without its Consent, shall be deprived of it's [*sic*] equal Suffrage in the Senate.

Article VI

All Debts contracted and Engagements entered into, before the Adoption of this Constitution, shall be as valid against the United States under this Constitution, as under the Confederation.

This Constitution, and the Laws of the United States which shall be made in Pursuance thereof; and all Treaties made, or which shall be made, under the Authority of the United States, shall be the supreme Law of the Land; and the Judges in every State shall be bound thereby, any Thing in the Constitution or Laws of any State to the Contrary nowithstanding.

The Senators and Representatives before mentioned, and the Members of the several State Legislatures, and all executive and judicial Officers, both of the United States and of the several States, shall be bound by Oath or Affirmation, to support this Constitution; but no religious Test shall ever be required as a Qualification to any Office or public Trust under the United States.

Article VII

The Ratification of the Conventions of nine States, shall be sufficient for the Establishment of this Constitution between the States so ratifying the Same.

Done in Convention by the Unanimous Consent of the States present the Seventeenth Day of September in the Year of our Lord one thousand seven hundred and Eighty seven and of the Independence of the United States of America the Twelfth In Witness whereof We have hereunto subscribed our Names,

G.º Washington—Presid.ᵗ and deputy from Virginia

New Hampshire

John Langdon
Nicholas Gilman

Massachusetts

Nathaniel Gorham
Rufus King

Connecticut

Wm. Saml. Johnson
Roger Sherman

New York

Alexander Hamilton

New Jersey

Wil. Livingston
David Brearley
Wm. Paterson
Jona. Dayton

Pennsylvania

B. Franklin
Thomas Mifflin
Robt. Morris
Geo. Clymer
Thos. FitzSimons
Jared Ingersoll
James Wilson
Gouv. Morris

Delaware

Geo. Read
Gunning Bedford jun
John Dickinson
Richard Bassett
Jaco. Broom

Maryland

James McHenry
Dan of St. Thos. Jenifer
Danl. Carroll

Virginia

John Blair
James Madison, Jr.

North Carolina

Wm. Blount
Richd. Dobbs Spaight
Hu Williamson

South Carolina

J. Rutledge
Charles Cotesworth Pinckney
Charles Pinckney
Pierce Butler

Georgia

William Few
Abr. Baldwin

Attest *William Jackson* Secretary

IN CONVENTION MONDAY SEPTEMBER 17TH 1787

Present the States of

New Hampshire, Massachusetts, Connecticut, Mr. Hamilton from New York, New Jersey, Pennsylvania, Delaware, Maryland, Virginia, North Carolina, South Carolina and Georgia.

Resolved,

That the preceeding Constitution be laid before the United States in Congress assembled, and that it is the Opinion of this Convention, that it should afterwards be submitted to a Convention of Delegates, chosen in each State by the People thereof, under the Recommendation of its Legislature, for their Assent and Ratification; and that each Convention assenting to, and ratifying the Same, should give Notice thereof to the United States in Congress assembled. Resolved, That it is the Opinion of this Convention, that as soon as the Conventions of nine States shall have ratified this Constitution, the United States in Congress assembled should fix a Day on which Electors should be appointed by the States which shall have ratified the same, and a Day on which the Electors should assemble to vote for the President, and the Time and Place for commencing Proceedings under this Constitution.

That after such Publication the Electors should be appointed, and the Senators and Representatives elected: That the Electors should meet on the Day fixed for the Election of the President, and should transmit their Votes certified, signed, sealed and directed, as the Constitution requires, to the Secretary of the United States in Congress assembled, that the Senators and Representatives should convene at the Time and Place assigned; that the Senators should appoint a President of the Senate, for the sole Purpose of receiving, opening and counting the Votes for

President; and, that after he shall be chosen, the Congress, together with the President, should, without Delay, proceed to execute this Constitution.

By the unanimous Order of the Convention

G.º Washington—Presid.ᵗ

W. Jackson Secretary.

AMENDMENTS TO THE CONSTITUTION OF THE UNITED STATES

Amendment I [1791]

Congress shall make no law respecting an establishment of religion, or prohibiting the free exercise thereof; or abridging the freedom of speech, or of the press; or the right of the people peaceably to assembly, and to petition the Government for a redress of grievances.

Amendment II [1791]

A well regulated Militia, being necessary to the security of a free State, the right of the people to keep and bear Arms, shall not be infringed.

Amendment III [1791]

No Soldier shall, in time of peace be quartered in any house, without the consent of the Owner, nor in time of war, but in a manner to be prescribed by law.

Amendment IV [1791]

The right of the people to be secure in their persons, houses, papers, and effects, against unreasonable searches and seizures, shall not be violated, and no Warrants shall issue, but upon probable cause, supported by Oath or affirmation, and particularly describing the place to be searched, and the persons or things to be seized.

Amendment V [1791]

No person shall be held to answer for a capital, or otherwise infamous crime, unless on a presentment or indictment of a Grand Jury, except in cases arising in the land or naval forces, or in the Militia, when in actual service in time of War or public danger; nor shall any person be subject for the same offence to be twice put in jeopardy of life or limb; nor shall be compelled in any criminal case to be a witness against himself, nor be deprived of life, liberty, or property, without due process of law; nor shall private property be taken for public use, without just compensation.

Amendment VI [1791]

In all criminal prosecutions, the accused shall enjoy the right to a speedy and public trial, by an impartial jury of the State and district wherein the crime shall have been committed, which district shall have been previously ascertained by law, and to be informed of the nature and cause of accusation; to be confronted with the witnesses against him; to have compulsory process for obtaining witnesses in his favor, and to have the Assistance of Counsel for his defence.

Amendment VII [1791]

In Suits at common law, where the value in controversy shall exceed twenty dollars, the right of trial by jury shall be preserved, and no fact tried by jury, shall be otherwise re-examined in any Court of the United States, than according to the rules of the common law.

Amendment VIII [1791]

Excessive bail shall not be required, nor excessive fines imposed, nor cruel and unusual punishments inflicted.

Amendment IX [1791]

The enumeration in the Constitution, of certain rights, shall not be construed to deny or disparage others retained by the people.

Amendment X [1791]

The powers not delegated to the United States by the Constitution, nor prohibited by it to the States, are reserved to the States respectively, or to the people.

Amendment XI [1798]

The Judicial power of the United States shall not be construed to extend to any suit in law or equity, commenced or prosecuted against one of the United States by Citizens of another State, or by Citizens or Subjects of any Foreign State.

Amendment XII [1804]

The Electors shall meet in their respective states, and vote by ballot for President and Vice-President, one of whom, at least, shall not be an inhabitant of the same state with themselves; they shall name in their ballots the person voted for as President, and in distinct ballots the person voted for as Vice-President, and they shall make distinct lists of all persons voted for as President, and of all persons voted for as Vice-President, and of the number of votes for each, which lists they shall sign and certify, and transmit sealed to the seat of the government of the United States, directed to the President of the Senate;—The President of the Senate shall, in the presence of the Senate and House of Representatives, open all the certificates and the votes shall then be counted;—The person having the greatest number of votes for President, shall be the President, if such number be a majority of the whole number of Electors appointed; and if no person have such majority, then from the persons having the highest numbers not exceeding three on the list of those voted for as President, the House of Representatives shall choose immediately, by ballot, the President. But in choosing the President, the votes shall be taken by states, the representation from each state having one vote; a quorum for this purpose shall consist of a member or members from two-thirds of the states, and a majority of all states shall be necessary to a choice. And if the House of Representatives shall not choose a President whenever the right of choice shall devolve upon them, before the fourth day of March next following, then the Vice-President shall act as President, as in the case of the death or other constitutional disability of the President.—The person having the greatest number of votes as Vice-President, shall be the Vice-President, if such number be a majority of the whole number of Electors appointed, and if no person have a majority, then from the two highest numbers on the list, the Senate shall choose the Vice-President; a quorum for the purpose shall consist of two-thirds of the whole number of Senators, and a majority of the whole number shall be necessary to a choice. But no person constitutionally ineligible to the office of President shall be eligible to that of Vice-President of the United States.

Amendment XIII [1865]

Section 1. Neither slavery nor involuntary servitude, except as a punishment for crime whereof the party shall have been duly convicted, shall exist within the United States, or any place subject to their jurisdiction.

Section 2. Congress shall have power to enforce this article by appropriate legislation.

Amendment XIV [1868]

Section 1. All persons born or naturalized in the United States, and subject to the jurisdiction thereof, are citizens of the United States and of the State wherein they reside. No State shall make or enforce any law which shall abridge the privileges or immunities of citizens of the United States; nor shall any State deprive any person of life, liberty, or property, without due process of law; nor deny to any person within its jurisdiction the equal protection of the laws.

Section 2. Representatives shall be apportioned among the several States according to their respective numbers, counting the whole number of persons in each State, excluding Indians not taxed. But when the right to vote at any election for the choice of electors for President and Vice President of the United States, Representatives in Congress, the Executive and Judicial officers of a State, or the members of the Legislature thereof, is denied to any of the male inhabitants of such State, being twenty-one years of age, and citizens of the United States, or in any way abridged, except for participation in rebellion, or other crime, the basis of representation therein shall be reduced in the proportion which the number of such male citizens shall bear to the whole number of male citizens twenty-one years of age in such State.

Section 3. No person shall be a Senator or Representative in Congress, or elector of President and Vice President, or hold any office, civil or military, under the United States, or under any State, who having previously taken an oath, as a member of Congress, or as an officer of the United States, or as a member of any State legislature, or as an executive or judicial officer of any State, to support the Constitution of the United States, shall have engaged in insurrection or rebellion against the same, or given aid or comfort to the enemies thereof. But Congress may by a vote of two-thirds of each House, remove such disability.

Section 4. The validity of the public debt of the United States, authorized by law, including debts incurred for payment of pensions and bounties for services in suppressing insurrection or rebellion, shall not be questioned. But neither the United States nor any State shall assume or pay any debt or obligation incurred in aid of insurrection or rebellion against the United States, or any claim for the loss or emancipation of any slave; but all such debts, obligation and claims shall be held illegal and void.

Section 5. The Congress shall have power to enforce, by appropriate legislation, the provisions of this article.

Amendment XV [1870]

Section 1. The right of citizens of the United States to vote shall not be denied or abridged by the United States or by any State on account of race, color, or previous condition of servitude.

Section 2. The Congress shall have power to enforce this article by appropriate legislation.

Amendment XVI [1913]

The Congress shall have power to lay and collect taxes on incomes, from whatever source derived, without apportionment among the several States, and without regard to any census or enumeration.

Amendment XVII [1913]

Section 1. The Senate of the United States shall be composed of two Senators from each State, elected by the people thereof, for six years; and each Senator shall have one vote. The electors in each State shall have the qualifications requisite for electors of the most numerous branch of the State legislatures.

Section 2. When vacancies happen in the representation of any State in the Senate, the executive authority of such State shall issue writs of election to fill such vacancies: Provided, That the legislature of any State may empower the executive thereof to make temporary appointments until the people fill the vacancies by election as the legislature may direct.

Section 3. This amendment shall not be so construed as to affect the election or term of any Senator chosen before it becomes valid as part of the Constitution.

Amendment XVIII [1919]

Section 1. After one year from the ratification of this article the manufacture, sale, or transportation of intoxicating liquors within, the importation thereof into, or the exportation thereof from the United States and all territory subject to the jurisdiction thereof for beverage purposes is hereby prohibited.

Section 2. The Congress and the several States shall have concurrent power to enforce this article by appropriate legislation.

Section 3. This article shall be inoperative unless it shall have been ratified as an amendment to the Constitution by the legislatures of the several States, as provided in the Constitution, within seven years from the date of the submission hereof to the States by the Congress.

Amendment XIX [1920]

Section 1. The right of citizens of the United States to vote shall not be denied or abridged by the United States or by any State on account of sex.

Section 2. Congress shall have power to enforce this article by appropriate legislation.

Amendment XX [1933]

Section 1. The terms of the President and Vice President shall end at noon on the 20th day of January, and the terms of Senators and Representatives at noon on the 3d day of January, of the years in which such terms would have ended if this article had not been ratified; and the terms of their successors shall then begin.

Section 2. The Congress shall assemble at least once in every year, and such meeting shall begin at noon on the 3d day of January, unless they shall by law appoint a different day.

Section 3. If, at the time fixed for the beginning of the term of the President, the President elect shall have died, the Vice President elect shall become President. If the President shall not have been chosen before the time fixed for the beginning of his term, or if the President elect shall have failed to qualify, then the Vice President elect shall act as President until a President shall have qualified; and the Congress may by law provide for the case wherein neither a President elect nor a Vice President elect shall have qualified, declaring who shall then act as President, or the manner in which one who is to act shall be selected, and such person shall act accordingly until a President or Vice President shall have qualified.

Section 4. The Congress may by law provide for the case of the death of any of the persons from whom the House of Representatives may choose a President whenever the right of choice shall have devolved upon them, and for the case of the death of any of the persons from whom the Senate may choose a Vice President whenever the right of choice shall have devolved upon them.

Section 5. Sections 1 and 2 shall take effect on the 15th day of October following the ratification of this article.

Section 6. This article shall be inoperative unless it shall have been ratified as an amendment to the Constitution by the legislatures of three-fourths of the several States within seven years from the date of its submission.

Amendment XXI [1933]

Section 1. The eighteenth article of amendment to the Constitution of the United States is hereby repealed.

Section 2. The transportation or importation into any State, Territory, or possession of the United States for delivery or use therein of intoxicating liquors, in violation of the laws thereof, is hereby prohibited.

Section 3. This article shall be inoperative unless it shall have been ratified as an amendment to the Constitution by conventions in the several States, as provided in the Constitution, within seven years from the date of the submission hereof to the States by the Congress.

Amendment XXII [1951]

Section 1. No person shall be elected to the office of the President more than twice, and no person who has held the office of President, or acted as President, for more than two years of a term to which some other person was elected President shall be elected to the office of President more than once. But this Article shall not apply to any person holding the office of President when this Article was proposed by the Congress, and shall not prevent any person who may be holding the office of President, or acting as President, during the term within which this Article becomes operative from holding the office of President or acting as President during the remainder of such term.

Section 2. This article shall be inoperative unless it shall have been ratified as an amendment to the Constitution by the legislatures of three-fourths of the several States within seven years from the date of its submission to the States by the Congress.

Amendment XXIII [1961]

Section 1. The District constituting the seat of Government of the United States shall appoint in such manner as the Congress may direct:

A number of electors of President and Vice President equal to the whole number of Senators and Representatives in Congress to which the District would be entitled if it were a State, but in no event more than the least populous state; they shall be in addition to those appointed by the states, but they shall be considered, for the purposes of the election of President and Vice President, to be electors appointed by a state; and they shall meet in the District and perform such duties as provided by the twelfth article of amendment.

Section 2. The Congress shall have power to enforce this article by appropriate legislation.

Amendment XXIV [1964]

Section 1. The right of citizens of the United States to vote in any primary or other election for President or Vice President, for electors for President or Vice President, or for Senator or Representative in Congress, shall not be denied or abridged by the United States, or any State by reason of failure to pay any poll tax or other tax.

Section 2. The Congress shall have power to enforce this article by appropriate legislation.

Amendment XXV [1967]

Section 1. In case of the removal of the President from office or of his death or resignation, the Vice President shall become President.

Section 2. Whenever there is a vacancy in the office of the Vice President, the President shall nominate a Vice President who shall take office upon confirmation by a majority vote of both Houses of Congress.

Section 3. Whenever the President transmits to the President pro tempore of the Senate and the Speaker of the House of Representatives his written declaration that he is unable to discharge the powers and duties of his office, and until he transmits to them a written declaration to the contrary, such powers and duties shall be discharged by the Vice President as Acting President.

Section 4. Whenever the Vice President and a majority of either the principal officers of the executive departments or of such other body as Congress may by law provide, transmit to the President pro tempore of the Senate and the Speaker of the House of Representatives their written declaration that the President is unable to discharge the powers and duties of his office, the Vice President shall immediately assume the powers and duties of the office as Acting President.

Thereafter, when the President transmits to the President pro tempore of the Senate and the Speaker of the House of Representatives his written declaration that no inability exists, he shall resume the powers and duties of his office unless the Vice President and a majority of either the principal officers of the executive department or of such other body as Congress may by law provide, transmit within four days to the President pro tempore of the Senate and the Speaker of the House of Representatives their written declaration and the President is unable to discharge the powers and duties of his office. Thereupon Congress shall decide the issue, assembling within forty-eight hours for that purpose if not in session. If the Congress, within twenty-one days after receipt of the latter written declaration, or, if Congress is not in session, within twenty-one days after Congress is required to assemble, determines by two-thirds vote of both Houses that the President is unable to discharge the powers and duties of his office, the Vice President shall continue to discharge the same as Acting President; otherwise, the President shall resume the powers and duties of his office.

Amendment XXVI [1971]

Section 1. The right of citizens of the United States, who are eighteen years of age or older, to vote shall not be denied or abridged by the United States or by any State on account of age.

Section 2. The Congress shall have power to enforce this article by appropriate legislation.

Amendment XXVII [1992]

No law varying the compensation for the services of the Senators and Representatives, shall take effect, until an election of Representatives shall have intervened.

Marbury v. Madison and Miranda v. Arizona

MARBURY V. MADISON
1 Cranch 137, 2 L.Ed. 60 (1803)

[Thomas Jefferson, an Anti-Federalist (or Republican), who defeated John Adams, a Federalist, in the presidential election of 1800, was to take office on March 4, 1801. On January 20, 1801, Adams, the defeated incumbent, nominated John Marshall, Adams' Secretary of State, as fourth Chief Justice of the United States. Marshall assumed office on February 4 but continued to serve as Secretary of State until the end of the Adams administration. During February, the Federalist Congress passed (1) the Circuit Court Act, which, inter alia, doubled the number of federal judges and (2) the Organic Act which authorized appointment of 42 justices-of-the-peace in the District of Columbia. Senate confirmation of Adams' "midnight" appointees, virtually all Federalists, was completed on March 3. Their commissions were signed by Adams and sealed by Acting Secretary of State Marshall, but due to time pressures, several of the justices-of-the-peace (including that of William Marbury) remained undelivered when Jefferson assumed the presidency the next day. Jefferson ordered his new Secretary of State, James Madison, to withhold delivery.

[Late in 1801, Marbury and several others sought a writ of mandamus in the Supreme Court to compel Madison to deliver the commissions. The Court ordered Madison "to show cause why a mandamus should not issue" and the case was set for argument in the 1802 Term.

[While the case was pending, the new Republican Congress—incensed at Adams' efforts to entrench a Federalist judiciary and at the "Federalist" Court's order against a Republican cabinet officer—moved to repeal the Circuit Court Act. Federalist congressmen argued that repeal would be unconstitutional as violative of Art. III's assurance of judicial tenure "during good behavior" and of the Constitution's plan for separation of powers assuring the independence of the Judiciary. It "was in this debate that for the first time since the initiation of the new Government under the Constitution there occurred a serious challenge of the power of the Judiciary to pass upon the constitutionality of Acts of Congress. Hitherto, [it had been the Republicans] who had sustained this power as a desirable curb on Congressional aggression and encroachment on the rights of the States, and they had been loud in their complaints at the failure of the Court to hold the Alien and Sedition laws unconstitutional. Now, however, in 1802, in order to counteract the Federalist argument that the Repeal Bill was unconstitutional and would be so held by the Court, [Republicans] advanced the proposition that the Court did not possess the power."[a]

[The Repeal Law passed early in 1802. To forestall its constitutional challenge in the Supreme Court until the political power of the new administration had been strengthened, Congress also eliminated the 1802 Supreme Court Term. Thus, the Court did not meet between December, 1801 and February, 1803.]

[On] 24th February, the following opinion of the court was delivered by Mr. Chief Justice MARSHALL: * * *

No cause has been shown, and the present motion is for a mandamus. The peculiar delicacy of this case, the novelty of some of its circumstances, and the real difficulty attending the points which occur in it require a complete exposition of the principles on which the opinion to be given by the court is founded. * * *

1st. Has the applicant a right to the commission he demands? * * *

---

[a] C. Warren, *The Supreme Court in United States History* 215 (1922).

* * * Proof of the status of Marbury's commission not only involved circumstances within the Chief Justice's personal knowledge, it was furnished in the Supreme Court by Marshall's own younger brother who had been with him in his office when, as Secretary of State, he had made out the commissions."

Mr. Marbury, [since] his commission was signed by the President and sealed by the Secretary of State, was appointed; and as the law creating the office gave the officer a right to hold for five years, independent of the executive, the appointment was not revocable, but vested in the officer legal rights, which are protected by the laws of his country.

To withhold his commission, therefore, is an act deemed by the court not warranted by law, but violative of a vested legal right.[b] * * *

2dly. If he has a right, and that right has been violated, do the laws of his country afford him a remedy?

The very essence of civil liberty certainly consists in the right of every individual to claim the protection of the laws, whenever he receives an injury. One of the first duties of government is to afford that protection. * * *

The government of the United States has been emphatically termed a government of laws, and not of men. It will certainly cease to deserve this high appellation, if the laws furnish no remedy for the violation of a vested legal right. * * *

[W]here the heads of departments are the political or confidential agents of the executive, merely to execute the will of the president, or rather to act in cases in which the executive possesses a constitutional or legal discretion, nothing can be more perfectly clear than that their acts are only politically examinable. But where a specific duty is assigned by law, and individual rights depend upon the performance of that duty, it seems equally clear that the individual who considers himself injured, has a right to resort to the laws of his country for a remedy.[c] * * *

It remains to be inquired whether,

3dly. He is entitled to the remedy for which he applies? This depends on,

1st. The nature of the writ applied for; and,

2dly. The power of this court.

1st. The nature of the writ. * * *

[b]Consider Van Alstyne, *A Critical Guide to Marbury v. Madison.* 1969 Duke L. J. 1. 8: "[T]here is clearly an 'issue' of sorts which preceded any of those touched upon in the opinion. Specifically, it would appear that Marshall should have recused himself in view of his substantial involvement in the background of this controversy.

[c]Consider Redlich, *The Supreme Court—1833 Term,* 40 N.Y.U.L.Rev. 1, 4 (1965): "[T]he Court could have ruled that, since the President had the power to appoint the judges, he also had the power to deliver the commissions which was in a sense the final act of appointment. Viewed as a component of the act of appointment, the delivery of the commissions could have simply been considered as lying within the discretion of the President."

This writ, if awarded, would be directed to an officer of government, and its mandate to him would be, to use the words of Blackstone, "to do a particular thing therein specified, which appertains to his office and duty, and which the court has previously determined, or at least supposes, to be consonant to right and justice." Or, in the words of Lord Mansfield, the applicant, in this case, has a right to execute an office of public concern, and is kept out of possession of that right.

These circumstances certainly concur in this case.

Still, to render the mandamus a proper remedy, the officer to whom it is to be directed, must be one to whom, on legal principles, such writ may be directed; and the person applying for it must be without any other specific and legal remedy.

1st. With respect to the officer to whom it would be directed. The intimate political relation subsisting between the President of the United States and the heads of departments, necessarily renders any legal investigation of the acts of one of those high officers peculiarly irksome, as well as delicate; and excites some hesitation with respect to the propriety of entering into such investigation. Impressions are often received without much reflection or examination, and it is not wonderful that in such a case as this the assertion, by an individual, of his legal claims in a court of justice, to which claims it is the duty of that court to attend, should at first view be considered by some, as an attempt to intrude into the cabinet, and to intermeddle with the prerogatives of the executive.

It is scarcely necessary for the court to disclaim all pretensions to such a jurisdiction. An extravagance, so absurd and excessive, could not have been entertained for a moment. The province of the court is, solely, to decide on the rights of individuals, not to inquire how the executive, or executive officers, perform duties in which they have a discretion. Questions in their nature political, or which are, by the constitution and laws, submitted to the executive, can never be made in this court.

But [what] is there in the exalted station of the officer, which shall bar a citizen from asserting, in a court of justice, his legal rights, or shall forbid a court to listen to the claim, or to issue a mandamus, directing the performance of a duty, not depending on executive discretion, but on particular acts of congress, and the general principles of law? * * *

This, then, is a plain case for a mandamus, either to deliver the commission, or a copy of it from the record; and it only remains to be inquired whether it can issue from this court.

The act to establish the judicial courts of the United States authorizes the supreme court "to issue writs of mandamus, in cases warranted by the principles and usages of law, to any courts appointed, or persons holding office, under the authority of the United States."[d]

The secretary of state, being a person holding an office under the authority of the United States, is precisely within the letter of the description; and if this court is not authorized to issue a writ of mandamus to such an officer, it must be because the law is unconstitutional, and therefore absolutely incapable of conferring the authority, and assigning the duties which its words purport to confer and assign. * * *

In the distribution of [the judicial power of the United States] it is declared that "the supreme court shall have original jurisdiction in all cases affecting ambassadors, other public ministers and consuls, and those in which a state shall be a party. In all other cases, the supreme court shall have appellate jurisdiction."

It has been insisted, at the bar, that as the original grant of jurisdiction, to the supreme and inferior courts, is general, and the clause, assigning original jurisdiction to the supreme court, contains no negative or restrictive words, the power remains to the legislature, to assign original jurisdiction to that court in other cases than those specified in the article which has been recited; provided those cases belong to the judicial power of the United States.

If it had been intended to leave it in the discretion of the legislature to apportion the judicial power between the supreme and inferior courts according to the will of that body, it would certainly have been useless to have proceeded further than to have defined the judicial power, and the tribunals in which it should be vested. The subsequent part of the section is mere surplusage, is entirely without meaning, if such is to be the construction. If congress remains at liberty to give this court appellate jurisdiction, where the constitution has declared their jurisdiction shall be original; and original jurisdiction where the Constitution has declared it shall be appellate; the distribution of jurisdiction, made in the Constitution, is form without substance.

Affirmative words are often, in their operation, negative of other objects than those affirmed; and in this case, a negative or exclusive sense must be given to them, or they have no operation at all.

It cannot be presumed that any clause in the Constitution is intended to be without effect; and, therefore, such a construction is inadmissible, unless the words require it. * * *

The authority, therefore, given to the Supreme Court, by the Act establishing the judicial courts of the United States, to issue writs of mandamus to public officers, appears not to be warranted by the Constitution;[e] and it becomes necessary to inquire whether a jurisdiction so conferred can be exercised.

The question whether an Act repugnant to the Constitution can become the law of the land, is a question deeply interesting to the United States; but,

---

[d]§ 13 of the Judiciary Act of 1789 provided: "That the Supreme Court shall have exclusive jurisdiction of all controversies of a civil nature, where a state is a party, except between a state and its citizens; and except also between a state and citizens of other states, or aliens, in which latter case it shall have original but not exclusive jurisdiction. And shall have exclusively all such jurisdiction of suits or proceedings against ambassadors or other public ministers, or their domestics, or domestic servants, as a court of law can have or exercise consistently with law of nations: and original, but not exclusive jurisdiction of all suits brought by ambassadors or other public ministers, or in which a consul, or vice consul, shall be a party. And the trial of issues of fact in the Supreme Court in all actions at law against citizens of the United States shall be by jury. The Supreme Court shall also have appellate jurisdiction from the circuit courts and courts of the several states, in the cases hereinafter specially provided for: and shall have power to issue writs of prohibition to the district courts, when proceeding as courts of admiralty and maritime jurisdiction, and writs of mandamus, in cases warranted by the principles and usages of law, to any courts appointed, or persons holding office under the authority of the United States."

Consider Van Alstyne, supra. at 15: "Textually, the provision regarding mandamus says nothing expressly as to whether it is part of original or appellate jurisdiction or both, and the clause itself does not speak at all of 'conferring jurisdiction' on the court. The grant of 'power' to issue the writ, however, is juxtaposed with the section of appellate jurisdiction and, in fact, follows the general description of appellate jurisdiction in the same sentence, being separated only by a semicolon. No textual mangling is required to confine it to appellate jurisdiction. Moreover, no mangling is required even if it attaches both to original and to appellate jurisdiction, not as an enlargement of either, but simply as a specification of power which the Court is authorized to use in cases which are *otherwise* appropriately under consideration. Since this case is not otherwise within the specified type of original jurisdiction (e.g., it is not a case in which a state is a party or a case against an ambassador), it should be dismissed."

[e]Consider Van Alstyne, supra. at 31: "It can be plausibly argued, that the Article III division of judicial power between appellate and original jurisdiction served a useful purpose other than that insisted upon by Marshall. Had Congress *not* adopted the Judiciary Act of 1789 or taken any other action describing Supreme Court jurisdiction, the division itself would have provided a guideline for the Court to follow until Congress was inclined to act." See also id. at 30–33.

By Marshall's interpretation of Art. III, may Congress authorize the Court to exercise appellate jurisdiction in cases involving foreign consuls? See *Börs c. Preston*, 111 U.S. 252, 4 S.Ct. 407, 28 L.Ed. 419 (1884).

happily, not of an intricacy proportioned to its interest. It seems only necessary to recognize certain principles, supposed to have been long and well established, to decide it.

That the people have an original right to establish, for their future government, such principles as, in their opinion, shall most conduce to their own happiness, is the basis on which the whole American fabric has been erected. The exercise of this original right is a very great exertion; nor can it nor ought it to be frequently repeated. The principles, therefore, so established, are deemed fundamental. And as the authority from which they proceed is supreme, and can seldom act, they are designed to be permanent.

This original and supreme will organizes the government, and assigns to different departments their respective powers. It may either stop here, or establish certain limits not to be transcended by those departments.

The government of the United States is of the latter description. The powers of the legislature are defined and limited; and that those limits may not be mistaken, or forgotten, the Constitution is written. To what purpose are powers limited, and to what purpose is that limitation committed to writing, if these limits may, at any time, be passed by those intended to be restrained? The distinction between a government with limited and unlimited powers is abolished, if those limits do not confine the persons on whom they are imposed, and if acts prohibited and acts allowed, are of equal obligation. It is a proposition too plain to be contested, that the Constitution controls any legislative act repugnant to it; or, that the legislature may alter the Constitution by an ordinary act.

Between these alternatives there is no middle ground. The Constitution is either a superior paramount law, unchangeable by ordinary means, or it is on a level with ordinary legislative acts, and, like other acts, is alterable when the legislature shall please to alter it.

If the former part of the alternative be true, then a legislative act contrary to the Constitution is not law: if the latter part be true, then written constitutions are absurd attempts, on the part of the people, to limit a power in its own nature illimitable.

Certainly all those who have framed written constitutions contemplate them as forming the fundamental and paramount law of the nation, and consequently, the theory of every such government must be, that an act of the legislature, repugnant to the Constitution, is void.

This theory is essentially attached to a written constitution, and is, consequently, to be considered, by this court, as one of the fundamental principles of our society. It is not therefore to be lost sight of in the further consideration of this subject.

If an act of the legislature, repugnant to the Constitution, is void, does it, notwithstanding its invalidity, bind the courts, and oblige them to give it effect? Or, in other words, though it be not law, does it constitute a rule as operative as if it was a law? This would be to overthrow in fact what was established in theory; and would seem, at first view, an absurdity too gross to be insisted on. It shall, however, receive a more attentive consideration.

It is emphatically the province and duty of the judicial department to say what the law is. Those who apply the rule to particular cases, must of necessity expound and interpret that rule. If two laws conflict with each other, the courts must decide on the operation of each.

So if a law be in opposition to the Constitution; if both the law and the Constitution apply to a particular case, so that the court must either decide that case conformably to the law, disregarding the Constitution; or conformably to the Constitution, disregarding the law; the court must determine which of these conflicting rules governs the case. This is of the very essence of judicial duty.

If, then, the courts are to regard the constitution, and the Constitution is superior to any ordinary act of the legislature, the Constitution, and not such ordinary act, must govern the case to which they both apply.

Those then who controvert the principle that the Constitution is to be considered in court, as a paramount law, are reduced to the necessity of maintaining that courts must close their eyes on the Constitution, and see only the law.

This doctrine would subvert the very foundation of all written constitutions. It would declare that an Act which, according to the principles and theory of our government, is entirely void, is yet, in practice, completely obligatory. It would declare that if the legislature shall do what is expressly forbidden, such Act, notwithstanding the express prohibition, is in reality effectual. It would be giving to the legislature a practical and real omnipotence, with the same breath which professes to restrict their powers within narrow limits. It is prescribing limits, and declaring that those limits may be passed at pleasure.

That it thus reduces to nothing what we have deemed the greatest improvement on political institutions, a written constitution, would of itself be sufficient, in America, where written constitutions have been viewed with so much reverence, for rejecting the construction. But the peculiar expressions of the Constitution of the United States furnish additional arguments in favor of its rejection.

The judicial power of the United States is extended to all cases arising under the Constitution.

Could it be the intention of those who gave this power, to say that in using it the Constitution should not be looked into? That a case arising under the Constitution should be decided without examining the instrument under which it arises?

This is too extravagant to be maintained.

In some cases, then, the Constitution must be looked into by the judges. And if they can open it at all, what part of it are they forbidden to read or to obey?

There are many other parts of the Constitution which serve to illustrate this subject.

It is declared that "no tax or duty shall be laid on articles exported from any State." Suppose a duty on the export of cotton, of tobacco, or of flour; and a suit instituted to recover it. Ought judgment to be rendered in such a case? Ought the judges to close their eyes on the Constitution, and only see the law?

The Constitution declares "that no bill of attainder or ex post facto law shall be passed."

If, however, such a bill should be passed, and a person should be prosecuted under it, must the court condemn to death those victims whom the Constitution endeavors to preserve?

"No person," says the Constitution, "shall be convicted of treason unless on the testimony of two witnesses to the same overt act, or on confession in open court."

Here the language of the Constitution is addressed especially to the courts. It prescribes, directly for them, a rule of evidence not to be departed from. If the legislature should change that rule, and declare one witness, or a confession out of court, sufficient for conviction, must the constitutional principle yield to the legislative act?

From these, and many other selections which might be made, it is apparent, that the framers of the constitution contemplated that instrument as a rule for the government of courts, as well as of the legislature.

Why otherwise does it direct the judges to take an oath to support it? This oath certainly applies in an especial manner, to their conduct in their official character. How immoral to impose it on them, if they were to be used as the instruments, and the knowing instruments, for violating what they swear to support!

The oath of office, too, imposed by the legislature, is completely demonstrative of the legislative opinion on this subject. It is in these words: "I do solemnly swear that I will administer justice without respect to persons, and do equal right to the poor and to the rich; and that I will faithfully and impartially discharge all the duties incumbent on me as _____, according to the best of my abilities and understanding agreeably to the Constitution and laws of the United States."

Why does a judge swear to discharge his duties agreeably to the Constitution of the United States, if that constitution forms no rule for his government? If it is closed upon him, and cannot be inspected by him?

If such be the real state of things, this is worse than solemn mockery. To prescribe, or to take this oath, becomes equally a crime.

It is also not entirely unworthy of observation, that in declaring what shall be the supreme law of the land, the Constitution itself is first mentioned; and not the laws of the United States generally, but those only which shall be made in pursuance of the Constitution, have that rank.

Thus, the particular phraseology of the Constitution of the United States confirms and strengthens the principle, supposed to be essential to all written constitutions, that a law repugnant to the Constitution is void; and that courts, as well as other departments, are bound by that instrument.

The rule must be discharged.[f]

MIRANDA V. ARIZONA

Supreme Court of the United States, 1966.

384 U.S. 436, 86 S.Ct. 1602, 16 L.Ed.2d 694.
Mr. Chief Justice WARREN delivered the opinion of the Court.

* * *

Our holding will be spelled out with some specificity in the pages which follow but briefly stated it is this: the prosecution may not use statements, whether exculpatory or inculpatory, stemming from custodial interrogation of the defendant unless it demonstrates the use of procedural safeguards effective to secure the privilege against self-incrimination. By custodial interrogation, we mean questioning initiated by law

[f]Six days later, the Circuit Court Act Repeal Law was held to be constitutional, *Stuart v. Laird*, 5 U.S. (1 Cranch) 299, 2 L.Ed. 115 (1803). After *Marbury*, the Court did not hold an act of Congress unconstitutional until *Dred Scott v. Sandford*, 60 U.S. (19 How.) 393, 15 L.Ed. 691 (1857).

enforcement officers after a person has been taken into custody or otherwise deprived of his freedom of action in any significant way.[1] As for the procedural safeguards to be employed, unless other fully effective means are devised to inform accused persons of their right of silence and to assure a continuous opportunity to exercise it, the following measures are required. Prior to any questioning, the person must be warned that he has a right to remain silent, that any statement he does make may be used as evidence against him, and that he has a right to the presence of an attorney, either retained or appointed. The defendant may waive effectuation of these rights, provided the waiver is made voluntarily, knowingly and intelligently. If, however, he indicates in any manner and at any stage of the process that he wishes to consult with an attorney before speaking there can be no questioning. Likewise, if the individual is alone and indicates in any manner that he does not wish to be interrogated, the police may not question him. The mere fact that he may have answered some questions or volunteered some statements on his own does not deprive him of the right to refrain from answering any further inquiries until he has consulted with an attorney and thereafter consents to be questioned.

I

The constitutional issue we decide in each of these cases is the admissibility of statements obtained from a defendant questioned while in custody or otherwise deprived of his freedom of action in any significant way. In each, the defendant was questioned by police officers, detectives, or a prosecuting attorney in a room in which he was cut off from the outside world. In none of these cases was the defendant given a full and effective warning of his rights at the outset of the interrogation process. In all the cases, the questioning elicited oral admissions, and in three of them, signed statements as well which were admitted at their trials. They all thus share salient features—incommunicado interrogation of individuals in a police-dominated atmosphere, resulting in self-incriminating statements without full warnings of constitutional rights.

An understanding of the nature and setting of this in-custody interrogation is essential to our decisions today. The difficulty in depicting what transpires at

such interrogations stems from the fact that in this country they have largely taken place incommunicado.

* * *

A valuable source of information about present police practices, however, may be found in various police manuals and texts which document procedures employed with success in the past, and which recommend various other effective tactics. These texts are used by law enforcement agencies themselves as guides. It should be noted that these texts professedly present the most enlightened and effective means presently used to obtain statements through custodial interrogation. By considering these texts and other data, it is possible to describe procedures observed and noted around the country.

The officers are told by the manuals that the "principal psychological factor contributing to a successful interrogation is privacy—being alone with the person under interrogation."[2]

* * *

To highlight the isolation and unfamiliar surroundings, the manuals instruct the police to display an air of confidence in the suspect's guilt and from outward appearance to maintain only an interest in confirming certain details. The guilt of the subject is to be posited as a fact. The interrogator should direct his comments toward the reasons why the subject committed the act, rather than court failure by asking the subject whether he did it. Like other men, perhaps the subject has had a bad family life, had an unhappy childhood, had too much to drink, had an unrequited desire for women. The officers are instructed to minimize the moral seriousness of the offense, to cast blame on the victim or on society. These tactics are designed to put the subject in a psychological state where his story is but an elaboration of what the police purport to know already—that he is guilty. Explanations to the contrary are dismissed and discouraged.

* * *

The manuals suggest that the suspect be offered legal excuses for his actions in order to obtain an initial admission of guilt. Where there is a suspected revenge-killing, for example, the interrogator may say:

"Joe, you probably didn't go out looking for
this fellow with the purpose of shooting him.

---

[1]This is what we meant in *Escobedo* when we spoke of an investigation which had focused on an accused.

[2]Inbau & Reid. *Criminal Interrogation and Confessions* (1962), at 1.

My guess is, however, that you expected something from him and that's why you carried a gun—for your own protection. You knew him for what he was, no good. Then when you met him he probably started using foul, abusive language and he gave some indication that he was about to pull a gun on you, and that's when you had to act to save your own life. That's about it, isn't it, Joe?"[3]

Having then obtained the admission of shooting, the interrogator is advised to refer to circumstantial evidence which negates the self-defense explanation. This should enable him to secure the entire story. One text notes that "Even if he fails to do so, the inconsistency between the subject's original denial of the shooting and his present admission of at least doing the shooting will serve to deprive him of a self-defense 'out' at the time of trial."

When the techniques described above prove unavailing, the texts recommend they be alternated with a show of some hostility. One ploy often used has been termed the "friendly-unfriendly" or the "Mutt and Jeff" act:

"*** In this technique, two agents are employed. Mutt, the relentless investigator, who knows the subject is guilty and is not going to waste any time. He's sent a dozen men away for this crime and he's going to send the subject away for the full term. Jeff, on the other hand, is obviously a kindhearted man. He has a family himself. He has a brother who was involved in a little scrape like this. He disapproves of Mutt and his tactics and will arrange to get him off the case if the subject will cooperate. He can't hold Mutt off for very long. The subject would be wise to make a quick decision. The technique is applied by having both investigators present while Mutt acts out his role. Jeff may stand by quietly and demur at some of Mutt's tactics. When Jeff makes his plea for cooperation, Mutt is not present in the room."

The interrogators sometimes are instructed to induce a confession out of trickery. The technique here is quite effective in crimes which require identification or which run in series. In the identification situation, the interrogator may take a break in his questioning to place the subject among a group of men in a line-up. "The witness or complainant (previously coached, if necessary) studies the line-up and confidently points out the subject as the guilty party."[4] Then the questioning resumes "as though there were now no doubt about the guilt of the subject." A variation on this technique is called the "reverse line-up":

"The accused is placed in a line-up, but this time he is identified by several fictitious witnesses or victims who associated him with different offenses. It is expected that the subject will become desperate and confess to the offense under investigation in order to escape from the false accusations."[5]

The manuals also contain instructions for police on how to handle the individual who refuses to discuss the matter entirely, or who asks for an attorney or relatives. The examiner is to concede him the right to remain silent. "This usually has a very undermining effect. First of all, he is disappointed in his expectation of an unfavorable reaction on the part of the interrogator. Secondly, a concession of this right to remain silent impresses the subject with the apparent fairness of his interrogator."[6] After this psychological conditioning, however, the officer is told to point out the incriminating significance of the suspect's refusal to talk:

"Joe, you have a right to remain silent. That's your privilege and I'm the last person in the world who'll try to take it away from you. If that's the way you want to leave this, O.K. But let me ask you this. Suppose you were in my shoes and I were in yours and you called me in to ask me about this and I told you, 'I don't want to answer any of your questions.' You'd think I had something to hide, and you'd probably be right in thinking that. That's exactly what I'll have to think about you, and so will everybody else. So let's sit here and talk this whole thing over."[7]

Few will persist in their initial refusal to talk, it is said, if this monologue is employed correctly.

---

[3]Inbau & Reid, supra, at 40.

[4]O'Hara, *Fundamentals of Criminal Investigation* (1956) at 105–106.

[5]Id., at 106.

[6]Inbau & Reid, supra, at 111.

[7]Ibid.

In the event that the subject wishes to speak to a relative or an attorney, the following advice is tendered:

"[T]he interrogator should respond by suggesting that the subject first tell the truth to the interrogator himself rather than get anyone else involved in the matter. If the request is for an attorney, the interrogator may suggest that the subject save himself or his family the expense of any such professional service, particularly if he is innocent of the offense under investigation. The interrogator may also add, 'Joe, I'm only looking for the truth, and if you're telling the truth, that's it. You can handle this by yourself.' "[8]

* * *

Even without employing brutality, the "third degree" or the specific stratagems described above, the very fact of custodial interrogation exacts a heavy toll on individual liberty and trades on the weakness of individuals.

* * *

In the cases before us today, given this background, we concern ourselves primarily with this interrogation atmosphere and the evils it can bring. In No. 759, *Miranda v. Arizona*, the police arrested the defendant and took him to a special interrogation room where they secured a confession. In No. 760, *Vignera v. New York*, the defendant made oral admissions to the police after interrogation in the afternoon, and then signed an inculpatory statement upon being questioned by an assistant district attorney later the same evening. In No. 761, *Westover v. United States*, the defendant was handed over to the Federal Bureau of Investigation by local authorities after they had detained and interrogated him for a lengthy period, both at night and the following morning. After some two hours of questioning, the federal officers had obtained signed statements from the defendant. Lastly, in No. 584, *California v. Stewart*, the local police held the defendant five days in the station and interrogated him on nine separate occasions before they secured his inculpatory statement.

In these cases, we might not find the defendants' statements to have been involuntary in traditional terms. Our concern for adequate safeguards to protect precious Fifth Amendment rights is, of course, not lessened in the slightest. In each of the cases, the defendant was thrust into an unfamiliar atmosphere and run through menacing police interrogation procedures. The potentiality for compulsion is forcefully apparent, for example, in *Miranda*, where the indigent Mexican defendant was a seriously disturbed individual with pronounced sexual fantasies, and in *Stewart*, in which the defendant was an indigent Los Angeles Negro who had dropped out of school in the sixth grade. To be sure, the records do not evince overt physical coercion or patent psychological ploys. The fact remains that in none of these cases did the officers undertake to afford appropriate safeguards at the outset of the interrogation to insure that the statements were truly the product of free choice.

It is obvious that such an interrogation environment is created for no purpose other than to subjugate the individual to the will of his examiner. This atmosphere carries its own badge of intimidation. To be sure, this is not physical intimidation, but it is equally destructive of human dignity. The current practice of incommunicado interrogation is at odds with one of our Nation's most cherished principles—that the individual may not be compelled to incriminate himself. Unless adequate protective devices are employed to dispel the compulsion inherent in custodial surroundings, no statement obtained from the defendant can truly be the product of his free choice.

From the foregoing, we can readily perceive an intimate connection between the privilege against self-incrimination and police custodial questioning. It is fitting to turn to history and precedent underlying the Self-Incrimination Clause to determine its applicability in this situation.

II

We sometimes forget how long it has taken to establish the privilege against self-incrimination, the sources from which it came and the fervor with which it was defended. Its roots go back into ancient times. Perhaps the critical historical event shedding light on its origins and evolution was the trial of one John Lilburn, a vocal anti-Stuart Leveller, who was made to take the Star Chamber Oath in 1637. The oath would have bound him to answer to all questions posed to him on any subject. The Trial of *John Lilburn and John Wharton*,

---

[8]Inbau & Reid, *supra*, at 112.

3 How.St.Tr. 1315 (1637). He resisted the oath and declaimed the proceedings, stating:

> "Another fundamental right I then contended for, was, that no man's conscience ought to be racked by oaths imposed, to answer to questions concerning himself in matters criminal, or pretended to be so." Haller & Davies, The Leveller Tracts 1647–1653, p.454 (1944).

On account of the *Lilburn* Trial, Parliament abolished the inquisitorial Court of Star Chamber and went further in giving him generous reparation. The lofty principles to which Lilburn had appealed during his trial gained popular acceptance in England. These sentiments worked their way over to the Colonies and were implanted after great struggle into the Bill of Rights. Those who framed our Constitution and the Bill of Rights were ever aware of subtle encroachments on individual liberty.

* * *

The question in these cases is whether the privilege is fully applicable during a period of custodial interrogation.

* * *

This question, in fact, could have been taken as settled in federal courts almost 70 years ago, when, in *Bram v. United States,* 168 U.S. 532, 542, 18 S.Ct. 183, 187, 42 L.Ed. 568 (1897), this Court held:

> "In criminal trials, in the courts of the United States, wherever a question arises whether a confession is incompetent because not voluntary, the issue is controlled by that portion of the fifth amendment * * * commanding that no person 'shall be compelled in any criminal case to be a witness against himself.'"

* * *

Because of the adoption by Congress of Rule 5 (a) of the Federal Rules of Criminal Procedure, and the Court's effectuation of that Rule in *McNabb v. United States,* 318 U.S. 332, 63 S.Ct. 608, 87 L.Ed. 819 (1943), and *Mallory v. United States,* 354 U.S. 449, 77 S.Ct. 1356, 1 L.E.2d 1479 (1957), we have had little occasion in the past quarter century to reach the constitutional issues in dealing with federal interrogations. These supervisory rules, requiring production of an arrested person before a commissioner "without unnecessary delay" and excluding evidence obtained in default of that statutory obligation, were nonetheless responsive to the same considerations of Fifth Amendment policy that unavoidably face us now as to the States.

* * *

Our decision in *Malloy v. Hogan,* 378 U.S. 1, 84 S.Ct. 1489, 12 L.Ed.2d 653 (1964), necessitates an examination of the scope of the privilege in state cases as well. In *Malloy,* we squarely held the privilege applicable to the States, and held that the substantive standards underlying the privilege applied with full force to state court proceedings.

* * *

Aside from the holding itself, the reasoning in *Malloy* made clear what had already become apparent—that the substantive and procedural safeguards surrounding admissibility of confessions in state cases had become exceedingly exacting, reflecting all the policies embedded in the privilege, 378 U.S., at 7–8. The voluntariness doctrine in the state cases, as *Malloy* indicates, encompasses all interrogation practices which are likely to exert such pressure upon an individual as to disable him from making a free and rational choice. The implications of this proposition were elaborated in our decision in *Escobedo v. Illinois,* 378 U.S. 478, decided one week after *Malloy* applied the privilege to the States.

Our holding there stressed the fact that the police had not advised the defendant of his constitutional privilege to remain silent at the outset of the interrogation, and we drew attention to that fact at several points in the decision, 378 U.S., at 483, 485, 491. This was no isolated factor, but an essential ingredient in our decision. The entire thrust of police interrogation there, as in all the cases today, was to put the defendant in such an emotional state as to impair his capacity for rational judgment. The abdication of the constitutional privilege—the choice on his part to speak to the police—was not made knowingly or competently because of the failure to apprise him of his rights; the compelling atmosphere of the in-custody interrogation, and not an independent decision on his part, caused the defendant to speak.

A different phase of the *Escobedo* decision was significant in its attention to the absence of counsel during the questioning. There, as in the cases today, we sought a protective device to dispel the compelling atmosphere of the interrogation. In *Escobedo,* however, the police did not relieve the defendant of the anxieties which they had created in the interrogation rooms. Rather, they denied his request for the assistance of counsel, 378 U.S., at 481, 488, 491. This heightened his dilemma, and made his later statements the product of this compulsion.

* * *

It was in this manner that *Escobedo* explicated another facet of the pretrial privilege, noted in many of the Court's prior decisions: the protection of rights at trial. That counsel is present when statements are taken from an individual during interrogation obviously enhances the integrity of the fact-finding processes in court. The presence of an attorney, and the warnings delivered to the individual, enable the defendant under otherwise compelling circumstances to tell his story without fear, effectively, and in a way that eliminates the evils in the interrogation process.

* * *

III

Today, then, there can be no doubt that the Fifth Amendment privilege is available outside of criminal court proceedings and serves to protect persons in all settings in which their freedom of action is curtailed in any significant way from being compelled to incriminate themselves. We have concluded that without proper safeguards the process of in-custody interrogation of persons suspected or accused of crime contains inherently compelling pressures which work to undermine the individual's will to resist and to compel him to speak where he would not otherwise do so freely. In order to combat these pressures and to permit a full opportunity to exercise the privilege against self-incrimination, the accused must be adequately and effectively apprised of his rights and the exercise of those rights must be fully honored.

It is impossible for us to foresee the potential alternatives for protecting the privilege which might be devised by Congress or the States in the exercise of their creative rule-making capacities. Therefore we cannot say that the Constitution necessarily requires adherence to any particular solution for the inherent compulsions of the interrogation process as it is presently conducted.

Our decision in no way creates a constitutional straitjacket which will handicap sound efforts at reform, nor is it intended to have this effect. We encourage Congress and the States to continue their laudable search for increasingly effective ways of protecting the rights of the individual while promoting efficient enforcement of our criminal laws. However, unless we are shown other procedures which are at least as effective in apprising accused persons of their right of silence and in assuring a continuous opportunity to exercise it, the following safeguards must be observed.

At the outset, if a person in custody is to be subjected to interrogation, he must first be informed in clear and unequivocal terms that he has the right to remain silent. For those unaware of the privilege, the warning is needed simply to make them aware of it—the threshold requirement for an intelligent decision as to its exercise. More important, such a warning is an absolute prerequisite in overcoming the inherent pressures of the interrogation atmosphere. It is not just the subnormal or woefully ignorant who succumb to an interrogator's imprecations, whether implied or expressly stated, that the interrogation will continue until a confession is obtained or that silence in the face of accusation is itself damning and will bode ill when presented to a jury. Further, the warning will show the individual that his interrogators are prepared to recognize his privilege should he choose to exercise it.

The fifth Amendment privilege is so fundamental to our system of constitutional rule and the expedient of giving an adequate warning as to the availability of the privilege so simple, we will not pause to inquire in individual cases whether the defendant was aware of his rights without a warning being given. Assessments of the knowledge the defendant possessed, based on information as to his age, education, intelligence, or prior contact with authorities, can never be more than speculation; a warning is a clearcut fact. More important, whatever the background of the person interrogated, a warning at the time of the interrogation is indispensable to overcome its pressures and to insure that the individual knows he is free to exercise the privilege at that point in time.

The warning of the right to remain silent must be accompanied by the explanation that anything said can and will be used against the individual in court. This warning is needed in order to make him aware not only of the privilege, but also of the consequences of forgoing it. It is only through an awareness of these consequences that there can be any assurance of real understanding and intelligent exercise of the privilege. Moreover, this warning may serve to make the individual more acutely aware that he is faced with a phase of the adversary system—that he is not in the presence of persons acting solely in his interest.

The circumstances surrounding in-custody interrogation can operate very quickly to overbear the will of one merely made aware of his privilege by his interrogators. Therefore the right to have counsel present at the interrogation is indispensable to the protection of the Fifth Amendment privilege under the system we delineate today.

* * *

The presence of counsel at the interrogation may serve several significant subsidiary functions as well. If the accused decides to talk to his interrogators, the assistance of counsel can mitigate the dangers of untrustworthiness. With a lawyer present the likelihood that the police will practice coercion is reduced, and if coercion is nevertheless exercised the lawyer can testify to it in court. The presence of a lawyer can also help to guarantee that the accused gives a fully accurate statement to the police and that the statement is rightly reported by the prosecution at trial.

An individual need not make a pre-interrogation request for a lawyer. While such request affirmatively secures his right to have one, his failure to ask for a lawyer does not constitute a waiver. No effective waiver of the right to counsel during interrogation can be recognized unless specifically made after the warnings we here delineate have been given. The accused who does not know his rights and therefore does not make a request may be the person who most needs counsel.

* * *

Accordingly we hold that an individual held for interrogation must be clearly informed that he has the right to consult with a lawyer and to have the lawyer with him during interrogation under the system for protecting the privilege we delineate today. As with the warnings of the right to remain silent and that anything stated can be used in evidence against him, this warning is an absolute prerequisite to interrogation. No amount of circumstantial evidence that the person may have been aware of this right will suffice to stand in its stead. Only through such a

warning is there ascertainable assurance that the accused was aware of this right.

If an individual indicates that he wishes the assistance of counsel before any interrogation occurs, the authorities cannot rationally ignore or deny his request on the basis that the individual does not have or cannot afford a retained attorney.

* * *

Denial of counsel to the indigent at the time of interrogation while allowing an attorney to those who can afford one would be no more supportable by reason or logic than the similar situation at trial and on appeal struck down in *Gideon v. Wainwright*, 372 U.S. 335, 83 S.Ct. 792, L.Ed.2d 799 (1963), and *Douglas v. People of State of California*, 372 U.S. 353, 83 S.Ct. 814, 9 L.Ed.2d 811 (1963).

In order fully to apprise a person interrogated of the extent of his rights under this system then, it is necessary to warn him not only that he has the right to consult with an attorney, but also that if he is indigent a lawyer will be appointed to represent him. Without this additional warning, the admonition of the right to consult with counsel would often be understood as meaning only that he can consult with a lawyer if he has one or has the funds to obtain one. The warning of a right to counsel would be hollow if not couched in terms that would convey to the indigent—the person most often subjected to interrogation—the knowledge that he too has a right to have counsel present. As with the warnings of the right to remain silent and of the general right to counsel, only by effective and express explanation to the indigent of this right can there be assurance that he was truly in a position to exercise it.

Once warnings have been given, the subsequent procedure is clear. If the individual indicates in any manner, at any time prior to or during questioning, that he wishes to remain silent, the interrogation must cease. At this point he has shown that he intends to exercise his Fifth Amendment privilege; any statement taken after the person invokes his privilege cannot be other than the product of compulsion, subtle or otherwise. Without the right to cut off questioning, the setting of in-custody interrogation operates on the individual to overcome free choice in producing a statement after the privilege has been once invoked. If the individual states that he wants an attorney, the interrogation must cease until an attorney is present. At that time, the individual must have an opportunity to confer with the attorney and to have him present during any subsequent questioning. If the individual cannot obtain an attorney and he indicates that he wants one before speaking to police, they must respect his decision to remain silent.

This does not mean, as some have suggested, that each police station must have a "station house lawyer" present at all times to advise prisoners. It does mean, however, that if police propose to interrogate a person they must make known to him that he is entitled to a lawyer and that if he cannot afford one, a lawyer will be provided for him prior to any interrogation. If authorities conclude that they will not provide counsel during a reasonable period of time in which investigation in the field is carried out, they may refrain from doing so without violating the person's Fifth Amendment privilege so long as they do not question him during that time.

If the interrogation continues without the presence of an attorney and a statement is taken, a heavy burden rests on the government to demonstrate that the defendant knowingly and intelligently waived his privilege against self-incrimination and his right to retained or appointed counsel. *Escobedo v. State of Illinois*, 378 U.S. 478, 490, n. 14, 84 S.Ct. 1758, 1764, 12 L.Ed.2d 977. This Court has always set high standards of proof for the waiver of constitutional rights, *Johnson v. Zerbst*, 304 U.S. 458, 58 S.Ct. 1019, 82 L.Ed. 1461 (1938), and we reassert these standards as applied to in-custody interrogation. Since the State is responsible for establishing the isolated circumstances under which the interrogation takes place and has the only means of making available corroborated evidence of warnings given during incommunicado interrogation, the burden is rightly on its shoulders.

An express statement that the individual is willing to make a statement and does not want an attorney followed closely by a statement could constitute a waiver. But a valid waiver will not be presumed simply from the silence of the accused after warnings are given or simply from the fact that a confession was in fact eventually obtained. A statement we made in *Carnley v. Cochran*, 369 U.S. 506, 516, 82 S.Ct. 884, 890, 8 L.Ed.2d 70 (1962), is applicable here:

> "Presuming waiver from a silent record is impermissible. The record must show, or there must be an allegation and evidence which show, that an accused was offered counsel but

intelligently and understandingly rejected the offer. Anything less is not waiver."

Moreover, where in-custody interrogation is involved, there is no room for the contention that the privilege is waived if the individual answers some questions or gives some information on his own prior to invoking his right to remain silent when interrogated.

Whatever the testimony of the authorities as to waiver of rights by an accused, the fact of lengthy interrogation or incommunicado incarceration before a statement is made is strong evidence that the accused did not validly waive his rights. In these circumstances the fact that the individual eventually made a statement is consistent with the conclusion that the compelling influence of the interrogation finally forced him to do so. It is inconsistent with any notion of a voluntary relinquishment of the privilege. Moreover, any evidence that the accused was threatened, tricked, or cajoled into a waiver will, of course, show that the defendant did not voluntarily waive his privilege. The requirement of warnings and waiver of rights is a fundamental with respect to the Fifth Amendment privilege and not simply a preliminary ritual to existing methods of interrogation.

The warnings required and the waiver necessary in accordance with our opinion today are, in the absence of a fully effective equivalent, prerequisites to the admissibility of any statement made by a defendant. No distinction can be drawn between statements which are direct confessions and statements which amount to "admissions" of part or all of an offense. The privilege against self-incrimination protects the individual from being compelled to incriminate himself in any manner, it does not distinguish degrees of incrimination. Similarly, for precisely the same reason, no distinction may be drawn between inculpatory statements and statements alleged to be merely "exculpatory." If a statement made were in fact truly exculpatory it would, of course, never be used by the prosecution. In fact, statements merely intended to be exculpatory by the defendant are often used to impeach his testimony at trial or to demonstrate untruths in the statement given under interrogation and thus to prove guilt by implication. These statements are incriminating in any meaningful sense of the word and may not be used without the full warnings and effective waiver required for any other statement. In *Escobedo* itself, the defendant fully intended his accusation of another as the slayer to be exculpatory as to himself.

The principles announced today deal with the protection which must be given to the privilege against self-incrimination when the individual is first subjected to police interrogation while in custody at the station or otherwise deprived of his freedom of action in any significant way. It is at this point that our adversary system of criminal proceedings commences, distinguishing itself at the outset from the inquisitorial system recognized in some countries. Under the system of warnings we delineate today or under any other system which may be devised and found effective, the safeguards to be erected about the privilege must come into play at this point.

Our decision is not intended to hamper the traditional function of police officers in investigating crime. See *Escobedo v. State of Illinois*, 378 U.S. 478, 492, 84 S.Ct. 1758, 1765. When an individual is in custody on probable cause, the police may, of course, seek out evidence in the field to be used at trial against him. Such investigation may include inquiry of persons not under restraint. General on-the-scene questioning as to facts surrounding a crime or other general questioning of citizens in the fact-finding process is not affected by our holding. It is an act of responsible citizenship for individuals to give whatever information they may have to aid in law enforcement. In such situations the compelling atmosphere inherent in the process of in-custody interrogation is not necessarily present.

In dealing with statements obtained through interrogation, we do not purport to find all confessions inadmissible. Confessions remain a proper element in law enforcement. Any statement given freely and voluntarily without any compelling influences is, of course, admissible in evidence. The fundamental import of the privilege while an individual is in custody is not whether he is allowed to talk to the police without the benefit of warnings and counsel, but whether he can be interrogated. There is no requirement that police stop a person who enters a police station and states that he wishes to confess to a crime, or a person who calls the police to offer a confession or any other statement he desires to make. Volunteered statements of any kind are not barred by the Fifth Amendment and their admissibility is not affected by our holding today.

* * *

IV

* * *

In announcing these principles, we are not unmindful of the burdens which law enforcement officials must bear, often under trying circumstances. We also fully recognize the obligation of all citizens to aid in enforcing the criminal laws. This Court, while protecting individual rights, has always given ample latitude to law enforcement agencies in the legitimate exercise of their duties. The limits we have placed on the interrogation process should not constitute an undue interference with a proper system of law enforcement. As we have noted, our decision does not in any way preclude police from carrying out their traditional investigatory functions. Although confessions may play an important role in some convictions, the cases before us present graphic examples of the overstatement of the "need" for confessions. In each case authorities conducted interrogations ranging up to five days in duration despite the presence, through standard investigating practices, of considerable evidence against each defendant.

* * *

Over the years the Federal Bureau of Investigation has compiled an exemplary record of effective law enforcement while advising any suspect or arrested person, at the outset of an interview, that he is not required to make a statement, that any statement may be used against him in court, that the individual may obtain the services of an attorney of his own choice and, more recently, that he has a right to free counsel if he is unable to pay. A letter received from the Solicitor General in response to a question from the Bench makes it clear that the present pattern of warnings and respect for the rights of the individual followed as a practice by the FBI is consistent with the procedure which we delineate today. It states:

"At the oral argument of the above cause, Mr. Justice Fortas asked whether I could provide certain information as to the practices followed by the Federal Bureau of Investigation. I have directed these questions to the attention of the Director of the Federal Bureau of Investigation and am submitting herewith a statement of the questions and of the answers which we have received.

"'(1) When an individual is interviewed by agents of the Bureau, what warning is given to him?

" 'The standard warning long given by Special Agents of the FBI to both suspects and persons under arrest is that the person has a right to say nothing and a right to counsel, and that any statement he does make may be used against him in court. Examples of this warning are to be found in the *Westover* case at 342 F.2d 684 (1965), and *Jackson v. U.S.*, [119 U.S.App.D.C. 100] 337 F.2d 136 (1964), cert. den. 380 U.S. 935, 85 S.Ct. 1353.

" 'After passage of the Criminal Justice Act of 1964, which provides free counsel for Federal defendants unable to pay, we added to our instructions to Special Agents the requirement that any person who is under arrest for an offense under FBI jurisdiction, or whose arrest is contemplated following the interview, must also be advised of his right to free counsel if he is unable to pay, and the fact that such counsel will be assigned by the Judge. At the same time, we broadened the right to counsel warning to read counsel of his own choice, or anyone else with whom he might wish to speak.

" '(2) When is the warning given?

" 'The FBI warning is given to a suspect at the very outset of the interview ***, as shown in the *Westover* case, cited above. The warning may be given to a person arrested as soon as practicable after the arrest *** but in any event it must precede the interview with the person for a confession or admission of his own guilt.

" '(3) What is the Bureau's practice in the event that (a) the individual requests counsel and (b) counsel appears?

" 'When the person who has been warned of his right to counsel decides that he wishes to consult with counsel before making a statement, the interview is terminated at that point, *Shultz v. U.S.*, 351 F.2d 287 ([10 Cir.] 1965). It may be continued, however, as to all matters *other* than the person's own guilt or innocence. If he is indecisive in his request for counsel, there may be some question on whether he did or did not waive counsel. Situations of this kind must necessarily be left to the judgment of the interviewing Agent.

* * *

" '(4) What is the Bureau's practice if the individual requests counsel, but cannot afford to retain an attorney?

" 'If any person being interviewed after warning of counsel decides that he wishes to consult with counsel before proceeding further the interview is terminated, as shown above. FBI Agents do not pass judgment on the ability of the person to pay for counsel. They do, however, advise those who have been arrested for an offense under FBI jurisdiction, or whose arrest is contemplated following the interview, of a right to free counsel *if* they are unable to pay, and the availability of such counsel from the Judge.' "

The practice of the FBI can readily be emulated by state and local enforcement agencies. The argument that the FBI deals with different crimes than are dealt with by state authorities does not mitigate the significance of the FBI experience.

The experience in some other countries also suggests that the danger to law enforcement in curbs on interrogation is overplayed. The English procedure since 1912 under the Judge's Rules is significant. As recently strengthened, the Rules require that a cautionary warning be given an accused by a police officer as soon as he has evidence that affords reasonable grounds for suspicion; they also require that any statement made be given by the accused without questioning by police. The right of the individual to consult with an attorney during this period is expressly recognized.

The safeguards present under Scottish law may be even greater than in England. Scottish judicial decisions bar use in evidence of most confessions obtained through police interrogation. In India, confessions made to police not in the presence of a magistrate have been excluded by rule of evidence since 1872, at a time when it operated under British law. Identical provisions appear in the Evidence Ordinance of Ceylon, enacted in 1895. Similarly, in our country the Uniform Code of Military Justice has long provided that no suspect may be interrogated without first being warned of his right not to make a statement and that any statement he makes may be used against him. Denial of the right to consult counsel during interrogation has also been proscribed by military tribunals. There appears to have been no marked detrimental effect on criminal law enforcement in these jurisdictions as a result of these rules. Conditions of law enforcement in our country are sufficiently similar to permit reference to this experience as assurance that lawlessness will not result from warning an individual of his rights or allowing him to exercise them. Moreover, it is consistent with our legal system that we give at least as much protection to these rights as is given in the jurisdictions described. We deal in our country with rights grounded in a specific requirement of the Fifth Amendment of the Constitution, whereas other jurisdictions arrived at their conclusions on the basis of principles of justice not so specifically defined.

* * *

V

* * *

Therefore, in accordance with the foregoing, the judgments of the Supreme Court of Arizona in No. 759, of the New York Court of Appeals in No. 760, and of the Court of Appeals for the Ninth Circuit in No. 761 are reversed. The judgment of the Supreme Court of California in No. 584 is affirmed. It is so ordered.

* * *

Mr. Justice HARLAN, whom Mr. Justice STEWART and Mr. Justice WHITE join, dissenting.

* * *

The earliest confession cases in this Court emerged from federal prosecutions and were settled on a nonconstitutional basis, the Court adopting the common-law rule that the absence of inducements, promises, and threats made a confession voluntary and admissible. *Hopt v. People of Territory of Utah,* 110 U.S. 574, 4 S.Ct. 202, 28 L.Ed. 262; *Pierce v. United States,* 160 U.S. 355, 16 S.Ct. 321, 40 L.Ed. 454. While a later case said the Fifth Amendment privilege controlled admissibility, this proposition was not itself developed in subsequent decisions. The Court did, however, heighten the test of admissibility in federal trials to one of voluntariness "in fact," *Ziang Sung Wan v. United States,* 266 U.S. 1, 14, 45 S.Ct. 1, 3, 69 L.Ed. 131 and then by and large left federal judges to apply the same standards the Court began to derive in a string of state court cases.

This new line of decisions, testing admissibility by the Due Process Clause, began in 1936 with *Brown v. State of Mississippi,* 297 U.S. 278, 56 S.Ct. 461, 80 L.Ed. 682, and must now embrace somewhat more than 30 full

opinions of the Court. While the voluntariness rubric was repeated in many instances, the Court never pinned it down to a single meaning but on the contrary infused it with a number of different values. To travel quickly over the main themes, there was an initial emphasis on reliability, e.g., *Ward v. State of Texas,* 316 U.S. 547, 62 S.Ct. 1139, 86 L.Ed. 1663, supplemented by concern over the legality and fairness of the police practices, e.g., *Ashcraft v. State of Tennessee,* 322 U.S. 143, 64 S.Ct. 921, 88 L.Ed. 1192, in an "accusatorial" system of law enforcement, *Watts v. State of Indiana,* 338 U.S. 49, 54, 69 S.Ct. 1347, 1350, 93 L.Ed. 1801, and eventually by close attention to the individual's state of mind and capacity for effective choice, e.g., *Gallegos v. State of Colorado,* 370 U.S. 49, 82 S.Ct. 1209, 8 L.Ed.2d 325. The outcome was a continuing re-evaluation on the facts of each case of *how much* pressure on the suspect was permissible.[9]

Among the criteria often taken into account were threats or imminent danger, e.g., *Payne v. State of Arkansas,* 356 U.S. 560, 78 S.Ct. 844, 2 L.Ed.2d 975, physical deprivations such as lack of sleep or food, e.g., *Reck v. Pate,* 367 U.S. 433, 81 S.Ct. 1541, 6 L.Ed. 2d 948, repeated or extended interrogation, e.g., *Chambers v. State of Florida,* 309 U.S. 227, 60 S.Ct. 472, 84 L.Ed. 716, limits on access to counsel or friends, *Crooker v. State of California,* 357 U.S. 433, 78 S.Ct. 1287, 2 L.Ed.2d 1448; *Cicenia v. La Gay,* 357 U.S. 504, 78 S.Ct. 1297, 2 L.Ed.2d 1523, length and illegality of detention under state law, e.g., *Haynes v. State of Washington,* 373 U.S. 503, 83 S.Ct. 1336, 10 L.Ed.2d 513, and individual weakness or incapacities, *Lynumn v. State of Illinois,* 372 U.S. 528, 83 S.Ct. 917, 9 L.Ed.2d 922. Apart from direct physical coercion, however, no single default or fixed combination of defaults guaranteed exclusion, and synopses of the cases would serve little use because the overall gauge has been steadily changing, usually in the direction of restricting admissibility.

* * *

I turn now to the Court's asserted reliance on the Fifth Amendment, an approach which I frankly regard

---

[9]Bator & Vorenberg, *Arrest, Detention, Interrogation and the Right to Counsel,* 66 Col.L.Rev. 62. 73 (1966): "In fact, the concept of involuntariness seems to be used by the courts as a shorthand to refer to practices which are repellent to civilized standards of decency or which, under the circumstances, are thought to apply a degree of pressure to an individual which unfairly impairs his capacity to make a rational choice."

as a *trompe l'oeil.* * * * Historically, the privilege against self-incrimination did not bear at all on the use of extra-legal confessions, for which distinct standards evolved; indeed, "the *history* of the two principles is wide apart, differing by one hundred years in origin, and derived through separate lines of precedents. * * *" 8 Wigmore, Evidence § 2266, at 401 (McNaughton rev. 1961). Practice under the two doctrines has also differed in a number of important respects.

* * *

Having decided that the Fifth Amendment privilege does apply in the police station, the Court reveals that the privilege imposes more exacting restrictions than does the Fourteenth Amendment's voluntariness test. It then emerges from a discussion of *Escobedo* that the Fifth Amendment requires for an admissible confession that it be given by one distinctly aware of his right not to speak and shielded from "the compelling atmosphere" of interrogation. From these key premises, the Court finally develops the safeguards of warning, counsel, and so forth. I do not believe these premises are sustained by precedents under the Fifth Amendment.

The more important premise is that pressure on the suspect must be eliminated though it be only the subtle influence of the atmosphere and surroundings. The Fifth Amendment, however, has never been thought to forbid *all* pressure to incriminate one's self in the situations covered by it. On the contrary, it has been held that failure to incriminate one's self can result in denial of removal of one's case from state to federal court, *State of Maryland v. Soper*, 270 U.S. 9, 46 S.Ct. 185, 70 L.Ed. 449; in refusal of a military commission, *Orloff v. Willoughby*, 345 U.S. 83, 73 S.Ct. 534, 97 L.Ed. 842; in denial of a discharge in bankruptcy, *Kaufman v. Hurwitz*, 4 Cir., 176 F.2d 210; and in numerous other adverse consequences.

* * *

The Court appears similarly wrong in thinking that precise knowledge of one's rights is a settled prerequisite under the Fifth Amendment to the loss of its protections. A number of lower federal court cases have held that grand jury witnesses need not always be warned of their privilege, e.g., *United States v. Scully*,

2 Cir., 225 F.2d 113, 116, and Wigmore states this to be the better rule for trial witnesses. See 8 Wigmore, Evidence § 2269 (McNaughton rev. 1961).

* * *

A closing word must be said about the Assistance of Counsel Clause of the Sixth Amendment, which is never expressly relied on by the Court but whose judicial precedents turn out to be linchpins of the confession rules announced today.

* * *

The only attempt in this Court to carry the right to counsel into the station house occurred in *Escobedo*, the Court repeating several times that that stage was no less "critical" than trial itself. This is hardly persuasive when we consider that a grand jury inquiry, the filing of a certiorari petition, and certainly the purchase of narcotics by an undercover agent from a prospective defendant may all be equally "critical" yet provision of counsel and advice on the score have never been thought compelled by the Constitution in such cases. The sound reason why this right is so freely extended for a criminal trial is the severe injustice risked by confronting an untrained defendant with a range of technical points of law, evidence, and tactics familiar to the prosecutor but not to himself. This danger shrinks markedly in the police station where indeed the lawyer in fulfilling his professional responsibilities of necessity may become an obstacle to truthfinding.

* * *

What the Court largely ignores is that its rules impair, if they will not eventually serve wholly to frustrate, an instrument of law enforcement that has long and quite reasonably been thought worth the price paid for it. There can be little doubt that the Court's new code would markedly decrease the number of confessions. To warn the suspect that he may remain silent and remind him that his confession may be used in court are minor obstructions. To require also an express waiver by the suspect and an end to questioning whenever he demurs must heavily handicap questioning. And to suggest or provide counsel for the suspect simply invites the end of the interrogation.

* * *

While passing over the costs and risks of its experiment, the Court portrays the evils of normal police questioning in terms which I think are exaggerated. Albeit stringently confined by the due process standards interrogation is no doubt often inconvenient and unpleasant for the suspect. However, it is no less so for a man to be arrested and jailed, to have his house searched, or to stand trial in court, yet all this may properly happen to the most innocent given probable cause, a warrant, or an indictment. Society has always paid a stiff price for law and order, and peaceful interrogation is not one of the dark moments of the law.

* * *

The Court in closing its general discussion invokes the practice in federal and foreign jurisdictions as lending weight to its new curbs on confessions for all the States. A brief résumé will suffice to show that none of these jurisdictions has struck so one-sided a balance as the Court does today. Heaviest reliance is placed on the FBI practice. Differing circumstances may make this comparison quite untrustworthy,[10] but in any event the FBI falls sensibly short of the Court's formalistic rules. For example, there is no indication that FBI agents must obtain an affirmative "waiver" before they pursue their questioning. Nor is it clear that one invoking his right to silence may not be prevailed upon to change his mind. And the warning as to appointed counsel apparently indicates only that one will be assigned by the judge when the suspect appears before him; the thrust of the Court's rules is to induce the suspect to obtain appointed counsel before continuing the interview. Apparently American military practice, briefly mentioned by the Court, has these same limits and is still less favorable to the suspect than the FBI warning, making no mention of appointed counsel.

The law of the foreign countries described by the Court also reflects a more moderate conception of the rights of the accused as against those of society when other data are considered. Concededly, the English experience is most relevant. In that country, a caution as to silence but not counsel has long been mandated by the "Judges' Rules," which also place other somewhat imprecise limits on police cross-examination of suspects. However, in the court's discretion confessions can be and apparently quite frequently are admitted in evidence despite disregard of the Judges' Rules, so long as they are found voluntary under the common-law test. Moreover, the check that exists on the use of pretrial statements is counter-balanced by the evident admissibility of fruits of an illegal confession and by the judge's often-used authority to comment adversely on the defendant's failure to testify.

India, Ceylon and Scotland are the other examples chosen by the Court. In India and Ceylon the general ban on police-adduced confessions cited by the Court is subject to a major exception: if evidence is uncovered by police questioning, it is fully admissible at trial along with the confession itself, so far as it relates to the evidence and is not blatantly coerced. Scotland's limits on interrogation do measure up to the Court's; however, restrained comment at trial on the defendant's failure to take the stand is allowed the judge, and in many other respects Scotch law redresses the prosecutor's disadvantage in ways not permitted in this country. The Court ends its survey by imputing added strength to our privilege against self-incrimination since, by contrast to other countries, it is embodied in a written Constitution. Considering the liberties the Court has today taken with constitutional history and precedent, few will find this emphasis persuasive.

In closing this necessarily truncated discussion of policy considerations attending the new confession rules, some reference must be made to their ironic untimeliness. There is now in progress in this country a massive re-examination of criminal law enforcement procedures on a scale never before witnessed. Participants in this undertaking include a Special Committee of the American Bar Association, under the chairmanship of Chief Judge Lumbard of the Court of Appeals for the Second Circuit; a distinguished study group of the American Law Institute, headed by Professors Vorenberg and Bator of the Harvard Law School; and the President's Commission on Law Enforcement and Administration of Justice, under the leadership of the Attorney General of the United States.[11] Studies are

---

[10]The Court's *obiter dictum* notwithstanding, there is some basis for believing that the staple of FBI criminal work differs importantly from much crime within the ken of local police. The skill and resources of the FBI may also be unusual.

[11]Of particular relevance is the ALI's drafting of a Model Code of Pre-Arraignment Procedure, now in its first tentative draft. While the ABA and National Commission studies have wider scope, the former is lending its advice to the ALI project and the executive director of the latter is one of the reporters for the Model Code.

also being conducted by the District of Columbia Crime disclaimer, the practical effect of the decision made today must inevitably be to handicap seriously sound efforts at reform, not least by removing options necessary to a just compromise of competing interests. Of course legislative reform is rarely speedy or unanimous, though this Court has been more patient in the past. But the legislative reforms when they come would have the vast advantage of empirical data and comprehensive study, they would allow experimentation and use of solutions not open to the courts, and they would restore the initiative in criminal law reform to those forums where it truly belongs.

Glossary

(Number in parentheses indicates the chapter in which the term is introduced.)

administrative warrant—A search warrant issued to check private premises for compliance with local ordinances. (10)

adversarial judicial system—A legal system such as that used in the United States, which places one party against another to resolve a legal issue, stipulating that only in an actual conflict will a judicial body hear the case. Also called adversary system. (2, 12)

affirm—A court agreeing with a lower court's decision. (4)

affirmative action—Programs created to spread equal opportunity throughout the diverse American population. (5)

amendments—Changes to a constitution or bylaws. (1)

American Dream—The belief that through hard work anyone can have success and ample material possessions. (5)

amicus brief—A "friend of the court" brief submitted by a person not a party to the action but interested in the outcome. (2)

Anti-Federalists—Colonists who opposed a strong federal government. (1)

appellate jurisdiction—Describes a court authorized to review cases and to either affirm or reverse the actions of a lower court. (2)

arraignment—Usually the first court appearance by a defendant during which the accused is advised of his or her rights, advised of the charges and given the opportunity to enter a plea. (12)

arrest—The detention of an individual; the taking of a person into custody in the manner authorized by law for the purpose of presenting that person before a magistrate to answer for the commission of a crime. (9)

articulable facts—Actions described in clear, distinct statements. (8)

asset forfeiture—The seizure by the government, without compensation, of money and property connected with illegal activity. (13)

bail—Money or property pledged by a defendant for pretrial release from custody that would be forfeited should the defendant fail to appear at subsequent court proceedings. (13)

balancing test—A position taken by the appellate courts to balance the needs of society for law and order and for effective law enforcement against the privacy rights of individuals. (6)

beachheading—The unconstitutional approach of purposely withholding the *Miranda* warnings until after a confession is obtained and then giving *Miranda* to re-ask the question. (11)

bifurcated trial—A two-step trial for capital cases. The first step is determination of innocence or guilt; the second step is determination of whether to seek the death penalty. (13)

Brady Rule—The suppression by the prosecution of evidence favorable to an accused upon request violates due process when the evidence is material either to guilt or to punishment, irrespective of the good faith or bad faith of the prosecution. (12)

brief—A summary presented to the court that describes the manner in which each side in a legal contest thinks the laws should apply to the facts of the case. To brief a case is to outline its pertinent facts. (4)

bright line approach—Determining the reasonableness of an action according to a specific rule that applies to all cases, in contrast to the case-by-case method. (8)

caption—The title of a case setting forth the parties involved. For example, *Smith v. Jones*. (4)

case law—Common law approach, so named because it is based on previous cases. Law that is set in prior cases brought before the courts and that provides a legal precedent that future cases may rely upon in making decisions on similar facts. Case law may make new law or serve to define or clarify legal questions. As a term in American law, it is synonymous with common law. (2)

case-by-case method—Determining the reasonableness of an action by considering the totality of circumstances in each case, in contrast to the bright line approach. (8)

certiorari—Latin for "to be informed." The Court uses this term to state which cases it will hear. Legal shorthand might simply state: "cert granted." (3)

charters—Businesslike agreements to establish a cooperative government. (1)

citizen's arrest—The detention by a nongovernment agent of one accused of an illegal act, with such detention being authorized by state statutes. (9)

civil wrongs—See torts.

"clear and present danger" test—The test of whether words are so potentially dangerous as to not be protected by the First Amendment. Replaced by the "imminent lawless action" test. (6)

"clear and probable danger" test—The test of whether the gravity of the evil discounted by its improbability justifies an invasion of free speech necessary to avoid any danger. (6)

codified law—Law specifically set forth in organized, structured codes such as the U.S. criminal code, state statutes or local ordinances. Also called statutory law. (2)

commercial bail—Using the services of a bail bond person to post a defendant's bail for a fee. (13)

common law—Early English judge-made law based on custom and tradition; a legal system that, as in the United States, decides present cases on past decisions. It also refers to judge-made or case law, as differentiated from statutory or constitutional law. As a term in American law, it is synonymous with case law. (2)

compacts—Documents with primarily a religious purpose in establishing how a community or colony chooses to govern itself. (1)

comparative law—Comparing and contrasting laws to expand understanding of law and legal theory (2)

compensatory damages—Reimbursement of the plaintiff for actual harm done, such as for medical expenses or lost business. (13)

compulsory process—Permits a defendant to require witnesses to appear in court, usually under the issuance by the court of a subpoena. (12)

concur—Agree with a lower court's decision but for a different reason. (4)

concurrent jurisdiction—Two or more courts authorized to hear a specific type of case. (2)

concurring opinion—Agreeing with the majority. (3)

conflict theory—Holds that laws are established to keep the dominant class in power, in contrast to the consensus theory. (2)

consensus theory—Holds that individuals in a society agree on basic values, on what is inherently right and wrong, and that laws express these values, in contrast to conflict theory. (2)

conservative—Decisions that favor the government's interest in prosecuting and punishing offenders over recognition or expansion of rights for individuals. (3)

constitution—A system of basic laws and principles that establish the nature, functions and limits of a government or other institution. A constitution provides a broad framework on which other laws are constructed. (1)

constitutionalism—A belief in a government in which power is distributed and limited by a system of laws that must be obeyed by those who rule. (1)

contemporaneous—A concept that holds a search can be incident to an arrest only if it occurs at the same time as the arrest and is confined to the immediate vicinity of the arrest. (10)

contextual discrimination—Describes a situation in which racial minorities are treated more harshly at some points and in some places in the criminal justice system but no differently than whites at other points and in other places. (5)

continuum of contacts—The almost limitless variations of contacts between the public and the police that illustrate how justification for police action increases as their reasons for thinking criminal activity is afoot build; how an individual's conduct can lead to sufficient probable cause and justify police in arresting the person, using force if necessary. (8)

contraband—Anything that is illegal for people to own or have in their possession, for example, illegal drugs or illegal weapons. (10)

conventional Fourth Amendment approach—Viewing the reasonableness clause and the warrant clause as intertwined, that is, all reasonable searches require a warrant. (8)

corporal punishment—Causing bodily harm through physical force, for example, whipping, flogging or beating. (13)

court trial—When a case is heard before only the bench (or judge) without a jury. (12)

crimes—Acts defined by federal or state statute or local ordinance that are punishable; wrongs against the government and the people it serves. While an individual has been victimized, the real victim is considered to be society itself, in contrast to a tort, which is a wrong against an individual. An act could be both a crime and a tort. (2)

curtilage—The portion of property generally associated with the common use of land, for example, buildings, sheds, fenced-in areas and the like. The property around a home or dwelling that is directly associated with the use of that property. Because there is a reasonable expectation of privacy within the curtilage, it is protected by the Fourth Amendment. (10)

custodial interrogation—Questioning by law enforcement officers after a person has been taken into custody or otherwise deprived of freedom of action in any significant way. (11)

de facto arrest—When a reasonable person would believe they are not free to leave while in the presence of the police, whether or not they have been told they are under arrest, have been handcuffed or are physically restrained. (9)

delegated powers—Powers of the national government, both enumerated and implied by legal authority, delegated or entrusted to the national government by the states and the people. (14)

demurrer—A request that a suit be dismissed because the facts do not sustain the claim against the defendant. (7)

detainer—Document filed against inmates who have other criminal charges pending against them, ensuring their appearance before the prosecuting jurisdiction for the next trial after their current sentence is complete. (12)

detention tantamount to arrest—Middle ground that is technically short of an arrest but more than a simple stop. (9)

dictum (plural dicta)—The statement by a court that does not deal with the main issue in the case, or an additional discussion by the court. (4, 7)

discrimination—An action or behavior based on prejudice. (5)

dissenting opinion—A justice's opinion that disagrees with the majority decision of the court. (3)

double jeopardy—A prohibition against the government from trying someone twice for the same offense. (11)

due process—The Fifth and Fourteenth Amendments' constitutionally guaranteed right of an accused to hear the charges against him or her and to be heard by the court having jurisdiction over the matter. It is the idea that basic fairness must remain part of the process, and it provides rules and procedures to ensure fairness to an individual and to prevent arbitrary actions by government. (5, 11)

entrapment—The act of government officials or agents (usually police) that induces a person to commit a crime that the person would not have otherwise committed. (11)

equal protection of the law—A constitutional requirement that the government give the same legal protection to all people: like people must be treated in like ways. (5)

establishment clause—Clause in the First Amendment that states: "Congress shall make no law respecting an establishment of religion." That is, it cannot create a national church. (6)

exclusionary rule—Judge-made case law promulgated by the Supreme Court to prevent police or government misconduct. It prohibits evidence obtained in violation of a person's constitutional rights from being admissible in court. (8)

exclusive jurisdiction—The only courts that can hear specific cases. (2)

exigent—Emergency. (10)

federalism—A principle whereby power is shared by the national government and the states; the Tenth Amendment provision reserving for the states those powers not granted to the federal government or withheld from the states. (14)

Federalists—Colonists who favored a strong federal government. (1)

free exercise clause—Clause in the First Amendment that declares: "Congress shall make no law . . . prohibiting the free exercise [of religion]." (6)

fresh pursuit—A situation in which police are immediately in pursuit of a suspect and may cross state jurisdictional lines to make an arrest of a felon who committed the felony in the officers' state and then crossed the border into another state. (9)

frisk—A reasonable, limited pat down search for weapons for the protection of a government agent and others. A less intrusive search than a full search, but one that is still regulated by the Fourth Amendment. It is not automatically permitted with a stop, but only when the agent suspects the person is armed and dangerous. Any evidence or contraband may be seized. (8)

fruit of the poisonous tree doctrine—Evidence obtained as a result of an earlier illegality (a constitutionally invalid search or activity) must be excluded from trial. (8)

functional equivalent—Equal or essentially the same. (10, 12)

furtive conduct—Questionable, suspicious or secretive behavior. (8)

general jurisdiction—Courts having the ability to hear a wide range of cases. (2)

good faith—Officers are unaware that they are acting in violation of a suspect's constitutional rights. A standard by which one is assumed to have acted honestly in carrying out a legal duty. (8)

grand jury—A group of citizens who determine whether sufficient evidence exists to send an accused to trial. (11)

Great Compromise—The agreement reached in drafting the Constitution that gave each state an equal vote in the Senate and a proportionate vote in the House. (1)

harmless error—Involves the admissibility of involuntary confessions: If no harm results, the confession should be admissible. Also, if the preponderance of evidence suggests a defendant's guilt, any "tainted" or illegal evidence not crucial to proving the case against the defendant will not cause the case to be dismissed. (8, 11)

hearsay—Testimony made in court about something heard outside of court offered as proof of the matter asserted; a statement made by someone other than the person who actually said it. (12)

holding—The rule of law applied to the particular facts of the case and the actual decision. (4)

hot pursuit—The period during which an individual is being immediately chased by law enforcement. A period that influences Fourth Amendment search and seizure concerns; the person to be arrested knows an arrest is about to be made and is actively trying to escape it. (9)

"imminent lawless action" test—A three-part test that the government must meet if certain communication is not to be protected by the First Amendment: (1) the speaker subjectively intended incitement; (2) in context, the words used were likely to produce imminent, lawless action; and (3) the words used by the speaker objectively encouraged and urged incitement. This test replaced the "clear and present danger" test. (6)

incorporation doctrine—Holds that only the provisions of the Bill of Rights that are fundamental to the American legal system are applied to the states through the due process clause of the Fourteenth Amendment. Also known as selective incorporation. (5)

indictment—A formal accusation of a defendant, usually by a grand jury, that sends the defendant on to trial for prosecution. (11)

indigent—Poor, unable to afford a lawyer. (12)

inevitable discovery doctrine—Exception to exclusionary rule deeming evidence admissible even if seized in violation of the Fourth Amendment when it can be shown that the evidence would have inevitably been discovered through lawful means. (8)

information literacy—Online research skills that include identifying issue, narrowing topic, locating data, discerning fact from fiction and presenting material in an academic and/or professional manner. (4)

Jim Crow laws—Laws that strictly segregated blacks from whites in schools, restaurants, streetcars, hospitals and cemeteries. Such laws passed in the American South in the 1800s to discriminate against blacks by restricting certain liberties were accepted by the Supreme Court until 1954, when separate was no longer considered equal. (5)

judicial activism—Allowing judges to interpret the Constitution and its amendments. (6)

judicial review—The power of a court to analyze decisions of other government entities and lower courts. (3)

jurisdiction—The authority of a legislative body to establish a law, the authority of a particular court to hear certain types of cases, or the authority a law has over a specific group of people. Three levels of jurisdiction are federal, state and local. (2)

jury nullification—ability of a jury to acquit a defendant even though they believe that person is guilty; occurs because the jury either feels the circumstances make it unfair to convict or they disagree with the law. (12)

just compensation—The requirement that property owners be paid fair market value by the government when government takes their property. (11)

law—A body of rules promulgated (established) to support the norms of a society, enforced through legal means, that is, punishment. (1)

legal citation—A standardized way of referring to a specific element in the law, with three basic parts: a volume number, an abbreviation for the title and a page or section number. (4)

legal opinion—See opinion.

liberal—Decisions that are pro-person accused or convicted of a crime, pro-civil liberties or civil rights claimants, proindigents, pro-Native Americans and antigovernment. (3)

limited jurisdiction—Restriction of the types of cases a particular court might hear. (2)

lineup—Occurs when the victim or witness is shown several people, including the suspect. (12)

litigious—A tendency toward suing; a belief that most controversies or injurious acts, no matter how minor, should be settled in court. (8)

Loyalist—A colonist who did not support the boycott of British goods in the colonies and who still paid allegiance to the British monarchy. Also called a Tory. (1)

magistrate—A judge. (8)

Mayflower Compact—Signed on November 11, 1620, by 41 passengers aboard *The Mayflower*; this document is considered to be the first formal document by the Pilgrims establishing a self-determining government upon arriving in the area of New England. (1)

militia—An armed group of citizens who defend their community as emergencies arise. (7)

minutemen—Colonial soldiers. (1)

mootness—Exists when the issues that gave rise to a case have either been resolved or have otherwise disappeared. (2)

National Reporter System—A private publisher's compilation of case law throughout the United States, organized by regional court systems. (4)

nightcap(ped) warrant—Issued when officers wish to execute a warrant at night because that is when the suspected illicit activity is primarily occurring. (8)

no-knock warrant—Issued when officers want to make an unannounced entrance because they are afraid evidence might be destroyed or officer safety requires it. (8)

nonincorporated amendments—When an amendment has not been made applicable (incorporated) to the states under the Fourteenth Amendment. (7)

opinion—A written statement by a judge that provides a description of the facts; a statement of the legal issues presented for decision, the relevant rules of law, the holding and the policies and reasons that support the holding. (3)

ordinances—Laws or codes established at the local level, that is, the municipal or county level. (2)

original jurisdiction—Courts authorized to hear cases first, try them and render decisions. Often called trial courts. May also apply to the U.S. Supreme Court. (2)

Patriot—A colonist who supported the boycott of British goods in the colonies and who owed allegiance to America rather than to the British monarchy. Also called a rebel. (1)

penal codes—Criminal codes or laws. (2)

penumbra—A type of shadow in astronomy with the principle extending to the idea that certain constitutional rights are implied within other constitutional rights. (8, 14)

peremptory challenges—A specific number of allowances given to each side in a case so that they may assert to remove a potential juror for any reason whatsoever. (12)

petition for certiorari—Request that the Supreme Court review the decision of a lower court. (2)

plain feel—Items felt during a lawful stop and frisk may be retrieved if the officer reasonably believes the items are contraband and can *instantly* recognize them as such. (10)

plain touch—Same as plain feel. (10)

plain view—Unconcealed evidence that officers see while engaged in a lawful activity may be seized and is admissible in court. (10)

pluralism—A society in which numerous distinct ethnic, religious or cultural groups coexist within one nation, each contributing to the society as a whole. (1)

police power—Goes beyond criminal law and refers to the government's right to create rules and regulations pertaining to health, safety and welfare, which includes such areas as zoning, fire, building inspections, education, health, gambling and safety regulations. (9)

popular literature—Publications written for the layperson, for example, *Time* or *Newsweek*. (4)

preferred freedoms approach—A position that stresses that civil liberties are to take precedence over other constitutional values because they are requisite to a democracy. Under this approach, the burden lies with the government to prove clear and present danger exists when a freedom is limited. (6)

prejudice—A negative attitude regarding a person or thing. (5)

preliminary hearing—A critical stage of criminal proceedings when it is determined if probable cause exists to believe a crime has been committed and that the defendant committed it. (12)

pretext stop—Stopping a vehicle to search for evidence of a crime under the guise of a traffic stop. (9)

preventive detention—The right of judges to consider the potential criminal conduct of those accused of serious offenses and deny bail on those grounds. (13)

primary information sources—Raw data or the original information. (4)

prior restraint—A restriction on publishing certain materials; rare in the United States and most other democratic countries. (6)

privilege—A claim that is not legally protected, in contrast to a right. (5)

pro se—Appearing in court without an attorney, representing oneself. Latin meaning "for himself." (12)

probable cause—Stronger than reasonable suspicion. The sum total of layers of information and the synthesis of what the police have heard, what they know and what they observe as trained officers. (8)

procedural due process—Constitutionally guaranteed rights of fairness in how the law is carried out or applied. (11)

procedural law—How the law is to be enforced, for example, how and when police can stop people. (2)

professional literature—Publications written for the practitioner in the field, for example, *The Police Chief*, *Police* or *Corrections Today*. (4)

prohibited persons—Individuals to whom, under the Gun Control Act, it is forbidden to sell firearms. (7)

promulgate—Publish or announce officially a law or rule; to make law through a legal process. (2)

proportionality analysis—In essence, making the punishment fit the crime. Sentences must be proportional or directly related to the crime committed. (13)

protective sweep—A limited search made in conjunction with an in-home arrest when the searching officer possesses a reasonable belief based on specific and articulable facts that the area to be swept harbors an individual posing a danger to those on the arrest scene. It is not a full search of the premises but a cursory inspection to determine if anyone else is present. (10)

public safety exception—Allows officers to question suspects without first giving the *Miranda* warning if the information sought sufficiently affects the officers' and the public's safety. (11)

punitive damages—Fines above and beyond the actual economic loss to punish the defendant in a civil trial. (13)

Quartering Act—Passed by Parliament in 1765, requiring colonists to feed and shelter British troops in America. (1)

racial profiling—The process of using certain racial characteristics, such as skin color, as indicators of criminal activity; acting on personal bias. Illegal race-based enforcement of the law. (5)

ratify—Approve a constitutional amendment. (1)

"rational basis" test—The standard for analyzing not only First Amendment claims by prisoners but also other constitutional claims as well, containing these four criteria: (1) there must be a rational connection between the regulations and legitimate interest put forward to justify it; (2) alternative means of exercising the right must remain open to prison inmates; (3) the regulations must have only a minimal impact on correctional officers and other inmates; and (4) a less restrictive alternative must be available. (6)

reasonable—Sensible, rational, justifiable. (8)

reasonable expectation of privacy—The Constitution does not provide an absolute right to be free from government intrusion, only *unreasonable* interference. (8)

reasonable suspicion—An experienced police officer's hunch or intuition, based on observed unusual conduct, which leads him reasonably to conclude that criminal activity may be afoot. (8)

reasonableness Fourth Amendment approach—An interpretation of the Fourth Amendment that sees the reasonableness clause and the warrant clause as separate issues. (8)

recesses—Periods when the Supreme Court does not hear cases but rather considers administrative matters and writes opinions. Also, breaks taken during the course of the trial. (3)

remand—Return a case to the lower court for further action. (4)

remoteness—Regarding the unreasonableness and unlawfulness of searches of seized luggage or other personal belongings not immediately associated with the arrestee's body or under his or her immediate control if the search is distant in time and place from the arrest and, as such, is no longer an incident of the arrest, and if no emergency exists. (10)

reserve powers—Powers retained by the states. (14)

resolution—A formal statement by a legislative body holding less authority than an ordinance or law; a referenced proposition of law. (6)

reverse—Overturn the decision of a lower court. (4)

reverse discrimination—Giving preferential treatment in hiring and promoting to women and minorities to the detriment of white males. (5)

right—A legally protected claim, in contrast to a privilege. (5)

ripeness doctrine—Invoked when a case comes to court too soon, preventing the court from getting prematurely involved in a case that may eventually resolve through other means. (2)

ROR—Released on their own recognizance, meaning that the court trusts defendants to show up in court when required. No bail money is required. Also called RPR. (13)

scholarly literature—Publications written for those interested in theory, research and statistical analysis, for example, *Justice Quarterly*. (4)

search—An examination of a person, place or vehicle for contraband or evidence of a crime. (8)

secondary information sources—Information based on the raw data or the original information, such as periodicals, treatises/texts, encyclopedias and dictionaries. (4)

seizure—A taking by law enforcement or other government agent of contraband, evidence of a crime or even a person into custody. (8)

selective incorporation—Holds that only the provisions of the Bill of Rights that are fundamental to the American legal system are applied to the states through the due process clause of the Fourteenth Amendment. Also known as the incorporation doctrine. (5, 14)

shepardizing—Using the resource *Shepard's Citations*, published for each set of official volumes of cases, indicating whether a case's status has changed. (4)

showup—When only one individual is shown to the victim or witness. (12)

sittings—Periods during which the Supreme Court hears cases. (3)

social contract—A philosophy proposed by French historian-philosopher Montesquieu, whereby free, independent individuals agree to form a society and to give up a portion of their individual freedom to benefit the security of the group. Durkheim described this social solidarity as a society's "collective conscience." (2)

Stamp Act—Passed by Parliament in 1765, it required stamps to be purchased and placed on legal documents such as marriage licenses and wills, and several commodities, including playing cards, dice, newspapers and calendars. It was repealed in 1766. (1)

standing—The right to object to the unreasonableness of a search or seizure because of a reasonable expectation of privacy and to claim a violation of other constitutional rights. In constitutional law, it must involve a case or controversy and an actual interest in the matter of dispute to bring a case or to argue a legal issue in court. (2, 10)

stare decisis—Latin for "to stand by decided matters." A legal principle that requires that precedents set in one case be followed in cases having similar circumstances, thus assuring consistency in the law. (2)

status offenses—Offenses deemed to be illegal when committed by juveniles because of their age, which are not unlawful for adults, such as smoking, drinking and curfew. (2)

statutory law—Law set forth by legislatures or governing bodies having jurisdiction to make such law. Also called codified law. (2)

stop—A brief detention of a person, short of an arrest, based on specific and articulable facts for the purpose of investigating suspicious activity. (8)

strict construction—A rigid interpretation of a law not likely to expand the specifically set forth law of the particular statute, particularly in expanding the intent of that law. (3)

string cites—Additional legal citations showing where a case may be found in commercial digests. (4)

subpoena—Requires an individual to appear in court to testify or to bring documents or other physical evidence to the court. (12)

substantive due process—Requires laws themselves to be fair. (11)

substantive law—Establishes rules and regulations, as in traffic law. (2)

suits at common law—Legal controversies arising out of civil law as opposed to criminal law. (14)

sunset clause—A set ending time for legislation that is not renewed to prevent old law from remaining on the books. (7)

supremacy clause—Constitutional doctrine that federal law will reign when there is conflicting state law (U.S. Const. Art. VI, Paragraph. 2). (1)

Terry **stop**—An officer with articulable reasonable suspicion may conduct a brief investigatory stop, including a pat down for weapons if the officer has reason to suspect the person is armed and dangerous. (8)

torts—Civil wrongs by one individual against another, with the remedy most often being either an order by the court for particular action or compensation, in contrast to crimes, which are wrongs against society. (2)

totality of circumstances—The principle upon which a number of legal assessments are made, including probable cause; the sum total of factors leading a reasonable person (officer) to a course of action. (8)

treatise—A definitive source of material written about a specific topic or area of study. (4)

unenumerated rights—Rights not specifically listed in the Bill of Rights. (14)

USA PATRIOT Act—Legislation that significantly improves the nation's counterterrorism efforts by (1) allowing investigators to use the tools already available to investigate organized crime and drug trafficking, (2) facilitating information sharing and cooperation among government agencies so they can better "connect the dots," (3) updating the law to reflect new technologies and new threats and (4) increasing the penalties for those who commit or support terrorist crimes. (11)

venue—The geographical area in which a specific case may come to trial, and the area from which the jury is selected. (2, 12)

voir dire—The process of questioning potential jurors to determine their impartiality. (12)

voluntariness test—A determination as to whether one willingly and knowingly relinquished his or her constitutional rights, without pressure to do so, assessed by two factors: (1) the police conduct involved and (2) the characteristics of the accused. A determination that considers the totality of circumstances in assessing whether consent was obtained without coercion or promises and was, therefore, reasonable. (10)

waiver—A purposeful and voluntary giving up of a known right. (11)

waiver test—Citizens may waive their rights, but only if they do so voluntarily, knowingly and intentionally. The waiver is what makes the subsequent action reasonable. (10)

wingspan—The area within a person's reach or immediate control. (10)

zones of privacy—Areas into which the government may not intrude. (14)

Author Index

Subject Index